Egypt, Islam, and the Arabs

STUDIES IN MIDDLE EASTERN HISTORY

Bernard Lewis, Itamar Rabinovich, and Roger Savory, *General Editors*

Israel Gershoni and James P. Jankowski

EGYPT, ISLAM, AND THE ARABS:

The Search for Egyptian Nationhood, 1900–1930

EGYPT, ISLAM, AND THE ARABS:
The Search for Egyptian Nationhood, 1900–1930

Israel Gershoni
James P. Jankowski

In cooperation with the Dayan Center and the
Shiloah Institute for Middle Eastern and African Studies,
Tel Aviv University.

New York Oxford
OXFORD UNIVERSITY PRESS
1986

Oxford University Press

Oxford New York Toronto
Delhi Bombay Calcutta Madras Karachi
Petaling Jaya Singapore Hong Kong Tokyo
Nairobi Dar es Salaam Cape Town
Melbourne Auckland
and associated companies in
Beirut Berlin Ibadan Nicosia

Published by Oxford University Press, Inc.,
200 Madison Avenue, New York, New York 10016

Oxford is a registered trademark of Oxford University Press

Library of Congress Cataloging-in-Publication Data
Gershoni, I.
Egypt, Islam, and the Arabs.
(Studies in Middle Eastern history)
"In cooperation with the Dayan Center and the
Shiloah Institute for Middle Eastern and African
Studies, Tel Aviv University."
Bibliography: p. Includes index.
1. Nationalism—Egypt. 2. Egypt—Politics and government—1882–1936.
3. Egypt—Relations—Arab countries.
4. Arab countries—Relations—Egypt.
I. Jankowski, James P., 1937– . II. Title.
III. Series: Studies in Middle Eastern history (New York, N.Y.)
DT107.8.G37 1986 320.5'4'0962 86-5221
ISBN 0-19-504096-1 (alk. paper)

2 4 6 8 10 9 7 5 3 1
Printed in the United States of America
on acid-free paper

To
Mary Ann
and
Shoshi

Preface

This is a study of nationalism in modern Egypt. Nationalism is an elusive concept, the subject of considerable—and inconclusive—theoretical discussion. If a working definition is needed, we define nationalism as a perception about political community: that nations are a natural social formation, that they are the object of the ultimate political loyalty and allegiance of their peoples, and that they have an inherent right to autonomy and self-determination within the world assembly of nations. This perception finds tangible expression in ideological movements that are devoted to the realization of new political orders: the reorganization of certainly the political but often also the economic, social, and cultural life of the community defined as the nation.[1]

As the major framework of group loyalty in modern times, nationalism is a state of mind as well as a pattern of behavior. In the first instance nationalism is the product of human thought, a perceptual rather than an objective entity. But it is always pointed toward the realization of itself in actuality, toward translating its ideal concepts into objective reality outside human consciousness. It is also a vision of collective self-realization: how a group wills its becoming. Nationalism is thus both an ideological construct and a practical way of life. Its abstract doctrines are usually accompanied by a programmatic emphasis on the achievement of national goals in the real world.

As an ideology, nationalism is a comprehensive interpretation of past, present, and future. Its concepts have their roots in an idealized past and point toward the realization of an equally glorious future. But its main concern is the here and now; its attitude toward other times is centered on the question of how they can be utilized for the purposes of the present. To be sure, nationalist ideology requires objective elements existing outside human consciousness: territory, race, language, kinship, religion, history, and the like. But without the manipulation of these factors by human consciousness and will, no nationalism exists. Natural factors are only the raw material of nationalism; consciousness and will are the engines responsible for its creation and perpetuation. Unless they are filtered through human consciousness and will, these objective elements possess no historical significance: only consciousness and will imbue territory, race, language, kinship, religion, or history with "national" meanings. The human intellect thus defines the relevant elements of human identity and loyalty and gives natural factors their relative importance as components within systems of collective identification and allegiance. In the process, consciousness and will transform these objective elements, giving them new meaning; hence territory becomes "patrie," race becomes "nation," language and history become "national culture," and so forth. The collective consciousness of a specific group of people, their identification of themselves as a collective unity or "nation," their common determination to act in order to realize collective aspirations: these are the factors defining national entities in the first instance and accounting for their subsequent development.[2]

The study of nationalism needs to concern itself with three interlocking dimensions. The first is an understanding of the perceptions that constitute nationalism: the ideas and patterns of thought that make up specific nationalist ideologies. The second is the interplay of nationalist ideas and nationalist actions: how nationalists attempt to realize their values in the real world. The third is the perpetual interaction and reciprocal influence of nationalist ideas and actions, on the one hand, and the external historical conditions in which nationalists find themselves, on the other: how historical circumstances influence nationalist doctrines and behavior, as well as how these ideas and actions shape the course of historical evolution.

Following these principles, this study has three overlapping concerns. The first is to examine how Egyptians perceived their own collective identity and affiliations from the turn of this century to the early 1930s. The second is to analyze how Egyptians tried to realize their nationalist beliefs in the world around them. The third is to describe and explain the encounter between nationalist perceptions and actions, and changing historical conditions.

This work proceeds on the basis of several assumptions about historical inquiry. Perhaps the most basic of these is that there are crucial interrelationships between the intellectual life of a society and its political development. An adequate understanding of both the emergence of nationalism in modern Egypt and its complex evolution over time demands that attention be given to the complex connections between ideas of the world and behavior in the world.

On the one hand, one cannot comprehend either the origins and meaning of intellectual constructs or their spread, change, and historical importance without examining the specific historical context (particularly institutional-political, but also socioeconomic) in which they emerge, exist, and evolve. As John Higham put it, ideas occur in "a context of other happenings which explain them,"[3] and thus the historian who concerns himself with the ideas of a society must of necessity also concern himself with the social context of thought. Thought can be studied apart from its social context, but the result is not history in the proper sense of the term.

On the other hand, the political behavior of people in a given society can be understood only in relation to the intellectual context in which political action occurs. Hence we do not restrict ourselves to a purely political approach to the history of nationalism in Egypt, an approach that views political behavior as a pragmatic response to circumstances devoid of any conceptual constraints or preconditions. In our view the political interests and goals of a community and the political activities undertaken to realize the same cannot be treated as nonconceptual phenomena shaped only by the imperatives of the moment. In regard to nationalist action in particular, aims and policies are defined and adopted by nationalists in the light of their nationalist worldview and values. Political behavior is often if not always motivated by ideological considerations, and therefore worldviews and values are an integral component of any explanation of political developments.

In sum, political occurrences are in part dependent on a structure of concepts and values into which they "fit" and which in turn "explain" them. Just as "ideas and symbols do not exist apart from social [or economic, or political] reality out there," so they help to define that reality: "they [ideas and symbols] are the means by which we perceive, understand, judge, and manipulate that reality; indeed, they create it."[4] From this perspective, in addition to the study of nationalist ideas in and of themselves, our focus is upon the use to which such ideas were put in Egypt: how they shaped national interests and goals; how they were diffused and embodied in political, social, and cultural institutions; how they helped to dictate national policies in education, literary life, and economics; in sum, how "intellectual habits and intellectual inventions shaped historic developments by setting the terms in which groups or generations of men conducted their lives."[5]

This study does not follow the purely "internal" approach to the history of ideas, the prophet of which was Arthur O. Lovejoy.[6] Intellectual history that analyzes "unit-ideas" detached from their sociopolitical context and insists on the autonomy and integrity of the text, although certainly legitimate for some purposes, does not seem to us a fruitful approach to the study of nationalism per se. First, the systems of nationalist ideas that emerged in Egypt in this period were both the product of their time and place and oriented toward shaping their society: neither universal nor timeless in nature, these ideas were intimately linked to their setting. Second, the many transformations in Egyptian nationalist orientations over time, the emergence and diffusion of new orientations as well as the decline of old ones, cannot be understood without a discussion of their broader context: the historical context of ideas is crucial to the analysis of change in ideas. Third, the exclusively internal approach seems to us to sterilize the historical process, making it the study of "high" ideas isolated from other nonideological processes of history. The internal approach all too often seizes upon the key concepts of leading thinkers over a long period of time, presuming that historical realities were not critical for the development of these concepts. This exclusive concern for the inner dynamics of "formal" and more systematic thought is particularly inapplicable to the study of nationalist ideas, which by definition are "informal," less systematic, and more programmatic in character. Finally, the internal approach leads one to neglect the impact of ideas on the real world. As historians, we believe that ideas are important for what they *do* as well as for what they *are*.

We hope, too, that our analysis avoids the reductionism of the exclusively "external" approach to intellectual history, one that makes ideas purely a function of circumstances, or thought merely instrumental to action in the social sphere. We believe that context can explain much but not all of the history of ideas: ideas are not merely echoes of social processes or forces, "reflections of something else that is inherently more important."[7] Although the historical context is vital to explaining the origins and much of the evolution of a system of thought, it cannot fully account for the specifics or the quality of a complex body of speculation. Once set in motion by society, thought has its own internal dynamics. Just as ideas cannot be analyzed exclusively in terms of themselves, neither can they be understood only as a product of external circumstances.[8]

Beyond this partial autonomy of ideas, we hold that ideas are worthy of systematic historical examination for two additional reasons. The first is that the context-text relationship is not unidirectional, with the flow of influence always proceeding from context to text: although the context is essential to an historical understanding of a text, it is also true that the context is illuminated by the text. The second is simply that the production of ideas is a form of human endeavor fully as deserving of historical study as human political, economic, or social behavior.

We have attempted to find a synthesis of the internal and the external approaches. On the one hand, we deal separately both with Egyptian nationalist thought considered as a partially autonomous construct with its own internal coherence, and with Egyptian national politics analyzed in terms of their own inner dynamics. On the other hand, our study constantly emphasizes the "connections between thought and deed" or "how the structure of mind connects with the stuff of experience."[9] To stress the connections between intellectual and political developments of course does not imply that the relationship is a simple, a mechanistic, or a determinist one: just as political interests and actions are not derivative of ideological systems, so the latter are not solely a reflection of, or a rationalization for, political realities. But it is to insist that there is a vital bond between the ideas of men and their actions, and that the study of one demands careful attention to the other.[10]

In the specific context of Egypt in the early twentieth century, we examine both Egyptian nationalist thought and Egyptian political behavior. It is our view that nationalism in Egypt has too often been treated in predominantly political terms (that is, in terms of the anti-British and anti-Western struggle for political independence), to the neglect of the involved cultural and intellectual dimensions that developed in the process first of Egypt's realizing national liberation from foreign domination, next of its defining a self-image, and finally of its clarifying a proper relationship with the world around it. Although studies of Egyptian thought in the modern period have often been attuned to the social context within which thought develops, too frequently they have avoided analysis of how that thought influenced the world of politics. Therefore, what we have attempted in this study is to explain the relationships among Egyptian conditions, the Egyptian worldview, and Egyptian political activity in regard to national issues.

Another emphasis or orientation of this study is its focus on the temporal development of Egyptian nationalist ideas and behavior. Neither the theory nor the practical policies of Egyptian nationalism were static phenomena, defined in final form at a particular point and continuing unchanged thereafter. Rather, both underwent enormous development and alteration after their initial formulation in the early years of this century. Given this dynamism of the history of Egyptian nationalism, one of our primary concerns is to describe and explain the successive stages, and sometimes even the substantive transformations, through which nationalist ideas and policies in Egypt passed. As R. G. Collingwood once phrased it, "to trace the process by which one historical phase turns into the next is the business of every historian who concerns himself with that phase."[11] In terms specific to Egypt, our intention is to portray and analyze the shift from the more traditionally rooted Egyptian-Ottoman-Islamic nationalist orientation dominant in Egypt up to World War I to the new Egyptian territorial nationalist *weltanschauung* which gained ascendency among the educated Egyptian public after the war. To explain the collapse of the first and the predominance of the second, both considered in relation to changing historical circumstances of the time, is the main subject of this study. The later erosion of an exclusive Egyptian territorial nationalism and the development of a more externally oriented sense of nationalism, both of which occurred over the course of the 1930s and 1940s, will be considered in a subsequent volume.

Yet another orientation of this study is its attempt to examine a wider universe of thought than has generally been the case in studies of nationalism in modern Egypt. Two assumptions are involved here. The first concerns the social nature of political attitudes and ideas. Following Karl Mannheim, we hold that the content and the development of a body of thought is most fruitfully conceived as the result of a group process:

> [I]t is not men in general who think, or even isolated individuals who do the thinking, but men in certain groups who have developed a particular style of thought in an endless series of responses to certain typical situations characterizing their common position.
>
> Strictly speaking it is incorrect to say that the single individual thinks. Rather it is more correct to insist that he participates in thinking further what other men have thought before him.[12]

If this is the case, it follows that the historian's primary concern must be with *collective* attitudes and ideas, with the concepts held in common by groups of people within a given society. While it goes without saying that no society is reducible to one group of thinkers or one body of opinion, nonetheless the historian's main focus must be upon those attitudes and intellectual constructs which to a greater or lesser extent are shared by at least some of the individuals making up that society. "Extraordinary" Egyptian thought is thus not our concern, nor is the "deviant" thought of certain individuals, no matter how intellectually impressive it might be. Rather, our attention will be turned to the mainstream (more realistically, the mainstreams) of nationalist thought in Egypt: by definition more ordinary, usually less impressive, but also dominant within Egyptian society.

To say that our concern is with collective thinking and opinion rather than with individual speculation is not to say that we believe ourselves to be dealing with an impersonal body of concepts that transcend the influence or control of individuals. On the contrary, concepts originate in the minds of individuals, are elaborated upon by individuals, and are accepted, modified, or rejected by individuals. These individuals have a specific identity shaped by specific circumstances, both of which will be the subject of our concern. We do assume, however, that these individuals were not totally isolated figures but were in communication with other individuals, responding to the ideas of others and in turn having some impact upon the speculation of others. It follows that one cannot comprehend the ideas of an individual without coming to terms with the collective or the "discursive" context of thought shared by the society or the subsector of society in which that individual lived and thought. Only through understanding the reciprocal influences of different individual minds in the same "community of discourse" can the ideas of individuals be fully appreciated.[13]

Our second assumption relates to the issue of how best to ascertain the collective opinion or schools of opinion found in a particular society. Robert Darnton has identified four possible categories of historical inquiry into ideas based on the type and range of evidence being examined:

> the history of ideas (the study of systematic thought, usually in philosophical treatises), intellectual history proper (the study of informal thought, climates of opinion, and literary movements), the social history of ideas (the study of ideologies and idea diffusion), and cultural history (the study of culture in the anthropological sense, including worldviews and collective *mentalités*).[14]

Of these four possibilities, this study is oriented toward the second and the third levels of inquiry. Although it does not deal with the popular attitudes and opinions of the uneducated Egyptian masses whose collective *mentalité* can be recaptured—if at all—only through the extensive utilization of Egyptian oral folklore, proverbs, and traditions, neither is it restricted to the consideration of the formal nationalist philosophies of Egypt's most famous and most brilliant thinkers (although it does deal with these as one aspect of Egyptian nationalism). Rather, its emphasis is upon something midway between the leading edge of Egyptian thought and the opinions of the Egyptian masses. It examines the writings of a broader range of nationalist theoreticians and political publicists than has been considered in most previous studies of Egyptian nationalism. Looking at a larger number of Egyptian writers about nationalism, including many whose opinions were clearly derivative and some whose ideas had little intrinsic consistency and/or merit, provides a surer appreciation of Egyptian nationalist views than that afforded by the analysis of the opinions of a selected group of presumably "representative" writers.

In attempting to reconstruct a fuller range of Egyptian nationalist thought and behavior, we give attention to the rational and pragmatic aspects of Egyptian nationalist opinion as well as its more emotional and sentimental dimensions. Both calculation and feeling bulked large in Egyptians' discussions of what their "nation" was as well as what its proper orientation and policies might be. Where pragmatic and instrumental arguments often prevailed in the discussion of specific national policies, more basic nationalist orientations were usually justified in terms of sentiment and emotion. Much of the dissemination and diffusion of nationalist concepts in particular can be appreciated only in the context of such subjective factors, since Egyptian nationalist writers often employed highly emotional language and played upon the subjective feelings of the educated Egyptian public in an effort to promote their ideas. Because one of our particular concerns is with the circulation and diffusion of nationalist ideas and policies—how originally marginal concepts over time become the ideological mainstream of a society—we pay special attention to the emotionally colored and psychologically appealing arguments used to popularize and spread Egyptian nationalist concepts.

Attention to subjective factors is also essential to penetrate to the deeper levels of meaning inherent in any historical subject. If the purpose of historical research is to produce an account that "not only tells what happened and how and why it happened but makes it happen again for the reader," then to accomplish this the historian

> must pay attention to the affective tone of general ideas and to their concrete manifestations in language, literature, art and popular myth. He must realize, for example, that every world view involves an emotional as well as an intellectual apprehension of nature.[15]

Thus we concern ourselves not only with an investigation of the "rational" dimensions of Egyptian nationalist thought and behavior, but additionally we repeatedly consider the "irrational" feelings, urges, and motives that gave that nationalism its emotional force and personal meaning.

The fundamental level of meaning and behavior that our study hopes to identify is something akin to what R. G. Collingwood termed the "absolute presupposition" in metaphysics: those basic concepts which are often unconscious within a population, which are taken for granted and demand no formal justification, and which underlay and give structure to all subsequent, derivative thought and action concerning a particular subject.[16] In terms of the discipline of history, we accept John C. Greene's view that "the primary function of the intellectual historian is to delineate the presuppositions of thought in given historical epochs and to explain the changes which those presuppositions undergo from epoch to epoch."[17] As Greene is quick to note, the identification and explanation of such presuppositions is a complex procedure:

> It becomes apparent, moreover, that there was not just *one* pattern of thought in the epoch, but that there were several, some dominant, the others subdominant, incipient, or vestigal. These general modes of thought often coexisted in the mind of a single individual even when they were not entirely compatible with each other. They manifested themselves simultaneously in a single paragraph of his writings. They were not the particular views of particular individuals or even of particular groups of individuals; they were tendencies or patterns which the intellectual historian, aided by hindsight, discerns in the thought of the age.[18]

Most of Greene's observations concerning the variety and interrelatedness of fundamental presuppositions apply in regard to Egyptian nationalist thought in the first half of the twentieth century. There was not one fundamental Egyptian presupposition concerning nationalism, but several; while one was dominant, others were subdominant, incipient, or vestigal; despite their formal incompatibility, such overall assumptions concerning nationalism did coexist in the mind of the same individual and find expression in the same writings; and the general patterns of nationalist thought in Egypt, although in part discernable to their contemporary authors, as a whole were collective tendencies or orientations ascertainable only in retrospect.

The integration of the intellectual and the political history of nationalism, the analysis of patterns of consciousness and thought combined with the examination of patterns of political action, the attempt to penetrate into more ordinary levels of attitude and opinion, and the delineation of the changing relationship of the dominant and the subdominant nationalist presuppositions of different periods—we view all these as necessary to the reconstruction of a more comprehensive portrayal of nationalist orientations in modern Egypt. From such an approach, we hope to demonstrate the complexity, the dynamism, the vitality, and the centrality of nationalism in twentieth-century Egyptian history.

Tel Aviv I. G.
Boulder, Colorado J. P. J.
June 1986

Acknowledgments

We wish to express our gratitude to the many institutions that provided assistance for this study: the American Philosophical Society; the American Research Center in Egypt and its Directors, Mr. John Dorman and Dr. Paul Walker; the Council on Research and Creative Work and the Committee on University Scholarly Publications of the University of Colorado; the Egyptian National Library (*Dar al-Kutub al-Misriyya*), particularly Mr. Salah 'Abd al-Sabur; the Institute of Behavioral Science of the University of Colorado; Professor Shimon Shamir and the Kaplan Chair in the history of Israel and Egypt, Tel Aviv University; and the United States–Israel Educational Foundation directed by Mr. Dan Krauscop. We express our appreciation to Professor Itamar Rabinovich and Mrs. Edna Liftman of the Dayan Center and the Shiloah Institute for Middle Eastern and African Studies not only for their support but also for creating a favorable and friendly atmosphere for conducting research. Professors George Pilcher and Boyd H. Hill of the Department of History of the University of Colorado were helpful chairmen as well as supportive friends, and Ms. Sandy Marsh was a very accommodating administrator. Professor Zwi Dvoretsky, Dr. Shabtai Gairon, and Mrs. Bilha Gus of the Institute of Advanced Studies at the Hebrew University of Jerusalem were most cordial and cooperative during our stay as Fellows of the Institute.

The vital task of typing and revising a long and often-vexing manuscript was ably performed by Ms. Marsh, Ms. Margaret Benshoff-Holler, Ms. Veta Hartman, Ms. Patricia D. Murphy, and Mr. Bert Rashbaum. Invaluable editorial assistance was provided by Ms. Nancy Lane, Ms. Joan Bossert, Ms. Catherine Clements, and their staff at Oxford University Press. We thank them all.

Many friends and colleagues have provided information, advice, and stimulation. Professor Emmanuel Sivan was kind enough to invite us to participate in the Seminar on Contemporary Arab Ideologies at the Institute for Advanced Studies of the Hebrew University of Jerusalem in 1981–1982: both he and the other participants in the seminar, Pierre Cachia, C. Ernest Dawn, Yehoshaphat Harkabi, Charles D. Smith, and Matti Steinberg, provided valuable criticisms and helped us refine our ideas about nationalism and Egypt. We are grateful to Professor Shimon Shamir of Tel Aviv University for his advice and constructive criticisms. Martin Kramer, Jacob Landau, Thomas Mayer, the late Richard P. Mitchell, Yehoshua Porath, Yosef Sadan, Ahmad Zakariya al-Shaliq, Sasson Somekh, and Ehud Toledano were all most helpful in giving us materials, stimulation, and support. Jamil 'Arif, Husayn Fawzi, and Hafiz Mahmud were gracious and responsive informants in our interviews with them. Y. Alper, H. Kutcher, and M. Neguib Girgis provided valuable assistance in assembling and translating materials. Our thanks go to Rachel Yorman for preparing the index.

This study would have been impossible without the patience, support, and love we both received from our families. Our greatest debt by far is to them.

Contents

EGYPT, ISLAM, AND THE ARABS

Dov Ben Ami

The Revival of Egypt **by Mahmud Mukhtar**

Introduction: Nationalist Tendencies in Egypt, 1900–1914

Many of the political, socioeconomic, and intellectual developments that have generated modern crises in national identity occurred earlier in Egypt than in other regions of the Islamic Middle East. Politically, Egypt became progressively more independent of all but nominal Ottoman authority over the course of the nineteenth century, leading educated Egyptians to reconsider the subject of Egyptian political affiliation and allegiance. In the socioeconomic sphere, the transformation of Egyptian economic relationships and social structures resulting from Egypt's integration into the modern world economy eroded older, more localized focuses of identity and loyalty. The eventual development of a new Westernized elite influenced by contemporary European ideas concomitantly provided alternative concepts of community to those being dissolved by time and change.

The result of those changes was to make the question of collective identity problematic for educated Egyptians. To a degree apparently unparalleled in the past, Egyptians began to rethink the nature and the boundaries of their community; in brief, of their nation. There was no clear-cut answer to this new dilemma of identity. As was the case in Arab society as a whole, three alternative focuses of loyalty vied for preeminence among Egyptians in the "liberal age" of the late nineteenth and early twentieth centuries.

> First in order of time there was "religious" nationalism: the assertion that all who adhered to the same religion should form a single political community.
>
> The second type of nationalism was that which was most familiar in the old and settled countries of Western Europe: territorial patriotism, a sense of community with all who shared the same defined piece of land, rooted in love for that land itself.
>
> The third . . . of the three kinds of nationalism was ethnic or linguistic, based on the idea that all who spoke the same language constituted a single nation and should form one independent political unit.[1]

The first significant speculation over the issue of national identity in modern Egypt occurred in the late nineteenth and early twentieth centuries. It was only in the 1860s and 1870s that a new Egyptian elite was emerging in sizable numbers and had been sufficiently influenced by recent changes in Egyptian politics and society to be inspired to reconsider the nature of its political community. The impetus for such reconsideration was greatly reinforced by the economic and political crisis of the late 1870s and early 1880s, when several groups of native Egyptians coalesced into a political movement challenging the position of the Khedival dynasty, the established Ottoman ruling elite, and European finance capitalism in Egypt. The defeat of that movement and the British Occupation of the country in 1882 at first stifled public nationalist discussion. The issue of Egyptian national loyalties surfaced again and became a matter of considerable attention only in the early years of the twentieth century, when political conditions inside and outside Egypt (internally, rising anti-British sentiment and the creation of formal political parties as a vehicle of political expression; externally, the 1908 constitutional revolution in the Ottoman Empire, several international crises threatening the Empire, and the emergence of a visible Arab nationalist current in Western Asia) provided the setting and the occasion for educated Egyptians to debate the question of their political allegiances.

We turn now particularly to the years from 1900 to 1914, when discussion of the respective merits of an external Ottoman-Islamic, a local Egyptian, and a regional Arab nationalist orientation for Egypt became for the first time a major issue for the educated Egyptian public.

The Ottoman-Islamic Orientation

The nature of the traditional "Islamic" identity of Muslims is not as straightforward an issue as it sometimes is assumed to be. For all the theoretical unity of Islam, historic Islam (that is, Islam as practiced by Muslims over time) has been a very broad and diverse phenomenon. Lacking both a centralized structure and a uniform body of dogma and ritual, Muslim society has long been composed of a multiplicity of local groups (villages, tribes, quarters), legal/educational schools, occupational guilds, mystical hierarchies, and regional polities, all overlapping and coexisting with each other. Through the course of Muslim history, Muslims have given their loyalty to various of these structures. While some sort of identification with Islam in general may be presumed at least for the elite, it is the individual's local group, school of law, guild, brotherhood, or regional power network that often seems to have been the most meaningful unit of affiliation and allegiance for both the elite and the masses. In political terms, substatal institutions frequently seem to have attracted the loyalty of Muslims more than did the remote and often oppressive state that might be formally sovereign over a given geographic area.[2]

In the nineteenth century, however, the relative insignificance of the traditional Muslim state vis-à-vis other Muslim institutions as a focus of Islamic identity was reversed. From one side, nonstatal organizations lost much of their vitality under the impact of modern change. The village was deprived of many of its functions as well as its communal solidarity, the religious educational system forfeited its monopoly over learning, the law schools gave up much of their control over daily life, and the brotherhoods beginning to atrophy—all losing a good part of their intellectual appeal to the best and the brightest in the face of rival and apparently more dynamic alternatives. From the other side, the state gradually increased its power and its appeal, extending its authority into spheres of life it had previously left untouched and benefiting from the dissemination of Western political concepts that emphasized the centrality of the state as the focus of identity and loyalty in the modern world.

In most of the Middle East throughout the nineteenth century, the state meant the Ottoman Empire. Although its real power had faded greatly through the seventeenth and eighteenth centuries, in the nineteenth the Empire definitely increased its authority and consequently its meaningfulness for the populations remaining under its dominion. From the late nineteenth century the Ottoman government itself gave increasing attention to the Islamic dimension of its sovereignty, asserting the claim of its Sultan to be regarded as the traditional leader or Caliph of the entire Muslim community and promoting the necessity for Muslims everywhere to rally around the Ottoman Sultan/Caliph in collective self-defense against the European menace threatening to engulf the whole Muslim world.[3] In part because of its "ardent undividedness," which made it appear an authentic, uncompromising opponent of Western imperialism, this new "pan-Islamic" ideology and appeal on the part of the Ottoman Empire met with a considerable response by Muslims both within and outside the Middle East.[4] In much of the Islamic world by the beginning of the twentieth century, identity as a Muslim had come to mean political solidarity with the Ottoman Empire and manifested itself in declarations of allegiance to its Sultan/Caliph, acceptance of its theoretical authority as an alternative to final subjection by Europe, and support for it in the international crises in which it was involved.

Egyptian intellectual speculation and political activism during the first period when nationalist sentiment was allowed to manifest itself freely in Egypt—that is, during the literary efflorescence and nationalist ferment of the 1870s and early 1880s—was marked by a mixture of attitudes toward the Ottoman Empire. On the intellectual level, loyalty to the Ottoman state already seems to have been overshadowed by the expression of locally oriented Egyptian territorial patriotism. The writings of the most important Egyptian thinker of this period, Rifa'a Rafi' al-Tahtawi, contain both traditional Muslim views of the community of believers in Islam and the newer notion of the existence of an Egyptian nation defined by territory and transcending religion. But it was the latter referent that received the greatest emphasis from Tahtawi, the land of Egypt being the object of his concern and the primary focus of his allegiance.[5] In the political realm, however, the 'Urabi movement of the early 1880s was more Ottomanist. While occasionally expressing resentment against both "Circassians" and "Turks" and the effects of their long domination over Egypt, the leaders of the 'Urabi movement repeatedly expressed their loyalty to the Ottoman Sultan, "the Sultan of the Islamic Milla," emphasized their desire to see "Islamic-Ottoman Egypt" continue under formal Ottoman sovereignty, and declared their struggle as being one of maintaining Islamic unity in the face of the threat of European domination.[6] Perhaps more significantly, popular sentiment during the heady days of nationalist activism in 1881–1882 seems to have been strongly Islamic in inclination, with 'Urabist journals calling for Egyptian solidarity with the Ottoman Sultan/Caliph, the Muslim religious leadership of Egypt doing the same and eventually putting the anti-British struggle in the context of Muslim Holy War, and popular sentiment dubbing the 'Urabist forces "the party of God" [*hizb Allah*].[7]

The political circumstances of Egypt after the defeat of the 'Urabi movement and the British Occupation of Egypt in 1882 reinforced an Ottoman orientation for many Egyptians. Although it may be too strong to maintain that "the British Occupation of Egypt in 1882 was the direct cause of the appearance of the summons to Islamic unity" in Egypt,[8] nevertheless that Occupation imbued the Ottoman connection with both a nostalgic sheen and a perceived utility that it had not previously possessed. Loyalty to the Ottoman Sultan/Caliph was one of the few possible avenues of resistance to British domination; at the same time, the diplomatic support of the independent Ottoman state was seen as a potential lever to be used against the British presence in the Nile Valley.[9] Post-1882 Egyptian pro-Ottomanism was thus the product of two powerful impulses: religious allegiance to the Islamic community on the one hand, and the liberation of Egypt from European imperialism on the other. Generated by dual imperatives and consequently of appeal, although for different reasons, to Egyptians who defined their political identity in either religious or territorial terms, an orientation toward the Ottoman Empire flourished in Egypt between 1882 and 1914.

One convenient barometer of Egyptian public opinion is the poetry of the period, much of which is heavily political in content. Many of Egypt's leading poets of the 1882–1914 period wrote verses extolling the Ottoman Empire, praising its reigning Sultan 'Abd al-Hamid II, and calling on their fellow Egyptians to be loyal to both. Whether the occasion was the report of anti-Ottoman intrigue by the Arabs of Western Asia, the ferment caused by the constitutional movement within the Ottoman state after 1908, the Italian invasion of Libya in 1911, or the Balkan Wars of 1912–1913, the position taken by most of Egypt's leading poets was to defend the territorial integrity and continued existence of the Ottoman Empire as well as to call for Egyptian support for it in its travails.[10]

The fullest and most important opinions about Egyptian national identity formulated during the period of the British Occupation were the views advanced by the leaders of the political parties formed in the decade immediately preceding World War I. The concepts put forth by the chief spokesmen of two of these parties in particular—the "Nationalist Party" [*al-hizb al-watani*], founded by Mustafa Kamil, and the "Party of the Nation" [*hizb al-umma*], whose leading theoretician was Ahmad Lutfi al-Sayyid—are doubly important for an understanding of the evolution of nationalist orientations in modern Egypt. The views of these two parties as articulated by Mustafa Kamil and Ahmad Lutfi al-Sayyid were the culmination, the most elaborate and cogent expression, of Egyptian nationalist attitudes as they had evolved over the preceding decades. Moreover, the ideas of Kamil and Lutfi were enormously influential in later years; much of Egyptian nationalist thinking in the period between the revolutions of 1919 and 1952 was largely the further refinement of the basic positions first propounded by these two leaders in the years immediately preceding World War I.

Mustafa Kamil is best remembered as a passionate exponent of Egyptian territorial patriotism and a vehement opponent of the British Occupation. But he was also a steadfast advocate of Egyptian solidarity with the Ottoman Empire. In abstract terms, his speeches and writings spoke both of "the Egyptian nation" [*al-umma al-misriyya*] and "of the Islamic nation" [*al-umma al-islamiyya*].[11] He perceived no conflict in giving allegiance to both: "for every living nation there are two great obligations; the obligation towards its religion and its creed, and its obligation towards its *watan* and the land of its fathers."[12] The Ottomanist inclinations of Kamil and his fellow Watanists have been traced to two complementary sources. One was a residual, largely emotional tendency to see Egypt as an inseparable part of the Muslim community and Islamic civilization and an almost unconscious conceptualization of reality in traditional Muslim terms (despite the fact that the Watanists gave formal priority to secular concepts of national identity).[13] The other was a more contemporary and practical thrust: the tendency to view the modern world in terms of two antagonistic camps (sometimes East-West, sometimes Muslim-Christian), to perceive the former as being under assault from the latter, and to assume that Eastern/Muslim survival in the modern world demanded Eastern/Muslim solidarity.[14]

Impelled in the same direction by both "shared religion" and "shared interest," the Watanists were consistent advocates of Egyptian political collaboration with the Ottoman Empire.[15] In 1898 Kamil published a study of *The Eastern Question* in which he warned of the dangers to the Islamic community represented by European designs on Ottoman territory and called on all Muslims to give political support to the Ottoman Sultan/Caliph.[16] In the years that followed, other Watanists repeated the summons for Egyptians to be loyal to "the Sacred Caliphate," obedience to the Sultan/Caliph in one instance being made a "religious obligation" for Egyptians.[17] In 1906 Mustafa Kamil and his journal *al-Liwa'* supported the Ottoman claim to administrative rights over territory in the Sinai Peninsula (the Taba dispute), rejecting the interpretation of the British-dominated Egyptian government that the territory in question was administratively part of Egypt and maintaining the Empire's legal sovereignty over all of Egypt.[18] In the following year, the newly formed Watani Party had as part of its program the summons to Egyptians to "strive to strengthen the relations of cordiality, the bonds, and the integral connection between Egypt and the Sublime State."[19]

After his untimely death in 1908, the successors of Mustafa Kamil at the helm of the party continued and indeed intensified this political orientation toward the Ottoman Empire, welcoming the constitutional revolution of 1908 and sending a delegation to Istanbul in 1909 to scout the possibility of formal Egyptian representation in the restored Ottoman parliament. Eventually, upon the ouster of the party's chief, Muhammad Farid, and its publicist, Shaykh 'Abd al-'Aziz Jawish, from Egypt in 1911, the two Watanist leaders progressed to Constantinople, where they entered into collaboration with the Ottoman regime for the purpose of promoting clandestine opposition to the British presence in Egypt.[20]

The Ottoman orientation of Kamil and his Watanist colleagues was not unconditional, however. Kamil himself often located his advocacy of a continued Egyptian connection with the Ottomans in the potential utility of that bond for the liberation of Egypt from the British Occupation. In his own words,

> we [Egyptians] are concerned more than others with the integrity of the Ottoman Empire, because the integrity of its domains is the foundation upon which our legal rights against the action of the English is based. We must not forget that whatever we demonstrate which has to do with the support of Turkey is viewed and considered by us as part of the Egyptian cause against the English.[21]

Most important in this regard were the qualifications concerning Egyptian internal harmony and external independence with which Watanists hedged their verbal pro-Ottomanism. On one level, Mustafa Kamil refused to allow his Ottoman orientation to drift into a religiously based nationalism: his position was that both Egyptian Muslims and Egyptian Copts were "one *umma,* indeed one family," and that nothing should be allowed to disrupt their national unity in the service of the homeland to which they both belonged.[22] Nor did his pro-Ottomanism extend to his desiring the renewal of effective Ottoman political authority over Egypt: he angrily rejected the accusation of his opponents that he wished to expel the British from Egypt in order to restore direct Ottoman rule over the Nile Valley.[23] While the Watanist outlook was a pluralistic one incorporating both devotion to the Egyptian nation and allegiance to the Islamic community as represented by the Ottoman Empire, it was Egypt that came first: as Mustafa Kamil put it in 1906, "our love for Egypt takes precedence over everything else. . . . We wish Egypt to be for the Egyptians."[24]

Far different attitudes toward the Ottoman Empire were voiced by Ahmad Lutfi al-Sayyid, chief spokesman of the Umma Party and editor of its newspaper, *al-Jarida,* in the years before World War I. Lutfi unambiguously rejected the idea of a continuing Egyptian political bond with the Ottoman Empire. Perhaps the most fundamental reason for his anti-Ottomanism was his conviction that religiously based solidarity was contradictory to the territorially rooted and largely secular nationalism he so strongly espoused: "It [religious loyalty] is incompatible with the sacred Egyptian slogan, 'Egypt for Egyptians.' "[25] But beyond this, Lutfi held that interest or utility was the only proper basis of political action, and the interests of Egypt as he defined them would not be served by a partially religious orientation toward the Ottoman Empire, which could divide Muslim and Copt within the country at the same time that it might set off a hostile "pan-Christian" reaction in Europe.[26] Given these perceptions of the theoretical flaws and the practical dangers of the Ottoman-Islamic orientation, Lutfi's writings are studded with criticisms of the pro-Ottoman pan-Islamic trend of the early twentieth century. The objective reality of the movement was sometimes denied, being credited only to "the brain of *The Times* correspondent in Vienna"; the concept of the entire Muslim world constituting a political unit was decried as "an imperialist principle" useful primarily for facilitating renewed Ottoman domination over other Muslim regions; and Egyptians were enjoined to "repudiate today as they have in the past, any accusation of religious bigotry, i.e., 'Pan-Islamism and fanaticism.' "[27]

In practical terms, Lutfi supported the British-backed position that asserted Egyptian control over the Taba region in Sinai in 1906; it was the pro-Ottoman agitation within Egypt over this issue that in part prompted Lutfi and his associates to undertake the publication of *al-Jarida* as "a purely Egyptian paper" that "aims at defending Egyptian rights and interests."[28] In subsequent years *al-Jarida* formally acknowledged the technical sovereignty of the Ottoman Empire over Egypt, but it generally argued against the implementation of measures such as Egyptian representation in the restored Ottoman parliament or Egyptian participation in Ottoman fundraising endeavors, which would have had the effect of linking Egypt more closely to the Ottoman regime.[29]

Lutfi's most notable opposition to the Ottoman connection came during the

Italo-Ottoman War over Libya in 1911–1912. On the theoretical level, he argued for the "absolute neutrality" of Egypt in the conflict: "the sovereignty of Turkey did not bring Egypt any advantage, nor cause it any harm," and so there was simply no point in Egyptians becoming involved in support of Ottoman causes such as the war.[30] Privately, Lutfi developed a plan for Egyptian negotiations with the British in order to attain Egyptian independence from the Ottoman Empire during the war. Discussions among Lutfi and other Egyptian leaders concerning such a scheme went as far as planning for the dispatch of a delegation ("the first *wafd*") to go to Great Britain to negotiate, before the opposition of Lord Kitchener aborted the entire project.[31]

The depth of pro-Ottoman sentiment on the popular level in prewar Egypt is very difficult to estimate, given the absence of all but the most impressionistic data about Egyptian public opinion. British officials in Egypt differed in their assessments of Egyptian attitudes toward the Ottomans. At the time of the dispute over Taba in 1906, Lord Cromer reported that, during his prolonged tenure in Egypt, he had never seen Egyptian Muslim sentiment as aroused over an issue as it was over Taba, while another official at the British Agency in Cairo warned of the possibility of an anti-British outbreak of violence because of the dispute.[32] In contrast, the Director of British Military Intelligence in Egypt asserted at the same time that "the vast majority [of Egyptians] would do all in their power to assist the Turk out of the place—religion or no religion."[33]

We need assume neither a uniform nor a totally consistent attitude toward the Ottoman Empire and its Sultan/Caliph even among Muslim Egyptians. At one end of the spectrum of opinion, members of the emerging native landed elite whose economic position and social standing were being consolidated under the British Occupation may well have shared what one of their younger spokesmen, Muhammad Husayn Haykal, later recalled as his own childhood feeling of "a dark image of the rule of the Turks," a perception that Ottoman domination had been oppressive and constricting for Egypt and Egyptians.[34] At the other extreme were those Egyptians such as the Watanist Ahmad al-Badawi who asserted the "first duty" of Egyptians to be to "hold fast to the Holy Caliphate" and who called on his countrymen to demonstrate their "support for the Commander of the Believers" in Constantinople. For such Egyptians, Ottoman sovereignty was indisputably legitimate, and continuing Egyptian allegiance to the Sublime Porte was a religious obligation.[35] Nor was it impossible to combine a negative view of the "Turks" with a sense of loyalty to the state they had created. The blend of both sentiments in one individual was captured best in an anonymous letter sent to Lord Cromer at the time of the Taba dispute in 1906:

> As men we do not love the sons of Osman; the children at the breast know their works, and that they have trodden down the Egyptians like dry weeds. But as Moslems they are our brethren; the Khalif holds the sacred places and the holy relics. Though the Khalif were as hapless as Bayazid, cruel as Murad, or mad as Ibrahim, he is the shadow of God, and every Moslem must leap up at his call as the willing servant to his master, though the wolf may devour his child while he does his master's work. The call of the Sultan is the call of the faith.[36]

On the political level, the Egyptian public demonstrated considerable support for the Ottoman Empire in regard to various diplomatic and military crises in which it was involved in the last decades of its existence. In 1892, when Egyptian and Ottoman authorities first disputed the question of Egyptian versus Ottoman administration of territory in Sinai, the Muslim journalist Shaykh 'Ali Yusuf and the Coptic editor Mikha'il 'Abd al-Sayyid both defended the Ottoman claim to control over the disputed area.[37] Similarly, during the Ottoman-Greek crisis and war of 1897, 'Ali Yusuf organized a subscription campaign in the pages of his journal *al-Mu'ayyad* to raise contributions in support of the Ottoman war effort.[38] Egyptian sympathy with the Ottoman position, which was demonstrated in the controversy over the Taba area in 1906, has already been mentioned.

The greatest surge in pro-Ottoman activity within Egypt prior to World War I occurred in relation to the Italo-Ottoman War of 1911–1912.[39] Emotional appeals for Egyptians to support their sovereign in the fighting in Libya came from spokesmen of the Watani Party as well as from many of Egypt's leading poets.[40] Sympathy for the Ottomans was paralleled by the expression of considerable anti-Italian sentiment, including calls for the commercial boycott of Italians within Egypt, the dismissal of Italian teachers from Egyptian schools, and an anti-Italian demonstration in Alexandria occasioned by the news of the (temporary) Ottoman recapture of Tripoli.[41] Committees to provide financial support and medical assistance for the Ottoman war effort emerged in Egypt, the Egyptian Red Crescent Society indeed owing its inception to the desire of Egyptians to organize medical assistance for Ottoman forces and their Arab allies, and public fundraising drives collected thousands of pounds for the purchase of supplies for the Ottoman cause.[42] Although the British authorities attempted to isolate Egypt from the conflict by prohibiting the use of Egypt as a staging area by the Ottomans or the participation of Egyptians in the fighting, nonetheless arms and supplies were smuggled to Ottoman forces from Egypt, and both an Egyptian medical mission and Egyptian military volunteers went to Libya to aid in the anti-imperialist struggle.[43] Compared to all this, Ahmad Lutfi al-Sayyid's articles calling for Egyptian neutrality in regard to the war expressed an isolated opinion quite out of tune with the rest of Egyptian public opinion, and soon prompted his colleagues in the Umma Party to pressure him into temporarily stepping down from the editorship of *al-Jarida* because of public resentment over his anti-Ottoman attitude.[44]

On the whole, it seems that an orientation toward the Ottoman Empire and the Islamic *umma* that it was felt to represent was still accepted by most politically active Egyptians in the early years of the twentieth century. It was not always produced by religiously based or pan-Islamic tendencies but often by more instrumental, Egypt-centered perceptions that an Ottoman connection would be useful in the achievement of the purely Egyptian goal of terminating the British presence in Egypt. Nor was solidarity with Egypt's Ottoman sovereign unreserved: even champions of the Ottoman bond such as Mustafa Kamil had definite limitations in terms of how far they wished to see Egypt's ties with the Ottoman Empire develop in practice. But however mixed the motives or hedged by reservations, allegiance to the Ottoman Empire was a factor capable of generating both intellectual commitment and positive action in pre-World War I Egypt. The Ottoman Empire had been part of the Egyptian universe for too long to be jettisoned even in the face of Egypt's autonomous development over the nineteenth century; after 1882, it also came to be seen as a potentially useful part of the international environment by many Egyptians.

Egyptian Territorial Nationalism

As the preceding discussion has noted, Egyptian pro-Ottomanism flourished in the period from 1882 to 1914 at least in part because of its perceived utility in regard to another nationalist orientation existing in Egypt. This was the concept of Egyptian territorial nationalism or patriotism; identification as part of a geographically distinct, historically unique Egyptian nation rooted in the Valley of the Nile. Produced both by the separate political and advanced socioeconomic development of Egypt during the nineteenth century and by the powerful example of European doctrines of territorial patriotism, a locally based, Egypt-centered sense of identity and allegiance developed in the late nineteenth and early twentieth centuries, particularly among those segments of the Egyptian elite most directly involved in Egypt's autonomous development.

The first explicit, self-conscious expressions of modern Egyptian patriotism date from the 1860s and 1870s. As has been noted, the object of the political and social speculations of the leading Egyptian thinker of that period, Rifa'a Rafi' al-Tahtawi, was clearly the land and people of Egypt conceived as a distinct unit. Emotionally, his attachment to Egypt has been described as "a warm personal feeling," a love of the land of the Nile and a pride in its glorious past that led him to compose a number of patriotic poems [*wataniyyat*] as well as to write two histories of the country.[45] Using *watan* in the sense of the French *patrie,* he repeatedly enjoined Egyptians to feel and to demonstrate "love of country" [*hubb al-watan*] for their homeland of Egypt.[46] Despite the otherwise traditionalist tenor of his political thought, Tahtawi's concept of what being born in Egypt meant had definitely secular connotations: arguing for the existence of "a natural brotherhood . . . over and above the brotherhood in religion" between all Egyptians, he maintained that regardless of their differing religious affiliations, Egyptians should collaborate together in working for the betterment of Egypt.[47] Tahtawi was perhaps the first modern Egyptian writer to view the entire civilized history of Egypt as a continuum and to formulate an embryonic theory of an Egyptian national character that extended from the ancient Egyptians to his contemporaries: "the physical constitution of the people of these times is exactly that of the peoples of times past, and their disposition is one and the same."[48] Pharaonic Egypt came in for repeated praise in his historical works, being characterized by phrases like "mother of the world" or "epitome for the rulers of great kingdoms."[49]

The nationalist attitudes of the leaders of the 'Urabi movement of the early 1880s were less exclusively Egyptianist than has sometimes been assumed. As Alexander Schölch has recently shown, the movement's famous slogan "Egypt for the Egyptians" [*misr lil-misriyyin*] meant more a native Egyptian participation and sharing in power and privilege with the established Turko-Circassian elite than the total replacement of the latter by the former, and the intellectual formulations of the movement's spokesmen demonstrate no developed concept of a secular national state limited to Egypt; rather, their sense of feeling for Egypt and its people was "embedded in, and subordinated to, the feeling of belonging to the Ottoman-Islamic league."[50]

Sentiments of Egyptian patriotism were not extinguished by the British Occupation of Egypt in 1882. If anything, they were reinforced by the deepening process of Westernization among the Egyptian elite, by the more obvious de facto separation of Egypt from the Ottoman Empire under British domination, and by the conscious promotion of locally oriented, non-Ottoman tendencies by the British authorities in the later years of the Occupation. Although the former flourished in good part in reaction to the British presence while the latter grew partially in response to British stimuli, nonetheless both the pro-Ottoman and the local Egyptian orientations appear to have increased in the period between 1882 and 1914.

Sentiments of Egyptian patriotism were expressed in their fullest form in the publications of the political movements of the immediate prewar period. With Mustafa Kamil, the concept of Egyptian patriotism reached almost mystical dimensions. The emotional quality of his Egyptian patriotism is caught in this excerpt from a speech of 1907:

> Those ignorant and bereft of understanding say that I am irresponsible in my love of it [Egypt]. How can an Egyptian be irresponsible in his love for Egypt? Indeed, however much I love it, it does not approach the degree to which its beauty, its glory, its history, and its deserving majesty enjoin for it.
>
> Oh you critics, look at it, contemplate it, acquaint yourselves with it. Read the pages of its past, and ask visitors to it from the ends of the earth: has God created any *watan* higher of station, finer of nature, more beautiful in character, more splendid in antiquities, richer in soil, clearer in sky, sweeter in water, more deserving of love and ardor than this glorious homeland?
>
> The whole world answers you with one voice: Egypt is the world's paradise, and the people which live in it and inherit it is the noblest of people if they glorify it, but guilty of the greatest of crimes against it and against themselves if they are not diligent regarding its rights and [if they] surrender its greatness to the foreigner.
>
> If I had not been born an Egyptian, I would have wished to become one.[51]

In Mustafa Kamil's presentation of the history of Egypt, the aspects that received the greatest emphasis were those which pointed to the uniqueness of the country, the unity of its population, and the majesty of its past. Kamil maintained the historical continuity of the population of Egypt, specifically denying that the bulk of Egyptians might be of external Arab descent and asserting rather that both Egypt's Muslims and Copts were "one family" descended from the ancient Egyptians.[52] A constant refrain in Kamil's writings and speeches was the role ancient Egypt had played in the world: it was Egypt that had "witnessed the birth of all [other] nations, and brought forth civilization and culture for the whole human race."[53] His prescriptions for modern Egypt flowed logically from his image of Egyptian history. A major theme in his speeches was the need for Egyptian internal unity to match the "harmony" and "concord" that he believed to have existed in the Egyptian past: thus he asserted that "Muslims and Copts are one people [*sha'b wahid*] united by [a common] patriotism, customs, manners and means of livelihood, and never will it be possible to cause a division between them."[54] Externally, just as he presented Egypt as a center of world civilization in the past, so he called for his country to play a leading role in the contemporary world. As a speech of 1902 put it:

> I have no doubt that all of you, as I do, wish Egypt to be a free country with the light of knowledge and learning spread throughout all her territories from Alexandria to the sources of the Nile; and that she become, as she once was, the cradle of moral and cultural greatness, the dispenser of civilization throughout the lands of the East.[55]

Politically, Mustafa Kamil's fervent Egyptian patriotism did not preclude a tactical Egyptian allegiance to the Ottoman Empire. But there is no question that it was his definition of himself as an Egyptian and his belief in Egypt as a unique nation that were the more vital determinants of his thought and action. On the theoretical level, he saw territorial nationalism as the most effective of all political bonds: as he put it in a speech in Alexandria in 1897, "patriotism [*al-wataniyya*] is the most noble bond for individuals, and the [most] solid basis for the establishment of powerful states and lofty kingdoms."[56] In practical terms, both his preoccupations and the blind spots in his political outlook were shaped by the Egypt-centered nature of his thought. He was obsessed with British imperialism, which directly affected Egypt, but relatively unconcerned about the parallel imperialism of France in North Africa (as he hoped to use the French as a lever against the British in Egypt) and about the consequences of Ottoman dominion in Arab Asia, where it was beginning to produce a sense of Arab separatism.[57] On the whole, the most important referent for Mustafa Kamil was clearly the land of Egypt defined in territorial terms: as Albert Hourani summarized the thrust of his thought, "it is 'Egypt,' 'my country' *(biladi)* which is the god of Kamil's worship."[58]

The first formulation of an exclusively Egyptian and thoroughly modern territorial nationalism unencumbered by residual Ottoman-Islamic overtones came from the pen of Ahmad Lutfi al-Sayyid in the years before World War I. The *umma* or nation in his view was a living organism, a natural unit produced by the inescapable human needs of the species. In one article he likened the nation to a family: just as the bond between brothers was based on the common interests, similar manners, and "identical upbringing" that they shared, so "the solidarity of two brothers in Egyptianness is based on exactly the same factors."[59] Being a natural unit, the nation has an inherent right to autonomy and liberty: "The *umma* is that civic association [*al-ijtima' al-madani*] which is a product of nature and one of its creations. It has the right to life and freedom, just as every individual possesses these natural rights."[60] Lutfi's theory did not limit membership in a nation to those born into it. In the Egyptian case, immigrants to Egypt were also to be considered Egyptians as long as they gave their loyalty to Egypt and assumed their duties toward the country: "The Egyptian community [*al-jam'iyya al-Misriyya*] consists of ethnic Egyptians [*al-Misriyyin al-asliyyin*] and other new elements of foreign origin who have made Egypt their permanent residence and the theater of their activities, so that it has very quickly become the repository of their wealth and their home for the present and the future."[61]

Like other Egyptian patriots, Lutfi praised Egypt's Pharaonic heritage and role in human history. But where his presentation of the Egyptian past went well beyond that of others of his generation was in his concept of the existence of a distinct Egyptian national character. In his view all of the Egyptian past was a unified whole, with modern Egypt being the outgrowth of that past.[62] Building off this belief in the continuity of Egyptian history, he expounded the idea of a homogeneous Egyptian people possessing their own unique characteristics:

> No one has any doubt that we are a nation distinct from any other by virtue of qualities peculiar to us, and which possibly no other nation shares with us. We have our own peculiar color, our own peculiar tastes, and a single, universal language. And we possess a religion which most of us share, ways of performing our activities, and a blood which is virtually one flowing in our veins, while our fatherland has clearly defined natural boundaries which separate us from everyone else.[63]

Much of Lutfi's journalistic output in the prewar period was an insightful delineation of that Egyptian national character as it was reflected in the songs, sayings, and speech of the people of Egypt. Consistent with his belief in a specific and distinct Egyptian character, he advocated the "Egyptianization" of various aspects of Egyptian life: of Arabic through the blending of the classical language with the colloquial dialect of Egypt, and of education through making Arabic the language of instruction in those schools where English had displaced it. Lutfi even advocated "Egyptianizing contemporary Western civilization" in Egypt by giving it "a truly Egyptian cast" that would be more suitable to the Egyptian mentality.[64]

Lutfi's political positions were thoroughly congruent with his theoretical presentation of Egypt as a distinct and unified nation. Within Egypt, he was a firm advocate of the political unity of Egypt's different religious communities in one nation as well as of the complete separation of religion from politics. When Muslim-Coptic tension began to surface in Egypt in the years preceding the war, Lutfi argued that the two major religious groups within the country "comprise the body of a single nation;"[65] to his fellow Muslims, he counseled the necessity of avoiding religiously based politics and the obligation of "the Muslim majority to extend the hand of tolerance and solidarity to their brethren."[66] Externally, Lutfi repeatedly maintained that the supreme loyalty of all Egyptians should be given to Egypt. He specifically rejected any dual loyalties for Egyptians: "we absolutely reject any attachment to any other homeland but Egypt, whatever our origin—Hijazi, Nubian, Turkish, Circassian, Syrian, or Greek."[67] The rhetorical question he posed at the conclusion of an article distinguishing between the Egyptian and Ottoman national personalities clearly indicated the exclusive nature of his Egyptian territorial nationalism: "When will we be content that we are Egyptians before anything else?"[68]

For all the theoretical consistency and the humane spirit demonstrated in the nationalist writings of Ahmad Lutfi al-Sayyid, it is doubtful if more than a handful of his Egyptian contemporaries of the early twentieth century accepted the exclusively Egyptian nationalist orientation found in them. Undoubtedly, much of the educated elite of Egypt had an Egyptian territorial orientation as *one* component of their nationalist outlook: as we have seen, allegiance to the land and people of Egypt was certainly shared by the leading rival of Lutfi and his Umma Party, Mustafa Kamil and his Watanist followers. But Lutfi's insistence on Egypt as the *sole* focus of the political loyalty of Egyptians was, as indicated in our discussion of pro-Ottoman sentiment in prewar Egypt, rejected by the Watanists, by other leading political voices in Egypt, and apparently by much of the educated public of Egypt. The importance of Lutfi's ideas about Egypt lies not in their immediate impact upon his contemporaries, which was minimal, but in their influence upon later generations of Egyptians. When the prewar constellation of political circumstances was irreversibly shattered by events during and after World War I, an atmosphere more conducive to the dissemination of concepts of territorial nationalism was created. Correspondingly, it was Lutfi's brand of Egypt-centered, exclusively territorial nationalism that became dominant among much of the Egyptian elite under the new Egyptian parliamentary monarchy in the 1920s and 1930s. The eventual impact of Ahmad Lutfi al-Sayyid upon Egyptian nationalist thought is indicated well by the sobriquet applied to him in post-World War I Egypt: *ustadh al-jil,* "teacher of the generation."

Egypt and Early Arab Nationalism

Of the three nationalist orientations—Ottoman-Islamic, local Egyptian, or Arab—that vied for the allegiance of Egyptians in the "liberal age," the third was by far the weakest in the period prior to World War I. Educated Egyptians could not totally neglect the Arab dimensions of their culture and history, of course. Arabic had been the language of most Egyptians for a millenium, and Egyptian writers were leaders in the literary "revival" [*nahda*] of Arabic as well as in the periodic debates over the possible alteration of its structure and its script which occurred in the late nineteenth and early twentieth centuries.[69] But in *national* terms—that is, with reference to Egypt defined as a distinct community and the political behavior that flowed from that self-definition—educated Egyptians overwhelmingly divorced themselves from both the neighboring Arab world and the nascent Arab nationalist movement in the years preceding World War I.

Establishing the degree to which educated Egyptians identified themselves as "Arab" in the late nineteenth and early twentieth centuries is problematic. To be sure, occasional allusions to an Arab affiliation for Egypt and its people can be found in the writings and speeches of prominent Egyptians of the period. Such references need to be viewed with caution, however: as will be demonstrated shortly, some of those who used such phrases also manifested a considerable sense of hostility toward their Fertile Crescent Arab "brothers" who were resident in Egypt. Particularly in the poetry of the pre-1914 period, such references to the Arabs appear to have been little more than literary conventions demanded by the aggressively classicist tenor of the *nahda* in its earliest phases.[70]

Most relevant in this context is the sense of distinctiveness, of superiority, and sometimes of hostility expressed by native Egyptians toward other Arabs in the late nineteenth and early twentieth centuries. This sense in part produced by specific Egyptian conditions of the period. Immigrants from other Arab lands, many from non-Muslim minorities, who came to Egypt in the nineteenth century were generally well-educated and ambitious. As such, many of them prospered and became prominent in their new homeland; in commerce, in the British-influenced bureaucracy, and in the cultural and publishing fields, non-Egyptian Arabs over time assumed a place of importance disproportionate to their numbers within the population at large. In addition to providing unwanted competition for native Egyptians in these fields, the Syro-Lebanese immigrants to Egypt were often pro-British as well, serving the Occupation in the bureaucracy and publicly supporting it as beneficial for Egypt.

Not suprisingly, all this eventually kindled considerable native Egyptian resentment against the Syro-Lebanese community in Egypt. As early as 1890 the Egyptian government attempted to prohibit the employment of "Syrians" in the Egyptian bureaucracy, only to be prevented from doing so by the British, who arranged a compromise whereby those resident in Egypt for at least fifteen years would be allowed to enter government service.[71] 'Abd Allah al-Nadim may have referred to Egypt and Syria as "twins," but in the early 1890s he also attacked the Syrians in Egypt as "intruders" [*dukhala'*] who exploited Egypt economically and who supported the British Occupation.[72] From time to time Muhammad 'Abduh was heard to complain of the domination of Egypt by "Europeans and Syrians, strangers from every land," and to object that his friend Lord Cromer was being "led by the nose by certain Syrians."[73] From more conservative Muslim circles came attacks on the purported anti-Islamic views of the predominantly Christian Syrians, such as those directed at the historian and novelist Jurji Zaydan, which questioned his credentials as an interpreter of Arab-Muslim history and which prevented his appointment as an instructor at the Egyptian University.[74] Mustafa Kamil called for the acceptance of Arab and other migrants to Egypt within the Egyptian nation as long as they were loyal to Egypt, but he is also on record as having referred to the Syrian Arabs as "intruders" in Egypt as well as "traitors" [*khawana*] to the Ottoman Empire, and also of accusing them of having repaid Egypt's hospitality with "ingratitude and hate."[75] Even that most liberal and tolerant of Egyptian nationalists, Ahmad Lutfi al-Sayyid, whose theoretical position was to advocate the fusion of all residents in Egypt in one Egyptian nation, nonetheless occasionally expressed resentment against the position of the Syrian Arab community in Egypt.[76]

If such were the feelings of educated Egyptians toward the equally cultured Arab immigrants to Egypt from the Fertile Crescent with whom they shared the same language and life style, what can we anticipate concerning their view of more traditional Arabs such as the nomadic Bedouin? Here the prevailing attitude seems to have been one of aloofness, superiority, and often outright contempt. Two British observers as different in their views of Egyptians as Lord Cromer and Wilfred Scawen Blunt at least concurred concerning "the dislike entertained by the dwellers in the Valley of the Nile to those of the desert" and that "no love was ever yet lost between Bedouin and Fellah."[77] An Egyptian proverb cited by Cromer makes an illustrative comparison between Egyptian attitudes toward Ottoman Turks and Arab Bedouins: "Better the tyranny of the Turk than the justice of the Bedouins."[78] The Watanist *al-Liwa',* justifying construction of a railway in the Hijaz because of the difficulties produced for pilgrims by "the savagery of the Bedouin" of Arabia, genuinely reflected the suspicion harbored by sedentary Egyptians for Arab nomads.[79] Perhaps the most graphic statement of the sense of superiority felt by educated Egyptians toward Arabs generally was the attitude reported of visitors to the famous salon of Princess Nazli by Sir Ronald Storrs: "Indeed, I heard more than once on the lips of her ministerial visitors the expression (anomalous in the greatest Arabic-speaking country) of *Pis Arabler,* 'Dirty Arabs.' "[80]

In terms of the political identity and allegiance of educated Egyptians, it was Egyptian territorial nationalism and/or an Ottoman-Islamic orientation that monopolized Egyptian loyalties prior to World War I. Through the entire nineteenth century, there had been little occasion for any Egyptian political identification with the neighboring Arab regions. With an Arab nationalist movement beginning to take shape only in the last decades of the century, one known in Egypt at first only on the basis of fragmentary and ambiguous rumors, there was simply no visible Arab focus for Egyptians to sympathize with. A partial Arab nationalist orientation has sometimes been attributed to the 'Urabi movement on the basis of the occasional use of the terms "Arab" or even "Arabism" [*al-'uruba*] by its publicists and its leaders' attempts to establish contacts with Arabs elsewhere.[81] The characterization seems erroneous, however: its origins may go back to the Khedive Tawfiq's efforts to discredit the movement with the Ottoman authorities by branding it as an Arab separatist movement in association with anti-Ottoman currents of discontent in the Fertile Crescent in the early 1880s, and its validity is contradicted by other references in which leaders of the movement explicitly denied any intention to create a new Arab political unit.[82]

After 1882, the difference between British imperialism in the Nile Valley and continuing Ottoman rule in Arab Asia presented the peoples of the two regions with fundamentally different political problems. Even in the years immediately prior to World War I, when Arab nationalism finally did emerge as an organized force in the Fertile Crescent provinces of the Empire, any Egyptian tendency to become associated with it was greatly diminished by that movement's own exclusion of Egypt from its purview. An Egyptian connection with the early Arab nationalist movement was hardly promoted when the chairman of the Arab Congress meeting in Paris in 1913 denied an Egyptian who was present the right to address the assembly or when he later declared that the Congress was restricted to Arabs from the Arab Ottoman provinces to the east of Egypt.[83]

There was very little sympathy expressed by notable Egyptians for the separatist, anti-Ottoman activities of Sharif Husayn of Mecca or for the aspirations of the Fertile Crescent Arab organizations seeking Arab autonomy within the Ottoman Empire in the early years of the twentieth century. Thus the occasional references to Arab political currents made by Egyptian poets were uniformly hostile to any hint of Arab separatism from the Ottomans.[84]

The leadership of two main Egyptian political parties of the prewar period, the *al-Hizb al-Watani* and the *Hizb al-Umma,* were also generally antagonistic to the emerging Arab movement. In 1898 Mustafa Kamil's *The Eastern Question* attacked the idea of an Arab Caliphate as a British-inspired scheme for sowing dissension in the Ottoman Empire, and his antipathy to Arab separatist tendencies if anything increased as he came to give greater emphasis to the Ottoman bond as a potential counterweight to the British presence in Egypt.[85] Mustafa Kamil's successors at the helm of the Nationalist Party were definitely opposed to Arab separatist trends when these appeared more openly in the years after 1908. The party's publicist, Shaykh 'Abd al-'Aziz Jawish, throughout his career a vehement advocate of Muslim solidarity and political collaboration, wrote articles attacking Arab political activities that were critical of the Ottomans and called on Arabs to remain loyal to their Sultan/Caliph.[86] In 1911 the party's leader, Muhammad Farid, wrote an unflattering account of the new Arab nationalist movement, attributing the desire for Arab autonomy in the Fertile Crescent in part to the ambitions of the local Arab elite to gain greater access to government office, in part to British machinations aimed at weakening the Empire "so that they can set up an Arab Caliphate in its stead which they would place in the hands of slaves of greed and avarice, [thus] making their rule over the Islamic world complete."[87]

The most significant action by Nationalist Party leaders concerning the prewar Arab nationalist movement was an explicit rejection by the Party's Administrative Council of the suggestion made by the pro-Arab activist 'Aziz 'Ali al-Misri that the Party support Arab aspirations for autonomy within the Ottoman Empire: according to Muhammad Farid's diary, the Council discussed the suggestion at length, but eventually "we refused to cooperate [with Misri] in his work, after we explained to him the disadvantages of dividing the two races within the state."[88]

Lutfi al-Sayyid, the leading spokesman of the Umma Party, was equally unsympathetic toward prewar Arab nationalist currents. In 1911, an article in his *al-Jarida* addressed "The Arab Question." While admitting that the Arabs were underrepresented in the Ottoman Parliament, Lutfi viewed current Arab-Turkish political tensions as an internal Ottoman matter that should be amicably resolved. His disinterested advice on the subject was that, rather than forming parties and undertaking anti-Ottoman agitation, the Arabs should study the Ottoman Constitution and attempt to rectify their grievances within the Ottoman framework.[89] In the same year, when two Syrian notables came to Egypt to promote (in Lutfi's words) "the annexation of Syria to Egypt," Lutfi was opposed to the idea, characteristically because "I did not see it as being in the interest of Egypt."[90] Lutfi continued to oppose Egyptian involvement in Arab affairs up to World War I, in 1912 terming both pan-Islam and "Arab unity" [*al-ittihad al-'arabi*] as being "delusions and fancies," and in 1913 asking the rhetorical question: "Is not an Egyptian who asserts his affiliation with Arabdom or Turkdom proving that he despises his fatherland and his people?"[91] Thus the two leading political trends in prewar Egypt were in substantial agreement in seeing Egypt as uninvolved in the early phases of the Arab nationalist movement as well as in demonstrating an appreciable reserve about the value of that movement as a whole.

There are only two prominent Egyptian political figures for whom a significant involvement in early Arab nationalism has been demonstrated. The first of these was the Khedive of Egypt from 1892 to 1914, 'Abbas Hilmi II, who promoted an Arab Caliphate presumably to be headed by himself. The notion of an "Arab" Caliphate vested in the (originally non-Arab) Egyptian ruling family appears to go back to the days of the Khedive Isma'il: in the turmoil of the late 1870s, Isma'il is reported to have encouraged publications challenging the Ottoman title to the office suggesting the creation of an alternative Caliphate situated in the Arab world.[92] Apparently forgotten in Egypt during the reign of the compliant Khedive Tawfiq, the idea reappeared after 'Abbas Hilmi's accession in 1892. 'Abbas's agents were reported to have been actively promoting the concept of an Arab Caliphate in the Fertile Crescent, the Arabian Peninsula, and even in East Africa in the late 1890s.[93]

The Khedive's Arab intrigues accelerated after 1900. Within Egypt, his spokesman Shaykh 'Ali Yusuf of *al-Mu'ayyad,* who in the 1890s had belittled rumors of any association between the Khedive and an Arab Caliphate, changed his tune by the early 1900s. In several articles between 1907 and 1909 he championed Arab autonomy against measures of Ottoman centralization and promoted Egypt's suitability as the site of a new Arab Caliphate.[94] Khedival agents were in contact with Arab nationalist organizations in greater Syria in the years immediately preceding World War I, propagandizing in favor of an Arab Caliphate and/or an Arab state headed by the Egyptian Khedive.[95]

Thus there is no doubt that ʻAbbas Hilmi II was involved in the early encouragement of Arab separatist trends in the two decades preceding World War I. But his was an involvement of a particular type. ʻAbbas's maneuvers among the Arabs stemmed from personal/dynastic rather than from ideological imperatives. They were aimed at furthering his own political prestige and authority as well as providing him with a useful counter in his involved relations of formal dependence upon the Ottoman Sultan, rather than at furthering Arab autonomy or separatism for its own sake. His lack of real commitment to Arab aspirations appears most clearly in the especially devious role he played in regard to the Italo-Ottoman War in Libya in 1911–1912. While publicly supporting the Ottoman cause, he was rumored secretly to be acting in collusion with the Italians in exchange for financial considerations within Egypt, both serving as a conduit for Italian bribery of Arab tribal contingents and attempting to encourage Ottoman/Arab capitulation to Italian forces.[96] In sum, ʻAbbas Hilmi was certainly involved in Arab politics and the inception of Arab nationalism before 1914, but it was hardly then a nationalist involvement.

The involvement of the other prominent Egyptian associated with pre-1914 Arab nationalism, ʻAziz ʻAli al-Misri, was of a more committed nature. Of Circassian ancestry but born in Egypt, Misri was an Ottoman army officer who served with distinction in the Yemen and in the Libyan war. Possibly one of the founders of the first Arab secret society of the Young Turk period, *al-Qahtaniyya,* he became active in the years immediately prior to World War I in the establishment of a secret society of Arab army officers, *al-ʻAhd.* Early in 1914 he was arrested by the Ottoman authorities, tried in secret for his involvement in Arab political agitation, and sentenced to death, but eventually released through the intervention of the British.[97] Although Misri was regarded by later generations of Arab nationalists as one of the heroes of early Arab nationalism, recent research has shown that Misri's ideas and activities were not as thoroughly Arabist as the nationalist myth assumes. It is possible that he was one of the promoters of ʻAbbas Hilmi's Egypt-centered Caliphal schemes for Khedival aggrandizement in Arab Asia, and Misri's own concepts of the Arab future envisaged Arab autonomy under the protective umbrella of Ottoman sovereignty rather than aiming for full Arab independence from the Sublime Porte.[98] Most importantly for our purposes, his active participation in the emerging Arab nationalist movement was virtually sui generis for an Egyptian in the pre-1914 period. While he became a popular figure in Egypt, he was known for his military role as an Ottoman "hero of Cyrenaica" rather than for his Arab-oriented political activities, and his attempt to involve the Nationalist Party in supporting the Arab cause was, as we have already noted, rejected by that organization.

Apart from the activities of ʻAbbas Hilmi and ʻAziz ʻAli al-Misri, there is only incidental and largely inconsequential mention of Egyptians involved in Arab political affairs before World War I. In Constantinople exiled Egyptian leaders were in contact with Arab nationalist groups, but as counselors and sometimes as critics of their political activities, not as full participants in Arab maneuvers toward autonomy and/or separatism.[99] Perhaps the most conclusive indication of the degree of Egyptian isolation from early Arab nationalism comes from a numerical compilation of individuals cited in the major histories of Arab nationalism as having been involved in Arab political organizations before 1914: of the 126 persons whom Professor C. Ernest Dawn was able to identify as participants in Arab nationalist or proto-nationalist groups up to 1914, only one (presumably 'Aziz 'Ali al-Misri) was Egyptian by origin.[100]

Thus, on the eve of World War I, two major nationalist orientations were being expressed by educated Egyptians. One was an Egyptian-Ottoman orientation that blended local Egyptian patriotism with a wider Ottoman allegiance. Possibly because it combined the sentiment of a quasi-traditional loyalty to the Islamic *umma* with a more recently elaborated concept of allegiance to the Egyptian *watan,* this appears to have been the most widely accepted nationalist orientation among educated Egyptians in the early years of the twentieth century. The other nationalist orientation was characterized by a more exclusive Egyptian territorial patriotism that viewed Egypt as a distinct entity and advocated its autonomous development. Although it appears to have been restricted to a small minority of even the educated elite of Egypt before World War I, this orientation was the embryo of the nationalist outlook that was to become prevalent after the war and the transformations it brought to the Middle East.

In contrast to their espousal of Egyptian Ottomanism or Egyptian territorial nationalism, Egyptians neither shared nor helped to shape the sense of Arab nationalism that was beginning to develop in the early years of the century. The emergence of Arabism in Egypt had to await both the collapse of the Ottoman orientation that was its direct competitor for Arab loyalties and the erosion of the Egyptian territorial nationalism that at first preempted Egyptian allegiance to Arabism after the elimination of Ottomanism.

I

THE SHAPING OF A "NEW EGYPT": WORLD WAR AND NATIONAL REVOLUTION, 1914–1926

1

Egyptians, Ottomans, and Arabs during World War I

World War I confronted Egyptians with major questions relating to nationalism. The wartime circumstances of the replacement of Ottoman by British sovereignty, the state of war between their old and new masters, and later the emergence of an active nationalist movement among their Arab neighbors to the East all combined to present Egyptians with new national relationships and possibilities. The manner in which Egyptians responded to these new conditions and options sheds considerable light on how Egyptian nationalist conceptions had developed by the second decade of the twentieth century.

Egyptian Pro-Ottomanism during World War I

The available evidence indicates that, at the start of the war in particular, Egyptian opinion favored the cause of the Central Powers and the Ottoman Empire against that of the British and their Allies. Recollections of an initial Egyptian sympathy for the Germans and Ottomans can be found in the memoirs both of Egyptians and of British officials conversant with Egyptian affairs. Significantly, that there was an inclination toward the Ottoman and German war effort is reported both by those Egyptians who shared the sentiment, such as Muhammad Farid or ʻAbd al-Rahman ʻAzzam, and by those who did not, such as Salama Musa or Muhammad Husayn Haykal.[1]

This attitude was the product of various factors. Part of it undoubtedly lay in Egyptian perceptions of the past record and present capabilities of the leading Central Power, Imperial Germany. Prior to the war Germany had acquired, with Egyptians as with others, a reputation both for military efficiency and for sympathy to Muslim causes in general and the Ottoman Sultan/Caliph in particular.[2] Perhaps most important in operative terms were the early military victories of German arms on both the Western and Eastern fronts, which led Egyptians to anticipate the inevitable victory of the Central Powers over the Allies.[3] The belief in German military prowess led to such phenomena as a staunchly anti-British member of the Watani Party, Mustafa al-Nahhas, apparently being so convinced of the prospect of German-Ottoman military success in their attack on the Suez Canal that he had to be taken on a tour of Canal defenses by the local British official in order to convince him that the attack had been repulsed.[4]

A more fundamental motive was primarily religious in nature: the allegiance given by Muslim Egyptians to the Ottoman Empire and its Sultan/Caliph. The power of the religious bond is testified to by both the British and Egyptians. British evaluations throughout the war accepted as given "the well-known sympathy of the masses of the people to the Turkish Khalifate."[5] Despite British promptings, Egyptian religious leaders refused to issue *fatwas* critical of the Sultan/Caliph or his agent the (ex-)Khedive in the months immediately following Ottoman entry into the war.[6] While the reference to the Caliph in Friday prayers was altered from one of hoping for his "victory" to a less militant wish for his "success," in the mosques the prayer for the Caliph is reported to have been more enthusiastically received than that for the new Sultan imposed on Egypt by the British.[7] Egyptian poets continued to write, if not to publish, poetry in praise of the Ottoman Sultan/Caliph during the war years.[8] The almost unconscious coupling of the Ottomans with Islam on the popular level is seen in the slogan heard in Cairo in the early months of the war, when Egyptians anticipated the triumphant arrival of an Ottoman army symbolically led by 'Abbas Hilmi: "Allah Hayy . . . 'Abbas Jay" ("God Lives . . . 'Abbas is Coming").[9] How deep-seated was Ottoman allegiance on the part of religiously inclined Muslim Egyptians appears most clearly in the account of a wartime conversation between Sultan Husayn Kamil and members of the Egyptian religious hierarchy contained in the memoirs of Muhammad al-Ahmadi al-Zawahiri. When asked by the Sultan as to the reason for Egyptian sympathy with the Ottomans and as to whether it was "religious" or "patriotic" in nature, Zawahiri recalls his puzzlement and that of his fellow *'ulama'* at the question itself: of course there was no national connection between Egypt and "Turkey," while "from the religious angle there was a sacred bond between us and Turkey, namely that of the existence of the Caliphate in it, and that sufficed as a reason binding Egyptians to it or at least sympathizing with it."[10]

Overlapping with this religious loyalty to the Ottomans was a more narrowly Egyptian motive for desiring their victory: the expectation that Ottoman/German triumph would result in the end of the British Occupation of Egypt. Later memoirs by Egyptians couple the two factors of residual allegiance to the Ottoman Empire with the Egyptian hope for the ouster of the British as the two primary motives behind Egyptian pro-Ottomanism; thus, many Egyptians awaited Ottoman success, "some of them out of love for the state of the Caliphate, and some out of hatred for the British Occupation and in the belief that the victory of Turkey would bring nearer the day of liberation from this occupation."[11] Egyptians' admiration for German efficiency, expectation of Germany's eventual success, religious loyalty to the Ottomans, and hope of Egyptian deliverance from British domination were not in conflict with each other; rather, they converged in producing a widespread sentiment of sympathy for the wartime opponents of Great Britain.

Egyptian support for the Ottoman cause appears to have run highest and to have been potentially most serious in late 1914 and early 1915, when the military course of events in Europe favored the Central Powers and when the Ottomans were known to be mounting a military expedition to attack the Suez Canal. This force received the active assistance of exiled Egyptian nationalist leaders. Even before his deposition as Khedive in December 1914, 'Abbas Hilmi issued a proclamation calling on Egyptians to welcome and assist the Ottoman expedition;[12] he also negotiated at length with the Ottoman authorities over his symbolic leadership of the force, but without success because of the mutual suspicions existing between himself and the Unionist regime.[13] The exiled Watani party leaders led by Muhammad Farid also offered their assistance to the Ottoman campaign, dispatching a delegate to accompany the expedition, and at least a few younger Egyptians then outside the country volunteered their services to the force.[14] Within Egypt there are vague reports of "an underground movement in favor of Turkey" and equally cryptic claims in later memoirs of Watani Party adherents meeting to plan a pro-Ottoman uprising that would erupt in conjunction with the Ottoman assault on the Canal; but no details of these activities are available.[15] The Ottomans themselves apparently put considerable stock in Egyptian assistance for their Egyptian campaign: the commander of the Ottoman force, Jemal Pasha, claims to have placed part of his hopes for success in an Egyptian uprising that would have been sparked by his attack on the Canal and which would have facilitated Ottoman victory over the British garrison in Egypt.[16]

Expectations of significant Egyptian internal assistance to the Ottoman war effort were never realized. Certainly part of the reason why pro-Ottoman activism did not materialize in Egypt was the security measures taken by the British authorities, which included the declaration of martial law, the expulsion of potentially pro-Ottoman foreigners from Egypt, the internment or exiling of several hundred Egyptian nationalists, and pressure on the Egyptian religious authorities to issue proclamations calling upon Egyptians to refrain from political activity and to maintain law and order.[17]

But there may also have been a more abstract element in the Egyptian passivity in regard to the Ottoman war effort in the early months of the war: Egyptian ambivalence as to the possible consequences of a successful Ottoman invasion of Egypt and whether it would only mean the replacement of one arbitrary and alien regime by another. Cynic though he was, Sir Ronald Storrs' summary of the attitude of Egyptian Muslims toward the Ottomans at the start of the war probably has some validity: " 'We wish the Turks all success—from afar,' the last portion of the benizon receiving the accent."[18] Although many Egyptians undoubtedly sympathized with the Ottoman cause in 1914, it was an abstract sympathy tempered by practical considerations.

Whatever the precise blend of reasons, no significant Egyptian assistance for the Ottoman war effort materialized in the early phases of the war. British evaluations of the Egyptian domestic scene in late 1914 emphasized that "acquiescence and tranquillity" still obtained after the outbreak of Anglo-Ottoman hostilities, that "the religious issue . . . remained dormant," and that "perfect tranquillity . . . continued to prevail" in Egypt in spite of the war and the declaration of a British Protectorate over Egypt.[19] Rather than turning on the British, the Egyptian Army units stationed along the Canal actively participated in its defense against the Ottoman assault of February 1915.[20] Behind the lines no anti-British uprising occurred in Egyptian cities, perhaps because the Egyptians planning for such activities had been waiting for Ottoman military success along the Canal before taking action in support of the Ottoman cause.[21] Additional internments and exiling of Egyptian pro-Ottoman sympathizers occurred in the wake of the repulse of the Ottoman attack along the Canal, further diminishing the prospects of pro-Ottoman activism in Egypt.[22] It was the manifest impossibility of undertaking meaningful pro-Ottoman activity within Egypt by 1915 that prompted an activist Egyptian nationalist like the young 'Abd al-Rahman 'Azzam, who in 1914 had been involved in Watanist plans for internal resistance, to flee Egypt for Libya in 1915, where he participated in the Sanusi operations in the Western Desert in 1915–1916.[23]

There is little evidence of pro-Ottoman activity within Egypt after 1915. The Ottomans and their German allies continued to dispatch agents to Egypt for the purposes of intelligence-gathering and subversion, but the apprehension of many Egyptian pro-Ottoman sympathizers by the British severely limited the possibilities of anti-British activism.[24] The second major Ottoman attack on the Suez Canal defenses, that of August 1916, was apparently unaccompanied by any expectations or any efforts to organize anti-British activity within Egypt itself. Thereafter, Egyptian hopes for liberation from the British via the agency of the Ottomans must have diminished when the fortunes of war shifted and the Allies went on the offensive into Palestine and Syria. While British reports in later years of the war continued to indicate considerable Egyptian passive sympathy with the Ottoman Empire and its Sultan/Caliph, they also emphasized that "Egypt has remained perfectly quiet and has scarce given any cause for anxiety" during World War I.[25]

The attitudes of Egyptian political leaders and groups toward the war and the combatants in it were not monolithic, of course. By 1914, an intellectual break with Ottoman/Islamic loyalties had already been achieved by the ideologues of the Umma Party, and this group demonstrated little concern for the Ottoman cause during the war. In the period between the outbreak of the European war in August and the Ottoman entry into the conflict in November, the position of the party's journal, *al-Jarida,* was that Egypt had no realistic option but to support the British in the war in view of Britain's position of dominance in the country;[26] Ahmad Lutfi al-Sayyid, the journal's editor, is also reported to have refused to allow his disciple Muhammad Husayn Haykal to express his own, more reserved attitude that Egypt should opt for a position of neutrality between the Allies and the Central Powers.[27] Privately, Lutfi approached the Egyptian Prime Minister Husayn Rushdi and the Foreign Minister 'Adli Yakan to suggest that Egypt offer to enter the war on the side of Great Britain in exchange for a British recognition of formal Egyptian independence from the Ottoman Empire. While Rushdi and Yakan were receptive to the idea, going as far as to submit the offer to the British for their consideration, the British did not respond favorably, and the idea (like the plan for formal Egyptian independence that Lutfi had offered during the Ottoman-Italian war a few years before) died.[28]

Wartime censorship from November 1914 onward presumably limited Lutfi and *al-Jarida* in what they could and could not say, but certainly the journal's public stance was supportive of the Allied cause and critical of the Ottoman one. In December 1914 *al-Jarida* wrote of the declaration of the British Protectorate over Egypt as "a great revolution" and expressed its hope that it would portend "a glowing future" for the country.[29] It presented the parallel termination of Ottoman sovereignty as not inimical to Egypt's true interest in attaining self-rule and was silent on the deposition of 'Abbas Hilmi II as Khedive while praising his replacement, Sultan Husayn Kamil.[30] When the first Ottoman expedition advanced on Egypt in early 1915, *al-Jarida* was contemptuous of the Ottoman endeavor, emphasizing the difficulties of a successful advance across the desert of Sinai and predicting the expedition's failure when it came up against the British forces entrenched along the Suez Canal.[31]

The best indication of the nature—and the limitations—of wartime Egyptian pro-Ottomanism comes from a consideration of the attitudes and activities of those Egyptian political leaders who were not under British control during the war. Considerable information is available about two such individuals: the Watani Party leader, Muhammad Farid, who was in exile from Egypt from 1911 to his death in 1919, and Khedive 'Abbas Hilmi II, who had been in Constantinople when war began, was first refused permission to return to Egypt and then deposed as Khedive by the British upon their declaration of a Protectorate over Egypt, and who spent the rest of his life in exile in Europe. Their bridges burned by the British, both Farid and 'Abbas Hilmi attempted to make common cause with the Ottomans and the Central Powers. Their mutual relations were stormy, however, marked by suspicions and cross-purposes on all sides. Insofar as the wartime dealings of the two men speak to the question of Egyptian national orientations during World War I, they testify primarily to the thoroughly unideological outlook of 'Abbas Hilmi and the only instrumentally Ottomanist position of Muhammad Farid.

'Abbas Hilmi's actions show the overwhelming concern of the ex-Khedive to have been his personal position. Although he originally cooperated with the Ottoman war effort, issuing a proclamation calling on Egyptians to assist the Ottoman forces in their liberation of Egypt from British control, by the end of 1914 his relationship with the Ottoman authorities had soured, and he left Constantinople to spend most of the war years in Central Europe.[32] From there he dealt with various parties: with the Ottomans to define the terms of his return to their territory and the resumption of his role in assisting their war effort; with the Germans to obtain their intercession on his behalf with their Ottoman allies in exchange for his aiding German propaganda efforts; with the British for a reconciliation that would at least guarantee his continued possession of his personal properties in Egypt; and with Arab political leaders in the apparent hope of carving out a domain for himself in Arab Asia to replace the one he had lost in Egypt. His contacts with the Arabs demonstrate best the personal/dynastic nature of the ex-Khedive's wartime activities: whereas in 1915–1916 he offered his services to the British to assist them in generating an anti-Ottoman revolt by the Arab state,[33] by the time he had reached a new accord with the Ottomans and returned to Constantinople in 1917 he was reported to be working to encourage anti-British sentiment among the Arabs in exchange for his being appointed Ottoman "Viceroy" in the Hijaz in place of the rebellious Sharif Husayn.[34]

There was a division of opinion concerning the relative merits of a narrower Egyptian versus a wider Ottoman/Islamic orientation on the part of Watani Party leaders in exile during World War I. A group of party leaders headed by Shaykh 'Abd al-'Aziz Jawish (originally non-Egyptian) were more Ottoman and

Muslim than Egyptian in outlook, concerning themselves with the needs of the Muslim community as a whole, viewing Egypt as a subordinate part of the Ottoman state, and being unconcerned with Egypt's longstanding position of autonomy within the Empire.[35] Muhammad Farid and those around him, in contrast, emphasized Egyptian rights and needs over those of her titular suzerain. Farid himself was most distrustful of the intentions of the Young Turk regime concerning Egypt, fearing the restoration of "despotic" Ottoman rule over Egypt and that the Young Turks wished to "eat Egypt."[36] He demonstrated a typically Egyptianist sense of superiority to the Ottoman "Turks," maintaining that "we are much more advanced than they" and asserting that Egyptians would not accept the reimposition of any form of autocratic Ottoman rule.[37] To prevent this from occurring, in his wartime dealings with the Ottoman government Farid persistently attempted to obtain guarantees of internal Egyptian autonomy in exchange for his collaboration with the Ottoman war effort.[38] He also exhibited a willingness to negotiate with the British toward the same end. The best indication of the instrumentally Ottomanist orientation of Muhammad Farid is that, as the prospect of Ottoman victory in the war faded, Farid began to think in terms of the necessity of a rapprochement with the British as long as they would recognize Egyptian internal autonomy and establish a representative regime in the country. By August 1916, although admitting "despair" over the failure of the second Ottoman invasion of Egypt, Farid and his colleagues nonetheless "all began to think that the best path is to reach agreement with them [the British] for granting Egypt a constitution."[39] Thus the core concern of the Watani Party leader was what would happen to his country as a result of the war, rather than with the fate of the Ottoman Empire or its Sultan/Caliph.

Egypt and the Arab Revolt, 1916–1918

Toward the middle of the war, the outbreak of the anti-Ottoman, pro-Allied Arab Revolt in Western Asia added a new element to the nationalist configurations visible in the Middle East. To be sure, the Arab Revolt and the national movement it represented were not of direct relevance for Egypt: Egypt had been excluded from the proposed boundaries of the independent Arab state envisaged by the Sharif Husayn of Mecca in his negotiations with the British prior to the uprising, and neither he nor other leaders of the emerging Arab movement included Egypt in their political desiderata in the movement's few heady years of growth and apparent success from 1917 to 1919. But the challenge posed by the Revolt to the Ottoman Empire and to its politico-religious leadership presented Egyptians with new questions concerning both their Ottoman suzerain and their Arab neighbors.

A report by Sir Ronald Storrs devoted specifically to the initial Egyptian reaction to the news of the Arab Revolt emphasized Egyptian surprise at the phenomenon and the inability of much of Egyptian opinion to absorb an Arab uprising against the Muslim Ottoman Empire into their worldview. Rumors denying the veracity of the announcement of the revolt or minimizing it as merely a maneuver by the Sharif of Mecca to extract financial benefits from the British apparently circulated in intellectual circles, while the popular reaction was described by Storrs simply as one of "incredulity" at the thought of Arab revolt against the Ottomans.[40] A considerable Egyptian skepticism about the likely significance of the uprising was reported by Storrs, with some Egyptians portraying it as only the latest phase in the chronic tribal instability found in the Arabian Peninsula. Nationalist elements in Egypt were reported to be definitely hostile to the Revolt's leader, characterizing Sharif Husayn as "a rebel against the Khalif, and a servile instrument of the English,"[41] an image of the Sharif that was to be repeated frequently by Egyptians in later years. A second evaluation of the early Egyptian reaction to the Revolt written by Storrs a few days later questionably claimed more support for the Revolt than he had originally perceived, stating that "a considerable portion of the Egyptian people is in sympathy with the movement."[42] But this report also emphasized the confusion of Egyptian opinion at the news of the revolt, concluding with the prediction that "the great mass of the populace has adopted a waiting attitude."[43]

A mixture of uncertainty tinged with uneasiness is visible in early Egyptian press commentary on the Arab Revolt. By far the main emphasis in initial Egyptian press reporting on the Arab Revolt was in justifying the Arab resort to revolt to the Egyptian public. This was done largely by expounding on the previous evils and inequities of the incumbent Ottoman government. Thus the "Unionist" (Young Turk) leadership was repeatedly denounced for various policies and actions attributed to it before and during the war: for its political repression of Arab nationalist sentiment in the Fertile Crescent; for its Turkish nationalist orientation and its alleged attempt to Turkify the peoples of the Empire; for its recent executions of Arab leaders in Syria and Lebanon; and in particular for its purported antipathy to Islam.[44] The theme of the irreligious and anti-Islamic character of the Young Turk regime was raised in most major articles dealing with the Arab Revolt in mid-1916. The Unionists were accused of attempting to "change the Islamic faith from its original course," which had been "on the basis of Arab nationality";[45] Ottoman Turkish custody of the Islamic Holy Places was rejected in favor of that of the Arabs;[46] and the authority of Muslim leaders and *'ulama'* in Egypt and elsewhere was cited as favorable to the Arab Revolt.[47] Given these various oppressions of the Young Turks, Arab rebellion was thus justified as being the product of recent Ottoman policies of "destruction, division, and expulsion" (the last a reference to the Armenian tragedy) or as "a natural result of the evil of Turkish rule and more specifically of the corruption of the principles of the Unionists, their tyranny, their oppression, and their desire to kill the Arab spirit and to Turkify the Arabs."[48] Thus the Arab Revolt was presented as neither anti-Ottoman nor anti-Islamic in the true sense of either term, but merely as the inevitable and necessary outcome of the anti-Ottoman and anti-Islamic deviations of the evil regime currently in control of the Empire and the Caliphate.

On the whole, the Egyptian press gave less attention in mid-1916 to the emerging Arab movement than it devoted to the errors of the current Ottoman regime. The Arab Revolt was also less than a burning issue in the Egyptian press in 1916. It was treated as a wartime development marginal to the more momentous events occurring in Europe at the same time. While of some potential significance for the course of the war, the Arab Revolt of 1916 was originally regarded neither as a major development in the conflict nor as an event involving Egypt directly. As the British High Commissioner in July 1916 summarized early Egyptian responses to the Revolt, "on the whole news [of the Revolt] has so far been received with comparatively little interest or comment."[49]

The marginality of the Arab Revolt to Egypt and Egyptian opinion appears to have persisted for the duration of the war. When the British in late 1916 feared the imminent collapse of the Revolt, reports from their officials in Cairo estimated that such a collapse would not influence the British position in Egypt in any significant manner.[50] A lengthy report on "Egypt and the Arab Movement" in the summer of 1917 estimated that, save for some "Ottoman Arabs" in Egypt who supported the movement and those elements of "Turkish extraction" in the country which were opposed to it, "Moslem opinion in Egypt as a whole continues to be entirely apathetic to the Arab movement for independence."[51] By March 1918, a meeting of British officials in Cairo that was devoted to analyzing the current situation in the Arabian Peninsula was assuming the unpopularity of the Arab Revolt in Egypt: as High Commissioner Sir Reginald Wingate summarized Egyptian sentiment in the context of discussing a possible attempt by Sharif (now King) Husayn to assume the title of Caliph, any such gambit "would be received coldly in Egypt, where the Sharifian movement had gained little sympathy."[52]

Within a few weeks of his rising against the Ottomans, Sharif Husayn requested the British to dispatch units from the Egyptian Army to assist his disorganized tribal levees in their warfare against the Ottoman garrisons in the Hijaz.[53] The initial responses of both the British and the Egyptian authorities to Sharifian requests for Egyptian military aid indicate the same mixture of scepticism and suspicion as appears in other data on early Egyptian attitudes to the Arab Revolt. British evaluations of the request referred apprehensively to the "pro-turkish [*sic*] feeling" to be found in the Egyptian Army officer corps, Egyptian lack of enthusiasm at the prospect of fighting in the deserts of Arabia in collaboration with tribal contingents, and the potential unpopularity of such a dispatch of troops with the Egyptian public.[54] From the Egyptian ministry of Husayn Rushdi came a request to disguise any Egyptian military assistance to the rebels in Arabia by sending troops only as "volunteers" dressed in native garb rather than in Egyptian uniform.[55] Egyptian Army units were eventually sent to the Hijaz, where they served in the field through the later years of the war. But they apparently felt little kinship with their Arab allies once in Arabia. T. E. Lawrence reported an attitude of disdain for the more backward Arabs on the part of the Egyptian forces aiding the Arab Revolt:

> They were fighting the Turks, for whom they had a sentimental regard, on behalf of the Arabs, an alien people speaking a language linked to their own, but appearing therefore all the more unlike in character, and crude in life.[56]

A similar sense of remoteness from events in Arab Asia can be seen in the attitudes of Egyptian political leaders toward the Arab Revolt. To be sure, there was some abstract sympathy with Arab grievances and Arab aspirations expressed by Egyptian political leaders. Muhammad Farid, for example, believed that the anti-Ottoman intrigues of the Arabs of the Fertile Crescent were justified by the anti-Arab actions of the Young Turk regime, which had treated the Arabs "like dogs."[57] Similarly, Sa'd Zaghlul is reported to have advised the young Arab Army officer Nuri al-Sa'id to work for the Arab Revolt, speaking of those who did so as the pioneers of a better Arab future.[58] But this occasional sympathy with the Arab movement on the part of Egyptian politicians did not contain any sense of Egyptian connection with or involvement in the Arab cause.

The relationship to the Arab Revolt of those two Egyptian leaders who had been involved in Arab politics before the war, ʻAbbas Hilmi II and ʻAziz ʻAli al-Misri, was in neither case an intimate one. The ex-Khedive remained in contact with Arab leaders in the peninsula from his exile in Europe during the early years of the war, among other things corresponding with Amir Faysal, the son of Sharif Husayn, in 1915, and in early 1916 reportedly dispatching emissaries to Mecca to meet with the Sharif himself.[59] But there is no evidence of his being involved in the genesis of the Arab Revolt in 1915 and 1916. By late 1917, when he had reached agreement with the Ottomans and returned to Constantinople, ʻAbbas Hilmi is reported to have been entrusted with the task of suborning the Arab rebels from their alliance with the Allied Powers. To this end he was apparently given considerable funds from the Ottoman government and promised an eventual appointment as Ottoman deputy in Arabia, should he be successful in attracting the Arabs back into the Ottoman fold.[60] But as had been the case in 1915 and 1916, there is no evidence that the ex-Khedive was successful in influencing the direction of the Arab movement in the later years of the war.

ʻAziz ʻAli al-Misri's connection with the Arab movement during World War I was more direct than that of ʻAbbas Hilmi, but ultimately equally as devoid of positive results. Misri's direct involvement in the Arab Revolt occurred shortly after its outbreak in mid-1916. He was appointed Chief of Staff of the Sharifian armed forces in September 1916, in which capacity he attempted to train and to organize the motley forces at the disposal of the Revolt.[61] His service with the Arab Revolt lasted but a few months, however; in March 1917 he left the Sharif's service and returned to Egypt, from whence he soon made his way to Spain, where he spent the later part of the war.[62] Considerable uncertainty surrounds the end of his active collaboration with the Arab Revolt. His own later recollections emphasized residual Ottoman and anti-imperialist motives: a wish to maintain some links between the Arabs and the Ottoman Sultan/Caliph (a questionable recollection in light of his earlier approaches to the British for an Arab state "independent of Turkey"); an apprehension that the Revolt could only pave the way for European dominance of the region; and a desire to arrive at a rapprochement between Arabs and Turks that would satisfy the aspirations of both.[63] Contemporaneous British materials provide a somewhat more cynical interpretation of his break with Sharif Husayn and the Arab Revolt. Misri himself was apparently soon frustrated by the inefficiency of the Arab forces and by "the impossibility of doing anything serious with the Shereef and his sons";[64] his obvious disillusionment soon led to rumors in the Arab camp that he was requesting an independent command from the British and possibly even considering negotiations with the Ottomans for an end to the Revolt.[65] On the other side Sharif Husayn soon came to fear, perhaps not without reason, that "Aziz Bey had not changed his Committee [of Union and Progress] spots and might set himself up as Enver (or even betray them to the Turks)."[66] Whatever the precise relationship between Misri and Sharif Husayn may have been, what is clear is that Misri's involvement in the Arab Revolt during World War I was both short and unproductive.

For all his involvement in the Arab nationalist movement before and during the war, Misri's own attitude toward the Arabs was one of less than full identification. In a lengthy conversation with Sir Ronald Storrs in October 1916 when both were in the Hijaz,[67] Misri is reported to have made sharp distinctions between the "Arab races" found in different regions of the Arab world. In his view the people of Baghdad were "really the most intelligent and advanced of all"; the Syrians may have been more sophisticated, but they also had "less real brain and character"; the Arabs of Tripolitania were backward but also possessed great potential for development; and in the Peninsula the Arabs of the Yemen were "greatly superior" to those of the Hijaz, "generations of a better diet being the possible reason." In this characterization of different Arab groupings Misri reportedly not only separated Egyptians from other Arabs but also recommended "with all his strength against the inclusion of Egypt in any Arab Empire or Confederation." If Storrs' report is a true reflection of Misri's opinions in 1916, it is instructive for its explicit separation of Egypt from Arab nationalism on the part of the one Egyptian who had been deeply involved in the nascent Arab movement.

An Evocation of the Popular National Mood, 1917–1918

The foregoing discussion of pro-Ottoman sentiment in Egypt during World War I applies primarily, of course, to the political leadership of the country and to the small segment of the population involved in its political movements. There is very little evidence available as to the attitudes toward the war or other political subjects held by the generally inarticulate mass of Egyptians. British censorship ensured that popular pro-Ottoman sentiment went unreported in the press; the memoirs of notable Egyptians do not comment on the opinions of the mass of Egyptians save in the most general of ways; and British evaluations also focus primarily on organized or elite opinion.

There is one later source, however, which consciously attempts to capture and recall the popular mood of the mass of Egyptians during the war. This is *Bayna al-Qasrayn,* the first volume of the famous trilogy of historical novels by Najib Mahfuz, which portrays the lives of one fictional Cairene family from World War I through World War II. Based on the author's own memories as well as his extensive research conducted in the 1940s, and concerned with depicting the political attitudes as well as the personal lives of "average" Egyptians, Mahfuz's fictionalized social history provides an insight into that middle level of Egyptian society between the upper strata, whose ideas and actions are known through their writings, and the lower classes, whose personal reactions to national events remain unknown.[68]

Set in the period between October 1917 and April 1919, *Bayna al-Qasrayn* covers both the last year of World War I and the initial stages of the postwar nationalist revolt. In Mahfuz's reconstruction, the national identity and loyalty of middle-class Egyptians were not in question during the concluding stages of World War I. Until the end of the war, the Ottoman Empire, the Sultan/Caliph, and the deposed and exiled Ottoman representative, Khedive 'Abbas Hilmi II, were still the primary objects of Egyptian allegiance. The intensification of the British presence during the war served only to reinforce an Egyptian orientation toward the traditional framework of Empire–Sultan/Caliph–Khedive. A significant shift in Egyptian national self-perception begins to occur only toward the end of *Bayna al-Qasrayn*—in 1919, when the anti-British uprising of March and April indicated an undermining of the hegemony of the Ottoman-Islamic framework of identity and its replacement by a local Egyptian national identity among the urban middle classes portrayed in the novel.

At the heart of the political attitudes of the characters in the novel lies dismay over both the ouster from Egypt of its leading anti-British figures and the apparent defeats suffered by the Ottomans in the war. In a passage near the beginning of the novel describing the family's reaction to the death of Sultan Husayn Kamil and the accession of Ahmad Fu'ad, even the apolitical mother Amina expresses the hope that "Our Lord God may restore to us our liege [*Afandina*] 'Abbas."[69] Her politically inclined son Fahmi gives more vehement expression to the same sentiment at one point, hoping that "the Germans and accordingly the Turks will emerge victorious" in the war, and thus that "the Caliphate will regain its former glory and that Muhammad Farid will return home."[70] The Watanist leaders Mustafa Kamil and Muhammad Farid—one dead, the other in exile—still remained Fahmi's heroes: when made aware of his father's personal debauchery, Fahmi finds the news as incredible "as if he had been told that Muhammad Farid had turned traitor to the mission of Mustafa Kamil and sold himself to the English."[71] In Fahmi's view, "the most important thing is that we rid ourselves of the English nightmare and that the Caliphate regain its pristine greatness so that we will find our way opened."[72]

Even when the war ends, the members of the 'Abd al-Jawad family do not rejoice. Rather, the Allied victory over the Central Powers and the Ottoman Empire is a bitter disappointment. Ottoman defeat is interpreted as having destroyed all hopes for the assertion of the power of the Sultan/Caliph and for the return of 'Abbas Hilmi and Muhammad Farid to Egypt. The unfavorable outcome of the military struggle seemed to make it unlikely that Egypt could be liberated from the British yoke in the near future; yet without the assistance of the Ottoman Empire and the Caliphate, there is little chance of expelling the British from Egypt.[73] On the other hand, an independent Egyptian nationalist struggle against the British on behalf of a separate Egyptian nation does not occur to any of the characters in the novel. Even Fahmi, who in 1919 becomes a fervent supporter of the Egyptian Revolution and who loses his life in the process, does not conceive of an independent Egyptian nationalist movement at the end of the war in late 1918. His musings on the day of the armistice indicate the power of the traditional Ottoman orientation throughout the First World War:

> The Germans defeated! Who could have imagined that! There is no hope now that 'Abbas or Muhammad Farid will ever come back. Above all, the hopes of the Caliphate are dashed. The English star is still in the ascendant, while ours is sinking. Everything is in His hands.[74]

Developments in Egyptian Territorial Nationalism during the War

In spite of the prevalent pro-Ottomanism of Egyptian popular opinion during World War I, nonetheless there was some development of the alternative Egyptian territorial nationalist orientation that had been fostered by Ahmed Lutfi al-Sayyid and the Umma Party's journal *al-Jarida* in the prewar period. Lutfi himself dropped out of Egyptian politics early in the war, becoming Director of the Egyptian National Library, and *al-Jarida* ceased publication forever in June 1915.[75] *Al-Jarida*'s nationalist orientation lived on, however, in a new journal that commenced publication in May 1915, *al-Sufur [The Unveiling]*. Although clearly representing a peripheral attitude at the time, the modernist outlook expressed in this journal included further contributions to the territorial nationalist school of thought that was to become dominant after the war.[76]

The wartime writings of one Egyptian intellectual in particular, Muhammad Husayn Haykal, were especially important in relation to the development of the Egyptian territorial nationalist perspective. In 1916, Haykal published a series of articles on the Egyptian modernist Qasim Amin in *al-Sufur*.[77] Formally a biographical tribute to Amin, at a deeper level the articles offered a powerful new interpretation of the basis and nature of the Egyptian collective. Using the life of Amin as his starting point, Haykal developed a theory of the relationship between the environment of Egypt and the Egyptian nation which profoundly influenced later Egyptian territorial nationalism.

Haykal's analysis of Qasim Amin and the Egyptian environment that had shaped him was based on several methodological premises. Haykal conceptualized history primarily in collectivist terms, as the evolution of groups such as nations, races, or cultures. According to this assumption, humans are social animals whose achievements find expression in collective frameworks. Thus society or the nation is the proper subject of historical inquiry. An individual's accomplishments can be comprehended and explained only as representing part of the collective historic accomplishment of his group. History properly understood is the study of national cultural units, with the biographies of individuals (such as Qasim Amin) of value only insofar as they reflect and personify the collective biography. The rise and fall of kings, their wars and power struggles, are merely external manifestations, temporary and in flux, of the collective life of their nations, which is the core and driving force of history. The development of nations is thus shaped not by individuals but by deeper and more permanent factors: "their temper, their customs, their beliefs, their hopes." It is on the basis of these patterns that "regimes, kings, and wars" develop.[78]

A second assumption of Haykal was that "objective research" in literature, art, folklore, and every other product of the human imagination is possible only through a thorough comprehension of the physical as well as the socio-psychological environment in which these forms are born and developed. A work of art, for example, is not generated in artistic isolation. It is not born from within its creator's own world of thoughts and private imagination, nor is it the fruit of his totally independent and unfettered initiative. "It is a mistake," claimed Haykal, "to study a work of literature as if it were a self-sufficient product."[79] Rather, its creator and his artistic world are themselves a consequence of physical influences from the environment and external social forces. These forces mold both creator and creation in their image; hence, the uncovering of a literary work's "societal sources" and "spiritual structures" is the key to understanding the work. Neither the creator nor his creation can be understood if they are "arbitrarily" isolated from their total setting, or if one attempts to comprehend them from the perspective of only one limited aspect of this setting.[80] In sum, then, the study of the natural, social, and mental environments and of the historical conditions, customs, and emotions to which they give rise is the only means by which all human activity, including literature, can be understood.[81]

The historical theories of Hippolyte Adolphe Taine (1828–1893) had a seminal influence on these postulates about society and history propounded by Haykal during World War I. Haykal quoted at length from the works of this noted French literary historian and philosopher, and a decade later admitted that he had studied Taine's writings in depth prior to writing the series on Amin.[82] Taine's approach merits examination, for it offers the key not only to an understanding of Haykal's territorial nationalist concepts but also to much of the territorial nationalist thought that became so prevalent in Egypt during the postwar national era.

Reacting to the subjective aspects of nineteenth-century romanticism, Taine was an absolute determinist who believed that objective conditions totally dominate the realm of ideas. Human development is completely governed by immutable natural forces. The latter automatically and mechanistically shape the mental characteristics of both individuals and human collectives. Neither the individual nor the group create their ideas or control the destiny of their development: rather, both are imprisoned in the mold that shaped them and whose characteristics they inevitably reflect. Because social and intellectual matters are determined by material conditions, Taine held that the study of society and ideas is capable of attaining the same precision as is achieved in the natural sciences. The laws of history and morals are as capable of quantification and measurement as are the laws of biology and physics.[83] Hence Taine's approach to the study of human affairs, eventually termed naturalism,[84] demanded the application of the methods and techniques of the natural sciences to the study of culture, literature, the arts, and all other products of the human imagination.

According to Taine's determinist philosophy, "race" [*la race*], "milieu" [*le milieu*], and "moment" [*le moment*] are the three great forces shaping culture, literature, art, belief systems, social norms, and collective perceptions. A complete analysis of race, milieu, and moment, Taine posited, would assure a "complete" and "objective" knowledge of man's entire mental behavior and of his culture in all its manifestations.[85] Taine's concept of "race" is not purely or even primarily biological and should not be identified with later racialist theories. Race for Taine was what the Hegelian school called *Volksgeist,* the spirit or the genius of a particular nation.[86] Taine's "milieu" is a straightforward concept. In brief, it is the totality of physical conditions in which a nation is born and lives—its environment or combination of soil, landscape, climate, and social institutions characteristic of a specific place.[87] "Moment" to Taine was in fact the spirit of the age, the *Zeitgeist,* the particular mental climate of opinions, beliefs, and ideals dominant at a given point in time within a collective unit.[88] Unlike race and milieu, which as soon as they crystallize become almost entirely static, the moment is changeable. However, even though the "spirits of the moment" change from one period of time to another, they also come to possess a cumulative force: successive moments become interwoven into a single totality, and this totality constitutes a factor of great influence in shaping the present and the future.[89]

Muhammad Husayn Haykal enthusiastically accepted both Taine's rigid determinism and the specific concepts of race, milieu, and moment as the operative factors in the shaping of history. It is not difficult to appreciate why Haykal was so taken by Taine's theories. Taine furnished Haykal with a comprehensive social philosophy capable of offering "objective" foundations for the impulse driving him to create an Egyptian territorial nationalist theory. Now he could postulate the Nile Valley's own race–milieu–moment as the primary and exclusive force that had formed the Egyptian nation and its distinctive personality. Moreover, through this philosophy Haykal could establish the relationship between the thought of an individual, such as Qasim Amin, and Egypt's special environment. Thus he could demonstrate the intimate relationship between the territory and environment of Egypt, on the one hand, and the development of a specific Egyptian spirit or "mentality," on the other.

In "Qasim Amin," Haykal expounded the specifics of his Egyptian territorial nationalist theory on the basis of Taine's formula of race–milieu–moment.[90] Haykal distinguished between "the natural milieu" [*al-wasat al-tabi'i*] or "the natural environment" [*al-bi'a al-tabi'iyya*], which were none other than Taine's "milieu," and "the social milieu" [*al-wasat al-ijtima'i*] or "the social environment" [*al-bi'a al-ijtima'iyya*], which was Taine's "race" or *Volksgeist.*[91] Although it was "the natural milieu" that created the basic nature and temper of the nation, it was "the social milieu" that formed its belief system, the perceptions and opinions prevailing in a given society.[92] To these was added "the spirit of the age" [*ruh al-'asr,* occasionally replaced by *al-wasat al-zamani*], which of course was Taine's "moment." Haykal limited his discussion of "the spirit of the age" to the climate of opinion and modes of thought that prevailed in Egypt in the late nineteenth and early twentieth centuries and formed the spiritual world of Qasim Amin and his generation. In Haykal's scheme, however, "moment" was of lesser importance than were "race" and "milieu," and he devoted less effort to its explication.[93]

What was the specific natural environment of Egypt? Haykal maintained that the Nile Valley had been blessed with climatic-topographic traits that could not be found in any other environment. First, the Nile Valley was a well-defined, self-contained, and isolated unit. It functioned as an independent entity, free of external influences. To the west, east, and south it was surrounded by huge deserts that formed an effective barrier between it and its neighbors. The desert blocked out any "external" or "foreign" climatic influences that could affect the special conditions obtaining within it. To the north, the Nile Valley was bordered by the Mediterranean Sea, which set it off from northern climatic zones. The Valley was split along its length by the Nile River itself, and this gave it its unique shape: a long, narrow strip of green characterized by great homogeneity over all its length and standing in sharp contrast to the desolate yellow of the desert on either side of it.[94]

The almost complete geographical isolation of the Nile Valley and the perpetual flow of the great river down its center created unique climatic conditions. Protected from sudden shifts of weather by its location and with its flat terrain, lacking topographic contrasts, the Nile Valley was blessed with a moderate, comfortable, and relaxed climate. The almost total absence of rain or snow as well as relatively minor variations of temperature from season to season reinforced its "eternal tranquillity."[95] This unique physical and climatic environment was, Haykal emphasized, thousands of years old. Its unchanging nature was attested to also by the character of the flora and fauna found in the Valley. Nurtured in such a distinct environment, the Valley's plants and animals faithfully reflected its special traits of homogeneity, inner harmony, moderation, and above all its "calm," best described by the word *sukun.*[96] Nature shaped life in the Nile Valley. The quiet flow of the river's water, their predictable flooding and ebbing, strengthened and stabilized the moderate rhythm of life in the Nile Valley. The river broke the harshness of the desert and blunted the cruelty and roughness of what otherwise would be a wilderness. It created a prevalent mood of softness, gentleness, benevolence, and quiet majesty throughout the settled lands of Egypt.[97] Most importantly, Haykal also saw the human dimensions of Egypt as being marked by the same tranquil qualities. In their lifestyle, Egyptians radiated the calm and tranquillity they absorbed from their natural milieu.[98] Haykal summarized the main thrust of his analysis of the Egyptian natural milieu with the assertion that

> it is this milieu which has embraced everyone who has settled in the Nile Valley for hundreds and thousands of years; it is this milieu which created in its own image all the living things and the human beings who reside in it; and neither the humans nor the [other] living things have had but the slightest influence upon it.[99]

Yet Haykal was also careful to emphasize that the inescapable environment of the Nile Valley had a less pleasant side to it as well. Through the congruence of its elements, which thereby mutually reinforced each other, it forced upon everything within it unity, conformism, and obedience to the same general pattern. In a sense, it enslaved flora, fauna, and humanity alike under its rigid regime of sameness. Those things which could not accept its uniformity of life and blend into the harmony it imposed, which chose to rebel and thus to violate the order it had established over the millenia, were destroyed or expelled from the Nile Valley.[100]

What was the corresponding social milieu, the "race" or *Volksgeist,* of Egypt? Here too Haykal was convinced that "the inhabitants of the Nile Valley share certain features which have distinguished them since primeval times; features of their bodily structure and, similarly, of their mental and moral makeup." Moreover, "all these features were created by this natural milieu in which Egyptians live."[101] Thus the link between the natural milieu and the social milieu was that of the link between the creator and his creation. Inevitably, the calm and moderation that characterized the physical environment of the Nile Valley left their imprint on the intellectual and emotional makeup of the Egyptian people, on their manners, morals, and culture.[102]

For Haykal the Nile Valley's remarkable placidity and stability were clearly discernable in the national character of Egyptians. In his far from flattering portrait of his countrymen, their behavior was marked by the same tendency toward acceptance and submissiveness as was apparent in the natural world of Egypt. Most striking and regrettable was the absence of any wish to change and progress on the part of Egyptians. Rather, the people of the Nile Valley immortalized the past, venerated the continuity between the generations, and submitted blindly to the customs and habits passed on to them by their ancestors. Continuity, not change, was the supreme value of their lives. Even when circumstances changed for the worse and they were beset by political upheaval or economic distress, Egyptians still tried to maintain their existing way of life. Rather than seeking change, they learned to make do with little, to get out of their environment the minimum necessary for survival, and to wait, passively and patiently, for times to change for the better.[103]

These unfortunate traits of the Egyptian national character, Haykal felt, explained the apathy and the uninvolvement of the Egyptian people in politics. The many changes of regime that had occurred in Egypt over the millenia, the rise of one dynasty or the fall of another, had never touched the people of the country. Egyptians had never thought of themselves as having a share in any regime or as being obligated to take part in its struggles. In Haykal's view all of Egypt's rulers, the Pharaohs as well as those who followed them, did not derive from "the genuine inhabitants of the Nile Valley."[104] Just as they had demonstrated no interest in deposing old rulers, Egyptians had always displayed a willingness to accept the yoke of new regimes: similarly, they had been utterly indifferent to everything involving political administration and organization. Once a particular contender for power had triumphed and become ruler, Egyptians submitted to him: almost immediately and automatically he received their mandate to rule.[105]

But even rulers were subjects—subjects of the Nile Valley. Haykal was constantly amazed by the enormous power of the environment of Egypt. Not only were the mass of Egyptians under its controlling influence, but even the fate of rulers and elites was determined by it. Egypt's rulers, most of whom had come to the country from abroad, had themselves quickly submitted to the dominant natural milieu and social setting. All invaders of the country had been assimilated to it, their descendants gradually losing their former characteristics and taking on the distinctive traits of the Nile Valley. This included their absorption of the prevalent tendency to submit to a life of calm and tranquillity. Here, Haykal claimed, was the explanation for the fact that only rarely had deposed political forces risen up to challenge their successors.[106]

Haykal was convinced that at the heart of the Egyptian national character lay a "natural submissiveness pressed deep within the Egyptian soul."[107] This dominant trait "colors all dispositions and beliefs which come in contact with it."[108] Its influence had extended from the realm of politics to that of culture and religion, causing all the various religions that had come into Egypt to assume determinist and fatalistic features in the Egyptian setting. The collective Egyptian temper had an unchallenged belief in predestination. Not only had "external" forces, influences, and rulers entering Egypt totally failed to alter this national trait, but their assimilation to it had in fact provided clear-cut proof that this fatalism was irremediably rooted within the collective Egyptian personality.[109]

Haykal's findings on the Egyptian natural environment and national character led him to a clearly ambivalent position, one that to a considerable degree also prevailed in the thought of the Egyptian territorial nationalists and modernists of the 1920s who came to share much of his outlook. On the one hand, he obviously admired and took pride in the solid, well-defined, and unique Egyptian national character as it had taken form in the environment of the Nile Valley. Haykal the territorialist, the discoverer of the national "spirit" and the would-be shaper of a new Egyptian collective image, could be positive about the national character of Egyptians. The Egyptian personality was a genuine, well-defined independent phenomenon; as such it deserved to serve as the basis of a distinct Egyptian national identity.

On the other hand, Haykal could not ignore what he perceived as the predominantly negative and retrogressive content of the Egyptian national character. In his portrayal it was dominated by traits of conservatism and fatalism, an inherent tendency toward submissiveness and resignation, and the fundamental abhorrence of the idea of change and progress. The modernist, the positivist (in the Comtian sense), and the reformer in Haykal could not easily accept his own conclusions. He was all too well aware of the defects and drawbacks of such a national character, and he was critical of it. But, within the terms of his own argument, there was little he could do about it; hence the pessimistic tone that accompanies his description of the role played by Qasim Amin and other modernist intellectuals, himself included, in Egyptian society.[110]

The dilemma confronting Egyptian intellectuals like Haykal was an almost insoluble one. In fine, the same Egyptian national character that Haykal was excited to discover and analyze in order to prove its uniqueness was blocking the path to the revival and the modernization of Egyptian society. Indeed, Haykal—and even more his disciples—was soon to find that his task as the discoverer of the distinctive Egyptian national character was far simpler and more attractive than his other job, the thankless and nearly impossible one of modifying and improving those national traits which he himself, as a territorial nationalist, believed to have crystallized over thousands of years.

In these wartime articles, Muhammad Husayn Haykal laid much of the foundation for the Egyptian territorial nationalist orientation that was to become dominant in Egypt as a result of the dramatic changes that occurred in Egypt after the war. The fact that he was in a minority school of opinion at the time should not detract from either the novelty or the importance of his ideas. In purely intellectual terms, Haykal brought an entirely new dimension to Egyptian territorial nationalism through his assimilation and dissemination of the environmentally determinist approach of Hippolyte Taine. It was the Taine-Haykal conceptualization of territorial nationalism that would characterize the Egyptianist outlook when it was at its most pronounced in the 1920s. With his view of the intellectual as a social reformer entrusted with the national mission of providing his nation with a new and more correct collective self-image, Haykal also served as the model for the activist role assumed by many Egyptian intellectuals in the postwar era. Both the ideas and the role model developed by Haykal in the near-underground conditions of World War I would soon become the central feature of Egyptian territorial nationalist intellectual activity.

2

The Revolution of 1919 and Its Aftermath: the Apotheosis of Egyptian Nationalism

Egypt experienced its first modern "revolution" immediately after World War I. Beginning in 1918 with peaceful maneuvers by Egyptian politicians toward terminating the recently declared British Protectorate, in 1919 it escalated into widespread protest and violence directed against the British presence in Egypt. The uprising of 1919 was followed by three years of complicated Anglo-Egyptian negotiations aimed at reconciling British imperial interests with Egyptian national aspirations. A resolution of sorts came in 1922–1923 with a unilateral British declaration of Egyptian independence and the institution of a parliamentary monarchy on the one hand, and a continued British political and military presence to safeguard British interests on the other.

In retrospect, the Egyptian Revolution of 1919 was far from being a revolution in the classic meaning of the term. Its leadership was largely drawn from the native Egyptian elite (albeit from newer, rurally based strata rather than the Ottoman-derived element that had dominated political life in the nineteenth century).[1] It was primarily a political phenomenon, aiming at no socioeconomic transformation of class structure and as a result achieving none (the rural risings of 1919 were quickly repressed and were not repeated; the main economic aspiration of the nationalists was to seek to create a native Egyptian capitalist sector parallel to the foreign one that had dominated the economy to that time).[2] Most important, even its political achievements were limited to a greater measure of (but by no means total) independence from Great Britain, which continued to maintain both military forces in the country and influence over Egyptian affairs. But to many of the Egyptians who participated in the Revolution of 1919, these limitations were either irrelevant or temporarily overlooked. At the time, Egyptians perceived it as a genuine revolution.

For our purposes, what is most important about the Revolution of 1919 is its unambiguously *territorial* nationalist character. Throughout, the statements and actions of its leaders were phrased in terms of Egypt's existence as an historic nation and her right to full national independence. Correspondingly, the words and deeds of its leaders ignored both the older alternative focal point for Egyptian political loyalty—the religious bond that had previously been symbolized by the Ottoman Empire—and the newer potential alternative for allegiance embodied in the emerging Arab nationalist movement.

Three factors in particular account for the exclusively territorial nationalist orientation that marked the Egyptian Revolution of 1919. The first is the ideological background of the leadership of the dominant movement in the Revolution, the Wafd. The Wafd's leadership in its early years was drawn primarily from older notables who in the prewar period had been associated with the Umma Party and its concepts of secular, separatist Egyptian nationalism. Sa'd Zaghlul himself had been a member of the Umma Party before the war; five of the Wafd's seven founding members had been associated with it; and included in that group was the leading ideologue of the Umma and of territorial nationalism, Ahmad Lutfi al-Sayyid.[3] As such, the Wafd largely continued and elaborated on the Egyptianist orientation that its leaders had developed before the war. In contrast, the Watani Party, which had championed an Ottoman-Islamic orientation prior to World War I, was little involved in the Revolution: with its organization shattered, its leaders expelled between 1910 and 1915, and part of its remaining leadership rapidly co-opted by the Wafd, it played an insignificant role in the ferment of the immediate postwar period and languished throughout the parliamentary period as a minor force in Egyptian politics.[4]

But prior inclinations alone are not enough to account for the postwar ascendancy of the territorial nationalist ideal. Also involved in the triumph of Egyptianism after the war were those new factors which led more and more Egyptians, including previously pro-Ottoman followers of the Watani Party, to accept the territorial nationalist ideas of the old Umma and the new Wafd. Here two elements seem to be most important. The more obvious and probably the more basic was the outcome of World War I. The defeat of the Ottoman Empire by 1918 and its subsequent transformation into an Allied puppet regime in 1919–1920 simply eliminated the Ottoman option as a realistic and viable political alternative for Egyptians. As with other former Ottoman subjects, including the Turks themselves, Ottoman defeat left Egyptians no alternative but to develop nationalist concepts and options along other lines.

The second new factor was the popularity of concepts of popular sovereignty and national self-determination by the end of World War I. Such ideas received an enormous impetus from two developments occurring in the last years of the war: the Russian Revolution of 1917, which appeared to portend the obsolescence of the prewar imperial order, and the speeches of President Woodrow Wilson of the United States in 1918, which forcibly expounded the theoretical basis of a new international system. A new vocabulary of the sovereignty of the nation and of its inalienable right to self-determination was sweeping the world by 1918. The trend was apparent to Sir Mark Sykes (himself an architect of one of the most old-fashioned of the secret imperial agreements concluded during the war) by the spring of 1918:

> The consent of the governed and the consent of the world are essential to any form of foreign influence or control over an emancipated people. . . . Keren-

> sky's disappearance and the advent of the bolsheviks have made a decided difference in world affairs. President Wilson's voice is now the important one and the ideas that do not fit in with his speeches won't have much influence on the peace conference.[5]

However illusory these expectations were demonstrated to be in the actual postwar settlement, nonetheless it was widely anticipated in many areas that they would provide the guidelines for the new international structure emerging out of the war. In Egypt, the concept of national self-determination led Egyptians to believe that both the old Ottoman order based on multinational loyalties and the imperialist domination that ran counter to the idea of self-determination would become obsolete in a postwar world system presumably designed along Wilsonian lines. The thrust of Wilsonian language was to cut against any form of supranational imperial order and to encourage the belief that a new, independent Egyptian polity characterized by popular sovereignty would find acceptance in the postwar settlement.[6]

The Egyptianist orientation of the Revolution of 1919 was already apparent at the famous meeting of 13 November 1918 between High Commissioner Sir Reginald Wingate and three Egyptian leaders (Sa'd Zaghlul, 'Abd al-'Aziz Fahmi, and 'Ali Sha'rawi), which in the nationalist imagination has always been regarded as the start of the revolutionary sequence. Although the conversation was devoted as much to the mitigation as to the total elimination of British rule, nevertheless the Egyptian leaders were definitely thinking in terms of Egypt as a unit free from any external national affiliation. They are reported by Wingate to have asserted that "Egypt is perhaps the most ancient race in the world"; that Egyptians "have a glorious past and have shown themselves capable of independent government"; and that it was only " 'just and right . . . that all self-respecting people should struggle for their national independence.' "[7]

What was implicit at the meeting of 13 November was soon made explicit. The charter of the Wafdist movement drafted in late November 1918 clearly reflected the new Wilsonian language of popular sovereignty and national self-determination: basing its authority on "the will of the people of Egypt," at this time the new movement unambiguously pledged itself to strive for "the complete independence of Egypt" [*istiqlal Misr istiqlalan tamman*]. The same charter mentioned no possible external affiliations for Egypt.[8] In early December the Wafd decided to attempt to internationalize the Egyptian question through appealing to the victorious Allied Powers for Egyptian independence and for Egyptian participation in the postwar peace conference that was to convene in Paris in early 1919. Inherent in the attempt to gain Egyptian admittance to the peace conference was the concept of Egypt as a separate national unit fully as deserving of participation in the shaping of the postwar world as were other national units that had aided in the Allied war effort.[9]

The first extensive theoretical statement of Egyptian historical distinctiveness and national uniqueness on the part of the new Wafd is contained in a manifesto concerning Egypt's national aspirations that was drawn up by the movement in January 1919 for presentation at the peace conference.[10] Its section devoted to the nature of Egypt and its people began by emphasizing the country's recent Western orientation, going as far as to quote the famous aphorism attributed to the

Khedive Isma'il to the effect that Egypt was no longer in Africa but had become part of Europe ("Mon pays n'est plus en Afrique, il fait partie de l'Europe"). It went on to attribute a particular and distinct national character to the people of Egypt, including the traits of intelligence, seriousness, and moderation as well as a remarkable ability to assimilate those foreign elements which had entered the country through its long history. In its view, the population of Egypt now formed "a single and unique race, perfectly homogeneous in its physique as in its mentality and its manners." It was on the basis of this indisputable historicity and distinctiveness of the Egyptian nation, combined with the natural right of all nations to independence, that the Wafd made its request for the complete independence of Egypt to the world community and the peace conference. The nascent theory of Egyptian national character and uniqueness found in this Wafdist document of 1919 is an indication of the degree to which the movement had, even in the first months of its nationalist struggle, absorbed the concepts of Egyptian territorial nationalism that had been elaborated before World War I and that were reinforced by the war and its results.

The idea of Egyptians as "a single and unique race" was more than a theoretical construct on the part of the Wafd. It found tangible expression in the largely successful attempt of the movement to unite all native Egyptians, the Muslim majority as well as the Coptic Christian minority, in an explicitly secular Egyptian nationalist movement. From its beginnings as an organized body in the winter of 1918–1919, the Wafd included both Muslim and Coptic notables in its leadership.[11] The uprising of March and April 1919 was marked by extensive Muslim-Coptic collaboration in anti-British demonstrations, including the appearance of Coptic and Jewish leaders in meetings held at al-Azhar, and marred by little intercommunal tension between native Egyptians.[12] To be sure, continuing nationalist protest and demonstration occasionally did boil over into peasant or mob attacks on Christian minorities within Egypt, particularly against the Copts in some rural areas and the Armenian community in urban Egypt;[13] but on the ideological level the Egyptian nationalist movement's exclusive focus on the external enemy did prove to be a powerful cement uniting Egypt's different religious communities together in a common national struggle.

Through the revolutionary years of the early 1920s, the Wafd continued to unite Muslims and Copts in a common nationalist movement. The speeches of its leader Sa'd Zaghlul denied that the religious or other differences between Egyptians possessed any relevance for their nationalist struggle, asserting instead "the union of the cross and the crescent" in the Wafd.[14] Copts continued to occupy a prominent place in the leadership and cadre of the movement: two of the six Wafdist leaders deported with Zaghlul to the Seychelles in 1921 were Copts, as were four of seven Wafdist activists condemned to death in the same year for their anti-British activities.[15] When the Egyptian Constitution was being drafted in 1922–1923, the movement's Coptic leaders and the organization as a whole opposed the concept of a separate electorate for the Copts, preferring the integration of all Egyptians in one electorate.[16] Although Coptic-Muslim cooperation was soon to fray in the hurly-burly of electoral politics from the mid-1920s onwards, for a few brief years the subsuming of religious differences in one secular Egyptian nationalist movement was to a considerable degree a reality.

The Egyptian Revolution and the Ottoman Empire

The preeminent goal of the postwar Egyptian Revolution was attaining "complete independence" for Egypt. What the phrase meant to Egyptians was a refusal to accede to any formal limitations, internal or external, substantive or symbolic, on Egyptian sovereignty and the right to national self-determination. Not the least of the components of complete independence was the demand for final termination of the centuries-old link between Egypt and the Ottoman Empire.

The dominant organization in the Revolution of 1919 was of course the Wafd, and it was a body unambiguously devoted to the elimination of all vestiges of the Ottoman connection. The Wafd's charter, drafted in late November 1918, had specified its primary aim as the achievement of complete independence for the country, making no mention of any external solidarity, and the "authorization" [*tawkil*] that it solicited from the Egyptian public in the winter of 1918–1919 and upon which it based its authority similarly cited "the independence of Egypt" as the goal of the movement.[17] In its official statements that discussed the question of the relationship of Egypt to the Ottoman state, the Wafd consistently took the position that World War I had ended any Egyptian connection with the Ottoman state. On one level, the movement justified Egyptian independence on Wilsonian grounds: because Egypt was a well-defined, homogeneous national unit and "because independence is a natural right of nations."[18] In addition to this, it based its demands for independence on the historical arguments that Egypt had been striving to free itself from alien Ottoman domination since the nineteenth century, when only the intervention of the European powers in 1840–1841 had prevented the country from gaining its independence on the field of battle, and that in practical terms the recent war had finally "broken the last link connecting Egypt to Turkey" when the British had made Egypt a Protectorate in 1914.[19] In the Wafdist view, to all effects and purposes Egypt had become liberated from Ottoman sovereignty in 1914 and, since the new Wilsonian principle of self-determination prohibited the imposition of foreign rule upon a people against its will, neither the Ottoman Empire nor Great Britain had any legal basis for dominance over Egypt.[20]

Eventually the Wafd added to its legal arguments the fact that the emerging successor of the Ottoman Empire, the new state of Turkey, itself renounced any claim to sovereignty over Egypt. During the Lausanne Conference, which negotiated the final treaty of peace between Turkey and the Allies in 1922–1923, the (unofficial) Wafdist delegation maintained that because Turkey's Ottoman predecessor had been the only state possessing internationally recognized sovereignty over Egypt, Turkey's renunciation of the same meant that "Egypt and the Sudan have become in law a completely and perfectly independent state."[21]

The lesser political movements that emerged during the years from 1919 to 1923 adopted and followed the exclusively territorial nationalist orientation set by the Wafd. Thus the shortlived "Egyptian Democratic Party," formed in early 1920, specified as the first principle in its program that it would work for "the internal and external independence of Egypt," making no mention of the former Ottoman bond and offering cooperation in an international organization to maintain world peace as the only external affiliation it would accept for Egypt.[22] The "Egyptian Socialist Party," established in 1922, demonstrated a more internationalist flavor congruent with its socialist orientation, pledging to work for the liberation of all peoples oppressed by imperialism; but it also had as its first goal the narrower aim of the liberation of "the entire Nile Valley." Understandably, its program made no reference to the Ottoman Empire.[23] The most important organization other than the Wafd to emerge during the 1918–1923 period was the Liberal Constitutionalist Party, formed in October 1922. It too had an exclusively territorial nationalist orientation, specifying "working to complete the genuine independence of Egypt" as the first principle in its program and neglecting any mention of any Ottoman or other external affiliation for Egypt.[24]

The most striking indication of the triumph of the territorial nationalist concept during the Revolution of 1919 comes from the postwar position of the Watani Party. Despite their prewar championing of the Egyptian connection with the Ottoman Empire, the Watanists also came to regard the Ottoman bond as null and void after the war. Although at least one prominent Watanist, Mustafa al-Shurbaji, still argued for a continued connection between Egypt and the Ottomans, much of Watanist opinion by 1919 had adopted arguments based on national self-determination and called for "complete independence" for Egypt and the Sudan.[25] As early as April 1919, the official Watanist position as put to the Paris peace conference was that the Ottoman claim to sovereignty over Egypt had been nullified by wartime developments and thus that Egypt and the Sudan should be recognized as fully independent.[26] By 1922–1923, the position taken by the Watanist delegation sent to the Lausanne conference was to demand the "complete independence of all of the Valley of the Nile" and to base that demand on the same quasi-historical arguments employed by the Wafd: that Egypt had been striving to free itself of Ottoman domination for nearly a century and would have done so in 1840 but for European interference; that both the Ottoman government and the European powers had implicitly recognized the existence of an Egyptian nation in the various special provisions concerning Egyptian autonomy to which the international community had agreed since the mid-nineteenth century; and that the recent Turkish renunciation of any claim to sovereignty over Egypt confirmed that Egypt was totally free of any external affiliation.[27] This postwar Watanist abandonment of the Ottoman connection testifies both to the partially instrumental basis of their earlier pro-Ottomanism and to the degree to which the war had transformed the international milieu in which Egyptians lived.

On the whole there was less pro-Ottoman sentiment visible in Egypt after the war than the prewar pro-Ottomanism manifested by many Egyptians would have led one to expect. A noteworthy feature of the political activities of Egyptian leaders during the Revolution is the apparent absence of direct contact or collaboration with the Ottoman government. British reports occasionally spoke (vaguely) of continuing Ottoman sentiment or of "Young Turk" instigation of anti-British activity, but more considered British evaluations of the Egyptian nationalist movement in late 1918 and early 1919 came to the conclusion that it was oriented primarily toward Egyptian rather than Ottoman goals, that it was "national in the full sense of the word," and that it was equally "anti-British, anti-Sultanian, [and] anti-foreign."[28] Neither British nor Egyptian sources on the Revolution of 1919 indicate any direct contact between the Wafd and the Ottoman government (itself under the effective control of the Allies after the war). Upon the arrival of their "delegation" in Paris in April 1919, the leaders of the Wafd publicly emphasized the exclusively Egyptian nationalist character of their movement and disavowed any connection with now-discredited Young Turks.[29] A similar lack of collaboration seems to have characterized the relationship between the Wafd and the parallel Turkish nationalist movement emerging in Anatolia in the early 1920s. In 1920 Lord Allenby was able to find no evidence to corroborate press reports of a financial connection between the Egyptian and the Turkish nationalist movements, and in 1922 visits to Ankara by both the Wafdist and Watanist delegations to the Lausanne conference were coldly received by the new Turkish government, which refused to support Egyptian admission to the peace talks.[30]

Egyptians do not seem to have been greatly concerned with the fate of their erstwhile sovereign, the Ottoman Empire, after World War I. British evaluations of Egyptian opinion in 1920, when the Allies were shaping their plans for the partition of the Ottoman state, reported a low level of Egyptian interest in the subject. Although some groups in Egypt (the old Turkish aristocracy with its Ottoman connections, the religious class with its orientation toward the Ottoman Sultan/Caliph, Watanist elements with prior ties to the Young Turk regime) were reported to have had a greater interest than did other Egyptians in the fate of the Ottomans, and although in general terms Egyptian opinion is reported to have largely disapproved of Allied intentions for partitioning Ottoman territories, condemnation of Allied plans by educated Egyptians, while "frequent," was also "rarely passionate."[31] Most telling is the Egyptianist filter through which most Egyptians appear to have viewed Ottoman developments. Thus the relationship of Allied plans to the formal status of Egypt and the possible continuation of an Egyptian tribute to the Ottoman state are reported to have concerned Egyptian opinion more than the intrinsic merits of the overall postwar settlement with the Ottoman Empire.[32] The combined effect of Ottoman wartime defeat with the postwar impact of Wilsonian concepts of national self-determination was noted in a British report on Egyptian opinion in June 1920: "It is clear that Egyptian sentiment in favour of Turkey has been much diminished by the spread of modern Nationalist theories and the realization that the Ottoman Empire is no longer a military power."[33]

The rise of a Turkish nationalist movement in Anatolia from 1920 onward introduced an additional consideration into the postwar Ottoman situation but does not seem to have altered the Egyptian tendency to view events in the dying Ottoman Empire as secondary and peripheral to what was occurring in Egypt. British reports in late 1922 on the Egyptian reaction to the victories of the nationalist forces led by Mustafa Kemal indicate a general Egyptian sympathy for the Turkish nationalist movement but no sense of direct Egyptian involvement in the Turkish struggle. Mustafa Kemal and his movement were receiving considerable adulation in Egypt by 1922. Egyptians sent messages of congratulation to the Turkish nationalists for their victory over the Greeks;[34] committees in support of the Kemalists emerged at al-Azhar;[35] Mustafa Kemal himself came in for praise in both the Egyptian press and in the verses of Egyptian poets;[36] and in general the British had "no doubt that the greatest enthusiasm and satisfaction prevails [*sic*] amongst all classes over the Kemalist victories."[37] Nor did this sympathy for the Turkish nationalist movement fade when on 1 November 1922 that movement deposed the Ottoman Sultan and in effect wrote *finis* to the Ottoman polity: even after the end of the Ottoman era, British reports were still observing that "there is a good deal of pro-Kemalist enthusiasm and propaganda in Egypt."[38]

What are most interesting about this Egyptian pro-Kemalist sentiment of the early 1920s are the interpretations of Egyptians concerning what was happening in Anatolia. In Egyptian conservative and religious circles, the Turkish nationalist victories were read in heavily Islamic terms. It was the victory of the nationalists as Turkish Muslims that was emphasized by many of Egypt's leading poets; Mustafa Kemal himself was compared to the Muslim heroes Khalid ibn al-Walid or Salah al-Din and his military victories to the battle of Badr.[39] When the Kemalists' vigorous struggle against Western domination was contrasted to the collaboration of the Sultan's regime at Constantinople with the Allies, even such a poet as Ahmad Shawqi, who had been vehemently pro-Ottoman before the war, was led to extol the virtues of the Turkish nationalists over the supine Ottoman regime and to criticize the Sultan's hostility to the nationalists.[40] To a religious leader such as Shaykh Muhammad Shakir of al-Azhar, it was the success of the Turks as a Muslim people that mattered: Mustafa Kemal was "a model for four hundred million Muslims" in comparison to the Ottoman Sultan, who had betrayed Islam by his capitulation to Allied dominance.[41] Privately expressed opinions in Egyptian religious circles may have been even stronger, reportedly anticipating that Mustafa Kemal would follow his victories in Anatolia with the launching of a religious war on behalf of other Muslim countries occupied by the Allied powers.[42] Thus much Egyptian sympathy for the Kemalists was based on a misapprehension that, since the successes of the Turkish nationalist movement were victories by Muslims against their non-Muslim opponents, they would bode well for Islam and for other Muslims in the future.

But even in Egyptian religious circles, the motivation behind pro-Kemalist sentiment was at least partially Egypt-oriented. What is emphasized in contemporary British evaluations on the subject is that it was because Mustafa Kemal was expected to "liberate Egypt" from the British yoke that religiously inclined Muslim Egyptians called for Egyptian support for the Turkish nationalist movement in 1922.[43] In one scenario current in Egyptian religious circles at the time, Mustafa Kemal was expected to follow his successes in Anatolia by first reconquering Thrace, then by liberating Syria from the French, from whence he would "invade and enter Egypt as a conqueror. Consequently it is unnecessary to worry about the election of a Parliament, or about the return of ZAGHLOUL, as KEMAL will redeem his promise [*sic*] to bring ZAGHLOUL back himself."[44] What such farfetched expectations concerning Turkish intentions indicate is that the support they received in Egypt came at least in part because of what Egyptians perceived the Kemalists might be able to do for Egypt itself.

The Egyptian Middle Class between Ottomanism and Egyptianism

There is little direct evidence as to the attitudes of most of the Egyptian population toward the Ottoman Empire and its collapse after World War I. British evaluations of the popular position toward the Ottomans after the war are contradictory. One British observer with long experience in Egypt concluded in January 1920 that, since "the defeat of the Turk was synonymous with the defeat of the religion of the Egyptians . . . the defeat of the Turk was certainly resented"; another British report only two months later came to the contrary conclusion that the Egyptian peasantry was "indifferent" to the fate of the Ottoman Empire and generally had "no sympathy for the Turk."[45] The physical evidence is inconclusive. There are reports of the Ottoman flag being raised in some of the rural areas in which anti-British uprisings were occurring in March 1919;[46] but a recent analysis of Egyptian rural unrest in 1919 has concluded that the main thrust of peasant activism was directed toward local autonomy or was even anti-statist in nature rather than explicitly pro-Ottoman.[47]

Some appreciation of the popular mood in urban Egypt in 1918–1919 can be gained from the detailed portrait of Cairene life provided in *Bayna al-Qasrayn.* Najib Mahfuz's novel is by no means a simple backwards projection of later nationalist myths onto his family of "average" Egyptians. The ʻAbd al-Jawad family are not dedicated Wafdists from the start, nor do they demonstrate any trace of the Pharaonic orientation that developed only after the Revolution and would have been incongruous in 1918–1919. Rather, Mahfuz's characters show considerable initial hesitance about the emerging nationalist movement as well as an appreciable lingering loyalty to the old order represented by the Ottoman Empire and the Nationalist Party.

At first, it is difficult for the family members to accept the new national movement and leadership emerging in 1918–1919. Zaghlul is only dimly known and his associates even less so. The fact that they had never belonged to the Watani Party greatly diminishes their standing in the eyes of the family. Suspicions exist initially concerning the intentions and the integrity of the leaders of the Wafd; it is rumored that Zaghlul is actually the instrument of the British.[48] Through the early phases of the Revolution of 1919, all members of the family continue to demonstrate a strong attraction for the nationalist heroes of the prewar period. When hearing of the visit of Zaghlul, ʻAbd al-ʻAziz Fahmi, and ʻAli Shaʻrawi to the British High Commissioner in November 1918, the son Fahmi instinctively measures the initiative against Watani Party precedents, praising Zaghlul because he had not thought that any Egyptian leader was capable of such boldness after the exile of the leadership of the national movement "headed by Muhammad Farid."[49] When another son, Yasin, grieves over the exile of Zaghlul in March 1919, he inevitably connects the event to the earlier exile of Watani Party leaders by the British: "it is terrible that all our men, ʻAbbas, Muhammad Farid, and Saʻd Zaghlul, are scattered far away from our homeland."[50] The constant measurement of the national leadership against the retrospective image of virtue and sacrifice possessed by the previous generation of leaders is symbolized best in the comment of the youngest son in the family, Kamal, when looking at the pictures of ʻAbbas Hilmi, Mustafa Kamil, and Muhammad Farid that hung in their home: "they are more handsome than Saʻd Zaghlul Pasha."[51]

Whatever their initial uncertainties, the Revolution of 1919 eventually affects everyone in the ʻAbd al-Jawad family: "no one could claim that the Revolution had failed to change at least one aspect of his life."[52] Responses obviously differ from individual to individual. At one pole is the mother, Amina, whose traditionalist worldview simply precludes modern nationalist sentiment. Attached to the older Watanist leadership because of its loyalty to the Ottoman Empire and correspondingly uncertain of the new national movement unsanctified by a connection with the Caliph, she feels that any nationalist struggle against the mighty British is doomed to failure.[53] Another pattern is that demonstrated by her apolitical and irreligious son, Yasin. Although he is at first sceptical about the Wafd' capabilities, eventually the frenetic activism of March 1919 leads him to marvel at the power of the Egyptian nation: "I would never have imagined that such a fighting spirit lay hidden in our people."[54] He is surprised at his own susceptibility to "real Egyptian patriotism" in light of his previous indifference to politics, and gives testimony to the power of the situation to sweep even the uncommitted along with the general current:

> I found myself in a surging sea of people and in an atmosphere of electrifying enthusiasm. So, completely forgetting myself, I merged with the crowd. And you can believe me when I tell you that I was as jubilant and enthusiastic and hopeful as anyone could ever be.[55]

The mixture of feelings with which "average" Egyptians reacted to the Revolution of 1919 is exemplified best in the attitudes of the father of the family, al-Sayyid Ahmad ʻAbd al-Jawad. Sentimentally nationalist—and Nationalist—since his youth, at the close of the war his nationalist expectations had been destroyed and he was reconciled to submission to British rule.[56] Yet he too is soon swept up in the events of 1918–1919. Gradually he and his middle-age cronies in the neighborhood of *Bayna al-Qasrayn* came to support the Wafd ("all Pashas"); its development and progress became the main subject of conversation during the daily get-togethers in ʻAbd al-Jawad's shop; and the leaders of the new movement came to be accepted as the legitimate heirs of the older Watanist leadership and the Ottoman symbol, ʻAbbas Hilmi.[57]

After several months of nationalist agitation, by March 1919 al-Sayyid ʻAbd al-Jawad and his friends in *Bayna al-Qasrayn* are Wafdist sympathizers. The British exiling of Zaghlul and his associates—"even the greatest Pashas"—is termed a "calamity."[58] The dramatic news of the release of the Wafdist exiles in April 1919 reinforces al-Sayyid's Egyptian nationalist orientation. He is swept up in the spontaneous demonstrations that fill *Bayna al-Qasrayn,* and his ambivalence and anxiety are replaced by enthusiasm and expectation:

> The age of fear and bloodshed is over, isn't it? Saʻd is now free and master of himself. He is probably on his way to Europe now. Only a step or a word separates us from independence.[59]

The "revolution" apparently over, al-Sayyid is now willing to glory in the nationalist activities of his son Fahmi, which he had previously opposed for personal reasons. Not only does he anticipate his friends' praise for Fahmi's "patriotism and courage," he also voices the supposition that had he himself still been a youth, unencumbered by the responsibilities of middle age, he too would have been an active supporter of the Revolution.[60]

The most prominent feature of Najib Mahfuz's detailed portrait of middle-class Egyptian reactions to the Revolution of 1919 is the initial dissonance between the nationalist orientation of the Egyptian political elite and the attitudes of the populace in whose name they spoke. In the early phases of the Revolution, elite and mass wanted very different things. Where the new nationalist leadership of the Wafd rejected the Ottoman connection as obsolete and useless by the end of the war in late 1918, most Egyptians still looked to the Empire and the Sultan/Caliph for deliverance; where the new leadership represented an alternative to the prewar political establishment of the Khedive and the Nationalist Party, the masses wished to see the new as an extension of the old. In the wake of World War I, there was a lag between what the Egyptian political elite perceived to be desirable and what the Egyptian masses hoped would occur. Only after the violent events of March and April 1919 were the majority of Egyptians wrenched from their traditional Ottoman orientation and a measure of harmony restored between the outlooks of the national leadership and their putative popular clientele. Although the nationalist agitation and turmoil of 1919 eventually did prod these "average" Egyptians away from their previous Ottoman loyalties, the process was clearly one in which they were reacting to the nationalist initiatives undertaken by the political elite.

Egypt and Arab Nationalism after World War I

As the leaders of the Revolution of 1919 saw Egypt as totally separate from its former Ottoman suzerain, so they perceived no direct connection between their movement and the parallel nationalism developing in neighboring Arab lands. On the programmatic level, the manifestos and declarations of Wafdists, Watanists, and lesser political parties in the revolutionary period simply ignored any direct relationship between Egypt and the Arab nationalist movement in Western Asia. An examination of some of the speeches of Sa'd Zaghlul indicate that, other than incidental references to Egyptians as "the sons of Pharaonic civilization and of Arabic civilization" or to the praiseworthy participation of Egyptian Bedouin Arabs in the nationalist movement, the preeminent leader of the Revolution paid no attention either to the Arab dimension of Egypt or to a possible connection between Egyptian and Arab nationalism.[61]

Nor were there significant practical links between the Egyptian and Arab nationalist movements after World War I. The Wafdist delegation in Paris in 1919 is reported to have declined to collaborate with an embryonic "Society of Eastern Nations" that was taking shape among non-European delegations to the peace conference on the grounds that its own mandate from the Egyptian people related only to the independence of Egypt.[62] The only formal connection between Egypt and the Arab nationalist movement in Western Asia after World War I appears to have been the seconding of an Egyptian Army officer to serve as Minister of War for the Sharifian government in the Hijaz in 1919–1920. This was a connection arranged by the British, however, and one that lasted only until mid-1920, when the officer resigned his post because of tension with King Husayn.[63] Perhaps the most poignant expression of Egyptian remoteness from Arab affairs after World War I is the picture painted by Sir Ronald Storrs of the exiled King Faysal of Syria on his way to Europe via Egypt in 1921: accorded no formal reception either by the Egyptian government or the Egyptian nationalist movement, "at Qantara station he awaited his train sitting on his luggage."[64]

Rather than seeing any affiliation between the postwar Egyptian and Arab nationalist movements, leaders of the Wafd in particular expressed a definite sense of superiority over the Arabs of Western Asia as well as a considerable feeling of resentment over the perceived favorable treatment accorded Arab as opposed to Egyptian nationalism by the Allied Powers in 1918–1919. This was apparent as early as the meeting of Egyptian leaders with Wingate on November 13, 1918, when one of the Egyptians spoke acidly of Egyptians "consider[ing] themselves far more capable of conducting a well-ordered government than the Arabs, Syria, and Mesopotamians to whom the Anglo-French Governments have granted self-determination."[65] The complaint was repeated frequently in the following year, when Arab representatives were allowed to proceed to Paris and Egyptian requests to do the same were rejected by the Allies. Thus Egypt was held to be "vastly superior" to areas such as the Hijaz, Arabia, Syria, and Lebanon (as well as to Eastern European states such as Greece, Serbia, and Rumania), and so certainly fitted for participation in the peace conference;[66] and the presence of a delegation from the remote and backward Hijaz was made the justification for an "infinitely more developed" Egypt to be represented at Paris as well.[67] The voicing of Egyptian resentment against favorable treatment of the Arabs appears to have been more than a convenient argument: as Sir Ronald Graham put it in April 1919, "there is no doubt that Egyptian amour-propre has been wounded by the absence of Egyptian representation at the Peace Conference, when India and, still worse, the disliked and despised Bedouin of the Hedjaz have been represented."[68] Eventually the Egyptian nationalists were to elevate the preference given the Arabs of Western Asia to one of the causes of the emergence of an active Egyptian nationalist movement after World War I:

> Another cause of encouragement to us was the recognition of the independence of our brothers of the Hedjaz, who speak the same language as ourselves and are of the same religion as most of us. The Arabs of the Hedjaz did not have before a separate political existence like ourselves. In fact, within a century, they were under our political control. . . . Was it illogical for us to expect from the British Government, in view of the oft-repeated assertions of its members, treatment at least as generous as that accorded to the Arabs of the Hedjaz?"[69]

Despite the apparent recognition of the Hijazis as "brothers" who shared language and religion with Egyptians, nonetheless the thrust of the presentation is clearly one of Egyptian superiority over the Arabs of the Hijaz and of Egyptian pique over the unjust preference granted the more backward over the more advanced.

Opinion in Egypt was not uniformly hostile to the Arab nationalist movement that flourished in the Fertile Crescent immediately after World War I. Although the continuing British censorship of the Egyptian press was particularly careful to control material on such topics as French activities in Syria-Lebanon that might be offensive to Britain's French ally or pan-Arab and pan-Islamic currents that might have adverse repercussions within Egypt, the Egyptian press was able to comment, in "moderate" and noninflammatory terms, on events in the Fertile Crescent.[70] The prominence of Syro-Lebanese publicists in Egyptian journalism at the time ensured that much of that coverage would be sympathetic to Arab nationalist aspirations and developments. When the ultimate clash between France and the Arab government at Damascus developed in the summer of 1920, most of the Egyptian press, both its Syrian-run and native wings, was reported to have been sympathetic to the Arab cause. Leading newspapers protested the highhanded and arbitrary division of the Fertile Crescent between Britain and France,[71] criticized the hasty French use of force against the Arab nationalists,[72] and lamented that "the policy of self-determination does not apply to eastern nations" and that "freedom has geographical and racial limits."[73]

But the sympathy demonstrated in Egypt with the Arab nationalist cause in 1920 had its own limits. It was the Syrian-run Egyptian press that took the lead on the issue and gave it the greatest attention.[74] Other than occasional appeals in Syrian-run papers for medical assistance to be dispatched from Egypt to Syria,[75] there seems to have been no sense that Egypt was either involved in or able to influence events in Syria. Nor was Egyptian interest in the defeat of a parallel nationalist movement particularly intense: as a British evaluation put it, the Franco-Arab clash of arms in Syria in July 1920 "evoked little excitement outside local Syrian circles, and no serious attempt has been made to arouse anti-European feeling in this connection."[76]

There was one Egyptian leader who did not share the general Egyptian disinterest in Arab nationalist issues in the immediate postwar period—the same figure who prior to the war had concerned himself in a major way with political currents in Arab Asia, the (now ex-) Khedive ʻAbbas Hilmi. In the early 1920s, ʻAbbas Hilmi undertook various gambits to extend his personal influence into Arab Asia. In Constantinople in 1920, he offered his services to the Ottoman government as an intermediary between the Ottomans and the Arab nationalists in the Fertile Crescent; there is no indication that the Ottomans found the offer worth pursuing.[77] By 1921 he was in secret contact equally with Arab nationalists in Syria, with the French, and with the British, trying to gain a sphere of authority for himself in Syria. To the Syrians he suggested the idea of union with Egypt in place of the French Mandate, with himself as ruler;[78] to the French he apparently offered himself as an anti-British counterweight to the pro-British King Faysal recently installed at Baghdad;[79] and to the British he recommended that the best way of maintaining their dominance in the Middle East would be through a system of alliances among the various Arab regions and Egypt, to be headed by "an Egyptian prince" knowledgeable in Arab affairs.[80] By 1922–1923 the ex-Khedive had made his way to Lausanne, where various nationalist figures had assembled in order to try to influence the Middle Eastern peace settlement. There he was reported to have been engaged in efforts to organize a "Supreme Oriental Revolutionary Society" uniting Egyptian, Indian, and Arab nationalists in a common anti-imperialist front.[81]

None of ʻAbbas Hilmi's maneuvers were successful. The French never acted toward making him King of Syria (although they were to toy with the idea again in subsequent years); the British knew him too well to try to make him their surrogate in the East; and nothing is heard of the "Supreme Oriental Revolutionary Society" after 1923. But the ex-Khedive's activities do carry some implications for the nature of Egyptian nationalism after World War I. They testify to the marginality of the Arab world for Egyptians during the 1919 Revolution; the only Egyptian efforts at involvement in Arab politics after the war were these attempts of a deposed Egyptian ruler to find a dominion in Syria to replace the one he had lost in Egypt. It is noteworthy in this respect that ʻAbbas Hilmi came under attack from other exiled Egyptians for his dabbling in Arab affairs: In late 1921 Nationalist Party activists in Europe, led by ʻAbd al-Hamid Saʻid, pressured him to abandon his Arab scheming and to concentrate on Egyptian affairs,[82] and at Lausanne in 1922–1923 the unofficial Wafdist delegation and the same Nationalist exiles opposed his grandiose efforts to create a general anti-imperialist league.[83]

Egypt and the Sudan: The Unity of the Nile Valley

The one partial exception to the exclusive focus upon Egypt by Egyptian nationalists during the Revolution of 1919 is in their attitude toward the Sudan. Certainly Egyptian nationalists had as one of their leading goals the restoration of political unity between Egypt and the Sudan. The general principle of the unity of the Nile Valley was a consistent demand of Egyptian nationalists from 1919 onward; it was insisted upon in appeals made to the peace conference in 1919,[84] in negotiations between Egyptian leaders and the British in 1920–1921,[85] by the unofficial Egyptian delegations sent to the Lausanne Conference in 1922–1923, and in initial drafts of the new Egyptian Constitution of 1923, at least until British pressure forced the removal of a constitutional reference to the Egyptian monarch as "King of Egypt and the Sudan."[86] Although neither the theoretical status of the Sudan as an Anglo-Egyptian Condominium nor the practical control of Great Britain over the region was changed by the Revolution of 1919, Egyptian nationalists continued to insist that the Sudan was an integral part of Egypt in the years to come. As an early resolution passed by the first Parliament of independent Egypt in 1924 put it, it was an "eternal principle" of the Egyptian nation that "the Sudan is an inseparable part of Egypt."[87]

But there were practical and ideological limitations to this rhetorical insistence on the unity of Egypt and the Sudan, limitations that show the concept to have been in large measure only an extension of the Egypt-centered nationalist orientation of the 1919 Revolution as a whole. The unity of the Sudan with Egypt was not referred to in the first statements of the emerging Wafd in late 1918 but was added to its program only in January 1919, when Sa'd Zaghlul asserted that the two regions were "inseparable" and that all of the Wafd's demands applied to the Sudan as well as to Egypt.[88] In practical terms, Egyptian leaders tended to view the independence of Egypt as taking priority over the question of Egyptian-Sudanese unity. Both Zaghlul in his negotiations with Lord Milner in 1920 and 'Adli Yakan in his with Lord Curzon in 1921 were willing to defer the Sudanese issue for resolution until the matter of Egypt's own status had been determined.[89] Similarly, the Wafd did relatively little to develop political linkages with the population of the Sudan, establishing few contacts with Sudanese in the years from 1919 to 1924.[90]

From a practical standpoint, the insistence of Egyptians on the unity of Egypt and the Sudan was a heavily instrumental concept, one based not on any metaphysical identity between the two regions or on the ethno-historical unity the peoples of both, but rather on the necessity of Egyptian control over the Sudan in order to assure the security and prosperity of Egypt itself. Thus Prime Minister 'Adli Yakan at one point was willing to accept the British position in the Sudan in exchange for Egypt's being given priority in the allocation of Nile waters;[91] Husayn Rushdi, when President of the Constitutional Commission in 1922–1923, referred to the Sudan as "life itself" because of its control over the Nile;[92] and in Sa'd Zaghlul's view the Sudan was "more necessary to Egypt than was Alexandria."[93] Although Zaghlul sometimes offered defenses of the Egyptian claim to the Sudan based on abstract principles of nationalism such as the presumed Egyptian descent of much of the population of the Sudan, arguments to the effect that "possession of the Sudan means rule over Egypt"[94] seem to have been more vital to him. That Egypt was the gift of the Nile was not only the view of Herodotus: Egyptian nationalists knew so as well. It is difficult to quarrel with the conclusion of Tariq al-Bishri that, in spite of the frequent rhetorical commitment of Egyptian leaders to integral unity of Egypt and the Sudan, still "the Egyptian patriotic movement was solely Egyptian, and its Wafd Party was exclusively Egyptian," and thus that "the independence of the Sudan with both of them was one of the effectuations and the consummations of the independence of Egypt."[95]

The Triumph of the Egyptian Nationalist Orientation

If the programs and policies developed by Egyptians in the course of their Revolution of 1919 and the early 1920s rejected all external links save that of Egyptian mastery over the Sudan, the upshot of the turmoil of the postwar period was the consolidation of the newly created Egyptian nation-state that resulted from the Revolution. In brief, the results of the Revolution of 1919 served as a tremendous reinforcement for the exclusively Egyptian-centered territorial nationalist orientation, a buttressing of the tendency that viewed Egypt and the Nile Valley as a distinct national entity.

The primary result of the Egyptian Revolution of 1919 was of course the achievement of technical if not complete Egyptian independence: Great Britain's unilateral renunciation of her Protectorate over Egypt in February 1922, then the proclamation of Egyptian independence and of his own assumption of the title of King by Sultan Ahmad Fu'ad in March 1922, followed by the drafting of a constitution and electoral law in 1922–1923. In none of these developments, which marked the emergence of the Egyptian parliamentary monarchy, was there any expression of external political affiliations for the newly independent state. The proclamation of 15 March 1922 announcing that "Egypt constitutes a sovereign and independent state" made no mention of the Ottoman Empire or the Islamic and Arab worlds.[96] The Constitution promulgated on 19 April 1923 was equally Egypt-oriented, declaring in its first article that "Egypt is a sovereign state, free and independent," and referring to Islam and the Arabs only in Article 149, where Islam was declared to be the religion of the state and Arabic its official language. The Sudan was mentioned, but only in the context of deferring the matter of the Constitution's applicability to the Sudan to the future.[97]

From a broader perspective, World War I and its settlement created a new age in the Middle East, the age of the territorially defined nation-state. An independent Turkey arising out of the ashes of the Ottoman Empire, a reinvigorated Iran undertaking parallel measures of Westernization under General/Shah Reza Pahlavi, and—not least—a largely independent Egypt continuing the impressive economic and cultural development that it had begun in the nineteenth century: all this seemed to vindicate, in the eyes of many educated Middle Easterners, the view that the territorially based nation-state was the proper and necessary form of polity to adopt for any people desirous of becoming "modern." In the Middle East as in much of the world in the 1920s and well into the 1930s, the territorially defined nation-state was king. It was certainly so in Egypt, where geography, socioeconomic developments, and the political course of events in recent years all conspired to separate Egypt from the Muslim and Arab areas around it.

3

Egypt and the Caliphate Question, 1924–1926

Although the Egyptian Revolution of 1919 was unquestionably the major development of the postwar period contributing to a reshaping of Egyptian nationalist orientations, it was not the only influence shaping the postwar dominance of territorial nationalism in Egypt. An additional factor of considerable importance was the simultaneous destruction of the Ottoman Empire. The impact of the end of the Empire extended through most of the Muslim world. On the political level, the elimination of the Ottoman Sultan/Caliph deprived the pan-Islamic movement of both its organizing force and its only viable focal point. From the early 1920s onward, there was no obviously preeminent leader in the Muslim world around whom other Muslims could rally, and the search for a replacement for the Ottoman Sultan/Caliph was to preoccupy much of Muslim opinion as well as many individual Muslim leaders in subsequent years. In intellectual terms, the destruction of the Ottoman polity and its traditional institutions raised fundamental questions concerning the normative political order. From the broadest perspective, the developments of 1914–1924 transformed the political world in which ex-Ottoman Muslims lived: rather than being the subjects, nominal or real, of a Muslim state in which reality was at least theoretically congruent with the traditional Islamic worldview, they became either the wards of European overlords or the citizens of new national states based on very different political concepts.

The Caliphate Question in Egypt, 1924

Of all the events of this period relating to the Ottoman Empire and its Sultan/Caliph, the development of greatest significance for Egyptians was the Turkish abolition of the Caliphate in March 1924. As we have seen, the rise of the Turkish nationalist movement in the early 1920s was generally regarded favorably in Egypt; its anti-imperialist successes were interpreted as boding well both for Islam and for other Muslims.[1] Even the separation of the Caliphate from the

Sultanate in late 1922 does not seem to have had a major impact upon Egyptians. Although the majority of opinion in the country is reported to have regarded the measure as a mistake on the part of the Turkish authorities, through 1922 and 1923 the British conclusion was that the new, reduced Caliphate had been accepted by Egyptian Muslim opinion.[2]

With the Turkish abolition of the Caliphate in March 1924, however, the contradiction between historic Islam and modern Turkish nationalism became unmistakable. The impact of the Turkish action upon the rest of the Muslim world was immediate.[3] In Egypt perhaps the most widely expressed initial response to the Turkish abolition of the Caliphate was shock at the abrupt termination of such a hallowed Muslim institution. Egyptians of a traditionalist orientation in particular seem to have felt a personal sense of loss and dismay over the end of the Caliphate: as the poet Ahmad Shawqi put it, "India is grief-stricken and Egypt mournful, weeping over you with flowing tears."[4] But even in more secular circles, the event was portrayed as being of major symbolic importance, one that marked the passing of an historical epoch for the Muslim world.[5] This sense of shock on the part of Egyptians was not generated by any perception of the meaningfulness of the Caliphate in their lives: what was lamented was the extinction of an important symbol, "the only remainder of the glory of Islam" in the past and in the present the only bond, however intangible, still linking Muslims throughout the world in one Islamic community.[6]

The Turkish government came in for a great deal of criticism in Egypt because of its abolition of the Caliphate. In political circles the strongest denunciations came from the Watani Party, which had had an historic orientation toward the Ottoman Empire. The Watani spokesman Amin al-Rafi'i repeatedly inveighed against the Ankara government for its "evil decision," for its callousness to the Caliph 'Abd al-Majid who during his brief tenure as Caliph had remained loyal to the new state of Turkey, and for the "terrorist measures" it was employing in its campaign against the Ottoman legacy in Turkey.[7] Muhammad Husayn Haykal in the Liberal Party's *al-Siyasa*, otherwise sympathetic to the new regime in Turkey, chided the Turks for impulsiveness and immoderation in the pace of change in Turkey in comparison to Egypt's more gradual process of modernization, which had been able to harmonize between "the necessities of the present and the requirements of religion."[8] But it was in religious and conservative circles that the Turks came in for the most vehement criticism. Conservative poets who had previously praised Mustafa Kemal now turned against him, explicitly because of the obviously anti-Islamic tenor of his policies by 1924.[9] To religiously inclined Egyptians in particular, the action of the Turkish authorities was "the most repugnant crime against Islam in the history of Islam."[10]

Much of Egyptian opinion at first rejected the validity of the Turkish abolition of the Caliphate and continued to recognize the exiled 'Abd al-Majid as Caliph. Publicists of both a religious and a secular orientation held that the Caliphate was the joint concern of all Muslims of the world, and thus that no body representing only a portion of Muslim opinion could take action on it unilaterally.[11] The initial reaction of most of the religious class in Egypt was to regard the Turkish abolition of the Caliphate as invalid and to consider their previous oaths of allegiance to 'Abd al-Majid as still in effect. This was the position taken in March 1924 by several prominent individual *'alims,* by both formal and ad hoc groupings of *'ulama'* that issued statements on the subject, and eventually by the Shaykh al-Azhar, who on March 15 officially declared the Turkish abolition of the Caliphate to be illegitimate and thus null and void.[12] This position of nonrecognition of the Caliphate's abolition was one that diminished in popularity over time, however, both because of the progressive unreality of the stance in the face of Turkish determination and because of the intrusion of domestic political considerations such as King Fu'ad's presumed desire to attain the Caliphate for Egypt and for himself.[13]

An equally widespread Egyptian attitude toward the Caliphate issue in March 1924 was disdain for the pretentions of King Husayn of the Hijaz to the Caliphate. Across the political spectrum, Egyptians refused to accept King Husayn's assumption of the Caliphate. The Liberals belittled his popular support; Sa'd Zaghlul denied his suitability for the position because of the British influence under which his kingdom had been created and was maintained; Amin al-Rafi'i of the Watani Party was contemptuous of him because of his ties to the British, indeed seeing the latter as the inspiration behind his claim to the Caliphate; and Egyptian *'ulama'* shared the perception that the King of the Hijaz was the creature of the British and thus lacked the requirement of political independence necessary for a valid Caliph.[14] As Lord Allenby reported to his government at the time, King Husayn's claims were seen in Egypt as "arrogant and absurd" as well as being caused by "British instigation;"[15] as such, they never received any significant support from Egyptians.

With the Caliphal claims of 'Abd al-Majid and King Husayn regarded as progressively unrealistic and from the start absurd, Egyptian opinion concerning the Caliphate soon moved toward two other solutions for the question of the fate of the institution in the light of the Turkish action of March 1924: convening a general Muslim conference or congress to discuss the future of the Caliphate, and bringing the Caliphate to Egypt. The idea of convening a general Muslim congress to discuss the Caliphate issue was one that antedated the abolition of the office, going back to 1923 when it had been raised as a possibility by the Turks themselves.[16] It surfaced again in March 1924 when the deposed 'Abd al-Majid himself suggested a Muslim conference on the Caliphate in his first public statement from exile.[17] Within a few days of the abolition of the Caliphate, the Egyptian press began to discuss such an assembly, generally seeing a definite need for a general congress to address what had now become an urgent issue in the Muslim world. A frequently expressed Egyptian viewpoint in these discussions was that Egypt, with its central geographical position, its preeminent religious institutions, and its considerable degree of political independence would be the Muslim country best suited to organize and to host such an assembly.[18] By mid-March the concept of a general Muslim conference in Egypt was being promoted by both individuals and ad hoc organizations, and appeals were being directed to both Prime Minister Sa'd Zaghlul and to King Fu'ad to lend official support to the idea.[19]

Parallel to the idea of convening a general Muslim congress in Egypt to discuss the Caliphate question came the notion of bringing the Caliphate to Egypt. Immediately upon the Turkish abolition of the Caliphate, suggestions appeared in the press first of Egypt as a possible "refuge" for the Caliphate,[20] then of the possibility of the establishment of a new kind of Caliphate in which

King Fu'ad might serve as the presiding officer of a "permanent Islamic council" in which all Muslim peoples would be represented.[21] Articles in *al-Muqattam* in particular promoted the idea of King Fu'ad as Caliph, both on the basis of his Majesty's presumed suitability for the post and because of Egypt's unique blend of geographical, cultural, and religious advantages as the site of the Caliphate in the modern world.[22] Before long a lead editorial in *al-Ahram* was expounding at length on Egypt as the seat of the Caliphate, arguing that it would benefit both Egypt and the Islamic world as a whole to see the Caliphate established in what was "the biggest and most advanced Islamic state."[23]

With these suggestions of a general Muslim congress in Egypt and Egypt as the seat of the Caliphate, we enter the realm of what P. J. Vatikiotis had described as "a miserably political issue," that is, the currents and countercurrents between Egyptian political forces concerning the Caliphate issue.[24] Given the prestige, both internal and external, which was bound to accrue to any Muslim leader accepted as Caliph, it was inevitable that the Caliphate question would become caught up in the maelstrom of Egyptian domestic politics.

The official position concerning the Caliphate on the part of independent Egypt's first popularly elected government, the Wafdist ministry of Sa'd Zaghlul that had come to office in March 1924, was one of noninvolvement by the secular government of Egypt in what was an international religious issue.[25] From the start Zaghlul apparently saw no alternative but to accept the Turkish action as a *fait accompli* and to proceed forward from it.[26] There are indications that the Wafdist ministry itself briefly entertained the idea of gaining the Caliphate for King Fu'ad and Egypt. The Egyptian Cabinet is reported initially to have found the prospect of King Fu'ad as Caliph an attractive one for Egypt on the grounds of the international prestige and leverage (vis-à-vis Great Britain in particular) that Egypt would obtain from the support of Muslims throughout the world.[27] In mid-March it was publicly announced that Zaghlul had discussed the Caliphate question with the King, and the King himself later claimed that Zaghlul had spoken at length with him "endeavouring to persuade him to accept the Caliphate."[28]

King Fu'ad's own intentions regarding the Caliphate are questionable. Both before and after the Turkish abolition of the institution, he repeatedly denied any desire to gain the Caliphate for himself.[29] As will become apparent in our discussion of the evolution of the Caliphate issue in Egypt, however, there is considerable circumstantial evidence to indicate that the King's denials of Caliphal aspirations were less than candid and that he both hoped for and worked to attain the Caliphate for himself in the mid-1920s.

The first official moves toward involving Egypt in the Caliphate issue were taken by the Egyptian religious establishment. As has been noted, the initial tendency among Egyptian *'ulama'* was to disavow the legitimacy of the Turkish abolition of the Caliphate and to continue to recognize 'Abd al-Majid as Caliph. This position changed over time, however, as various individuals and groups both within and without the religious class came to perceive the futility of continued loyalty and to call instead for an Egyptian initiative to organize a congress to discuss the Caliphate question.[30] The movement toward a general Muslim conference in Egypt became an official one on 25 March 1924, when the leadership of the Egyptian corps of *'ulama'* met and adopted a series of resolutions concerning the Caliphate. The most important of these were withdrawal of Egyptian recognition of 'Abd al-Majid as Caliph on the grounds that his had been a restricted and thus an invalid Caliphate since its inception in 1922, and a summons to other Muslim countries to send representatives to meet in Cairo in a year's time "in order to consider upon whose shoulders the Islamic Caliphate ought to be placed."[31]

An institutionalized and eventually Palace-backed effort by the Egyptian religious establishment to organize a general Muslim congress on the Caliphate in Egypt developed through the remainder of 1924. Invitations to attend the congress were dispatched in the name of the Shaykh al-Azhar to hundreds of individuals and organizations throughout the Muslim world.[32] Within Egypt a secretariat, an administrative council, several branch committees in provincial cities, and a journal devoted to promoting the idea of a congress were established under the leadership of officials of the Azharite hierarchy.[33] Although the initial activity of the Azharite establishment in promoting the congress may have been undertaken on its own initiative,[34] the movement soon acquired the support of the Egyptian Palace. The Palace-linked official of the Ministry of Waqfs and later Royal Chamberlain, Hasan Nash'at, traveled to Alexandria, Tanta, and other provincial cities to encourage the establishment of branch committees of the congress; funds were given by the same Ministry to the organizers of the congress to support their activities; and it was certainly the assumption of knowledgeable Egyptians that the doings of Nash'at, the Ministry, and the *'ulama'* were undertaken with the knowledge and approval of King Fu'ad.[35]

But the campaign for a general Islamic congress, with the apparent intention of its sponsors to see King Fu'ad selected as Caliph, did not go unopposed in Egypt in 1924. There were obvious factors, ranging from practical considerations concerning the uses to which the King might put the office to more theoretical questions about Egypt's suitability as the seat of the Caliphate and the possible implications of the Caliphate for Egypt's domestic political structure, which prompted many Egyptians to resist the idea of bringing the Caliphate to Egypt. Egyptian *'ulama'* themselves were not of one mind on the matter: some continued to acknowledge 'Abd al-Majid as Caliph even after the official hierarchy had denied the legitimacy of his Caliphate,[36] and one *'alim* openly accused his colleagues of subservience to King Fu'ad and as a result was hauled before the Grand Council of *'ulama'* on charges of insulting al-Azhar (he was acquitted).[37] More sustained opposition to the Azhar-based and Palace-backed campaign came from a body calling itself the "Supreme Caliphate Committee," which had been formed in March 1924. Headed by the Sufi Shaykh Muhammad Madi Abu al-'Aza'im and supported by Prince 'Umar Tusun as well as by elements from the Watani Party, its initial position was to insist on continued recognition of 'Abd al-Majid as Caliph, pending the convening of a congress that it was trying to organize in competition with that being undertaken by the Azhar hierarchy.[38] Restricted from public organizing and propagandizing from May 1924 by a Wafdist ministry at first suspicious of the Shaykh's associations, it continued private efforts to counter the Azhar committee and apparently had some effect in making Muslim opinion outside Egypt skeptical about the aims of official efforts toward a congress.[39]

The most significant domestic opposition to the Azhar campaign for the convening of an Islamic congress in Egypt came from Egypt's secular political parties. Shortly after the Azhar decision to organize such a conference on March 25, the Liberal Party journalist Mahmud 'Azmi addressed an open letter to Prime Minister Zaghlul questioning the constitutionality of the King of Egypt becoming Caliph and thus presumably assuming responsibilities and obligations beyond the confines of Egypt.[40] Zaghlul himself soon came to question the wisdom of the idea. In April 1924 he is reported to have told Wafdist deputies of his reservations about an Islamic congress in Egypt, and by June he was publicly expressing great skepticism about the possibility of restoring the Caliphate.[41] By the second half of 1924, as the King increasingly came to be perceived as the backer of the congress idea, the Wafdist ministry took direct action to inhibit Azharite efforts to organize such an assembly. The Ministry of the Interior prohibited government officials from participating in the local caliphate committees being established by the *'ulama';* Hasan Nash'at was dismissed from his post in the Ministry of Waqfs because of his involvement in promoting the congress; and later, after its fall from power, the Wafd covertly subsidized the rival committee headed by Shaykh Abu al-'Aza'im in order to block the Palace-backed efforts at a congress.[42]

It is questionable, however, if internal resistance was decisive in producing the delays that beset the campaign for convening a congress on the Caliphate in Egypt. External Muslim opposition to the idea seems to have been the crucial factor that prevented the congress from convening in March 1925, as its sponsors had originally planned. Much of the rest of the Muslim world was apprehensive about the efforts on behalf of King Fu'ad that were likely to be put forth at a Caliphate congress meeting in Cairo, and the responses of Muslims elsewhere to the invitations to the congress were marked by hesitance and requests for further clarifications concerning the aims and procedures of the congress before they would agree to participate in it.[43] It is also possible that the King himself may have been less interested in pursuing the Caliphal gambit by the end of 1924, by which time the Wafd had been ousted from office by a British ultimatum and a Palace-dominated ministry headed by Ahmad Ziwar had come to power. Whatever the reasons, on 25 January 1925 the Azhar Caliphate Committee, citing as its justifications the unsettled circumstances of Egypt where parliamentary elections were scheduled as well as the external complication of a Sa'udi-Sharifian war in the Hijaz, announced the postponement of the Cairo congress on the Caliphate until sometime in 1926.[44]

The 'Ali 'Abd al-Raziq Controversy, 1925

Although the Azharite promoters of the congress idea continued consultations and negotiations with Muslims outside Egypt after this announcement, no significant developments concerning a congress in Egypt occurred through the rest of 1925. It was not a year devoid of controversy about the Caliphate, however. The main development of 1925 relating to the Caliphate was the uproar raised by the publication of a small book written by a hitherto obscure judge in the religious court system. Shaykh 'Ali 'Abd al-Raziq's *Islam and the Bases of Rule* [*al-Islam wa Usul al-Hukm*] was a radical assault on both the specific position of the Caliphate and the traditional Muslim understanding of the nature of Islamic political institutions, and as such it generated one of the major religious-political controversies of the entire interwar period in Egypt.[45]

The essential thesis of 'Ali 'Abd al-Raziq's work was that there was no legitimate basis for the Islamic Caliphate. On the theoretical level, his examination of the *Qur'an* and the *Sunna* had failed to reveal any clear foundation for the institution; in his view the scriptural sources were either silent or hopelessly ambiguous on the subject of the leadership of the Islamic community after the Prophet.[46] Historically, he found the actual Caliphate to have imposed on the *umma* by force or guile since the first generation after Muhammad. Based on the desires of men rather than the words of God, the Caliphate as a whole had been a pernicious institution for the Muslim community, "a plague for Islam and Muslims, a source of evils and corruption."[47] Unjustified in theory and undesirable in practice, the Caliphate was an office with which Islam and the Muslim world could easily dispense.

Beyond this attack on the Caliphate, 'Abd al-Raziq went on to analyze the proper "bases of rule" in Islam. In the Shaykh's view, Muhammad's prophetic function had been solely spiritual, to lead men to religious truth and living. Although he had established a community, it was not to be confused with a state. To achieve its religious goals the *umma* did not need to be politically unified: the "Arab unity" forged by the Prophet had been a religious but not a political form of unity, the Arabs forming "diverse nations" both in the time of the Prophet and afterward; by extension, the existence of separate states coexisting within the body of believers would be compatible with the existence and the aims of the religious community.[48] Beyond his discussion of the political institutions of Islam, the broader point of 'Ali 'Abd al-Raziq's analysis was that the political and other institutions of the contemporary Muslim world did not need to be defined and restricted by the traditions of the Muslim past, and that the modern Muslims were free to arrange their affairs on the basis of "the most modern of what the human intellect has produced."[49]

'Ali 'Abd al-Raziq's book was a drastic and dramatic manifestation of the Western-oriented modernism that flourished in Egypt in the 1920s. Most obviously, the work attempted to provide a straightforward answer to the soul searching among Muslims over what should be done about the Caliphate after its abolition by the Turks: it should be forgotten. The book called instead for the complete separation of "church" and "state" in Islam, explicitly in regard to the traditional political institutions of the Muslim community but also implicitly in regard to the entire legal system of the *Shari'a* (the book insisted that the juridical system of the *Shari'a* was not traceable to the Prophet).[50] Through its denial of the historicity and thus the validity of traditional Muslim political institutions, the general thrust of the work was to legitimize the new Egyptian nation-state that had recently emerged: in 'Abd al-Raziq's view, there was nothing in Islam to prevent the political division of the Islamic world into national units to which Muslims would give their political allegiance. The book's conclusion was a sweeping assertion of the Europeanized perspective that characterized much of the Egyptian elite in the 1920s: look to the West, young man, for that which is "modern."

Inextricably intertwined with these theoretical points were practical considerations. 'Ali 'Abd al-Raziq's own political sympathies were Liberal; his family was prominent in the leadership of the Liberal Party.[51] In the some one hundred and fifty references to *"mulk"* and *"sultan"* in 'Ali 'Abd al-Raziq's book, most of which were critical of the evils of individual rule in Muslim history,[52] there were obvious comparisons to the regime of royal autocracy that had recently emerged in Egypt as well as implied warnings of the danger of increased tyranny that could result if the King strengthened his position by acquiring the Caliphate. Certainly many Egyptians interpreted the book as a political attack on the King and his Caliphal aspirations; as a contemporary evaluation in the press put it, "that which is meant in this is the Egyptian throne, the Egyptian crown, and its incumbent King Fu'ad."[53]

Given this context, the book aroused a storm of controversy in Egypt in 1925. The two parties most upset by the book were 'Abd al-Raziq's colleagues in the *'ulama'*, whose traditional worldview it assaulted, and the King, whose autocratic ambitions it threatened. Its publication was soon followed by hostile critiques on the part of the royalist press and by both individual *'alims* and groups of *'ulama'* disturbed by its author's views.[54] Formally in response to the complaints of the *'ulama'* but apparently prompted by royal pressure as well, the Shaykh al-Azhar eventually arraigned 'Ali 'Abd al-Raziq before the Grand Council of *'Ulama'* on charges that can be most cogently characterized as the divergence of 'Abd al-Raziq's views from the traditional understandings adhered to by his peers (for instance, his making Islamic law "a spiritual law" only, denying a political content to Muhammad's prophetic mission, and criticizing the religious basis of the Caliphate of Abu Bakr and the other Rashidun Caliphs).[55] On 12 August 1925, 'Ali 'Abd al-Raziq was found guilty of holding the impermissible views ascribed to him in the indictment and accordingly was dismissed from membership in the corps of *'ulama'*.[56]

Among the political parties, both the Watani Party with its historic Islamicist tinge and the new Unionist [*Ittihad*] Party recently created as the instrument of the Ziwar ministry and the Palace roundly condemned 'Abd al-Raziq and the views he had expressed in his book.[57] The controversy posed more difficult choices for Egypt's two leading parties, the Wafd and the Liberals. Sa'd Zaghlul is reported to have disagreed personally with 'Abd al-Raziq's position, terming the latter "ignorant in the principles of his religion" and approving of his being disciplined by the religious establishment.[58] Moreover, the partisan inclination of Wafdist leaders in the political wilderness of 1925 was to see in the controversy a useful wedge that could be used to split their Unionist and Liberal rivals.[59] Thus the initial tendency in the Wafd was to attack 'Abd al-Raziq for his defamation of Islam and to use the furor over the book to condemn their Liberal opponents for heretical views and even for out-and-out atheism.[60] But the Wafdist position in the dispute changed over time. Perhaps because the public debate clarified the dangers for freedom of thought raised by the case, and perhaps because of a realization of the implications of the case for their struggle with the Palace, in the later phases of the controversy the Wafdist press tended to criticize the trial of 'Abd al-Raziq as a threat to freedom of thought in Egypt.[61]

In spite of the Liberal Party's current participation in the Palace-oriented ministry of Ahmad Ziwar, the leading defenders of 'Ali 'Abd al-Raziq came from the ranks of this party. In part this was undoubtedly due to the connections of the 'Abd al-Raziq family with the party. But it appears to have had a more abstract basis as well. 'Ali 'Abd al-Raziq's book, with its attacks on individual and arbitrary rule, was indeed part and parcel of the Liberal political outlook. Impelled in the same direction by both personal and ideological considerations, in 1925 the

Liberal press and publicists defended ‘Abd al-Raziq against the official persecution he underwent, criticizing the disciplinary proceedings against the Shaykh on the dual grounds that the corps of *‘ulama’* lacked jurisdiction to take action that might affect the position of a state employee (‘Abd al-Raziq held a post in the *Shari‘a* court system, and his ouster from the corps of *‘ulama’* would necessarily entail his dismissal from his state post), and that the constitutional guarantee of freedom of expression possessed by every Egyptian under the Constitution of 1923 was being infringed by the proceedings against ‘Abd al-Raziq.[62]

Primarily because of the dilemma created for the Liberals by their support of ‘Abd al-Raziq while participating in a Palace-backed ministry that had to take action against him, the hearing and disciplining of ‘Ali ‘Abd al-Raziq was of considerable significance for the course of Egyptian politics. By law, ‘Abd al-Raziq's ouster from the corps of *‘ulama’* meant dismissal from his post as judge in the *Shari‘a* courts as well, since only members of the corps could be so employed. But the Minister of Justice who had jurisdiction over ‘Abd al-Raziq as a court official was ‘Abd al-‘Aziz Fahmi, President of the Liberal Party. Fahmi prevaricated over dismissing ‘Abd al-Raziq from his judgeship; the Prime Minister, probably under Palace pressure, in turn requested Fahmi's resignation; and eventually Fahmi and the two other Liberal ministers in the government did resign in protest over the issue.[63] This was the beginning of the end for the Palace-backed ministries that had ruled since the fall of the Wafd in late 1924. Recoiling from affiliation with the Palace, the Liberals now joined forces with the Wafd and the Watanists, and pressure by this combined opposition led to the holding of elections in May 1926 that saw a Wafdist majority returned to Parliament.

The political crisis that began with the ‘Abd al-Raziq controversy may also have had important consequences for the Caliphate question in Egypt. It has been suggested that, with Palace-dominated government on the way out by the winter of 1925-1926, King Fu'ad may once again have perceived it to be to his political advantage to play the Caliphate card in an effort to bolster his position vis-à-vis his domestic rivals.[64] An external incentive to action on the issue also existed by the end of 1925. This was the intention of the new Sa‘udi state in the Arabian Peninsula, announced in October 1925, to convene an international Islamic congress in Mecca. Although intended primarily to discuss the status of the Holy Cities in the wake of their conquest by the Sa‘udis, there was no guarantee that the still unresolved matter of the Caliphate would not be addressed at this gathering outside of Egypt and thus be less amenable to Egyptian influence.[65] Whatever the reasons, Egyptian hesitation on the Caliphate question ended in February 1926, when a meeting of the Azhar Caliphate Committee resulted in the announcement that the general Islamic congress intended to resolve the matter of the Caliphate would convene in Cairo in May 1926.[66] With this decision of early 1926, the Caliphate issue once again obtruded into Egyptian public life.

The Cairo Caliphate Congress of 1926

The resurfacing of the idea of a Caliphate congress in Cairo provoked considerable opposition within Egypt. Even prior to the public announcement by the Azhar Caliphate Committee in February 1926, forty *‘ulama’* of al-Azhar had signed a petition opposing the idea of bringing the Caliphate to Egypt as long as the country remained under foreign influence and the *Shari'a* was not the law of the land; the government is reported to have tried to suppress the petition and to have investigated its signees.[67] The official Azhar Committee's declaration in February 1926 was followed by counter-declarations by the Abu al-'Aza'im Caliphate Committee, which opposed the idea of a congress in Egypt while the country was "under English domination" and which supported the alternative Islamic congress being organized in independent Sa'udi Arabia as a more suitable venue for the resolution of the issue.[68] In the party press, the Wafdist *al-Balagh* expressed the view that the Caliphate would be inappropriate for Egypt in its present circumstances of only partial independence, and also that the installation of the institution in Egypt might adversely affect the country, becoming another international issue like the Suez Canal that would provoke perpetual foreign intervention in the affairs of Egypt.[69] The Liberal *al-Siyasa* argued, as it had in regard to the 'Ali 'Abd al-Raziq controversy of 1925, that the religious hierarchy lacked authority in questions affecting Egypt's public life; the only body competent to take binding action on the Caliphate in Egypt was Parliament itself, and the matter should be left to it.[70] Egypt's leading secular parties thus saw the convening of a Caliphate congress in Egypt as being, as one British report put it, "neither in the interests of Islam nor in those of Egypt."[71]

Reaction in other Muslim lands in 1926 was often just as negative. The foreign contacts undertaken by the Azharite organizers of the congress since 1924 had failed to garner much external support for the assembly. The domestic Egyptian opponents of the congress had addressed much of their activity and propaganda to Muslims outside Egypt, "endeavouring to convince them that it will not serve the purpose of Islam to get King Fuad elected Caliph."[72] This internal opposition combined with the native inclinations and justified suspicions of Muslims elsewhere to produce only a tepid foreign response to the summons to a Caliphate congress in Cairo. The position of thoroughly or partially secularized regimes such as those in Turkey and Iran was predictably hostile; the imperial powers, Great Britain and France, while doing little to discourage, also did not encourage attendance by their colonial subjects as a conclave that could only result in further complicating the situation in the Islamic world; most significantly, Muslim leaders and organizations in populous Muslim lands such as India and Indonesia, or central ones such as Syria and Palestine, remained leery of participating in a conference that seemed to them to be motivated by the dynastic interests of the otherwise un-Islamic ruler of Egypt.[73]

This domestic and foreign opposition to the congress soon placed its organizers on the defensive and eventually led to a significant reduction in the planned scope of the assembly. As the negative reaction became apparent, the King himself is reported to have told Egyptian religious leaders that he had no aspirations to become Caliph.[74] On 25 April 1925, only three weeks before the opening of the congress, the Azharite organizing committee decided to alter the nature of the congress. Whereas the original summons to the congress of March 1924, reiterated in February 1926, had specified that it would undertake the selection of a new Caliph, an exposition by Shaykh Muhammad Mustafa al-Maraghi on how conditions in the Muslim world had changed since 1924 provided the formal justification for the committee's substitution of a program of investigation for one of selection. Instead of choosing a Caliph, a congress agenda consisting of determining the nature and necessity of the Caliphate and the possibility of reinstituting it at some future point in time was adopted at the meeting of 25 April.[75]

When the Cairo Caliphate Congress finally met in May 1926, about forty individuals from fourteen different countries were recognized as formal participants by the organizers of the meeting and attended one or more of its four sessions. The congress was technically an unofficial one, with none of the participants formally representing their governments. The largest number of participants naturally came from Egypt, followed by a sizable group of notables from neighboring Palestine. Among the important Muslim lands without any representation at the Congress were Turkey, Iran, and Afghanistan; the one delegate from India and the two from Indonesia did not represent their country's largest organizations of *'ulama'*, which had decided not to attend the congress. Almost half of the accredited participants represented only themselves, while the remainder, with the exception of the Egyptian delegation, spoke only for marginal organizations in their home countries.[76]

The Congress held only four sessions (on 13, 15, 18, and 19 May 1926). On the whole the sessions were, in Lord Lloyd's words, "stormy and, from the first, ineffectual."[77] Procedural wrangles took up an inordinate amount of time, particularly among the Egyptian organizers of the congress and the Arab delegates from the Fertile Crescent. First the foreign delegates protested over the intended secrecy of the proceedings, although to no avail; later procedural wrangles included debates over an elected versus an appointed deputy chair and the claim by foreign delegates that the minutes of the session were being doctored by the Egyptian organizers. Nonreligious issues obtruded into the Congress as well: the Fertile Crescent delegates called for the congress formally to go on record in protest against French repression in Syria, and despite the Egyptian preference to avoid doing so, a resolution attacking French actions in Syria was adopted in the final session.[78] Debate over procedural and peripheral matters was so extensive that delegates came to protest the "anarchy" of the congress and to threaten to withdraw from participation if disputes continued as they had.[79]

On the central substantive issue of the Caliphate, the proceedings of the congress were singularly unproductive. Although the affair's Egyptian organizers had by May 1926 abandoned hope of actually selecting a Caliph at the congress, they wished to keep the door open to a future Caliphal election as well as to the possibility of King Fu'ad's attaining the office. A group of foreign delegates led by the Tunisian reformer 'Abd al-'Aziz al-Tha'alibi were more skeptical about the general feasibility of resurrecting the Caliphate and more hostile to measures or resolutions that might ease the way for Fu'ad's assuming the office in the future.[80]

Much of the work of the Congress was undertaken by three committees. One was concerned with procedural matters, the second with the theoretical questions of the nature and the necessity of the Caliphate, and the third with the practical issue of the actual prospects for reestablishing the institution. The second committee, which was dominated by Egyptians, reaffirmed a traditionalist view of the Caliphate as an indispensable feature of the faith and as an office combining both religious and temporal functions.[81] The third committee, of which only one Egyptian was a member, concluded that the restoration of the Caliphate was "incapable of realization at the present time, in view of the situation in which Muslims find themselves," and went on to recommend the maintenance of a central committee of the congress in Cairo and the creation of branch committees in other Muslim lands in order to work for creating conditions that would allow the revival of the Caliphate at some future time.[82] The pessimistic though realistic tone of this last report did not suit the Egyptian organizers of the congress when it was read at the last session, with the result that the Egyptians succeeded in attaching to it a rosier addendum stating that the Caliphate was "capable of realization," presumably in the near future.[83] By this session it was clear to the Egyptians that little that was positive would come from the congress; they therefore took the lead in adjourning it on May 19, four days before its scheduled close, and before it might result in any action that would (as an Egyptian participant put it) prove detrimental either to Islam or to Egypt.[84]

The Cairo Caliphate Congress was less than enthusiastically received by Egyptian public opinion. Prior to its convening, it was accorded less attention in the press than the inherent importance of its subject merited, a function both of the presumed tarnished motives of its sponsors and the fact that Egyptian opinion was preoccupied with the parliamentary elections scheduled for 22 May.[85] With the exception of Palace organs, press comment once the congress convened was largely negative. Even the nonpartisan *al-Ahram* found occasion to criticize the organizational incompetence of its promoters and the unproductiveness of its sessions.[86] The party press had a field day with its mismanagement, the Liberal *al-Siyasa* emphasizing the anarchy that marked the sessions of the congress and the Wafdist *Kawkab al-Sharq* calling it a "joke" perpetrated on the Muslim world by "the men of religion in Egypt."[87] While the partisanship of these latter comments is obvious, it was the contemporary British evaluation that "on the whole, the Opposition criticisms probably reflect fairly accurately the state of Egyptian public opinion."[88]

As another report of the British High Commissioner put it, the Cairo Caliphate Congress was "a fiasco."[89] It failed to restore the Caliphate, the intention of its sponsors when it was originally planned in 1924; to pave the way for a later reestablishment of the institution, the reduced aim of its organizers by its convening in 1926; or to lead to an Egyptian assumption of the office, the probable goal of at least some of its promoters throughout the mid-1920s. Nor was it followed by anything positive. It had adjourned on 19 May with a resolution to reconvene in Cairo in a year's time as well as to establish a permanent secretariat in Egypt and branch committees elsewhere to prepare for the future, but none of this seems to have occurred.[90] It appears that neither the central committee nor the branches were created, and certainly there was no subsequent congress in Cairo. The Azharite Caliphate Committee itself seems to have become inoperative after the congress of 1926, a victim of its members' incompetence and of the apparent abandonment of the Caliphal gambit by the monarch who had earlier supported their activities.

Islam and the Political Order in Egypt, 1924–1926

The debates over the Caliphate issue in Egypt in the mid-1920s provide a mirror in which the attitudes of educated Egyptians on the general subject of the proper relationship of Egypt to the Islamic community are reflected. Two features stand out most prominently in these discussions. The first is the lack of Egyptian consensus concerning the Caliphal institution. Egyptians differed radically on the substantive questions—the possibility of actually reviving the institution, the nature and functions of any reestablished Caliphate, and not least Egypt's role in the restoration of the office—which made up the Caliphate issue in the mid-1920s. The second noteworthy aspect of the Egyptian outlook apparent in the disputes over the Caliphate was the degree to which purely Egyptian considerations were the public justification for positions and actions on the Caliphate question. Whatever the ultimate determinants of their views (religious, national, or personal), Egypt's leaders rationalized their positions and actions in terms of the needs and interests of the newly created Egyptian national state.

It should be noted that there is no absolute sociological division apparent within Egyptian public opinion over the Caliphate and related issues in the mid-1920s. Although there was obviously a tendency for members of Egypt's religious class of *'ulama'* to voice more traditionalist appreciations of the Caliphate and the *umma* and for the country's political leaders and publicists to express more secular and Western-influenced conceptualizations, it is nonetheless very difficult to cluster individuals into distinct groups in terms of their views on Islam and the political order. The blurring of intellectual lines is exemplified best in the fact that the "point man" for political secularism in the 1920s, 'Ali 'Abd al-Raziq, was by education and training a member of the religious establishment. Sometimes the attitudes of otherwise traditionalist spokesmen show considerable penetration of nontraditional concepts. As Albert Hourani has noted, even one of 'Ali 'Abd al-Raziq's strongest critics, Shaykh Muhammad Bakhit, accepted the liberal ideas that "the source of the Caliph's power is the *umma*" and that Islam meant "democratic, free, consultative government," thus casting his defense of the Caliphal institution in distinctly modern terms.[91] Similarly, distinctions between an Egyptian and a Muslim identity appeared in the statements of *'ulama'*, such as the position of Shaykh al-Azhar in 1926 that it was "in our capacity as Muslims, not as Egyptians, [that] we wish a Caliph."[92]

On the other side, leaders of the secular political establishment sometimes demonstrated relatively traditionalist understandings of the Caliphate or the place of religion in political life. Sa'd Zaghlul, for example, is reported to have adhered to the position that the Caliphate did combine both "temporal and spiritual authority" and to have felt that 'Ali 'Abd al-Raziq's attempt to divide the two spheres was thoroughly unjustified in the Islamic context.[93] From a similar perspective the Wafdist *Kawkab al-Sharq* may have criticized the proceedings against 'Abd al-Raziq as unwarranted from the standpoint of the Egyptian state, but it also held that "the *'ulama'* were not wrong in their judgement" that the book was a misinterpretation of Islam.[94]

One point on which there was at least surface agreement amongst Egyptian opinion in the mid-1920s was the acceptance of the idea of a Caliphate as necessary and desirable. With but a few exceptions, educated Egyptians of differing political and cultural inclinations spoke in favor of the restoration of a Caliphate of some sort after the Turkish abolition of the office in 1924. This was implicit in the nature of the original debate concerning the most suitable claimant to the office in 1924; what was debated was who and how, not whether.

Undoubtedly the most important exception to this consensus on the desirability of the Caliphal institution was Shaykh 'Ali 'Abd al-Raziq's attack on the historicity of the Caliphate in 1925. But it needs to be emphasized that 'Abd al-Raziq's position was a very isolated one. There seems to have been practically no one in Egypt in 1925 who cared to agree in public with the Shaykh's radical interpretation of Islam. When other Egyptians did come to the defense of 'Abd al-Raziq during the proceedings against him in the summer of 1925, it was on constitutional rather than theological grounds that they did so. From the Liberal *al-Siyasa,* from secularist journals like *al-Hilal* and *al-Muqtataf,* and eventually from the Wafdist *al-Balagh* and *Kawkab al-Sharq* came assertions of every Egyptian's right to freedom of expression under the Constitution of 1923—but very little or no agreement with the substantive views about Islam that the Shaykh had propounded in his book.[95]

Much the same pattern was evident at the time of the Cairo Caliphate Congress in 1926. For all the invective directed against the congress in the partisan press in May 1926, there seems to have been no direct attack upon the idea of the restoration of the Caliphate. The goal of the congress was widely accepted as worthwhile, however retarded its actual implementation might be as a result of the mismanagement of the organizers of the Congress.[96] It is an arguable point whether this near-unanimity on the idea of the Caliphate was always the true inclination of all the authors who voiced it or merely a politically obligatory stance in light of the Caliphate question's being, as Sa'd Zaghlul is reported to have told Muhammed Husayn Haykal, "a sensitive one with the masses" in the 1920s.[97] Even if sometimes dissimulative, the publicly voiced consensus on the idea of the Caliphate testifies to the hold of the office upon the Egyptian public.

As soon as we move beyond mere endorsement of the concept of the Caliphate, however, we find radically different opinions about the nature, the functions, and the significance of the office. Most Egyptian *'ulama'* appear to have adhered to generally traditionalist conceptions of the Caliphate, the community, and the nature of political power in Islamic society. The articles by *'ulama'* in the Egyptian press at the time of the Turkish abolition of the office in March 1924 expounded the historic Islamic view of the Caliphate as a necessary, unitary, and combined religious and temporal office.[98] The meeting of Egyptian *'ulama'* of 25 March 1924 that called for an Islamic congress on the Caliphate to be convened in Egypt spelled out the traditionalist interpretation in perhaps its most official form in Egypt. Defining the Caliphate as a "general leadership in matters of religion and of this world" and specifying that the jurisdiction of the office extended to Muslims everywhere, the manifesto insisted that "the Caliph has absolute discretion to dispose of his subjects' affairs" and that "all power must derive and proceed from him."[99] The Caliph was thus made what he had theoretically been in the distant past: the ultimate sovereign of the Muslim world, whose authority extended to both religious and temporal affairs and to whom all "regional rulers" were ultimately responsible.[100] Similar traditionalist conceptions of the Caliphate continued to be expounded within the ranks of the Egyptian religious class in the years that followed. In reactions to 'Ali 'Abd al-Raziq's book, the aspects of the latter's views that were singled out for attack by his colleagues within the corps of *'ulama'* were 'Abd al-Raziq's division of authority between the religious and the political spheres, on the one hand, and his denial of a political role for the Prophet and the Companions, on the other. Thus the seven charges on which 'Abd al-Raziq was arraigned before the Grand Council of *'Ulama'* in August 1925 were all of a legal and historical nature: two accused him of making the *Shari'a* into a purely spiritual system of law; three asserted that he had misinterpreted the nature of Muhammad's prophetic mission; and two maintained he had besmirched the reputation of the early Caliphs.[101] The substantive positions in the judgment eventually rendered against the Shaykh were both traditionalist in content and categorical in tone: Islam indeed included "principles, devotions, and practices for improving the affairs of the world as well as [concerning] the Hereafter"; it had done so since the time of the Prophet, and 'Abd al-Raziq had been wrong to deny the same propositions.[102]

Such interpretations were put forward again by Egypt's leading religious officials at the time of the Cairo Caliphate Congress in 1926. Even before the congress convened, one of its key organizers, Shaykh Muhammad Faraj al-Minyawi, spoke out against a secularizing outlook that was defining a restored Caliphate in terms of the Caliph's being little more than the chairman of an elected Muslim assembly. Minyawi denounced such ideas as "a European system foreign to Islam" and maintained the necessity for the Caliph to possess "all his *Shari'a* rights" in regard to both religious and temporal affairs.[103] The Committee established at the congress to examine the theoretical aspects of the Caliphate held that the Caliphate was a necessity in Islam, without which the Muslim would die "ignorant" of the principles of the faith. Its nature was to provide "a general leadership of the religion and of this world," with religious and temporal aspects both falling under its jurisdiction; and just as the human body possesses only "one heart," so there could be only one Caliph.[104]

In the debates of the Congress, Shaykh Muhammad Bakhit probably expressed the viewpoint of most of the Egyptian delegates when he said it was only "heretics" who thought of the Caliphate as an "exclusively spiritual" office.[105] The timeless quality of the political thought of the majority of the Egyptian religious establishment appears most clearly in the statement of Shaykh Muhammad al-Ahmadi al-Zawahiri explaining the position taken by the committee of the Caliphate congress reporting on the theoretical aspects of the Caliphal institution: "We feel that the application of the general principles of religion ought to be subject to no exceptions; and we consider that there is no occasion to establish new conditions in deference to the exigencies of the age."[106]

Conceptions of the Caliphate and the Islamic community held by educated Egyptians outside the religious class were often markedly different from those found among the *'ulama'*. One obvious distinction was the greater sense of realism regarding the Caliphal institution expressed by non-*'ulama'*. In contrast to the insistence of religious leaders on the historical efficacy of the Caliphate and the possibility of restoring it as a vital institution in the modern world, commentators from the political arena more readily recognized the powerlessness that had long characterized the office. As Ahmad Zaki put it in 1926, "in the twentieth century the Caliphate has become more a symbol than a reality."[107] Admitting the realities of the contemporary situation, secular observers thus tended to see any continuing role for the Caliphate in symbolic rather than practical terms—as a potential moral authority within the Muslim world for some,[108] as a desirable symbol of the religio-cultural unity of Muslims for others.[109]

In the analyses of the possible nature and functions of a revived Caliphate which were expressed in secular circles within Egypt in the mid-1920s, quite modified and modernized views of the role of the Caliphal institution can be found. Concepts of a radically changed Caliphate were in the air throughout the Muslim world by the 1920s; writers in various Muslim lands perceived a need to make the office more congruent with contemporary ideas of limited and responsible government.[110]

The most detailed Egyptian exposition of a modernized Caliphate came in a book published in France in 1926 by the Egyptian jurist 'Abd al-Razzaq Ahmad al-Sanhuri. Its title alone was indicative of the author's evolutionary approach to the topic: *Le califat: son évolution vers une société des nations orientale.* Sanhuri's basic thesis concerning the Caliphate was that a "regular" (that is, traditional) Caliphate could not now be reestablished, given current conditions in the Muslim world.[111] What he advocated in its place was the creation of a "society of oriental nations" composed of the independent Muslim states that (among other things) would strive to revive the Caliphate at some future point in time. It was Sanhuri's view that the presiding officer of such a league could be recognized as "provisional" Caliph, pending the restoration of the full Caliphal institution.[112] Similar ideas of the Caliph as a glorified chairman of the board were voiced in Egypt in the same year: *al-Muqattam* speculated on the prospect that the Cairo Caliphate Congress might foreshadow a "society of Islamic or Eastern nations," and *Kawkab al-Sharq* expressed the alternative hope that the Islamic Congress that met in Mecca in June–July 1926 might mark the inauguration of a "league of Islamic nations" or "organization of the Caliphate" that would annually assemble representatives from different Muslim lands for the discussion of common problems.[113] What is most interesting about these suggestions from the perspective of nationalism in Egypt is the degree to which they implicitly recognized the division of the Muslim world into separate national states and concentrated on creating a mechanism for the periodic collaboration of the distinct units of which it was now composed.

The acceptance of the division of the *umma* into separate nation-states was stated explicitly in the commentary of Egyptians of a secularist orientation concerning the Caliphate in the mid-1920s. This was the premise of Muhammad Husayn Haykal's first commentary upon the abolition of the Caliphate in March 1924 when, despite his judgment that the Turkish action had been precipitate and injudicious, he nonetheless called for an Egyptian position of noninterference in the question, since "we Egyptians who demand to rule ourselves by ourselves and who insist upon no interference in our affairs by others cannot, either logically or politically, interfere in the affairs of others."[114] Wafdists were equally explicit in disavowing religious nationalism and asserting the primacy of the nation-state by 1924. As Ahmad Hafiz 'Awad put it in the first issue of the Wafdist *Kawkab al-Sharq* in September 1924, the idea of "Islamic patriotism" was outmoded, as each Muslim country had now become "a unique *watan* with unique politics and unique circumstances."[115] A similar belief in the historical ascendancy of the modern nation-state underlay Sanhuri's position: the reestablishment of a traditional Caliphate was impossible in his view precisely because "nationalist and separatist tendencies" were increasing "day by day" among the peoples of the Muslim world.[116]

The manner in which the Egyptian press treated the Caliphate question in the mid-1920s clearly demonstrates that the prime concern of Egyptians involved in the political life of the country was with the national implications of what was, formally at least, a religious issue. The coverage accorded the Caliphate in the wake of the Turkish abolition of the office in March 1924 followed a similar pattern in many of Egypt's leading newspapers: their editorialists addressed most of their attention to the political dimensions of the event. Thus, when Amin al-Rafi'i in the Watanist *al-Akhbar* analyzed the abolition of the Caliphate in March 1924, it was the political consequences of the event that he emphasized: that it was not to the national advantage of the Turks to forfeit the sympathy of other Muslims through an attack on Islam, and that the abolition of the institution could open the door to the sponsoring by one or another of the European powers of an alternative Caliphate that would merely be "a plaything in their hands."[117] Muhammad Husayn Haykal's analyses of the event also used the Caliphate question to draw primarily political conclusions. One of his editorials found the "lesson" of the Turkish action for Egypt to be the dangers of one-man rule such as that of Mustafa Kemal in Turkey (an obvious reverence to Sa'd Zaghlul in Egypt in 1924); another criticized the rival Wafdist government for not taking an official position on the issue and for not working for the immediate convening of an Islamic congress to discuss the Caliphate.[118]

The same primacy of the political and the national held true after March 1924. It was implicit in the debates that raged over 'Ali 'Abd al-Raziq's book and hearing in mid-1925, the Shaykh's supporters choosing to defend him on the strictly political grounds of the threat to constitutional guarantees of freedom of expression and the danger (of religious authority extending into the civil realm) posed by the proceedings undertaken against him by the Azharite hierarchy. Similarly, at the time of the Cairo Caliphate Congress in May 1926, it was the political implications of the assembly that were the main focus of attention in the secular press of Egypt. *Kawkab al-Sharq* made explicit the political and nationalist prism through which most partisan opinion in Egypt viewed the Caliphate issue in the mid-1920s: "the Caliphate is a political question before it is a religious one, and it concerns the government and Parliament before it concerns the learned men of religion."[119] A statement such as this from a journal that otherwise gave considerable attention to Muslim issues indicates a significant transmutation of perspective from the traditional Muslim view that *din* and *dawla* are twins.

When we consider the content of the views held by Egyptian political commentators on the Caliphate issue in the mid-1920s, the most notable feature is their focus on Egypt both in terms of the virtues that qualified it to play a leading role in the resolution of the crisis produced by the Turkish abolition of the institution, and in terms of how the country's prestige and national interests would benefit from or be injured by involvement in the Caliphate issue. "We do not see a land more suitable for the Caliphate and more fitting as its center than Egypt," *al-Muqattam* was editorializing within a few days of the Turkish abolition of the office.[120] In the weeks that followed, the idea of Egypt's unique qualifications for leading the way on the Caliphate issue became a theme frequently expounded upon in most of the secular press. The reasons why Egypt was particularly fitted to take the lead on the question were fairly standard by 1924: the country's central geographical position in the Islamic world; the presumed leading role played by Egypt in Islamic history; Egypt's contemporary preeminence in Islam as the largest Arabic-speaking country and the seat of a great Muslim religious institution such as al-Azhar; and the country's general level of cultural advancement, which qualified her to lead the rest of the Muslim world.[121] Conversely, those who opposed Egypt's organizing an Islamic congress or becoming the site of the Caliphate did so primarily on the political grounds that the country was unsuited as the seat of the Caliphate as long as any vestige of foreign domination continued: "free yourselves first and then choose a Caliph," as one Wafdist put it in 1925.[122] The Egyptianist tone of superiority found in commentary on the Caliphate question in 1924 is illustrated by *al-Ahram's* editorial comment on the meeting of *'ulama'* of 25 March: claiming that "the eyes of the Islamic world are directed to Egypt," the journal called on Egyptians to "work and prepare the arrangements for the congress in a manner compatible with the dignity of Egypt and its exalted place in the Islamic world in particular and in all of the civilized world in general."[123]

The same theme of Egypt's advantages and advanced position vis-à-vis other Muslim lands continued to find expression throughout the mid-1920s. It was voiced by both religious and political leaders: by Shaykh al-Minyawi in the pages of the Azhar Caliphate Committee's official journal extolling Egypt as "one of the greatest Islamic states in point of progress, civilization, riches, and prosperity;"[124] by the Liberal *al-Siyasa*'s deploring the Egyptian government's decision (later reversed) not to attend the Islamic congress in Mecca in 1926 because such nonattendance would be contrary to Egypt's position as a leader and a "model" for other Muslim lands;[125] and by the Wafdist *Kawkab al-Sharq*'s recommending Egypt as the seat of any permanent council of Muslim states that might result from the same congress on the grounds that "Egypt is the heart of Islam and the carrier of its banner."[126] However pro-Palace, Liberal, and Wafdist spokesmen differed on the precise terms of their country's involvement in international Islamic affairs, they all shared the same nationalist pride in Egypt's relative advancement vis-à-vis other Muslim lands.

Not all Egyptian political commentators regarded their country's involvement in the Caliphate issue as desirable, however. What needs noting here is the degree to which critics of the effort to organize a Caliphate congress in Egypt framed their criticisms of the endeavor in terms of its perceived negative implications for the Egyptian nation. The nationalist filter through which politically minded Egyptians viewed the Caliphate issue appears particularly clearly at the time of the Cairo Caliphate Congress in 1926. A variety of reasons why the convening of the congress would not be in the national interest of Egypt were put forth in the party press during the months preceding the congress. These ranged from purely internal arguments concerning the damage an Egyptian Caliphate might produce for the country's fragile constitutional order to externally oriented analyses of the negative impact the Caliphate could have for Egyptian foreign relations, with the Caliphate compared to the Suez Canal as a source of unwanted foreign interference in Egyptian affairs.[127] In most of these partisan critiques of the Congress, it was the needs of Egypt rather than those of Islam that were the basis for opposition to the convening of the congress on Egyptian soil.

One of the most detailed critical analyses of the idea of Egypt seeking to play a leading role in Islamic affairs in general and in the Caliphate question in particular was that offered by the Wafdist journalist 'Abbas Mahmud al-'Aqqad at the time of the opening of the Cairo Caliphate Congress. The point of 'Aqqad's article was to offer several "reasons for caution" about the entire campaign for the restoration of the Caliphate in which the Egyptian religious establishment had played such a prominent role.[128] After political criticisms of the royalist and absolutist inclinations of the clerical organizers of the congress, 'Aqqad's more abstract critique of the Egyptian campaign for the revival of the Caliphate was based on the movement's adverse implications for Egypt itself. On one level, involvement in the Caliphate question could impose external political responsibilities on the country, despite the fact that the parliamentary authorities had not opted to assume those burdens; on another, it would not be to Egypt's benefit to antagonize other Muslim states through pursuing the Caliphate for Egypt itself. In general, it would be of no advantage to the country to become involved with "imperialist states and foreign plots" over the Caliphal institution. 'Aqqad's conclusion breathed a spirit of isolation that genuinely reflected the Wafd's skepticism about Egyptian involvement in Islamic (and Arab) issues throughout the 1920s: "we fear that the Caliphate will become a new lasso over the shoulders of Egypt, by which British policy will draw it to humiliate itself and to humiliate other Eastern peoples."[129]

The extent to which the national interests of Egypt had become the primary criterion for the attitudes and actions of the country's political leadership by the 1920s can be illustrated by remarks made by the two preeminent figures in Egyptian public life during the decade, Sa'd Zaghlul and King Fu'ad. When asked his opinion on the Caliphate issue in June 1924, Zaghlul evaluated the hope of reviving the Caliphate as one of those "utopian goals" that, however sincerely desired by much of Muslim public opinion, would nevertheless be a counterproductive effort that could only "thwart effective policies" within the nation-states into which the Muslim world was now divided.[130] Five years later, when King Fu'ad maintained to the British that he had not actively aspired the Caliphate in earlier years, he rationalized his alleged reluctance to seek the office in terms of the Caliphate's undesirable implications for Egypt: "acceptance [of the Caliphate] would bring to Cairo every rapscallion in Islam, [and] would make him the butt of every kind of petition."[131] However questionable the candor of the latter comment in the light of other evidence concerning Fu'ad's ambitions in the mid-1920s, what is important is that the national interests of Egypt were made the standard for justifying their position vis-à-vis the Caliphate by both Egypt's first premier and her first king.

The Egyptian campaign to revive the Caliphate ended with the failure of the Cairo Caliphate Congress of May 1926. But the Congress fiasco marked more than the end of that two-year effort; it also signified the close of over a decade of rapid transformations in Egyptian political institutions, perceptions, and loyalties. Between 1914 and 1926, the old political universe in which Egyptians had lived before World War I crumbled around them. The war years destroyed the physical basis of the Ottoman system of which Egypt had for so long been a component part, and the postwar settlement completed the total liquidation of the Empire. What the controversy of the mid-1920s over the Caliphate confirmed was that there would be no re-creation of part of the Ottoman legacy elsewhere, no continuation in a setting other than the Ottoman of the symbolic focal point for Muslim allegiance that had been represented by the Caliphate. By 1926 the Ottoman religious-political order was dead.

Parallel to the death of the old came the birth of a new political universe, one marked by very different characteristics. In physical terms the multinational Ottoman Empire was replaced by several new national political units more or less independent; in theoretical terms the nation and the sovereignty of its people now assumed the positions previously held by the *umma* and the divinely ordained *Shari'a.* For Egyptians (perhaps less than for Turks, but certainly more than for Arabs), territorial nationalist concept received an enormous boost from the Egyptian Revolution of 1919 and the creation of the formally independent Egyptian parliamentary monarchy in the early 1920s. Where the old order had died, a new Egypt had seemingly been born.

As a result of both the death of the old and the birth of the new, the political alternatives before Egyptians narrowed. Whereas before 1914 it had been possible and even attractive for Egyptians to be both Ottoman and Egyptian, to be loyal to both their Caliph and their country, by the mid-1920s the first component in each of these pairs had vanished. The Ottoman/Islamic option of the past was gone, its central institutions eliminated and its possible terms in need of reformulation (as was to occur from the 1930s onward) to become meaningful in the post-Ottoman, post-Caliphal world. In the 1920s a potential Arab option had yet to emerge (as too it was to do from the 1930s onwards), given the differences in conditions still dividing Egypt from the rest of the Arab world and the setbacks that the Arab nationalism of Western Asia had suffered in the postwar settlement. By the mid-1920s and for several years thereafter, there seemed to be but one political path before Egyptians: to be Egyptian, to think Egyptian, and to act Egyptian.

II

THE INTELLECTUAL RESPONSE: THE IDEOLOGY OF EGYPTIAN TERRITORIAL NATIONALISM

4

Egyptian Intellectuals and the Formation of a New National Image

The Intellectual as Creator of a Collective Image

It seems almost banal to note that human beings read into the world their own needs, inclinations, and presuppositions. "It is our needs," Nietzsche tells us, "that interpret the world for us."[1] In a similar vein, Kenneth Boulding maintains that human behavior is not influenced directly by reality per se but by the image that human beings have of reality.[2] Ernst Cassirer comes to much the same conclusion in his *An Essay on Man.* What Nietzsche terms "needs" and Boulding calls "images," Cassirer defines as "symbols" or a "symbolic system." Man is an "animal symbolicum" living in a "symbolic universe," Cassirer argues: he "does not live in a world of hard facts. . . . He lives rather in the midst of imaginary emotions, in hopes and fears, in illusions and disillusions, in his fantasies and dreams."[3]

To be sure, there is normally some relationship between image and reality, between our apprehension of the world and the world itself. Although the image is not a photograph and therefore not an exact reproduction of reality, there is usually some resemblance between the two. But it is the image that matters. Once an image crystallizes, it comes to possess its own importance, its own reality. Human beings perceive reality as it were "indirectly," through their image of it, and they operate in accordance with their image rather than with reality itself. As Boulding put it, "behavior depends on the image" we possess of the world; "it is this Image that largely governs my behavior."[4]

Obviously, the image is not completely static. It is subject to modification or revision, sometimes even radical revision. Changes in reality or new information that we receive from reality can lead to modifications in our image of it. When such new "outside messages," to use Boulding's term, impinge on our image, the latter may be modified or reorganized.[5] However, even when the image is revised or modified, the influence exercised by this altered image upon our thought and behavior patterns is just as great as the influence of the original image. In sum, without the constant formation and reformation of images or the projection of a symbolic system upon the world, we cannot grasp the world. To paraphrase Nietzsche, our images are what interpret the world for us; they provide us with the conceptual framework for action.

But of course there are various kinds of images.[6] Our main concern is not with the private images of individuals but rather with the collective image developed and possessed by a society or by specific groups within it. When we speak of a collective image we mean a *Weltanschauung*—a total worldview, an overall image of social reality that approaches what Karl Mannheim called the "total conception of ideology."[7] In any large social unit, there is not a single collective image but rather various images possessed by the groups, sectors, or subcultures into which society is subdivided. As is the case with individuals, groups and societies also behave in accordance with their collective image(s) of reality. The preceding qualifications about the correlations of image and behavior by and large may be said to apply to collective images as well as to individual ones.

The creation and dissemination of such collective images of reality is a more complex process than the genesis of individual images. Every collective or (to use Boulding's term) "public" image of course begins in the minds of individuals and only becomes public as it is transmitted and shared throughout a given society.[8] In this process of the inception and diffusion of public or collective images, the role of a society's intellectuals is critical.

The crucial difference between intellectuals and others in a society seems to lie in the self-image of the former. Intellectuals often share an idealized concept of their role in relation to the existing collective image held by their society. What appears to set intellectuals apart is their refusal to accept existing collective images and their conscious attempt to formulate new ones for themselves and their society. Intellectuals do not passively accept the prevalent image of the world around them and merely act in accordance with it: more often, they seek to alter and reshape the collective image of their time and place. Of course, intellectuals do not always succeed in this self-appointed task. It is not necessarily the success of their endeavors but rather their incessant attempts to reshape the image of their community that set intellectuals apart from the rest of society.

In some ways, intellectuals are more free than others, possessing a self-view that makes them more willing to tamper with both images and the social realities upon which they are based. They are not totally free, however. There is always a finite range of possibilities from which the constituents of any new image may be drawn. As Edward Shils observed of the activity of intellectuals in general, "the process of elaborating and developing further the potentialities inherent in a system of beliefs entails some degree of rejection of the inherited tradition."[9] Yet, while this "range of rejection of the inherited varies greatly, it can never be complete and all-embracing."[10] Rather than total dismissal of a tradition, "the act of rejection practically always is an act of observance and development of an alternative stream of tradition, sometimes one which has been buried for a long time."[11] The "stock" of potential materials for a new collective image may be quite extensive, containing elements from a long and varied historical legacy as well as from prolonged contacts with other cultures in the world; in other cases it may be much more restricted, both temporally and spatially. But within these broad limits there is always some scope for those who think of themselves as intellectuals to pick and choose from the past and the present in order to construct a new image for themselves and their future.

The nature of a collective image and its development may be illustrated by a consideration of the examples of Ahmad Lutfi al-Sayyid and Muhammad Husayn Haykal. Their thinking was notable for its refusal to accept the existing collective image of Egypt. The current Egyptian self-image that had been passed down through the generations and was unconsciously accepted by modern Egyptians was viewed by them as incorrect on the one hand and dysfunctional on the other. In terms of the former, it presented an ahistorical and false picture of the Egyptian past and present; in terms of the latter, it was a static and antiprogressive portrait that threatened to block the evolution of Egypt in the future.

Their new collective image of Egypt possessed the opposite qualities. First, it was assumed by them to be the correct image of Egypt, an image that captured the true essence of the country and eliminated the incorrect elements of the present collective image. Secondly, it was dynamic rather than static, progressive rather than antiprogressive. Assuming their image of Egypt to be fully congruent with change and modernization, they believed that its resurrection and dissemination throughout Egyptian society was the indispensible prerequisite of Egyptian development. In sum, they believed that Egypt needed a collective image that was both valid and valuable.

The new collective image developed by these two figures and later elaborated by their Egyptianist disciples was not invented *ex nihilo.* Despite its utopian elements, it was not entirely the product of their imaginations. There was a relationship between the ideal image they envisaged for Egypt and Egyptian realities. In their delineation of the components of their new image of their country, Egyptian nationalist intellectuals assumed that many potentialities or latent elements (in Shils's terminology, "an alternative stream of tradition") for a new collective image were already present in the Egyptian heritage. They perceived their own role as one of transforming these potential or latent components into tangible reality. Yet, in the process of actualizing these latent components of a new Egyptian collective image, Egyptianist intellectuals also reorganized them, introduced new themes and motifs to them, and most importantly lent them a dynamic and operative character that they had previously lacked. In many cases one such latent image was selected, actualized, and extended; but this occurred only at the expense of other latent or actual components of Egyptian life whose social significance was intentionally minimized or obscured.

Muhammad Husayn Haykal is a useful case in point. When Haykal formulated the territorial component as the exclusive determining factor in the Egyptian collective image, he was fastening onto a latent component of Egyptian reality that he himself knew was largely beyond the consciousness of Egyptian society in its current historical situation. By reformulating and reorganizing the territorial principle, Haykal sought to bring this latent component to the surface—to make it manifest in order to afford it its natural and central status as the foundation for the ideal collective image that Egypt deserved. Yet at the same time Haykal ignored, rejected, or downplayed other elements that could have formed part of a collective image: on the one hand, the previously dominant Islamic/Ottoman elements that had shaped the collective consciousness of most Egyptians up to that time; on the other, the latent Arab linguistic and cultural elements that other Egyptian intellectuals were later to emphasize.

Egyptian territorial nationalist intellectuals in general shared the self-view that defined their own role as being that of "making manifest what is latent."[12] They also sought to elaborate and to inculcate an ideal collective image of Egypt through the selection and emphasis of the territorial elements of the Egyptian heritage while sharply downplaying its nonterritorial components. In their view, only this redefined and primarily Egyptianist image of Egypt could serve as the foundation of a new ideology for their country. Their new image was, above all, action oriented. It was not meant to reflect existing Egyptian reality; rather, it was intended to shape a new Egyptian reality.

In many ways, Egyptian nationalist intellectuals of the 1920s shared the premises and conclusions that J. L. Talmon has identified as characteristic of modern totalitarian democracy. Like their earlier European counterparts, they also appear to have postulated the existence of "a preordained, harmonious, and perfect scheme of things, to which men are irresistably driven, and at which they are bound to arrive."[13] They too created a new image for their country "by thinking not in terms of men as they are, but as they were meant to be, and would be given the proper conditions."[14] They possessed that powerful sense of mission that runs in avant-garde intellectual circles and posits that "[t]hose conditions would be brought about by the vanguard of the enlightened, who know the real will of the people and their ultimate wish, which the people themselves are as yet unprepared to formulate."[15] This perception of the mission of the intellectual, of cogitation as a sacred vocation, was not dissimilar from that observed by de Tocqueville on the part of French intellectuals of the *ancien régime:* "They believed in themselves. . . . In short, they had a fanatical faith in their vocation—that of transforming the social system, root and branch, and regenerating the whole human race."[16]

This all-embracing view of the place of the intellectual made the efforts of Egyptian territorial nationalists of the 1920s a much more sweeping endeavor than merely the redefinition of Egyptian national identity. The problem they posed for themselves in the wake of the Revolution of 1919 was not merely "who are we?" or even "what is Egypt?" This was part—but only part—of their concern. The decisive question preoccupying them was a broader one: "What do we seek and aspire to make of ourselves as Egyptians, or to make of our Egypt, and what materials and potential do we and Egypt possess in order to bring this goal about?" Correspondingly, the answers to this larger question were not to be found only in the formation of a new Egyptian identity. They rested in a far deeper and more comprehensive process: the formation of a totally new collective image that would result in a revolutionary change in the worldview of Egyptians and the actual condition of Egypt. The problem of identity and its solution thus formed but one component of a more ambitious intellectual effort to create a new image for Egypt that could lead to the transformation of Egyptian reality in all spheres of life.

When do human beings feel the need to disassociate themselves from an old collective image and to create a new one? Can we identify periods in history during which the need to establish collective images is stronger and more urgent than at other times? Generally speaking, it may be argued that the desire to create new images is greatest in times of change and uncertainty, whereas during periods of relative stability, when the sense of historical continuity and collective self-confidence are strong, such an impulse is weak or absent. Profound structural crises, severe political and social upheavals, fundamental social changes, the resultant loss of stability and self-confidence, a collective sense of the collapse of an old order and of the impending advent of a new era—these are the elements that characterize those transitional periods of history during which human beings, and particularly intellectuals, feel impelled to try to establish a new collective image for their society.

Drastic historical turning points of this sort give the intellectuals of a society the sensation that a severe incompatibility has arisen between the collective image and the social norms of the old order on the one hand, and the new objective circumstances of a rapidly changing world on the other. The old collective image was created under conditions that are ceasing to exist, and it is not consonant with the emerging historical configuration. Intellectuals believe that the new conditions taking shape before their eyes urgently require the formulation of a new collective image. Hence they develop one, and simultaneously call upon their society to adopt the new image extended to it in order that it may thereby enter into the new order even as it is being born. We can find a dialectical relationship between those basic structural crises which result from the destruction and disappearance of an old order, and the urge of intellectuals to formulate and promulgate a new collective image congruent with an emerging new order. Indeed, the more profound the crisis and the sense of change, the greater the fervor to create a new collective image.

In the Middle East, the collapse of the Ottoman Empire during and after World War I seems to have created precisely this sort of historical transition period. Its destruction, with all the political ramifications that accompanied it, had a profound effect upon all the former subjects of the Empire. The postwar collapse of the old Ottoman order and the emergence of the new national one is thus our point of departure from a general theoretical discussion to a more specific exploration of the thought and activities of Egyptianist intellectuals in the particular historical context of the 1920s, the decade immediately following the disappearance of the traditional Ottoman configuration.

The Revolutionary Temper of Egypt in the 1920s

What may be termed the Egyptian intellectual upsurge of the 1920s must be viewed first and foremost as an aggressive response to the drastic historical transformation that occurred in Egypt after the war and especially in the Revolution of 1919. An important feature of the Egyptian *zeitgeist* of the 1920s was the idea that Egypt was experiencing "revolution." As we have already noted, the Egyptian Revolution of 1919 hardly merits comparison with classical modern revolutions. But in considering images, it is perception rather than reality that is the critical issue; and here there is little doubt that in the 1920s many Egyptians, both intellectuals and others, firmly believed that they had just witnessed "revolutionary" events and were living in a "revolutionary" age. One major set of developments was that which had occurred in the region as a whole, particularly the collapse of the Ottoman Empire and the emergence of a new Middle East. The other key processes were domestic: the Revolution of 1919, the nationalist struggle of the early 1920s, and the subsequent establishment of a new political regime in Egypt. These external and internal changes provided both the stimulus and the setting for intellectuals' efforts to create a new collective image for Egypt.

The Collapse of the Ottoman Empire and the Emergence of Turkey

For much of the educated population of Egypt, the fall of the Ottoman Empire served as incontestable historical evidence that the curtain had been run down on the traditional Ottoman/Islamic framework of loyalty and allegiance. With the collapse of Ottoman institutions came the fading of old images, symbols, and ideals as well. The traditional world picture of Egyptians had been smashed. Correspondingly, certain Egyptians felt an intense urge to create a new world picture in place of the old.[17]

One specific prod to the expectation of the impending emergence of a new order was the rapid and successful development of modern Turkey as the successor to the Ottoman imperial structure. Perhaps more than any other country in the 1920s, the Turkey of Mustafa Kemal (Ataturk) served Egyptianist intellectuals as concrete historical proof of the fundamental changes occurring in the region. Turkey showed them the "natural" direction that Middle Eastern history was taking, from a supranational and religiously based imperial order to a largely modern, secular, territorially based national one. The radical reforms carried out by the new Kemalist regime, the pronounced Western orientation it adopted, and the total rebellion it proclaimed against Ottoman/Islamic tradition all fired the imagination of Egyptianist intellectuals. More than anything else, they were captivated by the attempt to create an entirely new national cultural image for Turkey, one that derived its symbols and contents solely from Turkish rather than Islamic elements.[18] The reinterpretation of Turkish history with the aim of recapturing the pre-Islamic Turkish past, the Turkification of art and literature in a manner that based both firmly on the modern Turkish language, and the identification of these changes with Western patterns struck responsive chords in Egyptianist intellectuals.[19] The creation of this new collective image, they believed, was redeeming Turkey from the shackles of the reactionary Islamic and Eastern tradition, opening it up to the modern West and thereby placing it on the road to renewal, progress, and enlightenment.[20]

In an essay of 1927 written after a visit to Turkey, Muhammad Husayn Haykal wrote at length in praise of what he termed "the Turkish renaissance."[21] In contrast to his earlier reservations concerning the abruptness, hence the disruptiveness, of the measures being undertaken by the regime in Turkey, Haykal now gave his unqualified support to Mustafa Kemal's radical reforms and to the revolutionary manner in which he had chosen to change Turkish society. Nor was Turkey alone: "the impact of this [Turkish] renaissance," Haykal wrote, "is not confined to the territory of Turkey alone, but is a renaissance of all Eastern peoples."[22] What was occurring in Turkey was destined to be of great significance for all of its former subjects, for its renaissance was "tearing down the old wall of tradition which had separated the peoples of the Ottoman Empire from progress and civilization for innumerable generations."[23] In a phrase so characteristic of the Westernizing orientation of the Egyptianist intellectuals in 1920s, he predicted that "the demolition of this dividing wall will open the way to the flow of civilization from West to East."[24]

Isma'il Mazhar was another great admirer of the Turkish Revolution. Mazhar found parallels between the Turkish and Bolshevik revolutions: where the latter represented a historical breakthrough for all humanity, the former constituted a breakthrough to the world of modernity and progress for Middle Eastern peoples.[25] One of the great strengths of the Turkish Revolution in Mazhar's view was its adoption of a clear-cut and progressive philosophy, a modern worldview that aimed at producing a basic mental and cultural change in the Turkish people: "the goal of the new Turkish philosophy is first of all to subjugate the Asiatic mentality and secondly to eliminate it in order that it will be superseded by the modern European mentality."[26]

For Egyptian nationalist intellectuals of the 1920s, Kemalist Turkey served as a model in several respects. First, it demonstrated that, to be progressive and fully part of the modern world, it was necessary to be culturally Western-oriented and to be willing to borrow extensively from Western civilization. Second, Turkey proved that a radical break with the more recent Islamic/Ottoman past and a corresponding reconstruction of a distinctive pre-Islamic past was both desirable and possible. Third, the Turkish experience in the 1920s pointed out the proper path to follow to attain the goals of modernity and nation building: that of a "revolution" that would alter all aspects of society suddenly and thoroughly. Finally, Kemalist Turkey was a continuous vindication of the territorial nationalist course that Egyptian intellectuals had chosen in the 1920s, a manifest demonstration of the premise that the only legitimate heir of the multinational Ottoman framework was modern state nationalism based on a specific territory and its unique historical heritage.

The Revolution of 1919: The Birth of the "New Egypt"

The impact of the collapse of the Ottoman Empire and the emergence of Turkey as a modern nation-state cannot alone account for the passion with which Egyptianist intellectuals of the 1920s sought to create a new collective image for Egypt. More important were internal Egyptian developments. It was the postwar political ferment and its perceived results that contributed more than anything else to the distinctive intellectual mood of Egypt in the 1920s. Although postwar events in the Ottoman Empire and Turkey were in part responsible for the belief that any new order would be national in form and Western-oriented in spirit, domestic developments were what produced the feeling that the content of this new order would necessarily be purely Egyptian. The nature and results of the Egyptian Revolution of 1919 primarily account for the distinctively Egyptianist character of postwar Egyptian thought. The numerous changes crowded into the five years between the popular uprising of 1919 and the installation of the Wafdist "ministry of the people" in 1924 were interpreted by Egyptianist intellectuals as a purely Egyptian national development—an authentic, spontaneous outburst of the Egyptian national soul, which was reawakening in order to restore the country to its former position of greatness and glory.[27]

Although the course of internal political developments was the decisive factor in the formation of this climate of opinion, other factors were significant as well.

Certainly one was the sensational discovery of the tomb of Tut-Ankh-Amon in late 1922. The timing of this discovery was very important, fitting perfectly into the sequence of revolutionary events occurring in Egypt at the time and thus greatly buttressing the distinctive Egyptian cast given to those events. It led inexorably to the expectation that Egypt was about to regain its unique national personality. In the process of being reborn, the young Egyptian nation was returning to its primordial Pharaonic essence.[28]

The classic literary statement of the sense of national revival present in Egypt in the 1920s is Tawfiq al-Hakim's novel *The Return of the Soul* [*'Awdat al-Ruh*].[29] No other work of the period gives such a vivid expression of the sense of "rebirth" alive in Egypt during the decade. For Hakim, the Revolution of 1919 marked the destruction of the decadent post-Pharaonic era of Egyptian history.[30] The Revolution had begun "the volcanic eruption" of the spirit of ancient Egypt; thus it was enabling Egypt to correct the course of its history, to disassociate itself from "false," "disappointing," pre-revolutionary Egypt, and to reestablish contact with its great Pharaonic past. What Egypt had been in the past, she was now becoming again: "a country which at the dawn of human history wrought the miracle of the Pyramids can never be at a loss to work another miracle, indeed many miracles!"[31]

Tawfiq al-Hakim explicitly identified March 1919 as the great turning point in modern Egyptian history. Just as March is the month of spring and rebirth in Egypt, so March 1919 was the month of national rebirth, the end of the long winter of Arab-Islamic domination that had been imposed upon the country and the coming of the spring of national renewal.[32] A central role in this reawakening of eternal Egypt was assigned to a personal redeemer, Sa'd Zaghlul, the "adored son" of Egypt, "the symbol of its hopes and sufferings," was made the embodiment and spokesman of the new spirit coming to life in contemporary Egypt.[33] A man of "true peasant stock," he was the representative of the last generation to live in slavery as well as of the first to be independent. Only a man of the countryside that had remained truly Egyptian over the generations of domination could serve as the savior of the nation.[34] He was a figure who inspired sacrifice in the entire nation. The continuity between ancient and modern Egypt in *'Awdat al-Ruh* was strikingly demonstrated in the comparison of Sa'd Zaghlul to the Pharaonic deity Osiris. Hakim compares Zaghlul's arrest and exile to Malta in March 1919 with the imprisonment and murder of Osiris: just as Osiris was resurrected after death and indeed symbolizes immortality, so too Zaghlul's return from exile is used to symbolize the eternity of Egypt and the inevitable success of its struggle for independence.[35]

Although it came as a complete surprise, the Revolution of 1919 united all Egyptians:

> Every group and community considered itself to have been the first to act, the first to feel the fiery new emotion. Yet no one understood that that sensation had arisen in all their hearts at the same time because they are all the children of Egypt [*abna' misr*] and they all have one heart.[36]

Through these protests of 1919, which involved every sector of Egyptian society, the Revolution of 1919 was presented as having recreated the Egyptian people as a single, homogeneous national body struggling for a common goal. Egypt itself was made not an abstraction but a living reality that transcended the factional loyalties and interests of its inhabitants and infused each of them with the same spirit.[37] The Egypt of Tawfiq al-Hakim was thus a glorious myth, one that reflected the sense of expectation that the events of the postwar years generated in Egyptianist intellectuals and which contributed to the new collective image of a revived, rejuvenated Egypt.

A later but equally valuable evocation of the mood of revolutionary breakthrough and awakening produced by the Revolution of 1919 is that provided in Najib Muhfuz's novel *Bayna al-Qasrayn.* The character who exemplifies the "new Egypt" in the novel is the son Fahmi. In Fahmi we find a highly developed Egyptian national consciousness expressed in militant national activism. Fahmi identifies completely with the new revolutionary spirit being forged in the Revolution. The national orientation he embodies is a purely Egyptian territorial nationalism. Fahmi also symbolizes the optimistic revolutionary temper of the post-1919 era in Egypt: the anticipation of the birth of a new Egypt and the faith of Egyptianist intellectuals in their own ability to create a new collective image for the country, one which would serve as a mechanism for its transformation. Unlike the other members of his family, Fahmi already perceives and expresses a new national image of another, ideal Egypt, Egypt as a distinct nation standing proud and self-confident, fighting for its rights, and willing to make great sacrifices for the sake of liberation and freedom. Fahmi's efforts to impart this revolutionary image of a new Egypt to the rest of his family lead to a great conflict with his father, a generation gap that Mahfuz makes a metaphor for the broader struggle between the traditional image of Egypt, which is dying, and the new, better image being born in the Revolution of 1919.

The nationalist ferment of late 1918 and early 1919 had an immediate impact on Fahmi: "patriotic talk set him dreaming the greatest dreams, by whose magic there appeared before his eyes a new world, a new homeland, a new home, a new people, all bursting with vitality and zeal."[38] His personal identification with the new nationalist movement is complete, leading him to decide to commit himself actively to participation in the struggle for Egyptian independence. "Duty to the homeland" becomes the most important thing in his life, transcending other concerns: by comparison with working for the Egyptian nation, everything else seems peripheral and unimportant.[39] He joins the nationalist activities of the Wafd, distributing revolutionary pamphlets inciting against the British Occupation.[40] On the first day of the demonstrations that marked the beginning of the Revolution, Fahmi is utterly intoxicated with patriotic fervor. Reality and fantasy become interwoven in his mind. He feels that he is experiencing a completely new life "fuller and more exalted" than anything he had experienced before.[41] Unstinting self-sacrifice, dedication to the homeland, and death for the sake of a "perfect national life" of grandeur and splendor—these become Fahmi's values in the tempestuous days of the Revolution of 1919.[42] He compares the Revolution to the eruption of a volcano: "there was bound to be an explosion to allow the release [of the desires] in his heart and in that of the homeland, an explosion like the eruption of a volcano that helps release the vapors accumulated underground."[43]

At the law school where he is a student, Fahmi immediately participates in a mass protest against the exiling of Zaghlul. With the other students, he shouts "Long live independence," "Down with the Protectorate," and "Long live Sa'd," noting that the last was "a new call. Everything seemed new that day."[44] The days that follow, when the Revolution continues and spreads to every part of urban and rural Egypt, only heighten Fahmi's sense of euphoria and exultation. He throws his whole being into the Revolution and enjoys every moment of it: "he hurled himself into the crowd with joyous intoxication and zeal, as if he were a stranger who had just found his long-lost relatives."[45] Egypt is being "resurrected" in the crowds that assemble daily "to go to battle with a sense of outrage that had long been repressed."[46] He himself is perfectly willing to die for his homeland and is even angry that he was not one of the "national martyrs" who fall in the early demonstrations: in his view, it is only fitting that "the sons [of Egypt] are the fuel of the Revolution."[47] He tells himself that "it makes no difference to me whether I live or die. Faith is stronger than death, and death is more honorable than humiliation."[48] Elsewhere he reflects contemptuously on the English who apparently believe that repression can end the Revolution: as he tells his brother Yasin, "this is really revolution. Let them kill as their barbarism dictates. Death can only enhance our life."[49] Thus the agonies of the Revolution are made into the birthpangs of the new Egypt, the suffering that leads to redemption.

Fahmi's involvement in the national cause brings an inevitable clash with his father. Al-Sayyid Ahmad 'Abd al-Jawad is upset because of the personal risks involved in nationalist activism, and he attempts to force Fahmi to desist from his involvement in the Revolution. But Fahmi, having savored the fruit of nationalist euphoria, refuses to give it up. In the face of his father's rage, Fahmi vows that "no power in the world can keep him from performing his national duty. He will never retreat one step. That time is gone forever."[50] What Mahfuz seems to be telling us is that the changes wrought by the Revolution in Fahmi and his contemporaries are irreversible, that they can never return to the traditional norms of the old order. The new national Egypt which Fahmi has committed himself to cuts him off forever from the ways of the old Egypt.

Fahmi's involvement in the Revolution ultimately leads to the result his father had feared. The climactic scene of the novel is set in April 1919, upon the sudden release of Sa'd Zaghlul and the other Wafdist leaders from their exile in Malta. Fahmi goes out to participate in the huge demonstration being held in honor of Zaghlul's release. The demonstration suddenly turns violent, however: British fire kills Fahmi in the process. Fahmi's last thought before his ironic death in a "peaceful" demonstration recall the sense of triumphant national rebirth and unity expressed earlier in Tawfiq al-Hakim's *'Awdat al-Ruh:*

> The great cavalcade moved. Its continuous waves surged forward chanting patriotic slogans. Then did Egypt seem to be a single demonstration, indeed one man, one slogan interminably advancing battalion after battalion.[51]

The great value of Najib Mahfuz's portrayal of the mental world of a young Egyptian revolutionary in 1919 is its fidelity to the conditions of 1919. While demonstrating a vibrant sense of a new Egypt being born, Fahmi and the rest of his family lack any Pharaonic dimension. His sense of Egyptian nationalism, though fully as fervent as that portrayed in *'Awdat al-Ruh,* is devoid of any perception of a linkage to the Pharaonic past of Egypt. Here Mahfuz seems to be reflecting Egyptian realities of 1919. The discovery of Tut's tomb, which historically was the greatest single factor in the emergence of Pharaonic mentality of the 1920s, had of course not yet occurred in 1919. Despite his own receptivity to the ideals of the Pharaonic school (his earliest works were Pharaonic historical novels),[52] Mahfuz makes every effort to be faithful to the perceptions of 1919.

But beyond this, Mahfuz's conception of the Revolution of 1919 is significantly different from that of Tawfiq al-Hakim. Where the latter perceived rebirth, the former saw only birth. Mahfuz did not see the spirit of the Revolution as signifying the resurrection of a prior Pharaonic spirit. Rather, for Mahfuz the Revolution of 1919 was a completely new historical starting point. The Egyptian nation and the national sentiment born in it were a totally new creation. Rather than a revival of the past, the Revolution from Mahfuz's perspective put an end to the past, specifically to Egypt's Ottoman/Islamic past. It marked the beginning of an entirely new present and future for Egypt—its modern and national epoch. The approaches of Tawfiq al-Hakim and Najib Mahfuz are both "revolutionary" in spirit as well as purely and exclusively Egyptian nationalist in content. Neither contains any significant Islamic, Eastern, or Arab elements. However, where the new national order of *'Awdat al-Ruh* is a return to the primordial Pharaonic past that had been lost, the new national order of *Bayna al-Qasrayn* is a creation *ex nihilo,* with no historical precedents. These two different but equally "revolutionary" approaches to recent Egyptian events can be found in the creative output of Egyptian nationalist intellectuals throughout the post-revolutionary period. Although Tawfiq al-Hakim's restorationist approach was the majority outlook and the more discontinuous perspective of Najib Mahfuz a minority position, both interpretations were expressed in the wake of the Revolution of 1919.

A final key feature of the Egyptian intellectual climate of the 1920s was the belief of Egypt's intellectuals that the Revolution of 1919 must and would be a cultural as well as a political phenomenon. According to this concept, the Revolution had to be extended from politics to the economy, the society, and above all to the realm of culture. In particular, a cultural revolution would transform the value system and the collective mentality of the Egyptian people, and thus would be the crowning achievement of the entire Revolution. These intellectuals eagerly drew parallels between their recent revolution and the French and Russian revolutions. Like the French philosophers of the eighteenth century and the ideologues of communism of the late nineteenth, contemporary Egyptian intellectuals of the early twentieth century had the historic task of establishing the philosophical and spiritual foundations that would allow the Egyptian Revolution to transform Egypt completely.[53]

In a retrospective essay of 1933 reflecting back on the intellectual mood of Egypt in the 1920s, Muhammad Husayn Haykal termed the dynamic intellectual activity that had begun from the Revolution of 1919 Egypt's "literary" or "cultural" revolution.[54] As had been the case in the classic European revolutions, Haykal thought, political independence would be incomplete unless accompanied by cultural independence and revival in the spheres of literature and art.[55] The achievements of the political revolution itself would be threatened in the long run if not followed by cultural changes. Cultural revolution would solidify and strengthen the political revolution, for only internal cultural changes protected a revolution from later challenge or destruction by hostile forces:

> This is due to the fact that literature and its course constitute the most authentic hallmark of a nation's civilization. Literature is the force which nothing else can vanquish or overcome as easily as an armed force can suppress political revolutions.[56]

The perception that the Revolution of 1919 was a total revolution, with its political dimension being but one manifestation of a far broader general transformation through which all Egyptian society was passing, was also expressed in Wafdist intellectual circles in the 1920s. In an editorial devoted to the unveiling of the monumental—and decidedly Pharaonic—sculpture, "The Renaissance of Egypt" [*nahdat misr*], in May 1928, 'Abd al-Qadir Hamza of *al-Balagh al-Usbu'i* developed the thesis that the Egyptian revival symbolized by the statue was not to be thought of merely as a political event. Hamza argued that the Egyptian Revolution, like the French Revolution, had released all the latent energies found within the Egyptian nation; thus, it heralded a general Egyptian renaissance in all spheres of life.[57] As Hamza interpreted the significance of the statue,

> this monument not only symbolizes the political revival [of Egypt], but its renaissance as a whole in its political, social, and intellectual aspects. For when the nation rose up in 1919 under the leadership of the late Sa'd Pasha, demanding its rights and independence, it undoubtedly cast off all constraints and forged ahead seeking progress in all its shapes and forms, very much like the French nation during its own great revolution.[58]

A more restrained assessment of the Revolution of 1919 and its impact upon Egyptian cultural life was that offered by the thoroughgoing modernist Isma'il Mazhar.[59] Mazhar took issue with the perspective that saw both the 'Urabi Revolt and the Revolution of 1919 as marking an intellectual renaissance in Egyptian life. Neither development, he contended, had made any deep impression on the intellectual and cultural life of Egypt.[60] In comparison to the earlier English and French revolutions, which had been "real" and "total" revolutions based upon the solid foundation of revolutionary new worldviews and which had had definite cultural as well as political programs, the 'Urabi Revolt and the Revolution of 1919 had been strictly political movements devoid of any cultural or philosophical content. But Mazhar was more optimistic about the future, assuming that a cultural and philosophical component could and would be added to the political revolution that had occurred in the recent past. The Revolution of 1919 had resulted in the proliferation of literary and scientific periodicals in the 1920s, in which respect the present era did resemble "that of the literary renaissance in England in the late eighteenth and early nineteenth centuries."[61] Mazhar entertained great hopes that these new cultural publications would initiate a cultural and scientific revolution in Egypt.[62]

The conception of the Revolution of 1919 as a "total" revolution was of course intimately connected with the aspiration of Egyptianist intellectuals to create a new and revolutionary collective image for their country. It was perceived as essential that new cultural images complement the political image of a new Egypt created by the Revolution. Only such a comprehensive and integrated collective image that would transform the Egyptian understanding of all aspects of their national life could succeed in disassociating Egypt from the false Ottoman-Islamic past and in restoring its genuine Egyptianist quality.

In this general atmosphere of intellectual vibrancy, special note needs to be made of the enormous power their new images had in shaping the activity of Egyptianist intellectuals. The "external" conditions that the new collective image anticipated had not yet coalesced. The new political order centered around an independent parliamentary monarchy that had begun to take shape in the early 1920s was still in its formative stages throughout the decade, with many of its characteristics not fully determined. The as yet undefined final shape of the new order allowed Egyptianist intellectuals to believe that many options were possible, and so encouraged them to give full rein to their imaginations. Perceiving Egypt to be in a "period of transition" or at "the parting of the ways" (the most frequently used terms being *'asr al-intiqal* and *muftaraq al-turuq*),[63] they held as crucial the image of the approaching future rather than that of the ephemeral present. The optimism, idealism, and naivété so prominent on the Egyptian intellectual scene in the 1920s can be appreciated only against this setting of an age that was believed to be transitional. The image of the "new Egypt" had not yet been tested against historical reality. For the time being, therefore, until later developments revealed the utopian elements in the image, the feeling that Egypt was marching forward triumphantly toward a perfect and uniquely Egyptian future could reign supreme.

Egyptianist Intellectuals and Their Publications

Who were the Egyptianist intellectuals of the post-1919 era?[64] In our view, it is useful to distinguish between two categories of territorial nationalist intellectuals active during the period. The first category is that of the intellectual "luminaries" of the age: the most creative and influential thinkers of a time and place, those whom Edward Shils has called "productive intellectuals" who "create works which extend and change their traditions."[65] They are the few intellectuals in a given society who address fundamental aspects of its worldview, who redefine basic elements of the same, and whose speculation is recognized by their contemporaries as seminal. They are the shapers of the "high culture" of their society, in the sense of its most abstract and comprehensive thought.[66] In view of the critical role of such intellectual luminaries, their thought should form the starting point of the examination of the intellectual history of a particular society and period.

In the Egyptian territorial nationalist school of thought dominant in Egypt after 1919, the following intellectuals appear to have been the most influential: Ahmad Amin (1886–1954); 'Abbas Mahmud al-'Aqqad (1889–1964); 'Abd al-Qadir Hamza (1880–1941); Muhammad Husayn Haykal (1888–1956); Taha Husayn (1889–1973); Isma'il Mazhar (1891–1962); and Salama Musa (1887–1958).[67] Husayn, Mazhar, and Musa were perhaps the most daring Egyptian intellectuals of the era, men whose writings repeatedly challenged received understandings and suggested new ways of viewing the world. Haykal, 'Aqqad, Hamza, and Amin (particularly the last two) were less dramatic in their ideas but were extremely influential journalists and commentators on social affairs. Of the seven, Muhammad Husayn Haykal deserves special mention: he was undoubtedly the most important formulator of the Egyptianist national orientation of the 1920s, and as such was the major source of influence on many of the Egyptian nationalist intellectuals who considered themselves his disciples. Four of these individuals were editors of major intellectual journals of the period (Haykal, *al-Siyasa al-*

Usbu'iyya; Hamza, *al-Balagh al-Usbu'i;* Musa, *al-Hilal* and later *al-Majalla al-Jadida;* Mazhar, *al-'Usur*), and thereby influenced Egyptian public opinion through what they chose—and did not choose—to publish. The seven were certainly among the most highly esteemed Egyptian authors of the period, regarded by their contemporaries (of similar nationalist and modernist views) as the leading pundits of Egypt in the 1920s. All save Hamza (a newspaper editor of note in the prewar period) achieved their preeminent status in the 1920s and early 1930s, when many of their most original and influential works were published. Their views were not universally accepted: indeed, Husayn, Musa, and Mazhar in particular were the subject of vehement attack by more traditionalist Egyptian intellectuals. Together, these seven figures developed most of the intellectual framework of the territorial nationalist orientation that flourished in Egypt after the Revolution of 1919.

But it is insufficient to deal solely with the intellectual luminaries of the Egyptian territorial nationalist school of thought. Fully if not more important in both the elaboration and the dissemination of Egyptianism were the "secondary" intellectuals of the period, those whom Muhammad Husayn Haykal defined at the time as "writers of the second rank" who followed the general approach laid down by the intellectual leaders of the age.[68] Shils characterized such secondary intellectuals as "reproductive intellectuals, who in turn diffuse, in modified form, the patterns of procedure and belief of the most creative workers in their respective fields."[69] A group usually much larger in size than that of the intellectual luminaries of a given culture or discipline, these secondary intellectuals generally think in less original and autonomous ways than those of the luminaries whose lead they often follow. Although not as creative as luminary intellectuals, such secondary or reproductive intellectuals are perhaps even more important than leading intellectuals in diffusing new ideas and molding the "common culture" or "moral unity of a society": "By means of preaching, teaching, and writing, reproductive intellectuals infuse into those sections of the population which are intellectual neither by propensity nor by role beliefs which they would otherwise lack."[70] Correspondingly, they may be of even greater significance to historians than are the leading thinkers of an era. It has been pointed out that

> [t]he tendencies of an age appear more distinctly in its writers of inferior rank than in those of commanding genius. These latter tell of past and future as well as of the age in which they live. They are for all time. But on the sensitive responsive souls, of less creative power, current ideals record themselves with clearness.[71]

The following chapters draw most heavily on the writings of approximately fifty Egyptian nationalist "writers of the second rank." Primarily journalists, academicians, and/or teachers, they were authors who repeated, occasionally extended, frequently vulgarized, but thereby popularized the new concepts being formulated primarily by the intellectuals in the luminary category. Based on their perception of themselves and their abilities, most did not claim to be the equals of the figures in the luminary group. Rather, they regarded themselves as the disciples of these luminaries. Where the luminaries were writing some of their most seminal and influential works in the 1920s and early 1930s, many of the authors in the secondary category were making only an initial appearance on the Egyptian intellectual scene at that time. (The distinction between luminary and secondary, as well as the respective roles of each in expounding and/or disseminating the Egyptianist worldview of the post-1919 era, will become clearer in the chapters that follow.)

Considered as a whole, the Egyptian territorial nationalist cohort of the post-1919 era was a diverse group. Intellectually, most of them possessed other commonalities besides their territorial nationalism, notably an aggressive modernism that made them vigorous proponents of the "new" [*jadid*] or of "innovation" [*tajdid*] and a European orientation that led them to regard the thought and practice of contemporary Europe as the model that Egypt needed to emulate.[72] But in terms of their background, socialization, and place in Egyptian society, there appear to have been few attributes shared by these territorial nationalist intellectuals.

The Egyptianist writers of the 1920s and early 1930s were of course defined by their birth in the late nineteenth or early twentieth centuries. None of the individuals in the group appears to have been born before 1880, the year of birth of both 'Abd al-Qadir Hamza and Ahmad Dayf; the youngest members of the group were Ahmad Husayn, Hafiz Mahmud, and Shuhdi 'Atiyya al-Shafi'i, all born in 1911. Not surprisingly, the major figures in the cohort were somewhat older, all born in the period from 1880 to 1891. Most of the secondary intellectuals seem to have been born between 1900 and 1910. A considerable gap of time and thus of life circumstances separated the oldest members of the group from the youngest, a factor that eventually contributed to the development of a significant difference in national orientation among the younger intellectuals. But in the 1920s and into the early 1930s, both Egyptian conditions after the Revolution of 1919 and the intellectual preeminence of the "generation of 1889" maintained a common nationalist worldview among all members of the group.

Apart from the commonality of birth within a particular period, other life circumstances of these Egyptianist intellectuals were disparate. Of the intellectual luminaries, two (Husayn and 'Aqqad) were born in Upper Egypt, two (Haykal and Musa) in Lower Egypt, and three (Amin, Hamza, and Mazhar) in Cairo. The majority of the secondary intellectual group appears to have been born in Cairo, Alexandria, or the Delta. In terms of religion, both Muslims and Christians expounded Egyptian territorial nationalism in the 1920s and early 1930s: the presence of several Copts and one Greek Orthodox Christian (Ibrahim al-Misri) in the group probably represents a somewhat higher percentage of Christians than that presumably found in the Egyptian population as a whole. This is not surprising, given both the relative educational advantages of Egyptian Christians and the nature of Egyptianist national orientation. It reflected the high degree of ideological consensus existing among Muslim and non-Muslim native Egyptian intellectuals in the 1920s, a consensus created by recent trends of secularism on the one hand and by the unified anti-British struggle represented by the Revolution of 1919 on the other.

The social origins of the group is a more elusive matter. Among the intellectual luminaries, two clearly had upper-class backgrounds (Haykal was from a landowning family of Lower Egypt, Mazhar from a wealthy Cairene family); two can be classified as being of lower-class origins (Husayn was the son of an agricultural worker, Amin that of a rural migrant to Cairo); and three (Musa, 'Aqqad, and

Hamza) probably may be categorized as middle-class. We do not have precise biographical data on all of the secondary intellectuals. Certainly the range was considerable: whereas Tawfiq al-Hakim was the scion of the Turkish aristocracy born in Alexandria and 'Abd al-'Aziz al-Bishri the son of a prominent Azharite shaykh, Husayn Fawzi's father was an agricultural engineer who had taken residence in Cairo, Ahmad Husayn's was an employee in the Ministry of Finance, and Ahmad Sabri came from a Bedouin family from the Sinai Peninsula. From the biographical materials available for some and from scattered references in their own works, most of the secondary group appear to have come from the broad middle strata of largely urban, Western-educated, professional or bureaucratic groups that had emerged in Egypt by the beginning of the twentieth century. The generic term for this segment of modern Egypt's population is the *afandiyya* (from the Ottoman Turkish *efendi* denoting literacy and/or state service, and in contrast to the *bashas* constituting the upper class).[73] By the interwar period, these middle groups within the Egyptian spectrum had come to regard themselves as the living embodiment of the Egyptian nation. In their own view the *afandiyya* were Egypt; it was they who "moulded public opinion and led the nation at times of crisis, set up its ideals and stamped it with its particular character."[74]

The educational background of this group of Egyptianist intellectuals is equally diverse. Of the luminaries, both Amin and Husayn studied at al-Azhar. More important was the partially European education of most of this luminary group; Haykal and Husayn studied in France, Musa in both France and England, Mazhar in England and later Germany. Hamza, 'Aqqad, and Amin, on the other hand, received their formal education within Egypt. The secondary intellectuals show the same educational diversity. As might be anticipated from the later secularizing outlook of most of the cohort, only a few passed through al-Azhar. Perhaps half of the group of secondary intellectuals received at least part of their formal education in Europe, the majority of those studying abroad doing so in that educational Mecca of the Egyptian elite in the early twentieth century, France. Whether educated within Egypt or in Europe, however, almost all of the group seem to have acquired a working knowledge of one or more European languages (usually English and/or French, occasionally German, and sometimes even classical Latin and/or Greek).

More similarities appear in the later careers of the group. By virtue of their contributing to the Egyptian periodical press, all may be classified as having been at least part-time journalists. But most were other things as well. Among the luminary category, Amin, Haykal, and Hamza were trained as lawyers (the first in the *Shari'a* court system, the latter two in the secularized courts). Husayn and 'Aqqad were academics (although the latter taught only briefly), whereas Musa and Mazhar devoted themselves to journalism. All save perhaps Amin were "men of letters" in the broadest sense of the term, intellectual gadflies who over their active careers read widely and wrote on a variety of subjects. The data on the secondary intellectuals seems to indicate a not dissimilar professional pattern. Several of the secondary group were lawyers and a few physicians; many taught at one time or another.

Not surprisingly, many in the group as a whole were involved in politics. Three of the luminaries played an active and important role in Egyptian politics in the 1920s (Haykal as a Liberal leader and the editor of the Liberal newspaper *al-Siyasa,* Hamza editing the Wafdist daily *al-Balagh,* and 'Aqqad serving as perhaps the main polemicist of the Wafd in the 1920s). Many of the secondary intellectuals were liberal sympathizers and contributors to its journals *al-Siyasa* and *al-Siyasa al-Usbu'iyya.* More important than the formal political differences within the group, however, were the more basic political similarities that united them. At least in this period, the substance of their political speculation was quite similar. Anti-traditionalism, a Western orientation, liberalism in the nineteenth-century sense of the term, an acceptance of change, and of course a commitment to Egyptian territorial nationalism: these were common themes found in the writings of most of these intellectuals in the 1920s and early 1930s. Moreover, at least in the optimistic years after the Revolution, when much seemed well in progress and more seemed possible in the future, they did not share the alienation from politics characteristic of many intellectuals in other places and periods. It was an era of cooperation among politicians and intellectuals, the parties reaching out to intellectuals for their support and service as spokesmen, the intellectuals by and large responding favorably and joining in the hurly-burly of partisan politics (with much of their least memorable expression being devoted to daily political issues). Whether Wafdist, Liberal, or other, Egyptian nationalist intellectuals differed on little that was fundamental.

But in terms of their background and socialization, relatively few common denominators can be identified among the leading Egyptianist intellectuals of the post-1919 era. To be sure, there were some: the obvious commonalities of Egyptian origin, birth between 1880 and 1911, and intellectual vocation. But the group as a whole otherwise included both Muslims and Christians in proportions not too dissimilar from the presumed national average; men of rural and urban, Upper Egyptian, Lower Egyptian, and Cairene birth; the children of large landowners and of poor rural migrants to the city (although the bulk of the group probably clustered within a broadly defined middle class); Azharites as well as European-educated intellectuals (but all influenced to some degree by European ideas); lawyers, teachers, and bureaucrats; and Wafdists, Liberals, and those who had dabbled with other parties (Haykal and Mahmud 'Azmi, for example were two of the founders of the short-lived Egyptian Democratic Party established in 1919; Ahmad Husayn and Hafiz Mahmud later were leaders of the Young Egypt Party of the 1930s.)

What united these men and allows us to define them as a group is, in brief, their ideas. At least for a time—from the early 1920s through the early 1930s—they expressed similar nationalist views. The Egyptianist school of the post-1919 period can best be analyzed "from inside out, *from* certain types of ideas *toward* certain categories of idea-articulators," in the words of J. P. Nettl; not by searching for "types of men who had ideas" but by focusing on the "types of ideas" expressed by men who were themselves of very diverse types.[75] The opposite functionalist approach, which proceeds from the analysis of institutions and roles and which makes ideology a variable of social structure, seems to us less useful in the case of post-1919 Egypt.[76] Egypt at the time was a society in flux, one lacking well-established institutions. The old order had been eroded by the developments of the nineteenth century, which had also created a new network of agencies and occupations. Neither old nor new institutions were particularly strong in the early twentieth century, the former being under assault and the latter still in the process of consolidation. Moreover, the recent Revolution of 1919 was seen as portending the start of a new age for Egypt, one in which both institutions and ideas would be transformed. In this situation of institutional restructuring and intellectual reorientation, the future mattered more than the past. It was a shared orientation toward the future and toward change, rather than a common social background or similarity of institutional role, which drew these men together. In a sense, the primary "institution" connecting the Egyptianist intellectuals of early twentieth-century Egypt was their ideas.

Given the diversity of social origin, educational experience, and institutional affiliation of this cohort of Egyptianist intellectuals, we are led to wonder what created their shared Egyptianist worldview. What seems to have been decisive in forging a common national perspective among people of such diverse circumstances was a combination of time and history. All born within the same time period and raised within the same Egyptian historical setting, they formed both a chronological "generation" and a distinct "generation unit." Karl Mannheim has defined these two constructs as follows:

> Youth experiencing the same concrete historical problems may be said to be part of the same actual generation; while those groups within the same actual generation which work up the material of their common experiences in different specific ways, constitute separate generation units.[77]

Intellectually, this group of Egyptians demonstrated that "identity of responses" to their historical situation stipulated by Mannheim as the prime criterion of a generation unit, "a certain affinity in the way in which all move with and are formed by their common experiences."[78] As Mannheim observed, not every potential generation (that is, group born in the same chronological time span) becomes a "generation unit" in actuality. The formation of the latter depends on the proper historical conditions, particularly on the rate of social change:

> When as a result of an acceleration of the tempo of social and cultural transformation basic attitudes must change so quickly that the latent, continuous adaptation and modification of traditional patterns of experience, thought, and expression is no longer possible, then the various new phases of experience are consolidated somewhere, forming a clearly distinguishable new impulse, and a new centre of configuration.[79]

What shaped this potential generation of Egyptians into an actual generation unit were the circumstances of Egypt in the late nineteenth and early twentieth centuries. Certainly the socioeconomic and cultural changes to which they were exposed were sweeping ones: a new economy, a new state, a new lifestyle, new schools, ideas, occupations, and roles all emerging shortly before or during their lifetime. It was in their youth that these changes helped to produce the Western-influenced and Egypt-oriented national outlook first articulated by the demi-generation of Mustafa Kamil and Ahmad Lutfi al-Sayyid, an outlook reinforced and intensified in the nationalist Revolution of 1919. Living in an age of change and either raised in the school of Egyptian territorial nationalism before World War I or seared by the nationalist flame after the war, this generation united in regarding Egypt as the primary focus of their loyalty as well as the overriding object of their intellectual speculation.

A few words need to be said about the period and the publications that we will be analyzing in detail in the following chapters. The high point of Egyptianist expression, and thus the period from which most of our data will be drawn, was the period from 1925 through 1933. The intellectual elaboration of new paradigms necessarily lags slightly behind the formative events giving birth to a new perspective. In the case of Egypt in the 1920s, the events underpinning the territorial nationalist orientation were the Revolution of 1919, the turmoil of the early 1920s, and the eventual creation of the new Egyptian parliamentary monarchy in 1922–1923. All of this had occurred by 1924, when the popularly elected government of Sa'd Zaghlul assumed office. With the uproar of the immediate postwar years ending by 1924, it became possible for Egyptian intellectuals to divert their attention from the narrowly political issues that had preoccupied them since 1919 to the broader issues of the meaning and the elaboration of the Egyptian nationalist outlook that had apparently triumphed in the political sphere. The relative freedom of expression available under the new regime also stimulated the establishment of many new outlets for intellectual speculation in the mid-1920s, including the publication of new journals of an Egyptian inclination. Thus the intellectual superstructure of the post-1919 Egyptian era did not take full shape until roughly a half-decade after the development of the political infrastructure on which it was based. It is between 1925 and 1933 that the territorial nationalist orientation was preeminent in Egypt and received its fullest elaboration.

The main publications in which the Egyptianist perspective was articulated may be listed quickly.[80] It needs to be emphasized that almost all the leading journals of an Egyptianist orientation were new to the 1920s and were themselves a tangible manifestation of the new nationalist era that Egypt was entering in the wake of the Revolution of 1919. The daily elaboration of the territorial nationalist outlook was to be found particularly in the newspapers of Egypt's nationalist parties: the Liberal *al-Siyasa* (established in 1922, edited by Muhammad Husayn Haykal and Mahmud 'Abd al-Raziq) and the Wafdist *al-Balagh* (established in 1923, edited by 'Abd al-Qadir Hamza). The theoretical articulation of Egyptianism occurred primarily in the weekly or monthly publications of opinion, whose content revolved around issues broader than those usually discussed in the daily press. There were six leading Egyptianist journals published in the 1925–1933 period. One was the older *al-Hilal;* still controlled by the Syrian Christian Zaydan family but edited from 1923 to 1929 by the vehemently Egyptianist Salama Musa, it (like most publications in Egypt in the 1920s) opened its pages to the dominant Egyptianist perspective. The two leading Egyptianist journals of the era were undoubtedly the weekly versions of the party papers *al-Siyasa* and *al-Balagh, al-Siyasa al-Usbu'iyya* and *al-Balagh al-Usbu'i,* both dating from 1926. It was particularly in the pages of the former that Egyptianism was expounded in the later 1920s and early 1930s, with most of the cohort of intellectuals, even some politically committed to the Wafd, contributing to it. The more radical cutting edge of the Egyptianist orientation was to be found in two smaller, less well-endowed journals, the monthly *al-'Usur* (1927–1930, edited by Isma'il Mazhar) and the monthly *al-Majalla al-Jadida* (1929–1944, edited by Salama Musa). The far extreme of Egyptianism was represented by *al-Fajr,* the short-lived weekly published by Ahmad Khayri Sa'id from 1925 to 1927. Together, these six journals of opinion constitute the main sources in which the Egyptian territorial nationalist orientation discussed in the following chapters was elaborated.

5

The Egyptian Nationalist Image of the Arabs

The Function of an Arab Counter-Image in Building a New Image of Egypt

In their efforts to create a new image for Egypt in the 1920s, Egyptianist intellectuals operated on two interrelated conceptual planes. The first was analysis and criticism of the existing but incorrect image of the nation. At the same time, they labored to construct a new and more correct image of their country in place of the previous false images. The two operations were complementary aspects of the same intellectual task: only through the destruction of the existing negative image of Egypt could a positive image of Egypt be created. The very process of constructing a new national image presupposed an in-depth discussion of the counter-image that for so long had prevailed in its place. Thus an analysis of the new, positive image of Egypt developed by Egyptianist intellectuals in the wake of the Revolution of 1919 requires an understanding of their efforts to demolish this counter-image which the new image was intended to replace.

In Egypt in the post-1919 era, the counter-image that served as a negative foil for Egyptian nationalist intellectuals was an Arab one. It was the Arab literary and cultural legacy, as well as constructs such as the "Arab mentality" or the "Arab personality"—all posited to be of foreign, non-Egyptian derivation—which were accused of having masked and/or distorted the authentic Egyptian characteristics of the nation. At its most extreme, the Arab counter-image was erected into an evil influence upon Egypt: it was Arabism that had prevented Egyptianism from manifesting itself and realizing its potential, and the removal of Arab traits found in Egyptian life was a necessary condition for the fulfillment of Egyptianism.

The construction of a negative Arab counter-image was vital to the formation of a positive image of the "new Egypt." It was only by emphasizing (and exaggerating) the alien, the traditional, and the reactionary elements of Arabism that Egyptianist intellectuals developed what they saw as the authentic and progressive elements of Egyptianism. Just as the "old" and "new" images were two sides of the same coin, so the aims of the analysis of each were inseparable: only by proving Arabism's weaknesses and thus the necessity of abandoning Arab traits and characteristics could Egyptian nationalist intellectuals realize their goal of the total Egyptianization of Egyptian life. The systematic demonization of the Arabs was an integral part of the reification of Egypt.

It must also be emphasized that this negative image of the Arabs was an intentional construct. Consciously created rather than unconsciously assumed, it was an image that Egyptian nationalist intellectuals sought to inculcate in all Egyptians. In their view, the Egyptian nation *had* to adopt a negative image of the Arabs in order to achieve its own renewal in terms of both the elimination of that which was alien and reactionary and a corresponding recovery of Egyptian authenticity.

Hence our own methodological approach. Because we are dealing with a conscious creation of Egyptian intellectuals, a contrived and instrumental image of Arabs and their culture, our task is not one of evaluating the validity or speciousness of the intellectuals' varied anti-Arab contentions. Rather, our objective is to describe and to analyze the range of Arab negative qualities presented in such great detail by Egyptianist intellectuals, always focusing on the intellectual meaning and emotional purport of this portrait for those intellectuals themselves. Our concern, in other words, is what Egyptian nationalist writings on the Arabs say about *Egyptians.*

The Issue: Separating Egyptian from Arab

In June 1933, shortly after the publication of his monumental novel *'Awdat al-Ruh,* Tawfiq al-Hakim addressed an open letter to Taha Husayn.[1] In it the figure who was perhaps the most creative literary spokesman of the new Egypt in the post-1919 era forcefully captured the central problem that preoccupied Egyptian nationalist intellectuals of the 1920s and early 1930s: how to establish a new collective image for Egypt that was based exclusively on purely Egyptian elements drawn only from the heritage of the Nile Valley, and which would thus suit the reviving nation in the aftermath of the Revolution of 1919.

Hakim lamented the absence of an autonomous Egyptian self-image: for much too long a time,

> [w]e could be compared to the unconscious; we had no awareness of self; we saw not ourselves but the long-gone Arabs; we sensed not our own being but theirs; the word "I/we" remained unknown to the Egyptian mind; the idea of the Egyptian personality [*al-shakhsiyya al-misriyya*] had not yet been born.

Hakim did admit that this situation was now changing. Thanks to the activities first of Ahmad Lutfi al-Sayyid and then of Taha Husayn and his generation of intellectuals, "Egyptian identity [*al-dhatiyya al-misriyya*] began to take on a clear, precise form not only in concepts of expression, but also in the style and the vocabulary employed. . . . We have now begun to sense and become aware of our being." Tawfiq al-Hakim saw the key to developing this distinctive Egyptian national consciousness in what he called "knowing ourselves," that is, in a deep understanding of the qualities of the Egyptian character "so that its importance becomes manifest to our generation." Egyptian society had not yet become aware of the full significance of being Egyptian: it still did not think, act, and live in a solely Egyptian way. Refusing to accept this situation, he demanded that Egypt realize her true essence and manifest the potential that hitherto had been obscured.

In addition to developing a thorough understanding of their Egyptian roots, traits, and national personality, Hakim also called upon Egyptians to become fully aware of the alien, non-Egyptian components that were presently found in Egyptian life. For him, the most prominent of these were its Arab components. As he put it, "our intermingling with the Arab spirit, this strange amalgam, has distracted us from the reality of our own spirit." The necessary precondition for Egyptian progress was "total and uncompromising liberation" of the nation and its people from all the "foreign" Arab elements that over the generations had become attached to the Egyptian personality. In his view of Egyptian history, Egyptian intellectual life for too long had been "reduced to imitating and copying—imitating Arab thought, and copying it." Thus the historic task of contemporary Egyptian intellectuals was to liberate Egypt from Arabism. Just as Ahmad Lutfi al-Sayyid had previously led the way to an awareness of the distinct Egyptian personality, so Hakim called on Taha Husayn to lead contemporary Egyptian intellectuals to realize this personality in actuality through the elimination of alien Arab elements from Egyptian life: "your first duty towards us is to separate one element from the other." Only by distinguishing what was Egyptian from what was Arab would Taha Husayn and his generation be able to say to Tawfiq al-Hakim and his generation that "we have shown you the way, now travel it yourselves." Hakim concluded his appeal to Husayn with a phrase that might stand as *leitmotif* for the nationalist thinking of this entire cohort of Egyptian nationalist intellectuals: "thus we have no choice but to know what an Egyptian is and what an Arab is."

The Dimensions of Arab Alienness

In the 1920s and early 1930s in particular, belief in the uniqueness of Egypt as well as its incompatibility with things Arab was a prevailing assumption among Egyptian nationalist intellectuals. Their nationalist thought started from the postulate of an immemorial Egyptian national character or "personality." Yusuf Hanna put it in this way:

> Every one of the world's nations has its own distinctive traits, and these are expressed in all the many and varied aspects of its life. The totality of these distinctive characteristics is that nation's "distinct personality," by means of which it is known and through which it distinguishes itself from other nations. . . . Egypt, too, has a distinct and well-defined national personality [*shakhsiyya qawmiyya*] of its own.[2]

A second basic premise of Egyptian nationalist intellectuals of the period was the conviction that complete Egyptian authenticity demanded purifying Egypt from all foreign elements. With reference to the Arabs in particular, the entire Arab heritage was viewed as the product of the Arab nation and character, both of which differed from those of Egypt. Therefore the attaining of complete national authenticity meant the complete separation of Egypt from Arabism and the Arabs; it meant Egypt's autochthonous development within the confines of her own distinctive culture and values.[3] The contrast between authentic Egyptianness and alien Arabism was stated by Hasan 'Arif in 1933:

> Whether or not Egyptians intermixed with the Arabs [in the past], the present people of Egypt are radically different from the Arabs in every way. The Egyptian is Arab neither in his [external] form, his mentality, his grasp of moral values and social life, his temperament nor his customs. The Egyptian nation possesses a self-contained personality which springs from its own environment and long history, which predates Arab history by thousands of years. The Egyptian nation's existence is independent of the Arabs, the Muslims, the Christians, and the entire world.[4]

For 'Arif, Egyptian acceptance of the thesis that Egypt was Arab would mean the loss of the country's distinctive identity and the immersion of its own national character in an alien Arab sea. Egypt's national will would be subordinated to that of the Arabs. In short, an Egypt with Arab characteristics would not be Egypt but a distortion of Egypt, a falsification of the nation's true essence and identity, a betrayal of her unique collective ego. An "Arab Egypt" was an abnormal condition from which the country needed to extract itself in order to be its purely Egyptian self.[5]

It was the Pharaonic heritage of Egypt that provided Egyptian nationalist intellectuals with the conclusive proof that Egypt was not, and could never be, Arab. Egypt's true national personality, they posited, had to be based on the unique "golden age" of Egypt represented by the Pharaonic era. The revolutionary new Egypt that was rediscovering its glorious legacy and drawing the inspiration for its contemporary renaissance from its ancient past could not be Arab. An Egypt marked by Arab traits would be denying its own unique heritage. In order to revive authentic Egyptian truths and values in the modern age, Egypt had to purge itself of the alien Arab characteristics found in it.[6]

Thus Hafiz Mahmud warned of the dangers to be found in the Egyptian connection with the Arabs and their culture. "After all, the Arab spirit is found only in the Arabian Peninsula," he responded to those who claimed that "we are Arabs merely because we speak Arabic."[7] In contrast to this, it was his contention that Egypt needed to be true to her own traditions and legacy rather than to any alien heritage:

> We as a human group are well aware that the home where we and our forefathers grew up is the one and only Egypt. It is our destiny that our collective consciousness, as it expresses itself genuinely, shall be influenced far more by the history of the Pharaohs than by the history of the Arabs.[8]

Mahmud was convinced that an Egypt that was Arab in its character would mean debasement, the denial of "the grandeur of distinctiveness" and the betrayal of "the greatness of her Pharaonic forefathers."[9] "Arab glory to the Arabs and Egypt's glory to the Egyptians," he declared.[10]

These widespread perceptions of a vital bond between ancient and modern Egypt found one of their most vehement statements in Nashid Sayfin's series "Egypt is Pharaonic, Flesh and Blood" of 1930.[11] Those who would clothe Egypt in Arab dress, Sayfin says, are guilty of distorting an ancient historic reality:

Egypt took shape as a distinctive national entity thousands of years before it came in contact with any of the elements constituting the Arab legacy. Did not the Pharaonic temples and monuments scattered the length and breadth of the Nile Valley provide "living," "objective" proof of the Pharaonic nature of the Egyptian people living in the valley?[12] Inquiring as to the possible effects of an Arabization of Egypt, Sayfin saw only ominous implications:

> Were Egypt to become Arabized . . . what would be her position *vis-à-vis* Tut-Ankh-Amon and the other Pharaonic kings who ruled Egypt, building her cities and constructing her temples while the rest of humanity were nothing but barbarians. . . . What would be Egypt's position *vis-à-vis* all these were she to become Arabized? Would she take pride in them, or become alienated from them?[13]

Perhaps equally important as the sense of alienness and unauthenticity of Arabism in Egypt to Egyptian intellectuals was the specific belief that Arabism was irreconcilable with the "age of renewal" underway in Egypt since 1919. The contemporary political, cultural, and social renaissance of Egypt was embodied in a return to the nation's authentic Pharaonic roots and in the consequent rebirth of the primordial Egyptian spirit. Egyptian renaissance could not possibly involve a return to "forged" Arab roots or a renewal of the "foreign" Arab spirit in Egypt. Arabism, as a foreign and external heritage, had no role to play in Egyptian revival. "Retrogressive" Arabism would only draw Egypt back into the pre-1919 "era of darkness," back to a distorted and decadent Egypt that lacked a sense of identity and was reactionary in society and culture.[14]

It was inconceivable to Egyptian nationalist intellectuals that in this era of national revival, Egypt would seek to create its national identity on non-national foundations. By their very nature external to the Nile Valley, these would negate Egyptian nationalism and prevent the formation of a unique Egyptian personality.[15] As Nashid Sayfin put it, there was no way to cultivate Egyptian national pride, aspire to independence, and glory in the heroic struggle of Sa'd Zaghlul and the Egyptian national movement as long as the claim that "Egypt is Arab" was still heard: "Egypt will gain no profit from independence and her renaissance will bear no fruit as long as she continues to assume a national identity not her own, and boasts a nationalism foreign to her."[16]

Others went further. Even at the close of the interwar period, Salah al-Din Dhihni held that the entire Revolution of 1919 had been inspired by a distinctive Egyptian and Pharaonic, rather than Arab, national consciousness. Had the Egyptians of 1919 thought and acted as Arabs, Dhihni maintained, there would never have been a revolution and the renaissance of Egypt would not have begun:

> When Egypt rose up, songs and ballads began to speak of "the children of the Pharaohs" or of "Egypt, Mother of the Pyramids". . . . Then the names of Ramses and Thutmose were on every tongue. But had Egyptians at that time asserted that they were "the children of the Arabs," or substituted for Ramses and Thutmose the names of Khalid ibn al-Walid or 'Amr ibn al-'As, or sung of the relics and ruins of Arabia, then there would have been no revolution to achieve independence.[17]

Thus the Egyptian national revolution itself negated any possibility of Egypt's being Arab. Revolution, independence, and cultural revival were purely Egyptian enterprises. Hence the nation's current task was to liberate herself of any fragments of Arabism that remained within her polity, her society, and her culture.

The Bases of Egyptian Anti-Arabism

In their struggle against this alien Arabism, Egyptianist intellectuals painted their portrait of the Arabs with the same brush they used to create their picture of Egypt. The same terms of reference through which they sought to understand the characteristics of an idealized Egypt were used in their detailed analysis of a demonized Arabism. The key terms in their analysis were "personality" [*shakhsiyya*] and "mentality" [*'aqliyya;* sometimes better translated as "mind"]. *'Aqliyya* meant the mental faculties and characteristics of the national collective; *shakhsiyya* combined these sentient components with the physical and racial characteristics of the nation. *Shakhsiyya* was thus the more comprehensive term. *Shakhsiyya* and *'aqliyya,* sometimes joined by the term *ruh* or "spirit," were seen as the key to comprehending the behavior patterns of any particular human collective.

In many respects *shakhsiyya* and *'aqliyya* were an elaboration of Muhammad Husayn Haykal's "social milieu" [*al-wasat al-ijtima'i*] (although Haykal and even his mentor Ahmad Lutfi al-Sayyid occasionally used the word *shakhsiyya*), or more remotely of what Hippolyte Taine had denoted by the term "race." Together, they were equivalent to the Hegelian *volksgeist,* the totality of specific characteristics particular to a group which simultaneously distinguished it from all other groups. Egyptianist intellectuals of the 1920s also adopted the position that the *shakhsiyya* of a given community was created and developed within a specific natural milieu. Since it was nothing but the creature of its homeland, the key to understanding the *shakhsiyya* of a particular nation was to be found in the comprehensive knowledge of the physical, climatic, and geographical characteristics of the environment in which it had taken form. With specific reference to the Arabs, Egyptian intellectuals thus posited an intimate bond between the *shakhsiyya* of the Arabs and the geographic environment that had nurtured them as a historic people. They also assumed that understanding the ramifications of the connection between the environment of the Arabs and their national "personality" would reveal the huge gap between the latter and the distinctive Egyptian milieu and "personality."

This environmental determinism derived from Haykal and Taine was not the only theoretical influence on Egyptian anti-Arabism. Four additional sources that may have been contributed to legitimizing the anti-Arab intellectual mood of Egypt in the interwar period deserve mention. First and most definite was the impact of contemporary theories concerning the Semitic race and the Semitic mind upon Egyptianist intellectuals. In particular, the ideas of Ernest Renan (1823–1892) concerning different racial groups and their characteristics achieved wide currency in Egypt by the early twentieth century. A collection of Renan's philosophical writings, including some dealing with race, was translated into Arabic and published in Cairo in 1929.[18] But the works of the greatest importance in nurturing anti-Arab currents of thought in Egypt in the 1920s were probably Renan's well-known pamphlet *De la part des peuples sémitiques dans l'histoire de la civilization* (1862) and his more comprehensive study *Histoire générale et système comparé des langues sémitiques* (1855).

Renan's essential position concerning the Semitic peoples was first that they were incurably inferior and backward in comparison to the Indo-European Aryans, and secondly that this inferiority and backwardness stemmed from inherent flaws in "the Semitic spirit" [*l'esprit sémitique*] and "the Semitic character" [*le caractère sémitique*].[19] Defects of "spirit" and "character" lay at the root of what Renan saw as the many negative behavioral traits of all Semitic peoples: their excessive sensuality and lust, their roughness and vulgarity, their narrowmindedness and lack of organizational ability.[20] Because of these fundamental flaws in their makeup, Renan asserted, the Semites had historically been inferior to the Aryans both politically and culturally.[21] Moreover, the Semitic spirit and character were permanently flawed because they faithfully reflected the defective biological inheritance of the Semitic race as a whole.[22] For Renan, Semitic inferiority was thus an objective scientific truth, a fact grounded in the same natural order of things that was also responsible for, and assured the continuance of, Aryan superiority and progressiveness.[23]

On the intellectual level it was the narrow subjectivism of the Semites, their ability to see the world only through themselves, which for Renan was the source of their one-sided concept of the universe: they succeeded in grasping its unity (hence their development of monotheism, which Renan saw as the Semites' only contribution to humanity), but proved completely incapable of understanding its variety, multiplicity, and complexity.[24] The ability to appreciate the many dimensions of events, the desire to search out their inner complexities and contradictions—these traits so typical of the Indo-European peoples—were nonexistent among the Semites, who in Renan's eyes suffered from a "fatal simplicity" [*fatale simplicité*].[25] Hence the total absence of mythology, the art of narrative, the fine arts, and great poetry in Semitic civilization.[26] Particularly notable by its absence was any Semitic affinity for philosophy and science. In Renan's own words, "l'esprit sémitique, il est de sa nature anti-philosophique et anti-scientifique."[27]

Of great importance was Renan's portrayal of the Arabs in particular as the quintessential Semitic people. This anti-Arab note running through Renan's writings on race was eagerly picked up by Egyptianist intellectuals searching for a theoretical basis for their own anti-Arab inclinations. In addition, they were flattered by the fact that the same philosopher who so "scientifically" had condemned the Semites and the Arabs as inferior was also fulsome in his praise of ancient Pharaonic Egypt, which he separated (along with ancient Babylon and Assyria) from the Semitic category. Stating that Egypt was neither Semitic nor Indo-European, he also asserted that "l'Égypte a eu une part considérable dans l'histoire de monde."[28] Clearly, Egyptianist intellectuals of the 1920s and early 1930s did not share the motives that had driven Renan to formulate his anti-Semitic and anti-Arab theories several decades earlier. Instead, it was Egyptian nationalist motives, the desire to create a distinctive and authentically Egyptian collective image, which undoubtedly influenced their adoption of Renan's theories. But there can be no doubt as to the impact of Renan's ideas upon them: with his anti-Arab views, he provided Egyptianist intellectuals with a "scientific" infrastructure upon which to base their call for the purification of Egyptian life from the Arab cultural heritage.

A second, more tentative, source of influence on the anti-Arab ideas of Egyptianist intellectuals of the 1920s and early 1930s may have come from within the

Islamic tradition itself. Here we refer to the Shu'ubiyya, the anti-Arab protest movement that had developed within intellectual and literary circles among the Mawali during the second and third Islamic centuries.[29] The Shu'ubiyya phenomenon emerged as a reaction to Arab superiority and dominance in early Muslim society. Its spokesmen rejected the Arab right to hegemony within the *umma* and called instead for equality between non-Arab and Arab Muslims regardless of ethnic origins. *Shu'ubi* authors ridiculed Arab claims to noble descent and racial virtues. Arab primitiveness was seen as the consequence of the nomadic, desert origins of the Arabs, and even the Arab contribution to the development of Islamic civilization was minimized in comparison to the contributions made by non-Arab Muslims, particularly the Iranians.[30]

Historically, the Shu'ubiyya glorified the ancient and non-Arab states and empires of the Middle East in order to reduce more recent Arab political ascendancy to what they felt to be more manageable proportions. Generally, they extolled the achievements of non-Arab peoples and races, positing that the Arabs had contributed to history only through imitating their regional predecessors.[31] The position of the Shu'ubiyya was that all these ancient peoples had achieved historic greatness while the Arabs were still in a state of primitive barbarism.[32] Moving from the past to the present, the *Shu'ubis* ridiculed Arab ignorance, simplicity, and cultural poverty, and presented the character and mentality of the Arabs in terms not too dissimilar from those of Renan, as lacking in cultural refinement and sophistication and marked by qualities of superficiality and externality.[33] It was the "Age of Ignorance," the Jahiliyya, which *Shu'ubis* saw as most representative of the true character of the Arabs, and as most faithfully embodying the weaknesses and inferiority of the Arabs as a collective.[34]

It is difficult to link the ideas of the Shu'ubiyya directly to the thought of Egyptianist intellectuals of a thousand years later. What is beyond doubt is that the anti-Arab argumentation of Egyptianist intellectuals of the interwar period is saturated with motifs and ideas resembling those of the earlier Shu'ubiyya. As we shall see shortly, notions of Arab cultural poverty, of the barrenness of the Arab legacy, and of the inherent primitiveness of the Arab character and mentality bulked large in the anti-Arab presentations of Egyptian "neo-*shu'ubis*" in the interwar years.

A third literary influence on Egyptian anti-Arabism came, rather paradoxically, from the writings of the most famous historian of the Arabs themselves. Ibn Khaldun's *Muqaddima* was widely known in Egyptian intellectual circles by the early twentieth century, and Egyptian intellectuals of an anti-Arab bent were able to find in it powerful arguments (perhaps all the more appealing because they came from an "Arab" pen) for their hostility to the Arabs. Of course they were selective in their use of ibn Khaldun. On the one hand, they studiously ignored the strengths and virtues that ibn Khaldun had seen as resting in the nature of Arab "desert life" [*badawa*]: the vitality, the courage, the heroism, the sense of mutual responsibility and group solidarity [*'asabiyya*] by which ibn Khaldun had explained the historical success of the Arabs.[35] What they seized on were two other notions of ibn Khaldun that better suited their anti-Arab inclinations. The first was his great methodological insight: that in order to understand the history of any group, one must study the environment, the physical, climatic, geographic, and social conditions in which the group had developed.[36] Obviously, this perspective intersected nicely with the parallel determinist influence deriving from modern European thought, an influence that implicitly separated Egypt from the rest of the Arab world. The second concept of ibn Khaldun that reinforced the Egyptianists' anti-Arabism was his emphasis on the cultural superiority of sedentary civilization [*'umran* or *hadara*] over the tribal lifestyle. Although urban civilization was often dominated and frequently nourished by the desert, it was nonetheless a more advanced state of life, the natural home of cultural refinement, of science, and of philosophy.[37] Thus it was the most original social theoretician of the Arabs who fed Egyptian inclinations to see Egypt as distinct from, and superior to, the Arabs.

A final source of influence on Egyptian anti-Arabism was a purely Egyptian one: the traditional negative image possessed by sedentary Egyptians of the nomadic Arabs inhabiting the deserts bordering the Nile Valley. The full range of nuances of this image have yet to be developed by modern scholarship. But there are enough references to its existence to posit it as a force in the anti-Arabism of Egyptianist intellectuals. In the popular mind of urban and rural Egyptians, the Bedouin seem to have been stereotyped as ignorant, brutal primitives who lived by tyrannizing the *fallahin* and exploiting agrarian, sedentary culture.[38] The image assumed a never-ending conflict between barbarism and civilization. Perhaps most important in regard to this stereotype was the almost unconscious tendency to equate the nomadic Arabs of the desert with the Arabs as a whole, an equation that as late as the 1930s led Egyptians to use the word "Arab" to mean "uncivilized Bedouin."[39] In the hands of Egyptian intellectuals already hostile to things Arab, the nomadic/Arab stereotype was a potent weapon. Elaborating on the latent image, they extended the negative characteristics applied to the Bedouin of Egypt to encompass all Arabs and everything Arab—the Arab "mentality," "personality," civilization, and legacy. Thus a portion, a relatively insignificant portion, of the Arab community came to stand as surrogate for the whole, with resultant Egyptianist oversimplification concerning the diversity and the richness of the whole.

The Nature of the Arab Mentality and Personality

The drive for Egyptian authenticity was not the only reason given by Egyptianist intellectuals as underlying their demand for a total break with the Arabs and Arabism. The Arabs not only represented something alien to Egypt, but also were marked by negative and undesirable national characteristics that had injured Egypt in the past and would continue to do so in the future. Thus the complete separation of Egypt from things Arab was not merely an act of distinguishing between the foreign and the genuine, but additionally an exercise in separating the bad from the good.

What lay behind the congenital defects of the Arab "personality"? Egyptianist intellectuals were convinced that at the heart of Arab backwardness was the natural milieu in which Arab collectivity had taken shape, the geographic and climatic environment that had formed the Arabs as a people. This, of course, was the Arabian Peninsula. Just as the fertile Nile Valley was a positive and beneficial influence on the Egyptian character and mentality, so the wild and barren Arabian Peninsula must have been the source of all that was defective in the Arab mind and personality. In the Egyptianist perception, the Arabs could never dissociate themselves from their peninsular roots. The original nomadic lifestyle of the Arabs, with its distinctive social norms and customs, had indelibly marked the Arab national character.[40] Assuming an inescapable, deterministic relationship between environment on the one hand and human characteristics on the other, Egyptianist intellectuals tended to perceive all Arabs, past and present, in terms of the original pre-Islamic, *jahili* Arab community. At the center of the negative Egyptianist image of the Arabs was early Arab society in its nomadic and uncivilized state.[41]

Obviously, this deliberate restriction of what was essentially "Arab" to the customs and habits characteristic of the first phase of Arab history was intended to serve Egyptian nationalist interests. The portrayal of the Arabs as an indelibly primitive collective because of their nomadic origins emphasized the contrast between their culture and mentality, and the sophisticated civilization of the Egyptians, whose roots were in the sedentary milieu of the Nile Valley. Egyptian nationalist intellectuals inverted the values associated with the peninsular origins of the Arabs as a people: the same environmental influences that 'Abd al-Rahman al-Kawakibi and other Arab nationalist ideologues saw as the positive kernel of Arabism—the source of Arab purity, vigor, and strength—were perceived by Egyptianist intellectuals as the source of all that was lacking or warped in the Arabs and their culture.[42]

Both Arab culture and the Arab national personality were the product of the desert. The endless wastes of forlorn wilderness, the frightening emptiness, the scarcity of food and water sources, the imperative of perpetual wandering in the search for sustenance, the fundamental insecurity stemming from continual concern over the next day's nourishment, the absence of a sense of permanence and stability—these were the basic characteristics of the life imposed by the Arab natural environment. "The Arabs," emphasized Tawfiq al-Hakim in his analysis of their native environment, "are a nation which grew up in poverty the likes of which no other nation has known; a barren wilderness and waterless deserts which cause bloody conflict and an endless struggle for sustenance and life."[43]

Muhammad Husayn Haykal presented the Arab natural milieu in terms similar to those of Hakim. The Arabs had become a nation in the desolate expanses of the Arabian Peninsula during the Jahiliyya period, and it was these desert wastes that had shaped their character and mentality.[44] Their homeland was a "wasteland," an "empty wilderness" isolated from all of the great cultural centers of the ancient and medieval world.[45] Moreover, the Arab lifestyle was one of incessant instability, a perpetual movement over this endless wasteland. This migratory existence prevented them from coalescing into larger groups, constructing significant settlements, or establishing a durable society within a sedentary framework.[46] Haykal also emphasized that much the same situation "continues to prevail in the Arabian Peninsula to this very day."[47]

It was the environment of Arabia that had prevented the emergence of "a civilization which had stable foundations."[48] Here Haykal echoed ibn Khaldun: "civilization is one of the fruits of a human community in a sedentary setting."[49] But unlike ibn Khaldun, Haykal saw no continuity in the relationship between nomadic Bedouin life [*badawa*] and sedentary urban existence [*hadar*]. On the contrary, in his view sedentary culture and the nomadic lifestyle had nothing in common. Bedouin nomadism by its very nature was anti-civilizatory and could not serve as a reservoir or source of enrichment for developed human culture.[50] The Bedouin, with their chronic material poverty, could never put together the necessary accumulation of wealth needed to create a true civilization, and thus were doomed forever to remain civilizationless.[51]

Tawfiq al-Hakim was also convinced that their nomadic past had stamped the Arab national character. The outlook and values of nomadism were etched deep into the Arab mentality and had prevented Arabs from developing a distinctive civilization of their own. The lack of a sedentary environment and consequently the absence of developed cultural life, he asserted in a manner reminiscent of both Renan and ibn Khaldun, were the most prominent collective characteristics of the Arabs, making their outlook on life the ultimate antithesis of the sedentary perspective of "fanatic attachment" to the soil that characterized Egyptians.[52] As Hakim maintained:

> The Arabs feel everything but constancy. And how would they know constancy when they have no land, no past, and no cultivated sedentary civilization [*'umran,* a term also employed by ibn Khaldun]? [They have] only countries born of circumstance rather than rooted organically in the land. After all, without land there is no constancy, and without constancy no contemplation, and without contemplation no mythology, no broad imagination, no deep thought or sense of construction.[53]

In terms of its specific traits, the Arab "personality" as presented by Egyptianist intellectuals was marked by an inherent "simplicity."[54] They frequently sketched the personality and mentality of the Arabs in the image of the *badu,* the man of the desert: physically tough, primitive, coarse, given to bodily pleasures and lusts yet desiring the attractions of the civilized world beyond the desert. One of the harshest pictures of this type was that of Tawfiq al-Hakim in 1933. For him, the Arabs dreamed perpetually of "that life of pleasure" found in civilized, sedentary societies.[55] In doing so, their focus was solely on the material and the grossly sensual: "[t]he Arab nation is one whose total existence is a dream about the pleasures of life and of [physical] satiation. . . . The Arabs' entire thought and art revolve around the indulgence of the senses and the material."[56] Yet, since they had not been raised and nurtured in civilized society, the Arabs were unable to internalize its values or to absorb its riches except in the most superficial of ways. When the Arabs did come in contact with civilized society, they quickly and avariciously seized only its "momentary pleasures."[57] Although they had conquered various advanced societies and come into contact with great civilizations, still they had "grabbed so quickly that they only skimmed the cream from the surface."[58] Their nomadic character, rooted deep within them, led the Arabs to absorb only the superficial and the marginal outer layer of the civilizations they had overrun.[59]

Further fundamental flaws of the collective Arab mentality in the eyes of Egyptianist intellectuals were in its lack of realism and its inclination to the fantastic. The Arab imagination was not a mature, creative imagination like that of Egyptians, a source of cultural constructiveness and artistic productivity. Rather, it was a wild, primitive imagination, an imagination of the senses and the instincts. The product of the Arab imagination was always an escape from the harsh and cruel realities of their background, a fantasy where everything was ideal but also always beyond their reach. It was a flawed imagination that created mirages in a vain attempt to obtain what was lacking in the real world. Arab intellectuals deluded themselves with journeys into the unreal and the impossible. The existence and function of this fantasy world could only be understood, Egyptianist intellectuals theorized, against the backdrop of the poverty that had shaped the Arabs. Thus to Haykal it was the terrible material deprivation of the Arab past, their endless wandering and remoteness in the desert, which had "created the Arab as a creature of fantasy who scarcely recognizes the intricacies of genuine reality."[60]

To Egyptian nationalist intellectuals a basic feature of the Arab mind was its inferiority in comparison to the Aryan mind. 'Abbas Mahmud al-'Aqqad was captivated by the racial theories of European philosophers and sociologists, particularly those of Ernest Renan.[61] He assumed a dichotomy between the backward, inferior Semites and the advanced, superior Aryans, and fully accepted the idea that an immense gap separated Semitic from Aryan thought processes and modes of expression. In his view, there was simply no way to bridge the differences between the "Semitic mentality" and the "Aryan mentality."[62] The natural environment that had shaped the Arab character as well as the language and history deriving from that background had all "conspired to make the Arabs a nation without imagination."[63] Similarly Taha Husayn, who usually did not participate in the denigration of the Arabs, in this instance took for granted what he termed "the orientalists' theory" positing fundamental differences between "the Semitic mind" and "the Aryan mind."[64] While the former as personified by the Arabs was "superficial," being satisfied with outer manifestations only, the latter as personified in the French in particular "penetrates always to the heart of the matter."[65] Another enthusiastic Egyptian adherent of Renan's ideas as well as of his naturalist-racist view of the Arabs was Muhammad Ghallab. Ghallab posited that "Arab-Semitic culture" was manifestly inferior to "Indo-Germanic culture." The Arabs as a whole were characterized by Ghallab as being "narrow-minded," "short on imagination," and marked by "primitive thought processes" as well as an "inferior mentality."[66]

Another major negative trait that Egyptianist intellectuals discovered in the desert-shaped collective personality of the Arabs was the absence of a sense of historical time and importance. Broadly phrased, the Arabs were devoid of historical consciousness. They were a collective of nomadic wanderers through time who had no sense of connection with particular eras, with specific events, or with shared historical achievements. Their contribution to the historical legacy of humanity, whether measured in splendid physical remains or in notable spiritual achievements, was negligible. In Tawfiq al-Hakim's striking metaphor, "the role of Arab civilization in the symphony of the human race is like that of a scherzo in a Beethoven symphony—a tune, short, pleasing, and sweet!"[67]

Muhammad Husayn Haykal's critique of the historical poverty of the Arabs focused in particular on the pre-Islamic era of Arab history. Well after Egypt, Greece, Rome, and other historical nations had developed great civilizations, no real historical development had occurred among the ancient Arabs. The period of the Jahiliyya did bear witness to the bravery and fortitude of the Arabs as a people; "as for its civilization and scientific and artistic manifestations, however . . . the history of the pre-Islamic Arabs has nothing to tell us."[68] Even after the rise of Islam, the Arabs of the Arabian Peninsula continued to lack an historical consciousness.[69] Haykal's general conclusion was that nomadism cannot provide the ground for the development of historical consciousness; the latter is the exclusive product of civilized society. The Arab nation's ahistoricism, Haykal concluded, "derives from its bedouin lifestyle which is the foundation of its existence."[70]

Paradoxically, however, this absence of an historical awareness among the Arabs did not mean that the Arabs neglected their past. On the contrary, one of the characteristics of the Arab ahistorical frame of mind was a fixation upon and a glorification of one specific segment of the past, the era of the founders of Islam [*al-salaf*]. The era of the Prophet Muhammad and the early Muslims was the exclusive concern of the Arabs, apparently representing all that was significant in history to them.[71] History was thus not a dynamic process to the Arabs: rather, the Arab concept of the past was a fossilized one, an exclusive focus on a remote era in which the Arabs had flourished and which never really ended. The Arab tendency to worship this particular piece of the past, to sanctify it, and to try to preserve its patterns resulted in a closed and sealed history. The ahistorical mentality of the Arabs dismissed the idea of dialogue between the past, on the one hand, and the present and future, on the other. Their history was a monologue from the past, and the past alone. To them the past was a static as well a stagnant entity—a frozen model that the present and the future were obligated to idolize, to imitate, and to perpetuate.[72]

In the eyes of Egyptianist intellectuals, this static Arab perception of history was reactionary. It asphyxiated history by embalming it in the archaic framework of a mutely worshipped past. Rather than living in the present with their eyes turned toward the future, the Arabs lived in an illusory museum of petrified images of their past, a past that, in their presumption of its immortality, was in actuality absurd.[73] Some Egyptian intellectuals analyzed the Arab focus on the *salaf* in terms reminiscent of Nietzsche's concept of "antiquarian history."[74] The Arab sense of history, they claimed, did not see its purpose as one of advancing the present through an understanding of the past. Rather, it tended to embalm and mummify the present in the image of the past. Rather than harnessing and using the past for the sake of the present, the Arab approach buried the present in the sarcophogus of the past.[75] It was designed to perpetuate the past, not to rejuvenate it. In short, the Arab "antiquarian" historical perception allowed the dead to rule over the living; in so doing, it stifled life and change.[76]

The writings of Salama Musa in the 1920s offered perhaps the most vehement analysis of the Arab ahistorical and antiquarian mentality.[77] For Musa, when the Arabs studied their history, it was not out of genuine desire to understand it in depth; rather, their aim was solely to enhance their "national pride by means of exalting the venerable forefathers [*al-salaf*]."[78] For the Arabs, the study of the past was not a means of creating a better present and future; instead, the present and the future were perceived merely as an extension and a continuation of the past. Musa felt that such a concept of history was ultimately a cul-de-sac, for it was based on a flawed concept of the course of human evolution and so would result in enriching neither the present nor the future.[79]

It was in modern psychology that Musa found the explanation for the inner drive behind the anti-historical, petrified Arab sense of history. In his view, the Arabs were attempting to "flee" their dismal present through their addiction to the presumably more perfect era of the *salaf.* The constantly changing realities of the modern world, which the Arab personality by its very nature was not adapted to, was replaced by the "fortified shelter" of a more glorious and more perfect past.[80] Musa saw this Arab desertion of the contemporary world as evidence of a collective psychosis, indeed of the infantilism of the Arab personality. His own terms for it were trenchant: "the history complex" [*murakkab al-ta'rikh*] and "the ancestors complex" [*murakkab al-salaf*].[81] To Musa, this withdrawal into an illusory past that could never return was incompatible with modernity and progress. The fact that "the ancient has a sacred status among the Arabs" was in his eyes counterproductive, leading to the tyranny of the past over the present.[82]

'Abbas Mahmud al-'Aqqad shared Musa's critical view of the Arabs as fixated on the ancient and the archaic. Arabs' worship of "the dead in preference to the living" also appeared to 'Aqqad to be a compulsive phenomenon, a ritual required in order to achieve collective self-assertion and self-esteem.[83] Also like Musa, 'Aqqad ascribed this Arab characteristic to the desert milieu in which the Arab personality had been formed and had assumed its values: "the Arabs assiduously clung to the old and preferred the dead to the living simply because they were desert tribes, and as such tended to venerate ancestry and to stress clannishness."[84]

This perceived anti-historical mentality of the Arabs was of course held to be utterly contradictory with the currents of revival and progress sweeping Egyptian society in the 1920s. The obvious imperative for Egyptians was that they must divest themselves of any remnants of a mentality both alien and reactionary. Thus Salama Musa called on Egyptians to shake off the Arab mentality that was inhibiting their own natural renaissance and development. The Arab personality and mentality were simply antithetical to all that was both true to Egypt and desirable for it:

> Our task now is to break with the [Arab] past and to outline a new course for the future, because the spirit of this past is out of harmony with our spirit. . . . We must awaken ourselves by detaching ourselves from the *salaf.* We seek to live. In our souls there burns a noble passion for development and an overpowering drive towards glory.[85]

In similar language, 'Aqqad distinguished between the Arab mentality with its archaic elements and the future-oriented, progressive outlook of twentieth-century Egyptians, calling on his countrymen to "put an end to [thinking about] our past Arab centuries lest we ourselves be asphyxiated by the dust of these centuries."[86]

Both the assortment of negative traits found in the Arab personality and the fundamental contradiction between it and the genuine Egyptian personality found vivid literary expression in Tawfiq al-Hakim's *'Awdat al-Ruh.* The novel creates a series of polarities between that which is genuinely Egyptian and that which is basic to the Arab. The language is of course symbolic and metaphoric, one Egyptian *fallah* personifying ancient, civilized Egypt, one Bedouin Arab serving as the embodiment of the rootless and primitive Arab nation. Nonetheless, the conflict between the son of the desert and the child of the soil is made into an eternal clash between the irreconcilably opposed Arab and Egyptian national "personalities."

When the hero Muhsin arrives with his parents for a short vacation at their farm near Damanhur, he is delighted once again to meet the *fallahin* who till the family's lands. Muhsin greatly admires these "simple" *fallahin.* He identifies with their rural lifestyle, their modes of expression, and their lighthearted joy for life, as well as envying their permanence on the land and their love for it.[87] But there is also a darker side to Egyptian rural life, represented not by the *fallahin* but by an Arab character. Muhsin quickly learns of continual disputes between the peasants and the "Arab" [*al-a'rab*] watchmen who earn their living by guarding the farm and its lands from outside marauders. In an encounter with the Arab guard 'Abd al-'Ati, the latter is presented in the worst possible light. Because of a family dispute, 'Abd al-'Ati is seen cursing and berating a young *fallah,* 'Arjawi, even threatening to kill him on the grounds that "Arab honor" has been insulted.[88] Muhsin's inquiry concerning the broader implications of this local argument illustrates the attitude of superiority and contempt that Hakim believed to be characteristic of Arabs toward the Egyptians:

Muhsin	And so, 'Abd al-'Ati, is the Arab better than the *fallah?*
'Abd al-'Ati	And how is that, sir? Is the Arab like the *fallah*??!
Muhsin	What is the difference between the two?
'Abd al-'Ati	You say how is that, sir? Why, the Arab is noble.
Muhsin	And the *fallah* is not noble?
'Abd al-'Ati	The *fallah* is a slave and the son of a slave. We are Arabs. We cannot agree to mix with him.[89]

Reflecting upon this unpleasant episode, Muhsin's own contrasts between the Egyptian peasant and the Arab nomad were all to the advantage of the former. Where the *fallah* was characterized by "his goodness, his calm, his love of peace [which] all are the hallmarks of civilization and stability," the Arab was still "known for his wild traits, love of war, vengeance and bloodletting, all the relics of a barbaric, primitive life."[90] Where the peaceful Egyptian led "a social, civilized life," that of the Arab was still "a barbaric, nomadic, wilderness life."[91] Most important was Muhsin's conclusion about honor and nobility—that the sedentary, peace-loving civilized traits of the Egyptian "bespeak noble origins, not slavery, not meanness inherited by a slave the son of a slave."[92] Muhsin's conviction of the superiority of the Egyptian *fallah* over the Arab nomad was expressed even more strongly in his concluding thoughts about the Arabs and *fallahin:* "the *fallah* is superior to the Arab. He is nobler than the Arab. He is better than the Arab."[93]

The harsh image of the Arab presented in *'Awdat al-Ruh* may derive in part from the *fallahin*'s own traditional negative perception of the Bedouin Arabs living along the edges of the Nile. But it is more than that as well. In Hakim's eyes, it was the intellectual's task to reorganize this largely latent and unfocused image into a vivid public perception. It was his task to teach Egyptians who they really were and who they were not, as well as to make them aware of their own Egyptian potential and how to realize it. This is why even Muhsin at one point was forced to admit that, in comparison to the Arabs portrayed in the novel, the *fallahin* did lack a proper awareness of their roots and their nobility. Whereas the Arabs had inherited an awareness of their "origins" and the evolution of their lineage from generation to generation, the Egyptian *fallahin* needed to be made aware of the same.[94] For Hakim, the latent rural image was but the point of departure for the creation of a much more self-conscious Egyptian self-image.

The Arabs and Islam

The negative image of the Arabs prevailing among Egyptian nationalist intellectuals in the post-1919 period was not without its problem areas. Perhaps the greatest of these was the Arab relationship to Islam. If the Arab national character was so primitive that civilized life and thought was beyond its reach, how had the Arabs produced the Prophet Muhammad, the Islamic faith, and one of humanity's most impressive civilizations?

Egyptianist intellectuals who did attempt to deal directly with the issue of the Arab relationship to Islam tended to base their arguments on a combination of *shu'ubi* motifs and a quasi-racial approach resembling that of Renan. Thus, while they did not deny that the Arabs had established Islam and had been the people to propagate its message throughout the world, the Arab contribution to all that was civilized and valuable in historic Islam was minimized and defined as negligible. The approach was to emphasize the speed with which other peoples had supplanted the Arabs within the Islamic community and should be credited with the great achievements of Islamic civilization.

Shu'ubi themes were echoed in the writings of Isma'il Mazhar. Mazhar found the term "Arabic civilization" [*al-hadara al-'arabiyya*] totally unacceptable; in his view the only proper term for historic Islam was "Islamic civilization" [*al-hadara al-islamiyya*], which he maintained "partakes not at all of Arabism except in the language."[95] Although he later qualified this position, grudgingly admitting that some Islamic phenomena had been "colored by Arabism," he nonetheless attempted to restrict these to as narrow a range as possible, itemizing the direct Arab contribution to Muslim development as "the *Qur'an,* the law of personal status, and the regulations for religious observances between man and God."[96] All other aspects and institutions of Islamic civilization had been contributed or developed by Syrians, Egyptians, Iraqis, Persians, Greeks, and Byzantines. In the blossoming of Islamic civilization, the Arab contribution had been limited to the preparatory stage only: the political unification of all these "great" cultural heritages in a single unit and thus the creation of the necessary condition for their eventual integration in a cultural synthesis.[97]

A fuller version of this approach came from the pen of Muhammad Husayn Haykal. In a 1925 article on "The Arabs and Islamic Civilization,"[98] Haykal attempted to provide an answer to the general question of the Arab role in the development of Islamic civilization. As he saw it, at the start of Islamic history, "the Arab Muslims left the Arabian Peninsula without a civilization."[99] It was their early conquests that first brought the nomadic Arabs into contact with sedentary civilization and its arts and sciences, "those things which the Arabian Peninsula had never known."[100] Haykal's main emphasis was on the brevity and the marginality of the Arab impact on the civilized societies that they had conquered. Given the sensual bent that Haykal presumed to be inherent in the Arab national character, the Arabs themselves were portrayed as quickly surrendering to a life of ease and pleasure. Becoming absorbed with the material comforts offered by their new conquests and finding satisfaction in corporeal delights, the Arabs had soon lost their nomadic vigor, strength, and *esprit de corps.*[101]

Like Isma'il Mazhar, Haykal also believed that the Arab role in the development of Islamic civilization was largely one of creating favorable conditions for cultural efflorescence rather than one of making its own creative contributions to that civilization's complex of ideas and institutions. Thus the Arabs were termed the "instrument of communication" among the cultures and peoples of the regions they had conquered.[102] By creating a unified political and administrative framework from Iran to Spain, the Arabs set the stage for the emergence of a new cultural synthesis in the Near East. But other than their initial structural contribution to this process, the Arab role was marginal. "Only a handful of the Arab conquerors themselves," Haykal asserted, "took part in these intellectual and artistic efforts [forging Islamic civilization], although all [these efforts] were accomplished at their command and under their supervision."[103] The Arabs themselves played no role in the process. The new literary genres and poetic forms of Islamic literature were imported from the outside and adapted to Arabic by non-Arabs. Similarly, it was these writers who composed the great literary works of early Islam such as *Kalila wa Dimna,* The Thousand and One Nights, and the story of 'Antar.[104]

Thus the Arab role in the evolution of Islamic civilization was limited by Haykal to the merely structural one of providing the political and linguistic shell within which the genius of others was to flourish. But Haykal went further than this, attributing little true significance even to this instrumental Arab contribution to Islamic history. To his mind, the integration of the different cultures and traditions of the Near East into a single Islamic civilization was not a particularly difficult task. After all, since antiquity these cultures had all shared an identical geographic, climatic, and mental milieu. The eventual creation of one Islamic civilization was therefore seen by Haykal as a simple, almost an inevitable, process based on the "natural proximity" of all the peoples, cultures, and collective mentalities existing since before Islam in the Near East and the Mediterranean basin.[105]

No less anti-Arab was Salama Musa's analysis of the Arab role in the development of Islamic civilization. The substantive tendency of his writing was to attribute to the Arabs and to "Arab culture" [*al-thaqafa al-'arabiyya*] many of the weaknesses he believed were found in Islamic civilization. In contrast with the previous authors we have considered, Musa felt the Arab influence on Islam was appreciable, but it was also thoroughly negative.[106]

Musa was vehement in his disapproval of any attempt to inculcate the political ideas of historic Islam, with their roots in early Arab political practice, in the minds of Egyptian youth. The Arab-Islamic political heritage had been marked by "anachronistic institutions" as well as "corrupt and dictatorial regimes" throughout its history, and as such was completely antithetical to a modern and liberal education aimed at developing an Egyptian younger generation oriented toward the West, progress, and modern values.[107] Islam's presumedly "totalitarian" governmental forms repeatedly came under attack by Salama Musa. Even at their best, he asserted, Islamic regimes were harsh, dictatorial, and unprogressive. He was particularly intent on demolishing what he saw as the myth of the inherently democratic and representative nature of Islamic politics. He chose rather to emphasize the antidemocratic and authoritarian strands, in his view primarily derived from Arab practices, which he found in Islamic political culture. "It is not in the interests of our constitutional regime to praise and extoll [the Caliphs] Harun al-Rashid or al-Ma'mun, for each was a despotic ruler in no way different from 'Abd al-Hamid [II] whom the Young Turks deposed."[108] Generalizing from these specifics, it was his position that "even during its best and most progressive periods, Arab government was despotic."[109] Musa denied that Islam incorporated the idea of "consultation" [*shura*] into its political life; even the Caliph 'Umar ibn al-Khattab "consulted no one" in making his decisions.[110] Consultation had never been institutionalized in Islamic government and remained unrealized in the despotic political tradition of Islam.

Perhaps Musa's fundamental concern was what the defects and weaknesses of the Arab-Islamic political tradition had meant for Egypt. In general terms, Musa viewed the Arab conquest of Egypt and the ensuing Islamic era as an historical catastrophe that had brought cultural and social disaster upon Egypt and its people. The Arabs and Islam had severed Egypt from its natural Egyptian identity based on the Nile Valley alone. Egypt had been forcibly annexed to a wider Arab-Islamic world, and one to which her own cultural traditions were completely foreign. Since the Arabs and after them Islam had no sense of "nationalism," the Arab conquest of Egypt and the country's subsequent Arabization and Islamification had deprived her of her own true national identity and consciousness.[111] The Arabs had systematically eliminated the "patriotic sentiment" previously characterizing Egypt and destroyed the distinctive sense of national awareness that had existed for millenia in the Nile Valley: "Egyptian nationalism had become submerged in the Islamic environment and its civilization masked by the Arab *badawa* [Bedouin culture]."[112]

What was cloaked in the garb of rational analysis with Haykal and Musa became dogmatic assertion in the writings of Tawfiq al-Hakim. Hakim was so thoroughly convinced of the worthlessness of Arab culture that he did not bother to attempt to explore its possible contribution to Islamic civilization. As far as he was concerned, the nomadic Arabs could not contribute anything either to the Islamic faith or to Islamic civilization. Indeed, at heart the Arabs had remained pagans and even were basically antagonistic to the idea of monotheism. They had never been real Muslims in the sense Egyptians were.[113] Hakim supported this extreme position by maintaining that the Islamic religion had completely detached itself from its Arab origins. It had shed its tribal and nomadic ritual elements, over time taking on all the attributes of a universal monotheism with a highly developed moral code, law, and theology. For Hakim, from the moment Islam had become a genuine monotheism it had lost its Arab character and had become foreign to the primitive Arab personality. "The Arabs," Hakim proclaimed, "always opposed religion whenever it interfered with their drive to satisfy the passions inbred in their nature."[114] In Hakim's *'Awdat al-Ruh* Shaykh Hasan described Arab irreligiousness in even more vehement terms: "They have no religion and no belief. They know no compassion and no Islam."[115]

Perhaps the most elaborate attack on the Arab role in history came in Isma'il Mazhar's systematic critique of what he termed "the Arab thought process." As we have seen, Mazhar generally minimized the Arab role in the development of Islamic civilization. In one crucial sphere, however—that of thought and thought processes—he felt that what he perceived as the backwardness of Muslim worldviews and philosophical speculation was a direct consequence of the decisive influence of the Arabic language and Arabic culture on historic Islam. This influence, Mazhar emphasized, was totally negative.[116]

Mazhar's philosophical point of departure in his analysis of the components of Arab-Islamic thought was positivistic. He was a great admirer of Auguste Comte's theory of three evolutionary stages—the theological, the metaphysical, and the scientific—in the development of human thought.[117] In examining the evolution of the Arab mentality from his positivistic viewpoint, it immediately became clear to Mazhar that the Arabs had never developed beyond the early stages of human intellection. A close look at the Arab mentality's components convinced him that the Arabs had never progressed to the third or scientific stage of thought. Arab thought through its entire history had been locked into earlier, more primitive stages of evolution. Its approach to reality had always remained theological and metaphysical rather than scientific.[118]

The underdevelopment of the Arab mentality was particularly apparent to Mazhar in what was called the "Arab philosophy." To begin with, Mazhar contended, Arab thought contained no original philosophical speculation. If for no other reason, "Arab philosophy" did not deserve its name.[119] Lacking imagination and the power of invention, all Arab thought was based on imitation. True, the Arabs had absorbed a few philosophical motifs through intermediaries: Jews, Nestorians, the pagans of Harran. But they themselves had never developed their own independent philosophical system based on their own speculation and free of religious elements. In this sense, Mazhar claimed, neither al-Farabi, ibn Rushd, nor ibn Sina had ever established a school of philosophy. Mazhar also denied the appelation of philosophical school to Islamic religious groups or trends such as the Mu'tazilites, the Ash'arites, or Sufism: in his view these movements were "theological schools that sought the support of philosophy."[120] In the final analysis, "the concept of philosophy remained an individual concept among the Arabs."[121] New philosophical schools did develop in Europe after the Renaissance and with the rise of secular and rationalistic thought—but only in Europe. Arab-Islamic civilization had not been influenced by these later developments. Thus there was a "fundamental difference" betwen the European mind, which had attained the scientific stage of intellectual evolution, and the Arab mind, which remained frozen at the metaphysical stage.[122]

It was this complete absence of rationalist and positivist thought processes that to Mazhar explained the paucity of pure scientific production among the Arabs. At best, one could find a few Arab writings in the fields of medicine, chemistry, and botany. But these were the exceptions that proved the rule: the underdevelopment of the Arab intellect and its fundamentally unscientific nature, which remained grounded in theological and metaphysical thought patterns.[123]

Like the anti-Arab writing of so many of his contemporaries, Mazhar's harsh analysis of the supposedly inferior nature of the Arab mentality was an instrumental one meant to serve his own exclusivist Egyptian nationalism. It was aimed at proving that Arab thought processes and the culture developing out of those, since they were antipositivist and reactionary, were a threat to Egypt's revival and advance toward modernity. Mazhar repeatedly maintained that the current renaissance of Egypt had to based on modern, scientific European-oriented thought. It needed to adopt rationalist and positivist thought processes that were free of all theological or metaphysical tendencies. With the optimism typical of the era, he concluded by affirming that Egyptians had now chosen the proper path, one that would lead to "an exit from the darkness of the hidden [= metaphysical] methodology toward the light of the positivist [= scientific] methodology."[124]

Toward an Aryan/European Affiliation for Egypt

One way for thoroughly committed Egyptianist intellectuals to deny any Egyptian connection with the civilization and mentality of the "Asian" Arabs was to postulate a more palatable alternative affiliation for Egyptians. Since Egyptians were not really linked to the Arabs, with what regions, peoples, or civilizations were they instead affiliated?

The more frequent answer given by wholeheartedly Egyptian nationalist intellectuals was to link Egypt to its northern neighbors. Perhaps the most famous proponent of the idea of Egypt's having Mediterranean or European affinities was Salama Musa. To him, Egypt was part of the West rather than the East:

> [A]s my knowledge of the East increases, so does my aversion to it and my feeling that it is foreign to me; as my knowledge of Europe increases, so does my love and attachment for it and my feeling that I am part of it and it is part of me.[125]

Musa employed quasi-religious language to deny any Eastern affiliations for Egypt and to insist that its natural links were with the West: "I am a disbeliever [*kafir*] in the East, a believer [*mu'min*] in the West."[126] On the basis of these feelings, he called his fellow Egyptians to the historical obligation of shedding their present "customs acquired from Asia" and to the parallel necessity of "adopting the customs of Europe."[127] In his view, Egyptians needed to become "out-and-out Europeans" [*Awrubiyyin salihin*].[128] A considerable part of Musa's speculation of the 1920s was devoted to expounding upon this thesis of Egypt's similarity to Europe.[129]

For both Salama Musa and Dr. Muhammad Sharaf, the assertions that "Egyptians are not Semitic" and that "Egypt is a non-Eastern nation" could be demonstrated equally on the grounds of geography, biology, and culture. Through a detailed comparison of the physical characteristics, social customs, language, and material culture of Egyptians with those of other peoples, they concluded that the closest affiliations of Egyptians lay with the peoples of Europe rather than those of Asia. Musa and Sharaf were also apparently the first to develop the position that Egypt was part and parcel of "Mediterranean" civilization, and through that an inseparable part of Europe.[130] As a physician, Sharaf brought the presumed evidence of medicine to prove the point:

> [I]n terms of its origins, modern Egypt is ancient Egypt. Any [medical] examination of the blood confirms that modern Egypt is not African or Asian but European; i.e., belonging to the peoples who live around the Mediterranean Sea.[131]

Others based the non-Arabness of Egypt more on historical evidence. Thus, for Muhammad Ghallab it was the modern science of Egyptology that offered conclusive and "scientific" proof of the absolute distinction between Egypt and the Arabs/Semites. As he explained it, "until the mid-nineteenth century people confused Egypt with the Semitic nations."[132] Thanks to the Egyptologists, it was now appreciated that "Egypt is a nation which emerged on the banks of her Nile and among her mountains surrounding it. There is nothing to link her with the Asians, nor a common nexus tying her to the Nubians, nor strands of kinship connecting her to the North Africans."[133] Egypt was utterly unlike the "Semitic nations" with their "limited imaginations and narrow thought processes"; indeed, Egyptology had proved the existence of a great Egyptian literary tradition, a noteworthy and distinctive Egyptian philosophy, and Egypt's world-historical role as "teacher of the world" and even "master of the universe."[134] Like Salama Musa, Ghallab was convinced that these findings of modern Egyptology also left no doubt that Egypt's closest affiliations, both in spirit and in history, were with the Indo-European race and the Hellenic-Mediterranean-Western cultural and intellectual tradition.[135]

In contrast to the Mediterranean orientation of Musa, Sharaf, and Ghallab, Tawfiq al-Hakim found considerable affinity between the texture of Egyptian civilization and that of India. In his view, Egypt and India were twin civilizations manifesting similar qualities of spiritualism, tranquillity, peacefulness, stability, and permanence.[136] Blessed by nature with material abundance, both possessed the similar spiritual boons of a humanistic outlook and a universalist orientation. Hakim went on to contrast these common Egyptian and Indian characteristics with the very different traits found in Arab-Semitic civilization: "It is completely absurd for us to expect to find in all of Arab civilization any sort of inclination towards matters of the spirit and the intellect in the way in which Egypt and India grasp the terms spirit and intellect."[137] To Tawfiq al-Hakim, "there is not the shadow of a doubt in my heart that Egypt and the Arabs are diametrically opposed: Egypt is spirit, calm, permanence, constructiveness; the Arabs are material, haste, transience, superficiality."[138]

Arabic Literature

Arabic literature [*al-adab al-'arabi*] occupied a central place in the negative image of the Arabs held by Egyptian nationalist intellectuals in the 1920s. Their definition of that "literature" was an extremely broad one, comprising all of the artistic faculties, all the areas of artistic expression (prose and poetry, architecture, music, the visual arts), and also the concepts, ideals, and creativity reflected in these genres.[139] In line with their general approach to the Arabs and their culture as a whole, the negative image of Arabic literature that they presented was consciously structured as the mirror image of their idealized perception of Egyptian artistic expression, which at the time was usually termed Egypt's "national literature" [*al-adab al-qawmi*].

Egyptianist intellectuals of the 1920s followed the Taine-Haykal line of environmental determinism in their analysis of Arabic literature. They posited that it must be understood in terms of the physical environment that had shaped the totality of the national personality of the Arabs. Arabic literature was viewed as a territorially determined reality, a kind of spiritual reproduction of the material setting in which it had developed. The three primordial forces of *race–milieu–moment*—the nomadic Bedouin "race," the barren deserts of Arabia, and the *Zeitgeist* of the pre-Islamic Jahiliyya period—had created both the external forms and the internal essences of Arabic literature. Egyptian nationalist intellectuals repeatedly emphasized that Arabic literature could not be understood and explained primarily in terms of post-*jahili,* Islamic developments, but rather had to be comprehended in terms of the primitive disposition of the nomadic Arabs among whom it had first taken shape. Arabic literature could not escape its formative period. Indeed, it was defined by, and existed only within the constraints of, the form and content it had first assumed in the Jahiliyya period. It was in this presumed timelessness of Arabic literature, of course, that Egyptian intellectuals found the cause of that literature's backwardness. The ultimate purpose of this reductive sort of analysis of Arabic culture is clear; by squeezing all of Arabic literature into a *jahili* mold while denuding it of any later civilized dimensions, Egyptianist intellectuals emphasized both its inferiority and its unsuitability for Egypt.

In the Egyptian nationalist portrayal of its nature, traditional Arabic literature was suffused with the primeval desert landscape of the Arabian Peninsula. Niqula Yusuf, who took as axiomatic that "natural environment" and "psychological environment" together were the determinants of literature, held that "Arabic literature is an Asian literature, the product of the desert."[140] In his view, its function was to serve as a "photographer of bedouin life and the Arabs' way of living, with its meagre grazing lands of dry pasture, [its] bazaars, tents, camels, remains of destroyed camps, courtyards, and dungheaps."[141] This literature represented only the uncivilized, wandering Bedouin, being nothing more than "a collection of the bedouins' vain songs of self-glorification [*fakhr*], of fanaticism [*hamas*], and of the bitter satire [*hija'*] which they pour upon their despised neighbor."[142] In sum, Arabic literature defined in this fashion was the primitive expression of a simple people who had never known the artistic achievements of civilization.[143]

Tawfiq Mikha'il Tuwaij and 'Abbas Mahmud al-'Aqqad shared the perception that Arabic literature was simple and uncivilized. Tuwaij asserted Arabic literature was only "a reproduction of nomadic life," its theme being Bedouin daily activities centered around their herds and their tents.[144] 'Aqqad was particularly negative in his critique of Arabic literature, explaining its weaknesses in terms of the immutable stamp that it bore of the Jahiliyya period. Again and again, he emphasized that Arabic literary production was imbued with the atmosphere of the desert and that it gave expression only to the nomadic spirit. Camels, tents, and "the vast, endless desert wastes" were virtually its only themes.[145]

Muhammad Husayn Haykal also viewed Arabic literature primarily as an expression of the nomadic mentality of the Arabs. Concentrating on Arabic poetry in particular, he saw as its central motif the eternal struggle waged by the Bedouin against the harsh conditions of the desert. Poetry was particularly important in this endless Arab struggle for survival; it was the Bedouin's defense against the cruelty of nature.[146] Through poetry, the Bedouin drew upon his and his tribe's spiritual resources in order to "overcome the afflictions of fate and the vicissitudes of time."[147] However, the desert's central role in the nomadic struggle for existence had had its effects on Arabic poetry itself. Like the nomadic lifestyle of the Arabs, Arabic poetry cannot be harmonized with nature. Rather, it perpetually fights the desert, protesting the suffering inflicted by nature upon the Arab. It is "constantly at the ready to fight and to overcome nature."[148]

The *jahili* essence of Arabic literature was a theme developed at length in the writings of Ahmad Amin.[149] Amin held that the content of Arabic poetry was fundamentally *jahili* in nature, its raison d'être being the description of the vanished landscapes and conditions of the Jahiliyya period. Throughout the entire Islamic period, Arabic poetry had remained true to its original nature; not even its diffusion into lands very remote and different from the Arabian Peninsula had altered its *jahili* form and content.[150] *Jahili* motifs and metaphors, Amin maintained, continued to form the backbone of Arabic literary expression in modern times as well.[151]

To Amin, the dominance of the "*jahili* spirit" over Arab writers of all eras resulted in literature that was anachronistic and grotesque. With their images and metaphors locked into *jahili* patterns, the imaginations of such writers were equally restricted by the Arab past. Thus one finds that, even though the airplane had supplanted the camel, Arab-oriented writers stubbornly continued to employ the image of the camel as well as metaphors appropriate to the camel's actions in order to deal with the airplane.[152] Moreover, even this fixation on the motifs of the Jahiliyya was in large part artificial. In reality, the lost world of the Jahiliyya was unknown to contemporary Arab writers, yet they behaved as if it were real. "The [Arab] intellectuals," Amin asserted, "talk about what they do not know, project images of what they do not see, and spin narratives about what they do not understand."[153]

Based on his extensive knowledge of traditional Arabic literature, Amin criticized in depth what appeared to him to be the total subjection of that literature to the time and place of its birth. It represented a cult of the desolate and barren wilderness; the worship of a primitive nomadic lifestyle; a blind addiction to *jahili* heroes and events; and an intellectual intoxication with the mood of loneliness and melancholy characteristic of the environment of the desert.[154] The reason for this archaic orientation on the part of Arabic literature was clear to Amin: it was the determinist influence of the environment upon artistic expression. Originally, all this had been a genuine reflection of the conditions of Arab life, and so had resulted in an authentic and even an impressive literary product. But to continue with the same subjects and images in lands and eras vastly different from pre-Islamic Arabia was clearly an absurd exercise in the eyes of a modernist such as Ahmad Amin.[155]

Egyptianist intellectuals saw their particular mission as one of revealing the astounding poverty of this nomadic literature and in exposing its lack of real cultural virtue. They invested a great deal of effort in attempting to demonstrate that Arabic literature was an uncivilized and primitive art form, a conglomeration of a few ill-related motifs that had not yet developed into a mature and cohesive literature. In this area as in many others, it appears to have been Muhammad Husayn Haykal who first laid down the guidelines other Egyptianist intellectuals would follow in their treatment of Arabic literature.[155] The gap between it and the literary works produced in ancient Egypt, Greece, and Rome (Haykal frequently coupled these in contrast to Arab culture) was a fundamental one. One simply could not find in the shallow poetry of the Arabs the same "epic dimension" detailing the glory of victory and the agony of defeat, the heroic energy and dynamism "that you can find in Homer's *Iliad*."[156] Neither did Arabic literature have the elements of "religious or pagan philosophy" expressing a civilized society's speculations concerning the eternal, or anything resembling meditations about time, life, death, and the hereafter "like you can find in the traditions of the Egyptians, the Greeks, and the Romans."[157] Haykal further maintained that Arabic literature lacked entire literary genres: the art of the narrative tale, the epic, and the drama, which were so superbly developed in the literatures of Greece and Rome and were even known in Egypt—all were completely foreign to Arabic literature.[158] Similarly, Arab artistic expression in its broadest sense was particularly lacking in "the fine arts" [*al-funun al-jamila*]: music, painting, sculpture, and the like.[159]

In Haykal's view, the only genre found in Arabic literature was the erotic love poetry of the *ghazal,* which had originated in the Jahiliyya and been refined in the Ummayad period. Yet even the *ghazal* was not true, realistic love poetry. Rather, it was a sensual, primitive poetry of an idealized format in which the poet pined for a lover once known but now abandoned. Haykal ascribed this naive and unrealistic love poetry to psychological causes rooted in the poet's material existence. Unfamiliar with the luxuries of life, the early Arab poet "could experience only woman. Hence he bestows upon her all [the content of] his mind and heart and all the figures and images which he perceives and grasps."[160]

Views similar to those of Haykal concerning the innate poverty of Arabic literature were voiced by many Egyptian intellectuals. Ahmad Amin saw in the *ghazal* one of the keys to understanding the "internal essence" of Arabic literature. He too felt this "essence" was devoid of true literary merit because of its desert origins.[161] Although Hafiz Mahmud attempted to moderate his colleagues' completely negative attitude toward Arabic literature, maintaining that it was not completely lacking in the art of narrative in view of the "splendid historical tales" found in the *Qur'an,* nonetheless Mahmud was forced to admit that "throughout most of its history the Arab imagination has been unable to achieve a true capacity for the novel."[162] The group of younger writers of the "Modernist School" [*al-Madrasa al-Haditha*] associated with the journal *al-Fajr* in the mid-1920s were more vehement in their negative opinions of Arabic literature. They repeatedly expressed their distaste for the "Arabic literature of the nomads," which had never flowered forth with its own schools of painting, architecture, sculpture, music, and the like.[163]

Two of the harshest critics of Arabic literature in Egypt in the 1920s were Salama Musa and his disciple, Ibrahim al-Misri. Musa viewed Arabic literature as a "blindly imitative" art form that ignored and consequently falsified reality.[164] Rather than taking as its objective the fostering of change and growth, it had dedicated itself to the preservation of a fossilized and archaic past. Thus it was not surprising that Arabic literature possessed neither drama, painting, nor sculpture. All that could be found in the artistic expression of the Arabs were *jahili* poetic motifs dedicated to the recollection of a lost era: the erotic introduction [*nasib*] of the ancient Arabic *qasida;* the poet's lyric to his imaginary lover [*ghazal*]; the panegyric to a patron [*madih*] or the elegy to the dead [*ritha'*]; or bitter satirical attacks on the enemy and his tribe [*hija'*]. Musa insisted that all these forms reflected the same primitive and anachronistic mood characteristic of Jahiliyya period itself, a temper fundamentally contradictory to that of the dynamic, progressive modern era.[165]

Another important aspect of Arabic literature to Salama Musa was its emphasis on form over content, on the external and superficial over the internal and essential. Voicing a view held by many Egyptianist intellectuals, he saw Arabic literature as a whole as displaying a clear preference for verbal expression [*lafz*] over meaning [*ma'na*].[166] In Arabic poetry, he stated, the criteria for evaluating the worth of a literary work were its decorative features and external polish, its technical virtuosity and the mastery of intricate rhyme schemes that the piece demonstrated. This central characteristic of Arabic poetry made it little more than "a collection of verbal expressions rich in strong sounds but poor in significant meaning."[167]

Musa, like other Egyptianist intellectuals, was convinced that this emphasis on pretty yet hollow rhetoric, on form over content, could be ascribed to the inherent poverty of the "bedouin language" of the Arabs. In his view Arabic was a language of unsophisticated primitiveness created as the medium of expression of a poor and simple community existing in conditions of privation. "The Arabic language," Musa stated in summary of his position, "is a bedouin tongue that barely functions when confronted with the kinds of advanced civilization that we are currently living in."[168]

Musa's discussions of the poverty of Arabic artistic expression gave special attention to the absence of an architectural tradition among the early Arabs.[169] Although the "civilized nations" such as the Egyptians, the Greeks, and the Romans had developed architecture to the point where it had become an integral part of their way of life, the Arabs had never expressed any affinity for the building arts. Impressive temples, statuary, or well-organized cities were simply absent from the culture of the early Arabs, "who were wandering tribes that never knew the art of building."[170] It was typical of both Salama Musa and of his generation to explain the collective defect of the Arabs in environmental terms. If the Arab imagination was artistically backward and primitive, it was so because it had been shaped in the backward and primitive natural milieu of the desert. Monumental architecture was simply not suited to the desert environment in which the Arabs had lived. Complex architectural design and large-scale *objets d'art* were dysfunctional for the nomadic lifestyle of the early Arabs, hence had not developed within the Arabic tradition.[171]

To Ibrahim al-Misri, the poverty of Arabic artistic expression was explainable primarily in terms of the superficiality and shallowness of the Arab "mind." In his discussion of Arabic literature, what emerged as the most promient mental characteristic of the Arabs as a people was their inability to analyze and to synthesize. To Misri, Arab conceptual and integrative abilities were extremely limited. The Arab writer or artist was incapable of creating true literature or art, instead being content with a fragmentary, truncated expression of concepts. Rather than creating a complete, integrated poem, the Arab poet composed isolated stanzas; similarly, in prose Arab writers preferred "a fancy phrase or a few appropriate rhetorical flourishes" to coherent, interconnected narrative.[172]

The inclination of Arab artists and writers toward the partial was linked by Misri to a further mental shortcoming, Arab preference for form over content. Here Misri's analysis was very close to that of Salama Musa. As Misri saw it, Arab artists were capable of pretty phrases and rhetorical virtuosity but lacked any appreciation of the internal essence of things.[173] The symmetrical rhyme and strict meter that had characterized the poetry of the Jahiliyya period and had changed but little in the Ummayad and Abbasid periods reflected this particular defect of Arabic poetry. The conventions of the genre demanded that a single rhyme should be used throughout an entire poem, thereby unifying the poem and making it "a single verbal sound."[174] But to Misri, this rigid uniformity was "proof" of the "natural primitiveness" and "deep-rooted barbarism" of Arabic culture.[175]

Misri went beyond mere criticism of the style of Arabic poetry, however, maintaining that Arabic poetry in particular was "an anti-art, i.e., an anti-life literature."[176] In several respects, it lacked the essential ingredients of true literature. As a Bedouin creation, it was subservient to restricted literary canons appropriate only to desert conditions. Strong in verbal acrobatics, in content it was spiritually empty. It was prone to the exaggeration and thus the falsification of life, describing human character and behavior in unreal metaphors. It focused on a fantasy world that removed it even further from reality. Perhaps most important was what it did not do: it avoided describing and analyzing the workings of human conscience and the tensions of the human spirit. As Misri trenchantly summarized the value of early Arabic verse, "poetry is one thing and reality another."[177] Misri's interpretation of the reasons for this backwardness of Arabic literature was essentially similar to the analyses of other Egyptian nationalist intellectuals of the interwar period. It was the Arab personality itself that explained the poverty and inner emptiness of Arabic artistic expression: "the Arab is intensely sensual, always seeking to satisfy his senses, alaways on the move, ever restless, and consummately skillful at exploiting his physical capabilities in obtaining pleasure and his mental strengths in the pursuit of transitory enjoyment."[178]

Perhaps the most comprehensive and multifaceted critique of Arabic literature offered by an Egyptian intellectual in the 1920s was that of 'Abbas Mahmud al-'Aqqad. To 'Aqqad, the "nomadic *jahili*" language of the Arabs simply lacked the capacity for prose composition.[179] From the Jahiliyya period until the present, 'Aqqad maintained, Arabic had been "the language of rhetoric and speech and not the language of writing."[180] Arabic literature had assumed a central style of expression, that of rhetoric or *balagha,* in its formative pre-Islamic years, and it had never transcended the limitations of that mode of expression. The main problem of Arabic literature lay in the nature of *balagha* itself, which was merely intuitive improvisation, a verbal form emphasizing eloquence at the expense of content and meaning. The Arab rhetorician took great pains to express himself in an ornate style consisting of short, rushed, repetitive fragments of speech; but these verbal flourishes were inconsequential in their content.[181]

In 'Aqqad's judgment, the tragedy of Arabic literature was that this purely rhetorical mode of expression developed in the Jahiliyya period had become the characteristic style of Arab writers ever since. Until the present, Arabic literature had not freed itself of the influence of *balagha.*[182] The rhetorical mode in which Arabic literature was locked had never permitted the Arabs to develop a genuine prose genre suitable for extended exposition and thus capable of bearing a "great message."[183]

The absence of prose from the Arabic literary tradition was taken by 'Aqqad as a decisive indicator of the poverty of Arabic literature. Drama, the novel and novella, the short story—all of these genres were alien to Arabic literature. The reason for this fundamental deficiency lay in the circumstances of Arabic literature's birth in the Jahiliyya period, when a "prose style" [*uslub al-nathr*] was absent from Arab expression.[184] Arabic literature lacked a capacity for "lengthy, detailed writing, or the composition of thorough and elaborate research studies full of meaning and information."[185] The absence of a prose tradition indicated a variety of inherent defects in Arabic literature to 'Aqqad, including an inability to attain internal harmony and unity, an inclination toward partial rather than comprehensive analysis, and a general orientation toward the simplistic, the superficial, and the banal.[186]

Whatever the absence of an Arabic prose tradition might signify, for 'Aqqad the poverty of Arabic literature was most fully revealed in the content of Arabic poetry. Like other Egyptian nationalist intellectuals, 'Aqqad assumed that the essential defects of Arabic poetry derived from its lack of change and development since the formation of its basic canons in the Jahiliyya period. In his view, the ancient Arabic *qasida,* with its basically nomadic motifs and concerns, had remained the central foundation for Arabic poetry until the present.[187] The strict symmetrical verse [*nazm*] so characteristic of the poetry of the Jahiliyya continued to dominate in Arabic poetic expression, and this style was seldom more than "scattered verses united by a single rhyme within which the poet skips from one subject to another and then back again, without any recognizable uniformity of method and without logical order."[188] A comparison of Arabic with English poetry (which 'Aqqad esteemed highly) allowed him to highlight the defects of the "*jahili* poetry" of the Arabs. Where Arabic poetry was provincial, oriented to the Arab tribe and articulated within the tribal context, English poetry was universal in its scope and appeal; where Arabic poetry was noted for its exaggerated "sensuality" [*hiss*] and was based on "sensual description" [*wasf hissi*], English poetry was oriented toward spiritual concerns and inner feelings, and above all gave full rein to human "imagination" [*khayal*].[189]

'Aqqad's analysis of the inner structure and themes of Arabic poetry was one of the most detailed of any Egyptianist intellectual of the period. As he presented it, the Arab poet envisaged the outside world he was describing by means of a direct "sensual picture" [*sura mahsusa*] rather than through an "inner picture" [*sura batiniyya*].[190] Consequently, the verbal portraits painted in Arabic poetry were "simple and primitive," emphasizing the physical dimensions of their subject.[191] In its content, Arabic poetry was characterized by "wit" [*dhaka'*] but lacked the more profound quality of "imagination" [*khayal*].[192] Strongly influenced by nineteenth-century English Romantic theories of literary criticism, 'Aqqad held that "wit" was the antithesis of true "imagination," reflecting quite contrary tendencies and talents: simplicity rather than depth, fragmentation rather than organic unity, accident rather than order.[193] Because of this inner superficiality, Arabic poetry was incapable of achieving that "organic unity of the poem" which in 'Aqqad's view was one of the characteristics of true literature. Arabic poetry, ever faithful to its original *jahili* character, consisted of fragments or even of structurally unrelated single lines of verse; but in its emphasis on the sensual and its facile cleverness, it was unable to fuse separate ideas into a coherent whole.[194]

Like Salama Musa and Ibrahim al-Misri, 'Aqqad decried the complete absence of an artistic tradition in the visual arts in early Arab culture. The Arabs had manifested a certain facility for "technical ornamentation" [*zukhruf handasi*] in the past, but had demonstrated little capacity for architecture and the building arts in a broader sense.[195] Arab visual art was marked by ornamentation for its own sake—"ornamentation devoid of any link to life."[196] Extravagant and flashy decoration expressed in vivid and clashing colors were the basis of the visual arts of the Arabs. Above all, Arab visual art lacked one of the most important and appealing features of genuine visual art—naturalistic representation.[197]

'Aqqad reserved a special place in his negative portrayal of Arabic literature and art for the role of myth in Arab culture. Echoing the racialist conceptualizations of later nineteenth-century European thought, 'Aqqad maintained that the "Arab-Semitic mind" was not blessed with a mythological capability or a natural facility for expressing itself in myth such as was possessed by other races from the ancient Egyptians to the Aryan Indians, Greeks, and Romans.[198] He related this to the "sterility of the imagination" among Arabs and other Semites: where more creative peoples created their myths from the power of their "imagination" [*khayal*], the Arabs created theirs out of their "sensations" [*hawass*].[199] Since imagination was clearly superior to sensation as a basis for creativity, Arab mythology was thus of inferior quality to that of more gifted peoples. The Arabs were incapable of creating archetypes that spoke to the eternal human condition in the same way that the Aryan mind, with its rich imagination, had been able to develop. 'Aqqad attributed this shallowness of myth in Arabic literature to the fact that the Arabs' "pseudo-myths" were the product of "intuition" [*hads*] rather than being inspired by "imagination."[200] Intuition was a faculty derived from the senses and thus clearly inferior to genuine imagination, which was rooted in the intellect.[201]

The Egyptian nationalist critique of Arabic literature and art found its most extreme expression in the articles of Tawfiq al-Hakim. From the substantive aspect, Hakim added little that was new to the critical analyses of other Egyptianist intellectuals. Yet with his eloquence of expression and his attitude of thoroughgoing disdain for everything Arab, he went far beyond them. Other Egyptianist intellectuals at least made a pretext of offering a measured analysis of Arab artistic shortcomings; Hakim merely stated his contemptuous conclusions concerning the "nomadic *adab*" of the Arabs.

The central and most obvious expression of the artistic incompetence of the Arabs in the eyes of Tawfiq al-Hakim was their complete inability to create "artistic harmony."[202] The Arabs simply lacked the capacity for uniting partial or separate components into a comprehensive and integrated artistic whole. Indeed, they were incapable of even distinguishing between the partial and the separate, on the one hand, and the complete and the unified, on the other. "The Arab mentality [*al-'aqliyya al-'arabiyya*] does not perceive the requisite artistic unity for a great work of art."[203] Rather than working toward a harmonious, integrated composition, Arabic literature was "satisfied with a single verse, or a single proverb or expression, or melody or ornament."[204] In general, the Arabs "restrict the entire function of art to [the display of] physical opulence and the gratification of sensual pleasures."[205]

The lack of a capacity for artistic integration also explained Arab shortcomings in architecture. Like Salama Musa and 'Abbas Mahmud al-'Aqqad, Tawfiq al-Hakim felt that the Arabs lacked the ability to design and construct elaborate compositions in both the literary and the physical spheres. Among the Arabs, the "art of ornamentation" [*fann al-zukhruf*] had had taken the place of true architecture; decoration had replaced construction; ornamental aesthetics substituted for architectural aesthetics: "Arab architecture . . . in my opinion is nothing but ornamentation. . . . To the Arabs, everything is ornamentation."[206]

Arab literature, both poetry and prose, also suffered from the limitations of the Arab mentality. Like the visual arts, Arabic verbal expression had never attained true artistic maturity comparable to other world literatures. The Arabic tradition lacked epopeia, in Hakim's view; it was indeed anti-epic poetry. Arabic verse was "a pleasing jingle" and sometimes was imaginative in verbal terms; "but beyond that, it is neither poetry nor art."[207] In terms of genres, it lacked both narrative and drama:

> It is a mosaic of words and meaning, an "arabesque" [*arabisk*] of expressions and phrases. Thus every *maqama* of al-Hariri is like the porch of the mosque of al-Mu'ayyad. It is a fine geometrical form, studded with gold and silver.[208]

Arabic literature as a whole lacked extended compositions that developed a single subject in detail. Most books written by Arabs were no more than collages, eclectic collections of materials on various subjects. These compendia gathered something concerning every subject their authors might stumble across and put these fragments together in one book—a few aphorisms, a bit of ethics, a touch of religion, something to amuse the reader, a little poetry and a little prose.[209]

Arab music was also nothing more than "a vocal arabesque" [*arabisk sawti*].[210] In its monotonous repetition of the same melody, it lacked the rich and subtle vocal harmony produced by an ensemble of voices or instruments such as was found in the Greek or Egyptian musical traditions. The Arabs did not really understand the nature of music, which like architecture belonged "to the symbolic rather than the figurative arts."[211] Like all Arab artistic expression, Arabic music lacked inner depth: "The Arabs turned music into a pleasure for the ear—no more, no less—just as they made architecture no more and no less than a pleasure to the eye."[212]

Nor did Arabic painting and sculpture escape the tyranny of the sensual orientation that exercised its sway over all other Arabic artistic expression. To Hakim, Arabic painting was intended "simply for decorating or beautifying books and manuscripts."[213] Painting and sculpture were alien to the Arabs "in view of the fact that these artforms demand of their practitioners a deep sense of general symmetry and harmony born of extended contemplation of the inner consciousness of seeing the whole in the part and the part in the whole—something the Arabs do not have."[214]

Thus the negative image of the Arabs developed by Egyptianist intellectuals in the post-1919 era found its most elaborate expression in their views about the Arabic artistic heritage. From the Egyptianist perspective, the Arab character could neither create nor enjoy any kind of genuine literature, art, or music. The Arabs and artistic creativity were a contradiction in terms.

Assault on the Alien and the Archaic

For Egyptian nationalist intellectuals of the interwar period, the central purpose of their criticism of Arabic literature and art was to demonstrate their alienness to Egypt and to reveal the considerable damage they had done to native Egyptian artistic creativity. It was not only the poverty of Arabic literature that necessitated its total rejection by Egyptians; equally important was its absolute incompatibility with the distinctive spirit of Egypt as a nation. Hence the supreme task of Egyptian writers, artists, and musicians in post-1919 "revolutionary" Egypt was to liberate Egyptian literature from the yoke of this "nomadic" influence, to purge Egypt of the foreign Arab influence that had attached itself like a parasite to the body of Egypt. So long as Arabic *adab* ruled in Egypt, there was no chance for an Egyptian literary and artistic renaissance, and no possibility of creating an independent and original Egyptian national culture.

The basic principles of this approach were set forth in 1925 by the radical journal *al-Fajr* [*The Dawn*], which had as its goal " the realization of intellectual independence for Egypt" and which defined itself as "the journal of destruction and construction."[215] To the younger intellectuals of the "Modernist School" [*al-Madrasa al-Haditha*] associated with this periodical, the creation of a new Egyptian culture demanded the two complementary processes of "destroying and building—destroying the reactionary and the corrupt while building the necessary good."[216] In their view, the realization of Egyptian authenticity required not merely the separation of what was Egyptian from what was Arab; in addition, it necessitated the forcible destruction of the alien and imperialist culture that had been imposed upon Egypt by the Arabs.[217]

Ahmad Durini Khashaba epitomized the Egyptianist "revolt" against Arabic literature:

> [W]e are revolting against all of Arabic literature because it is a worthless and defective literature as well as a foreign one, and because for thirteen hundred years, since it invaded our country following the Islamic conquest, it has not succeeded in inspiring even one Egyptian writer to produce some new input [of value] for our lives. . . . Arabic literature has not benefited a single Egyptian. . . . This is a sterile literature useless to us. Hence it would be incorrect for it to serve as our literary guide along the new path which we have resolved to follow.[218]

In a similar vein, Niqula Yusuf asserted that there was a total "contradiction" between "territorial literature" and the "nomadic desert literature" of the Arabs, a people who have "neither links nor kinship ties with us."[219] Ibrahim al-Misri was also convinced that the subjugation of Egyptian literary expression to the canons of Arabic literature had effaced Egypt's native personality.[220] Speaking for many Egyptian nationalist intellectuals of the 1920s, Misri maintained that "Egyptian literature has remained, up to the beginning of the twentieth century, a literature of imitation and copying."[221]

This insistence on the alienness of the Arab literary tradition led many Egyptian nationalist intellectuals of the interwar period to make a frontal attack upon their more traditionalist and Arab-oriented rivals on the Egyptian literary scene. Contemptuously referring to such writers as "the school of the ancients" [*madhhab al-qadim*] or "the school of tradition" [*madhhab al-taqlid*], modernist authors repeatedly condemned traditionalists for their subjugation to foreign literary models, their perpetuation of alien artistic canons, and their failure to create a genuinely Egyptian literature and art.[222] Their criticisms of the traditionalist poets Ahmad Shawqi and Hafiz Ibrahim were particularly aggressive. The neoclassicism of Shawqi and Ibrahim, their attempt to revive both the style and the subject matter of classical Arabic verse through the use of identical meter and rhyme schemes as well as the duplication of the metaphorical richness and sentimentality of classical poetry, came under sharp attack from modernist critics. The neoclassicist poets were accused of falling under the sway of the alien "Arab mentality," of having been seduced by the superficial charms of the nomadic poetry of the Jahiliyya period, which was the foundation of all Arabic verse.[223]

Ibrahim al-Misri was especially vehement in his criticism of Arab-oriented Egyptian poets. Angrily condemning them for their conformity to archaic conventions, he termed their poetic output "irrelevant" to contemporary Egyptian needs.[224] Neoclassicist poetry was a vain attempt to rediscover a lost world. The intoxication of some Egyptian poets with *jahili* themes was based on a "foolish delusion" that only in the nomadic traditions of the early Arabs could "the stimulus to all forms and types of poetic genius" be found.[225] To Misri, such poets were absurdly dogmatic in adhering rigidly to previously determined structure, meters, and rhymes. Theirs was an art that "reveals a freezing of the thought processes, a feebleness of the forces of invention, and the enjoyment of a kind of spiritual stagnation."[226] To read Arab neoclassicist poetry was to Misri only to see once again those "defects of the Arab mentality" which were so apparent in the poetry of the Jahiliyya period.[227]

No less aggressive were Salama Musa's repeated attacks on those Egyptian writers who "blindly follow" the style and subject matter of *jahili* poetry. Musa was convinced that modern Egyptian literature must totally reject the influence of that "early Arabic literature which is, over and above all, a literature of the Middle Ages."[228] It simply could not serve as an inspiration for modern Egyptian society, which was utterly different "from the society which held sway in Damascus a thousand years ago."[229] For Musa, Arabic literature was incompatible with modernity and progress: "Arabic *adab* prevents literature from renewing itself. It causes the writer to look backward, seeking inspiration in the past, rather than looking hopefully to the future or confidently to himself."[230]

To Tawfiq Mikha'il Tuwaij, the foreign literature of the Arabs had been created for "a different national collective" and reflected "a different life" from that of Egypt; as such, it could not "harmonize with the taste of the modern Egyptian."[231] Echoing one of the prevalent complaints of Egyptianist intellectuals in the 1920s, Tuwaij lamented that Arabic literature received too much attention in Egyptian secondary schools and at the Egyptian University, while the study of "ancient and modern" Egyptian literature was neglected in the same institutions.[232] It was regrettable that Egyptian schools continued to teach Arabic literature "even though it is foreign to us, and despite the fact that its image world is one of bedouin life with which we are completely out of touch."[233] In a similar vein Ahmad Durini Khashaba asked, "[W]hy must we study the life of a *jahili* nation which is still locked into the remote past, a nation whose conditions we know to have been ugly and insignificant, before we study our own life?"[234]

Muhammad Husayn Haykal was another leading critic of Arab-inspired, traditionalist writing in contemporary Egypt. Although his comments lacked the militant tone that characterized the critiques of Misri and Musa, nonetheless his substantive conclusions were similar to theirs: that Arabic literature was too underdeveloped in its forms, too archaic in its spirit, and too alien in its essence to serve as a central source of inspiration for modern Egyptian writers and artists.[235]

Thus he attacked what he felt to be the "shameful surrender" of a number of contemporary Egyptian writers to the forms and themes of traditional Arabic literature, accusing them of blind imitation of Arab patterns and approaches "even though this imitation violates their nationalism and even more their personality, and even though it makes them nothing more than mouthpieces who constantly repeat what the ancient Arabs said."[236]

Ahmad Amin also developed the theme of the alienation of Arabic literature from the needs of modern Egyptian society. Amin believed that Arabic *jahili* literature was irrelevant to the conditions of twentieth-century Egypt.[237] Traditional Arabic literary patterns were inappropriate for contemporary Egyptian schools, indeed acting as a barrier to artistic expression. When, for example, Egyptian teachers tried to develop the facility for artistic expression in their students, the use of traditional Arabic models actually impeded the process.[238] Arabic literature's primitiveness, narrowness, and lack of relevant creative genres prevented Egyptians from achieving artistic truth. Thus the classroom teacher had to fall back on Western literature, which at least contained some of the modern literary styles and techniques necessary to appreciate the modern world. In contrast, Arabic literature lacked both the conceptual tools and the substantive insights into the human condition that contemporary Egyptians needed:

> [I]n Arabic literature, when [the student] is compelled to study a selection of the works of Jarir, al-Farazdaq, al-Akhtal, or a selection of *maqamat* by al-Badi', al-Hariri, or the like—nothing of this depicts even a single aspect of the social reality in which he lives, or anything like it, nor even [offers] any penetrating idea which might produce a broader perspective. Thus he completes his study of this literature without developing a love for it; at best, he remains indifferent to it.[239]

In Amin's eyes, both teachers and students were in an absurd situation, one in which the entire goal of the study of literature was being missed. Egyptians were obliged to graze in foreign literary fields in order to escape the "punishment" of studying an irrelevant "*jahili* literature" which inhibited them from reaching literary and artistic truth.[240]

Ahmad Amin was convinced that the solution to this sorry situation was in the adoption of radical measures designed to liberate the Egyptian educational system from the grip of Arabic literature. Thus he proposed the elimination of "the study of *jahili* literature and everything resembling it" from the Egyptian secondary curriculum; pupils should no longer have to "waste their time" in the study of a literature that, because it did not speak to their background and condition, was liable to destroy their literary taste before it had even been formed.[241] Amin argued that the study of early Arabic literature should be restricted to the higher levels of education, being taught in the Arabic language departments of the Egyptian University, al-Azhar, and *Dar al-'Ulum*. There, Arabic literature could be studied as a purely academic subject, "just as archeologists study ancient remains and historians study ancient history."[242]

Egyptian nationalist intellectuals' campaign against Arab-inspired literature and Arab-oriented writers in Egypt culminated in 1929–1931 in the vitriolic attacks of the thoroughly Egyptianist *The New Journal* [*al-Majalla al-Jadida*] against both journalists of non-Egyptian Arab origin and native Egyptian writers with

Arabist inclinations. On one level, Salama Musa and his colleagues associated with *The New Journal* denounced what they defined as "the rule of foreign Syrians over Egyptian journalism."[243] It was their contention that Syrian-born journalists had exploited the considerable development that had taken place in the journalistic profession in Egypt since World War I in order to assume a leading role in the Egyptian press. The situation in the Egyptian press was an "abnormal" one in which the most important and influential newspapers and periodicals were under the ownership and editorship of journalists of Syrian or Lebanese extraction.[244] An original Egyptian literature could not develop and prosper in a press controlled by non-Egyptians. Only native Egyptian ascendancy in all areas of communication in Egypt could assure fulfillment of the ideal of an independent and original Egyptian literature.[245]

The New Journal's contributors assumed the existence of "a life and death struggle" between native Egyptian writers and these Syrian journalists.[246] Each possessed fundamentally different concerns. Whereas the native Egyptian writer was a patriot who regarded journalism in particular and literature in general as tools for realizing Egyptian interests, progress, and independence, the detached Syrian worked only for the advancement of his own narrow economic interests, abandoning journalistic responsibility in order to satisfy private desires. It was this counterproductive asymmetry between native Egyptian and foreign Syrian that provided the theoretical basis for *The New Journal*'s demands for the exclusion of non-Egyptians from journalism in Egypt. The periodical appealed to the Egyptian public to cease the purchasing or reading of publications "held in foreign ownership."[247] In the name of "pure Egyptianism," it demanded that Egyptians refrain from "turning journalism into a non-Egyptian industry," instead imploring Egyptians to support the native-run Egyptian press.[248] Reading the "foreign" newspapers published in Egypt would only lead to the absorption by Egyptians of "views that true [Egyptian] nationalism cannot accept," since the writers in these journals were themselves foreign to Egypt and its needs.[249] In general, journalism in Egypt needed to become "an Egyptian industry whose Egyptianism is boundless," rather than a "Syrian industry" devoid of true Egyptian national spirit.[250]

No less aggressive was *The New Journal*'s parallel offensive against Egyptian-based writers of Syrian and Lebanese extraction who promoted an Arab-Islamic orientation in Egypt. Authors such as Rashid Rida of *al-Manar,* Muhibb al-Din al-Khatib of *al-Fath,* and the literary critic Mustafa Sadiq al-Rafi'i were accused of constituting "dens of reaction" within Egypt and of working against the contemporary Egyptian literary renaissance.[251] Their Syrian origins, Arab identifications, and allegiance to Muslim principles were seen as making them enemies of the new Egypt, men who were doing all they could to oppose the beneficial trends of secularization, Westernization, and Egyptianization currently at work in Egyptian society. The reactionary nature of their message was affirmed by its religious orientation, by its efforts to associate Egypt with "inferior Eastern nations such as India or Java," and by their resistance to the attempts of "patriotic Egyptians" to model Egypt "in the image of progressive European nations like Germany and England."[252]

This Manichean dichotomy between "them"—"foreign Arabs" in Egypt as well as writers of an Arab-Islamic inclination—and "us"—native Egyptian intellectuals—was perhaps the most extreme manifestation of the general anti-Arab mood that reached its peak by the end of the 1920s. The demonization of Arabic literature and culture led to the demonization of Egyptian writers of an Arab orientation, whose most prominent representatives were journalists and authors of Syro-Lebanese origin. This process was fed by particular economic and political circumstances of the day, including the cessation of publication and the unemployment of journalists because of the Great Depression and the authoritarianism of the Sidqi regime of the early 1930s, as well as the perception that the Syrian newspapers were either puppets of or too accommodating toward that regime. Nonetheless, the attacks of Salama Musa and *The New Journal* were an authentic reflection of the desire of Egyptian nationalist and modernist intellectuals to break with their country's Arab past and to create an Egyptian future for it. Only by denouncing both Arab influences and the Arabs themselves could these nationalist intellectuals achieve a breakthrough toward the creation of a distinctively Egyptian literature, culture, and national image.

6

The Egyptianist Image of Egypt: I. Environment and the Nation

In revealing the defects of Egypt's negative Arab counter-image, Egyptian nationalist intellectuals of the 1920s were paving the way for the elaboration of a more positive national image. They asserted that this alternative image was Egypt's genuine and proper one, an embodiment of a natural synthesis of the conditions of the Nile Valley and the people who had inhabited it for thousands of years. Repeatedly and enthusiastically quoting Herodotus, Egyptianist intellectuals held that Egypt was indeed "the gift of the Nile" and could be understood only as a unique national entity with its own geography, history, and culture.[1]

The creation of this new national image was to be accomplished through an intellectual comprehension of all the latent capabilities and spiritual potential inherent in the land and its people. Through the rediscovery and actualization of the "true eternal essence" embodied in Egypt, through the "renormalization" (as some intellectuals phrased it) of the Egyptian people, Egypt would return to its natural state. There existed a real Egypt buried deep within the Egyptian collective subconscious, and it was the task of Egyptian nationalist intellectuals to bring it to the consciousness of Egyptians and from there into living reality, while simultaneously purifying both Egyptian national consciousness and Egyptian reality of the false Arab/Islamic image that had prevailed for so long.[2]

For these intellectuals, Egypt's return to her nature meant a return to separate national existence. In their eyes, only independent national status could assure that the country would realize her authentic personality and character. The new national image would also provide Egyptian society with a suitable framework for renewal and modernization. That is, Egyptian nationalist intellectuals of the 1920s assumed a correlation between the realization of Egyptian authenticity and the attainment of modernity: only the return of Egypt to her genuine national identity and consciousness would create the conditions required for the development of a progressive, dynamic nation-state marching inexorably into the modern age.[3]

As the foundation for this new Egyptian national image, Egyptianist intellectuals of the 1920s developed four collective sub-images. The first was a *territorial image* demonstrating that the unique environment of the Nile Valley was the determining influence in the development of a distinctive Egyptian personality. It was the Nile Valley that had given the Egyptian national character its unique traits and its separate identity, making of Egypt and its people a unit different from all other lands and peoples. The second was an *historical image* indicating that all Egyptians, those of the past as well as those of the present and future, possessed a distinct collective history and shared a single historic destiny. In sum, the course of Egyptian history over the past several millenia had forged the inhabitants of the Nile Valley into one historical entity and had created a collective historic experience of uninterrupted continuity. The third was a *Pharaonic image* aimed at revitalizing the "natural bond" between modern, post-1919 Egypt and ancient Pharaonic Egypt. The Pharaonic heritage of Egypt was assumed to be the country's only authentic national heritage. Correspondingly, the hidden Pharaonic dimensions of Egyptian life had to be uncovered in order to "Pharaonize" Egyptian culture, literature, art, and social life through the reintroduction of genuine Egyptian motifs deriving from the Pharaonic period. And the fourth was a *cultural image* proving that Egypt had an independent national culture separate from that of the Arab and Muslim legacy—distinctive literary traditions, myths, philosophies, genres, and even language, all of which derived from the environment and history of the Nile Valley. The intellectuals' ultimate aim was to revitalize this authentic Egyptian cultural heritage and to make it into the substantive content of modern Egyptian artistic life.

The Territorial Imperative: The Nile Valley as Shaper of the Egyptian Personality

> The individual does not exist by himself. His existence derives from the environment [*al-wasat*] in which he lives. Only a complete understanding and knowledge of the natural milieu [*al-bi'a al-tabi'iyya*], the social milieu [*al-bi'a al-ijtima'iyya*], the historic condition [*al-hala al-ta'rikhiyya*], and the beliefs, customs, thoughts, emotions, and trends which flourished under their influence—all these and only these can enable us to understand the writer, poet, philosopher, or any other person linked to the collective, influenced by it, and affecting it.[4]

This statement written by Muhammad Husayn Haykal in 1921 is a direct continuation of the social philosophy developed by Haykal during World War I. At the same time it defines the prevalent attitude of the entire generation of post-1919 Egyptianist intellectuals toward a proper understanding of their society. Hippolyte Taine's formula "race–milieu–moment," reformulated by Haykal as "milieu–race–moment," attained tremendous popularity among this generation. The assumption of the existence of a determining link between man and nature, between human traits and physical factors—most specifically between the national character and cultural personality of a people, on the one hand, and the particular geographic and climatic conditions in which they lived, on the other—was a central operating principle for Egyptianist intellectuals in the 1920s.

We must be careful, however, to avoid misleading interpretations. We are not dealing here with an internal dynamic of ideas flowing in a direct and autonomous stream from Taine and Haykal to the post-1919 generation of Egyptian nationalist intellectuals. The philosophical maxims of this determinist and mechanistic approach could not have been accepted so readily, had these concepts not met certain of the Egyptianists' expectations and desires. The intellectual mood of the new era emerging from the Revolution of 1919 absorbed this approach so enthusiastically because it provided an explanation of Egypt that matched the temper of the times. First and most importantly, the environmental determinism of Taine and Haykal gave these intellectuals a single explanatory factor, seemingly more fundamental and comprehensive than any other compatible with the nationalistic, secularist, and modernist mood of the decade, which could distinguish Egypt from all other lands, peoples, and cultures. By positing environment as a primordial force more basic than any other to human development, they made Egypt and its people a unique and unified entity.

In addition, the approach was a mechanism capable of liberating Egypt from all external forces or foreign elements: because Egypt's environment made her unique, everything that came from outside the Nile Valley was *ipso facto* alien. An Egypt distinct, independent, and homogeneous: the environmental approach provided all these characteristics for the new nation-state that had emerged in the wake of World War I. Environmentalism thereby became the sacred goddess of Egyptian nationalist intellectuals in the 1920s, the paradigm with which they could understand, liberate, and Egyptianize all aspects of Egyptian life. Thus it is not the independent "internal" development of ideas that explains the sudden popularity of the territorial nationalist worldview, a perspective that from all evidence had been peripheral even among Egyptian intellectuals before the First World War, in post-1919 Egypt. Rather, it was the revolutionary transformation in both regional and Egyptian conditions during and after the war that created a new pattern of expectations and aspirations with which this worldview was congruent.

How are nations formed in their environmental crucibles? Egyptianist intellectuals employed environmental determinism to understand Egypt and its uniqueness. Wherever humans are, they argued, it is their continued presence within the confines of a specific region, with its special physical configuration, which over time makes the people of that place into a distinct collective or "nation."[5] Moreover, not only does the nation owe its very existence to the territory it inhabits; territory also holds the key to the nation's nature and constitution. Since no two places are identical, two national groups cannot be so either. From its territory the nation was thus assumed to derive its special physical, social, and mental traits as well as its distinctiveness from all other territorially defined nations.[6]

A representative statement of the environmental determinism prevalent among Egyptian nationalist intellectuals in the 1920s may be found in the introduction to Ahmad Sabri's Pharaonic play, *The High Priest Amun* [*Kahin Amun*].[7] Within specific geographical units, Sabri asserted, "it is nature that creates the nationality of peoples [*qawmiyyat al-shu'ub*] and that impresses its special stamp upon them."[8] Natural forces, both geographic and climatic, acted like "corrosive acid" upon humans, etching upon them the characteristics that distinguish human groups from each other.[9] According to Sabri, individual human beings became one national organism under the influence of nature, over time undergoing chemical and biological changes that eventually made them both similar to each other and distinct from all others.[10] Ahmad Husayn's opinion of 1930 demonstrates the degree to which environmental determinism had become a total, overarching philosophy for Egyptian nationalist intellectuals:

> Man is the product of his environment. It is this environment which forms and nurtures him. It gives him his color, body structure, and blood. Moreover, it shapes his particular character and sensations. This is the influence of the environment upon man and in consequence inevitably on the social collective [as well]. This decisive influence is one of nature's laws.[11]

The general argument of intellectuals like Sabri and Husayn was the basis for a more specific argument touching directly upon Egypt. While territory was the father of nationality for human beings in general, nowhere had territory defined a nation more definitively than in the case of Egypt. The Nile Valley was one of the most pronounced and distinct of all geographic environments. Its shape and boundaries were clear-cut: a level and fertile lowland enclosed by a broad sweep of either deserts or seas. The distinction between the green valley and the yellow desert or blue sea was unmistakeable. Egypt was thus viewed as the archetype of nations, a collective unit more deeply and thoroughly distinguished by nature than any other nation.[12] The natural rhythms of Egypt also made the Nile Valley an independent and self-contained climatic entity. It was assumed to function according to its own laws, free of the influence of external physical factors. Egypt's climate was inevitably reflected in the flora, fauna, and humanity living in the Valley. The self-contained nature of Egypt, its sense of stability and perpetuity, the gentleness of its climate, all created homogeneity among the forms of life found in the Nile Valley.[13]

The distinctive and homogeneous natural unit of the Nile Valley had existed from time immemorial. Its unique geographical and climatic conditions had existed when Egyptian civilization began; they formed the backdrop to the lengthy Pharaonic era; and they had continued to prevail in Egypt up to the present.[14] It was inevitable that the people of this distinct land would also be influenced by this unchanging environment. Both the individuals living in the Nile Valley and the social collective that was Egypt were assumed to have possessed essentially the same character even in historical eras thousands of years apart.[15] The parallelism between an immutable Egyptian environment and an unbroken national tradition received perhaps its most definitive expression by Muhammad Husayn Haykal:

> If you will also remember that the natural environment of the Nile Valley has not changed for thousands of years, and that it is this same natural environment which refines languages, beliefs and psyches; that those who have invaded and settled in Egypt for countless generations have lost all their old racial characteristics and yielded to the power of the natural environment, becoming [Egyptians] just as if their fathers and forefathers had lived in Egypt since Pharaonic times; if you will recall all of this, you will become convinced that there is a firm psychic bond between modern Egypt and ancient Egypt.[16]

Together, the distinctiveness and permanence of the environment of the Nile Valley explained why the Nile Valley alone was the creator of the Egyptian nation. The Egyptian nation was a collective unit making all the children of the Valley—past, present, and future—one unified and cohesive national organism. The Nile Valley had shaped one "Egyptian mentality" [*al-'aqliyya al-misriyya*], one "Egyptian spirit" [*al-ruh al-misri*], one "Egyptian genius" [*al-'abqariyya al-misriyya*], one "Egyptian civilization [*al-hadara al-misriyya*], one "Egyptian culture" [*al-adab al-misri*], or, in the phrase intended to embody all these, one "Egyptian personality" [*al-shakhsiyya al-misriyya*].[17] These uniquely Egyptian essences in turn created "Egyptian patriotism" [*al-wataniyya al-misriyya*], the love of the Egyptian people for their immemorial homeland, and "Egyptian nationalism" [*al-qawmiyya al-misriyya*], the identification of Egyptians with their perduring human collective.[18]

At this point it is necessary to note a second external source of inspiration, parallel to the influence of the ideas of Hippolyte Taine, upon the environmental determinism prevalent among Egyptian nationalist intellectuals in the 1920s. These are the sociological and anthropological writings of Gustave Le Bon (1841–1931). Several of Le Bon's more important works had been translated into Arabic by Ahmad Fathi Zaghlul as early as the first decade of the twentieth century, when they gained considerable popularity among Egyptian intellectuals. New editions of Le Bon's writings appeared in the territorial nationalist atmosphere of the 1920s.[19]

In particular, the section of Le Bon's *Les premières civilizations* (Paris, 1889) devoted to ancient Egypt, which appeared in an Arabic translation in 1924, had a direct influence upon the nationalist speculation of Egyptianist intellectuals.[20] Following Taine, in this work Le Bon developed the argument that "environment" [French *milieu;* Arabic *bi'a*] and "race" [French *race*; Arabic *jins*] constituted the "primitive forces" that had formed Egyptian civilization and determined its specific character.[21] More generally, Egyptianist intellectuals took from Le Bon the concept that nations possess their own distinct personality. Each national collective has a character, mentality, and soul that can be ascertained objectively and scientifically. Like any individual, any nation is governed by a "dominant character" bequeathed to it by its ancestors and ultimately determined by the physical and psychological milieu in which they lived.[22] Le Bon emphasized both the autonomy and the power of national character. From the moment it takes shape, national character is an independent force. It is the operative determinant in the historical development of the nation, giving it its distinctive identity, forming its culture and life style. Furthermore, the collective national character is more powerful and thus takes precedence over the individual characters of its members; the children of the nation, rather than influencing their nation's personality, share and are shaped by it.[23]

Although ignoring the pro-Arab strands in Le Bon's other writings, Egyptianist intellectuals of the post-1919 period relied extensively on Le Bon's conceptual scheme. Thus Niqula Yusuf argued that "nations, like individuals, have personalities within which are embodied their character traits, temperament, spiritual heritage, and modes of social life."[24] Similarly, 'Abbas Mahmud al-'Aqqad held that all of a nation's traditions and customs, folklore and myths, literature, art, and language were only the concrete external manifestations of one perduring essence, which he termed "the national personality" [*al-shakhsiyya al-qawmiyya*].[25] Yusuf Hanna defined national personality in specifically Egyptian terms. The Egyptian national personality was "a distinct personality" [*shakhsiyya bariza*] that embodied "the totality of the distinctive characteristics and traits" of the Egyptian race and culture forged within the Nile Valley.[26]

The desire of Egyptian nationalist intellectuals to endow Egypt with its own distinct and independent national personality unquestionably led them to an extremely deterministic position. The territory of the Nile Valley was elevated to the rank of the preeminent factor in Egyptian development. The dependence of individual Egyptians on the environment of Egypt was presented as a priori and absolute.[27] National personality was made a function of nature, and individuals did not violate the laws of nature. Rather, man and his society were an extension of the natural order found in Egypt, with their thoughts, emotions, and behavior only manifestations of the inexorable determinism of nature over all orders of life: vegetable, animal, and ultimately human.[28] This relentless linkage between nature and national characteristics led to a situation for some intellectuals in which human belief systems were nothing more than cognitive maps of the physical environment in which they were found. Wherever a particularly stable and unchanging environment prevailed, as in Egypt, human thought was also assumed to be immutable, merely mirroring its environment. To Tawfiq al-Hakim, Egypt was a "classic case" of human intellection reflecting physical environment:

> There are in Egypt enduring world views which have barely changed from the era of ancient myths until the present. This is because they are tied to the innermost essence of this earth, deriving their inspiration from the soul of the clay of this fertile valley and from the spirit of this eternal Nile. For man's world views, his beliefs, his religions and his superstitions are generated by the forms of life which surround him.[29]

Hasan Subhi also viewed the human intellect's submission to the power of nature as predetermined and absolute. The flow of time, of history, had brought only insubstantial changes to the enduring realities of Egypt. It was as if time had had to adapt to the constancy of the Egyptian environment. "Life in Egypt," Subhi wrote, "in all its variety of forms is subordinate to the phenomena of nature which are barely touched by the passage of time."[30] Time itself obeys the environment in Egypt, with the pattern of historical change in the Nile Valley mirroring the stability and tranquillity of the Egyptian physical setting.[31] In a similar vein, Shuhdi 'Atiyya al-Shafi'i developed the thesis that Egypt had a "clear and distinct nature," all of whose component parts are well established and defined. No wonder that

> we find a solid resemblance and link between the mental life of modern Egypt and that of her ancient Pharaonic sister. For nature has never changed in Egypt: her illuminating sun, her effusive Nile, her clean skies, stark deserts, and fertile soil, everything that inspired Pharaonic man, his religious beliefs and his civilization, still exists just as it was!!"[32]

The determinist scheme that postulated a fundamental and eternal dependence of Egyptian character/mentality/personality upon the Egyptian environment was stated most categorically by Ahmad Husayn:

> What determines man therefore is not his genetic origins but his environment and his specific circumstances [of life]. The Egyptian who lived thousands of years ago is the Egyptian of today just as he is the Egyptian of tomorrow. For the elements which shaped him yesterday are those that shape him today, and it is they that will shape him in the future as long as the Nile is the Nile and the heavens are the heavens.[33]

It needs to be emphasized that the environment did not affect individuals separately in this determinist theory of territorially derived nationalism. Rather, nature treated all individuals in a similar way, stamping all members of the national collective with one group personality. The Egyptian nation was not a voluntary association that Egyptians could join or leave according to their personal whim: it was rather an impersonal reality imposed by nature on the individuals who composed it.[34] Renan's concept of nationalism as a "plébiscite de tous les jours" was thus rejected by these intellectuals. As Mahmud 'Izzat Musa explained it, "nationalism is not created by man. It is part of the essence of every Egyptian, created in him and living inside him, yet never buried with him but rather remaining for eternity after him."[35] The relationship between the individual and his national personality was therefore asymmetrical and unidirectional: the latter shaped the former, but the former had little influence over the latter. The individual had neither the capability to escape the influence of his national personality nor the power to alter the stamp that it had placed upon him.[36] Muhammad Zaki Salih stated the point most forcefully in 1927:

> National character is not the totality of the characters of individuals, but rather derives from the national spirit [*al-ruh al-qawmiyya*] that influences individuals more than it is influenced by them. It impresses its stamp on individuals and is not stamped with their impress. [For] it derives not only from the present generation, but from the generations of times past. It is the result of thousands of years of history that weigh so heavily on the individual. We [Egyptians] did not inherit from our forefathers only their possessions and their blood, but also their inclinations, sensations, and passions. These tendencies remained latent in the individual or the collective, and transferred from generation to generation.[37]

Egyptianism in School Textbooks

The extent to which this environmentally grounded concept of nationalism permeated Egyptian intellectual life in the 1920s can be seen in the textbooks in civics education [*al-tarbiyya al-wataniyya*] written and published in Egypt during the second half of the decade. These textbooks—the means whereby the educated elite passed on their understandings of reality to their children—obviously reflect the mental climate of the period. In doing so, they bear witness to the wide diffusion of an exclusivist, territorially based nationalism at the time.[38]

The civics textbooks of the 1920s were designed to give pupils a fundamental understanding of the new Egyptian state. The national objective served by the teaching of civics was explained as the desire to inculcate in Egyptian students "the willingness to bring happiness to their nation and to exalt their homeland"; to achieve these goals, pupils needed to "appreciate fully that they are sons of the [Egyptian] homeland, that they have no pride save in her and no life save in her life."[39] Another textbook defined its aim as "disseminating instruction among all classes and selecting curriculum topics that will create out of the Egyptian masses a single nation aware of its rights and obligations and assuming its proper place among the nations [of the world]."[40]

A central place in these textbooks was given to the study of nationalism. All the texts defined the nation in territorial terms. The emergence of the nation was presented as a function of living within a particular physical environment. With specific reference to the Egyptian nation, the textbooks made a deliberate attempt to inculcate the concept of Egypt as a distinct and territorially based nation-state. They explicated at great length the ideas of the Egyptian homeland and Egyptian patriotism, Egyptian nationalism and the Egyptian nationalist movement. Particular emphasis was given to the components constituting the Egyptian nation.

In the first civics textbook published in the 1920s, the "nation" [*al-umma*] was described as "a group of people most of whom derive from a single origin [*asl wahid*] and who are united by common traditions, characteristics, interests, and aspirations."[41] The elements [*al-'anasir*] making up the nation were defined as "unity of origin" [*wahdat al-asl*], "unity of traditions" [*wahdat al-taqalid*], "unity of character traits" [*wahdat al-akhlaq*], and "unity of aspirations and hopes" [*wahdat al-amani wa al-amal*].[42] "Unity of origin establishes the historical basis of the nation, while the unity of traits of character and the unity of aspirations form its cultural basis."[43] The book emphasized that all the factors that shaped the nation were the product of the extended residence of the population in "a single environment" [*bi'a wahida*].[44] The natural environment was thus made into the primary element forging the unity of the nation. It was the environment that gave people a common origin. Hence the nation was not created in the consciousness of a single generation alone; rather, it personified the consciousness of many generations. According to this textbook the nation could also be termed "the solidarity of the generations" [*tadamun al-ajyal*].[45]

Another civics text defined the specific Egyptian nation in similar territorial terms: "that large group of people composed of families and individuals native to the Egyptian region [*al-qutr al-misri*] is called the Egyptian nation [*al-umma al-misriyya*]."[46] In this text the elements making up the Egyptian nation were presented as first and foremost "unity of character traits" [*wahdat al-akhlaq*], followed by "unity of interests" [*wahdat al-masalih*] and "unity of aspirations" [*wahdat al-amani*].[47] This text also traced these unities among the people of the nation to the long-term effects of a common environment: "the unity of origin of the nation and its extended collective life in one region [*iqlim wahid*] make individuals similar to one another in their national disposition and character traits."[48]

A third civics textbook from the 1920s contains an even sharper formulation of the territorial nationalist conception. "The nation," it asserted, "is a group of people living in a specific locality [*buq'a min al-ard*] whose individuals are bound by a single civilization, common interests, and identical feelings."[49] The book emphasized that race and language were not essential elements in the creation of a national entity:

> In any event, "unity of race" [*wahdat al-jins*] and "unity of language" [*wahdat al-lugha*] are today not an important factor in the formation of a nation. Note for example the Swiss nation, which is composed of three racial elements, Germans, French, and Italians, each of which speaks its own language. Similarly, the United States is a single nation composed of various races derived originally from the nations and peoples of Europe.[50]

The text then went on to argue that it was the concentration of a group of people within the same territory that was the crucial factor producing common goals, identical patterns of behavior, and shared social norms.[51] The text offered a detailed definition of the essence of the Egyptian nation and a description of its historical evolution that is worth quoting at length:

> *The Egyptian Nation:* Egypt is the gift of the Nile, in whose fertile valley the Pharaonic nation, the creator of the greatest of ancient civilizations, was established. It was on the shores of this blessed river that the Pharaonic Egyptians dwelt in peace and tranquillity. Generation after generation they prospered and multiplied. Other elements of different hues eventually intermingled with them. These came as conquerors or arrived as mercenaries or immigrants—Romans and Greeks, Arabs and Africans, Turks and Circassians.
>
> And all—after they had found refuge in the land of Egypt, inhaled her air, drunk the water of her Nile, partook of her many bounties, and sheltered themselves beneath the clear blue dome of her sky—all mingled with the Pharaonic element. When all intermingled, all differences of blood and racial solidarity vanished. They became one nation [*umma wahida*]. . . . Thus one and all were cast in an Egyptian mold and nothing else, bound to each other by common characteristics and tied by the bonds of shared traditions. Their characters became homogeneous, their sensations similar, and their temperaments alike.[52]

False Bases of Nationalism

From the permitted we learn the forbidden. It is striking to note that in these civics textbooks of the 1920s, the Arabic language and Islam (the latter considered either as a religion or as a civilization) are assigned no role whatsoever in the formation of the Egyptian nation and the definition of its national personality. They are simply omitted as possible elements creating either nations in general or Egypt in particular. The Egyptian national personality was presented as a territorially derived reality existing above and beyond the influence of Arabic and Islam. Not content merely to emphasize Egypt's territorial essence while neglecting any possible Arabo-Islamic impact on Egypt, many Egyptianist intellectuals attached great importance to the detailed explication of the reasons why language and religion were not integral elements in the creation of the Egyptian nation and the shaping of its national specificity.

The rejection of language and religion as constitutent factors in the shaping of nations flowed naturally from the Egyptian acceptance of the "milieu–race–moment" formula as the exclusive key to understanding social reality. Ahmad Husayn echoed the views of his teachers and his textbooks when he proclaimed that "religion and language are not factors that determine nationality."[53] His prime example was the American one: the people of the United States might "adhere to Christianity and speak English. Yet can we say that the Americans are English?"[54] Similiarly, Egyptians were Egyptians and not Arabs "because we live in Egypt and not in the Arabian Peninsula."[55] Husayn's utter dismissal of language as a constituent of nationalism appeared in his declaration that "we are no more Arabs than we are English."[56]

Husayn's peer and colleague Hafiz Mahmud was equally vehement. His argument was that the identity of any nation was determined solely on the basis of the land it inhabited and the environment that shaped it, not on the basis of the language its members spoke. Therefore Egyptians, though they spoke Arabic, were not Arab, "just as the American, though English-speaking, is American, and the Australian, though he speaks the same language, is neither English nor American."[57] This rejection of linguistic nationalism was also expressed by Ibrahim Ibrahim Jum'a:

> It is plain to me that the environment we have inhabited since becoming speakers of Arabic is not Arab. We all know clearly that, despite the intermingling of the Egyptian and Arabic races, and despite the Egyptian language having succumbed to Arabic, we were created as a distinct nation with a mentality and nature completely different from the Arab mentality and nature.[58]

Even Emile Zaydan, the second-generation Egyptian owner and editor of *al-Hilal,* accepted this nonlinguistic concept of nationalism. In a detailed analysis of "the components of nationalism" in which he discussed territory, race, religion, and history, he concluded that language played no significant role in the formation of nationalism. Language

> in and of itself is not sufficient for the creation of national spirit [*al-ruh al-qawmiyya*]. The English and the Americans are two distinct peoples despite their common language. Similarly, Egypt, Syria, Algeria, and all the other Arab countries each have an independent existence even though they share the Arabic language.[59]

The Egyptian nationalist dismissal of religion as a possible component in nationalism was based on two arguments, one specific to Islam and the other applicable to all religions. The first was the assertion that Islam was a universal rather than a particularist religion; as such, its appearance was directed to all humanity, and it made no distinctions between different nationalities. The second argument was that modern realities had rendered religion anachronistic as a focus for collective identity; in contrast with previous periods of history that had been religious in ethos, the modern era, secular in spirit, recognized only secularly based nationalisms as legitimate. The *leitmotif* of this rejection of religion as a basis for nationalism was the slogan "religion is for God and the homeland for all" [*al-din li-Allah wa al-watan lil-jami'*].[60]

Hafiz Mahmud, for example, vigorously rejected the possibility that Islam held any national significance for Egyptians. In his view, Islam was the religion of individuals who believed in Allah and maintained ties of moral—but not political—solidarity with other Muslims throughout the world. "Religion is for all human beings wherever they are," he proclaimed.[61] Thus he dismissed the possibility of a religiously based nationalism out of hand. He also denied that an "Arab spirit" had, through Islam, penetrated Egypt and made the people of Egypt into an Arab-Islamic nation.[62] After all, the Prophet Muhammad had brought "a universal mission for all humanity"; under no circumstances should his mission be identified with Arabism or restricted to the Arabs alone.[63] Thus the allegiance of most Egyptians to Islam did not mean that they had accepted an Islamic national identity: their Muslim identity was a universal one unrelated to their continuing national identity.[64] Egyptian nationalism was a secular phenomenon, as distinct from Islam as it was separate from any other religion. It neither challenged nor undermined religion. Correspondingly, religion need not interfere in national matters or constitute an obstacle in the formation of a secular, progressive national personality and culture.[65]

Even more negative in his attitude toward religion was Salama Musa. Christian by background plus a dedicated positivist and secularist by education, Musa assumed that nationalism was the historic successor of religion as the primary focus of man's identity and loyalty. Inexorable laws of human evolution had made secular nationalism into the exclusive legitimate framework of political organization as well as social progress.[66]

Musa blurred the historical differences in the evolution of the societies of Christian Europe and the Islamic Middle East. He argued that since the Reformation—which he considered "a national-social revolution more than a religious revolution"—the societies of the West had become liberated from the bonds of religious loyalty and had adopted national allegiances in their place. A "total distinction" had been made between religion and the nation-state in modern Europe.[67] Musa was convinced that a similar historical process had been occurring in the Middle East since the beginning of the nineteenth century. As a result of the sweeping transformations that had taken place in the region over the past century, the status of religion as the primary focus of identity had been undermined. As in Western Europe, new historical conditions had produced territorial nationalism. "The patriotic bond" [*al-rabita al-wataniyya*] had thus replaced "the religious bond" [*al-rabita al-diniyya*] as the basis of collective identity.[68]

Given this view of modern history, Musa opposed any attempt to make religion part of national life or to base nationalism even in part upon a religious component. Similarly, the notion of a religious community having a "national essence"—that is, the attempt to provide religion with a national dimension and to claim the existence of "religious nationalism"—was denounced by Musa. Any mixing of religion and nationalism, any desire to provide the nation with religious foundations, appeared to him to be both anachronistic and dangerous. It was an attempt to roll back the wheels of history. "We children of the twentieth century," he declared, "are too advanced to rely on religion as a [national] bond unifying us."[69] Musa also directly attacked the pan-Islamic ideal. The collapse of the Ottoman Empire during World War I had given the *coup de grâce* to pan-Islam, shattering the myth of the unity of the Muslim *umma.* Musa also viewed the pan-Islamic hope of reconciling nationalism and religion, of finding a *modus vivendi* for the two, as being in conflict with the laws of human evolution and as representing a challenge to the progress of humanity. "In promoting Islamic unity [*al-jami'a al-islamiyya*]," he warned, "we are lagging behind contemporary times by nearly a thousand years."[70] Progress meant nationalism, and nationalism by its very nature was post-religious and secular.[71]

Musa therefore called for the total separation of nationalism and religion. In his view, "the religion of the future is individualistic religion [*diyana fardiyya*] and not collective religion [*diyana jama'iyya*]."[72] Musa sought to excise from the scope of religion all public authority, be it political, social, cultural, or educational, and to make these matters the concern of the nation-state alone. Only the complete reduction of religion to the level of the individual would ensure that loyalty to religion would not contradict loyalty to the nation. Harmony between nationalism and religion could be guaranteed best by their complete separation: religion needed to recognize the superior jurisdiction of nationalism in its role as the modern focus of collective identity, and nationalism needed to respect religion's status as the individual's spiritual guide.[73]

Egyptianist intellectuals did not limit this nonlinguistic, nonreli
of nationalism to Egypt alone. They extended it beyond the Nile Va
an image of their Arab neighbors that mirrored their image of Egyp
to the concept of one Arab people with a unified historical lega
writers presented the vision of a polycentric and multi-hued Arab wo ... which, following the model of Egypt, individual nation-states with distinctive territorial identities had taken form. Local uniqueness rather than all-Arab homogeneity was assumed to be the true existential situation of the Arab-speaking lands. Hence it was the construction of separate Arab nation-states, each with its distinct national existence and personality, which was the preferred regional ideal. Through the creation of such a world of separate Arab nations, not only would the region return to its natural state, but the existence of an independent Egyptian state would also be legitimized.

Such is the portrait of the Arab world and inter-Arab relations drawn by Tawfiq al-Hakim in 1933.[74] Hakim did not totally ignore the linguistic and cultural brotherhood "existing objectively" among all speakers of Arabic.[75] Yet in his view this did not obviate the deep-rooted individual existence of each Arab national unit. Since each Arab nation was a distinct entity, he argued that each needed to emphasize the unique traits that characterized it and it alone:

> It must comprehensively investigate its distinctive personality in [the context of] its long history. The Egyptian, ancient Egypt and the eras followed it; the Syrian, Phoenicia and successive periods; the Iraqi, Babylonia and the historical eras which preceded and followed it; and so on. [Therefore] each of the [Arab] nations must recover, from the bowels of the earth upon which it lives, the virtues of its character and all the treasures locked in its past.[76]

The fact that each Arab land had its own existence and personality did not mean the total isolation of the Arab states from each other. On the contrary, Hakim accepted the abstract principle of inter-Arab cooperation and solidarity. But he did so in Egyptianist terms. Interaction between the Arab lands meant a dialogue among separate nations defined on a territorial basis, among a related family of nonetheless independent individuals:

> I call for Egyptianism, Iraqiism, Syrianism, and so forth, not in order to create disunity but rather [to promote] union; not out of fanaticism, but out of love. For on the day when a solid personality flowers for each of us, then will mutual cooperation and unification increase among us.[77]

The alternative idea of total Arab unity that would dissolve national distinctiveness and destroy local variety was seen by Hakim as a serious danger to the progress and prosperity of all Arabic speaking peoples. "Our complete submergence within the personality of the remote Arabs is inconceivable because it contradicts the nature of things."[78]

A fuller image of a pluralistic Arab world was presented by Muhammad Husayn Haykal.[79] The geographical proximity and cultural similarity of the Arab lands in Haykal's view had never blurred the specific character derived from a unique environment that each possessed. The road to rehabilitating these particular national personalities rested in the renewal of the pre-Islamic cultural heritage of each. Convinced that each separate national unit had its own potential "specific ilization," Haykal felt the same had to be renewed and cultivated in order to serve as the authentic foundation of the nation's modern life. The Arab lands needed to be liberated from the reign of "foreign" civilizations—Arab, Ottoman, most recently European—through the revitalization of their distinctive "national civilizations."[80] For every territorial unit in the Arab world, he claimed, there was a "specific national identity" anchored in the cultural consciousness of the people who had inhabited the area for millenia, and it could be brought to life again only through careful attention to the distinct historical tradition of each Arab land.[81]

Later, Haykal asserted that Egypt's experience with its own "Pharaonic personality" must serve as the model for the renaissance of other Arabs. Every Arabic-speaking national collective needed to follow the Egyptian path of looking into its past and reconstructing it in its entirety, thereby providing the only sure basis for building an authentic and solidly rooted present and future for the nation. Past, present, and future were all linked to place: just as the modern Egyptian nation was returning to its original Pharaonic spirit and character as defined by the conditions of the Nile Valley and drawing from them its inspiration, so Syrians, Iraqis, an other Arab peoples must rediscover their unique, territorially defined heritages and use them to construct their distinct national identities.[82] Thus, just as he had done to his fellow Egyptians, he repeatedly reminded other Arabs of the truth that "he who has no past has neither present nor future"; admonished Syrians to look to their Phoenician roots for guidance and Iraqis to search for inspiration in the Assyrian, Babylonian, and even earlier eras; and generally advised his readers that the past civilizations of the Arab lands had the power "to reach out to us in time just as they are linked to us in space."[83] Haykal envisaged an optimistic future for the new multinational Arab order that would result from each Arab nation's rediscovery of its own past and personality. Although it would be a world of equal nation-states each aware of its own individuality and jealous of its uniqueness, nonetheless it would not lack for fertile dialogue and genuine cooperation. Indeed, he predicted "a strong spiritual union" among the Arab peoples of the future, one that ultimately would lead all the peoples of the region to develop a prosperous civilization "compared to which all the civilizations known to now will become insignificant."[84]

Thus Hakim, Haykal, and others like them insisted on the application of the Egyptian territorial model to the rest of the Arabic-speaking world. Through the elevation of environment to the rank of supreme determinant of human development and the corresponding postulate that different territories created different heritages, they were able to negate the effect of either the Arabic language or the Islamic religion as factors in the forming of nations and the shaping of national personalities. Territory was made the exclusive framework for the construction of national existence and development. Egypt and the new national image they were creating for it was to be the vanguard for the other Arab lands, showing them the proper path to national consciousness and realization. The result was to be a new regional order that would be modern in nature, in accordance with sound nationalist principles derived from enlightened Europe. The new polycentric regional order would replace the obsolete one based on religious principles, which the Ottoman Empire had represented. Recognizing the uniqueness—both spatial and temporal—of every nation in the Middle East, the new order would emphasize local identities and ensure the independent existence of each.

7

The Egyptianist Image of Egypt: II. Toward an Egyptian Territorial History

Frequently during the 1920s and early 1930s, Egyptian nationalist intellectuals charged that the history of Egypt was not being studied "as it actually was." Egypt's historical image, they complained, was distorted by two "foreign" elements: Arab-Islamic historiography and the Western historiography of European orientalists. Each in its own way, these two traditions had obfuscated the distinctive nature of Egyptian history, creating a "counterfeit portrait" of the history of the people of the Nile Valley.[1] To this indictment was added that of the unconcern of Egyptians themselves regarding their past, of the general acceptance and sometimes even the participation of Egyptians in the creation of this false image of Egyptian history.[2]

Muhammad Husayn Haykal complained bitterly that "to date, our country's history has not been set down by a judicious historian and in a truly scientific way."[3] More specifically, Haykal charged that Egyptian history had been neither researched nor recorded "as a national history," as the story of the Egyptian people inhabiting an Egyptian environment over thousands of years.[4] What was incorrectly presented as Egyptian history was nothing but the chronicle of the "foreign" rulers, peoples, and cultures that had entered the Nile Valley from outside and dominated the people of Egypt. As written in the past, Egyptian history was "the history of those foreign conquerors who humiliated our fathers and grandfathers."[5] Haykal lamented that "we do not know the history of this homeland of ours in its authentic shape, but rather [in terms of] what the despotic rule of others has done to it."[6] The severity of the distortion of Egypt's true history was accentuated in Haykal's view by the fact that this "counterfeit history" was still serving as "the official history which we were taught [in the schools] and which our children are taught today."[7]

Similar criticisms can be found in the writings of Muhammad 'Abd Allah 'Inan. He asserted bitterly that any interest in Egyptian history had been left either to Arab-Islamic historians or to Western historians. Both groups had subjugated the writing of that history to their own ideological interests and had made it serve the political and cultural forces in whose name they acted.[8] They bore the responsibility for the fact that Egyptian youth today were ignorant of Egypt's history and her unique mentality. Under their influence, entire periods of Egyptian history were "still concealed from our eyes by a curtain of darkness."[9] Like Haykal, 'Inan also protested against this false interpretation of the past "being forced upon schoolchildren today."[10] 'Inan called upon his fellow Egyptian intellectuals to free themselves of the "stifling yoke" of this false history and to fight against it. Only through the rediscovery of Egypt's true "national history" [*al-ta'rikh al-qawmi*] could the "noose" of this incorrect image be removed from the neck of Egypt.[11]

First and foremost, the struggle for a genuine Egyptian "national history" had to be waged against those official educational institutions in which the foreign and false historiographical approaches had embedded themselves. Haykal, 'Inan, and other Egyptian nationalist intellectuals condemned Egyptian schools for allowing non-Egyptian approaches to history to dominate the study of the Egyptian past. The curricula of these institutions were repeatedly criticized for giving preference to the study of European or Islamic history and for presenting the history of Egypt and its people either as only a part of the history of the Arabs and Islam or, in other instances, as a byproduct of Mediterranean and Western history. This improper emphasis in the practice of history in modern Egypt had created the absurd situation in which Egyptian students seeking to know the special history of their own country had to leave Egypt and to study its past in foreign educational institutions and universities.[12] Muhammad Husayn Haykal in particular rebelled against this anomalous situation, defining it as a "shame" and a "disgrace" for Egypt. Its toleration by Egyptians during the early years of the development of higher education in Egypt in the period before World War I was understandable; but in the post-1919 period of national "renaissance," it could no longer be accepted.[13] Thus Egyptianist intellectuals of the 1920s shared a common outrage over the disparity between the new national image of Egypt that was being formulated in the post-1919 era and the unacceptable image of the country's past that continued to be dominated by a non-Egyptian, foreign perspective. An Egypt in the process of revival deserved a rediscovered history, a new collective image based on a proper understanding of the nation's heritage. In sum, a new present and future demanded a new sense of the past.

Egyptianist intellectuals formulated the national need for a new history in terms of emancipation and rehabilitation. Egyptians had to free their collective memory of the burdens of foreign histories, purify their historical awareness of externally imposed images, and recover a distinct Egyptian collective memory that could serve as the solid foundation of a new national consciousness. To write Egyptian history "as it actually was" meant reconstructing the history of Egypt in a fashion that displayed its "territorial essence"—that is, the millenial and paramount bond between the Nile Valley and the people of Egypt.[14] As Haykal stated the argument, the history of a nation was "the generations who preceded us and the souls who lived in the very same milieu in which we live today." It was imperative that contemporary Egyptian intellectuals, representing "the last in a long chain of Egyptian generations," revitalize the link between these generations and thereby recreate the organic historical unity of the Egyptian nation.[15]

The task of recreating a proper understanding of Egyptian history was perceived by these intellectuals as essential for the construction of a new national reality. Haykal formulated this axiom very clearly. The study of the past and the cultural legacy found in it, he stated, "is considered by all civilized nations to be one of the foundations of nationalism, . . . a powerful and productive tool for creating nationalism."[16] History played a crucial role in forming national consciousness and consolidating a sense of collective allegiance. It provided historical legitimacy for a nation in the process of revival, demonstrating the durability of the national personality.[17] Hence the role of the nationalist historian was to write history in the interests of nationalism. It was his duty to present "national history" as the story of the development of the social collective within its particular environment. Only through the writing of a genuine national history would Egypt obtain the correct, authentic, and distinctive Egyptian past it deserved.[18]

The Principles of an Egyptian National History

The development of a new historical image for Egypt did not remain a utopian dream for these Egyptian nationalist intellectuals. Rather, they translated their premises into operative terms, formulating various methodological principles and historiographic guidelines for the writing of a genuinely national history for Egypt. The flood of directives for the reinterpretation of history put forth during this period amounted to a relatively unified historiographic scheme that *in toto* offered a revisionist theoretical framework for studying the history of the Nile Valley and the historical development of its people. Within this general scheme we can discern six central concepts that underlay the paradigm for the rediscovery of Egypt's national history.

Time is Anchored in Place

The new national history was founded on a specific concept of time in which time was made an exclusive function of place. The physical environment or milieu was held to determine the nature of any given period or moment. It was the environment that dictated the rhythm of the flow of time. Time was contained, as it were, within the bounds of geography, and had to obey the determinist laws of nature prevailing within the environment.[19] In the specific case of Egypt, it was maintained that Egypt's life had been shaped by a "territorial clock." Whatever periodization might be applied to the country's long history, all these moments occurred in the Nile Valley. This commonality of place united successive periods of time in one historical entity. Thus continuity rather than change was seen as the essence of Egyptian history; Egypt's "eternal life" was interpreted as having experienced only incidental changes over the millenia.[20]

Tawfiq al-Hakim's writings offer a concrete expression of this territorial conception of time. It was Hakim's position that time and place together were the two forces that had shaped the Egyptian philosophical outlook.[21] Egyptian thought for thousands of years had revolved around the "immense struggle" between man, time, and place. Whereas "the Greeks were obsessed with fate and destiny" (here Hakim indulged in his favorite comparison between Greeks and Egyptians), "the Egyptians are obsessed with time and place [*al-zaman wa al-*

makan].” Indeed, Egypt’s *raison d’être* as a nation was to master time and place and to make them both subordinate to the will of Egypt.[22] In Hakim’s view, Egypt was capable of overcoming time through its geographical and human resources. The organic continuity of life in the Nile Valley and the permanence of the “Egyptian spirit” deriving from its rootedness in that environment were viewed as stronger than time.[23] It was this subjugation of time to place that to Hakim opened the possibility of renewal. Because it was embedded in a well-defined environment, revival was an essential characteristic of Egypt. The Egyptian outlook had always been marked by the “expectation of the victory over time and space. This victory finds its expression in resurrection.”[24]

This concept of the possibility of transcending the limits of time and of restoring the essence of the past was shared by other Egyptianist intellectuals. They also assumed a unique Egyptian capacity for revitalizing the past, for restoring the magnificence that had characterized Egypt in its past “golden age.” The durability and power of the Egyptian environment, they felt, ensured that time would repeat itself in Egypt. The course of history had not altered Egypt; rather, again and again it had merely revealed the same “true mythic essence” persisting throughout.[25]

The notion of the perennial revitalization of one perduring Egyptian essence was central to the theoretical scheme of the new national history. As conceived by these Egyptianist intellectuals, territorial time meant the elimination of the absolute distinction between past and future. It enabled Egypt periodically to renew itself, to recapture the country’s youthful vigor. In this sense, Egypt was eternally young.[26] From this perspective, time did not mean unavoidable destruction and loss; history was not necessarily a process of irreversible decadence. The wheels of time were not moving inexorably in one direction that could never be reversed. In this territorial concept of time, history contained the potential for death and for rebirth. At least for Egypt, national rebirth and rejuvenation were just as possible as national decline and eclipse. At its root, the concept that time was subordinate to place made possible the building of the present and future on the basis of the past.[27]

Thus Tawfiq al-Hakim argued that for Egypt “resurrection” [*ba‘th*] was embedded in the physical structure of the Nile Valley. The river’s even flow, the predetermined annual sequence of high and low water, were for Tawfiq al-Hakim but two signs of the unique rhythm of time in Egypt. It was this regularity that produced moments of revival:

> Every year the Nile lives and dies once. Death and rebirth. Rebirth followed by death. . . . From this Nile myths of resurrection [*asatir al-ba‘th*] have emerged. The idea of eternity developed in this beautiful and even timeless land. It [Egypt] is the source and origin; it is the source to which one returns. We die upon it and return to it. Death, then life, then death. Thus forever and ever. Neither death nor life stop. This is the essence of the Nile.[28]

Hakim was convinced that the idea of rebirth was a fundamental trait of Egypt, one of its “enduring ideas” that reappeared continually in Egyptian history.[29] For Hakim as for other Egyptian nationalist intellectuals, the idea of periodic national revival was an integral part of Egypt’s life as well as one of the most prominent features of the Egyptian historical experience. "Resurrection is the anthem of eternal Egypt, sung every year by the Nile, the plants, the birds, the heavens—and the poets."[30]

The Unity of Egyptian History

The second historiographic principle underlying the new national history derived directly from the first. This was the theory that all Egyptian history, despite its apparent multiplicity of eras and diversity in regimes and cultures, was a single, unitary, and indivisible whole. This again was traced to the unique nature of the physical environment of the Nile Valley, whose enormous, irresistible power was credited with shaping an organic historical unity among the diverse elements coming into contact with it. All the peoples of the Nile Valley—the dead, the living, and those yet to come—were inevitably subject to identical geographic, climatic, and social influences. A reservoir of distinctively Egyptian experiences had accrued gradually in the collective consciousness of successive generations, creating a common collective memory for all Egyptians. Each generation drew its memories from this collective reserve while simultaneously adding a new layer to it.[31]

This organic Egyptian history enjoyed autonomy from external or foreign influences. It was governed and determined by the endogenous mechanisms, both environmental and social, of the Nile Valley alone. The determinism of nature created determinist laws for Egyptian history. While imprisoning Egyptian evolution within rigid limits, these laws also liberated Egyptian history from the effects of external forces or events. External historical pressures coming to bear upon Egypt were held to be inevitably absorbed into the temporal pattern imposed by the more powerful environment of the Nile Valley.[32] Egyptian history was thus overwhelmingly the story of the interaction between the Egyptian human collective and its physical surroundings, an internal and unending dialogue between Egyptian man and his homeland. Compared to this dominant relationship, the interplay of Egypt and the world beyond the Nile Valley was a secondary process.[33]

Given these assumptions about Egyptian history, the national historian's function was viewed as one of revealing and reestablishing the unity of the Egyptian past and present. Haykal defined this task as the revealing and the reconstruction of "the firm psychological link" [*al-ittisal al-nafsi al-wathiq*] between ancient and modern Egypt, "the same firm psychological link which makes Egypt an eternal and imperishable historical unity."[34] Thus the national historian had to demonstrate the millenial continuity of Egyptian history. In the process, he would recreate the vital bond between the golden age of the Pharaohs and the new golden age of the contemporary national era.[35] In a similar spirit, Salama Musa maintained that "it is impossible for us to understand a nation except in terms of its historical unity."[36] Neither particular aspects nor specific periods of Egypt's long history were the proper object of the study of national historians, he argued; rather, it was the complete reconstruction of Egypt's unique territorial past. "In order to comprehend the political factors which govern our affairs," he wrote, "it is imperative that we study our history in its entirety."[37]

The Historical "Law of Assimilation"

The environmental determinism and unity that characterized Egyptian history in turn produced the third axiom of Egyptian nationalist historiography. This was the historical "law of assimilation," according to which all the peoples, languages, religions, and cultures that had come into contact with the Nile Valley and its inhabitants were held to have succumbed to the physical and spiritual superiority of Egypt. Rather than being "external forces" influencing or altering the Egyptian personality, they were brought under its sway and assimilated into it, losing their original identity as they were reshaped in an Egyptian image, and eventually becoming an integral part of Egypt and the Egyptian collective. Invaders such as the Hyksos, the Persians, the Nubians, the Greeks, the Romans, the Byzantines, the Arabs, and the Mamluk and Ottoman Turks were all held to have had not the slightest effect on the stability and strength of the Egyptian national personality. Instead, that personality had stamped its characteristics upon them, Egyptianized them, and made them subject to Egyptian historical patterns.[38]

Muhammad Husayn Haykal provided perhaps the clearest formulation of this law of historical assimilation. In his view, outsiders coming to Egypt inevitably "acclimatized themselves to our country, intermixing with us and becoming part of us, in fact all becoming Egyptians themselves. Their first nationality completely vanished."[39] To Haykal, the "fusion" [*indimaj*] of non-Egyptians was a central process of Egypt's long history.

> Egypt's history from the Pharaohs to the contemporary period is the history of the fusion [*ta'rikh al-indimaj*] between all those who sought to invade Egypt and the inhabitants of Egypt. . . . They assimilated by virtue of the atmosphere [*jaww*] of this valley, . . . the Hyksos, the Greeks, the Romans, the Arabs, the Mamluks, all became Egyptians who accepted the authority of Egypt and who completely embodied the spirit of the Nile Valley.[40]

The above premises in turn engendered three additional historiographic principles.

Falsity of Periodization

The proponents of Egyptian territorial history rejected any periodization of Egyptian history. They regarded the division of Egyptian history into separate periods as an invention of foreign historiographies intended to destroy the historical unity of Egypt and its people. The belief that Egyptian history could be divided into unrelated Pharaonic, Greek, Roman, Arab, Ottoman, or other periods was a false one. It denied the "eternal truth" of the indivisible unity of Egyptian history, ignoring the "objective" internal factors that made the history of Egypt a seamless web.[41]

Here again, Muhammad Husayn Haykal's formulation was the most important and influential one.[42] Haykal complained that even "well-intentioned historians" of Egypt had erred in "classifying Egypt's history by periods to which were given the names of non-Egyptian nations."[43] Haykal criticized this periodization of Egyptian history as an arbitrary reduction of Egyptian history to "the history of the rulers of Egypt."[44] He belittled this approach as treating Egyptian history in non-Egyptian, external terms. It was peoples and not ruling dynasties, the underlying society and not the political superstructure, the national personality rather than the ruler's traits, which were the essence of history and which should shape its content.[45]

Like Haykal, other Egyptianist intellectuals saw the assimilation of all external forces into the Egyptian personality as empirical proof of the indivisibility of Egyptian history. They also emphasized that the task of the national historian was to Egyptianize the Egyptian past by shattering the superficial periodization imposed on it from the outside in order to expose the deeper layers constituting its fundamental organic unity. The Egyptian national historian had the obligation of showing that both the Egyptian social milieu and the Egyptian personality had remained unchanged since the Pharaonic era, and that these constants were the hard kernel of Egyptian history.[46]

The Centrality of the Egyptian People in History

Egyptianist intellectuals rejected interpretations of history that focused on the role and importance of the individual in the historical process. Rather, they adopted a positivist historical approach that emphasized the central role of impersonal forces in the shaping of history. Egyptian history was not properly the chronicle of rulers, kings, or dynasties but rather of the collective, impersonal forces that had shaped its course: material geographic and climatic features; social structures and cultural constructs; and the enduring patterns of behavior derived from these. As Salama Musa put it in reference to the theories of Herbert Spencer, "history must include all strata of the nation and investigate the entirety of material, religious, economic, and similar conditions."[47] In an inversion of the great-man approach of Carlyle, the Egyptian nation as a whole was the only "hero" in Egyptian history, and Egyptian history was its collective biography.[48] The nationalist historian was directed to turn his attention away from the temporary and meaningless ephemera of dynastic history and instead to put the Egyptian people at the center of the historical stage. His nationalist function was thus to emphasize the centrality of Egyptian collective national forces in each and every chapter of Egyptian history.[49]

The Unbroken Independence of the Egyptian Nation

The historical permanence of the Egyptian national personality in turn ensured the continuing internal independence of the Egyptian nation. Egyptianist intellectuals sought first of all to dispel the false conception that held that "the Egyptian people remained controlled by foreign nations from the end of the Pharaonic period onwards."[50] This distorted image of Egyptian history had been fostered deliberately by the imperialist school of Egyptian history and was intended to legitimize the continuation of imperialist domination over the country. It presented Egyptians as an inherently submissive and subjugated people. Continuously under the rule of foreigners, for millenia Egypt had never enjoyed independence. Scholars of the imperialist school were accused of belittling even the Egyptian desire for independence and liberty, maintaining that "the Egyptian people had never known [national] dignity for which they would be prepared to sacrifice themselves, and have never accorded [national] pride a significance for which they would be prepared to struggle."[51]

Egyptianist intellectuals responded to these claims by asserting the Egyptian nation's "eternal independence." "The history we know," declared Ibrahim Jalal, historian and Director of the Egyptian Department of Numismatics, "bears witness to the fact that Egypt tasted the sweet joy of independence through long periods and for many generations."[52] In a similar vein Muhammad Husayn Haykal maintained that "Egypt repeatedly achieved her independence throughout generations and centuries in which she offered a model of power and strength."[53] In refutation of the view of 'Abd al-Rahman al-Rafi'i, Haykal interpreted the popular uprising against the French Occupation in 1798 as a modern manifestation of "a national behavior pattern" thousands of years old, in which the Egyptian nation had always struggled for liberation from foreign conquerors.[54] Similarly, a textbook by Tawfiq al-Mar'ashli described the "correct way" to teach Egyptian history as the story of Egypt's perennial striving for independence and her "repeated heroic struggles" to attain national liberation. For Mar'ashli, this perpetual desire for liberty and struggle for independence constituted the "true essence" of the history of the Egyptian people.[55] For Taha Husayn, Egypt's national vitality and its desire for independence was a perpetual feature of the country's history from the Pharaonic period to the contemporary era of national revival:

> The Egyptian nation may have slumbered, but it has not faded away. Neither nationalist sentiment nor [the desire for] popular acclaim induces me to deny that the Egyptian nation ever died during any period of its long history. . . . Neither did it lose its independence for thousands of years. And if it may have lost it periodically, it by no means forgot that independence. . . . I hereby declare: the Egyptian nation did not die, and the proof of it is that it is still alive; it feels, it senses, it reasons, and it struggles for its existence.[56]

Egypt's independence was also preserved because the foreign rulers governing her eventually became Egyptianized. In the Egyptianist view, the success of foreigners in ruling over Egypt and its people for any length of time was explained by the fact that their activities gradually became inspired by "Egyptian national motives and impulses." Their very Egyptianness was the ultimate source of their strength and greatness.[57] "If it came to pass that a foreign king became an independent ruler over Egypt," Tawfiq al-Mar'ashli maintained, "then she [Egypt] clung to him until she turned him into an Egyptian who loved Egypt and desired to make her inhabitants happy." Ptolemies, Fatamids, Ayyubids, Mamluks: all became Egyptianized in spirit, to the point where their goal became the same "complete independence" [*istiqlal tamm*] desired by contemporary Egyptian nationalists.[58]

The Outlines of Egypt's National History

The formulation of this theoretical framework for Egyptian historiography in purely territorial terms was an impressive methodological achievement. In a relatively short span of time, Egyptianist intellectuals had developed a coherent set of historiographic principles to serve as the basis of a revisionist interpretation of the totality of Egyptian history. Their achievement, however, remained primarily on the theoretical level: during the period under consideration, only partial attempts were made to translate these principles into historical practice and to apply them to the rewriting of the specifics of Egyptian history. There was a considerable gap between the new schemata, on the one hand, and the reinterpretation of Egyptian history actually accomplished by Egyptianist historians, on the other. With this qualification in mind, we shall now examine those works which did attempt to offer an essentially territorial interpretation of Egyptian history based on the new theoretical framework. The following, then, is an attempt to summarize the territorial nationalist interpretation of Egyptian history as presented by several of its leading exponents in the later 1920s and early 1930s.

Not surprisingly, a central place in the territorial interpretation of Egyptian history was reserved for the long Pharaonic age. The Pharaonic era as a whole and the time of the New Kingdom of the Eighteenth, Nineteenth, and Twentieth Dynasties in particular were presented as both the formative epoch of Egypt and its most glorious phase or "Golden Age" [interchangably *al-'asr al-dhahabi* or *al-'ahd al-dhahabi*]. The Egyptian nation had taken its distinct and most perfect form under the Pharaohs, when its unique national personality crystallized.[59] Egypt's place as one of the leading countries of the world was established in the Pharaonic era.[60]

Particular emphasis in this interpretation of the Pharaonic age was placed on the world-historical role of ancient Egyptian civilization. The greatest achievement of the Egyptian nation was presented as its role as pacesetter for the evolution of the entire human race. At the dawn of human history, Tawfiq al-Mar'ashli asserted, "Egypt preceded all the nations of the earth in founding a civilization whose brilliance radiated forth over a span of forty centuries."[61] A civics textbook of the period emphasized the debt of contemporary European civilization to Pharaonic Egypt: the Egypt of the Pharaohs "was that civilization that the Persians, the Greeks, and the Romans took and made into the foundation of their civilizations [and] upon which was built the civilization of present-day Europe."[62]

Just as significant in the eyes of these territorial nationalist historians was the Pharaonic era's contribution to establishing the basic patterns of Egyptian history. In their view, it was Pharaonic Egypt that had served as the prototype for the development of all of Egypt's distinct national traits. In general terms, the Pharaonic period was frequently alluded to as the embodiment of all later Egyptian history.[63] More specifically, it was seen as the crucible in which the several characteristics of Egypt's unique territorial historical pattern had first developed; the organic unity of Egyptian history, the law of assimilation of foreign elements, and the central role of the Egyptian people themselves in the country's history were all traceable to the Pharaonic age. But perhaps most important to these nationalist intellectuals, and certainly more relevant to their times, was the Pharaonic period as a model of Egyptian independence. As 'Abd al-'Aziz al-Bishri put it in his civics textbook, "Egypt was a mighty and independent country for more than 5000 years."[64] Thus in their treatment of the major episode of foreign domination during the Pharaonic era, that of the Hyksos, Egyptianist intellectuals emphasized the "heroic struggles" of the people of Egypt against the alien rule, the rapid expulsion of the foreign invader from Egypt, and the fact that the ouster of the Hyksos heralded the splendors of the New Kingdom.[65] This Egypt, nationalist intellectuals protested to those who would distort its history, was hardly an "Egypt that for most of its history was under foreign rule"; rather, this was the first truly independent nation in the world, the affairs of which were in the hands of a regime that was the peer of any of its contemporaries.[66]

The territorial nationalist interpretation could not avoid the question of the decline of ancient Egypt under the later Pharaonic dynasties. In dealing with this issue, Egyptianist historians placed their emphasis on the internal decadence spreading throughout Pharaonic society rather than on the inherent power of the external forces that entered Egypt from the outside. In their view it was internal decline that brought about the Persian conquest of Egypt and the establishment of foreign Persian rule over Egypt at the close of the Pharaonic era.[67] But the Persian interlude received little attention from these historians. The true historical significance of the decline of Pharaonic Egypt was that it paved the way for the conquest of the country by Alexander of Macedon in 332 B.C., a conquest that opened a genuinely new era in Egyptian history.

The conquest of Egypt by Alexander the Great did not break the continuity of Egyptian history. Although the Greek conquest did constitute a turning point in the sense of ending the millenial domination of Pharaonic civilization over Egypt, nonetheless the course of history after Alexander's entry into Egypt only reaffirmed the validity of the territorial historical perspective for Egyptianist historians. This perspective was authenticated by the course of political events after the Greek conquest: Alexander's own rule over Egypt lasted only a few years, and the dynasty founded by Ptolmey I Soter, which succeeded Alexander in Egypt, soon came under the sway of the spirit of the Nile Valley and made Egypt a state as independent as its Pharaonic predecessors.[68]

Thus Muhammad Husayn Haykal described the relationship between the first Ptolmey and Egypt as one of mutual dependence that benefited both sides: "Ptolmey became an independent ruler through Egypt, and Egypt became [an] independent [state] through him."[69] The territorial interpretation presented the entire Ptolemaic dynasty that ruled Egypt between Alexander and the Romans as an independent Egyptian polity. Moreover, its independence stemmed from its having become Egyptianized, absorbing the "Egyptian mentality" and working for the furtherance of Egyptian national interests.[70] As Ahmad Husayn saw Egyptian history under the Ptolemys, these Greek conquerors "assimilated astonishingly well to Egyptian nationality." They adopted Egyptian beliefs, dressed like Egyptians, and took Egyptian names. Their "enlightened rule" was exercised "for the good of Egyptians and the glory of Egypt." Thus the Ptolemys became "Egyptian kings in blood, flesh, and thought. They ruled Egypt for the Egyptians."[71]

No less important in the view of Egyptian nationalist historians was the fact that the Ptolemys quickly restored Egypt to "her leading position among the nations of the world."[72] The dynasty "consolidated Egyptian sovereignty and restored to her and to her civilization the glory of the Pharaohs."[73] Egypt became a universal cultural power under the Ptolemys. Their city Alexandria was referred to as the "Mecca" of the Hellenistic world.[74] It was in Alexandria, Haykal noted, that "the materialist philosophy of the Greeks fused with the spiritual philosophy of Egypt. From this union there grew a unique Egyptian philosophy, the philosophy of the Alexandrian school."[75] Thus it was the blending of the genius of the Greeks with the equally impressive Egyptian national character which was responsible for the cultural achievements of the Ptolemaic period.[76]

Egypt's Roman epoch was presented far less enthusiastically in the territorial historical interpretation. The six centuries between the Roman and Arab-Islamic conquest of Egypt did not offer the proponents of national history the same manifestations of Egyptian autonomy and greatness as they found in earlier periods. The Romans eliminated Egypt's independent national status. The Nile Valley became a Roman province and was subordinated to the broader imperial interests of the Caesars.[77] Roman policy was portrayed as oppressive of native Egyptians, the source of Egyptian resentment and continued tension between rulers and ruled. Local and national rebellions occurred repeatedly: only the cruelest repression enabled the Roman governors to maintain their rule "at sword's point" over the land of the Nile. First Rome and then Byzantium systematically attempted to suppress the "impulse to national liberation" that the Egyptian people continued to demonstrate throughout the period.[78]

Egyptian nationalist historians made a clear distinction between the "Ptolemaic type" and the "Roman type" of rule over Egypt. The former was the more usual pattern of foreign rule. It was a pattern in which external forces conquered the country but were successful in ruling it only because they assimilated to it, coming under the sway of Egypt's territorial history. Adopting Egyptian customs and eventually becoming Egyptian, their rule became devoted to the advancement and prosperity of Egypt itself. The secret of their success was their own "surrender to the power of the strong Egyptian character"[79] and their consequent willingness to "assume Egyptian nationality and merge into it."[80] From this surrender came victory: "thus the Macedonians, the Mamluks, and the Fatimids who opted for Egyptian nationality enjoyed glory and security."[81]

The latter type of rule was represented by those "external forces" (first the Persians, later the Romans and Byzantines) who clung to their foreign identity and refused to assimilate to Egypt. Remaining always alien to the country and its people, they were compelled to rule both "by recourse to violence and oppression such as is the case under martial law."[82] Their failure derived from "their attempt to fight the Egyptian character," an attempt that pitted Egyptians against their domination.[83] Thus "the Persians, the Romans, and the Byzantines who spurned Egyptian nationality knew no peace and could pacify Egypt only through violence, subjugation, theft, and brute force."[84]

How to fit the spread of Christianity in Egypt during the Roman-Byzantine period did not pose a serious problem for Egyptianist historians. Its rapid dissemination among the populace of Egypt was attributed in large part to the Jewish roots of Christianity, Judaism itself being viewed as "linked in many ways to early Pharaonic religion."[85] Christianity thus picked up on many of the concepts and ideals of ancient Egypt. They also argued that its ready reception by Egyptians had to be understood with reference to Egyptian resentment against the oppressive rule of the Romans and Byzantines. It was "Roman oppression" that caused the Egyptian masses to turn to a religion that preached "brotherhood, peace and tolerance" and offered solace for "the deprived, the miserable, and the downtrodden."[86] Moreover, the Monophysite variety of Christianity that became dominant in Egypt was opposed to the orthodoxy of the alien Byzantine establishment. Thus Egypt's religious history in the Byzantine era was seen as one phase in its longer nationalist struggle. This opposition of a native Egyptian form of Christianity to a foreign Byzantine one was also viewed as being of great historical importance: it was the hatred of the Monophysite Egyptian masses for Byzantium and its official religious dogmas that were credited with an important role in the collapse of Byzantine rule and the Arab conquest of Egypt in the seventh century.[87]

The Arab-Islamic period of Egyptian history was the object of special attention by the formulators of the territorial school of Egyptian history. Egypt's incorporation into the Arab and Muslim community from the seventh century onward presented the most serious challenge to their vision of the unity and continuity of Egyptian history. Had the people of Egypt not been totally Arabized and Islamified, becoming Arabs and Muslims in every sense? If this was the case, was the seventh century not the beginning of a "new history" for the people of the Nile Valley and an irreparable break with their pre-Islamic "ancient history"?[88]

Egyptian nationalist historians replied to these questions with a categorical negative. They devoted their efforts to proving that the Arab-Islamic period of Egyptian history was no more than another phase in the unbroken development of the Egyptian national personality, a continuation of Egypt's territorial history that remained within the parameters first defined in the Pharaonic era. Two general arguments were put forth in substantiation of this interpretation. The first presented the Arabs as foreign conquerors of Egypt similar to other peoples who had invaded the Nile Valley. Originally alien overlords, they soon were conquered by Egypt itself, bowing before the innate superiority of the Egyptian national personality and assimilating to Egyptian culture and society. The second line of attack presented the largely independent Muslim states that emerged in Egypt from the ninth century onward as historic proof of the rapid recovery of the Egyptian personality from foreign conquest, and of Egypt's resumption of an independent position among the polities of the region.

The thesis that the Arabs first came to Egypt as foreign conquerors but were eventually overcome by the power of the Egyptian national personality and thus assimilated themselves to its territorial patterns was one of the most widely held convictions of the post-1919 period. There was hardly an Egyptianist intellectual who did not voice this argument in one form or another. The position contained an important subthesis within itself: that the Arabic language and the Islamic religion brought to Egypt by its Arab conquerors had been absorbed by the Egyptian people only after both had undergone a process of Egyptianization.

Two intellectuals who developed these points in some detail were 'Abbas Mahmud al-'Aqqad and Taha Husayn. 'Aqqad viewed the Arabs as "enemies" who had been resisted by Egyptians. To him, theirs was but one in a long series of "foreign invasions" that marked Egypt's recent history. Forerunners of the Turks, the French, and the English, the Arabs had sought to dominate Egypt, to end its independence, and to alter its national identity. But they only aroused the independent spirit of the Egyptian people, prodding it into a violent national resistance against the foreigner.[89] Taha Husayn viewed the Arab conquest of Egypt in similar terms. The Arab invasion to him was but one instance of a cyclical historical pattern that had become an integral part of Egypt's national history. For thousands of years the Egyptian people had been subjected to "a variety of injustices" and "all sorts of hostility" from foreigners: Persians, Greeks, Romans, Arabs, Turks, the French, and finally the English.[90] The Arab conquest indeed had been the most dangerous of these foreign conquests. It had threatened Egypt's independent historical existence by turning Egypt into a peripheral province of a larger empire whose center of gravity was far removed from the Nile Valley. But the innate desire for freedom embedded deep within the Egyptian character had provoked Egyptians' resistance against their Arab conquerors just as it had inspired them to rise up against other "external dangers."[91] Husayn was also convinced that his British contemporaries faced the same historic destiny—to be cast out of Egypt by its people.[92]

Egyptianist historians presented the struggle between Egyptians and Arabs and the eventual victory of the former over the latter in terms of rival national personalities. Over time, the Arabs in Egypt had had their original nomadic national personality supplanted by an Egyptian one; their nomadic characteristics had vanished and were replaced by purely Egyptian collective traits, thought patterns, and modes of behavior. As Hafiz Mahmud explained the fate of the Arab conquerors of Egypt, "[t]he Arabs are a group of people who entered Egypt as foreigners but who lived there as Egyptians . . . when Egypt came in contact with them she swallowed their Arabism and was able to Egyptianize them completely."[93] A civics textbook of the 1930s presented much the same idea: "the Arabs (like the Turks) arrived in Egypt as conquerors . . . they blended into the original local population, the Copts, and out of this mixture was formed a single nation, the Egyptian nation."[94] Ahmad Husayn viewed the Arabs as the most powerful foreign force that had threatened the independence and distinctiveness of Egypt. It was because of the threat this force represented that the failure and the eventual Egyptianization of the Arabs in Egypt constituted the clearest historical proof of the invincible assimilative power of the Nile Valley.[95] In his view, the unique "Egyptian vitality" [*al-hayawiyya al-misriyya*] had been responsible for Egypt's absorption of all foreign conquerors, the Arabs included.[96] His conclusion was that

> it is completely absurd to claim that Egypt is Arab, or that Egyptian blood has become Arab; its absurdity is confirmed by science and by history. The contemporary Egyptian is Pharaonic by nature—so Pharaonic in his blood that no other blood has been able to overcome or influence this.[97]

Additional proof of the assimilation of the Arabs to Egypt was found by Egyptianist intellectuals in the profound transformations that had taken place in both the Arabic language and the religion of Islam after their arrival in the Nile Valley. Both originally alien to Egypt, both were nonetheless Egyptianized after their introduction into Egypt.[98] Indeed, the only reason they became prevalent in the land of the Nile was because they had conformed to the Egyptian mentality and personality. In the crucible of the Egyptian environment, Arabic and Islam adapted themselves to the linguistic patterns and modes of belief which had prevailed throughout Egyptian history. This reformulation was the condition of their acceptance by Egyptians. One of the clearest statements of this view was made by Ahmad Husayn:

> There remains the question of religion and language, the question which causes some to believe that we have to be [considered] Arabs. Yet the truth is that this very religion and language constitute further proof that everything in Egypt cannot be other than Egyptian. . . . For the Arabic language in Egypt became an Egyptian language [*lugha misriyya*] in its idioms and metaphors, its images and expressions. In sum, this is an Egyptian language in which you sense the

Egyptian temperament [*al-mizaj al-misri*], and in which you feel the simplicity and graciousness of the Egyptian. The same can also be said of religion. Islam in Egypt is an Egyptian religion [*din misri*] in harmony with the Egyptian psyche [*al-nafsiyya al-misriyya*] and with Egyptian customs and traits.[99]

Muhammad 'Abd Allah 'Inan's writings on the history of Egypt deal at length with the "historic confrontation" between the Egyptian national personality and the language and religion of the Arab invaders of Egypt. 'Inan addressed the issue in the wider context of the development of Egyptian nationalism [*al-qawmiyya al-misriyya*]. In his view, Egyptian nationalism had existed since the dawn of history. None of the foreign conquerors of Egypt had been able to destroy or to disrupt the Egyptian sense of nationalism; it had been "always a latent force" resisting foreign rulers of the country.[100]

An Egyptian sense of nationalism characterized the country's Islamic era as well as earlier ones; it indeed held the key to an understanding of the historical development of Islamic Egypt. Despite the adoption of the Islamic religion and the Arabic language, for 'Inan the Egyptian national personality remained the central force inspiring the minds of Egyptians. Thus Egypt "may have received certain innovations—Islam and the Arabic language—from her conquerors; but she [also] preserved her distinct national characteristics."[101] 'Inan took the argument as far as possible: "under Islam there emerged a Muslim Egyptian nation that was Arabic only in the language it spoke, but not in its particular racial or national characteristics."[102] Even the active participation of Egyptians in the further development of the cultural life of Islamic civilization did not mean that Egypt had lost its unique Egyptian national identity, or indicate a break in Egypt's ties to its ancient Pharaonic heritage:

Egypt in no way lost its Egyptian personality under different Islamic states. Indeed, this personality remained perpetually strong and distinct. It absorbed the states of its [Islamic] rulers and Egyptianized them.[103]

For 'Inan, not only had Islam failed to absorb Egypt into the greater *umma* or to stamp the country with an Arab-Islamic identity, but paradoxically it had afforded a new opportunity for the Egyptian personality to demonstrate its capabilities.[104] His conclusion about "Islamic Egypt" was a sweeping one: "we can see that everything in Islamic Egypt's history expresses the strength of her Egyptian personality and the force of her national vitality."[105]

Egyptianist writers were eager to point out the concrete manifestations of how the Arabic language and the Islamic religion had taken on an Egyptian coloring in Egypt. In discussing language, they found a fundamental difference between the Egyptian colloquial dialect [*al-'ammiyya*] and all other spoken dialects of Arabic, a difference that to them proved beyond doubt the Egyptianization of Arabic that had taken place in Egypt. In the view of Hasan Subhi, Arabic had never become more than the "official language" of the country employed by the ruling elite and used in administration and religious instruction.[106] On a more basic level, this "official language" had failed to supplant the Egyptian colloquial language as the medium of expression of the people at large.[107] "The essence of the Egyptian language" [*jawhar al-lugha al-misriyya*] had not changed in the least: throughout the entire Arab-Islamic period, the masses of Egypt had continued to speak their Egyptian dialect with all its "primordial Egyptian" expressions, structures, and idioms.[108] To Muhammad Lutfi Jum'a, the fact that an Egyptian visiting another Arab country was described as "Egyptian and not Arab" was the most convincing proof of the persistence of Egyptianness among Egyptians. The Arabic language, although providing a connecting link with other Arabic speakers, was not strong enough to cancel out an individual's identity as an Egyptian either in the eyes of other Arabs or to Egyptians themselves.[109] In Ahmad Husayn's view, Egyptians, Hijazis, and Moroccans were all Arabic-speaking peoples, but "what an enormous gap separates all three languages! The Egyptian can barely understand the Moroccan or the Hijazi when he speaks."[110] The key to this conundrum for Husayn lay in the fact that Arabic had lost its original homogeneity upon expanding into different geographical regions. It had been recast into several distinct dialects, each bearing the imprint of the territory and the territorially derived cultures of these various regions. The Arabic language had not changed Egypt; rather, the Egyptian environment and the national personality shaped by the milieu of Egypt had altered the very language of the Arab conquerors.[111]

The evolution of a distinctive Egyptian form of Islam received even greater emphasis from proponents of the territorial interpretation of Egyptian history. Muhammad Husayn Haykal dealt extensively with the "Pharaonic foundations" apparent in Egyptian popular Islam.[112] Haykal argued that many Pharaonic rituals and customs, such as marriage rites, circumcision practices, even hair styles, "are maintained in Egypt today just as they were six thousand years ago. Since the dawn of history through all the successive religions which have prevailed in Egypt, they have not altered."[113] Haykal attached particular importance to the fact that Pharaonic customs could be found continuing in both the Coptic and the Muslim communities in Egypt. His argument emphasized the unique features of death and burial customs in Egyptian Islam, which he held were unparalleled in any other Muslim country and which he traced to ancient Pharaonic burial practices.[114] Additional evidence of the continuing importance of Pharaonic religion in modern Egypt was also found in the practices of Egyptian Sufis, particularly in view of Sufism's hold upon much of the Egyptian peasantry. In Haykal's view it was not accidental that Sufi Islam focused on local saints [*awliya*] and celebrated their birthdays [*mawalid*]. Haykal saw these customs as clear Pharaonic survivals that had become internalized deep within the Egyptian national personality.[115]

A more emphatic statement of the same viewpoint was offered by Ahmad Husayn. In his view, Egyptian Islam had divorced itself completely from its Arab roots. Islam in the Nile Valley had taken on symbols, customs, and practices that derived directly from ancient Egyptian religion. The religious life of the Egyptian masses in particular was based on local Egyptian, sometimes even pagan, customs and traditions rather than on the "imported" tenets of orthodox Islam.[116] This could be seen in many features of Egyptian Islam. The mosques of Egypt that adhered to Pharaonic architectural principles; the local pilgrimages to the tombs of Sufi saints and the prayers recited there; the music that accompanied the reciting of the *Qur'an* in Egypt; the funeral arrangements, burial practices, and even the tombs found in Islamic Egypt: "all these are things that the [Islamic] religion does not recognize and indeed abhors."[117] They are found in Egyptian Islam, however, "because the Egyptian cannot absorb a religion except in a manner which is in harmony with his own disposition."[118]

Tawfiq al-Hakim attempted to demonstrate the local character of Islam in

Egypt from a different perspective. For him, the ascendancy of the Egyptian personality over the Islamic religion in Egypt manifested itself most clearly in the architecture of Cairo's leading mosques.[119] Unlike all other Islamic countries, mosques in Egypt were built according to the model of Pharaonic monuments, which themselves were completely alien to the primitive and puritanical nature of Islam. Their size, solidity, and breadth, their simplicity of line, their echoing of Pharaonic decorative motifs—all these were unusual in view of the total absence of an indigenous architectural tradition in Islam. What was called Islamic architecture really expressed the continuity of the Pharaonic artistic tradition within Islam in Egypt. The Egyptian architect could draw his inspiration only from "the history of his soul and his country": thus he had created "a personal art that has no connection with anything beyond this soul and this country."[120]

In literature as in art, Egyptianist intellectuals often found a uniquely Egyptian spirit persisting in what at first sight appeared to be an alien cultural body. For Taha Husayn, "the Egyptian personality" had continued to express itself within the Egyptian Arabic literature produced in Egypt: although weakened by Arabo-Islamic influences, it nonetheless "never died and was never effaced, but remained alive."[121] Similarly Muhammad Husayn Haykal praised the work of medieval poets such as al-Baha' Zuhayr and Jamal al-Din ibn Nubata for its distinctively Egyptian character, finding "the sweet spirit of the Nile flowing in this Arabic Egyptian poetry."[122] The most sweeping statement of the continuing vitality of the Egyptian national personality in Egyptian Arabic literature was Muhammad 'Abd Allah 'Inan's assertion that

> Arabic literature in Egypt [has] a deep Egyptian tone which distinguishes it from all other Arabic intellectual traditions in the East or the West. Thus the Arabic literature which developed in Egypt is Egyptian. It flourished and blossomed as Egyptian. The impact and influence of Egyptian society stamped it and guided it more than any other factor.[123]

In short, within a few years of its appearance in Egypt, Islam had become Egyptian national Islam. The perduring Egyptian national personality had succeeded in dissolving Islam's original characteristics and in replacing them with distinctively Egyptian traits. It was not Islam that had formed Islamic Egypt; rather, it was the Egyptian personality that had modified Islam and adapted it to the Egyptian milieu and to the character of the Egyptian nation. Thus the Islamic period of Egyptian history, more than expressing the strength of Islamic civilization, offered further evidence of the superiority of the Egyptian historical legacy and the unity of Egyptian territorial history.

Another way in which Egyptianist historians of the 1920s attempted to prove the centrality of the Egyptian national personality in determining the course of Egyptian history during the Islamic era was through a chronological survey of the course of Egyptian history from the Arab-Muslim conquest to the present. The general inclination of these historians was to deemphasize the importance of the early Islamic period of the conquests, the Ummayads, and the Abbasids. Instead, their discussions focused on the "Egyptian age" of Islamic Egypt: the long period from Ahmad ibn Tulun in the ninth century to Muhammad 'Ali and his descendants in the nineteenth, when Egypt had usually enjoyed autonomy within the larger Islamic community. This second period—by far the longest of Egypt's Islamic era—provided them with clear evidence of the subjugation of Islam and the Arabs in Egypt to the superior power of the Egyptian national personality.

Exponents of the territorial interpretation of Egyptian history attached little importance to the early Islamic centuries. They portrayed Rashidun (642–661), Ummayad (661–750), and early Abbasid (750–868) rule over Egypt as a transitional period, one that had left no impression on Egypt's territorial history. Eventually, the natural "impulse of nationalism" of the Egyptian people manifested itself to terminate this short-lived period of foreign rule.[124] What was important about these two centuries of early Muslim history in Egypt was their close, when "Egypt arose again fully and completely independent."[125]

In 868 Ahmad ibn Tulun was appointed Abbasid governor of Egypt; he rapidly established de facto autonomy from the dynasty at Baghdad. From the territorial perspective of Egyptian history, his reign marked a new "era of independent Egypt in Islam."[126] Egyptianist intellectuals praised the Tulunids for restoring Egyptian history to its normal territorial course. The autonomous regimes that followed the Tulunids—the Ikhshidids (935–969) but even more the Fatimids (969–1171) and the Ayyubids (1171–1250)—were also presented as having asserted Egyptian independence from centralized Islamic rule and having fostered Egyptian distinctiveness within the Muslim community. The assimilation of these dynastic groups to Egypt, the argument ran, eventually turned them into promoters of Egyptian national interests vis-à-vis other Muslim lands. Their assertion of Egyptian autonomy and their pursuit of purely Egyptian political interests were seen as another indication of the "continuing dominance" of the Egyptian national personality during the Arab-Islamic era.[127]

These Egyptian Islamic dynasties, particularly the Fatimids, were presented as having restored the political and cultural greatness of Egypt, which the early Islamic empire had threatened to destroy. Egypt's traditional status of primacy in the region was reasserted in the new form of cultural preeminence throughout the entire Muslim world. The city of Cairo and the great mosque-university of al-Azhar were both established in this period, the latter soon assuming "the highest standard among Islamic religious universities until this very day."[128] Far-reaching trade links connecting Egypt with the Italian republics developed in this period, bringing considerable wealth to Egypt and making the Egyptian economy the strongest and most developed in the region. This flourishing economic life was accompanied by a cultural renaissance that was reflected in the development of Cairo into one of the largest and most impressive cities of the Muslim world.[129]

Egypt's growing political power and position in the Muslim world were particularly pronounced in relation to the European Christian Crusades. The territorialist interpretation emphasized the "historic role of Egypt" in the successful Muslim resistance to Crusader invasion, indeed portraying Egypt as the savior of the *umma* at a crucial moment in its history.[130] Muslim success against the Crusaders was explained in Egyptian national terms. It was a demonstration not of Muslim sentiment and solidarity but of Egyptian nationalism, Egyptian power, and Egyptian preeminence within the Muslim community.[131] Only Egypt could have led the *umma* to victory over the "foreign conqueror."[132] The fate of the Crusaders was determined not by Islam but by Egypt, which had always been a "cemetery for all invaders."[133]

The proponents of the territorial interpretation of Egyptian history saw the lengthy Mamluk period (1250–1517) as the completion of the process of the reassertion of Egyptian independence and sovereignty during the Islamic era. To Muhammad Husayn Haykal, "the Mamluks even more than the Ayyubids became independent rulers by means of Egypt, and Egypt became independent by means of them."[134] The place of the Malmuks in Egyptian history was sometimes compared to that of the Ptolemys: both groups ruled Egypt for roughly three hundred years; both were characterized by "total assimilation" of the ruling elite through social contact and intermarriage; and both periods were ones of Egyptian greatness, power, and the resumption of Egypt's "classical status" as leader of the region.[135]

The accepted historiographical view of the Mamluks as an alien and oppressive elite was challenged by some Egyptianist historians. They argued that conventional wisdom about the Mamluks differentiated unfairly between the Mamluks as a foreign military elite, on the one hand, and the masses of the Egyptian people, on the other; that it presented an incorrect picture of the relationship between what it portrayed as brutal Mamluks and tyrannized Egyptians. Muhammad Husayn Haykal thus asked if historians were being fair to the Mamluks when they defined their period as "an era of tyranny in the history of Egypt."[136] He pointed out that ruling regimes everywhere at this time were "despotic regimes, for the idea of democracy was totally non-existent."[137] The issue of the Mamluks' supposed regime of oppression was an Egyptian "internal matter" from the nationalist perspective; it bore no relation to the Mamluks' own identification with Egypt and their readiness to struggle against any external force threatening the sovereignty and integrity of the country.[138] Ibrahim Jalal wrote in a similar vein, denying that the Mamluks were a different "nation" from Egyptians. Instead, he argued that "the Mamluks were not a nation, but rather individuals who took Egypt as a homeland, adopting and imitating her people's nature, character, language, sciences, temperament, and traditions as their model."[139] In his review of Egyptian history the Mamluks had "settled amidst the Egyptians, assimilated to them, intermarried with them, involved them in power, and shared all the country's resources with them."[140]

Because of their assimilation to the genius of Egypt, the Mamluk period was portrayed as a new golden age for the country. Politically, Egypt expanded south, west, and east; economically, Egypt became "the commercial crossroads between east and west";[141] culturally, history, geography, poetry, and architecture all flourished.[142] In sum, "their era was one of progress and prosperity. Science spread, the arts blossomed, industry flourished, and commerce was dynamic."[143]

It was equally important from the Egyptianist perspective that the impressive development of Mamluk Egypt came at a time of general Muslim decline. The collapse of the Abbasid Caliphate and the perceived decadence of Islamic civilization were contrasted with Egypt's political, economic, and cultural flowering under the Mamluks. Nor was Egypt's central role in Islamic history under the Mamluks neglected. At a critical moment in Islamic history, it was the Mamluks under Baybars who stopped the seemingly inexorable Mongol tide at 'Ayn Jalut in 1260 and who forced the Mongols back across the Euphrates. Thus was Islam saved from "the Tatar invasion."[144] For 250 years thereafter, it was the Mamluks of Egypt who ensured the continued existence of the Islamic *umma* in the face of repeated Mongol assaults. The symbolic expression of Egypt's evolution into the fortress of Islam, the unchallenged leader of the Islamic community, was the thirteenth-century shift of the Caliphate from Baghdad to Cairo. By becoming the seat of the Caliphate after 1258, Egypt took the place previously occupied by Damascus and Baghdad. Although the Caliphal institution in fact decayed under the Mamluks, who had no interest in restoring its strength, its very location in Egypt during the later medieval centuries signified Egypt's resumption of its historic position as an independent entity.[145]

What was perhaps most important about the Egyptianist treatment of the Mamluk period was the explanation given for the glory of the Mamluks. Egyptian territorial historians had a simple explanation for the contrast between Mamluk greatness and the decline of the rest of the Muslim world. Mamluk achievements derived from the power of the Egyptian environment rather than from Muslim or Turkish sources. It was the vitality of the Egyptian national personality, firmly anchored in the sureties of the Nile Valley and expressing Egypt's eternal aspiration for liberty and independence, which had defeated the Mongols and ushered in an era of Egyptian preeminence in the region and the *umma.*[146]

The territorialist interpretation of Egypt's Ottoman era followed logically from their portrayal of Egyptian independence and greatness under the Mamluks. The Ottoman conquest of Egypt in 1516–1517 was viewed as having at first arrested Egypt's development as a separate national community. The Ottoman success in conquering Egypt and in turning the country into an "Ottoman province" was explained by the fact that the Ottomans were a "great world power" comparable to Greece or Rome.[147] Muhammad Husayn Haykal indeed presented the Ottoman conquest of the Nile Valley as a kind of restoration of Roman rule. In his view, "the Turks ruled Egypt in the Roman fashion," meaning through a hard-handed policy aimed at subjugating Egypt and its people to the needs of Ottoman imperial interests and deriving maximum benefit from the exploitation of Egyptian resources.[148]

But, unlike the Romans' efficient provincial administration which succeeded in dominating Egypt for centuries, effective Ottoman rule over Egypt did not last long. From the perspective of Egyptianist historians such a decline was almost predictable, for "Egypt did not lose her Egyptian personality during the darkness of Turkish rule."[149] From the very beginning of their rule, the Ottomans had been unable to eliminate the power of the Mamluks. By the seventeenth century the Mamluks were recovering strength vis-à-vis the Ottomans and beginning to struggle openly for "the restoration of Egypt's sovereign power and independence."[150] By the start of the eighteenth century, the Mamluks had succeeded in supplanting Ottoman authority over Egypt. Significantly, they did so in alliance with the traditional leadership of the Egyptian people, the urban *'ulama'* and the rural *mashayikh.* Together, this coalition neutralized the Ottoman administration; the Ottoman governor "holed up like a prisoner" in the citadel in Cairo "without possessing authority over anyone or anybody in Egypt."[151]

The process of the transfer of power from Ottoman to Mamluk agents reached full fruition by the middle of the eighteenth century, when the Mamluks regained control of the administration of Egypt. By the later eighteenth century the *shaykh al-balad* 'Ali Bey was in revolt against the Ottoman Sultan, indeed going so far as to declare "the independence of Egypt."[152] Significantly, the title he was credited with assuming was *'Aziz Misr,* "the Mighty One of Egypt" (a term applied in the *Qur'an* to Joseph when he served as minister to the Pharaoh). Thus, two centuries after the Ottoman conquest, Egypt's naturalized "sons" the Mamluks were presented as having restored Egypt to the same independence and regional prominence she had enjoyed in the pre-Ottoman Mamluk period.[153]

Given the pro-Western bias implicit in the Egyptianist approach, the French Occupation of Egypt in 1798 was obviously seen as having opened a major new era in Egyptian history. The Mamluks themselves may have been badly battered by Napoleon's modern army of invasion; "but the Egyptians resisted strongly, until the affair ended with a complete [French] evacuation from the country."[154] Egyptian territorial historians argued that the Egyptian struggle against the French was a further manifestation of the perennial Egyptian desire for independence, merely the latest in a long succession of liberation struggles waged by Egyptians against "foreign imperialist forces."[155] They also maintained that the French Occupation, despite its brevity, had brought benefits for Egypt. It was the French who during their three years in Egypt brought Egypt into the modern era through introducing "the ideas of the French Revolution and the foundations of Western civilization."[156] Thus indirectly, by "opening the eyes of Egyptians to a new life," the French Occupation served as an "agent for the restoration of Egypt to her grandeur and strength."[157]

The French Occupation indeed paved the way for a new renaissance of Egypt, which was realized in the nineteenth century under the great Muhammad 'Ali and his successors. Egyptian territorialist historians heaped praise upon the reign of this founder of modern Egypt. On the external front, they noted, Muhammad 'Ali brought Egypt new power and influence through his creation of a modern Egyptian army and navy.[158] Under Muhammad 'Ali, "Egypt became a great empire with an army that defeated the Turks, the masters of war in Europe, and a navy that turned the Red Sea into an Egyptian lake and that ruled the eastern Mediterranean."[159] Thus Egypt's proper place as primary power in the Arab East had been reestablished.[160] On the domestic front, Muhammad 'Ali was credited with implementing a series of radical reforms in Egypt. In sum, Muhammad 'Ali and his successors opened Egyptian society to far-reaching processes of Westernization and modernization that again put the country on the path of enlightenment and progress.[161]

The achievements of Muhammad 'Ali and his successors, however, were realized at a heavy price: the massive entry of Europe into Egypt, which ultimately led to European occupation and the end of Egyptian independence. The tragedy of nineteenth-century Egypt was presented as the conflict between her "wondrous" growth and development, on the one hand, and "imperialist doctrine" that demanded the reduction of Egypt to subordinate status, on the other.[162] Despite all the efforts of Muhammad 'Ali's successors, especially the Khedive Isma'il, both to continue the development of the country and to reassert Egyptian independence, they were powerless against the pressure of imperialism, which, at the height of its power in the late nineteenth century, eventually brought about Egypt's occupation by Great Britain in 1882. Thus Egypt's nineteenth-century renaissance was cut short and replaced by another period of foreign domination over the Nile Valley.[163]

Modern Egyptian nationalism was of course seen as the historic response to the lamentable position in which Egypt found itself after 1882. Egyptian territorialist historians concluded their sketch of Egypt's new national history on an optimistic note. Reflecting the general mood of Egypt in the post-1919 era, they held that the nationalist movement of the late nineteenth and early twentieth centuries would again lead to Egyptian liberation and salvation. Not only was the most recent foreign occupation of Egypt, that of the British, being reversed, but the present nationalist era was also witnessing the rebirth of the immemorial Egyptian national personality. Once and for all, Egypt would return to her true Pharaonic nature, through which she would realize her full potential of Egyptian authenticity and world glory.[164]

In conclusion, it is important to recognize that the territorial approach to Egyptian history emphasized the Egyptian essence of each phase of the Islamic era while simultaneously challenging one of the fundamental assumptions of both traditional and modern Islamic historiography: the view that the Islamic community or *umma* was an indivisible whole that must be marked by mutual sympathy and solidarity among its different regions and peoples. This was the generally accepted view of Muslim reformers and revivalists in the modern period, from Jamal al-Din al-Afghani and Muhammad 'Abduh in the nineteenth century to Rashid Rida and the *Salafiyya* movements such as the Muslim Brotherhood in the twentieth. This concept had assumed that unity was the natural state of the *umma* and as such a prerequisite of the Arab-Muslim prosperity, power, and cultural flourishing that had characterized the early Muslim centuries. Correspondingly, the later division of the Muslim community into separate regional units was both abnormal and deleterious in its results for the quality of Muslim civilization.

The territorial nationalist historiographical approach inverted this conventional interpretation of Islamic history. Rather than lamenting those "periods of division" of the *umma* in which Egypt had been ruled by autonomous "Egyptian" Islamic dynasties, it presented these periods as both natural and beneficial for Egypt. Egypt's days of prosperity and glory during the Islamic era were seen as having commenced only when the political unity of the Islamic community collapsed: hence the indifferent or even antagonistic attitude of Egyptianist historians to the early centuries of Egyptian Islamic history. It was not unity but diversity that was deserving of praise in Muslim history: only through the political pluralism of the later Muslim centuries had the separate territorial entities of which the *umma* was composed been able to realize and express their proper historical distinctiveness. The true sequence of Islamic history was thus held to be not early unity/success followed by later disunity/failure, but rather the early submersion of different peoples and nations into an artificially unified *umma* followed by their eventual liberation and realization of their proper independence and national authenticity.

8

The Egyptianist Image of Egypt: III. Pharaonicism

Pharaonicism [*al-fir'awniyya*] may be defined as that body of opinion which postulated the existence of a unique and durable Egyptian national essence persisting from the Pharaonic era to the present. According to advocates of the theory, the people of contemporary Egypt were the direct descendants of the people of ancient Egypt and as such possessed the same essential characteristics, qualities, and potential. The first traces of Pharaonic concepts are visible in the thought of Egyptian territorial nationalists of the late nineteenth and early twentieth centuries.[1] However, only with World War I, the Egyptian Revolution of 1919, and the changes in Egyptian life resulting from both did the Pharaonic perspective reach conceptual maturity and receive widespread support from the educated elite of Egypt.

Pharaonicism was the emotional pivot of Egyptian territorial nationalism, the central conviction and aspiration that the other dimensions of nationalist thought were intended to illuminate and serve. The desire for Egyptianist intellectuals to see Egypt rediscover and revert to its authentic Pharaonic character; their belief that Egypt was both obliged and destined to be Pharaonic in its collective consciousness as well as its everyday life; their efforts to Pharaonicize Egyptian literature, art, and culture: all this testifies that Pharaonicism was more than an intellectual construct for its proponents. Its passionate tenor, the utopian visions embodied in it, and the messianic expectation that it could and would be realized in post-1919 Egypt made Pharaonicism the heart and soul of Egyptian territorial nationalism.

It is important to stress that Pharaonicism was not solely an intellectual theory. Pharaonicist intellectuals were not content with mere formulation of theoretical views about Egypt's Pharaonic nature or with the confinement of their ideas to intellectual circles. Rather, they constantly strove to realize and actualize the Pharaonic truths they were rediscovering. They gave a great deal of attention to disseminating the truths of Pharaonicism to the Egyptian public. In textbooks, newspaper articles, fiction, drama, poetry, and the visual arts, Egyptian nationalist intellectuals attempted to spread their enthusiasm for things Pharaonic to all educated Egyptians. Following Haykal's maxim that Egyptians needed above all to "know themselves," they saw their historical role as one of teaching the nation first to acknowledge its Pharaonic "essence" and then to live in accordance with it. Through their efforts, Pharaonicism became a tangible—if transient—feature of the historical development of Egypt in the post-1919 era.

The Biological Basis of Pharaonicism

The sources of the Pharaonic outlook were varied. Obviously, Pharaonicism derived in part from the Egyptian territorial nationalist ideas about geography and history that we have already discussed. But Pharaonicism was not based on these concepts alone. Pharaonicist theory added to these equally important elements the concept that a blood relationship linked ancient and modern Egyptians, creating both physical and mental similarities between them. Indeed, many of the irrational and mythological elements found in Pharaonicism may be traced to its partially racialist basis.

Salama Musa was a leading exponent of the racial basis of Pharaonicism. The thread that runs through all of Musa's Pharaonicist discussions is the assumption that biology was the central element establishing the unity of ancient and modern Egypt. To Musa, the racial bond between the Egyptians of the Pharaonic era and those of contemporary Egypt was a scientific truth that could be demonstrated empirically. This basic racial kinship, he maintained, was the source of those common characteristics in social structure, patterns of thought, and artistic expression that marked the history of the people of Egypt over the millenia. To "those among us who believe that the study of the Pharaohs will not prove useful to us because the bonds of language, religion, politics, society, culture, and the arts between us have been broken," his immediate response was that "this is a mistaken belief, for we have never ceased to be, first and foremost, Egyptians with respect to our racial composition. The same blood flows in our veins which flowed in the veins of our ancestors five thousand years ago."[2] In an article on "We the Egyptians," Musa again emphasized racial descent as the element creating the "familial unity" between the ancient Egyptians and the "modern Pharaohs." "We are a family living in this valley for more than ten thousand years," he asserted; there was not a single person born and raised in the Nile Valley "who does not have a drop of that same blood which flowed in the veins of Ramses, Khufu, Khaf-Re, and Akh-en-Aton."[3]

This belief in the physical connection of ancient and modern Egyptians was frequently voiced by Egyptian nationalist intellectuals. Marqus Samiqa, for example, went so far as to tell an audience of Egyptian students that "[a]ll of you are Copts. Some of you are Muslim Copts, others are Christian Copts, but all of you are descended from the ancient Egyptians."[4] Similarly, Nashid Sayfin asserted that "Egypt is Pharaonic [in] flesh and blood and will remain so forever."[5] In the opinion of Muhammad Zaki Salih, "the blood of Ramses has not ceased to flow in the veins of Egyptians. These are not the assumptions or fantasies of writers, but scientific truths which many scientists are now accepting."[6] Thus from the dawn of history until the present day, the "blood" of Egyptians had remained essentially the same. Despite all the turmoil in their past, Egyptians had been successful in maintaining their racial integrity. Rather than being swamped by groups of foreign origin, the racial stock native to Egypt had been able to maintain its purity, assimilating newcomers to the Nile Valley to itself and imposing its own traits upon them. In the Pharaonicist view, this biological continuity proved the maintenance of Egypt's Pharaonic essence over the millenia.[7]

The above assumptions were of course given a "scientific" basis by Egyptianist intellectuals with a claim to speak in the name of science. Thus the Egyptologist Hasan Subhi proclaimed the biological integrity of Egyptians since the Pharaonic period, asserting that the biological similarity of Egyptians over the ages outweighed the other changes that had occurred in Egyptian life. To him, the biological continuity of Egyptians counterbalanced the alterations that had taken place even in an area as vital as language:

> It is true that my language is Arabic and Turkish. But if you speak of blood, my blood—there you will find no other influence but that of Egyptianism [*al-misriyya*]. . . . My blood is your blood; it is the blood of every one of you; it bears no mark but that of Egyptianism.[8]

Speaking for Egyptian youth rather than for Egyptian science, Ahmad Husayn also insisted upon the "indestructibility" of Egypt's racial stock. For him, "the racial history" [*al-ta'rikh al-jinsi*] of Egyptians was the story of the biological assimilation of the successive invaders of the Nile Valley to the indigenous Egyptian population. Again and again, foreign groups entering Egypt gradually lost their original genetic characteristics and took on those of the native Egyptians.[9] Husayn extended the thesis of the genetic continuity of Egyptians to an assertion of their physical superiority over other races. To him, the "blood" of Egyptians was simply stronger than that of others:

> Egyptian blood has assimilated all the various types of blood of the peoples who have attacked it. It has always emerged the victor whenever it was mingled with other blood.[10]

What was true in general was also true of the Egyptian relationship to the Arabs:

> It is false to say that Egypt is Arab because Egyptian blood has become Arab. Science and history attest that it is false. The Egyptian of today is Pharaonic in his environment, Pharaonic in his blood which no other race has been capable of overwhelming or effecting.[11]

This biological continuity between the Egyptian past and present was also extended into the indefinite future by Husayn. "We asserted that the [current] inhabitants of the Nile Valley are its inhabitants of yesterday, and that it is they who will be its inhabitants of tomorrow—Pharaohs like Ramses and Thutmose."[12]

Perhaps the most influential version of the position that biology made modern Egyptians "Pharaonic" was presented by Muhammad Husayn Haykal. Together with Salama Musa, Haykal was the outstanding spokesman of the Pharaonic interpretation. Particularly important was his article of 1926 on "Modern Egypt and Ancient Egypt."[13] In this attempt to prove the "indivisible organic unity" between contemporary Egyptians and their ancient forebearers, Haykal expounded new Pharaonicist concepts that rapidly became the common property of the entire Pharaonicist school. The essay was frequently cited in the later writings of many other Egyptian Pharaonicist intellectuals.

Challenging the conventional wisdom of the day, which attributed an Arab or Islamic character to Egypt and which held that Egyptians were "completely different" from their Pharaonic ancestors, Haykal instead asserted the "eternal" nature of the connection between ancient and modern Egypt.[14] In his view, a fundamental factor creating this continuity between ancient and modern Egypt was biological descent. But it was the broader repercussions of the physical link that mattered most to him. Biology had forged a "firm psychological bond' that had unified Egypt and its people from the Pharaonic era to the present.[15] Egyptians needed to be made aware of both the biological connection and its cultural implications: "the blood which flowed in their veins flows in yours. [As a result,] those psychological stimuli which moved them move you."[16] Haykal admonished Egyptians in general:

> You are sentenced of necessity, willingly or unwillingly, to surrender to the heritage which has been bequeathed to you. If you should some day look into your heart and take stock of your actions, if you should some day examine your character, analyze your nature, and come to know your true temperament, you would discover that the essential nature of your ancestors has been passed on to you.[17]

Characteristic both of Haykal's approach and the later Pharaonicist outlook was the programmatic, action-oriented emphasis of this article. Perceiving himself as an instructor in Egyptian nationalism, Haykal called upon both his fellow nationalist intellectuals and the Egyptian public as a whole to realize the inherent Pharaonicism of Egypt by reconstructing their links with their Pharaonic forefathers. Speaking as a national guide, he asserted that "it is the privilege and the duty of Egyptians to recall all the hidden treasures of the Pharaohs in order to unite their past and their present."[18] Haykal went on to specify a number of areas to which Egyptians needed to direct their attention in order to revive the Pharaonic heritage. These included the collection and study of ancient Pharaonic literary texts; uncovering and understanding the similarities in the rituals, ceremonies, and customs of ancient and modern Egyptians; appreciating the common social norms and cultural traditions practiced by Pharaonic and post-Pharaonic Egyptians; and analyzing the considerable affinities between the language of ancient Egypt and the contemporary colloquial dialect spoken in the countryside. He placed his greatest emphasis on the need to attempt to identify and comprehend the "Pharaonic elements" persisting in contemporary popular Egyptian Islam.[19]

Thus the Pharaonicism of Muhammad Husayn Haykal had an instrumental quality. It not only illuminated the relationship between past and present but also was intended to shape the future. For Haykal, what once was would again be. Egypt's future was destined to be a Pharaonic one. Because it would be shaped by the inexorable pressures of the Egyptian environment and the equally inescapable force of the biological continuity between Egyptians, Egypt's future course of development had to be Pharaonic in essence. In Haykal's own determinist language,

> there is no way then to deny the firm psychological bond which links Egyptian history from its beginnings to the present [and] to the end of future ages which only history can comprehend. No matter how the means of subsistence may change; no matter how the railroads, ships, airplanes and other forms of trans-

> portation that the imagination of the world will invent may shrink the globe; no matter how the borders between nations will be erased and national sentiment may dwindle: this firm psychological bond will remain forever. As long as the Nile and the skies of Egypt exist, . . . as long as people dwell there and ancestors bequeath to their descendants the mental life which nature has bestowed upon them . . . this [national] character will forever remain as it was at the hour of its creation.[20]

The Pharaonicist Mood

More important than the theoretical underpinnings elaborated for Pharaonicism by Egyptian nationalist intellectuals was the emotional and often irrational aura surrounding the theory. First and foremost, Pharaonicism was a mood, a state of mind, rather than an abstract theory. Hence an appreciation of what it meant to its Egyptian adherents in the 1920s must address its subjective dimensions.

One specific event of the early 1920s that provided an enormous stimulus to the emerging Pharaonicism of the period may also serve as an illustration of its emotional tenor. This was Howard Carter's discovery of the tomb of the Pharaoh Tut-Ankh-Amon in 1922. The discovery of Tut's tomb lent itself to the promotion of Pharaonicism in several ways. First, its timing coincided almost perfectly with the culmination of the Revolution of 1919 in the establishment of a formally independent Egyptian nation-state during the years 1922–1923. Then there was the tomb itself. Discovered intact, untouched by time or bandits, its unprecedented treasures bore irrefutable witness to the wealth, sophistication, and splendor of the Pharaonic predecessor of the new Egypt. The figure of Tut added to the impact. Young, associated with the mighty Eighteenth Dynasty as well as with the reformist Al-Amarna Revolution of his father Akh-en-Aton (which was viewed as distinctly modernist in both the content of its thought and the style of its art), and surrounded by an aura of unrealized potential as a result of his early death, Tut-Ankh-Amon was a vivid symbol of both the glory of the past and the promise of the future. The discovery of the tomb of Tut at precisely the time when an old era of Egyptian submergence was giving way to the revival of the nation was seen as fortuitous for Egyptian history as well as for Egyptian archeology. The event itself was a symbol of the age, of Egypt's impending leap from the gloom of the Ottoman/Islamic era to the light of a new and authentically Egyptian epoch.[21]

The national significance of the discovery of the tomb of Tut-Ankh-Amon appears best in the ceremonial opening of Tut's tomb in March 1924. The event was deliberately timed to coincide with the inauguration of independent Egypt's first elected Parliament in March 1924. Ten days before the opening of Parliament, three trainloads of Egyptian and foreign dignitaries traveled from Cairo to Luxor to participate in the formal opening of the boy-king's tomb. On 6 March the King, deputies of the recently elected Parliament, members of the diplomatic corps, and High Commissioner Lord Allenby were given guided tours of the tomb and the riches assembled therein. As the official quality of the event makes clear, the ceremony was intended to express the identity of the Egyptian nation with its Pharaonic heritage.[22]

This was certainly the spirit with which it was received by the Egyptian public. *Al-Hilal,* perhaps the closest thing to an "establishment" journal at the time, extolled the openings of Tut's tomb and of Parliament as the two most important events of the month; where the latter represented "the beginning of a democratic, constitutional era in this country," the former had "directed attention to the glory of Pharaonic Egypt's civilized and sublime achievements."[23] Even more indicative of the impact of Tut and his tomb at the time was the poet Khalil Mutran's "Hymn to Tut-Ankh-Amon," which appeared in *al-Hilal* in June 1924. Originally Lebanese but resident in Egypt since the 1890s, the venerable Mutran had previously been pro-Ottoman in his nationalist inclinations.[24] Yet even he was prompted to compose an ode glorifying Tut, extolling the glories of eternal Egypt, and linking Tut with the new monarchy and the parliamentary regime:

> I am Pharaoh, Tut-Ankh-Amon am I,
> Lord of the Valley of the Nile, conqueror of foes!
> I am he through whom the worlds
> Does Egypt's glorious past magnify! . . .
> Egypt is still what it was when I belonged to her,
> The possessor of matchless glory,
> It gives me joy
> To see her as she was of old,
> That splendid standing esteemed throughout the world. . . .
> The history of Egypt is still what has been since antiquity,
> A history of advancement and excellence
> All of it [filled with] great achievements,
> And arts, and finery. . . .
> Her present age is my age
> All of it restoring renown and glory.
> Long live [King] Fu'ad on the throne,
> And that peerless leader Sa'd.[25]

Pharaonicist intellectuals frequently referred to the impact of the discovery of the tomb of Tut on their nationalist outlook. To Muhammad Husayn Haykal, the discovery of Tut's tomb was tangible evidence of the firm bond linking modern Egyptians to their Pharaonic ancestors. Every Egyptian, Haykal wrote later,

> applauded with delight the discovery of the antiquities of Tut-Ankh-Amon. Every one of us sang the praises of the civilization of the Eighteenth Dynasty for everything that we have had in common for millenia. Every one of us has thought, "if my forefathers had reached this loftiest of summits, the acme of civilization, why should we not reach the same heights?"[26]

Muhammad Zaki Salih was another Egyptian nationalist intellectual who possessed the firm conviction that the revival of "eternal Egypt" [*misr al-khalida*] was imminent. For him the role of Tut in this revival was a central one: Tut, he maintained, "confirms the rights of eternal Egypt and announces them to all corners of the world." Tut's contribution to the revival of Egypt could not be exaggerated:

> emerging from the depths of centuries and resurrected at the dawn of the Egyptian renaissance, he has become the best expression of modern Egypt's determination to realize its goal of national existence.[27]

The romanticism that marked Pharaonicism can best be illustrated through an examination of Pharaonicist accounts of visits made to the historic sites of ancient Egypt. Pharaonicist intellectuals of the 1920s made a personal pilgrimage to the various Pharaonic monuments situated in Upper Egypt the main method for expressing admiration for, and sense of continuity with, the Pharaonic heritage. The national revival of Egypt demanded direct contact with the Pharaonic legacy. For them, the idea of a pilgrimage to Upper Egypt and its Pharaonic splendors was not primarily an antiquarianist expression of nostalgia. It did not represent a flight from the imperfect and frustrating present to an idealized past, a lost paradise. On the contrary, it was their confidence in the present and their faith in the future that led Pharaonicist intellectuals to insist upon the necessity of such pilgrimages. The concept of the visit to Upper Egypt was thus practical and instrumental in nature. As 'Abbas Mahmud al-'Aqqad expressed the concept in 1924,

> those [Egyptians] who make the pilgrimage [*hajju*] to the tomb of Tut-Ankh-Amon go to it desiring life. . . . They come to unite one age with another, one world with another, to conquer three thousand years packed with emotions, multitudes of thoughts, and hosts of utopian dreams. They come searching for what is new and alive among the hidden treasures of the tombs and the remains of those who have passed away, not what is ancient and decayed in them.[28]

Of the many such pilgrimages to Upper Egypt undertaken during the 1920s, a consideration of three are sufficient to indicate the nature of the phenomenon. The first leading intellectual to undertake such a visit and to expound upon its influence on him was Muhammad Husayn Haykal. As early as December 1922, only a short time after the discovery of Tut's tomb, Haykal hastened to obey the dictates of his "Pharaonic conscience" by visiting Upper Egypt and touring the Pharaonic monuments located there. Haykal's account is noteworthy for its style as well as its content. Passionate in tone, filled with reverence for the subject he is describing, and focused on the subjective meaning of the Pharaonic past rather than its objective reality, Haykal's articles of 1922–1923 seem to have been the model for much of the distinctive jargon of post-1919 Pharaonicism.[29]

The tomb of Tut-Ankh-Amon was not the only site in Upper Egypt that drew Haykal's praise. In great detail, he described his "stunning encounter" with the entire complex of royal tombs in the Valley of the Kings.[30] The wall paintings and reliefs found therein particularly impressed him; to his mind, these looked as new after some four thousand years as if they had just been created.[31] This durability of Pharaonic art led him to meditate upon what he termed "the philosophy of eternalization" that in his view lay at the heart of the Pharaonic worldview. The enormous effort to overcome death that was represented in tombs and art alike was interpreted by Haykal in national terms as indicating a profound Pharaonic sense of responsibility to the nation, a feeling that the Pharaohs had to do all they could to bequeath their monumental achievements to successive generations of Egyptians.[32]

But it was his visit to the tomb of Tut-Ankh-Amon that was the emotional centerpiece of Haykal's account of his pilgrimage to Upper Egypt. His tone was incredulous in describing the contents of the tomb—all the profusion of wealth and talent, the jumble of unparalleled *objets d'art* packed into the tomb "leave the spirit stunned and at a loss in the presence of these wondrous sights."[33] Nor did this impression fade when he and his companions left the tomb; rather, it "became a part of us, [a part] which we feel, of which we are aware, about which we think, and which has an ineradicable effect upon our senses, consciousness, and thought."[34] As the splendor of the Egyptian heritage thus attached itself to the consciousness of those who had visited the tomb, they received an enormous reinforcement of their self-confidence and their faith in the ability of contemporary Egypt to recapture the greatness so evident in the tomb of Tut.[35]

The remainder of his tour of the Pharaonic monuments in the Luxor area only increased Haykal's sense of wonder at the splendor of Pharaonic Egypt. Of the various remains of ancient Thebes, it was the colossal temple complex of Karnak that impressed him most.[36] To Haykal Karnak represented "the holy of holies of ancient Egypt, the majesty of the past and the glory of history, the civilization which has passed from the earth yet is eternal, mankind at the height of its perfection."[37] His awe with "the incredible," as in the tomb of Tut, again produced a sense of helplessness and speechlessness in Haykal.[38] It was the inability of words to express his feelings when confronted with the wonders of Pharaonic Egypt which led Haykal to demand that every Egyptian make a similar pilgrimage in order to experience their majesty for himself.[39] Furthermore, Haykal maintained that contemorary Egyptians could not understand the modern world or realize their potential within it without becoming familiar first with the legacy of Pharaonic civilization:

> As a man of today you will never be able to accomplish anything whatsoever and will be retarded in your understanding of science, art, and the precision characteristic of your age until you have stood in the presence of these monuments which for hundreds of centuries have inspired humble admiration.[40]

As the latter passages indicate, Haykal's concern in these articles on his pilgrimage to the Pharaonic sites of Upper Egypt was not merely with the description of what he had seen. Rather, his deeper purpose was didactic: to present the contemporary implications, the relevance for modern Egyptians, of their Pharaonic heritage. Haykal held that the relationship between ancient and modern Egypt was not a one-sided one in which the present generation of Egyptians drew inspiration from its ancestors but those ancestors themselves were uninvolved in the process. Rather, he viewed the relationship between the two Egypts as one of dialogue in which both parties were actively involved.[41] Thus he asserted that, if contemporary Egyptians could discern the intentions of their ancestors, they would know that "Ramses was urging the Egyptians of today to regain the glory and grandeur which were Egypt's in the days of his power."[42] In turn, modern Egyptians had an obligation to "the immortal dead"; to follow in their footsteps, reviving the splendor of the nation to which they both belonged.[43]

Haykal employed various techniques to emphasize the unparalleled splendor of modern Egypt's Pharaonic heritage. One was to compare the achievements of Pharaonic Egypt with the better known ones of Classical Greece and Rome. When he did so, he obviously found the former to be by far the most impressive. Thus he criticized modern Egyptians who marveled at Greek and Roman art, informing them that they did so only out of ignorance; were they to see the art represented in the tomb of Tut, "their admiration for these [Greek and Roman] statues and paintings would diminish while their eyes, hearts, and minds would be captivated by this king of the Egyptian Eighteenth Dynasty."[44] Haykal contended that the Pharaonic legacy surpassed all others: "can you find a single monument in the whole world which would not be reduced, diminished and dwarfed by the recollection of the greatness of the temples at Karnak?"[45] He did not think so.

Such comparisons naturally led Haykal to a consideration of the relationship of Pharaonic Egypt and the rest of the world. Here his essential point was the world-historical impact of the Pharaonic achievement. The "golden age" represented by the Pharaonic era in Egypt had been a "golden age" of relevance for all humanity.[46] All mankind owed its civilization and progress to the example of ancient Egypt. Pharaonic Egypt had laid the foundations for advanced civilizations elsewhere: while other human societies were still primitive, Pharaonic Egypt had broken through to civilization, thus becoming the exemplar and archetype for the breakthrough to civilization in other regions at a later date. Egyptians needed to "realize that our forefathers are the fathers of art and that Egypt is the cradle of civilization."[47] Beyond this, Haykal asserted that Egypt was indeed "the zenith of civilization"; no later civilization ever reached the same level of achievement as had been represented by ancient Egypt.[48]

Haykal concluded these meditations on Egypt's Pharaonic heritage by coupling the historical mission of Egyptian civilization in the past with what he believed to be the universal mission of modern Egypt. Just as humanity had relied on the leadership of Egypt in ancient times, so it will not be able to progress in the present era "until Egypt shall again lead the way." Egypt had "the responsibility for leading the world along the path of progress and happiness," of once again becoming "the mother of civilization." Correspondingly, the rest of mankind needed "to accept Egypt's precedence and leadership in order to reach ultimate perfection."[49] This messianic expectation was to become a central feature of Pharaonicist thought.

Many other Egyptianist intellectuals visited the Pharaonic sites in Upper Egypt during the 1920s. One was ʿAbd al-Qadir Hamza.[50] Like other Pharaonicists, Hamza reported that his journey to Upper Egypt was a powerful and emotionally moving experience. His tone in describing the various sites he had visited was the usual one of awe combined with reverence. In particular, the remains of ancient Thebes fired his imagination. In his mind's eye, the city was resurrected as he gazed as its ruins:

> Thebes is standing in all its glory before me on the banks of the Nile, Thebes with all its palaces, streets, gardens, residents coming and going, its solemn processions moving on to the temples [to perform the religious rituals] to Osiris or Amon or Ra or other gods.[51]

Typical of his nationalist outlook was the significance he attached to the remains of Thebes; as he put it, "this Thebes has but a single meaning, the strength of the faith of a great nation."[52]

Description was not Hamza's main concern in writing about his trip, however. Description merely served as the setting for the national message that he wished to pass on from these "eternal remains" he had seen. He emphasized two concerns in this respect. First, he admonished modern Egyptians for what he perceived to be their indifference to their ancient heritage. He berated his contemporaries for in effect abandoning the Pharaohs to Western Egyptologists who "exploit them and enrich themselves while we sit by and look on from the sidelines."[53] In his view, there was a real danger that such indifference could lead to Egyptians' "losing the bond between our own time and that of these forefathers."[54] His second concern flowed from the first. This was the necessity for contemporary Egyptians to make the effort to visit Pharaonic sites. Visits to the remains of Pharaonic Egypt played a vital national role for Hamza:

> We Egyptians will be unable to recognize ancient Egypt or our forefathers who taught the Greeks and Romans and created the world's first civilization if we do not look at them through their monuments. We must look at their remains in order to fill our spirit with pride and power, in order to escape this [mentality of] inferiority which centuries of humiliation and slavery have created in us. We must visit them, fill our sight with them, hear with our own ears the acclaim of those from all over the world who make the pilgrimage every day, in order to realize that between us and them there exists a bond which has not been broken.[55]

Haykal and Hamza of course represent the Pharaonicism of an older stratum of Egyptian nationalist intellectuals. What of the Pharaonicism of the younger generation of educated Egyptians? Few passages in Egyptian nationalist literature capture the early outlook of this group better than Ahmad Husayn's recollections of his first visit to Upper Egypt as part of a school tour in December 1928.[56] In its vitalism and dynamism, Husayn's Pharonicism was significantly different from the more reflective mood found in Haykal or Hamza. But other similarities in tone and substance between his and his elders' accounts demonstrate how, at least during its heyday, Pharaonicism was an impressively cross-generational ideology that was accepted and shared by the entire chronological range of the educated Egyptian public.

Husayn's tour began with a visit to the Valley of the Kings. The paintings on the walls of the tombs particularly impressed him. He found it difficult to believe that these paintings had been painted "four thousand five hundred years ago."[57] After inquiring as to whether the paintings had been restored or retouched and informed that they had not, "the amazing truth" of their antiquity led him to burst forth with praise of "the miracle of the paints of ancient Egypt."[58] In his view, these ancient yet alive portraits were a symbol of the eternity and immortality of Egypt itself:

> The whole world is baffled by these magical paints which scorn time, sun, rain, heat, cold, and every other atmospheric phenomenon. They have laughed at all the forces of destruction, to this day remaining so brilliant that you would imagine that they had been done only yesterday. What a wonder![59]

This "miracle" of ancient Egyptian painting led Husayn to a comforting rhetorical question: "have not the sciences of modern centuries a long way to go before they understand the secrets of the arts and sciences of our ancient Egypt?"[60]

Pharaonic painting was not the only aspect of ancient Egypt that excited his wonder. The durability of Pharaonic mummies was another proof of both the continuity of eternal Egypt and its superiority to other civilizations. He scoffed at abortive modern attempts to duplicate the complex process of mummification: "in the context of twentieth-century science, that same wondrous ability to keep the body from perishing over tens of thousands of years [*sic*] seems an impossible process."[61] Husayn's conclusion was again a broader one: the inferiority of modern civilization to that of ancient Pharaonic Egypt. As he put it, his consideration of ancient Egyptian painting at Luxor suddenly led him to the realization that "these ancestors [of ours] knew the secrets and arts of nature in a manner in which we do not even know them today."[62]

The culmination of Husayn's journey to Upper Egypt was an evening visit to Karnak. Like Haykal before him, he admitted an inability to comprehend his own feelings when brought face to face with the marvels assembled there: "I was breathless in the face of majesty and sublimity which fill the heart with a feeling of grandeur and might."[63] As for Hamza at Thebes, for Husayn at Karnak past and present combined. The awesome impact of the site caused reality to blend into myth; Karnak became for him as alive as it had been in the past, an integral part of the Egypt of today:

> I no longer gazed at the pillars and monuments at Karnak with the feeling that they were relics, but as though they were a living thing speaking [to me]. I stood before the soaring obilisk and the pool and the hundreds of statues scattered all about. I stood as though commanded to do so. Indeed, every meter of this land, every inch of it, speaks to me of power and glory. I was envisioning the armies massed behind Thutmose and Ramses, armies which conquered the whole [known] world of the time. I was listening to their songs of victory and imagining the light which radiated from this spot. In short, I was resurrected, yes resurrected; I became a new man.[64]

The last sentence leads to the most important feature of his visit to Upper Egypt for Ahmad Husayn. This was its personal impact upon him. In a revealing passage, Husayn related how opening himself to "the glory of the forefathers" had produced in him a psychological revolution. Longings and aspirations of which he had previously been unconscious became utterly clear as a result of his trip to Upper Egypt:

> I felt rebirth growing and increasing in my soul and mind. . . . [T]hat day was an eternal day in my life . . . because it heralded the beginnings of the change in my soul and my entry into a new world.[65]

The change referred to was a simple but a momentous one: "upon my life I vowed to adore Egypt passionately; I was filled with ardor and fierce love of it."[66] What had happened to him as a result of his trip to Upper Egypt was held out by Husayn as a necessary model for all young Egyptians: just as he had been "resurrected" at Karnak, "in just this way must every youth in Egypt be resurrected. I was recreated in a new mold, and it is indispensible that every youth in Egypt be cast in a new mold."[67]

Both in his autobiography written in the 1930s and in a memoir penned some forty years later, Husayn consistently maintained that "that historic night at Karnak" had had a crucial impact upon his life.[68] He recalled being compelled to address his fellow students even while still at Karnak concerning the meaning of what they were seeing. His message was a powerful one:

> Behold, the present is no different from the past; the human spirit exists in every time and place. Its essence is never changed. . . . What is beyond a doubt is that

> the Nile flowed in the past as it flows today, that the stars shone in the past as they do today. Everything is just as it was.[69]

His point, of course, was the contemporary relevance of this continuity:

> The grandeur surrounding you is not foreign to you. Those who erected all this have bequeathed their power and firmness of will. Egypt which once carried the banner for all humanity is obligated to revive itself in order to return to its previous position. Finally, we must shake off the dust of our apathy and laziness. It is our duty to fill our souls with faith and determination. It is our duty to utilize our courage and strength. It is our duty to strive until we resurrect Egypt in all its power, glory, and greatness.[70]

For the Egyptian younger generation growing up in the Pharaonicist atmosphere of Egypt in the 1920s, the Pharaonic heritage was thus not a dead one with no relevance for their own life and time. Egypt possessed an eternal potential for greatness. The Egyptian younger generation, now reacquainted with the splendor of their ancestors and imbued with the spirit of that great age, had to assume their historic mission of the resurrection of Pharaonic Egypt. In discussing the enormous impact of his trip to Upper Egypt upon his own political career, Ahmad Husayn later put it this way:

> Since that night [at Karnak], I devoted my life to the revival of the glory of Pharaonic Egypt. I joined the partisans of Pharaonicism [*al-fir'awniyya*], and did even too much in this regard through appealing to people to take Pharaonic names—starting with myself. I took the name Ahmas . . . a shortening of my name Ahmad Husayn. I became obsessed with Pharaonicism. I became famous for my Pharaonic mania [*majnun al-fir'awniyya*].[71]

The Journalistic and Literary Dissemination of Pharaonicism

Pharaonic themes made up much of the content of Egyptian territorial nationalism. A concern for the achievements and greatness of Pharaonic Egypt found frequent expression in the leading Egyptianist journals throughout the 1920s and early 1930s. In addition, the period was the heyday of the production of Pharaonically inspired literature—that is, the drama, fiction, and poetry that took Pharaonic Egypt as its subject. Together, this Pharaonicist journalistic and literary production of the period attempted to provide a new content for the cultural life of the new, but yet very old, Egyptian nation.

The didactic quality of much of this Pharaonicist literature deserves emphasis. Pharaonicist intellectuals were not merely concerned with rediscovering Egypt's past as an intellectual exercise; rather, their more vital concern was to make the Pharaonic heritage a living source of inspiration for contemporary Egypt. Perhaps the most relentless of these intellectuals in his insistence on the relevance of ancient Egypt for modern Egypt was Salama Musa. Viewing himself as a popular educator, he saw the popularizing of Pharaonicist concepts as a vital national necessity:

> The study of the Pharaohs is propagandizing for the Pharaohs. We desire this propagandizing because it makes our historical personality complete, promotes our national honor, and enlightens us as to the sources and foundations upon which our civilization, i.e., the civilization of the world, is based.[72]

Musa judged the study of the Pharaonic era solely in terms of "its value for us"; the only reason for inquiry into ancient Egyptian history was that it was essential to the creation of "a modern Pharaonic Egypt."[73]

Among the most basic tools for the dissemination of Pharaonicist ideas were school textbooks. Civics textbooks produced for the schools of the new Egyptian state in the 1920s usually contained chapters or sections on the history and civilization of ancient Egypt.[74] In addition, textbooks dealing specifically with the Pharaonic period were also produced for use in the Egyptian school system. A summary of the contents of the chapters of one such work provides sufficient indication of their Pharaonistic thrust: the civilization and the various dynasties of ancient Egypt; the Pharaonic political system; ancient Egyptian beliefs and gods; Pharaonic architecture; Egyptian agriculture and commerce under the Pharaohs; the development of the ancient Egyptian military and its wars against "foreigners"; and Pharaonic arts.[75]

In the realm of Egyptian journalism, the Pharaonicist mood was apparent first in the visual symbols and contents found in the main nationalist journals of the period. The Liberal *al-Siyasa* and *al-Siyasa al-Usbu'iyya,* for example, used as their masthead the Pharaonic symbol of the winged solar disk of protection associated with the god Horus. Although the weekly *al-Siyasa al-Usbu'iyya* was not an illustrated journal in the strict sense of the term, pictures of Pharaonic objects or scenes frequently accompanied articles dealing with ancient Egypt. The visual aspects of Pharaonicism were even more conspicuous in the Wafdist *al-Balagh al-Usbu'i* and the modernist *al-Majalla al-Jadida,* both of which were given to the publication of multi-page photo essays concerning Pharaonic subjects. This visual emphasis on the Pharaonic legacy was paralleled by the textual content of the leading cultural journals of Egypt of the period. In *al-Balagh al-Usbu'i* of 'Abd al-Qadir Hamza, in *al-Siyasa al-Usbu'iyya* edited by Muhammad Husayn Haykal, in Salama Musa's *al-Majalla al-Jadida,* and in *al-Hilal* for which Musa served as editor for much of the 1920s, numerous articles on Pharaonic Egypt demonstrated the interest of Egyptianist intellectuals in virtually all aspects of Pharaonic life. Particularly in the pages of these three journals, Egyptianist secondary intellectuals filled in the details of the Pharaonicist perspective and contributed greatly to the popularity of Pharaonicism.

Not surprisingly, the science of Egyptology [*misrulujiyya*] came in for a great deal of attention in Egyptian cultural journals in the wake of the discovery of the tomb of Tut-Ankh-Amon. Articles devoted to Egyptology's scientific methods, to its historical development since the late eighteenth century, and to its most prominent discoveries were a standard item in Egyptian periodicals of the period.[76] A parallel type of contribution was interviews with Egyptologists (particularly with the younger generation of emerging native Egyptian archeologists) in which these scholars expounded on their work and its significance for modern Egypt.[77] The collections and operations of the massive Egyptian Museum in Cairo also formed a natural subject of interest in the Pharaonicist atmosphere that characterized Egyptian intellectual circles in the post-1919 era.[78] Egyptianist journals also provided regular coverage of official visits by the leaders of the new Egyptian government to archaeological excavations, presenting such visits as a tangible symbol of the bond between the ancient Pharaohs and the contemporary monarchy.[79]

Of the many dynasties that had ruled in Pharaonic Egypt, Egyptian cultural journals of the post-1919 era gave the greatest attention to the New Kingdom of the Eighteenth, Nineteenth, and Twentieth Dynasties. Particularly attractive to the temper of the times were figures associated with the shortlived Al-Amarna Revolution during the Eighteenth Dynasty: the modernism of the Pharaoh Akh-en-Aton ("one of the most innovative Pharaohs"), the beauty of his consort Nefertiti, and the youth of their son Tut-Ankh-Amon all received repeated attention from Pharaonicist intellectuals themselves enthused with modernism, beauty, and youth.[80] On a less contemplative level, the power and conquests of the great monarchs Ramses I and Ramses II of the Nineteenth Dynasty were cited to prove another equally important dimension of the glory of ancient Egypt.[81]

Pharaonic religious conceptions of course received attention in discussions of ancient Egypt. What is perhaps most interesting in the many articles by Pharaonicist intellectuals concerning ancient Egyptian religion is the contemporary slant given to the Pharaonic past. Sometimes the approach was defensive: to refute contemporary Western assertions that Pharaonic religion was exploitative of the Egyptian people,[82] or to emphasize the religious sincerity of the Pharaonic Egyptians and the vital nexus between their sincerely held religious convictions and their achievements in other fields.[83] The most frequently employed approach, however, was to assert the universal importance of early Pharaonic religious conceptions, analyzing how Pharaonic religion contributed to later religious systems and maintaining that "many ancient Egyptian articles of faith have become part of advanced modern religions."[84]

Salama Musa's arguments concerning the nature and importance of Pharaonic religious concepts and achievements provide an excellent example of the Egypt-centered quality of Pharaonicist discussions about ancient Egyptian religion. His general thesis concerning Pharaonic Egypt's role in the religious history of the world was simple but sweeping. It was Pharaonic Egypt that had originated advanced religious beliefs and disseminated them first through Judaism, then through Christianity, and finally through Islam.[85] The Pharaoh Akh-en-Aton was singled out as the key figure in the origins of sophisticated religious ideas in ancient Egypt; Musa credited him with reaching the point of "true monotheism" before the reactionary priesthood undermined his "monotheistic revolution."[86] Musa also attributed to Pharaonic Egypt both the development of the concept of an afterlife and the elaboration of a "universal treasury of myths" concerning the supernatural and how to manipulate it.[87]

Egyptian cultural publications of the post-1919 era gave great attention to Pharaonic artistic expression. Virtually every aspect of Pharaonic art, from painting and architecture to the design of furniture and clothing, came in for analysis.[88] The conclusion of an article on the construction and aesthetic qualities of the Pyramids illustrates the didactic emphasis that marked much of the Pharaonicist journalistic writing of the period: not only had the world of the Pharaohs "reached the heights of human achievements," but "the sources of its eternal life still throb through the inscriptions and pictures [of the Pyramids]."[89]

Pharaonic literature was another dimension of the ancient Egyptian heritage that was extensively treated in the cultural journals of the day. This was a particular subject of interest to one of the leading Pharaonicist intellectuals of the 1920s, Hasan Subhi, who devoted numerous articles to the language of ancient Egypt and the hieroglyphic script in which it was written,[90] to the analysis of the structure and content of Pharaonic poetry as well as the translation of Pharaonic poems into modern Arabic,[91] and, not least, to the relevance of this Pharaonic literature to contemporary Egyptian "national literature."[92] As might be expected, the thrust of much of the material dealing with this subject was the relentlessly didactic one of establishing the unbroken connection between Pharaonic and modern Egypt. Thus Subhi's "Living Expressions from the Ancient Egyptian Language" and an anonymous piece on "The Pharaonic Language" both had as their ultimate concern the resemblances between the language of the Pharaohs and modern colloquial Egyptian expression, and the corresponding need for contemporary Egyptians to acknowledge and build upon this linguistic continuity between past and present Egypt.[93]

The pragmatic intent undergirding much of the attention given to the Pharaonic legacy by Egyptian nationalist intellectuals in the post-1919 era was best expressed in their discussions of two aspects of Pharaonic Egypt: its grandeur and splendor [the most common terms employed were *majd* and *'azama*] vis à-vis other ancient societies, and its role in the development of the world as a whole. A frequent emphasis of articles on Pharaonic Egypt was the awesome effect Pharaonic monuments, ceremonies, and splendor most have had upon both Egyptians and outsiders privileged enough to view them.[94] Such articles were clearly tendentious, employing the ancient glory and power of Egypt as the inspiration for a more glorious and powerful Egyptian present and future. Like Muhammad Husayn Haykal before them, these authors saw themselves as the restorers of Egyptian national pride, which in turn would serve as the necessary basis for their contemporary nationalism. Ahmad Husayn made the point forcefully when he said that

> we are telling you about your Pharaonic Egyptianness because the secret of your greatness lies in it. We are telling you, believe that you are like your forefathers and that you must restore their glory. Oh Egyptian, believe in your greatness! By the living God you are mighty, great in your origins, great in your past, your present, and your future.[95]

But the world significance of ancient Pharaonic civilization, its decisive role in laying the spiritual and material foundations of human progress, was a subject of even greater fascination for Pharaonicist intellectuals. The concept that Egypt had played a world-historical role was one of the most frequently repeated themes in the Pharaonicist literature of the post-1919 period. Small wonder: for nationalist intellectuals obsessed with shaping a new image for Egypt, one that could restore the self-esteem and pride of the nation, this concept provided seemingly "objective" proof of both Egypt's innate cultural genius and its superiority over other national collectives.

Two sides of Egypt's role in the world at large received greatest attention in articles on the subject. On the one hand, these articles emphasized that the Egyptian contribution to human development had been an absolutely unique and unparalleled one. No other civilization or society remotely approached Egypt in its contribution to world history. On the other, the articles stressed the scope of the Egyptian contribution—that Pharaonic elements and influences could be identified in every "high culture" that had emerged in Asia, Africa, Europe, and the Americas. *Insaniyya* was the usual term for this universalism of the Egyptian contribution to humanity. Egypt's temporal precedence was denoted by such phrases as "Egypt, cradle of world civilization"; "Egypt, source of civilization"; "Egypt, mother of the world"; "Egypt, mother of civilization"; and "Egypt, mother of humanity."

The best example of the tendency to see Egypt as having been of seminal importance in world history is found in the writings of Salama Musa. For Musa, the history of Pharaonic Egypt formed a central part of the history of humanity. Egypt's temporal primacy in the development of civilization had made it the fount of civilization throughout the world. In specific terms, Egypt had been the first country to achieve the material breakthrough from primitive nomadic society to a more agricultural and complex form of social organization.[96] Musa's assumption was that civilization elsewhere had inevitably been influenced by ancient Egypt: "the Pharaohs are not only our forefathers; they are the ancestors of the world."[97] In more graphic terms, Egyptians were a "world people" and their history "universal history."[98]

Much of Salama Musa's historical writing of the period was devoted to the detailed demonstration of these general propositions. Individual articles developed the point for Iraq, where he attributed the origins of Sumerian civilization to Iraq's technological borrowings from Pharaonic Egypt, which in his view had developed prior to Sumer;[99] for the ancient civilizations of India, Central Asia, and Southeast Asia;[100] for Africa;[101] for Central America, where he traced the emergence of civilization to seaborne Egyptian influences;[102] and for the Semitic peoples of the Middle East.[103] He went as far as to assert important Pharaonic influences upon England, with one of his articles attempting an investigation of English geographical terminology in order to show Egyptian linguistic influence.[104] His point in the latter was both thoroughly Pharaonicist and utterly nationalist: "it is true that the English have occupied our country, but history confirms that we occupied their country two thousand five hundred years ago, and that our Egyptian names live on in their cities, rivers and gulfs."[105]

Younger Pharaonicist intellectuals echoed Musa's assertions. For Nashid Sayfin,

> Egypt is the cradle of civilization. . . . It is Egypt which invented the art of writing which became the soul of civilization and the secret behind its existence. It is Egypt which raised agriculture from its primitive phase to that of mechanized farming, and whose devices are still used in Egypt and elsewhere today. . . . It is Egypt which created the most perfect political regime of its day. It is Egypt alone which deserves the sole credit for being the first to introduce the traditions and symbols of monarchy. With its beliefs, Egypt paved the way for the other nations which followed it. It believed in the Day of Resurrection, the Day of Judgment, rewards and punishments, the fundamental articles of religion which no other people in the world prior to the Prophets had believed in save Egypt. . . . This is our Egypt, the noble Egypt of the Pharaohs.[106]

As usual, Ahmad Husayn was even more graphic and forceful:

> In ancient times, when mankind lived in caves and jungles and was close to the animals, the first civilization arose on the banks of the Nile. This was a civilization which put to shame every other civilization of the past and present. Thus Egypt took the hand of mankind thousands of years ago and led it out of the

jungle and into civilized habitations, out of barbarism into organized life, out of ignorance into knowledge.[107]

Pharaonicist intellectuals were able to find significant traces of Pharaonic influence almost everywhere. Salama Musa was able to find Pharaonic precedents for later intellectual developments as diverse as Judaic wisdom literature (the Biblical Book of Proverbs was "none other than the proverbs of the Egyptian Amenophis"), the Greek epics (much of Homer's *Iliad* "originated in Egyptian stories"), and both Greek and Arab aphorisms ("many of the proverbs and aphorisms which we believe were originated by the Arabs or the Greeks were in fact the creation of the Egyptians").[108] The "universal" concepts of Pharaonic Egypt were sometimes presented as the "spiritual source" of more contemporary intellectual currents as well. Salama Musa, for example, credited much of the thought of the modern European Enlightenment to Pharaonic inspiration. Without the intellectual achievements of the ancient Egyptians in regard to the mastery of nature, the Enlightenment would not have been possible.[109] Musa's own claims concerning the later reverberations of Pharaonic thought spanned much of modern history as well as much of the world. At one point, he asserted the influence of "Pharaonic ideas" on thinkers as diverse as Rousseau, Tolstoy, and Gandhi.[110]

Pharaonic Egypt's material contributions to the development of humanity came in for equal attention. Numerous articles in Egyptian cultural journals expounded on the ancient Egyptian invention or discovery of many basic features of material culture. Reading and writing; chairs, tables, and eating utensils; glass and glass vessels; public buildings and planned housing developments; the use of pillars in architecture; boats for transportation and trade; the use of gold in art and exchange; both democracy and an organized military; and the foundations of the sciences of astronomy, chemistry, biology, geography, and mathematics—all these and more were traced to ancient Egypt.[111] The thrust in such analyses was invariably to demonstrate both the temporal precedence of Egypt in regard to such aspects of civilization and its far-reaching impact on the rest of the world. In regard to any originally Egyptian developments that could possess both positive and negative implications, it was of course the former that were stressed. In Muhammad Lutfi Jum'a's "Egyptian Democracy in the Pharaonic Age," for example, Jum'a's concern was to refute the belief that the Pharaonic elite had enslaved and exploited the masses. In his view, the glorious achievements of the Pharaonic past were simply inconceivable without the existence of freedom and harmony in Pharaonic society; Pharaonic class divisions were termed "purely theoretical" and Pharaonic society was evaluated as having been "based on liberty, equality, and fraternity."[112] Jum'a went on to maintain that recent archeological and historical evidence demonstrated the influence of this first "democracy" on the more famous democracy of classical Greece: "the countries of the Greeks were themselves *poleis* similar in their political systems to those of the ancient Egyptians."[113]

The last point was particularly important to Pharaonicist intellectuals. Constantly aware of the historical significance accorded the civilizations of classical Greece and Rome in the subsequent evolution of Europe and by extension in the development of the modern West, they appear to have felt obliged to show that all humanity, Europeans included, was far more indebted to Pharaonic Egypt than to ancient Greece and Rome for the seeds of progress. In their view the Pharaonic heritage was the ultimate source of much of the inspiration of the Renaissance, the Enlightenment, and modern Europe's scientific and philosophical development in general. Their argument was a simple but powerful one: since Greece and Rome had drawn so much of their culture from Pharaonic Egypt, it was the latter that needed to be acknowledged as the true originator of civilization and the real source of its concepts and techniques.[114]

Again Salama Musa provides the best example of the trend. Musa's particular concern in his discussions of the place of Pharaonic Egypt in relation to the rest of the world was to promote Egyptian claims of primacy vis-à-vis its northern rival. Where Egypt was termed "the first cradle" of civilization, Greece was "the second cradle."[115] Egypt's contribution to world history in the areas of material life, art, and religion were evaluated as more important than those of Greece in commerce and philosophy. In addition, Musa credited much of Greek science, philosophy, literature, and art to Egyptian precedents, the elaboration of themes original to Egypt.[116] In turn, the Greek impact upon the rest of the world was in part the continuation of Egyptian influence: "the diffusion of Greek civilization is indirect evidence of the diffusion of ancient Egyptian civilization."[117] Greek civilization was thus not an "original creation" but rather a "further development" of the civilization of Pharaonic Egypt.[118]

What Musa developed for Greece 'Abd al-Qadir Hamza maintained for both Greece and Rome, arguing that the bulk of the cultural achievements of Greece and Rome were due to Egyptian inspiration. Citing Gustave Le Bon's *Egyptian Civilization,* Hamza asserted that "these two civilizations [Greece and Rome] were linked to Egyptian civilization; both of them copied all the elements of their life from its sciences."[119] Muhammad Zaki Salih offered a more sweeping version of the same argument:

> The Greeks, with all their gracefulness of expression and the noble thought processes which they have provided; the Romans, with all their forcefulness in administration and the high [example of] determination in government which they have furnished; and even the Anglo-Saxons, who exemplify vigorous greatness [today]—are all humble in the presence of eternal Egypt. They salute Egypt as a soldier salutes his commander or a pupil his teacher. And no wonder, since Egypt is the first teacher of all nations and peoples.[120]

The motive underlying this apologetic approach to history is obvious; Egyptian superiority to ancient Greece and Rome served as a powerful reinforcement for the feelings of national self-assertion and pride that were the root concern of the Pharaonicist impulse.

The purpose of this image of Pharaonic Egypt as the first teacher of humanity was not only to serve as a source of Egyptian national pride, however; many Pharaonicist intellectuals also looked to the future. They assumed that Egypt's post-1919 revival and the Pharaonic renaissance of which they were part would also bring the eventual return of Egypt to its former position of leadership and primacy in the world at large. Pharaonicism possessed a definitely messianic quality. At their most visionary, Pharaonicist intellectuals saw modern Egypt and its people possessing the same mission for all humanity that their forefathers had had; that of leading the way to further human progress. Such a world role was inherent in the nature of Egypt; Egypt had always had "a universal message for the world at large."[121] As the world's first civilization, it necessarily followed that modern Egypt would inevitably play a "major role in the advancement of contemporary civilization."[122] The past showed the way to the future. Thus for Salama Musa, the entire purpose of Egypt's contemporary Pharaonic revival was to "spur us on to return to the position of leadership of mankind which our forefathers held."[123] Ahmad Husayn put the messianic interpretation in stronger language, confidently predicting that, when Egyptians had successfully revived "our Pharaonicism . . . the whole world will rejoice in the new civilization which will be resurrected on the banks of the sacred Nile."[124]

One of the most sweeping philosophical statements on the chosen nature of eternal Egypt came in an editorial in *al-Siyasa al-Usbu'iyya* of 1928. It grounded Egypt's universal and continuing mission to mankind in both the history and the geography of the country. Because of its unique geopolitical location, from its inception Egypt had been literally the center of the world, the "eternal" crossroads at the heart of the great transformations that had occurred in the evolution of humanity.[125] In more metaphysical terms, Egypt had always been the cockpit of history, the site of the perpetual struggle between "light and darkness," "truth and falsehood," "right and wrong."[126] Egypt's mission was thus unending. Anchored in the natural order of the world, this mission derived from the very nature of the country. But it was also a world-historical role within the capabilities of Egypt. In the past, the country had proved itself more than competent in meeting the obligations imposed on it by its central location. Therefore, just as Pharaonic Egypt had been well aware of its special place and acted accordingly, so must modern neo-Pharaonic Egypt do the same.[127] The journal thus presented a messianic vision of eternal Egypt returning to its true place in the order of things, that of "the center of creation" and the beacon of progress for all the world. As the center of the cosmic struggle between good and evil throughout time, Egypt's present revival would again make the country the source of "light, truth, and guidance for East and West alike."[128]

The Pharaonic perspective naturally manifested itself in Egyptian literature of the post-1919 period. Pharaonic themes were particularly prominent in Egyptian drama and poetry, and were occasionally to be found in the nascent Egyptian fiction of the period as well. It was characteristic of the generally Pharaonicist mood of the times that even authors who were not Pharaonicist in their general orientation nonetheless periodically made Pharaonic Egypt the subject of their writings. While there is considerable scope for further research on this broad topic, here we wish to note some of the more important Pharaonicist literary compositions of the era.

One of the most striking uses of Pharaonic themes in post-1919 Egyptian literature occurred in the genre of drama. Several plays set in ancient Egypt and filled with admiration for its achievements were written and performed in Egypt in the later 1920s and early 1930s. One of the most illustrative of the genre was Ahmad Zaki Abu Shadi's *Akh-en-Aton, Pharaoh of Egypt* (1927). Here one of modern Egypt's most talented and most Pharaonicist poets recreated the febrile mood of the Al-Amarna period and the attempted religious, intellectual, and cultural revolution that it witnessed. Akh-en-Aton himself was repeatedly extolled as a "reformer" and a "revolutionary" for his sweeping innovations; his "heroic struggles" against the forces of conservatism and reaction embedded in the priestly class and the royal establishment received equal emphasis.[129] Characteristically, the author of the drama viewed Akh-en-Aton's goals and aims as the distinctively modern ones of peace, human brotherhood, and the welfare of society.[130] The sudden illness and death of this great reforming Pharaoh and the resultant failure of his "revolution" were naturally defined as an enormous loss both for Egypt and the world.[131] Abu Shadi summarized the conclusion of the drama as follows:

> The curtain falls on the end of the greatest of poets and thinkers, who grasped the significance of human brotherhood from the dawn of history . . . who sacrificed majesty and power in order to promote his sublime ideals and to diffuse his spiritual and intellectual creed.[132]

The loss was not total, however. Again in the words of the author, "he became a source of eternal inspiration for emissaries of peace throughout the generations."[133]

A parallel piece was Ahmad Sabri's play *The High Priest Amon: A Pharaonic Drama* (1929). This, too, had as its subject the radical religious revolution of the Pharaoh Akh-en-Aton. The attitude to the reforming Pharaoh and his measures of reform was suitably adulatory; his era was one of "artistic and expressive creativity."[134] Nor was the reaction to Akh-en-Aton's attempted reform presented as having totally erased his positive, progressive impact. Sabri saw both his aim of "kindling the [Egyptian] national spirit" and his policy of religious tolerance as having been adopted by later Pharaohs, as well as his ideas in a more general sense having become the "living legacy" of later generations of Egyptians.[135]

The Pharaonic age was often set to music. Two popular productions of the 1920s were *The Glory of Ramses* (1923) and *Tut-Ankh-Amon* (1924), both written by Mahmud Murad with music composed by Sayyid Darwish. Ahmad Husayn later testified to the considerable influence of the plays of Murad and Darwish upon the Egyptian younger generation that was coming to political awareness in the 1920s.[136] His secondary-school drama group staged both productions in the later 1920s. Husayn had been particularly impressed by *The Glory of Ramses.* When at Karnak, for example, overcome by the splendor of what they were seeing, the students had burst out singing Murad's and Darwish's songs: "suddenly we realized that we were repeating the entire script, melody after melody and word for word. We spent three hours at the gates of Karnak, chanting [the play's] songs of glory and pride."[137]

To this list of Pharaonicist dramas must be added Tawfiq al-Hakim's first two plays, *People of the Cave* (1933) and *Sheherazade* (1934). These two philosophical dramas dealt respectively with "the contest between time and man" and "the contest between man and space."[138] The fact that Hakim, who was later to become a prolific playwright, never returned to Pharaonic themes with the same single-mindedness as is found in these two early pieces indicates the power of the Pharaonicist mood of the period upon Egyptian creative expression up to the mid-1930s.

Pharaonic themes appeared in Egyptian fiction in the 1920s as well. Fictional treatments of the Pharaonic period were published in the genre of popular prose entertainment, such as the tale of [Queen] *Nafrat, or the Sweetheart of Pharaoh*

[*Nafrat aw 'Ashiqat Fir'awn*] (Cairo, 1928), an historical romance set in the Ancient Kingdom.[139] In the genre of the short story, Muhammad Husayn Haykal wrote several stories revolving around Pharonic motifs in the 1920s and early 1930s. Haykal's concern in these tales seems to have been to recreate the mythological inner universe of the ancient Egyptians in a manner that would allow modern Egyptians to share the emotional and spiritual world of their ancestors.[140]

The most famous work of fiction of the period dealing with Pharaonic themes was of course Tawfiq al-Hakim's *Return of the Soul* [*'Awdat al-Ruh;* written in 1927, published in 1933]. As we have seen, it gave voice to both the intensely anti-Arab mood of the post-1919 era and the passionate hope of Egyptian nationalist intellectuals for the contemporary revival of an authentically Egyptian spirit in the new Egypt. What needs emphasis here is its profoundly Pharaonicist quality. In part inspired by the ancient Egyptian myth of "rebirth" associated with the God Osiris, and making frequent use of the Pharaonic *Book of the Dead,* its symbolism centered on the theme of modern Egypt's current revival after millenia of national eclipse. In its vision of a new Egypt rising from the turmoil of nationalist revolution, *'Awdat al-Ruh* is perhaps the best literary manifestation of the Pharaonicist spirit of the post-1919 age in Egypt.[141]

Pharaonicism was expressed more frequently and more clearly in the production of Egyptian poets of the post-1919 era. In poetry more than in any other artistic genre, the prevalent modes of expression up to the 1920s had been conservative or at most neo-classicist. By the 1920s, however, even poets whose previous outputs had been predominantly traditionalist in style and content began to express the Pharaonic mood of the new era. Khalil Muftan, Ahmad Shawqi, Hafiz Ibrahim, Muhammad Wali al-Din Yakan, Muhammad 'Abd al-Muttalib, Ahmad al-Kashif, Ahmad Muharram, and (to a lesser extent) Isma'il Sabri to various degrees replaced their prewar espousal of Egyptian patriotism within a wider Ottoman-Islamic context with a postwar orientation to Egypt as an independent national entity. With regard to Pharaonicism in particular, the postwar poetry of Egypt's leading poets dealt with many of the same Pharaonic themes that preoccupied Pharaonicist intellectuals of the period, and expressed in poetic form much the same belief that the post-1919 era would mark the beginning of a new neo-Pharaonic period of Egyptian grandeur.[142]

No poet expressed the changing temper of the times better than the venerable Ahmad Shawqi, acknowledged doyen of Egyptian poets in the early decades of the twentieth century. Like other writers of the day, Shawqi too viewed Pharaonic Egypt as "the cradle of human civilization" that had provided the basis for later civilizations.[143] Also like others, he emphasized the role of ancient Egypt in the genesis of classical Greek and Roman civilization. The Pharaohs

> Were a luminous shooting star when earth was night,
> When human beings were lost and much astray
> By their light went Rome through the world—
> By their gleam did Athens derive its wisdom.[144]

In other poems Shawqi praised ancient Egypt as the source of human knowledge as well as the birthplace of monotheistic religion, which had brought humanity from savagery to enlightenment.[145] Specific poems of a Pharaonicist nature by the "prince of poets" included three compositions about King Tut and his tomb as well as poems about the Pyramids, the Sphinx, and Ramses II.[146] Like all Pharaonicists of the period, Shawqi's nationalist poetry constantly searched for the relevance of the glory of Pharaonic Egypt for contemporary Egypt. His poems called upon the youth of Egypt to draw self-confidence and vitality from "the greatness of the[ir] Pharaonic forefathers" as well as to emulate the human greatness and majesty apparent in the achievements of the Pharaohs.[147] Thus even the leader of prewar poetic neo-classicism and pro-Ottomanism expressed many of the Pharaonic views characteristic of Egyptian intellectuals in the post-1919 era.[148]

If older Egyptian poets of previously conservative views found themselves carried away with the Pharaonic mood of the 1920s, it is hardly surprising that younger Egyptian poets demonstrated a similar or even greater degree of enthusiasm for Egypt's Pharaonic heritage. As early as 1921, the controversial collection of modernist poems published by Ibrahim ʻAbd al-Qadir al-Mazini and ʻAbbas Mahmud al-ʻAqqad, *al-Diwan,* contained several Pharaonic poems.[149] In 1926 Ahmad Zaki Abu Shadi published a collection of his work entitled *The Land of the Pharaohs* [*Watan al-Faraʻina*], all of which was devoted to the adulation of the "glory of ancient Egypt," to praise of the monumental remains of Pharaonic art, and to expressions of desire for a revival of the golden age represented by Pharaonic Egypt.[150]

Even more illustrative of the Pharaonic outlook of the period is the poetry of young Egyptians who began to publish only in the wake of the nationalist Revolution of 1919. Such poets were even more deeply affected by the Pharaonic perspective than were their elders. Muhammad al-Asmar may serve as a representative of this demi-generation of youthful poets influenced by the Pharaonic outlook. In a composition of 1927, Asmar vividly contrasted the enormous differences between the Egyptian and the Arab cultural heritages. When considered in the context of the greatness of the Pharaonic ancestors of the Egyptian people, the poet argued, the achievements of the ancient Arabs were insignificant. Asmar disparaged the literary creativity of the two great Ummayad poets al-Farazdaq and Jarir. If only they had been aware of the earlier greatness of Pharaonic Egypt, he maintained, they would never have boasted of their Arab geneologies. As he stated the comparison,

> Oh thou Farazdaq . . .
> If only you knew who the Pharaohs were
> You would never have boasted, saying
> "These be my ancestors," in whom you take pride.[151]

Benchmarks of Pharaonicism

The Pharaonic mood that developed within Egyptianism in the post-1919 era did not remain at the same level through time. As we have noted, its emergence dates from the inauguration of the independent Egyptian monarchy and the parallel discovery of the tomb of Tut-Ankh-Amon in the early 1920s. It reached its height between perhaps 1924 and 1930, when the burgeoning press of a now-peaceful and seemingly progressive Egypt was filled with a chorus of praise for Egypt's ancient Pharaonic legacy. By the early 1930s, however, the Pharaonic mood began to fade in the face of the failures that "eternal Egypt" experienced after 1930 and the emergence of new stimuli to a broader sense of national self-definition that began to appear by the 1930s.

Two episodes of the late 1920s and early 1930s may serve to illustrate the brief popularity but eventual decline of the Pharaonic outlook. The first is the erection, the unveiling, and the public response to the colossal sculpture "The Revival of Egypt" [*nahdat misr*], which was meant to symbolize Egypt's rebirth after the Revolution of 1919. The second is the controversy surrounding the design of the tomb and the public monuments commemorating the leader of the Revolution, Sa'd Zaghlul.

The idea of the erection of a public monument to celebrate the contemporary "rebirth" of the Egyptian nation dates from 1919–1920. Under the impact of the Revolution of 1919, a promising Egyptian sculptor working in Paris, Mahmud Mukhtar (1891–1934), began work on a sculpture intended to commemorate the national revival of Egypt. He displayed a model of the same at a Parisian art exhibition in 1920, where it won a prize. Mukhtar's work and its favorable reception immediately impressed Egyptian nationalist leaders: in 1920 a campaign in the Egyptian press resulted in a public fundraising drive and the formation of a quasi-official committee (headed by former Prime Minister Husayn Rushdi) to finance and supervise the creation of a large-scale reproduction of Mukhtar's model. The monument was to be created from Egyptian granite quarried at Aswan in order to mirror the Pharaonic use of that stone. In 1922 huge blocks of raw stone were floated down the Nile, again in imitation of ancient Pharaonic practice. Mukhtar completed the statue itself in the square in front of the Cairo train station. Its style may be termed Pharaonic realist: a massive Sphinx-like figure next to which stands the several times life-size figure of an Egyptian peasant woman, one hand resting on the Sphinx's head, the other removing her veil as she gazes into the distance. The former figure was intended to represent the antiquity and perdurance of the Egyptian national heritage; the latter one symbolized both the Egyptian peasantry who embodied the authentic national character of Egypt and (in the gesture of the removal of the veil) the need for social as well as cultural modernism and liberation. The base carries, in Arabic and French, the name of the work: "Nahdat Misr"/"Le Réveil de L'Égypte."[152]

On 20 May 1928 an official ceremony was held to formally unveil "The Revival of Egypt."[153] It was meant to officially celebrate the process of Egypt's national rebirth over the preceding decade as well as to emphasize to the Egyptian public and the world at large the Pharaonic nature of that renaissance. In attendance were King Fu'ad, high court officials, the British High Commissioner Lord Lloyd, dignitaries from al-Azhar, and of course Prime Minister Mustafa al-Nahhas, all his ministers, much of Parliament, and the press. While the project as a whole was not an exclusively Wafdist initiative, there is little doubt that the Wafdist ministry in office at the time did all it could to exploit the occasion to its own advantage. All in all, the event was a Pharaonic—and a Wafdist—revel.[153]

The major address at the ceremony was delivered by Prime Minister Nahhas.[154] He began with the obvious praise for the sculpture and its creator, Mahmud Mukhtar. The latter was extolled for his successful effort at embodying "eternal Egypt" in art, for developing an artistic concept that united different aspects of Egypt's long history, and for providing a genuine artistic expression of the unceasing greatness and glory of the Egyptian nation.[155] He had even stronger words of praise for the statue itself. It was a symbol of

> the bond uniting different phases of Egyptian history, past, present, and future. It represents the glory of the past, the earnestness of the present, and the hope of the future. It represents a picture of young Egypt preoccupied with the Sphinx so that it may revive through her and she through it, directing its glance towards its old power and copying the glorious precedent of its reawakening. . . . If there is a single nation whose ancient past vindicates its current rebirth, that nation is Egypt.[156]

The remainder of Nahhas's speech demonstrated the diffusion of Pharaonicist phraseology from the intellectual into the political realm which had occurred over the course of the 1920s:

> Since ancient times [Egypt] has been the cradle of civilization and the source of human wisdom. Her glory evolved progressively through successive epochs until she became the master whose authority the entire world learned to venerate. . . . Civilization and wisdom spread from her to the Greeks, to Rome, to the radiant Arab state, and to Europe.[157]

Egypt's modern renaissance was set against this backdrop of past greatness. In Nahhas's view contemporary Egypt was renewing her Pharaonic greatness "with the absolute certainty that this remarkable vitality [demonstrated by history] had remained slumbering for thousands of years, hidden in our souls, never ceasing to exist."[158] The current process of national revival was so powerful that "awakening Egypt has achieved in a few years [that is, 1918–1928] what she could not previously achieve in many decades."[159] Nahhas's conclusion was a predictably optimistic one. Addressing his royal and notable audience with confidence, he informed them that "this revival shall remain, God willing and thanks to your patronage, the inspiration of the nation's determination."[160]

The remainder of the ceremony possessed much of the same Pharaonicist quality as that visible in Nahhas's speech. After a poem by Egypt's "national" and now Pharaonicist poet, Ahmad Shawqi, was recited,[161] King Fu'ad was asked to unveil the statue. At the King's command *Nahdat Misr* was officially unveiled. The ceremony concluded with Mukhtar standing next to his creation as the crowd of honored guests filed past and offered their accolades.[162]

Reaction in the Egyptian nationalist press to the unveiling of Mukhtar's *Nahdat Misr* was predictably enthusiastic. The cultural journal *al-'Usur* characterized the statue itself as "a unique work of art which speaks of the grandeur of thought [now] awakening in the soul of the Egyptian people and calling it to assume its rightful place among the peoples of the world in view of its eternal history."[163] While the Liberal *al-Siyasa al-Usbu'iyya* naturally gave less attention to the Wafdist aspects of the event, it nonetheless celebrated its Pharaonic content. Its editorial on the unveiling concluded by praising the ceremony for having brought together representatives of from all walks of life in an event that symbolized the unity of the Egyptian nation in "one soul, the soul of eternal, immortal Egypt."[164] Egyptian poets joined in the acclaim for the statue and its unveiling. In addition to Shawqi's poem read at the ceremony, Khalil Mutran composed an ode in honor of this sculptural "monument to Egypt's renaissance."[165]

The most glowing commentary about *Nahdat Misr* and its unveiling came from the Wafdist press. ‘Abd al-Qadir Hamza’s editorial on the event extolled Egypt’s celebration of “this monument which symbolizes its revival and elevates its name,” calling the statue itself “a national treasure in the care of the nation.”[166] In his view, the statue was not solely a symbol of the contemporary “revival” of Egypt, it was also “a sign of the continuous connection between modern Egypt in its revival and its progress and ancient Egypt, the leader of the world in civilization and progress.”[167]

A fuller analysis of the statue and its national meaning came from the pen of the Wafd’s leading ideologue, ‘Abbas Mahmud al-‘Aqqad. More elaborately than Hamza, ‘Aqqad presented *Nahdat Misr* as a “tangible reflection” of the “total revival” occurring in all spheres of Egyptian life in the wake of the Revolution of 1919.[168] ‘Aqqad lavished praise on the artistic excellence of Mukhtar’s work. But its spiritual meaning and significance impressed him even more. Like Hamza, ‘Aqqad saw *Nahdat Misr* as a reflection of the continuity of Egyptian history:

> Once again the stones of Egypt give expression to what the spirit of Egypt has imparted to them of her ancient past and her great expectations of the present. This is the greater significance embodied in the statue of revival created by the master Mahmud Mukhtar.[169]

‘Aqqad closed his article with a call for further artistic demonstrations of Egypt’s ongoing renaissance. *Nahdat Misr*

> will have no significance unless it is followed by additional testimonies beyond this one statue [which will give expression] to the meaning of national life. We cannot sincerely rejoice [in *Nahdat Misr*] unless it serves us as a prelude to other sculptural masterpieces placed in every square [of Cairo].[170]

Mukhtar’s statue was not the only monumental visual representation of Egypt’s contemporary revival to receive official endorsement and encouragement in the 1920s. A natural subject for memorialization was the leader of the Egyptian Wafd and the Revolution of 1919, Sa‘d Zaghlul.[171] Immediately after Zaghlul’s death in 1927, the Wafdist-Liberal coalition ministry of ‘Abd al-Khaliq Tharwat decided to purchase Sa‘d’s home, the headquarters of the 1919 revolution (popularly known as “the house of the nation” [*bayt al-umma*]), and to convert it into a national museum for the Wafdist leader. The Tharwat ministry also began planning for the construction of a neighboring mausoleum for Zaghlul and for the erection of two statues commemorating him in public squares in Cairo and Alexandria. What is important in the present context is that the latter three memorials to Zaghlul were conceived in a Pharaonic style: the mausoleum was designed to resemble a Pharaonic temple, and the two statues were to be sculpted, like *Nahdat Misr,* of Aswan granite and decorated with Pharaonic symbols. The official intent was clearly to make Sa‘d Zaghlul a symbol of “the Pharaonic spirit which throbs in Egypt.”[172]

The Wafdist government that held office from March through June 1928 naturally facilitated the early planning preparations for construction of the mausoleum and statues. But upon that ministry’s fall in June 1928 and its replacement by a Liberal regime, Zaghlul’s memorials fell victim to partisan politics. In spite of pledges to continue with the mausoleum, the government of Muhammad Mahmud first froze construction for nearly a year, then in May 1929 announced that financial exigencies made it impossible to continue with the project.[173] Only with the return of the Wafd to office in January 1930 was construction resumed on the mausoleum. At this time, however, the original consensus over this memorial to Zaghlul had evaporated. The expense of the project now came in for public criticism. So did its Pharaonic quality and its ostensible violation of Muslim principles of both form and content. In the words of a contemporary British report, the Liberal press "criticized as idolatrous the pharaonic style in which Zaghlul Pasha's mausoleum, at a cost of some 38,000 Egyptian pounds, is to be constructed, and challenged the government to seek a fetwa from the ulema on the matter." The Wafdist *al-Balagh* in turn "told the Liberals that they were not, and did not deserve to be, the defenders of Islam."[174] This episode of 1930, although brief and minor in and of itself, was a definite portent that the coming decade was to be less "Pharaonicist" in mood than the previous one had been.

Despite the public controversy and the fall of the Wafdist ministry in mid-1930, the mausoleum was completed in 1931.[175] Designed by Mustafa Fahmi, it is manifestly Pharaonic in spirit: a tall square structure of Aswan granite decorated with Pharaonic bas-reliefs externally, and internally a sarcophagus in Pharaonic style to hold the remains of the Wafdist leader. Even with the completion of the mausoleum, however, the actual transfer of Zaghlul's remains to his new resting place was obstructed by partisan considerations. Through the early 1930s, the anti-Wafdist ministry of Isma'il Sidqi repeatedly delayed the transfer of Sa'd's body to the mausoleum. Only upon the return of the Wafd to office once again in May 1936 did the project come to fruition. On 29 June 1936, Zaghlul's remains were transferred and reburied in the new mausoleum.[176] The comment of Zaghlul's first Wafdist biographer, 'Abbas Mahmud al-'Aqqad, captures both the Pharaonic design of this memorial to Zaghlul and the controversy that it aroused in the less Pharaonicist atmosphere of the 1930s: "It is an Egyptian structure abounding in simplicity and splendor, built in an ancient Egyptian style but nonetheless one which does not contradict Islamic principles."[177]

The story of Sa'd's two statues is a similar one. Although the idea of their creation and erection met with little or no opposition immediately after Sa'd's death, this did not remain the case as time progressed. Both the Liberal ministry of the late 1920s and the Sidqi regime in the early 1930s showed much less enthusiasm for their sponsorship than Wafdist governments had demonstrated. It was Sidqi who in 1930 officially canceled plans for their development under government auspices.[178] The creation of the statues themselves, executed by Mahmud Mukhtar in the early 1930s, apparently went unrewarded by successive non-Wafdist ministries up to the sculptor's death in 1934.[179] Once again, it was the return of the Wafd to office in 1936 that saw the project for the statues to Zaghlul completed. During its tenure in office in 1936–1937, Mukhtar's statues were finally placed in public squares in Cairo and Alexandria.[180] Both were again heavily Pharaonic in style. Carrying the image of Zaghlul in one case (Cairo) extending his hand in a gesture of protection, in the other (Alexandria) striding resolutely forward, their bases were decorated with reliefs celebrating Egyptian rural life, the Pharaonic heritage, and the nationalist movement that Zaghlul had led. Unlike *Nahdat Misr* or Sa'd's mausoleum, however, the statues were apparently received less than enthusiastically upon their public installation in the late 1930s. Even 'Aqqad was critical of their aesthetic shortcomings. In his view, they did not succeed in expressing the "human qualities, mental power, and moral generosity which made Sa'd great and deserving of immortalization."[181] 'Aqqad's verdict on the statues of Sa'd was very different from the one he had rendered on Mukhtar's *Nahdat Misr* a decade earlier: "Mahmud Mukhtar failed."[182]

'Aqqad's criticism of Mukhtar and his work was not purely aesthetic. This lukewarm response from a hitherto fervently Wafdist and Pharaonicist intellectual also reflected the new and in many ways anti-Pharaonic mood of Egypt by the 1930s. Even as Zaghlul's monuments were being officially erected and opened, they were becoming anachronistic relics of a disappearing age.

The fading of the Pharaonicist outlook is part and parcel of the development of the new Arabo-Islamic—and often vehemently anti-Pharaonic—tendencies that emerged in Egypt after 1930 and will be discussed in this context in a subsequent volume of this study. What needs emphasis here is the transience of the Pharaonic phase as represented in the response to the work of Mahmud Mukhtar. This particular juncture in modern Egyptian history needs to be noted carefully. Neither before the period of the 1920s and the early 1930s nor after it was a distinguished Egyptian national leader buried in a mausoleum designed to resemble a Pharaonic temple. Egypt's other national leaders of the modern era, from Muhammad 'Ali through Mustafa Kamil to Jamal 'Abd al-Nasir, have been buried in mosques. Zaghlul is the exception, and as such is a genuine reflection of the unique era of the 1920s in which he led the nation.

9

The Egyptianist Image of Egypt: IV. Toward An Egyptian National Literature

The concept of an Egyptian "national literature" [*al-adab al-qawmi*] or an "Egyptian literature" [*al-adab al-misri*] crystallized in the later 1920s and early 1930s. Its development was shaped by two features of the interwar Egyptian intellectual scene. The first was the emergence of Egyptian territorial nationalism as the predominant nationalist orientation in Egypt after 1919. Most Egyptian nationalist intellectuals of this period shared the basic premise that just as the creation of a new Egyptian national image demanded a new appreciation of the Egyptian environment and a reinterpretation of Egyptian history, so too it mandated the transformation of literary activity in Egypt. The development of a new Egyptian national literature was presented as an indispensable parallel to the creation of other components of Egypt's new national image: its territorial uniqueness, its distinctive history, its Pharaonic essence. A new national literature was seen as one of the necessary dimensions of the realization of modern Egyptian nationalism. It was impossible to speak of political independence and sovereignty, or of economic independence and the development of a national economy, without linking the cultural sphere to both of these. An authentic and autonomous national literature would reinforce political and economic independence.

The second feature of the intellectual climate of interwar Egypt that shaped the theory of Egyptian national literature was a more specific one: the antagonistic reaction against Arabic literature [*al-adab al-'arabi*] on the part of most Egyptian nationalist intellectuals. As we have demonstrated, most Egyptianist writers of the 1920s shared an antipathy for previous patterns of literary development in Egpyt. They viewed their cultural task as creating a new literature to take the place of traditional Arabic literature. In their view, the only way to escape from the constraints of traditional Arabic literature was to create a new Egyptian literature that would derive all its themes from the distinctive mileau of Egypt.

The creation of a new Egyptian national literature demanded intellectual activity on four levels. First, Egyptianist intellectuals had to develop a *theory* of national literature capable of defining its nature, functions, and content. Second, they had to formulate a practical *program* for the development of an Egyptian national literature—methods that would transform the theory into literary reality, and a scale of priorities for Egyptian writers to concentrate on in order to make theory into reality. Third, the practical creation of an original national literature involved the introduction of new literary *genres* in which the new national literature would manifest itself. Finally, the intellectuals also had to address the perplexing issue of precisely what kind of *language* should be employed to express that new national literature.

The Theory of National Literature

The original formulator of the principles of an Egyptian national literature was Ahmad Dayf. Dayf studied for his doctorate in Paris and completed his Ph.D. thesis in 1917; in his *Le lyricisme et la critique littéraire chez les Arabes,* the influence of the anti-Arab theories of Ernest Renan was clearly visible. From Renan Dayf adopted the concept that every people has a specific national and cultural character as well as a distinctive literary personality deriving from the natural environment in which that personality develops. Dayf also seemed to accept most of Renan's generalizations concerning the primitive and backward nature of Arabic literature in particular. Upon his return to Egypt Dayf became Lecturer in Arabic Literature at the Egyptian University, where he further developed these concepts.[1]

The statement of a need for a theory of Egyptian national literature was expounded by Dayf in his opening lecture of the 1918–1919 academic year delivered on 9 November 1918 (four days before the Wafd's visit to Wingate).[2] The main thrust of his address was the demand for a literature centered on Egypt:

> [W]e wish to have an Egyptian literature which will reflect our social state, our intellectual movements, and the region in which we live; reflect the cultivator in his field, the merchant in his stall, the ruler in his palace, the teacher among his students and his books, the shaykh among his people, the worshipper in his mosque or his monk's cell, and the youth in his amorous play. In sum, we want to have a personality in our literature.[3]

Dayf emphasized that it was not his intention to separate this new Egyptian literature from the Arabic literary legacy. But he still demanded the Egyptianization of Arabic literature in Egypt. "All that we aspire to is that we will have an Egyptian Arabic literature: Egyptian in its subjects and perceptions, Arabic in its language, rhetoric, and styles."[4]

Dayf repeated his thesis that Egypt had to develop for itself a literature with a definite national content in the 1920s, when he demanded an Egyptian literature that would "accurately portray [Egyptian] social life."[5] In his view the political, social, and ideological conditions of Egypt as they had developed after World War I needed to be made the central focus of this new literature. Here he reiterated the need for a new literature in Egypt, "an Egyptian type reflecting the Egyptian spirit and Egyptian life."[6] Like every nation, the Egyptian nation could not exist without giving expression to its own unique worldview and its perceptions of its particular conditions, or without exploring and discovering its own feelings and emotions as a nation.[7]

It was Muhammad Husayn Haykal who formulated the basic concepts of the theory of an exclusively Egyptian national literature. On 18 March 1925, Haykal published an article on "National Literature" [*"al-Adab al-Qawmi"*] in *al-Siyasa.*[8] This article proved to be a milestone in the development of the theory of an Egyptian national literature. Haykal started from the assumptions of Dayf concerning the need to modernize and Egyptianize Arabic literature in Egypt. But he went far beyond this. His philosophical background and theoretical bent led him to expand this idea into the call for a thoroughgoing reformulation of the nature of literary and artistic activity in Egypt.

Again following the approach of Hippolyte Taine, Haykal defined a genuine literature as the product of a specific natural environment, a particular race or people, and a specific time period. A truly creative figure could be understood only in light of his natural environment, his racial characteristics, and the climate of the age in which he lived and worked. Accordingly literature and art, writer and artist, needed to embody and to express the specific natural and human forces giving rise to their work—their environment, their people, and the spirit of their age.[9]

Applying the above axioms to contemporary Egypt, Haykal held that the country's literature and art must reflect the Egyptian natural environment, the national character of the Egyptian people, and the modern age. The relationship between natural environment and literature was for Haykal one of the absolute dependence of the latter on the former. Literature had no separate existence apart from the environment that had shaped it: on the contrary, literature was an extension of the environment that existed only to give artistic expression to the realities determined by the natural order. The symbiosis of Egypt, Egyptian man, and Egyptian time was the necessary subject matter of Egyptian literature and art. Therefore, the sole task of the national writer or artist was to give creative expression to the specific national forces behind him: "the soul of the writer as well as the thinking and inspiration pouring forth from him . . . [must be] a reflection of a particular age and a specific environment."[10]

Haykal also maintained that it was only through intensive interaction with his natural setting that the artist or writer could realize his full potential, or that any national literature and art could manifest its true genius. Haykal viewed the Greek and Roman classics as well as the achievements of modern European literature as the models that Egyptian national literature needed to emulate in the contemporary period. Ancient Roman and Greek as well as modern French, German, and English literature were for him genuine "national literatures" precisely because their creators were both the products and the supreme expressions of a particular place, a specific time, and a distinct people.[11]

In Haykal's view an Egyptian national literature would play a vital role in the national life of post-1919 Egypt. Besides being a crucial component of a modern Egyptian national culture, it would also be a major factor in the social integration of the Egyptian people. Haykal thought that a national literature could bridge the gap between two opposing groups on the Egyptian intellectual scene: the literary defenders of the "old" [*qadim*] and the advocates of the "modern" [*hadith*]. Optimistically anticipating that a new national literature would generate enthusiasm among both schools of thought, he hoped that it would be a factor of reconciliation, transforming the hostility between traditionalists and modernists into a new creative synthesis.[12]

Haykal's analysis then proceeded to address the crucial issue of the place of the existing Arab heritage in relation to contemporary Egyptian culture. On the basis of his perception of the Arab world as a mosaic of separate territorial nations, each "distinguished by its own special character autonomous of all its fellow-nations, the source of which lies in its natural environment and its climatic conditions," he concluded that each Arab country had its own "particular civilization" distinct from that of the other Arabic-speaking lands.[13] National literature was thus for Haykal a phenomenon specific to each Arab region and marked by its unique identity and character. The subjects, themes, and symbols of one Arabic literature were different from those of other Arabic literatures, in accordance with the differing environments characterizing each of the Arab countries.

Haykal did not deny that the Arabic language was the linguistic framework common to all the various Arabic national literatures. However, he also maintained that "these writers and poets do not reflect one distinct civilization."[14] Given this, the intellectual elites of each Arab country had to develop and promote their own national literature by emphasizing their own territorial literary characteristics and shaping their own independent literary personality, which would give autonomous identity to their literature. Their artistic and literary works had to reflect their country's natural landscape, its unique history, and its separate social realities.[15] Haykal concluded by calling on writers and artists of Egypt as well as of Syria, Iraq, Tunisia, Algeria, and Morocco to create for their individual nations specific national literatures that would mirror their unique circumstances.[16]

Haykal's statement of the need for a distinctive Egyptian national literature stimulated an intensive discussion concerning the formulation of a fuller theory of an Egyptian national literature in the late 1920s and early 1930s. Much of the theory and the program of this new national literature was primarily the creation of secondary Egyptian nationalist intellectuals; most of the active participants were disciples of Haykal and contributors to his journals *al-Siyasa* and *al-Siyasa al-Usbu'iyya.* In one sense, the concept of an Egyptian national literature became a vehicle for the literary self-assertions of these secondary intellectuals—the means for the expression of the nationalist worldview of a new literary generation, through which they attempted to carve out their own niche on the Egyptian cultural scene.

Eventually, a formal group evolved to promote the idea of an Egyptian national literature. "The Association of National Literature" [*Jama'at al-Adab al-Qawmi*] was active from 1929 through 1931. The main spokesman of the group was Muhammad Zaki 'Abd al-Qadir; also prominent in its activities were Muhammad al-Asmar, Mahmud 'Izzat Musa, Muhammad Amin Hassuna, Zakariya 'Abduh, and Mu'awiya Muhammad Nur. The activities of the group culminated in 1930 with the issuance of a public "summons" [*da'wa*] for the development of a new and distinctively Egyptian "national literature."[17]

The theory of an Egyptian national literature rested on two basic premises. The first was clearly stated by Ibrahim al-Misri: "every nation in the world has a distinctive literature."[18] The other was best expressed in the literary manifesto of the Association of National Literature: "literature is the portrait of life."[19] The first meant that since Egypt was indisputably a nation, it had to have a unique literature of its own; the second defined the content of that literature as a reflection of the life of the nation.

Egyptianist intellectuals applied the scheme of environmental determinism that they derived from Haykal and, through him, from Taine in a very mechanistic fashion. Since each nation was a territorially shaped reality, owing its existence and its subsequent development to the natural environment in which it had been born and then evolved, so its literature was the predetermined result of the synthesis of the natural environment and the human collective residing in it. Literary creativity depended entirely on the specific milieu in which it had originated and was nurtured, drawing its identity and personality from the all-powerful environment.

Implicit in this scheme was the belief in the specificity of individual nations and their literatures. Just as there were no two identical regions in the world, so there were no identical nations or national literatures. By its very nature, true literature was particularistic and territorial, deriving all its themes, subjects, and symbols from a specific milieu and giving voice to the realities of a specific place, people, and time. The *leitmotif* of Ahmad Dayf in 1926 that "national literatures differ from each other according to the difference in their [nations'] temperaments, customs, natural disposition, and social life" was accepted by other adherents of the approach as well.[20] Niqula Yusuf later elaborated the principle as follows:

> Thus the literature of nations is distinguished one from another according to the difference of their personalities. . . . Because social forms are not similar to each other and the characters of peoples do not resemble each other, and because environments, climates, and the inherited and acquired characteristics have their effects, so the literatures of peoples differ in their manifestations and orientations.[21]

But national literature was not merely a reflection of the nation; in turn, it had vital functions to perform for the nation. One was to develop the spiritual import, the idealistic aspects of natural and social forces. As Ibrahim al-Misri put it, literature had to comprehend and expound "the hopes and aspirations which reverberate in the soul of the nation"; without this spiritual dimension added to life by literature, life would lack meaning.[22] A second and related function of literature in national life was its role in developing national feeling. A national literature was an indispensible component in spreading nationalist sentiment and values among the population as a whole. Tawfiq Mikha'il Tuwaij stated the point as clearly as anyone: "the supreme goal of literature for which all nations aim is the strengthening of national feeling and the elevation of the prestige of the homeland and of everything related to it."[23]

These ideas concerning national literatures in general, their relationship to the environment, and their role in the development of national life were all of course applied to the specific case of Egypt. Egypt was put forth as a near-perfect example of how the symbiosis of a well-defined environment and a unique social order could generate a rich literary and artistic tradition. The unique scenes visible in the Nile Valley, its distinctive climate, its people with their particular cultural traits and especially with their impressive Pharaonic legacy: all these were presented as assets that provided Egyptian writers and artists with the ideal setting for the development of an original and sophisticated literature and art. Given this potential, a literary "genius" was inherent in Egypt: modern Egyptian literature had to liberate this genius buried deep within the Egyptian soul, restore it to life, and create a new Egyptian art from it. A world-class Egyptian national literature therefore existed in embryonic form; the role of "the national writer" [*al-adib al-qawmi*] was merely to draw it out of the collective national subconscious, to elevate it to the level of public awareness, and thereby to create an Egyptian literature that would be the equal of other great world literatures.[24]

An axiom of the theory of Egyptian national literature was that it should draw its inspiration overwhelmingly from Egyptian sources and materials. That Egyptian literature and art be above all *Egyptian* was a frequent demand on the part of Egyptianist intellectuals in the 1920s and early 1930s. Thus Ibrahim Ibrahim Jum'a called for Egypt to develop "a type of literature which will be firmly, genuinely, and clearly based on the Egyptian environment";[25] Salama Musa insisted that the Egyptian writer "make Egypt the arena of his literature and journalism, relying on its history, deriving guidance from its past, and seeking inspiration in its future in order to make its literature and journalism Egyptian";[26] and Muhammad Husayn Haykal gave fuller expression to the idea when he stated that

> [t]he best guarantee of the authenticity of the personality [*dhatiyya*] of the writer in his literature is that what he writes is related to his heart, his intellect, and all his life. This cannot be realized fully except when we describe our life, the life of our ancestors, the environment which nurtured us, and the heritage which is latent in us.[27]

Thus an Egyptian national literature had to be created out of the dialogue between the Egyptian writer and his environment, out of the interaction of Egyptian art and Egyptian reality. This of course presupposed that the Egyptian writer or artist knew his Egyptian background and had internalized its truths within himself. Niqula Yusuf expressed this point as follows:

> In order for Egyptian literature to be colored by genuinely national colors, it is clear that its stage must be the Egyptian environment and its breeding-ground a local soil. Therefore, the first and foremost duty of the Egyptian writer is to focus his concern on the depiction of Egyptian realities and all of the environments which surround them.[28]

Ideally, national literature was local literature. Its uniqueness and exclusiveness could be achieved only through its focusing on the Egyptian scene, Egyptian time, and Egyptian reality.[29]

Perhaps the most thorough and sophisticated formulation of the theory of an Egyptian national literature of the time was that propounded by Ibrahim al-Misri. Misri shared the view of other Egyptianist intellectuals that the central task of an Egyptian national literature was to rediscover and to reconstruct the vital relationship of Egyptians and their particular environment. But he went beyond most of his colleagues in seeing this as only one component of the development of a new literature in Egypt. Building on the formula of *race–milieu–moment,* Misri emphasized that the national writer needed to give equal attention to the influence of temporal factors in his writing. Misri defined the true national writer or artist as one whose work demonstrated three basic elements: first, an original and independent creativity; next, an intuitive consciousness of the distinguishing features of his particular environment; and third, a powerful awareness of "the spirit of the age" [*ruh al-'asr*].[30] The writer of true genius was one who simultaneously presented "a mirror of his environment and a portrait of his age"; who captured the essence of both his place and his time.[31] Misri's main point was thus that both a "consciousness of the environment" [*wa'i al-bi'a*] and a "consciousness of the age" [*wa'i al-'asr*] were preconditions for the creation of true literature and art.[32]

Beyond the obvious imperative of personal creativity, Misri held that consciousness of his environment was a vital faculty that the national writer had to demonstrate. By this he meant that the writer had to possess an intimate knowledge of his country's unique conditions. This demanded sensitivity to both nature and society, to the physical features as well as the social realities of his country. In portraying these environmental factors, the national writer or artist had to shape a realistic image of his nation. National literature was not a remote or abstract creation; it was a "living literature" [*al-adab al-hayy*] rooted in the daily life of a particular place and people.[33]

However, national literature also could not ignore the factor of time—the *zeitgeist* or "spirit of the age" in which it was created. The consciousness of the environment alone could not provide literature and art with another component that for Misri was no less critical. This was the modernist dimension. For him, "modernism" was the capacity of literature to meet the specific problems placed before man and society by the present. National literature in particular had to give expression to the profound impact of "the spirit of the age" upon the human spirit, to reflect the encounter between man and modernity.[34]

Misri warned his fellow Egyptian intellectuals that developing a consciousness of their Egyptian environment alone without simultaneously cultivating an equally acute consciousness of their time could lead to the confinement of Egyptian literature and art to parochial subjects and styles and its isolation from the main intellectual currents of the modern world. If this were to occur, Egyptian national literature would suffer the same fate as traditional Arabic literature. For Misri, the writer's awareness of the spirit of the age was the guarantee of a link between particularistic territorial elements and universalistic components in his literary output. The genius and greatness of Russian, German, French, and English literature in the nineteenth century lay in their ability to harmonize a specific national awareness with a broader consciousness of the age, thereby synthesizing their particularistic national qualities with a message of relevance and meaning for humanity in general. Egyptian writers and artists could and must follow the same path toward the creation of "this modern, living literature which includes the consciousness of both environment and time, and from which emanates a universal quality."[35] The young Egyptian writer needed to demonstrate two parallel capabilities: an orientation toward the wider world and a simultaneous maintenance of "his particular sources of inspiration and the essence of his Egyptian personality."[36]

By 1930, after several years of public discussion of the theory of national literature in Egypt, the reverberations of this discussion seem to have extended from intellectual circles to the Egyptian public in general. One indication of the broader impact of the theory by 1930 was the public response to the "summons" [*da'wa*] for the creation of an Egyptian national literature drafted by a group of

Egyptianist intellectuals and published in *al-Siyasa al-Usbu'iyya* in the summer of 1930.[37] The summons drew numerous letters of response, portions of fourteen of which were published in *al-Siyasa al-Usbu'iyya.*[38] Eleven of these enthusiastically supported the idea of creating a distinctively Egyptian national literature, with their authors voicing their willingness to join in the enterprise. Two of the respondents, while agreeing with the idea in general terms, qualified its anti-Arab and non-Western tone. One respondent (probably non-Egyptian from internal evidence in his letter) supported the concept of national literature but interpreted it in an Arab context, calling for the creation of one national literature for all Arabs.[39]

The tenor of the comments of the eleven who accepted the idea without reservations was undoubtedly influenced by the public discussion of the past several years, echoing many of the terms developed in it. The remarks of one student respondent demonstrate the impact the theory was having in Egyptianist circles by 1930:

> Literature must be a portrait of society in which the characteristics and customs of a people as well as the passions and desires found in their souls will appear. It must be a correct portrait of the age concerning [its] goals, thought, and power of expression. Why do we not have a national literature? Egypt is full of scenes like smiling fields, clear skies, and a shining sun, which can give inspiration to the thought of our writers, enhance their understanding, and from which they can draw inspiration. . . . Why should we rely on the literatures of other nations when it is more appropriate for us to rely on ourselves?[40]

A feature of the theory of Egyptian national literature that demands special emphasis is the theory's call for realism in literature. Above all, Eygptian national literature had to be completely realistic. The task of the national writer or artist was to describe Egypt as it really was, to present the natural and social life found in the Nile Valley as they appeared in reality. National literature had to strive for empirical, almost scientific, precision and objectivity. Muhammad Zaki 'Abd al-Qadir expressed the position well when he defined national literature as "the portrayal of Egyptian life and the presentation of all the passions and feelings which abound in it as they are."[41]

The demand for realism in literature and art was integrally connected to another imperative: naturalism in literature and art. For Egyptianist intellectuals, realism meant naturalism, the precise portrayal of the natural order and the social forms dependent upon it. The accurate description of the natural world and the exact reconstruction of man's relationship with nature were the overriding tasks of the national writer or artist. This conception of literature and art demanded the exclusion of the writer's or artist's personality from his creation. The mirroring of objective, external truths of nature and society rather than the expression of individual feelings was what was demanded in the creation of geniune literature and art.

Mahmud Taymur was a prominent spokesman of this call for realism and naturalism in Egyptian national literature. In his view, Egyptian national literature needed the development of "a realistic school" [*madhhab waqi'*] of prose narrative as one of its central components.[42] Egyptian fiction should be an accurate expression of the customs, feelings, and values of the Egyptian people. It needed to reflect "the true image of Egypt."[43] In Taymur's conception of literature, the task of the national writer was always to direct his attention toward real life and to give his readers a narrative that would mirror their own lives; thus "proper narrative brings life close to the reader and presents its experiences to him ready-made, understandable without the necessity of going deeper into them."[44]

A similar position on realism was taken by other exponents of the theory of an Egyptian national literature. Niqula Yusuf asserted the necessity for Egyptian literature to "paint" Egyptian life "in realistic and accurate colors, as is done in Russian literature, thus becoming a genuine mirror of Egyptian life."[45] Tawfiq Mikha'il Tuwaij said much the same thing when he stated that "we need that national writer who will develop our narrative literature, making it a true mirror of Egyptian life and the Egyptian environment."[46] The poet 'Ali Muhammad al-Bahrawi defined true poetry as poetry that consciously reflects a particular environment and time.[47] 'Aziz Talha provided perhaps the most useful summary of this demand for realism and naturalism in literature when he declared:

> The literary life of every nation is their realistic portrayal in a way in which you can feel their existence, their essence, and their appearance, their good and bad features, and the scope of their view of the entire world. If you know their literature, you virtually live in their time and environment.[48]

These views on realism and naturalism in national literature clearly reflect the impact of later nineteenth-century European ideas. They also reveal a paradox in the worldview of Egyptianist intellectuals. On the one hand, literary realism both in Europe and Egypt was a rejection of the tenets of the preceding Romantic orientation. Where Romanticism emphasized the expression of the writer's or artist's personal feelings and emotions, realism demanded the impersonal and dispassionate description of external reality. In form, realism broke with the Romantic reliance on the use of subjective symbols and metaphors, calling rather for a literature and art that described phenomena in a precise, scientific, "objective" manner. The realistic approach also marked a definite departure from the Romantic insistence on the need for the writer or artist to enter into an emotional dialogue with nature in order to comprehend its inner meaning; instead, realism predicated the necessity for the observer to remain separate and detached from the object of inquiry.[49]

On the other hand, a consideration of the general *Weltanschauung* of Egyptian nationalist intellectuals of the post-1919 era also reveals a definite positive impact of European Romanticism upon their thought. Their reification of the nation as a perduring entity; their attribution of unique characteristics, personalities, and mentalities to different nations; and not least their summons to the revival of Egypt's Pharaonic heritage: all these bear the imprint of nineteenth-century European Romanticism. How can we then explain what seem on the surface to be two antithetical trends: the realistic and naturalistic approach of Egyptianist intellectuals to literature and culture, and their romantic and vitalistic perspective on politics, society, and history?

In explaining the paradox, we need first to note that the Egyptian territorial nationalist orientation contained elements of realism and naturalism within itself. The emphasis of Egyptianist intellectuals on the environment and on its relationship with the national personality or character may be regarded as decidedly "realistic" elements existing within a broader romantic framework. The intellectuals' demand for realism in literature and art was made in order that this realism might portray and reflect their otherwise romantic image of Egypt. Moreover, the new Egyptian nationalism, which emphasized the collective nature of the nation's personality and will and which viewed artistic creativity as an instrument for the achievement of national goals, concomitantly rejected the romantic concept of art as a purely individual activity expressing the imperatives of the self conceived in isolation from the natural and social orders.

Additionally, the demand for realism and naturalism in Egyptian national literature needs to be understood and explained primarily in terms of the origins of the theory of national literature as a reaction and protest against the nature of traditional Arabic literature in Egypt. As we have seen, the image of Arabic literature among Egyptianist intellectuals was that of a decidedly romantic literature. In their view, Arabic literature was characterized by such romantic attributes as subjectivism, egocentrism, and an anti-social character. Its extreme antirealism, which amounted to escapism; its preference for the expression of instincts and sensations rather than the intellect and rationality; its imagination, which was given to surrealist fantasies; all the irrational pagan/*jahili* or religious/Islamic elements embedded in it; its satisfaction with expressing fragments of the truth while avoiding the greater unities of reality; and its general tendency to focus on the primitive and uncivilized world of the Bedouin nomad—it was against these perceived traits of Arabic literature that Egyptianist writers rebelled. They adopted the call for realism, naturalism, and the objective portrayal of the externals of reality as their methodological tools for combatting this romantic literary tradition, which had prevailed in Egypt for too long. Thus the antiromantic and anti-Arab mood combined with the race–milieu–moment formula embraced by Egyptianist intellectuals to make realism the central principle of Egyptian national literature.

The Program for the Development of an Egyptian National Literature

As had been the case with the other components of the new Egyptian national image formulated and promoted by Egyptian nationalist intellectuals, the theory of an Egyptian national literature had a practical dimension. As a creation intended to match Egyptian conditions, the new national literature was to be realized in practice—in the translation of the theory into Egyptian literary reality. Given this practical orientation, Egyptianist intellectuals attempted to formulate a detailed program that would direct the daily activity of the new generation of Egyptian writers and artists toward distinctively Egyptian modes of literary and artistic creativity. The credo of the new Egyptian national literature on the programmatic level was "the Egyptianization of literature" [*tamsir al-adab*]. The test of literary and artistic activity became its contribution to an original and distinctively Egyptian literature and art, one created by Egyptians for Egyptians, which drew its subject matter only from the land of the Nile, and which served the national renaissance of Egyptian nation.

The first programmatic issue facing the exponents of an Egyptian national literature was the relationship of that literature and other literary heritages. As we have emphasized, the Egyptianists strenuously rejected traditional Arabic literature as a basis for Egyptian national literature. Their attitude toward Western literature was more complex. There is no doubt that the demand for the creation of an Egyptian national literature was in part a reaction and protest against what they termed the massive invasion of Western literary influences into Egyptian cultural life, which had reached its zenith in the 1920s. They protested against what they viewed as an unconditional surrender to European literature and the sense of Egyptian inferiority *vis-à-vis* anything Western which it indicated. To them, this unrestrained emulation of Europe was a definite danger to Egypt and its national growth. If continued, it would inhibit original Egyptian creativity.

Criticism of the unrestrained translation of Western literature in Egypt was not new to the late 1920s and early 1930s. In the mid-1920s, the spokesmen of the short-lived Modernist School had leveled much the same complaint against the imitation of the West. Its journal *al-Fajr* contained vehement denunciations of what were called "the imitators–the propagandists of modernism who think with a Western mentality," and warnings that the influx of Western literary materials into Egypt would undermine efforts aimed at promoting authentic Egyptian literary creativity.[50] For the Modernist School, Westernized intellectuals who groveled before Western culture were no less misguided than "reactionary imitators" who thought in traditional Arab terms.[51] Both Arabic and Western literature were foreign to Egypt, and Egyptian nationalist writers needed to liberate themselves from the influence of both. Instead Egyptian writers needed to develop "an independent Egyptian mentality" in literature, separating themselves from the "Arab mentality" but also from the "Western mentality."[52] To the leading spokesman of the Modernist School, Ahmad Khayri Sa'id, genuinely Egyptian modernist writers had to be "united against the old [*al-qadim*] as well as against the false new [*al-jadid al-fasid*]."[53]

Denunciations of the extreme emulation of the West in Egypt also came from exponents of the concept of an Egyptian national literature. Thus Muhammad Zaki 'Abd al-Qadir criticized the cult of Western literature that was so widespread among the Egyptian elite by the end of the 1920s, challenging Egyptian "imitation of the West and taking from its literature," which found its practical expression in "the powerful movement of translation which dominates many of our writers and intellectuals."[54] "Today we are drowned in a sea of translation," he lamented.[55] Egyptians appeared to enjoy the taste of Western literature even though it was completely foreign to them; similarly, contemporary Egyptian authors were led to discuss subjects of which they knew nothing. The overall result was the imprisonment of Egyptian literary creativity in channels that had no social, historical, or genetic connection with Egypt.[56] Ibrahim al-Misri called for distinguishing Egyptian literature from Western models, maintaining that if Egyptians continued to be absorbed in the literary imitation of the West, the result would be "the effacing of our [literary] personality in a civilization which we do not really understand."[57]

At the same time, the proponents of an Egyptian national literature believed that that literature had to be modern and progressive. Given its function of liberating Egyptian creative life from the stagnation imposed upon it by traditional Arabic literary patterns, it had to become a dynamic agent of rapid modernization and development. In this role, it also needed to open itself to modern literary trends and influences coming from the progressive West. It had to draw at least part of its inspiration from modern European literary models, which themselves had succeeded in blending the parochial with the universal (modern Russian, German, French, English, or American literature were the examples usually cited). Thus modern Egyptian national literature had to walk a fine line between authenticity and emulation: while borrowing the tools and methods of modern creativity from Europe, it had to use these techniques to express purely Egyptian subjects and themes.[58]

Ibrahim al-Misri and ʻAbd Allah ʻInan were two advocates of this orientation toward national literature. Misri argued that "despite their present orientation towards a common international culture," this had not prevented the leading contemporary European literatures from "zealously preserving their own personalities."[59] ʻInan took much the same position: while assuming that Egyptians had to "rely on the West for obtaining the means of progress and development to which we aspire,"[60] he immediately added that "the West is incapable of giving us . . . national consciousness, national history, and national literature."[61] Like modern European nations, Egypt had its own national personality and historical consciousness, and thereby also its own national literature. While borrowing from the literary concepts of the West, this literature had to be based in its substance on Egyptian qualities derived from the distinctive Egyptian legacy. A truly dynamic and "modern" literature, ʻInan concluded, had to possess a particularistic "national spirit" as well, "for there is no living and glorious literature which is not based on this spirit."[62]

The operative conclusion of this approach to the West was that, to encourage original Egyptian literary and artistic creativity, Egypt must place limits on the volume of translated Western literary material and reduce its accessibility within Egypt. The formulators of the program for an Egyptian national literature emphasized that it was not their intention to stop translation totally and thus to isolate Egypt culturally from the West. Rather, what they demanded was that priority in cultural life be given to native Egyptian productivity over materials of foreign origin. Mahmud ʻIzzat Musa clearly expressed this approach when he argued that the new national literature that he and his colleagues were striving to create would liberate the innate powers of creativity embedded in Egyptians themselves from the domination of foreign literature. Thus, to create a "purely and genuinely national literature" Egyptians had to proceed in two directions at the same time: "on the one hand, the reduction of the stream of foreign literature to a limited amount; on the other hand, the revival of the national stream of thought in all its various dimensions."[63]

After thus defining the proper relationship of Egyptian national literature and modern Western literature, the formulators of the program for an Egyptian national literature proceeded to itemize the practical ways in which such a literature could be created. Three aspects of Egyptian life were considered possible sources of inspiration for an authentically Egyptian literature. The first was the ancient Pharaonic legacy of Egypt and its survivals in later eras; the second was the timeless component of the natural environment and landscape of Egypt; and the third and, in the end, the most important was the Egyptian people, in particular the Egyptian peasantry or *fallahin* of the Egyptian countryside.

The Pharaonic Legacy

Egypt's Pharaonic legacy was an obvious source of inspiration for an authentically Egyptian national literature. But it is significant that the idea of basing Egyptian national literature on Pharaonic precedents received relatively little attention from those Egyptian intellectuals who actually formulated the programmatic aspects of national literature. Their realistic and naturalistic approach to literature and art seems to have been the crucial factor behind this relative disinterest in the Pharaonic legacy. Pharaonicism seemed to many of them too romantic a source for the new Egyptian literature they desired, a factor that would only introduce irrational dimensions into a creative process they wished to keep realistic in character. Hence they were often skeptical of the possibilities of basing Egyptian national literature on the Pharaonic legacy, preferring to ground it in more tangible and concrete sources such as Egyptian nature and the Egyptian people. They also argued that an Egyptian national literature must be primarily modern in its inspiration: "it is necessary that the call [for a national literature] be oriented towards the creation of a modern Egyptian literature which derives its inspiration from our present life and current conditions."[64]

There were some Egyptianist intellectuals of the period, however, who tried to show that it would be possible to make the Pharaonic literary heritage part of the foundation for a new Egyptian national literature. Their essential argument was that there was no way to Egyptianize literature and art in Egypt without Pharaonicizing it as well. Only Pharaonicism could give Egyptian culture a truly national character. Thus Ibrahim Ibrahim Jum'a asserted that modern Egypt needed a "Pharaonic literature" [*al-adab al-fir'awni*] oriented toward reviving Pharaonic literary themes.[65] In his view, national literature had to reflect the continuum of national existence over the millenia, devoting itself to the description of "magnificent and fascinating Egypt from ancient times through medieval times to the modern age."[66] Similarly, Shuhdi 'Atiyya al-Shafi'i maintained that the role of modern national literature in Egypt was to present a picture of the ancient Pharaonic era, which had been the cradle of the Egyptian nation. Egyptian literature needed to reconstruct in detail the spiritual life of the ancient Pharaohs, with all its beliefs, arts, sciences, literary genres, thoughts, and emotions.[67] By and large, however, Jum'a and Shafi'i expressed a minority view; most Egyptianist intellectuals who considered the programmatic aspects of Egyptian national literature minimized the Pharaonic legacy, emphasizing instead more current sources of literary inspiration.

The Unique Environment of Egypt

A repeated theme in the writings of Egyptianist intellectuals was that the natural setting of Egypt had not received the attention it deserved in Egyptian literary activity. They were convinced that the new Egyptian national literature had to change this situation radically, making the natural scene of Egypt one of its main concerns. If "literature is the portrait of life," and if life could not be separated from the environment that had shaped it, so nature inevitably had to be a central concern of literary creativity.

In an article on the theme of "Enchanting Egypt and the Disrespect of Its Sons for Its Beauties," Muhammad Husayn Haykal called for his fellow Egyptian writers to take "the splendid beauty of the land of the Nile" as the central subject of their literary activity.[68] The Nile, which the ancient Egyptians had named "the greatest sea," was the indisputable heart of Egyptian life and as such should serve as the first source of inspiration for Egyptian literary creativity.[69] Beyond the river was the land of Egypt: the verdant strip of fertile land created by the river along its banks, then the huge desert that enclosed both river and farmland. These too should be a perennial source of inspiration for national literature. Haykal admonished younger Egyptian writers always to remember that "first and foremost, we Egyptians are surrounded by an enchanting nature," and that these natural scenes should become an inspiration in their work.[70]

Muhammad Zaki 'Abd al-Qadir also criticized the indifference of Egyptian writers toward the charms and attractions of the Egyptian natural scene. "Egypt is really beautiful," he wrote, "and it is amazing that we have not learned how to portray this beauty."[71] A genuine national literature for 'Abd al-Qadir was one based on an intimate relationship to nature, drawing both its subjects and its symbols from the natural scene:

> We have in Egypt an unequalled and fascinating countryside in which the imagination finds the most fertile inspiration. . . . We have a land, a sky, a river, and a landscape which endlessly repeat themselves, phenomena which achieve their most beautiful form in Egypt. . . . Finally, we have a life which is rich both sensually and intellectually. In sum, we have all the components of literature.[72]

Niqula Yusuf provided a more elaborate exposition of the view that the natural setting of Egypt deserved to become one of the major components of a new Egyptian national literature.[73] Yusuf went beyond the efforts of his colleagues in addressing first the methodological issue of how the writer or artist could achieve an accurate and valid portrayal of nature. For him, the answer was straightforward: realism and naturalism were the artistic concepts that had to inspire Egyptian writers and artists in their approach to nature. A true artistic representation of nature was its description, and that alone. In this extremely realistic approach to art, Yusuf was in part inspired by the work of John Ruskin. He accepted Ruskin's argument that the transformation of nature into art should not alter nature because nature in its very essence *was* beauty. Thus there was no need to add, or to remove, anything from nature; aesthetic truth was the exact reconstruction of that beauty. Any idealization, exaggeration, or symbolic presentation of the beauties of nature deviated from both truth and art.[74]

Having resolved the methodological issue to his satisfaction, Yusuf provided his fellow Egyptian national writers with a catalog of scenes upon which they could draw for inspiration in their work. In one article he examined the natural setting of Egypt: huge awesome deserts surrounded by equally vast and impressive bodies of water; a placid, restful climate characterized by a comfortable summer and a warm winter; beautiful sunrises and sunsets.[75] In another he surveyed the length of Egypt, finding "beautiful, artistic scenes" from the Mediterranean coast in the north to the Sudanese border in the south.[76] Yusuf summed up his ideas on nature as a source of art with an admonition to his fellow Egyptian writers that

> every Egyptian writer must now remember that, in giving a true and realistic portrayal of the scenes of his country in their simplicity, gentleness, and plainness, he is first redeeming his country and secondly [redeeming] its art. . . . The natural scenes of Egypt are many and beautiful, and they await the national writer who can eternalize their beauty.[77]

The Egyptian People and the Egyptian Peasantry

If the natural landscape of Egypt was one main source of inspiration for an Egyptian national literature, the human landscape of the country—the people living in the Nile Valley—had to be another central one. Literature and art that were truly the property of the nation had to mirror the life and ideas of the mass of Egyptians who had been ignored in traditional Arabic literature. A genuine national literature had to be "populist literature" [*al-adab al-sha'bi*] focused on those hidden classes whom literature and art had hitherto neglected. In this respect, one credo of the proponents of an Egyptian national literature in the post-1919 era was very similar to that held by many of the Russian intelligensia in the previous century: the summons of the *narodniks* for Russian writers and artists to "go to the people" for inspiration.

Numerous restatements of the *narodnik* cry to "go to the people" can be found in the writings of Egyptianist intellectuals concerned with developing the details of the new Egyptian national literature. Thus Yusuf Hanna asserted that the search for a genuine Egyptian literature naturally involved an examination of Egyptian rural life and the customs and ideas of the *fallahin.*[78] "The spirit of thc nation" was not an abstract or mystical concept to Hanna: it was rather a tangible reality, the essence of which was exemplified most completely in "country life" [*al-hayat al-rifiyya*].[79] There was no other way for the national writer or artist to portray this spirit of the nation save through understanding rural life and placing the central figure in Egyptian society, the *fallah,* at the core of his art.[80]

Tawfiq Mikha'il Tuwaij said much the same thing, stating that Egypt needed national writers who would go to the people, take inspiration from the folklore and oral sayings of the *fallahin,* and from these generate "an authentic Egyptian literature which describes Egyptian life and which is intimately connected to the Egyptian soil."[81] Ibrahim Ibrahim Jum'a similarly called for the creation of a new kind of "populist literature" [*adab sha'bi*] that would mirror the existential condition of the life of the Egyptian masses.[82] In 1930, Muhammad Zaki 'Abd al-Qadir phrased the demand in terms of the promotion of a new "rural literature" [*al-adab al-rifi*] that, by making the nation more aware of peasant living conditions, would thereby serve to assist in the improvement of those conditions.[83]

Salama Musa emphasized that the *fallahin* was the social group that had preserved intact the true spirit of Egypt over the millenia. In their mentality was to be found the "Pharaonic essence" of Egypt, the authentic spirit of the nation. As such, they had to become a major source of literary inspiration. Musa also maintained that loving attention to the life of the Egyptian peasantry would enhance literary creativity: only intimate contact with what was most authentic in Egypt could provide the spark for a genuine national literature. Both Musa's

Egyptianism and his populism were well exemplified in his ringing declaration that "[i]f you see a writer who is not concerned with the Egyptian *fallah,* this means only that he does not care for him. If he does not care for him, he also hates Egypt, for all of us are *fallahin.*"[84]

Ahmad Mahmud Sulayman expounded on another theme found in the populist approach to Egyptian national literature. This was the idea that the folklore of the Egyptian peasantry—their popular songs, tales, and humor, which had evolved spontaneously over the millenia—deserved to be an important source of inspiration for national literature.[85] The lower classes of Egypt were both "the majority of the nation" and its "most important pillar"; hence it would be absurd for the current literary and cultural revival in Egypt to ignore the rich materials, the musical, poetic, and narrative "treasures," found in the popular milieu.[86] Only intensive study of the folklore of the peasantry could integrate this authentically Egyptian material into the written literature of Egypt. If this was done, Sulayman maintained that Egyptians would find not only the "ideal way" to transform popular folklore into a basis for their national literature, but also the "proper means" for the advancement of the peasantry themselves.[87]

Niqula Yusuf expounded at length on many of these concepts. He too demanded that the Egyptian national writer become intimately acquainted with the nature of Egyptian rural life in order to make it a central subject of Egyptian national literature. Like Sulayman, he demanded that the Egyptian national writer study the rich popular folklore of Egypt, "which today is a true national literature in Egypt."[88] Yusuf gave greatest emphasis to the need for literature to capture the mental dimensions of the Egyptian peasantry. Yusuf's own interpretation of the mental traits characteristic of the *fallahin* was the typical urban mixture of admiration and condescension, stressing the *fallah's*

> calm character, his tendency towards submissiveness and fatalism, his reliance on God, his contentment with the meanness of his livelihood, his patience with all that is hateful in his life while hoping for the justice of God, . . . his inclination to humor, jesting, and banter, his aversion to wholehearted commitment to difficult and serious tasks, and his love of tolerance, the appreciation of others, self-criticism, and sarcasm.[89]

One of the most enthusiastic spokesmen of the populist approach was Ibrahim al-Misri. Misri completely identified the new national literature of Egypt with the folk tradition of the country. Misri began from the premise that the average, anonomous Egyptian had been ignored in literature until the present revival of an Egyptian national literature. But a nation that was trying to recreate its cultural personality and cultural identity could not ignore the "heart and soul" of its society.[90] The failure of traditional literature to become a true national literature, he argued, stemmed from the fact that Egyptian writers were oriented toward higher culture and did not know the peasant or the worker even though these categories made up much of the population of Egypt.[91]

Misri was convinced that the creation of an Egyptian national literature required that the common man be made the protagonist of literature. The life of simple Egyptians must be put at the center of the stage. Thus he called on writers to "study the life of the peasants and laborers who are the mass of Egyptian workers, and [to] depict their character, customs, their heroic daily struggle, their needs and requirements."[92] He appealed to his peers to "look to the city, the native worker [*al-'amil ibn al-balad*] and how he is loving, suffering, struggling. Go to the countryside. Drop your arrogance to the *fallah*!"[93] The programmatic solution for the development of an Egyptian national literature seemed very simple to Misri: go to the people.

Misri also attributed a revolutionary ability to transform society to this populist insistence on a focus on the common people. By learning and writing about the Egyptian lower classes, intellectuals would themselves assume a revolutionary position in society. By turning to the masses, the productivity of Egyptianist intellectuals would become "simultaneously a work of art and a work of revolution and reform."[94] Misri concluded his appeal for an Egyptian national literature with the assertion that

> our Egyptian literature will not realize itself save when we look closely at our people, when we infuse our culture with the spirit of our people, when we attempt to understand them through it [that is, their spirit] and to love them as the Russian writer loves his people, and when we come to appreciate that they, like all peoples, have a solid, glorious, and tangible personality which deserves to be immortalized in heroic art.[95]

It is important to point out that this populist approach in Egypt in the post-1919 era was not confined to the literary realm alone. It was but one aspect of the broader territorial nationalist worldview of Egyptianist intellectuals. It is hardly surprising that Egyptianist intellectuals attempting to shape a new national image should turn their attention to what was indisputably the most indigenous, the most unadulterated, the most "Egyptian" dimension of modern Egypt: its countryside and peasantry. The lifestyle of the *fallahin* was perceived as originally and distinctively Egyptian, and the *fallah* seen as the purest example of what it meant to be Egyptian. In the *fallah's* primitive, unchanging style of life, the genuine qualities of Egyptian civilization had been preserved and could be rediscovered after centuries of alien domination. The *fallah* was an Egyptian fossil in which the pristine and authentic nature of Egypt was revealed. Salama Musa stated this best in his declaration that "ancient Egypt or the Egypt of the Pharaohs is still alive among our *fallahin*."[96] Thus for Musa the "Pharaonic essence" of Egypt must be sought and could be found in the mentality of the peasantry; their beliefs, rituals, customs, myths, patterns of thought, and behavior embodied an ideal Egypt.[97]

These Egyptian *narodniks* worshipped the myth of the *fallahin.* Although some of the specifics of the traditional negative image of the *fallah* can be found in their writings, in normative terms they vehemently rejected the devaluation and scorn of the peasant found particularly in Arabic literature and to a lesser degree in Western treatments. Egyptianist intellectuals saw their role as one of rehabilitating the image of the *fallah,* of transforming him into a model for all Egyptians. The "authentic virtues" of Egypt could be seen only in the *fallah:* what was beautiful and noble in Egypt was embodied in its peasantry. Because his unbroken habitation along the banks of the Nile had rooted him almost organically in the soil of Egypt, the peasant was the real Egyptian. Both his modest lifestyle and his love of the land attested to his having been saved from the external influence and national degeneration that had afflicted other Egyptians over the millenia. Innocent and pure, living spontaneously and intuitively, knowing no artificiality or pretence, the Egyptian peasant was all that was best in Egypt.[98]

In line with their heavily environmental outlook, Egyptanist intellectuals maintained that the Egyptian peasant could best be understood through understanding the environment that had shaped his life and character traits. The peasantry had internalized the effects of the Egyptian natural setting over the generations. The unique and unchanging geographical structure of the Nile Valley, for example, was credited with giving the *fallah* his psychological stability and stoicism; a figure well aware of his firm roots in the soil of Egypt, he could face the difficulties presented by life with confidence. Similarly, the agricultural lifestyle and the village community in which he was embedded created a preordained and unquestioned life cycle that in turn was used to explain the peasant's personal placidity and calm.[99]

Egyptianist intellectuals either explained away or interpreted as strengths those presumed peasant traits which others had viewed negatively. Thus, while the power of the environment had produced an unchanging peasant lifestyle and the quality of peasant conservatism, the intellectual emphasized the benefits of peasant conservatism. It was viewed as nationally constructive, the secret of the preservation of the "Pharaonic essence" of Egypt by the *fallahin.* Egypt owed its amazing national continuity to peasant conservatism; had the *fallah* not clung fanatically to the ways of his ancestors and passed the same on to his descendants, much of what was authentically Egyptian would have been lost. On a different level, peasant humor was also extolled as a necessary mechanism of defense against the vicissitudes of life and as a means of externalizing the inevitable sorrows of life: the *fallah* survived through humor.[100]

Two presumed traits of the Egyptian peasant that received great emphasis were his family attachment and his realism and practicality. The *fallah*'s devotion to his family was extolled and given national overtones; the continuity of the Egyptian family was made a symbol of the continuity of the Egyptian nation.[101] The success of the Egyptian nation was linked in a different way to the assumed realism and practicality of the *fallah.* 'Abbas Mahmud al-'Aqqad expressed the concept concisely when he said that "the Egyptian [peasant] is a worker [*'amil*] in his life as well as he is practical [*'amali*] in his view of life."[102] To 'Aqqad, "the essential Egyptian mind is a realistic, practical mind."[103] Enclosed in his surroundings and capable of acting only within the constraints imposed by his environment, the Egyptian peasant was thus shielded from exposure to the radiation of foreign cultures. The implication was obvious: salvation from the alien and the inauthentic depended on the *fallah.*

The Egyptian peasant was thus made the repository of all that was virtuous and noble in the Egyptian nation. The nation could place its trust in the *fallah,* seeking guidance from his infallible intuition. Egyptian *narodniks* argued that it was both necessary and inevitable for the new Egyptian national literature to draw its inspiration from the Egyptian peasantry. If the creative mind sought to know the truths of Egyptian greatness, to understand the essence of the nation and to discover the reason for its durability, it must go to the people, mixing with them and through them understanding Egypt.[104]

The Genres of an Egyptian National Literature

Egyptian nationalist intellectuals gave considerable attention to discussing the specific literary and artistic genres that were needed to form the substance of an independent Egyptian culture. Their analysis focused on four genres in particular. Three of these—prose narrative, drama, and the fine arts—had to be created almost *ex nihilo* because of their absence from the traditional Arabic heritage in Egypt. As such they had to be in large part inspired by Western stylistic models, although always applied to and within the specific Egyptian national context. The fourth genre, poetry, could of course be found in the Arab tradition, but in the Egyptianists' view only in unprogressive and anachronistic forms. They therefore demanded the creation of a new Egyptian poetry that would be both open to Western stylistic influences and more appropriate to modern Egyptian life.

Egyptian Narrative

The question of how to develop a tradition of prose narrative that would be both distinctively Egyptian and yet thoroughly modern was one of the most acute issues addressed by intellectuals concerned with shaping a new Egyptian national literature. Perceiving fiction as "the central pillar of Western literature," they believed that modern Egyptian literature must also place this genre at the center of its creativity.[105] "The art of narrative," an editorial in the literary journal *al-Fajr* stated, "is the basic feature of literature."[106] They elevated the ability of a society to create "narrative literature" [*al-adab al-qasasi*] or "narrative art" [*al-fann al-qasasi*] into one of the vital tests of cultural achievement. Similarly, they insisted upon the development of the major subgenres of fiction in Egypt: the novel [*al-qissa*], the epic novel [*al-qissa al-tawila* or *al-riwaya*], the short story and novella [*al-qissa al-qasira* or *al-uqsusa*], and the descriptive sketch [*al-sura al-wasfiyya*].

Four criteria were stipulated for this new Egyptian narrative art. First, it had to be "national narrative" [*qissa qawmiyya*] or "local narrative" [*qissa mahalliyya*] in its content. This meant that the main concern of Egyptian prose narrative writers had to be to portray in detail the distinctive features of Egyptian life and the unique characteristics of Egypt and of Egyptians.[107] Second, within this authentically Egyptian orientation, fiction was called upon to focus on the social dimensions of Egyptian life. It must depict both rural and urban social life in Egypt, taking as its central subject the life of society rather than that of the individual.[108] Third, to achieve these two goals Egyptian fiction had to employ a realistic approach that concentrated on the accurate and factual description of external reality. Indeed, it was maintained that realism could manifest itself best in fiction.[109] The last criterion of the new Egyptian fiction was that it had to take much of its literary inspiration from modern European fiction. Nineteenth-century Russian, French, and (to a lesser degree) English literature received greatest emphasis in this context. Chekhov, Dostoyevsky, Turgenev, Tolstoy, and Gorky in Russia; Balzac, Flaubert, Hugo, Zola, Proust, Rolland, Anatole France, Gide, and de Maupassant in France; and from England Dickens, Scott, and Shaw: the works of all these writers were cited as appropriate models for Egyptian writers in their efforts to develop a modern narrative tradition in Egypt.[110]

Individual views concerning fiction were not this schematic, of course. Muhammad Husayn Haykal lamented what he called "the feebleness of the art of fiction" in the Arabic literary tradition.[111] He was an enthusiastic proponent of the idea that fiction had to become the central genre in a new national literature that could be influential in the social reform of modern Egypt. For him the Egyptian environment, with its variety of natural and human scenes, was itself "overflowing with the inspiration for fiction."[112] Haykal indeed believed that "the art of narrative" should become the focus of Egyptian national literature: fiction could present Egyptian social life and the aspirations and ideals of society more fully and concretely than poetry, the visual arts, or music.[113] Unlike many of his disciples, however, Haykal was not a proponent of the exclusively realistic approach to fiction. For him, the flourishing of different approaches, from the romantic to the realistic to the symbolic, held greater promise for the successful development of an Egyptian fiction of broad appeal in Egypt.

An impressive but iconoclastic interpretation of the place of fiction in Egyptian national literature was put forth by Ibrahim al-Misri. Misri also did not believe that modern Egyptian fiction should be exclusively realistic in its approach. On one level, he felt this was simply too narrow a formula for literature. On another, he held realism itself to be a superficial and mechanistic approach that could not reach or portray what was deeper and more complex in both man and society. He instead called upon Egyptian novelists to open their fiction to a broad range of literary stimuli, particularly to twentieth-century fiction, which demonstrated an awareness of modern symbolism and psychology. For him, writers such as Proust, Gide, Mann, and Huxley were the best models for modern Egyptian writers of fiction.[114] Misri also differed from his colleagues in calling for fiction to concern itself with the world of the individual and his revolt against the traditional bonds of society. Freud's impact upon Misri is very clear in his analysis of the true novelist as one who concentrated his attention on the inner dimensions of the human soul, "this part of the soul which is deeper, more secret, and more repressed."[115] The frontier of Egyptian fiction had to become the inner arena in which the individual struggled both with his own passions and with the traditional constraints imposed upon him by society. Such had been the subject matter of the greatest Western novelists like Dostoyevsky, Balzac, and Proust, and such had to be made the center of Egyptian fiction as well.[116]

Egyptian Drama

In the theory of Egyptian national literature, drama was conceived as an integral part of prose. This can be seen in the terms employed for the play, drama, and the theater. The general terms used to denote the genre of drama were "theatrical literature" [*al-adab al-masrahi*] or "the theatrical composition" [*al-ta'lif al-masrahi*]. A distinction was made between the writing of drama and the actual production of plays. Thus Egypt's leading Egyptianist playwright of the 1930s, Tawfiq al-Hakim, wrote that "the theatrical story [*al-qissa al-tamthiliyya*] is one of the forms of literature," distinguishing between the composition of the play and its production on the stage. In his view, the playwright could achieve artistic truth and greatness in writing plays "without needing the stage and the actors."[117]

The view of Egyptianist intellectuals concerning the proper subject matter upon which drama should be based fit in with their conception of the play as one of the several genres of prose. As with fiction, they argued that the Egyptian theater should have a nationalist orientation and content. Muhammad Amin Hassuna wrote of "the need for creating a local theater [*masrah mahalli*] nurtured by Egyptian tales which will become a true school of the people where they will learn about [Egyptian] life in a serious and effective way."[118] The program of the Association of National Literature of 1930 similarly proclaimed its purpose to be "orienting the Egyptian theater towards the national dimension, making it into an Egyptian theater in its spirit, its power, and its creativity".[119] Thus drama in Egypt, like Egyptian fiction, was conceived as having the ability to transmit to the Egyptian public both the realities of Egyptian daily life and the ideals to which society should aspire. Egyptianist intellectuals believed that drama could become an important agent in criticizing and thus eroding outmoded traditional norms as well as in shaping a new national consciousness for Egypt.[120]

The important place accorded drama and the theater in Egyptian national literature appears clearly in Muhammad Husayn Haykal's writings.[121] Haykal criticized the superficiality and quest for popular success that seemed to him to have characterized much of modern Egyptian drama. Too many Egyptian playwrights, he complained, interpreted drama as a facile, undemanding art form in which they merely titillated and aroused the emotions of "the primitive masses."[122] Haykal saw this popularization of the Egyptian theater as a reduction of the art of drama to an insignificant entertainment with no lasting social or cultural impact. His metaphor was to compare much of the current Egyptian theater to the puppet theater intended for the amusement of children. In place of this worthless type of drama prevalent in Egypt, Haykal called for the development of drama and theater that viewed their function as true art rather than mere entertainment and which would possess a clear and constructive national message. Such drama and theater would be able to assume the proper place of the genre in the building of a new Egyptian national consciousness. What he desired for Egyptian drama was that it become "an art which deserves the name of art."[123] Haykal called upon Egyptian playwrights to become much more serious in their approach to drama, enjoining them to view their craft "seriously and to consider it worthy of diligent and persistent effort."[124] Only such socially responsible drama, he believed, could fulfill the mission destined for drama in the national revival of Egypt: to improve the life of the nation and to contribute to its progress.[125]

Egyptian Fine Arts

Also in the development of an Egyptian "national art" [*al-fann al-qawmi*] or "the Egyptian fine arts" [*al-funun al-jamila al-misriyya*], Egyptianist intellectuals postulated the need for the introduction of new artistic principles and methods that would take their inspiration from both Egypt and the modern West. In the visual arts as opposed to literature, they placed great emphasis on deriving the subjects and the content of Egyptian art from the artistic tradition of ancient Egypt. The assertion of Muhammad Durini Khashaba that "ancient Egypt was an artistic nation [*ummat al-funun*]" captures the belief of Egyptianist intellectuals in the inherently artistic nature of their country.[126] At the same time, however, they also emphasized that the art of modern Egypt must be based on contemporary stylistic concepts and models. Thus Salama Musa vehemently rejected any possible connection between the Egyptian fine arts of the future and what he termed "backward Eastern [artistic] taste." Rather, in his view Egyptian art needed to emulate Western art: in the fine arts, "the way to deliverance is for us to orient ourselves totally towards the West and simultaneously to rid ourselves of all the Eastern arts."[127]

The most important group of writers who systematically addressed the question of the nature and place of the fine arts in modern Egypt was the Modernist School associated with the journal *al-Fajr* in the mid-1920s. The main theoretical thrust of the Modernist School was an attempt to combine modernism in artistic styles with Egyptianism as the substantive content of the Egyptian visual arts. The summons for Egypt to achieve intellectual independence, in the view of the Modernist School, could be accomplished in art only through the creation of a new visual artistic tradition inspired by modern Western artistic concepts but employing these in the depiction of distinctively Egyptian subjects and themes. Such a synthesis demanded a totally new art. The key terms "creativity" [*khalq*] and "originality" [*ibtikar*] in essence meant artistic modernity and Egyptian authenticity.[128] What Egyptian art needed was "a new Egyptian artistic mentality" and the development of "the Egyptian creative genius."[129] Stylistically, the artistic perspective of the Modernist School was largely realistic. Its ideal was naturalistic, figurative painting and sculpture that would portray Egyptian life in "rational" and unembellished terms. More subjective artistic approaches such as impressionism or expressionism had little influence on the school.[130]

The Modernist School also gave considerable attention to music.[131] Its approach to music was militantly modernist. Its adherents rejected the tonal system of traditional Arabic music as a basis for the music of modern Egypt, calling for the total elimination of what they term "outmoded, obsolete music" in Egypt.[132] In its place, they demanded the development of "original national music" for the reviving Egyptian nation.[133] In substance, this meant the adoption of the modern Western tonal system as well as the composition of Western-style classical works by Egyptians. At the same time, however, they called upon Egyptian composers to draw their musical themes from native Egyptian subject matter. If both procedures were followed, Egyptian music would be a national music with a distinct Egyptian coloring as well as an integral part of modern, universal music. The proper model for this "original national music" was the kind of music developed in nineteenth-century Eastern Europe. The Russian national music of Tschaikovsky, the Hungarian national music of Bartok, the Polish national music of Chopin, and the Czech national music of Dvorak were cited as the examples that Egyptian composers needed to emulate.[134]

Among prominent Egyptian nationalist intellectuals, 'Abbas Mahmud al-'Aqqad gave the greatest attention to the visual arts. He devoted many of his essays of the 1920s to the place of the visual arts in the cultural life of modern Egypt. He did so, however, only within the larger context of his general effort to grapple with the relationship of sensation and imagination, to understand the nature of aesthetics, and thereby to create a comprehensive theory of literature and literary criticism. Thus his discussion of art was only one component of a more ambitious intellectual enterprise.[135]

The premise of 'Aqqad's examination of the place of the visual arts in Egyptian life was their importance as an expression of the nation. Like literature, art was a factor making different nations distinct. Since both literature and art expressed the specific traits of a community, they were a true embodiment of its nature and spirit. In his view "art is a witness and a proof of the temperament of the nation, of its distinctive characteristics which science and industry cannot elucidate."[136] Moreover, for 'Aqqad the true test of the progress of a nation lay in its ability to develop and promote a sophisticated art: it was impossible to describe a nation as advanced if its arts were backward. Science might be the test of the material advancement of the nation, but art was the test of its emotional and psychological development. Given the above, for 'Aqqad it was ineluctable that Egypt would devote itself to the enhancement of its fine arts; only they could demonstrate its progress and revival. Thus he argued that the "artistic awakening" of Egypt must be encouraged by both official and voluntary means.[137]

'Aqqad's view of the visual arts differed in important ways from that of many other Egyptianist intellectuals. On one level, he opposed an emphasis on borrowing from ancient Pharaonic art. In general terms, he saw art as too dynamic and vibrant to be imprisoned in patterns developed in the past. More specifically, the themes of death and eternity so prominent in Pharaonic art to him seemed inappropriate as sources of inspiration for the art of modern Egypt.[138]

In addition, he was not an advocate of realism and naturalism in art. His vision of the evolution of art posited three successive stages of achievement. The first and simplest was that of "pure imitation," that is, realism in which the artist merely recorded what he saw with his eyes. In the second stage, the artist still copied reality but also expressed his own feelings and sensations in his art. The third and in 'Aqqad's view the highest stage was "the stage of originality [*ibtida'*] and of spiritual symbolism," where the artist expressed his own genius and generated something new from it.[139]

'Aqqad evaluated the development of the fine arts in Egypt in the 1920s on the basis of this schema of stages in art. His own fear was that Egyptian painting and sculpture in particular were becoming locked into the first, realistic phase of expression.[140] In contrast to many of his peers he called for more impressionist and symbolic, as opposed to realistic, Egyptian art. Realism as the highest aim of art was counterproductive to him: it could not express the unique talent, insight, genius, and creativity of the artist himself. He believed that national art should not stop at the stage of realism and the production of "natural pictures" [*suwar tabi'iyya*]. Instead he called for such realism to be only a transitional step toward the development of "symbolic pictures" [*suwar ramziyya*] created out of the artist's genius and imagination.[141]

In terms of specific artistic styles, 'Aqqad was convinced that Egyptian fine arts needed to adopt the perspective of impressionism [*al-ihsasiyya*].[142] French Impressionism in particular seemed to him the ideal model for the development of the fine arts in Egypt, although post-Impressionist European schools of art such as Neo-Impressionism and Expressionism also received his blessing as acceptable sources of emulation for Egyptian artists. An opening to Impressionism and its successors would give the fine arts in Egypt a progressive, modernist character that would be more in accord with the dynamic and pro-Western mood of post-1919 Egypt than would a purely realistic approach. On a more personal level, impressionism could liberate the artist from the slavery imposed by realism, allowing him to give full expression to his personality and genius. Through the adoption of the impressionist approach, the artist would become the master rather than the slave of his environment. At the same time, he would neither abandon nor ignore the influence of his environment, his society, and his time. These would of course continue to find expression in his art, but now they would be reflected through the prism of the artist's own personality and genius.[143]

Egyptian Poetry

Where fiction, drama, and the fine arts were seen as having begun to be modernized and Egyptianized prior to the Revolution of 1919 and were perceived as having made great progress since then, Egyptian nationalist intellectuals generally believed that most of the poetry written in Egypt, even the work of leading nationalist poets, had remained wedded to the styles and subject matter characteristic of traditional Arabic literature. They attempted to change this in two fundamental ways. First, they called for the Egyptianization of poetry in Egypt: the replacement of foreign Arab and Muslim literary themes and subjects with material drawn from the natural and social milieu of Egypt. Poetry in the new Egypt needed to become *Egyptian* poetry. Second, with their infatuation with the culture of the modern West, they also maintained that poetry in Egypt needed to be based on the new and exciting ways of poetic expression that had developed in the West in recent centuries. Poetry in twentieth-century Egypt also needed to become *modern* poetry. Thus modernism harmonized with Egyptianism were the two general principles underlying the Egyptian nationalist conception of Egyptian poetry.

Beyond their consensus on these two broad principles, however, Egyptianist intellectuals diverged on precisely how to make poetry in Egypt both modern and Egyptian. The opinion expressed by most Egyptianist intellectuals who considered the issue was straightforward: they called for the adoption of realism as the new model for modern Egyptian poetry. Realism was perceived as the most effective lever for eliminating the ornate, exaggerated, and pretentious emphasis characteristic of both classical Arabic poetry and the neoclassicism of the nineteenth century, which still provided the conceptual framework for most contemporary Egyptian poetry. Realism would make Egyptian poetry more flexible, less adorned with verbal flourishes, more substantive in content. Through all this it would become more real—a more exact, precise presentation of modern Egyptian scenes and events. Egyptianist intellectuals spoke of the need to create "prose poetry" [*al-shi'r al-qasasi* or *al-shi'r al-manthur*],[144] the subgenre that within a few decades was to become dominant in Egyptian poetry.

There were various declarations of this approach to poetry. Ibrahim al-Misri presented an ideal of poetic realism (which contrasted vividly with his nonrealistic approach to other genres of national literature) by calling on Egyptian poets to draw their poetic inspiration from the Egyptian countryside, to portray "Egypt's enchanting nature," and to devote their attention to the desires and emotions of both the rural and urban masses.[145] Niqula Yusuf's formula was for Egyptian poets to concentrate upon the beauties of their own country in their poetry, forgetting things extraneous to Egypt.[146] Speaking for the Association of National Literature in 1930, Muhammad Zaki 'Abd al-Qadir stated the intention of the Association to be the composition of "nationalist anthems" [*anashid qawmiyya*], making them as much as possible "a portrait of the hopes and aspirations of Egyptians."[147] 'Ali Muhammad al-Bahrawi, after calling on his fellow poets to write about Egyptian hopes and feelings, gave a moving description of what modern Egyptian poetry would look like:

> Egyptian poetry [written] on this basis would be that poetry which portrays Egyptian life in its original environment. It would interpret its feelings, express its inner emotions, sketch its highest ideals. At the same time it would be part of the universal poetry of humanity, for it would describe the sufferings which are one aspect of humanity as well as point out ideals for it.[148]

But realism was only one approach to a genuinely Egyptian and thoroughly modern poetry for Egypt. An alternative outlook blended elements of realism with an underlying romanticism. In this approach, the revolt against Arab classicism and Egyptian-Arab neoclassicism was expressed in terms very similar to the anticlassicist Romanticism found in Europe in the early nineteenth century. The object of this revolt was as much or more personal than national: to free the creative powers of the individual poet from the rigid patterns of previous Arabic poetry, thereby allowing him to express his own spirit as well as to elaborate on the spiritual dimension of humanity in general. The romantic approach, like the realistic one, was a reaction to the rigidity and artificiality of traditional Arabic poetry; but while the latter emphasized the description of the Egyptian milieu as the path to poetic creativity, the former stressed the liberation of the poet's genius as the road to a new and better poetry.

One of the two main advocates of this approach was Muhammad Husayn Haykal. Thoroughly disillusioned with Egypt's neoclassicist poetry, he called for the "total liberation" of the poetic imagination. His counsel to Egyptian poets was phrased in largely romantic terms. Only by giving voice to their own inner feelings and sensations would they, and poetry with them, be freed from the shackles of existing poetic conventions. A "revolution in poetry" [*thawrat al-shi'r*] was needed to parallel the "revolution in prose" [*thawrat al-nathr*] already underway, and to form a component in the more general "revolution in literature" [*thawrat al-adab*] demanded by the revival of the Egyptian nation.[149] It was not sufficient for Egypt to establish the right of "freedom of thought" [*hurriyyat al-fikr*], which he implied had been achieved in the 1920s and formed the foundation for recent progress in prose literature and art. In addition, Egypt needed to consolidate the right to "freedom of feeling" [alternatively *hurriyyat al-hass; hurriyyat al-'atifa; hurriyyat al-shu'ur*] that was the basis of poetic creativity.[150] The only path to the revolution in poetry he desired was for the most talented Egyptian writers to "strive for the freedom of feeling and sensation as they previously thirsted for freedom of thought and freedom of expression."[151] The new style of Egyptian poetry that Haykal envisaged demanded synthesis on two levels. The first was the combining of a realistic attention to the environment of Egypt and the qualities of its people with a romantic concern with the inner world of the poet. The second was the creative blending of the local spirit of Egypt with the humanism and universalism found in the best of modern poetry.[152]

'Abbas Mahumd al-'Aqqad offered an even more detailed program for the proper composition of Egyptian national poetry.[153] An admirer of nineteenth-century English Romantic poets in particular, his own poetic perspective was a thoroughly romantic one. ʻAqqad rejected what seemed to him to be the simplistic and mechanistic approach of the realists, according to which the primary role of the poet was to present an accurate and factual depiction of the external world. From his perspective ʻAqqad argued that the poet was neither a scientist nor an historian. Poetry by its very nature could not reconstruct reality "as it really was"; it rather depended on the personal involvement of the poet with reality.[154] Between the "subject"—the poet—and his "object"—the materials of his poetry—there was no clear separation. The poet's experience, imagination, and inner genius shaped the "object" in its own image.[155] The poet was an artist dealing with reality by means of his emotions and imagination, not through his "touch and sight." For the poet, reality per se did not exist at all: what did exist was the image of reality created by his own imagination.[156]

From this perspective, ʻAqqad also maintained that the poet was not merely the product of his environment or his age. As he put it, "the representation of the environment is not a prerequisite of poetic genius . . . since the great poet may be at variance with his environment."[157] The genius of the poet took him out of the constraints of time and place, enabling him to create a poetry that transcended a specific land or a particular generation. ʻAqqad similarly rejected the utilitarian approach to poetry, which viewed it as an instrument for achieving nonartistic goals. The poet betrayed his role as poet if he wrote his poetry with utilitarian considerations in mind. He must preserve his autonomy as a poet and make his poetry his fundamental concern. Poetry was an end in itself, not a means.[158]

Consequently, ʻAqqad differed dramatically from most other Egyptian nationalist intellectuals of the period in his view of the place of Egypt in the poetry of Egyptians. He vehemently disagreed with the prevalent interpretation that Egyptian national literature, poetry included, had to address national themes. He insisted instead that poetry possessed value and significance for the nation by virtue of its inherent qualities rather than because of its subject matter:

> Give us a poet who composes a poem by which he makes Egyptians love the flower, and I guarantee [that will give us] the greatest national benefit and the most genuine revival. . . . If a nation loves the flower, loves gardens, loves order and harmony, loves cleanliness and beauty, and loves constructive work and reform, it will not endure living in poverty, ignorance, and humiliation. Give us a poet who makes us familiar with a beautiful poem of love and I guarantee [that it will give us] a nation of upright men and women and excellent children.[159]

Where ʻAqqad did share the perspective of most Egyptian nationalist literary critics was in his belief in the need for a greater popular influence in the written poetry of Egypt. In his view, Egyptian poetry needed a firm basis in the folklore of the Egyptian *fallahin.* The native instincts of the Egyptian people had been preserved over the millenia in the popular songs of the *fallahin;* thus "the features of the authentic Egyptian spirit" as well as "the genuine Egyptian temperament" were to be found in the oral traditions of the masses.[160] In ʻAqqad's view, the problem was that the riches to be found in the popular tradition of Egypt had never been absorbed into the "official" written poetry of the country.[161] The ruling elite of Egypt had developed a "sterile official literature" often composed by non-Egyptian authors and intended to serve non-Egyptian purposes.[162] In place of this elitist and alien poetic tradition, 'Aqqad called for Egyptian poets to free their innate poetic instincts from this foreign overlay and to liberate the genius found in the Egyptian popular tradition from the shackles that had been placed upon it. Poets had to blend the popular folklore of Egypt with what was authentic and worthwhile in its written poetry in order to create a new poetry that would be both modern and Egyptian.[163]

The Issue of Language in Egyptian National Literature

One of the most difficult questions facing Egyptian nationalist intellectuals was that of the suitability of the Arabic language as a vehicle for Egyptian national literature. Even before World War I, the issue of the reform or modernization of Arabic had become a matter of discussion in Egypt. Suggested alterations in the language included the development of neologisms to supplement the antiquated vocabulary of Arabic, proposals for the simplification of the grammatical rules of traditional Arabic, and the demand for the "Egyptianization" [*tamsir*] of Arabic in Egypt through the blending of the colloquial spoken dialect of Egypt with the formal literary language.[164] One of the main proponents of altering the terminology and structure of Arabic was the liberal reformer Qasim Amin; the great prewar exponent of Egyptianization was the intellectual father of the territorial nationalist orientation, Ahmad Lufti al-Sayyid.[165]

In the post-1919 era, exponents of linguistic reform divided into two camps. The majority primarily picked up and refined earlier ideas of terminological and grammatical modernization. A smaller group was more radical, advocating these concepts while adding to them notions of the augmentation and/or partial replacement of written literary Arabic with the spoken colloquial of Egypt.[166]

Proponents of the reformist approach based their ideas of linguistic change on an evolutionary approach to language. They disagreed with one of the basic assumptions of earlier Arabic and Muslim writers on Arabic, that of the immutable status of the language of the *Qur'an*. Tawfiq Mikha'il Tuwaij expressed the premise well: "the means of writing must develop in harmony with social life, and change according to the changes of time and place."[167] From their secular and rationalist perspective, they conceived of language as an instrument intended to meet the basic human need of communication. In this sense Arabic was no different from other languages: it was an historical phenomenon rather than a divinely ordained one. As Hafiz Mahmud put it, Arabic was subject to "the law of change" that governed the universe: it was both proper and necessary for it to evolve over time. Since language was one of the most vital methods of human interaction, humans could not allow it to become obsolete or unsuitable for communication.[168]

The specific approach advocated by this reformist group was that of the internal modernization of Arabic to make it an efficient and dynamic vehicle for the expression of modern thoughts and concepts. In particular, they emphasized the need to simplify both the style and the structure of Arabic. Niqula Yusuf, for example, wrote of the need to "escape from the antique style" of Arabic, criticizing its ornateness and verbosity as well as quoting Qasim Amin's famous characterization of Arabic to the effect that " 'in other languages humans read in order to understand; but in the Arabic language one has to understand in order to read.' "[169] He called upon Egyptian writers to adopt "a realistic style" [*uslub waqi'*] that would convey their meaning simply and directly.[170] In terms of its structure, the reformists echoed the concept of Arabization through the coining of neologisms in order to make Arabic an appropriate instrument for dealing with the contemporary world.[171]

The ideas of Muhammad Husayn Haykal on changing the Arabic language may serve as an example of this reformist approach to the language issue. Haykal began from the usual premise of language as a dynamic phenomenon subject to the laws of evolution and change: "The Arabic language is a living entity [*ka'in hayy*]. So it has been, and so it always will be."[172] As this dynamic phenomenon, Arabic had to "absorb the civilization of humanity and become able to carry all the scientific, artistic, and literary products of the human intellect."[173]

To Haykal the first necessity was the simplification of Arabic. A recurrent theme in his discussions of language in general was that words were only "the external garment" worn by reality.[174] As such, they were always secondary in importance to the meanings they conveyed. Literature was not equivalent to its words but rather was the symbols, concepts, and understandings presented by those words. Thus style needed to take second place to meaning: if, in order to achieve a smooth transmission of ideas, it proved necessary to change the words and the structure of a language, so be it.[175] Applying this concept to his own age, Haykal maintained that modern literature could not rely on verbal richness or complexity. The most appropriate language for today was what he once termed the most "transparent" [*shaffafa*], thereby revealing its meaning to the reader as simply and directly as possible.[176] Haykal believed that a suitable modern national literature was "not based on the words and phrases that the writer employs as much as it is based on images and meanings."[177] Therefore, he called for developing "the literature of thought" [*adab al-fikr*] rather than "the literature of form" [*adab al-lafz*].[178]

In terms of specifics, Haykal believed that one of the best ways to simplify Arabic would be by discarding its desinential inflection [*i'rab*].[179] The second reform he advocated was the development of a more modern, scientifically adapted vocabulary by means of "Arabization" [*ta'rib*]. Here his definition of Arabization differed slightly from many of his fellow reformers. He advocated the acceptance of Western scientific and technological terms that were already entering contemporary Arabic usage, rather than insisting upon the sweeping development of equivalents based on indigenous Arabic roots.[180] Haykal maintained that only those writers who so adapted their language to "the spirit of the age" would be capable of producing a modern national literature for Egypt.[181] In a more general sense, Haykal also asserted that the reform of Arabic was a necessary aspect of Egyptian progress. As he phrased it, "language is one of the manifestations of life. Therefore, it must bear all of the images and ideas which the living wish it to bear, in the fashion in which the living wish to bear."[182]

If Haykal's ideas about the modernization of Arabic were fairly straightforward, his thoughts on the desirability of its Egyptianization were indecisive. He did call, in a general way, for the "Egyptianization" of literature in Egypt.[183] But it is unclear as to precisely what he meant by this. Earlier in the 1920s, Haykal did advocate at least the use of the colloquial dialect by characters in drama and fiction. He also maintained the right of the writer to choose the kind of language appropriate to his purposes, be it literary Arabic, Egyptian colloquial, or some combination of the two.[184] However, Haykal never seems to have proposed, in an unequivocal way, the substitution of the colloquial dialect for current literary Arabic as the means of literary expression in Egypt. Moreover, by the close of the 1920s he seems to have been convinced that the use of colloquial Egyptian Arabic could not solve the problems of contemporary literature in Egypt. Compared to the issues of style and spirit in prose and poetry which we have already discussed, he saw the matter of language as a secondary problem for Egyptian national literature.[185] In sum, Haykal never became a real advocate of the Egyptianization of the Arabic language in Egypt; he placed his emphasis for solving the problems of Arabic on its modernization rather than its Egyptianization.

Not all Egyptianist intellectuals of the 1920s were as restrained. A more extreme approach expounded by at least a few proponents of linguistic change in Egypt was that the sweeping "Egyptianization of language" [*tamsir al-lugha*] was a necessary precondition for the emergence of a distinctive Egyptian national literature. Tawfiq ʻAwwan stated the position clearly when he asked, "How can we write national literature in a language which is in no way our language!"[186] The essence of this more radical Egyptianizing approach was that as long as the Arabic language was the language of literature in Egypt, it would be impossible to achieve Egyptian authenticity and national independence in literature. Literary achievement was predicated on the authenticity of language: as Salama Musa put it, "our real disaster is that the Arabic language cannot serve Egypt and cannot revive it."[187] The use of Arabic inevitably reduced literature in Egypt to but one branch of general Arabic literature. Again Musa put it well:

> [L]iterary Arabic assimilates our Egyptian nationalism [to the Arabs] and makes it part of Arab nationalism. He who adopts literary Arabic absorbs the Arab spirit. He marvels at the heroes of Baghdad instead of absorbing the Egyptian spirit and learning the history of Egypt.[188]

Their theoretical solution for this dilemma was "the creation of an independent Egyptian language," one capable of expressing "the hopes and sorrows of the nation in the Egyptian tongue [*al-lisan al-misri*]."[189] In their view, the colloquial dialect of Egypt was equally a "refined" and a "progressive" language.[190] Most important, it was the authentic language of the Egyptian people. Given all these strengths, it had to take the place of the literary Arabic, which in their view was "a nomadic language."[191] Perhaps the most vehement formulation of the distinction between literary Arabic and the Egyptian colloquial was that offered by Tawfiq ʻAwwan: "Egypt has a language which is not the language of the Arabs. This language is the language which the people speak in all their conversations, all speaking it whether articulate or inarticulate, merchant or *fallah*, rich or poor."[192] Thus the right of the Egyptian colloquial dialect to become the basis of literature in Egypt was attributed to its "naturalness" [*tabiʻiyya*]:

> National literature demands first and foremost naturalness. Is it natural in any way that we address the *fallah* or the merchant in a language foreign to him! One of the most distinguishing characteristics of nationalism is the language in which the people [*qawm*] speak. If we really want to have a national literature, so we must write in the colloquial language![193]

Advocates of this radical approach were not totally utopian, however. Most of them realized that the thoroughgoing Egyptianization of Arabic that they desired was a revolution of such proportions that it could not be accomplished quickly. Therefore, their proposals were similar to those offered by Ahmad Lutfi al-Sayyid a generation earlier: for the blending of as much as was possible of the Egyptian colloquial dialect with the formal written language of Egypt. Specifically, this meant the incorporation of words, phrases, and even grammatical structures from the spoken into the written language. The radicals took ideas concerning the simplification of Arabic further than did the reformers; Salama Musa at one point suggested the elimination of almost all the inflection customary in the literary language.[194] In addition, they hammered on the need for Egyptian writers to employ colloquial Arabic extensively in dialogue.[195] Their general intention for the future evolution of Arabic in Egypt seems to have been that the written language used by Egyptians would become inspired more by colloquial usages than by present literary practice.[196]

It was characteristic of the Egyptianism of these exponents of radical change in Egyptian Arabic that they suggested the application of a similar process of linguistic change in other Arab regions. The creation of distinctive national languages grounded in the specific traits of the different Arab lands was for them an imperative throughout the Arab world. Again, Tawfiq ʻAwwan offered what may have been the strongest statement of this position:

> Egypt has an Egyptian language; Lebanon has a Lebanese language; the Hijaz has an Hijazi language; and so forth—and all these languages are by no means Arabic languages. Each of our countries has a language which is its own possession: so why do we not write it as we converse in it? For the language in which the people [*qawm*] of any region speak is the language in which they also write.[197]

A more elaborate variant of the same idea was put forth by Muhammad Amin Hassuna.[198] To him one of the central problems of national literature throughout the Arab world was that "the Arabic language is not the language of one people alone, but the language of [several] peoples and nations which write it and sometimes even speak it."[199] The solution of this problem of an artificial linguistic unity superimposed on top of national diversity was for the Arabs to follow the example of the Romance languages of Europe, that is, the eventual development of separate national languages out of the Arabic (=Latin) tradition. France, Italy, Spain, and Rumania had developed distinct national languages on the basis of their local environment and cultural traditions, languages that for Hassuna represented the proper synthesis of environment, people, and time, and which were thereby capable of giving correct expression to the unique characteristics and national consciousness of these peoples. In his view the same could and should occur among the Arab peoples, different national entities with their own locales and customs. Of course Egypt would lead the way in this process. Hassuna expected that eventually, after the dissemination of the Egyptian precedent of adopting the spoken language as the basis of written literature in Egypt, the Arabic-speaking world would be reshaped in the image of the Latin-speaking world; as a family of related nations possessing their own languages and literatures despite their common linguistic origins.[200]

With Hassuna's vision of a pluralistic Arab world composed of separate Arab nations with distinct national languages and cultures, we have come full circle in our discussion of the territorial nationalist image of Egypt. In sum, Egyptian territorial nationalist intellectuals wished to separate Egypt in virtually all dimensions—geography, history, culture, literature, even language—from its Arab and Muslim neighbors. Although the position proved easier to assert and to demonstrate in some areas (geography and history in particular) than in others (especially literature and language), what is worth mentioning in conclusion is the scope of the endeavor. The national image Egyptianist intellectuals wished to create for their "new" nation was applied to all spheres of nature and social existence. In their view, such a comprehensive isolation and reification of Egypt was vital in order to consolidate its national existence in the post-1919 era.

Egyptian "National" Literary Production

In the 1920s and early 1930s, considerable literary and artistic work inspired by the concept of an Egyptian "national literature" was actually produced in Egypt. In almost all literary and artistic genres we can find the beginnings of literary and artistic production that was moving in the direction demanded by the advocates of an Egyptian national literature. The following overview does not attempt to describe all the literary and artistic production of the period that followed "national" guidelines, nor does it attempt a critical literary analysis of this activity. Rather, its purpose is merely to demonstrate the range of nationalist literature and art produced in the post-1919 era as well as to give some of the more prominent examples of this production.

Fiction

Prose narrative was undoubtedly the most important area of national literary production in the 1920s and early 1930s. The precursor of much of the Egyptianist literature of the post-World War I period is a work published just before the war, Muhammad Husayn Haykal's story *Zaynab* (1913).[201] Frequently termed the first genuine novel written in Arabic, it foreshadowed later Egyptian nationalist narrative in at least three basic ways. First, it was realistic in approach; most of its text was devoted to the detailed description of the Egyptian natural scene as well as the characters and events whose actions are the subject of the story. Secondly, *Zaynab* was profoundly Egyptianist in spirit; subtitled "Countryside Scenes and Manners" [*manazir wa akhlaq rifiyya*], it is set primarily in an Egyptian village setting and is filled with lengthy and passionate descriptions of the beauties of the Egyptian countryside. Thirdly, *Zaynab* anticipated later Egyptian "national" literature stylistically: it is apparently the first work of Egyptian creative literature to employ the Egyptian colloquial dialect in the dialogue of its peasant characters. As H. A. R. Gibb summarized the significance of the work,

> it is impossible to deny to *Zaynab* the credit of being the first Egyptian novel, written by an Egyptian for Egyptian readers, and whose characters, settings, and plot are derived from contemporary Egyptian life.[202]

As Gibb noted, it is only with the publication of the second edition of *Zaynab* in 1929 (when its author was a renowned literary and political figure, when it had been selected as the basis for a film, and in the context of an already developed discussion of Egyptian "national literature") that the novel became widely known to the Egyptian reading public.[203] Its popularity and repute date from this time onward: henceforth, *Zaynab* was frequently referred to as the prototype for the Egyptian novel.[204]

It was in the medium of the short story rather than that of the novel proper that a distinctively Egyptian "national" fiction first found significant expression. Before and during World War I, some of Muhammad Husayn Haykal's short stories, such as his *Hadith Shabab* (1911) and *Hadith al-Shams* (1916), had attempted to deal with Egyptian society in a realistic fashion and had employed the Egyptian colloquial for the dialogue of the characters.[205] Muhammad Taymur (1892–1921) made the same use of the vernacular in some of the short stories he wrote prior to his premature death; he is also credited with beginning to move the short story in Egypt away from the didactic and artificial character it had hitherto possessed.[206] The short stories of 'Isa 'Ubayd (d. 1923) appearing in the immediate postwar years clearly reflected the impact of the Revolution of 1919 and the charismatic personality of Sa'd Zaghlul on Egyptian writers, and lay the basis for the Egypt-oriented short story.[207]

The major figure in the development of the Egyptian short story, however, was Muhammad Taymur's younger brother, Mahmud Taymur (1894–1973). Influenced by the work of de Maupassant and Chekhov as well as by that of his brother and 'Isa 'Ubayd, Mahmud Taymur transformed the short story in Egypt from a didactic essay relying almost exclusively on conversation among its characters into genuine fiction blending realistic description, character portrayal, and dialogue.[208] Taymur produced dozens of short stories in the 1920s. While many of these were first published in periodical form, their rapid republication in collections testifies to the popularity of his writings at the time. Especially noteworthy were two early collections of his short stories: *al-Shaykh Jum'a wa Qisas Ukhra,* which was praised as the basis of a new and modern Egyptian literature at the time of its publication in 1925, and *al-Shaykh Sayyid al-'Abit wa Aqasis Ukhra* (1926), which was also very popular with the Egyptian reading public.[209] Taymur's stories were the first of the genre to fit the canons of the then developing theory of Egyptian national literature: realistic in content and nationalist in tone, they fit the model of "national" literature almost perfectly. As such, Taymur's stories in the later 1920s and early 1930s served as the model for those intellectuals who were calling for the creation of a new, modern, and distinctively Egyptian fiction in Egypt.[210] In the view of Salama Musa in 1931, the contribution of Mahmud Taymur to the "realization of Egyptian nationalism" in the sphere of literature was comparable to the achievement of Mustafa Kamil in politics or that of Muhammad Tal'at Harb in economics: where Kamil had tried to realize Egypt's political existence and Harb its economic substance, Taymur had striven to realize the country's "literary essence."[211]

The second major short story writer of Egypt in the 1920s was Mahmud Tahir Lashin. Lashin's writing paralleled that of Mahmud Taymur in its realistic description, its local Egyptian orientation, its acute criticism of the flaws of contemporary Egyptian society, and its intensive use of Egyptian colloquial dialect.[212] The artistic culmination of early Egyptian fiction may have come in his short novel of 1934, *Eve Without Adam* [*Hawwa' bila Adam*], possibly the first novel in Arabic in which "the outcome appears as a natural development from the interaction of characters and their environment."[213]

Muhammad Husayn Haykal also contributed to the development of a distinctively Egyptian—and Egyptianist—style of short story. Haykal wrote several short stories in the late 1920s and early 1930s that were deliberately intended as "experiments in *al-adab al-qawmi*."[214] Although his stories did not make use of Egyptian colloquial in dialogue at this time, they clearly fit within the paradigm of "national literature" in terms of their realism, their attention to the Egyptian rural scene, their concern for analyzing and thereby correcting Egyptian social problems, and their optimism that these problems could and would be solved.[215]

Other short story writers of the 1920s whose Egyptocentric stories fit within the framework of Egyptian national literature included Muhammad Amin Hassuna, Muhammad Ra'fit al-Jamali, Ahmad Hanafi, 'Isa Muhammad al-Siba'i, and Muhammad al-Sarafi. In their focus on Egyptian natural scenes, Egyptian social conditions, and the contemporary national revival of Egypt, the popular tales of the above authors reinforced the Egyptianist perspective of the educated Egyptian public.[216] One of Muhammad Amin Hassuna's stories indicates the overwhelmingly Egyptianist bent of much of this popular entertainment. Entitled *Egypt the Free or Lion Cubs of the Revolution* [*Misr al-Hurra aw Ashbal al-Thawra;* Cairo, 1930], it was characterized by its author as "a contemporary romantic patriotic Egyptian tragedy."[217]

The initial forum for the publication of Egyptian short stories was the avant-garde cultural journal *al-Fajr* published by the Modernist School in the mid-1920s. Its special column of "Egyptian Stories" ["*Qisas Misriyya*"] that appeared in every issue published scores of new stories as well as critiques of modernist fiction in the two years of the journal's publication. Many of the early stories of Mahmud Taymur and Mahmud Tahir Lashin first appeared in *al-Fajr,* as both men were associated with the Modernist School at the time; other young authors whose early work appeared in the journal included Husayn Fawzi, Ahmad al-Sawi Muhammad, Sa'id 'Abduh, Yahya Haqqi, Isma'il al-Malaki, and the editor of *al-Fajr,* Ahmad Khayri Sa'id. Most of the fictional material appearing in the journal was also characterized by realism, a concern for Egyptian social issues, and the use of the colloquial dialect in dialogue.[218]

Two further benchmarks in the development of Egyptian narrative were the first volume of Taha Husayn's autobiography, *The Days* [*al-Ayyam:* first published in serial form in *al-Hilal* in 1926–1927; published in book form in 1929], and Ibrahim 'Abd al-Qadir al-Mazini's popular novel, *Ibrahim the Writer* [*Ibrahim al-Katib;* 1931]. Although the former is of course not a novel, its use of the third person for the narrative, its realistic portrayal of the author's early life, and its detailed and moving self-characterization all served to make it a major influence on the further development of the art of narrative in modern Egypt.[219] Perhaps most interesting about Mazini's novel from the nationalist perspective is the circumstances of its composition: it was written by this already well-known essayist and poet in response to a competition for new Egyptian novels prompted by the appearance of the second edition of Haykal's *Zaynab* and the interest in a new Egyptian fiction that it aroused.[220] Although its literary quality is often regarded as inferior to the best Egyptian fiction of the day, it too demonstrated the emerging nationalist nature of creative writing in its realism, focus on Egyptian society, and occasional use of the colloquial.[221]

The culmination of the movement toward an Egyptian national fiction was Tawfiq al-Hakim's *Return of the Soul* [*'Awdat al-Ruh*]. *'Awdat al-Ruh* shared many of the characteristics of a distinctively Egyptian fiction that we have noted in earlier works, particularly the realistic description of the Egyptian countryside and its inhabitants, the occasional criticism of contemporary Egyptian social conditions, and the use of the vernacular in dialogue. We have already discussed many of the additional dimensions that made it the prime example of the Egyptianist perspective, ranging from its anti-Arab tone to its idealization of the Egyptian *fallahin* to its concluding passages reveling in the nationalist Revolution of 1919.[222]

Drama

Numerous plays with a decidedly nationalist flavor were written and/or produced in Egypt from the mid-1920s onwards. Sometimes the inspiration came from other media, as with several of the short stories of the Taymur brothers that were recast in dramatic form.[223] Possibly the most renowned Egyptianist playwright of the 1920s was the venerable Ahmad Shawqi, whose nationalist dramas *The Fall of Cleopatra* [*Masra' Kliyupatra;* 1927] and *Cambyses* [*Qambiz;* 1931] both centered on the theme of Egyptian resistance to foreign conquest.[224] Not surprisingly, younger authors were even more committed to the use of Pharaonic or authentic Egyptian rural motifs in their plays of the 1920s. Along with the previously mentioned Pharaonic dramas of Mahmud Murad, which so impressed Ahmad Husayn, younger writers who wrote plays that either dealt with Egypt's ancient past or attempted to portray its contemporary society in a realistic fashion included Husayn Fawzi, Ibrahim Ramzi, 'Abbas 'Alam, and Ahmad Zaki Abu Shadi.[225]

Beyond this Egyptian nationalist drama, the 1920s and early 1930s also witnessed considerable organizational activity directed toward the establishment of an Egyptian national theatre. It is hardly coincidental that the famous theatrical troupe founded by Yusuf Wahbi in 1923, the year after Egypt received its formal independence, was named the "Ramses" Company.[226] A leading figure in the genesis of an Egyptian national theatre was Zaki Tulaymat. Sent by the Egyptian government to France in the mid-1920s to study theatre, in 1930 he became the first director of the short-lived "Institute for Dramatics" [*Ma'had al-Tamthil*] established under the auspices of the Egyptian Ministry of Education. Tulaymat's own views on drama included the advocacy of the blending of classical Arabic with the Egyptian colloquial dialect in Egyptian theatrical productions.[227] The culmination of this practical theatrical activity came in 1935, when the Egyptian "National Theatre" [*al-Masrah al-Qawmi*] opened in Cairo. Appropriately, its first production was Tawfiq al-Hakim's Egyptianist play *People of the Cave* [*Ahl al-Kahf*].[228]

The Fine Arts

"National" development appears to have been less pronounced in the sphere of fine arts. In the journals of the 1920s, one can find frequent mention of artists' groups and organizations that attempted to promote Egyptian fine arts. In the middle of the decade, the Modernist School associated with the journal *al-Fajr* served as the main forum for the encouragement of avant-garde styles in painting and music. In addition to the journal's frequent summons for the development of new and original Egyptian painting, some of the school's members were themselves painters whose work dealt with scenes of Egyptian life in a realistic manner.[229] Later in the decade, the most prominent artistic association of a nationalist nature was apparently the "Society of Imagination" [*Jama'at al-Khayal*]. The major themes of the painting of this group were Egyptian nature, the daily life of Egyptians, and occasionally Pharaonic scenes.[230] The society's most important painter was Mahmud Sa'id, whose realistic portrayal of contemporary Egyptian life received high praise from several leading Egyptian nationalist intellectuals.[231] In sculpture, the most prominent nationalist artist of the 1920s and early 1930s was Mahmud Mukhtar, whose sizable corpus of distinctively Egyptianist sculpture—Egyptian peasant women, Pharaonically inspired busts, figures from Egyptian village life, and his masterpiece of a woman facing the *khamasin* wind of Egypt—are the most striking visible expression of the Egyptianist era.[232]

Poetry

Set against the dramatic development of an Egyptian national fiction and the less pronounced but still appreciable nationalist production in the genres of drama and the visual arts, there was less artistic production of an Egyptianist quality in the field of poetry. By and large, Arabic poetry in Egypt even in the post-1919 era continued to be more traditional, and thereby less Egyptianist, in both its form and its content.

Two poetic trends of the 1920s and the early 1930s deserve mention in the context of Egyptian national literature, however. First, on the theoretical level a considerable movement of protest against the Arabic-inspired neoclassicism prevalent in Egyptian poetry since the later nineteenth century developed in Egypt after World War I. While not explicitly nationalist in character, it paralleled the Egyptian territorial nationalism of the period in its revolt against the Arab poetic canons of the past. Second, the subject matter of Egyptian poetry, as already noted, showed a partial change in the post-1919 era, with Islamic and Ottoman themes (particularly the latter) appearing less frequently and with local and purely Egyptian motifs occupying a more central place.

The new approach to Arabic poetry had begun to manifest itself just before World War I, particularly in the early writings of the three younger poets, Ibrahim 'Abd al-Qadir al-Mazini, 'Abd al-Rahman Shukri, and 'Abbas Mahmud al-'Aqqad, who self-consciously styled themselves as a new "School of Innovation" [*madrasat al-tajdid*]. Although Mazini and 'Aqqad eventually broke with Shukri, the group's modernist approach to poetry became a very influential one upon the publication of a two-volume work of literary criticism by Mazini and 'Aqqad, *al-Diwan,* in 1921. It is from the latter publication that the group and the outlook they represented acquired the name by which they have since been known, the *Diwan* Group.[233]

The literary emphases of the *Diwan* Group—their demand for the organic unity of a poem, their emphasis on meaning rather than form, and above all their insistence that poetry express the subjective feelings of the poet—paralleled the prevailing political Egyptianism of the post-1919 period. First, their vehement criticism of the barrenness and poverty of the Arabic neoclassicism still prevalent in Egyptian Arabic poetry at the time was both a reflection and a reinforcement of the anti-Arab mood that characterized Egyptian nationalist sentiment after World War I. Beyond this, their substantive suggestions concerning the writing of poetry were thoroughly congruent with the Egyptianist mood of the 1920s. Their emphasis on the central place of emotion and personal experience in poetry led them naturally to focus on the local scenes and life of their own country, which they themselves had witnessed and been moved by; their opposition to the rhetorical exaggeration found in earlier Arabic poetry and their summons to the use of direct and simple language was the poet's equivalent of the novelist's and dramatist's use of colloquial language; and their relentless insistence that the poet deal with contemporary reality in a realistic fashion obviously mirrored the modernism and realism characteristic of the theory of Egyptian national literature.[234]

In terms of the subject matter of postwar Egyptian Arabic poetry, the decade of the 1920s was the heyday of "patriotic" poetry in Egypt. Of the three great Arabic poets of the early twentieth century in Egypt, Ahmad Shawqi addressed Egyptianist themes as diverse as the 1918 meeting of Wafdist leaders with Wingate, which marked the beginning of the postwar movement for independence; the Milner Commission and Plan of 1919–1920; the exile, return, and personality of the Revolution's leader, Sa'd Zaghlul; and the need for national unity among Egyptian religious communities and Egyptian political parties. In addition, much of his poetry of the 1920s celebrated nonpolitical but indisputably Egyptian nationalist subjects: the establishment of *Bank Misr,* the opening of the new Egyptian University, and (as we have noted) Pharaonic themes such as the Sphinx, Pharaonic temples, and Tut-Ankh-Amon. The patriotic poetry of Shawqi [*wataniyyat Shawqi*] now became almost the official nationalist poetry of the new postwar era.[235]

Shawqi's poetic peer, Hafiz Ibrahim, appears to have published less overtly political poetry after World War I. But his postwar verse did deal with Egyptian natural scenes and Pharaonic themes.[236] The third leading Arabic poet writing in Egypt in the early twentieth century was Khalil Mutran. Although originally non-Egyptian, even he absorbed much of the Egyptian nationalist mood of the 1920s, composing poems on Egyptian natural and rural themes as well as occasionally Pharaonicist pieces such as his celebration of Tut-Ankh-Amon of 1924.[237] Other neoclassical poets of the postwar era largely followed the lead of these three dominant figures, replacing their earlier Ottomanist political sentiments with a focus upon the new nation-state of Egypt.[238]

Given the concern with Egyptian and frequently with Egyptianist subject matter apparent in the postwar writings of older Egyptian poets, it is hardly surprising that the work of younger Egyptian poets also reflected the prevailing Egyptian territorial nationalism of the era. 'Aqqad's postwar poetry both directly addressed political subjects (such as Zaghlul's return from exile in 1923) and dealt with Egyptianist themes such as the Pharaonic monuments of Egypt, the Nile, and the Egyptian countryside with its seasonal variations.[239] One of the most prolific younger poets of postwar Egypt and a major influence in the development of Egyptian poetry from the 1930s onward was Ahmad Zaki Abu Shadi; in the 1920s he produced both a collection of *Poems about Egypt* [1925] that expressed his nationalist views, as well as the previously cited collection *The Land of the Phar-*

aohs [1926] containing poems about Pharaonic Egypt.[240] In the journal *al-Fajr* in the mid-1920s, Ahmad Hilmi Salam and Ahmad Rami published poems based on local Egyptian subject matter; those of the latter occasionally employed the colloquial dialect for the speech of their characters.[241] Toward the end of the decade Muhammad al-Asmar, himself a member of the Association of National Literature of the early 1930s, composed "patriotic" poems that appeared in the Liberal *al-Siyasa al-Usbu'iyya.*[242]

The most vivid expression of the penetration of the Egyptianist perspective into Egyptian poetry in the post-1919 era was the development of a new subgenre of poetic production, that of the "national anthem" [*al-nashid al-qawmi*]. Numerous poets, both older and younger, turned to the task of composing anthems suitable for the inspiration of the citizenry of newly independent Egypt. The titles of the most famous are a sufficient indication of their Egyptian nationalist nature: Ahmad Shawqi's "Little Son of Egypt" [*Bunayya Misr*], Ahmad Muharram's "Egypt the Free" [*Misr al-Hurra*], and Sayyid Darwish's "My Country My Country" [*Biladi Biladi*].[243] The refrain of the last is worth quoting as a final illustration of the territorial nationalist orientation of Egyptian national literature: "My country my country—to you my love and my heart."[244]

III

IDEOLOGY IN ACTION: EGYPT, THE ARABS, AND THE EAST IN THE 1920s

10

Egypt and the Arab World in the 1920s

The intellectual currents analyzed in the preceding chapters did not exist in a vacuum. They developed in a particular political and socioeconomic milieu that they both reflected and affected. The ideology of Egyptian territorial nationalism gained ascendancy in the environment of the post-1919 era and thus can be understood and explained only in its specific context. But at the same time the Egyptianist worldview of the period also played a role in shaping new sets of attitudes and new patterns of behavior. In particular, the orientation of educated Egyptians toward neighboring regions can be appreciated only in light of the intellectual atmosphere of Egypt after the Revolution of 1919.

In this and the following chapter, the political ramifications of the predominantly Egyptianist and correspondingly anti-Arab mood that prevailed among the educated Egyptian public in the 1920s will be considered. This chapter examines how the Egyptian elite and the new state they controlled acted in regard to Egypt's Arab neighbors; the next chapter treats Egyptian attitudes and actions relating to the wider "Eastern" world.

Fundamental to an appreciation of the practical Egyptian relationship with the Arab world is an understanding of regional conditions at the time. Simply stated, the circumstances of the 1920s were not conducive to the development of a positive Egyptian relationship with neighboring Arab regions. For most of the nineteenth century, there had been a considerable difference in the pace of change occurring in Egypt and that taking place in other Arabic-speaking lands. Egypt's precocious modernization equally in the political, economic, and social spheres had itself contributed heavily to the sense of separate nationalism apparent in Egypt by the early twentieth century. This differential in development was pronounced in the 1920s prior to the deceleration in the rate of Egyptian modernization and the acceleration of the pace of development in other Arab regions, which eventually began to bring conditions in Egypt and the Arab world into greater equilibrium. Thus the contrast between an economically developed, culturally Europeanized, and politically independent Egypt that had just undergone a national "revolution," on the one hand, and an economically more underdeveloped, culturally less Westernized, and politically subjugated Arab world, on the other, was at its greatest in the 1920s. As we have demonstrated, the natural result of these tangible disparities was for Egyptian nationalist intellectuals to view Egypt and its people as something quite different from their Arab neighbors. In much the same manner, the disparities also led the political and economic leadership of Egypt to find little sense of community or shared interest linking Egypt to the Arab world.

Egyptian Economic and Cultural Collaboration with the Arab World

Despite the general detachment of educated Egyptians from the Arabs in the 1920s, the decade was not totally without Egyptian efforts aimed at increasing Egyptian interaction with the neighboring Arab world. As shall be shown shortly, this seldom extended to the political realm. But, in regard to the more innocuous spheres of economics and culture, there were various attempts to develop greater Egyptian-Arab cooperation even in the Egyptianist atmosphere of the 1920s.

Undoubtedly the most important exponent of Egyptian economic and cultural collaboration with the Arabs in the 1920s was Muhammad Tal'at Harb, the founder and first president of *Bank Misr.* Of Arab origin (the "Harb" tribe in Sinai), he had long demonstrated a greater concern for the Arabs than that shown by most Egyptians.[1] Although a committed Egyptian nationalist, he differed from most of his peers in viewing Egypt as an inseparable part of the Arab world in linguistic and cultural terms, and he believed that tangible benefits were to be had by both parties as a result of increasing Egyptian commercial links with its Arab neighbors.[2] Thus, on the basis of both cultural affinity and economic utility, he repeatedly advocated the intensification of Egyptian economic and cultural ties with the Arab world.[3]

Among Egyptian political publicists, exhortations to the Egyptian public to offer cultural assistance as well as economic aid to other "Eastern" (not exclusively Arab) peoples occasionally appeared in Wafdist publications; but on the whole, such notions remained little more than vague platitudes on the part of spokesmen for the Wafd in the 1920s.[4] The most detailed proposals for inter-Arab economic and cultural cooperation appear to have come from publicists associated with the Liberal Party. In 1927–1928 Muhammad Husayn Haykal wrote a series of articles advocating the development of closer cultural and educational ties between Egypt and its Arab neighbors. Among other things he called for preferential rules for the admission of Arab students to the new Egyptian University; for the dispatch of Egyptian educational missions to "Eastern Arab" countries; and for the convening of periodic conferences that would bring Arab intellectuals together for exchange of information and ideas.[5] Haykal's associate Mahmud 'Azmi went beyond the cultural realm to suggest a variety of measures that would promote greater economic as well as cultural integration of Egypt and the Arab lands of the Fertile Crescent. His proposals included educational coordination to create a common core curriculum for schools in Egypt and the Fertile Crescent; the promotion of inter-Arab trade through the lowering of tariff barriers between Arab countries and the granting of preferential trade status among them; the easing of visa requirements to facilitate travel and interchange; and the creation of a currency union between Egypt and the Mandated territories of the Fertile Crescent.[6] Nor were suggestions of Egyptian cultural outreach to the Arab world the preserve of liberals and westernizers such as Haykal and ʻAzmi in the 1920s: similar proposals for closer educational integration and the convening of conferences for Arab intellectuals came from more conservative figures as well.[7]

More important than the wish is the reality. Such proposals for Egyptian economic and cultural cooperation with the Arab world went largely unrealized in the 1920s. In the economic sphere, there are only a few projects of Egyptian-Arab collaboration dating from the 1920s. One that failed to develop was that of a group of Egyptian and Syrian-born notables (including Ahmad Shafiq, Shaykh Muhammad Bakhit, Muhammad Rashid Rida, and the Syrian financier Habib Lutf Allah) who in the mid-1920s attempted to obtain the concession to establish a National Bank, first in the Sharifian Kingdom of the Hijaz and then in the emerging Saʻudi state; the overthrow of the former and the fundamentalism of the latter doomed their efforts to failure.[8] A similar attempt by Ahmad Shafiq to establish an "Islamic company" for prospecting in the Arabian Peninsula was also rejected by the cautious ibn Saʻud.[9]

The financial expansion into Arab Asia that had eluded Shafiq and his associates in the Arabian Peninsula was at least partially achieved by *Bank Misr* in the Fertile Crescent. Talʻat Harb had high hopes of establishing branches of *Bank Misr* in both British-controlled Palestine and French-run Syria and Lebanon in the 1920s, and he made several trips to these areas between 1925 and 1929 in an endeavor to find local partners for such branches.[10] His efforts failed in Palestine, where local subscriptions were insufficient to meet the 49 percent of share capital envisaged by Harb for Palestinian investors.[11] His efforts in Syria were more successful: agreement on a joint venture between *Bank Misr* and Bank ʻIzz al-Din of Tripoli was reached in 1929, and the office of *Banque Misr-Syrie-Liban* opened in Beirut in 1930.[12]

Bank Misr's often cited penetration into the Arab world in the 1920s should not be exaggerated, however: this extension of its operations to Arab Asia came only at the end of the decade, well after it had opened its first foreign branch in Paris; the branch established in Syria and Lebanon was not a financial success, reportedly losing money through the early 1930s;[13] and its expansion into the Fertile Crescent was at any rate incomplete, as a Palestinian branch of the Bank was never created in the interwar period.[14] It should also be noted that its endeavors were private ones. As far as the Egyptian government was concerned, apparently the only official project of Egyptian economic involvement in an Arab country in the 1920s was an agreement of 1928 with the Saʻudi government for the provision of limited Egyptian assistance for the improvement of facilities for pilgrims in the Islamic Holy Cities.[15]

The limitations of Egypt's economic connections with the Arab world in the 1920s can be seen best in statistics. Since the nineteenth century, the economic linkages of an agriculturally based Egypt had been primarily with the industrial economies of the West rather than with its agricultural neighbors, and this continued to hold true in the 1920s. In 1928–1929, about 4 percent of Egyptian imports came from Arab Asia, whereas less than 2 percent of Egyptian exports went there; this was hardly a vital economic nexus between Egypt and the Arab East.[16]

A greater degree of Egyptian collaboration with the Arab world in the 1920s was realized in regard to the cultural sphere. The inauguration of significant cultural linkages between Egyptians and other Arabs in the modern period began in the 1920s. Modern Arab professional meetings date from 1926, when an Arab antiquities conference convened in Egypt; before the decade was over, similar periodic meetings of Arab doctors and Arab writers had been begun.[17] The same year witnessed the first organized tour of students from other Arab countries sent to Egypt.[18] An Arab cultural event of significance occurred in 1927, when Ahmad Shafiq and the Eastern Bond Society organized an international Arab conference honoring the poet Ahmad Shawqi. Attended by representatives from most Arab countries and receiving Egyptian royal patronage, it was the occasion of fervent declarations of Arab cultural similarity and solidarity.[19]

But these Egyptian-Arab cultural contacts of the 1920s also had their limitations. One was that as a whole, Egyptians were less enthusiastic about cultural interaction than were other Arabs. Whereas Arab student groups began to visit Egypt in 1926, it was 1929 before reciprocal Egyptian student tours to the Fertile Crescent were inaugurated.[20] Despite the hopes of its sponsors that the Shawqi celebration of 1927 would lead to institutionalized Arab collaboration in the codification and modernization of the Arabic language, further efforts by the Eastern Bond to organize an international Arabic language conference got bogged down in questions of precedence among Arab states and led to no permanent results.[21] Most importantly, even these private efforts at inter-Arab cultural collaboration received little or no support from the Egyptian government. Thus, in spite of the repeated appeals of Egyptian and Arab intellectuals, nothing appears to have been done to liberalize admission requirements for other Arabs into the Egyptian University. Similarly, Ahmad Shafiq's efforts to prod the then formally independent Arab regimes to discuss the coordination of educational curricula was supported in Iraq but flatly rejected by the Egyptian Minister of Education, the indisputably Egyptianist Ahmad Lutfi al-Sayyid.[22] Hence appeals for inter-Arab cultural interaction remained purely rhetorical in the 1920s. It was not until the 1930s that, in a changed political as well as cultural climate, such efforts at Arab cultural collaboration received official endorsement in Egypt.

Egypt's Political Relationship with the Arab World

In comparison to the occasional receptivity of Egyptians at least to ideas of Egyptian economic and cultural interaction with the Arab world, there was very little openness on the part of educated Egyptians to notions of political collaboration with Egypt's Arab neighbors. The concept of Arab "unity" per se was only infrequently discussed in Egyptian political circles in the 1920s, and what little opinion was voiced on the subject tended both to exclude Egypt from the terms of discussion and to be pessimistic concerning the possibilities of Arab unity. Looser ideas of Egyptian-Arab political cooperation for common ends were occasionally put forth by Egyptian publicists, but they were usually phrased in heavily instrumental and primarily Egyptianist terms.

The position of Egyptian nationalist writers concerning the issue of Arab "unity" as such was overwhelmingly negative in the 1920s and early 1930s. The idea of the Arabic-speaking peoples forming one interrelated unit was presented both as an outmoded concept in conflict with the "spirit" of the post-World War I world and an idea "contradictory" to the existence of the modern Egyptian nation-state founded on a territorial basis.[23] To Sami al-Jaridini, territorially based nationalism such as had developed in Europe was the ideal model both for Egypt and for other Eastern nations, and it was a concept fundamentally at variance with notions of Arab, Muslim, or Eastern unity. In his view, Arab unity in particular was "nothing but a sincere and well-intentioned fantasy which conflicts with reality in all its complexities"; anticipating Sa'd Zaghlul's famous comment made later in 1925, he dismissed Arab unity as "no more than the union of the weak with the weak. And what sum will you get by multiplying zero by other zeros?"[24] From Muhammad Lutfi Jum'a's opinion of 1922 that Arab unity would take "hundreds of years at least" to be realized, to *al-Ahram*'s view of 1930 that the creation of "a government unified in every sense of the word" was an impossibility for the Arabs in light of current political realities, articulate opinion in Egypt in the 1920s and early 1930s regarded Arab unity as unlikely.[25] Muhammad 'Abd Allah 'Inan captured the general disdain of Egyptian nationalists for Arabism in his characterization of Arab unity as "an imaginary aspiration devoid of any practical basis or foundation, . . . a mirage which the facts and circumstances of reality completely dissolve."[26]

Even those who believed that Egypt was culturally part of the Arab world did not extend their perception of Egypt's relationship with other speakers of Arabic to the political sphere. Muhammad Husayn Haykal, while writing of the lands of the "Arab East," Egypt included, as "one nation from the spiritual aspect," nonetheless spoke of the future political connection between the lands of the Arab East only as one of "unity . . . in goal and in desire."[27] Similarly Mahmud 'Azmi proposed only a program of Arab economic and cultural collaboration rather than the political unification that had been attempted but had failed during and after World War I.[28] Perhaps the clearest indication of Egyptian remoteness from ideas of Arab political integration may be obtained from a consideration of the views of Muhammad 'Ali 'Alluba, one of the leading supporters of Egyptian involvement in Arab affairs in the 1930s. In 1930, in a speech otherwise devoted to promoting the benefits of inter-Arab economic and cultural cooperation, 'Alluba explicitly defined such cooperation as desirable only if it remained "far removed from politics."[29]

Egyptians did not express much more enthusiasm for the more limited concept of political cooperation between the separate Arab states. When publicists in Egypt did suggest the possibility of Egyptian political collaboration with Egypt's neighbors in the 1920s, their proposals were usually not confined to the Arabs alone. The criteria for such collaboration were functional rather than national in this period, being suggestions for what were in effect informal anti-imperialist alliances directed not at the Arabs per se but to all the peoples of "the East" who shared the common problem of resisting the domination of the West.[30] Some proposals for specifically Arab political collaboration were put forth in Egypt, such as *al-Ahram*'s call for an anti-imperialist "alliance" of Arab states in 1924 or the suggestion made by *al-Balagh al-Usbu'i* in 1929 for "mutual agreement, cooperation, and the formation of a united front by the nationalist movements in Egypt, Palestine, Iraq and Transjordan" in order to oppose their common enemy, Great Britain.[31] As the last quotation indicates, however, these were proposals for the pragmatic political collaboration of separate Arab "movements" rather than the later Arab nationalist vision of one Arab nation seeking political fusion.

Two additional qualifications of these suggestions for Egyptian political cooperation with the Arabs put forth in Egypt at the time need to be made. First, such proposals were usually premised on the benefits that collaboration would bring for Egypt. As the Wafdist ‘Abd al-Rahman ‘Azzam put it in 1928, Egypt needed to “exploit [its] central position in the Arab world to a great extent in its relationship with all the Western nations so that these will know if Egypt is satisfied the Near East as a whole is satisified.”[32] The possibly apocryphal but nonetheless pithy remark once attributed to Zaghlul—that “Egypt controls the electric switch; if you push it, all the Arab lands follow”—captures the instrumental outlook that underlay much of the Egyptian attitude toward the Arab world in the 1920’s.[33]

Second, suggestions for greater Egyptian political interaction with the Arabs assumed Egypt’s primacy in any such interaction. When suggestions for Egypt to offer political, economic, or cultural assistance to its Arab neighbors were made, their tone was usually a patronizing one; such aid would give the Arabs “the knowledge and expertise which it [Egypt] has already achieved,” and thus would allow the Arabs to “take the same road which Egypt has taken.”[34] Cooperation with the more backward Arab world was a one-way street, a *mission civilisatrice,* to its Egyptian proponents in the 1920s; a “duty” imposed upon Egypt by cultural affinity, to the Wafdist *al-Balagh al-Usbu‘i;* a “burden of leadership” mandated by history, to the Liberal *al-Siyasa al-Usbu‘iyya.*[35]

At least as frequent as these functionalist and open-ended suggestions for regional political cooperation in this period, however, were outright Egyptian disavowals of the utility of such endeavors. Stated briefly, Egyptian nationalists believed that their new Egyptian nation needed to concentrate on its own affairs. Egypt had little or nothing to gain from involvement in the politics of the more backward Arab countries: on the contrary, such involvement would only waste precious energies that could be put to better use at home. In addition, entanglement in regional Arab politics would embroil Egypt in political adventures born of nostalgia but with little relevance to contemporary political realities and even fewer prospects for success.[36]

Representative of this general position were Husayn Mahmud’s criticisms of Egyptian participation in Arab political affairs as developed in a 1930 article on “Egypt and the Arab Countries.”[37] Mahmud enumerated a long list of utilitarian reasons that simultaneously buttressed the concept of an exclusively Egyptian political orientation and repudiated the notion of Egyptian involvement in Arab political life. Egypt was poor in natural resources. The manpower at the country’s disposal was limited. Struggling for her own national liberation from the British, Egypt needed to concentrate all her sparse resources, forces, and efforts within the Nile Valley and not disperse and waste them in the wider Arab arena. Beyond these pragmatic and Egyptocentric considerations, Mahmud perceived fundamental disparities among the different Arab countries. Egypt could not bridge the natural gaps separating the Arab lands. Mahmud’s conclusion on the Arab nations and Egypt’s relationship with them expressed the sense of exclusive Egyptian nationalism and “Egypt-firstism” prevalent in Egypt in the 1920s:

> The other Arab nations differ basically from one another in the degree of their development. Each has a distinctive local situation and its own unique problems. It is not in our interest to take upon ourselves the leadership of these nations.[38]

The Egyptian State and the Arab World

An obvious question concerning the actual foreign policy of the new Egyptian state in the 1920s relates to the degree to which Egypt was its own master. Egypt became formally independent in February 1922. However, given the facts that the unilateral British declaration granting Egypt independence at that time had also reserved major areas of domestic and foreign affairs for British supervision, and that the British continued to retain powerful levers for influencing Egyptian policy making, in reality Egyptian independence was far from complete. Although the precise degree of British influence and/or control over Egyptian foreign policy will become apparent in the analysis that follows, some preliminary awareness of the British-imposed constraints under which the Egyptian government operated is necessary.

In general terms, the Egyptian government possessed considerable freedom of action in regional affairs in the 1920s. To be sure, there were many spheres of foreign relations, particularly issues that touched upon British strategic interests in the Middle East or questions that might affect British relations with other major powers, where the British unquestionably interfered in Egyptian foreign policy either in the positive sense of requiring Egypt to do certain things or in the negative sense of forbidding actions that would have been opposed to British interests in the region. Even after allowing for the considerable measure of British control over Egyptian foreign policy, however, there were still large areas of regional international relations in which the British did not shape the substance of Egyptian foreign policy. In some cases, the issue at hand did not directly impinge upon British interests and so the Egyptians were left to their own devices; in other matters that did touch upon British interests, the British sometimes chose not to expend their sizable but nonetheless finite resources in pressuring the Egyptians; and there were yet other specific developments about which, for all their vaulted knowledge of things Middle Eastern, the British were simply in the dark as to the precise details of what the Egyptian government was doing in its relations with its neighbors. In sum, the British often influenced and sometimes even controlled the specifics of Egyptian policy making in the period of the parliamentary monarchy, but they did not do so consistently, and frequently the degree of their control over the Egyptian state was less complete than has generally been assumed.

An important preliminary observation about the actual foreign policy of Egypt in the 1920s was that it was oriented more toward the developed nations of Europe than toward Egypt's more "backward" neighbors. Thus independent Egypt established its first formal diplomatic relations with European states rather than with Arab or Muslim countries. Whereas diplomatic missions had been opened in London, Paris, and Rome by 1923 and in Berlin, Brussels, Madrid, Prague, and Athens by 1925, the only Middle Eastern states with which Egypt opened formal relations in the mid-1920s were Turkey and the short-lived Sharifian Kingdom in the Hijaz.[39] The conclusion of treaties of friendship and the inauguration of formal diplomatic relations with the fellow-Muslim states of Iran and Afghanistan did not occur until 1928.[40] In contrast, Egypt's formal relations with those few Arab lands that were technically independent were attentuated throughout the 1920s: relations with the Sharifian state in Arabia lasted only until 1924; formal relations with its Sa'udi successor were broken from 1926 to 1936;

and Egypt's first treaty with a technically independent Arab state was concluded only in 1931, when a Treaty of Extradition was signed with Iraq.[41]

The practical political relationship of the newly independent state of Egypt and the many political units into which the Arab world was divided in the 1920s of course differed according to the conditions existing in each Arab country. Some Arab areas were geographically and historically remote from Egypt, others both temporally and spatially closer to it; a few were independent, most under foreign domination; some paralleled Egypt in their recent development, while others shared little if anything of Egypt's recent pattern of evolution. But through these different relationships one common skein was apparent for the period from the emergence of a technically independent Egyptian state in 1922–1923 to the end of the decade: the absence of Egyptian policies aimed at promoting a common national bond between Egypt and its Arab neighbors.

Egypt and the Arab West

Throughout the 1920s the new Egyptian state had little official connection with the Arab regions to the west of Egypt. France was dominant in the Maghrib, and the policy of the Egyptian government in the 1920s was oriented toward establishing and consolidating good relations with France rather than toward promoting any Egyptian links with the indigenous Arab/Muslim population of French North Africa. Although the Egyptian public and press occasionally did express sympathy with Arab nationalist activities directed against French and Spanish imperial domination in the Maghrib, such as the ʻAbd al-Krim revolt in the Rif in the mid-1920s,[42] the Egyptian government avoided any official involvement in the politics of the Arab west. An indication of Egyptian acceptance of the colonial status quo in the Maghrib appears in relation to the participation of the Riffian delegation in the Cairo Caliphate Congress in 1926: when the Spanish government formally protested such a possibility, the Egyptian authorities bowed to Spanish pressure and refused to allow a delegation representing the Riffian rebels to enter Egypt.[43]

Independent Egypt's only significant political contact with an Arab land to the west of the Nile Valley in the 1920s was with neighboring Italian-controlled Libya. Here geography rather than ideology was the crucial variant that caused Egyptian involvement in Libyan affairs: Egypt shares a common border with Libya, and problems of geographical propinquity necessitated the formulation of practical Egyptian policies toward its Libyan neighbor.

In the mid-1920s, two issues concerning Libya became matters of public concern and controversy in Egypt. The first to develop was the issue of the use by Libyan opponents of Italian rule of Egyptian territory as a refuge and/or a base. In January 1924, the Italian government requested the government of Egypt to apprehend and surrender to the Italian authorities in Libya a number of Libyan Arabs currently in Egypt.[44] When the demnand became known in Egypt it generated considerable protest, "without distinction of party," over the possibility of the government's giving in to Italian pressure and failing to defend both the person of fellow Arabs resisting imperialism and the sovereign rights of newly independent Egypt.[45] Faced with the Italian demand from one side and public indignation from the other, the ministry attempted to compromise. On 24 February 1924, it announced that the individuals in question would neither be returned to Libya nor allowed to remain in Egypt; instead, they would have to leave Egypt for another refuge of their choice.[46] Thus the substance of the Italian demand (that Egypt not become a base of anti-Italian activity) was met while the appearance of Egyptian national honor was salvaged. What is of note in this early diplomatic incident in the new Egypt is the result, which placed Egypt's national interest in harmonious relations with Italy ahead of solidarity and support for Egypt's Arab neighbors.

The second issue involving Egyptian relations with Libya in the 1920s was more directly related to Egypt itself. This was the question of the Egypto-Libyan border. The desert boundary between Egypt and Libya had never been precisely demarcated while both were Ottoman territories, and a tentative Anglo-Italian agreement on the border line had not yet been finalized when Egypt became independent in 1922. Successive Egyptian ministries resisted Italian efforts to negotiate the boundary in the early 1920s; only in mid-1925, after Italy had forced the issue by its occupation of the disputed oasis of Jaghbub, did the ministry of Ahmad Ziwar enter into serious negotiations.[47] Impelled both by the desire for good relations with Italy and by its earlier preliminary border accord with the Italians, this was one issue in which the British government did intervene to shape the regional policy of "independent" Egypt, repeatedly pressuring the Egyptians to accept the Italian interpretation of the boundary.[48] In December 1925 the Egyptians did so, reluctantly concluding the Western Frontier Agreement that recognized Italian sovereignty over Jaghbub.[49]

Given the Egyptianist temper of the mid-1920s, the public reaction to the lingering dispute over the border in general and Jaghbub in particular was thoroughly oriented to the national honor and national interests of Egypt. The emphasis of press commentary in the dispute was overwhelmingly on the national rights of Egypt and how they had been violated, first by the Italian occupation of Jaghbub, then by the Ziwar ministry's acceptance of that occupation.[50] In the Wafdist press the disputed border territories were declared to be as much part of Egypt as were Cairo or Alexandria;[51] it was the ministry's "cession of sacred Egyptian soil" in the middle of the Sahara for which it was roundly condemned in December 1925;[52] and even the characterization of the agreement of December 1925 as an abandonment of Muslim rights that would "disgrace Egypt in the eyes of Islam" had as its operational referent the international prestige of Egypt.[53]

Egyptian Royal Ambitions in the Arabian Peninsula

Egypt had more sustained and more intense political contact in the 1920s with the Arab regions to the east of the Nile Valley. One stimulus to greater Egyptian involvement in the affairs of Arab Asia in the 1920s was the presence of a more visible Arab nationalist movement in that area. Although the aspirations of Arab nationalists still excluded Egypt in the 1920s, the existence both of independent states in the Arabian Peninsula with which Egypt had to interact and of nationalist groups in the Mandated territories of the Fertile Crescent, which consciously sought Egyptian sympathy and assistance in their struggle against the British and the French, served to pull Egypt into occasional involvement in the political affairs of Arab Asia.

Independent Egypt's first substantive contact with an Asian Arab state was with the short-lived Arab Kingdom of the Hijaz headed by Sharif/King Husayn. The formal Egyptian diplomatic relationship with the Kingdom of the Hijaz was of very brief duration. Although the government of Egypt wished to establish diplomatic relations and an Egyptian Consulate in the Hijaz as early as 1923, the British requested that formal Egyptian relations with the Hijaz await the regularization of British-Hijazi diplomatic relations.[54] As a result, the actual establishment of an Egyptian Consulate in Jidda did not occur until April 1925, only a few months before the extinction of the Hijazi Kingdom by the rival Sa'udi state.[55]

Nor was the informal relationship between Egypt and the Kingdom of the Hijaz a particularly harmonious one. In both 1923 and 1924, prior to King Husayn's abdication and the Kingdom's loss of Mecca to the Sa'udis in October 1924, serious disputes between the Egyptian and Sharifian governments occurred concerning the ceremonial *Mahmal* (decorated litter) and *Kiswa* (black brocade cover for the *Ka'ba*) that were sent annually as part of the Pilgrimage from Egypt. In 1923, the Egyptian attempt to send a medical mission along with the Egyptian Pilgrimage was interpreted by the sensitive regime in the Hijaz as a slur on its own health services: it refused entry to the mission, at which point the Egyptian government withdrew the *Mahmal*.[56] In the following year the terms of the medical services that would accompany the Egyptian Pilgrimage were negotiated in advance to the satisfaction of both governments, but tension arose when King Husayn attempted to remove the name of King Fu'ad from the *Kiswa*. The commander of the Egyptian Pilgrimage responded to the affront by making "slighting references to the Hijazis who, he recalled, had been trounced by the forces of Mohamed Ali a century before."[57]

An incident of late 1924 provides an excellent example of the marginality of Arab affairs in general to Egyptian nationalist opinion in the 1920s. As Sa'udi forces were overrunning the Hijaz in the fall of 1924, King Husayn's youngest son, Prince Zayd, passed through Egypt en route to London. In an interview in the press, he suggested that "Islamic" assistance rendered to his father would be most appreciated and expressed the hope that the government of neighboring Egypt would see its way to proffer assistance to the beleaguered Kingdom of the Hijaz. When reported in Egypt, Prince Zayd's remarks were interpreted as having been an appeal for Egyptian diplomatic, financial, or even military aid to be given to the Sharifian state.[58]

The idea of Egyptian intervention in the war in western Arabia provoked a storm of controversy inside Egypt. It was vehemently opposed by the major journals associated with Egypt's political parties. In the first instance, they argued that neither King Husayn nor the dynasty he had established were deserving of assistance. Although many Egyptians were apprehensive about the suitability of the Sa'udi regime as a custodian of the Islamic Holy Cities,[59] they were even more negative concerning Husayn and his regime. The King had "joined the ranks of the enemies of Islam" during World War I; he had also "fragmented the unity of the Arab nation" by his recent attempt to assume the office of the Caliphate; or he was simply "crazy" and his forced abdication justified.[60]

But beyond their longstanding animosity to King Husayn, Egyptian publicists maintained that neither Egyptian capabilities nor interests were such as to warrant intervention in Arabia in 1924. Editorials in *al-Balagh* and *al-Akhbar* argued that

Egypt was incapable of effective intervention, the former inquiring sarcastically how an Egypt that could not adequately liberate itself from the British was expected to extend its political power abroad, the latter maintaining that it was necessary for Egypt to cleanse its own house of "foreign occupation" before becoming involved in external disputes.[61] Intervention in Arabia was sometimes seen as serving British more than Egyptian interests by protecting the Sharifian client-state of Great Britain; it could possibly lead to an unnecessary Egyptian involvement in western Arabia in order to prop up a British protégé, or set an undesirable precedent for Egypt's future assumption of "the burden of defending the English Zionist colonies" in Palestine.[62]

The essential point in much Egyptian criticism of the idea of Egyptian intervention in the war in Arabia was that there was no Egyptian national interest at stake in the struggle. To 'Abbas Mahmud al-'Aqqad of the Wafd, the war in the Hijaz was simply of "no concern to Egypt," and involvement in it would bring "no benefit" to the country.[63] To Ibrahim 'Abd al-Qadir al-Mazini writing in *al-Akhbar,* the national interest of Egypt lay not in defending the Sharifians but in "the improvement of relations with the Najdis," which demanded no intervention in the Peninsula.[64] Of partisan Egyptian dailies, only the new *Kawkab al-Sharq* expressed the position that "events in the Hijaz can be considered as local Egyptian events" meriting Egyptian concern; its animosity to King Husayn, however, prevented it from advocating Egyptian intervention in the war on his behalf.[65] The Olympian tone of the Liberal *al-Siyasa* summarized the prevailing view of most indigenous Egyptian opinion toward the idea of Egyptian intervention in the Sa'udi-Sharifian war: *al-Siyasa's* position was that Egypt had no direct connection to this movement and thus that "we do not see any place for Egyptian interference in the affairs of these kingdoms and states in any official way."[66] The Sa'udi-Sharifian conflict in the Peninsula in 1924 was thus seen by the leaders of Egyptian public opinion through the prism of Egyptian concerns, and these involved the avoidance of Egyptian involvement in what was seen as a foreign controversy basically unconnected to Egypt or its national interests.

The rejection of the notion of an Egyptian role in Arabia was an attitude fully shared by the Wafdist ministry in 1924. Within a few days of the surfacing of the notion of Egyptian intervention in the Sa'udi-Sharifian war in October, it publicly announced a position of neutrality in the struggle, thereby effectively foreclosing the possibility of Egyptian intervention.[67] There is no record of the Zaghlul ministry's having undertaken any diplomatic initiatives in regard to the conflict in Arabia.[68]

This attitude of Egyptian noninvolvement in Arabian affairs did not extend through all official circles in Egypt, however. In contrast to the Wafd, the King and those associated with him appear to have perceived, in the conditions of turmoil obtaining in the Arabian Peninsula in 1924–1925, the possibility of extending Egyptian royal influence beyond the confines of Egypt. It is significant in this context that in October 1924, at the time of the controversy over possible Egyptian intervention in the Hijaz, the only quasi-official Egyptian approach to the British concerning such intervention came from an official of the Azharite religious hierarchy suggesting that the solution for the instability in the Hijaz would be to place the region under the authority of an international Muslim council, a proposal that obviously would have possibilities for Egypt and its Palace-linked religious establishment to play a significant role in the affairs of western Arabia.[69] Neither the Palace nor al-Azhar had an opportunity to develop a forward policy in Arabia in late 1924, when the incumbent Wafdist ministry was quick to repudiate the idea of Egyptian intervention in the Sharifian-Sa'udi struggle. But a year later, when the Wafd had been replaced by the royalist ministry of Ahmad Ziwar, the Palace could take action when the chance to become involved in Arabia once again arose.

In the summer of 1925, an increasingly desperate King 'Ali of the Hijaz sought financial and other assistance from the consuls of various foreign powers at Jidda. Among those he approached was the new Egyptian Consul, Salih 'Abd al-Rahman, apparently promising to support King Fu'ad's Caliphal ambitions in exchange for Egyptian financial aid and mediation on his behalf with the Sa'udis.[70] 'Abd al-Rahman, who apparently regarded Sa'udi power as a Russian-linked revolutionary threat to Egypt, extended 'Ali's approaches to a suggestion for the dispatch of Egyptian armed forces to the Hijaz to take control of the area and prevent Sa'udi conquest.[71] The Egyptian government did not go as far as to accept its agent's idea of armed intervention in Arabia, possibly because of British warnings not to go to that extreme.[72] But, aware that a successful Egyptian intervention in the Hijaz would bolster both Egypt's external prestige and King Fu'ad's claims to the Caliphate, it did mount a diplomatic initiative in Arabia in the fall of 1925.

In September 1925, Shaykh Muhammad Mustafa al-Maraghi was sent by King Fu'ad on a secret mission to Arabia. The ostensible goal of the mission was to arrange the terms of a negotiated settlement of the Sa'udi-Sharifian war.[73] But, as Martin Kramer's recent research in the Egyptian royal archives has shown, Maraghi's deeper purpose was to create an Egyptian sphere of influence in the Hijaz. In his discussion with King 'Ali in Jidda, Maraghi made demands that would have resulted in an Egyptian position in Arabia not dissimilar from that which the British tried to obtain in the Husayn-McMahon correspondence a decade earlier, including Egyptian supervision of security for the Pilgrimage, priority for Egyptians in technical appointments, and the general coordination of Hijazi with Egyptian foreign policy.[74] The hapless 'Ali had no choice but to concur with these sweeping Egyptian demands.[75]

Real power in Arabia, however, now rested with ibn Sa'ud. When he met with the latter in Mecca, Maraghi sought two things: first, acceptance of Fu'ad's claim to the Caliphate by ibn Sa'ud, then a local arrangement in the Hijaz that would provide for both local autonomy and international Muslim collaboration in the establishment of a new regime for the Holy Cities. The Shaykh's assumption apparently was that the historic Hijazi orientation toward Egypt in combination with Egyptian participation in the determination of Hijazi governance would result in Egyptian hegemony in western Arabia. According to Maraghi's report to King Fu'ad, ibn Sa'ud agreed to both principles in his discussions with the Shaykh.[76] Based on what he interpreted as a satisfactory Sa'udi response, Maraghi regarded his mission as a success: ignoring the interests of King 'Ali, whose appeals had sparked his journey, the Shaykh concluded his report to the King with the proud prediction that as a result of his endeavors, "it is probable that Egypt would have the greatest voice among the Islamic states, and the most influence, in the Holy Lands."[77]

But Maraghi grossly overestimated his achievements. Whatever ibn Sa'ud had promised the Shaykh in September, his actions after his conquest of the remainder of the Hijaz in December 1925 demonstrated no willingness to accept Egyptian preeminence in western Arabia. Rather than welcoming an Egyptian role in Western Arabia, in January 1926 ibn Sa'ud had himself declared King of the Hijaz. In essence, both Shaykh Maraghi and his royal sponsor had been had.

Perhaps partially because of a sense of having been gulled by ibn Sa'ud in 1925, King Fu'ad in particular demonstrated great hostility to the Sa'udi regime for the remainder of his life. The official Egyptian attitude of coolness and reserve toward the Sa'udi state, which was to prevail for most of the interwar period, was apparent as early as 1926 in relation to the Islamic Congress organized by the Sa'udis at Mecca in June–July 1926 to discuss local arrangements for the administration of the Holy Cities and the Pilgrimage. The Palace-linked Ziwar ministry had for long refused to participate in the Congress; the original Egyptian delegation in attendance was an unofficial one headed by Shaykh Muhammad Madi Abu al-'Aza'im, one of the leading Egyptian opponents of the movement for an Egyptian Caliphate.[78] Only after the Congress's convening in June 1926, when the Ziwar ministry had been replaced by a Liberal-dominated one that was both less subservient to the Palace and more aware of the need for Egyptian participation in the determination of matters pertaining to the Holy Cities and the Pilgrimage, was an official Egyptian delegation headed by Shaykh Muhammad al-Ahmadi al-Zawahiri appointed.[79]

When the official Egyptian delegation arrived in Mecca at the end of June, its participation in the Islamic Congress was limited. Reportedly instructed to avoid the discussion of political matters,[80] it temporarily withdrew from participation when the Congress did consider the question of borders between the Hijaz and Transjordan.[81] Its sole quasi-political intervention in the deliberations was unabashedly Egyptianist in nature, consisting of a vehement protest by Zawahiri against the separate use of the words "Egypt" and "the Sudan" in Congress proceedings and the ingenious suggestion that the term "Sudan" applied only to the non-Egyptian Sudan such as the Congo, a facesaving proposal that the Chair immediately accepted.[82] The Egyptian delegation was one of two delegations (that of the Yemen being the other) that refused to be bound by the contents of King ibn Sa'ud's message defining his policies in the future.[83] Thus in effect it avoided anything that could be construed as official Egyptian recognition of the newly expanded Sa'udi state.

An event occurring during the Mecca Islamic Congress wrote *finis* to the possibility of formal diplomatic relations between the Egyptian and Sa'udi governments. At Mina on 19 June, fundamentalist Wahhabis took offense at the music being played by the Egyptian escort of the *Mahmal.* When they began to assault the escort, the Egyptians opened fire, killing an estimated twenty-five Wahhabis and injuring scores more.[84] When a week later the *Mahmal* again became the object of a hostile Wahhabi demonstration, the Egyptian government on 30 June abruptly withdrew the *Mahmal* and its escort before all the Pilgrimage ceremonies had been completed.[85] Ibn Sa'ud apparently interpreted the incident as an intolerable remnant of foreign privilege within the territories of his new kingdom. Thus in the following year he attempted to impose strict conditions on the dispatch of the Egyptian *Mahmal,* among other things forbidding its accompaniment by an armed escort. The Egyptian government rejected these terms, and in 1927 and for a decade thereafter no Egyptian *Mahmal* was dispatched on the Pilgrimage.[86]

The trouble surrounding the *Mahmal* may have not been too displeasing to Egypt's monarch. It seems to have provided him with a convenient justification for not doing something he had been loath to do anyway, which was to establish formal diplomatic relations with the new Sa'udi kingdom that had been declared in January 1926. In an illuminating conversation with Arthur Henderson in August 1926, Fu'ad made the *Mahmal* incident the formal reason why Egypt could not yet accord diplomatic recognition to the Sa'udi state.[87] But his other remarks to Henderson reveal that the Egyptian monarch still had hopes of establishing Egyptian, and his own, dominance in western Arabia. He criticized the "fanaticism" of ibn Sa'ud and the Wahhabis, opined that this was making ibn Sa'ud "more and more unpopular," and stated that he himself had "no belief in the permanence of the present regime in the Hejaz." Fu'ad's ultimate intentions toward western Arabia and its Holy Cities in 1926 appear in his suggested solution for the instability that he anticipated would plague the region:

> In King Fuad's opinion there was only one solution for the Hejaz, namely, an Egyptian Governor on the same lines as for the Sudan. The Egyptian army was too large for the needs of Egypt, and two battalions might with advantage be sent to Jeddeh to keep order there. No other system would so surely guarantee the satisfactory control of the pilgrimages. He foresaw the closest co-operation for many years to come between England and Egypt. As the greatest Moslem Power, Great Britain should be the principal beneficiary of a regime which would ensure a well-ordered, sanitary and peaceful Haj.[88]

King Fu'ad's dreams of establishing an Egyptian political role in the Hijaz were utopian. The British immediately refused to sanction the approach for an Egyptian military occupation that the King had made in August 1926,[89] and the relative stability and order that the Sa'udi regime maintained thereafter provided no occasion for Egyptian political intervention in subsequent years. Yet although the King was too weak to take positive action in regard to Arabia, his position in Egypt was strong enough for him to prevent the regularization of Egyptian-Sa'udi relations. Until the eve of King Fu'ad's death in the spring of 1936, there were no formal diplomatic relations between Egypt and the Sa'udi state (renamed the Kingdom of Sa'udi Arabia in 1932). This was very much a personal policy of the Egyptian monarch, one he maintained in the face of repeated Sa'udi approaches toward the normalization of relations, in opposition to the feelings of much of Egyptian opinion and several Egyptian ministries that nonrecognition was counterproductive, and contrary to British perceptions that the situation of nonrecognition was the source of "a great deal of trouble to all concerned."[90] On the diplomatic level, the two largest independent Arab states of the interwar period existed in technical isolation from each other.

There is one other independent state in the Arabian Peninsula with which Egyptian "relations" need to be mentioned. This is the Yemen. As was the case with its larger neighbor to the north, there were no formal diplomatic relations between Egypt and the Yemen in the 1920s. The question of such recognition does not seem to have arisen until 1929, when the Imam Yahya dispatched a letter to King Fu'ad asking his assistance for Yemenis in Egypt.[91] Perhaps again seeing an opportunity for establishing an Egyptian position in Arabia, the King immediately dispatched a personal emissary to the Yemen on a good-will mission and considered the establishment of an Egyptian consulate in the Yemen.[92] In this case it was British pressure that dissuaded the Egyptian monarch from becoming involved in southwest Arabia: regarding Egyptian "interference" in the Yemen as both anti-British and anti-Sa'udi, the British cautioned Fu'ad that "Egypt has no interests" in the Yemen, hence needed no formal relationship with it.[93] King Fu'ad took the hint, immediately dropping the idea of establishing formal diplomatic relations with the Yemen.

These intermittent attempts to expand Egyptian (chiefly royal) influence in the political affairs of the Arabian Peninsula provide an excellent example of the absence of any sense of Arab nationalist sentiment among Egypt's political leadership in the 1920s. Spokesmen for Egypt's political parties strenuously opposed any Egyptian role in the Hijaz on the grounds that Egyptian national interests would not be served by such involvement; the King and his agents construed an Egyptian role in the Peninsula primarily in terms of royal prestige and influence; even an Arab-inclined journal such as *al-Ahram* (the only major newspaper favoring Egyptian intervention in the Peninsula in late 1924) justified its advocacy of an Egyptian forward policy in Arabia in terms of the "material and moral benefits and advantages" of such a policy for Egypt itself.[94] These episodes did not mark a challenge to the prevalent Egyptian territorial nationalism of the decade; rather, they reflected the primacy of that orientation among the Egyptian elite in the 1920s.

Syrian Mandate, Syrian Revolt, and Egyptian Response

The official position of the newly independent Egyptian government toward the French Mandate over Syria (including Lebanon) in the 1920s was one of accommodation with the indisputable reality of French hegemony. An agreement between the French and Egyptian governments regulating the status of Syro-Lebanese nationals resident in Egypt conferred at least indirect Egyptian recognition on the French Mandate. In effect the two governments divided jurisdiction over Syrians and Lebanese in Egypt; those only temporarily in the country were recognized by the Egyptian government as subject to French jurisdiction and diplomatic protection, and the French government in turn agreed that Syro-Lebanese "already established in Egypt" would come under the sway of the new Egyptian nationalities law then in the process of formulation.[95] Thus the government of Egypt acknowledged French authority over the persons of Syro-Lebanese traveling abroad, if not directly over Syria and Lebanon.

The central political event with respect to the Syrian Mandate in the 1920s was the Syrian Revolt of the mid-1920s. Revolt in Syria natually produced sympathy and support for the nationalist movement from the large and prosperous Syrian Arab community resident in Egypt by the 1920s. Both existing Syro-Lebanese organizations in Egypt and ad hoc committees brought into existence by the need to support the uprising in their homeland took the lead in publicizing the Syrian nationalist cause and in attempting to generate political and financial support for the rebels in the field.[96] The "innumerable telegrams" addressed by these bodies to international agencies and world public opinion calling for Syrian independence eventually generated formal protests from the French against Cairo's having become a "centre of malcontents and agitators" from Syria.[97] The central organizing body for this external assistance to the rebellion was the "Syrian-Palestinian Congress," which had its headquarters in Cairo: it may have raised £E 10,000 in Egypt alone in the mid-1920s for the support of the Syrian Revolt.[98]

But it was not only the Syro-Lebanese community in Egypt that came out in support of the Syrian rebels in late 1925. Much of native Egyptian opinion did so as well. Egyptian newspapers sent special correspondents to Syria to report on the struggle there; Egyptian poets wrote in praise of the Syrian rebels and lamented French acts of repression; and journals as diverse as the Syrian-run *al-Muqattam* and the Wafdist *Kawkab al-Sharq* called on Egyptians to render aid to the Syrian victims of the violence as it extended throughout much of Syria in the fall of 1925.[99] Material assistance from Egyptians soon was offered: an emergency committee to raise funds for Syrian relief was organized under the leadership of Prince 'Umar Tusun, and the efforts of one existing Egyptian organization, the Eastern Bond Society, are reported to have raised £E 1,200 within a short time of the French bombardment of Damascus for the same purpose.[100] By far the most prominent Egyptian to speak out publicly in support of the Syrian Revolt in 1925 was Sa'd Zaghlul, who on 5 November 1925 issued a "declaration to the nation" that publicly expressed Egyptian "sympathy for our suffering brothers" in Syria and condemned the French shedding of innocent blood in Damascus as a crime against humanity.[101] Zaghlul added his voice to those calling for Egyptians to contribute to Syrian relief and offered a personal donation of £E 100 for the purpose. Other Wafdist leaders followed Sa'd's lead, making their own contributions to Syrian relief; party publicists joined in the condemnation of France's actions in Syria.[102]

Egyptian sympathy for the Syrian nationalist cause in 1925 needs to be qualified and set in its proper context, however. Although there was considerable verbal and some material support for the Syrians in Egypt in 1925, there was no real sense of Egyptian involvement in the Syrian question expressed by Egyptians. Thus Sa'd Zaghlul's statement of 5 November, for all its justification of Egyptian concern with events in Syria on the grounds of "the firm bonds of history, language, religion, customs, and geographical propinquity" linking Egypt to Syria, nonetheless placed the Egyptian obligation of aiding the Syrians primarily on a humanitarian and universalist basis rather than on a more restricted nationalist one: "we think that this [financial aid] is the least that a neighbor must do for his neighbor, the least of what a man can give to his fellow man."[103] In his reply to a group of Syrians who visited him a few days later to thank him for his statement of support, Zaghlul similarly maintained that the sympathy he had voiced with the Syrian cause was no less than what "every Egyptian, indeed every Easterner, indeed every human being" should feel on account of the bloodshed occurring in Syria.[104] Perhaps most revealing about the Wafdist leader's attitude toward the Syrian issue in 1925 is what he was saying privately. According to his Wafdist colleague 'Abd al-Rahman 'Azzam, Zaghlul's declaration had come only at the prompting of 'Azzam. Even then the Wafdist leader had at first rejected the notion of making a public statement in support of the Syrians and Syrian relief. It was in his initial rejection of 'Azzam's request that Sa'd Zaghlul is supposed to have uttered the famous equation concerning the Arabs and the possibility of their realizing unity which has often been used to characterize the attitude of the entire Egyptian elite toward Arab nationalism in the 1920s: "If you add a zero and a zero and a zero, what is the result?"[105] Both the original derogation of Arab nationalism and the eventual expression of sympathy for the Syrian Revolt need to be noted.

On the official level, there is no record that the Egyptian ministry of Ahmad Ziwar spoke out publicly on the Syrian Revolt as the Wafd did in late 1925, or intervened diplomatically on behalf of the Syrian nationalists. Most importantly, the active concern of Egyptians with the situation in Syria was of brief duration, an aberration in the otherwise Egypt-centered attention of native Egyptian opinion throughout the 1920s. Occasioned by unusually dramatic events in Syria itself, Egyptian interest soon faded in intensity, resulting in no permanent Egyptian links with Arab nationalism.

Egypt and the Palestine Mandate in the 1920s

In view of Great Britain's continuing position of hegemony over Egypt, it is hardly surprising that the new Egyptian state accorded a more definite recognition to the British Mandates in Palestine and Iraq than it gave to the French Syrian Mandate in the 1920s. With the coming into effect of the Mandates in 1923 (Palestine) and 1924 (Iraq), the British government in October 1925 formally requested Egyptian recognition of "the special positiion of His Majesty's Government in the two territories in question."[106] In February of the following year, the ministry of Ahmad Ziwar granted such recognition. The note recognizing the two British Mandates contained no reservations concerning the Jewish National Home specified for the Palestine Mandate. It did, however, insist that the establishment of the Palestine Mandate should in no way affect the Egyptian-Palestinian boundary laid down in Egyptian-Ottoman negotiations in 1906, a reservation that the British accepted.[107] Both in its lack of concern with the Jewish National Home and in its determination to uphold Egyptian national rights, the Egyptian position toward the British Mandated territories accurately reflects the Egypt-oriented foreign policy of successive Egyptian ministries throughout the 1920s.

During this decade Egypt had only the most tenuous official relationship with the new Kingdom of Iraq. The British Mandate over Iraq precluded the establishment of official diplomatic relations between the two countries: it was 1930 before Iraq gained the capability to conduct her own foreign relations. Nor was there a close relationship between kings Fu'ad and Faysal: although the latter stopped in Egypt periodically when en route to Europe, his visits were not official ones, and his host in Egypt was the British Residency rather than the Egyptian Palace. It was only in December 1927, after an appeal by Hamid al-Basil of the Wafd, that the Egyptian Palace formally offered its hospitality to the Iraqi monarch during one of his trips through Egypt.[108]

The Palestine Mandate posed special problems for Egypt in the 1920s. One matter of periodic concern was the border between independent Egypt and Mandatory Palestine. Although Egypt had been responsible for the maintenance of law and order in the Sinai Peninsula since the nineteenth century, the precise border between Egypt and Palestine received final definition only in the twentieth century. As a result of the Egyptian-Ottoman dispute over possession of Taba in

1906, the border was officially designated as running along the line from near 'Aqaba in the south to Rafah in the north, with Egypt gaining "administrative possession" of Sinai west of that line. Nor was Egyptian authority over Sinai unquestioned thereafter: despite their formal acceptance of the 1906 line as the de facto border twenty years later, the British themselves held Sinai to be only administratively Egyptian. The combination of British suggestions that Sinai be made a British military base, and occasional articles in the British press asserting that the Peninsula was of little value to Egypt, prompted nationalist Egyptians to suspect a British intention to detach Sinai from Egypt and make it part of Palestine.[109] In 1927, such fears led Watanist deputies in the Egyptian Parliament to warn of a British plan to annex Sinai to Mandatory Palestine and to demand to know if the border had been definitively resolved.[110] A year later, the Wafdist *Kawkab al-Sharq* opposed the plans of the Muhammad Mahmud ministry to improve communications in Sinai, arguing that this would only serve British imperial interests.[111]

The larger issue complicating the Egyptian relationship with Mandatory Palestine in the 1920s and after was the emerging conflict of Arab and Jewish nationalism. In part this was due to outside instigation, as both Zionists and Palestinian Arab nationalists reached out to Egypt for backing of their respective positions. On the one hand, Zionist leaders were not unaware of the potential for support from the then Western-oriented and often anti-Arab elite of Egypt: repeatedly in the 1920s, Zionist officials contacted Egyptian notables, seeking Egyptian sympathy for their endeavors in Palestine and Egyptian mediation between themselves and the Palestinian Arabs.[112] On the other hand, the Palestinian Arab leadership looked to neighboring Egypt for support in both political and nonpolitical matters. Muslim religious authorities in Palestine sought Egyptian financial assistance for their central project of the 1920s, the restoration of the al-Aqsa Mosque in Jerusalem; Palestinian Arab political delegations visited Egypt seeking support for their opposition to both the British Mandate and the Jewish National Home; and the emerging dominant figure of Palestinian Arab politics, Muhammad Hajj Amin al-Husayni, traveled to Egypt several times in the 1920s to promote Egyptian backing for his religious and political activities.[113] In a sense, Egypt became a scene of a contest between the two rival nationalist movements in Palestine; each sought Egyptian support for the achievement of its aspirations.

Opinion in Egypt itself was not of one mind in regard to either the Zionist movement or the Palestine question. A recent study of the Egyptian press and the Palestine issue in the interwar period indicates varying tendencies among the leading newspapers of Egypt in the 1920s. Where the Wafdist *al-Balagh* regularly opposed Zionism as a religiously based and therefore retrograde nationalist movement,[114] the Liberal *al-Siyasa* was more accommodating to Zionist aspirations, calling for Arab-Jewish reconciliation in a secular Palestinian state,[115] and the pro-Palace *al-Ittihad* supported the aim of a Jewish National Home as articulated in the Mandate.[116] Even the Syrian-operated dailies *al-Muqattam* and *al-Ahram* differed on Palestine in the 1920s. The former was more sympathetic to Zionism and envisaged the evolution of a common Arab-Jewish *watan* over time; the latter usually supported Palestinian Arab nationalist demands and predicted the failure of the British-backed effort to establish a Jewish National Home in Arab Palestine.[117] Of all the major dailies of Egypt, only *al-Ahram,* already journalistically the best newspaper in Egypt, gave regular coverage to the internal affairs of the Jewish Yishuv in Palestine—a further indication of the general marginality of the entire Palestine issue for an internally oriented Egypt in the 1920s.[118]

On the practical level, throughout almost the entire decade of the 1920s the attempts of the rival nationalist movements in Palestine to win Egyptian sympathy and support had little success. Muslim Egyptians did contribute to the Palestinian project for the restoration of the al-Aqsa Mosque, with King Fu'ad leading the way with a personal donation of £E 5,000 and the Egyptian Ministry of Awqaf contributing an equal amount.[119] But the support of the Egyptian establishment for the project appears to have been less than enthusiastic. The King is reported to have prevented the creation of a permanent fundraising committee within Egypt for the project in 1923, and rumors of possible financial peculation and of the diversion of funds to political uses by the Palestinian organizers apparently cut into Egyptian contributions to the endeavor.[120] When the ceremonies celebrating the restoration occurred in Jerusalem in October 1928, the Egyptian government declined Palestinian invitations to send an official delegation and was represented only by the Egyptian Consul in Jerusalem.[121]

More significant was that there was virtually no official Egyptian support for the Palestinian Arab political cause during the 1920s. After formal Egyptian independence, the Egyptian government restricted its contacts with Palestinian Arab political leaders to a minimum. Although he met with King Fu'ad in 1923 and 1929, Hajj Amin al-Husayni was not received by Egyptian government officials on his trips of 1926, 1927, and 1928; indeed, on the first he was "completely ignored" by Ahmad Ziwar despite the fact that he was staying in the same hotel as the Prime Minister.[122] In the same year the Shaykh al-Azhar, Muhammad Abu al-Fadl al-Jizawi, is reported to have rejected Palestinian Arab appeals for a public statement in support of their political program on the grounds that political issues were beyond his sphere of authority.[123] There is no indication that successive Egyptian ministries either took a public stance in support of the Palestinian Arab cause or made approaches to the British concerning Palestine in the 1920s.

Indeed, the position of the Egyptian government and of those few Egyptian political leaders who did involve themselves in the Palestine issue in the 1920s if anything inclined in the direction of Zionism. Neither of the two dominant political figures of the decade, King Fu'ad or Sa'd Zaghlul, appears to have made a public commitment concerning the Palestine question at the time. Both appear to have kept an open mind on the subject; Zaghlul reportedly came close to meeting with Chaim Weizmann in 1924, and the King discussed Zionism with the Chief Rabbi of Egypt in 1928.[124] Other Egyptian political leaders of various orientations—among others, the cultural conservative Ahmad Zaki, the militantly secularist Mahmud 'Azmi, the veteran Arab nationalist 'Aziz 'Ali al-Misri, and even one Prime Minister of Egypt, Ahmad Ziwar—are reported to have met with Zionist emissaries and to have expressed sympathy with Zionist aspirations and/or a desire to mediate between Zionist and Palestinian Arab nationalists.[125] At least two of these figures, Ahmad Zaki and Mahmud 'Azmi, visited Palestine in the mid-1920s and reportedly spoke in favor of Arab-Jewish rapprochement.[126] Yet, like the contacts of Egyptian notables with Palestinian Arab leaders, the Zionist connections of individual Egyptian politicians were unproductive: there is no indication that they had any effect on bringing the conflicting parties in Palestine closer together.

For its part the Egyptian government took firm action against Palestinian Arab efforts to make Egypt the scene of protests against Zionism or to involve Egypt in the Palestine issue. Thus it arrested Palestinian Arabs demonstrating against Lord Balfour when he stopped in Egypt on his way to Palestine in 1925, and it periodically shut down the Palestinian-run journal *al-Shura* when it agitated too vehemently on the subject of Palestine.[127] In 1925 the government of Ahmad Ziwar accorded quasi-recognition to the Zionist endeavor when it sent a delegation headed by the Rector of the Egyptian University, Ahmad Lutfi al-Sayyid, to the ceremonies marking the opening of the Hebrew University of Jerusalem.[128] Although Lutfi's participation in the event was a relucant one (he declined to give an address at the ceremony lest it be construed as support for Zionism), and despite the fact that most of the Egyptian press used the occasion to express opposition to Zionism,[129] nonetheless the delegation's dispatch came close to official Egyptian endorsement of the Zionist enterprise. Such an endorsement was at least implicit in the Ziwar ministry's recognition of the British Mandate, including the obligation to develop a Jewish National Home, in the following year. Both the Egyptian presence at the opening of the Hebrew University and the Egyptian recognition of the Palestine Mandate drew criticism from the Palestinian Arab community and may have been a factor in the opposition of Hajj Amin al-Husayni to King Fu'ad's Caliphal ambitions in the mid-1920's.[130] It was Zionism, with its apparent modernism as well as its largely western and practically oriented leadership of the 1920s, which appealed most to the equally modernist and Westernized spokesmen of Egyptian territorial nationalism during the same decade.

The Palestine Disturbances of 1929

Both the relative indifference and the comparatively detached attitude of educated Egyptians toward the Palestine question which characterized Egyptian opinion in the 1920s were challenged at the close of the decade by the widespread violence that erupted in Palestine in the summer of 1929. The 1929 "Wailing Wall disturbances" produced an appreciable reaction in Egypt in the summer and fall of 1929. The general conclusion of the British at the time was that Egyptian "public opinion is definitely biased in favour of the Arabs as against the Jews,"[131] an evaluation confirmed by what other evidence is available. A variety of organizations in Egypt issued public statements and declarations in support of the Muslim position in the dispute over the Western Wall–al-Aqsa area, defending Muslim rights and actions in the controversy and protesting both Jewish activities and British policy in the Mandate. The concern expressed by many of these groups went beyond the purely verbal, extending to appeals to Egyptians to render financial support, medical assistance, and legal aid to the Palestinian Arabs. A considerable amount of such assistance was actually delivered in 1929–1930: although the suggestion of an Egyptian medical mission was rejected as unnecessary by the Palestinian Arab Executive,[132] the Young Men's Muslim Association (YMMA) collected several hundred Egyptian pounds for Palestinian Arab relief,[133] other groups raised lesser sums,[134] and Egyptian notables did proceed to Palestine in 1930 to represent the Supreme Muslim Council before the "Wailing

Wall Commission" of the League of Nations investigating the issue (Ahmad Zaki presented the historical side of the Muslim case, and Muhammad 'Ali 'Alluba offered the Muslim legal brief).[135]

But there are several limitations and special features of Egyptian concern with and involvement in the Palestine issue in 1929 that need to be pointed out. The first is that the organizations that took an active interest in the events in Palestine were overwhelmingly of two kinds: either Muslim religious organizations whose primary purpose was the defense and promotion of Islam (for example, the Young Men's Muslim Association, the Islamic Guidance Society, the Society of the Islamic Banner, and a presumably ad hoc "Egyptian Society for the Defense of the Sacred Enclosure and the Islamic Holy Places"),[136] or associations of foreign Arabs or Muslims resident in Egypt (such as the Syro-Palestinian Congress in Egypt, an Egyptian association of Javanese Muslims, or groups of Syro-Palestinian, North African, and Indian Muslim students at al-Azhar).[137] Only a few nonreligious Egyptian organizations said or did something about the Palestine controversy at the time of the violence of August 1929: the Eastern Bond Society, a group calling itself "the people and merchants of Old Cairo," and the Watani Party.[138] Most significant in this respect is that, with the exception of a Watani Party protest against British policy in Palestine sent to the League of Nations and an appeal by the party for Egyptian medical assistance to the Palestinian Arab community,[139] Egypt's secular political parties appear to have done nothing in relation to the Palestine issue in the wake of the disturbances of 1929—no meetings, no public protests, no appeals for assistance or involvement.

Nor did the Egyptian government become involved in the Palestine question as a result of the violence of 1929. A striking feature of the many protests and appeals about the controversy issued by groups and individuals in Egypt in late 1929 is that they were addressed either to public opinion in general, to "the Arab and Islamic worlds," or to specific recipients outside Egypt, such as the League of Nations, the British Prime Minister or High Commissioner in Palestine, or even President Herbert Hoover of the United States (protesting his statements on the question)—but none seem to have been sent to the Egyptian government to call for official Egyptian action in regard to the dispute. With Egyptian governmental involvement in the controversy in Palestine apparently unexpected by Egyptians, none seems to have occurred. There is no evidence that the ministries of Muhammad Mahmud and 'Adli Yakan in power in late 1929 or that of Mustafa al-Nahhas, which governed briefly in 1930, took a public stance or attempted to intervene in private with the British concerning Palestine; and the biographer of King Fu'ad stated that Egypt's monarch also preferred to avoid involvement in the issue, viewing it as "entirely a matter for the British government."[140] Apparently the only quasi-official Egyptian representation concerning the situation in Palestine in the wake of the violence of 1929 was that made by the Rector of al-Azhar, Shaykh Muhammad Mustafa al-Maraghi, in a "private memorandum" of September 1929 that warned that recent events in Palestine had "produced a very bad effect on the minds of Egyptian Moslems" and appealed to the British to "remove the causes of dispute in the Holy Places, whether religious or secular, and [to] restore the people to a state of peace."[141] The aloofness of at least part of the Egyptian establishment in the 1920s is illustrated by the bizarre suggestion made to a British official by Prince Muhammad 'Ali of the Royal Family after the 1929 disturbances: for a sum of perhaps £E100,000, the Muslim authorities in Palestine could be persuaded to *sell* the Western Wall to the Jews and thus resolve the controversy over its possession.[142]

Rather than taking action on behalf of the Palestinian Arabs in 1929–1930, the behavior of the Egyptian government regarding Palestine demonstrated a scrupulous concern for Egyptian neutrality on the issue. When the British in August 1929 requested the Egyptian authorities to check the dissemination of anti-Jewish material in the Egyptian press and to institute special security procedures to ensure against the possibility of anti-Jewish violence in Cairo, the ministry of Muhammad Mahmud was quick to comply.[143] In early 1930, Prime Minister Mustafa al-Nahhas refused to allow Palestinian Arab delegations that had been sent to Egypt to hold public meetings;[144] Nahhas's Minister of Finance, Makram 'Ubayd, rejected an appeal for assistance from the Palestinian Arab leader Jamal al-Husayni when the two met in London in April 1930;[145] and when out of office in late 1930, Nahhas similarly declined to respond affirmatively to similar Palestinian Arab requests for public support from the Wafd.[146]

Although Muslim and foreign Arab circles within Egypt did come out strongly in support of the Arab/Muslim cause in Palestine, the attitudes found in the Egyptian press at the time of the disturbances of 1929 were almost as removed and disinterested as those which had been expressed in regard to other Arab crises of the 1920s.[147] Most of the main newspapers of Egypt reported on events in the Mandate with a critical eye, refusing to accept one-sided reports coming out of Palestine from clearly committed sources on either side. Criticisms of the Palestinian Arabs sometimes appeared, such as *al-Muqattam's* chiding of the Arab Executive in Palestine for its exaggerated accounts of the violence.[148] The establishment newspapers of Egypt repeatedly appealed to both sides in the controversy to exercise moderation, calling for the restoration of law and order in the Mandate, for both Jews and Muslims to refrain from violence and to discuss their differences peacefully, and for the resolution of the crisis in such a way that the "Arabs and Jews [in Palestine] will live as they lived before, in serenity, undisturbed by troublemakers."[149]

There was a significant dichotomy, however, in the attitudes expressed by two different segments of opinion in Egypt toward the causes of the current crisis in Palestine and the possible manner in which that crisis might be resolved. The Muslim religious organizations, which accounted for most of the verbal support and material assistance given to the Palestinian Arabs in 1929, tended to see the recent tension in Palestine through a religious filter. In their statements, the central cause of the violence of 1929 was "Jewish" (rather than "Zionist") encroachment on the traditional status quo in the vicinity of al-Aqsa.[150] The "aggression" had come from "the Jews," who were sometimes accused of wishing to destroy the al-Aqsa Mosque in order to restore the Jewish Temple upon the same site,[151] and the situation could be resolved only through British and international recognition of continued Muslim possession of the religious sites in the disputed area.[152]

For the more secularized and nationally oriented spokesmen writing in the daily newspapers of Egypt, both the issues and the answers were different. Editorials were usually addressed more to the national than to the religious conflict existing in Palestine, positing the recent religious controversy as but part of a broader national clash between "Arabs" and "Zionists" produced by the attempt of the latter to implant a Jewish National Home in a region already populated by Arabs.[153] The solutions for the tension that were suggested in the Egyptian press similarly tended to carry a political emphasis. The immediate necessity was for the termination of large-scale Jewish immigration to Palestine and the abandonment of the "mirage" of creating a Jewish National Home there;[154] the long-range solution envisaged was the establishment of a "representative, democratic government" uniting Jews and Arabs in one state.[155] Finally, the image of Jews and Zionists presented in the daily press was more complex and more open than that found in the proclamations of Muslim religious organizations: distinctions were made between "Jews" and "Zionists" in analyses of the problems in the Mandate,[156] statements from both pro- and anti-Zionist Jews were published,[157] and it was maintained that the Jews of Egypt should be accorded the same freedom of expression in sympathizing with their co-religionists in Palestine as the Muslims of Egypt had in supporting the Muslim position in the controversy over the Western Wall–al-Aqsa area.[158]

The most interesting aspect of the attitude of Egypt's leading secular publicists at the time of the violence in Palestine in 1929 is the absence of any perception of a direct connection between events in Palestine and the affairs of Egypt, or of any belief that Egyptian national interests were affected by developments in the Mandate. Rather than seeing a connection between the violence in Palestine and the affairs of Egypt, Egypt's secular press perceived primarily a negative "lesson" to be learned from the disturbances: the necessity of avoiding sectarian conflict in Egypt. As one of *al-Muqattam*'s first articles on the disturbances put it, "nations are based on unity, and revive only when they have solidarity. . . . The [Egyptian] nation does not know any religion except the religion of patriotism."[159] Similarly, an editorial in the Wafdist *al-Balagh* used events in Palestine to caution its readers about the dangers of "religious controversy" in Eastern nations, advising that sectarian discord could only serve to weaken national causes by allowing "the imperialists" to maintain their control over their colonies on the pretext of protecting religious minorities.[160] Somewhat later *al-Ahram* devoted a lead editorial to refuting the opinion of *The Times* to the effect that the violence in Palestine marked a drift to religiously based nationalism in the Near East. The editorial's title is a sufficient indication of its thoroughly Egyptianist perspective: "Egyptians Before Anything Else; Religion Is for God and the Homeland Is for All."[161]

It was *al-Siyasa,* the journal of the Liberal Party, which was most explicit in maintaining that Egypt was not directly involved in the controversy in Mandatory Palestine and so should continue to remain aloof from it. In its first editorial on the violence of August 1929, appropriately entitled "The Incidents in Palestine and Egyptian Affairs: There is No Basis for Comparison," the paper attacked recent British press speculation that had offered events in Palestine as an example of the precarious position of minorities in the region and thus as a justification for Great Britain's maintenance of her position in Egypt. *Al-Siyasa* took issue with such an interpretation, arguing at length that there was no analogy between what had occurred recently in Palestine and what might occur in Egypt in the future.[162] This editorial was followed by others in a similar vein, one asserting that Eastern peoples needed to "refrain from religious or sectarian struggles which have become contradictory to the spirit of the age,"[163] another specifically stating that Egyptians were different from the Arabs of the Fertile Crescent in both their national circumstances and aspirations:

> It is necessary for our Arab friends to understand that the particular conditions and attitudes by which they are influenced in their comprehension of events and [their] estimate of situations are not found in the shaping of the Egyptian viewpoint, and especially that Egypt does not at any time wish to know these sectarian attitudes which are found at the depths of the Arab nationalist movements.[164]

Al-Siyasa's opposition to sectarianism in Egypt in 1929 led it to criticize not the local Jewish community, which on the whole had refrained from active involvement in support of their co-religionists in Palestine, but rather the Syro-Palestinian population in Egypt, which was playing a leading role in efforts to generate Egyptian sympathy and support for the Arab-Muslim cause in Palestine. Thus one of its editorials inveighed against unnamed "committees of residents in Cairo which occupy themselves with Arab causes," accusing these groups of working to create divisions between the religious communities of Egypt through their agitation concerning Palestine. Proclaiming that "Egypt will not under any circumstances accept being an arena for religious propaganda," the editorial declared an uncompromising sense of secular Egyptian nationalism: "the Egyptian national body contains, besides Muslims, the religious groups of the Christians and the Jews, and Egypt does not feel today and will not feel in the future anything except its distinct Egyptian nationalism."[165] *Al-Siyasa*'s hostility to Egyptian involvement in the Palestine question in 1929 is an authentic representation of the sense of separation from both Arab and Muslim affairs that characterized the outlook of Egyptian territorial nationalists throughout the 1920s.

Considered in context, the Egyptian reaction to the 1929 disturbances in Palestine did not reflect a major change in the Egyptianist orientation prevalent among the Egyptian elite after the Revolution of 1919. At the same time, however, it did indicate the beginning of the emergence of new forces and attitudes in Egyptian society and thought that later were to challenge the Egyptianist paradigm. The significance of the Egyptian reaction to the Wailing Wall disturbances lay not in the short run, when pro-Arab and pro-Muslim forces failed to influence the position of either the Egyptian establishment or the government of Egypt, but in the long run: as a portent of pressures that in the 1930s would begin to affect both the nationalist outlook and the political behavior of Egyptians.

11

"Easternism" in Egypt in the 1920s

Despite the dominance of an exclusivist Egyptian territorial nationalism in Egypt during the 1920s, World War I and the attendant collapse of the Ottoman Empire did not completely eradicate external, supra-Egyptian orientations and identifications in Egypt. The Ottoman Empire had been a part of the Egyptian mental universe for too long to allow for the total elimination of sentiments of sympathy and solidarity with the wider Islamic community that the Ottoman polity had come to represent. Even in the post-1919 period, some Egyptian publicists and intellectuals searched for an alternative to the now obsolete Ottomanism of the prewar period—an external orientation that would be congruent with their primary loyalty to the new Egyptian nation-state but would also allow them to feel a continuing sense of connection with other lands, peoples, and cultures.

The alternative that they came up with in the 1920s was a generalized "Eastern" identification. Generically known as "Easternism" [*al-sharqiyya*] or "the Eastern idea" [*al-fikra al-sharqiyya*], it consisted of concepts that postulated the similarity of various Eastern peoples and promoted closer cooperation among Eastern countries. Easternism was more nebulous than either Egyptian territorial nationalism, an Islamic orientation, or any sense of Arabism. As a consequence, it was also a more shallow, less meaningful concept. In one sense it represented a continuation of the prewar Ottoman/Islamic orientation that had prevailed in Egypt; in another it was an anticipation of the Arab regional orientation that was to take its place from the 1930s onward. The umbrella of Easternism was large enough to accommodate both Egyptian secularists and modernists, such as Mansur Fahmi or 'Ali 'Abd al-Raziq, and more conservative, Islamically inclined figures, such as Muhammad Rashid Rida, Ahmad Zaki, or Ahmad Shafiq. Perhaps because it was many things to many men. Easternism also proved to be a transitory concept, eventually giving way to ideas that aimed at the more precise and thus more realistic goals of Arab/Islamic solidarity and collaboration.

The Eastern Idea

Concepts of Eastern relatedness and solidarity were not new to Arab and Egyptian thought in the interwar period. The idea of the division of the civilized world into East and West had already been articulated by the first generation of Arab modernist thinkers in the decades prior to World War I. Definitions of the East and concepts of what unified it differed from thinker to thinker, however. Where political activists such as Jamal al-Din al-Afghani seem to have applied the term to all non-Western peoples threatened by a voracious Europe, more culturally oriented figures such as Jurji Zaydan appear to have used it as a synonym for the Arabic-speaking world; still others such as ʻAbd Allah al-Nadim seem to have restricted its usage to the territories and peoples of the Ottoman Empire.[1]

"East" and "Eastern" [*sharq*/*sharqi* or *sharqiyya*] continued to remain ambiguous terms in Egypt in the 1920s and 1930s. By some they were used to refer primarily to the Muslim world; the adjective Eastern was combined with Islamic into a compound phrase denoting the Eastern and Islamic region as an integral unit.[2] For others of a more secularist orientation the term East was combined with the adjective Arab and employed to indicate the Eastern Arab lands in western Asia and northeast Africa.[3] Perhaps the term's most prevalent usage was a rough, undefined synonym for the Near or Middle East, that is, for the preponderantly Muslim areas in northern Africa and western Asia.[4] East/Eastern were also used to denote what Europeans meant by the Orient, most of the Asian and African land mass.[5]

Nor was the exact relationship of the component parts of the East precisely defined. Occasionally enthusiasts of the Eastern idea went so far as to speak of "the Eastern nationalism" [*al-qawmiyya al-sharqiyya*] or of "the united nationalism" [*al-qawmiyya al-muttahida*] linking all of its regions.[6] But such a merging of the countries of the East was less common than referring to Eastern countries as separate units and distinguishing between a "particular nationalism" [*al-wataniyya al-khassa*] and a more diffuse "general nationalism" [*al-wataniyya al-ʻamma*].[7] The following statement of purpose by the journal *al-Siyasa al-Usbuʻiyya* on the anniversary of its third year of operation in 1928 illustrates the melange of referents to which East and Eastern could be applied:

> We do not need to remind our readers that the goal which *al-Siyasa al-Usbuʻiyya* aims at as a political newspaper has been and will always continue to be the strengthening of relations and the solidifying of connections between the countries of the Arab world and between all the Eastern countries, and the creation of the bond of solidarity, within the limits possible, between East and West. If *al-Siyasa al-Usbuʻiyya* is Egyptian in its establishment and its editing, nonetheless it is Arabic Eastern [*sharqiyya ʻarabiyya*] in its aims and its goals.[8]

The widest basis of an Eastern orientation in Egypt in the 1920s was an external and largely artificial one: the difference between all the lands and peoples of the East, on the one hand, and the well-defined, apparently homogeneous, and then dominant West, on the other. Easternism in this sense was derivative, a function not of intrinsic similarities or bonds among the individual units constituting the East but rather of their all being something *other* than the West. It was the contemporary polarity of Europe and all other regions of the world that could lead Egyptians who were otherwise oriented toward the West to see their country as part of the East. "Whether we like it or not, Europe considers us as standing shoulder to shoulder with the other Eastern peoples," said the Wafdist Leon Castro in an article of 1924 calling upon the Egyptian government to develop an active "Eastern policy."[9] In this sense, the East had meaning only in contrast to the West. As the former editor of the journal of the Eastern Bond Society phrased it in a retrospective essay of 1932 on "the Eastern idea," the concept denoted "Asia and Africa, and that in comparison to the Western idea which means Europe and America."[10] For such as 'Ali 'Abd al-Raziq, who used the term in this fashion, Easternism was admittedly "a broad, unnatural idea [*fikra 'arida ghayr tabi'a*] in which circumstances unifies them [the peoples of the East] in self-defense."[11] In this variant, the East was wholly derived from its Western opposite, a contingent identity resulting from the particular conditions of the recent past.

What was it about the West that had produced the East? In a political culture as diverse as that of Egypt, there were many interpretations of the relationship between East and West. Obviously, one very specific and concrete bond that linked Eastern regions and peoples together was the common threat represented by Western imperialism. In the colorful language of *al-Siyasa al-Usbu'iyya,* the East was one pole in "the violent battle between imperialism and freedom, or between the West and the East."[12] Unquestionably, one of the major purposes of Eastern solidarity was to strengthen all the East *vis-à-vis* the West. Eastern cooperation was thus defined as "a common course towards [attaining] the advantage and the power which the West had gained over the East."[13] The need to cooperate in defense against Western imperialism was often the overriding impulse behind Eastern solidarity for those who defined the term in broader Asian-African terms. When employed in the latter sense, the concept of the East anticipated that of the Third World of more recent times, denoting all those areas of the globe which were not part of the developed West and thus which shared the common fate of domination and exploitation by the West in the modern era.

This contingent concept of Easternism found in Egypt in the 1920s had severe limitations in terms of both its efficacy and its depth. Because it was primarily their common treatment by the dominant West that brought Eastern peoples together, their solidarity was a reactive solidarity of "weakness" rather than one of strength deriving from internal bonds.[14] By extension, the aim of Eastern cooperation was the restricted one of "a unity of goal which is that of demanding freedom from the covetous hand of Europe" rather than the achievement of more positive internal purposes.[15] This kind of Easternism was a broad concept, but it was also a shallow one.

Beyond the obvious political motive behind Easternism, there were cultural dimensions to the phenomenon as well. The root concern of a good deal of Egyptian Easternist thought in the 1920s was with the maintenance of Eastern cultural integrity and authenticity, the preservation of the heritage and historical legacy of Eastern peoples. Easternist writers often accepted as a given that the East and the West embodied different historical experiences, worldviews, mentalities, and characteristic modes of behavior. No real synthesis could be achieved between them. "The crux of the matter," wrote the President of the Eastern Bond Society, al-Sayyid 'Abd al-Hamid al-Bakri, "is that East is East and West is West."[16] Similarly Prince 'Umar Tusun, the leading royal supporter of Eastern activities and causes in Egypt in the 1920s, defined the gap between East and West as follows:

> That East is East and West is West is a truth confirmed by history and reality, by the past and the present. It is impossible to join them together save if humanity could rise above its present level and unite all people. But this is most unlikely, and hoping for it is an illusion.[17]

For those who divided the world into East and West on a permanent civilizational basis, the cultural threat represented by the latter was fully as important as the political one. The purpose of Eastern solidarity at its most basic level was "opposing one thing from the West, namely contempt for everything Eastern," and correspondingly defending the Eastern "personality" from those who sought to destroy it and to impose a totally Western stamp upon the peoples of the East.[18] Egyptian Easternist writers thus resisted the rampant processs of Westernization underway in Egypt in the 1920s. To them, what they termed "the Westernizing of the East" [*taghrib al-sharq*] was both wrong and harmful. Westernization was the worst kind of surrender to the West and to Western imperialism, for it assumed that the peoples of the East had no history, culture, and national spirit of their own that were worth preserving in the modern age. In opposition to such ultimate capitulation to the West, Egyptian Easternists called upon "the sons of the East" to rediscover and revive their distinctiveness and their identity based on the rich historical legacy of the East. Genuine progress and development for Eastern nations could come only through being true to their own Eastern nature; conversely, wholesale Westernization would be in conflict with an authentic revival in Eastern lands. Again as 'Umar Tusun put it, "blind imitation of Western civilization would be a non-independent renaissance which would not take account of the differences between us and the Europeans in character, customs, morals, and religion."[19]

For Egyptian exponents of this cultural sense of Easternism, the "Eastern idea" meant, first and foremost, an independent and non-Western course of revival and progress for the East, one that held the promise of both advancement and authenticity. A striking example of this outlook as well as an illustration of how the Eastern orientation of the 1920s served as a way station for an Islamic-Arab orientation in subsequent decades can be found in some of the earliest published writings of Hasan al-Banna, eventually the General Guide of the Society of the Muslim Brothers.[20] The main thrust of these early essays was to oppose what Banna termed "the doctrine of imitating Europe" [*fikrat al-taqlid al-urubbi*] that was "currently sweeping" the lands of the East.[21] It is important to note that Banna was not opposed to change and development as such, both of which were necessary in order to overcome "backwardness and stagnation."[22] What he did insist upon, however, was "genuine modernization" that would be "in harmony with the temper of the East."[23]

Hasan al-Banna's main attack in these articles of 1929 was directed against what he saw as the ideological and psychological conquest of the minds of the leaders of the East by the West. He criticized the rulers of Eastern countries, taking them to task for yielding to "the false illusion" of equating progress with the West and for behaving as if revival and modernization meant nothing but the complete Westernization of their societies.[24] Banna saw this asymmetrical cultural borrowing as fundamentally destructive in that one supposedly superior civilization inevitably dominates while the other, ostensibly inferior, in effect denigrates itself and thus "instills within itself the seeds of its own destruction."[25] The rulers of the East, Banna added in an ironic paraphrase of Rudyard Kipling, would do well to remember that "East is East and West is West—whether they like it or not."[26] Banna's lesson was plain:

> The leaders of the East had best divest themselves of this false doctrine, the doctrine of imitating Europe, and guide their nations on an original Eastern road . . . to greatness and revival. This goal should be the innermost desire of all and the basis for programs of Eastern reformation.[27]

In the generally pro-Western atmosphere of the 1920s, such deep-seated hostility to the West was the exception rather than the rule in Egyptian Easternist expression. More characteristic of the decade was an acceptance of the possibility of beneficial interaction between East and West in spite of cultural differences and political antagonisms. Even those who argued the need for Eastern solidarity and cooperation to face the menace of Western imperialism frequently perceived the East's best hope in defending itself against the West as resting in its ability to assimilate useful Western concepts and institutions selectively. Rather than outright rejection of everything Western, the East was called upon to be receptive to the best of the West. "Preserving what is best in the old [while] taking what is most beneficial from the modern" was the most prevalent Easternist viewpoint in the 1920s.[28] The writings of Easternist spokesmen cited Japan as the perfect example of the capacity of Eastern nations to select and adapt elements of Western civilization and to integrate them successfully into a non-Western heritage.[29]

On a more universal level, proponents of an Eastern orientation for Egypt sometimes presented the East-West dichotomy not as a contest in which one party's gain was the other's loss, but as a division that had the potential to be mutually beneficial for both parties as well as for mankind as a whole. This non-antagonistic sense of difference between East and West was expressed well by Mustafa 'Abd al-Raziq in an interview of 1930. On the one hand, 'Abd al-Raziq firmly maintained that "I do not want Egypt to become a piece of Europe. I want Egypt to remain a piece of Africa connected with Asia while simultaneously competing with the West in all that it has achieved in the way of science, civilization, and progress."[30] But at the same time, 'Abd al-Raziq believed that a prerequisite of Eastern development and progress was learning from the West: "I want Egypt to imitate the basics of Western civilization and to absorb them fully rather than just wearing them like a borrowed dress, so that the Nile Valley will become one of the agents of human progress."[31] Thus, in the relatively optimistic mood that characterized Egypt in the 1920s, an identification of Egypt with the East did not necessarily preclude fruitful contact with the West. As one of the leading spokesmen of Eastern cooperation of the 1920s, 'Abd al-Razzaq al-Sanhuri, put it in 1932, "the East is about to revive, but it will revive not to challenge the West, but to cooperate with it for the good of humanity."[32]

If the East took on meaning and reality largely in distinction from the West, it also existed only in concord with the concept of Egypt. The second generally accepted premise of the Eastern idea in Egypt was its harmonization with the territorial nationalism so dominant in Egypt in the 1920s. Virtually all of the

Egyptian proponents of Eastern solidarity and cooperation presented Easternism as a complement, rather than an alternative, to Egyptian nationalism. In the political sphere they overwhelmingly accepted the division of the East into separate political units or nations and promoted the cooperation of these parallel entities rather than calling for their replacement by a new, larger Eastern nation. At most, they maintained that Eastern collaboration was not incompatible with the separate local nationalisms found in individual Eastern countries:

> [I]t would be satisfying to the Eastern idea if there flourished in the regions of the East those various [nationalist] bonds and if every nation revived to fulfill its national rights . . . for whatever advances any nation or religion or language in the East advances the East as a whole.[33]

Where Egyptian supporters of the Eastern idea differed from other Egyptian nationalists of the decade, of course, was in their definition of Egypt as part of the East rather than as either an independent civilizational unit or an entity more closely linked to Europe and the Mediterranean than to Asia–Africa. A classic statement of Egypt's Eastern character was given, appropriately enough, by the President of the Eastern Bond Society, al-Sayyid 'Abd al-Hamid al-Bakri, in response to Salama Musa's contention that Egypt formed part of the European world of discourse. In Bakri's view the racial, cultural, linguistic, religious, and geographic connections between the land of the Nile and and the other regions of the East were overwhelming and had been the decisive factors in Egyptian development throughout history. Bakri listed numerous factors—the Arabic language, literature, and poetry prevalent in Egypt; the Islamic religion, customs, and behavioral norms characteristic of Egyptians; Egyptian music, clothing, building arts, modes of expression, and ways of thinking; even the presumed Semitic or Nubian racial origins of the people of Egypt—all of which provided "everlasting evidence" of Egypt's "Eastern" nature and identity.[34]

In the dual identity of Egyptians as Egyptians and as Easterners, it was Egypt that came first. It did so in two senses. First, Egypt was the primary concern even of those Egyptians who considered themselves advocates of the "Eastern idea." It was Egyptian independence, development, and progress that mattered most and took up most of their attention and activity. Moreover, Eastern interaction was often perceived in largely instrumental terms, as a means of advancing Egyptian interests. This was the self-evident purpose of calls to Eastern solidarity *vis-à-vis* Western imperialism. As *al-Siyasa* put it succinctly in one of its periodic declarations of devotion to the Eastern idea, "the *watan* first and all of the East second."[35] Alternatively, the achievement of a significant degree of Eastern cooperation, particularly in the political sphere, was sometimes perceived as dependent on the prior realization of the nationalist goals of the separate states of which the East was composed:

> When every Eastern nation has achieved what it can to become a true nation—well-ordered, united, cohesive, cast in one mold, and taking pride in its homeland and in its nationalism, then it will be easy to think about forming an Eastern League of Nations. . . . But for now, the formation of such a League even if feasible would be marked by an inherent feebleness and vulnerability which would quickly spread to the members which had created that League. So it would have no long-term consequence, nor for that matter be of much use.[36]

Thus for some the achievement of national aims was itself a prerequisite for the realization of broader Eastern goals.

Second, for virtually all its advocates Easternism was a secondary identification in the 1920s. The extent to which the Eastern idea was subordinate to that of the Egyptian nation appears best in the sentiments of Egyptian superiority and pride as well as the hopes for Egyptian leadership and cultural or political aggrandizement in the Eastern arena, which often accompanied expressions of the Eastern idea on the part of its Egyptian proponents. Great pride was taken in Egypt's perceived place as an (or even as *the*) cultural and political leader of the Eastern world. In an editorial in *al-Siyasa al-Usbu'iyya* calling for Egypt to facilitate educational exchanges with neighboring lands, the request was justified on the grounds that such exchanges would be "an opportunity to consolidate the position which Egypt has attained by right as the leader of the literary revival in the lands of the East."[37] Similarly, an editorial in the Wafdist *Kawkab al-Sharq* extolled Egypt's national movement as "the model and pattern for peoples of the East, from the Near to the Far East," and expressed the hope that Egypt could maintain its historic position as the "teacher" of other Eastern peoples.[38] Ahmad Shafiq's explanation of why the Eastern idea and the Eastern Bond Society developed in Egypt "before any of the other Eastern countries" summarized this sense of Egyptian leadership and *mission civilisatrice* felt by many of the advocates of the Eastern concept in the 1920s:

> It is an indisputable fact that Egypt is a lighthouse for the East and a lodestar for its inhabitants. For when all is said and done, there is no country in the East which has the characteristics of Egypt because of its location between three continents as well as the mild disposition of the Egyptians who consider every Easterner as a compatriot. . . . But above all, Egypt is a bridge, a meeting point between East and West, a catalyst bringing the two cultures together.[39]

The practical limitations of this largely derivative and thoroughly secondary orientation toward the East appear best from a consideration of the phenomenon's programmatic aspects. As was the case with proposals for inter-Arab cooperation throughout the 1920s, the furthest that advocates of Easternism were willing to go in regard to political interaction was to suggest the desirability of political consultation and cooperation among separate Eastern states. Ideas on the informal political collaboration of Eastern states in a political bloc, and even on the formal establishment of a "league" of Eastern nations analogous to the League of Nations, were expressed occasionally by proponents of the Eastern idea in Egypt in the 1920s.[40] The purpose behind such political collaboration was invariably defensive: the need to create "a powerful bloc which could stand in the face of European imperialism,"[41] for a "League of Eastern Nations" that could resist "the aggressions of the West and its plots."[42] A detailed proposal for such an "Oriental Society of Nations" was put forth in 1926 by 'Abd al-Razzaq al-Sanhuri in his book *Le califat, son évolution vers une société des nations orientale.* Arguing that Eastern nations were just as capable as Western ones of institutionalizing meaningful cooperation such as that found in the West-sponsored League of Nations, Sanhuri proposed the establishment of a league composed of "independent oriental states" that would promote peace and cooperation among Eastern nations through organizing subsidiary bodies to coordinate practical cooperation in specific spheres of life, such as labor affairs.[43]

Even Sanhuri's proposal for an Oriental Society of Nations, however, illustrates the conceptual and practical difficulties that the Eastern idea encountered in the 1920s. It was made in a work on the Caliphate, a specifically Islamic institution, with Sanhuri suggesting that such a league, once established, should work for the revival of the Islamic Caliphate.[44] Although Sanhuri recommended that such a provisional Caliphate should keep religious and political authority separate, nevertheless his Oriental League of Nations in effect would have been an Islamic League of Nations. It was also a very utopian proposal. As he himself concluded about the League, what Sanhuri was propounding was "a noble idea" rather than a feasible blueprint for immediate implementation.[45]

With the prospect of meaningful political cooperation between Eastern nations obstructed by political realities in the 1920s, supporters of the Eastern idea gave most of their attention to the possibilities for nonpolitical collaboration. The "spiritual unity" of the nations of the East was conceived as the catalyst for national revival. Through spiritual unity the East would emerge from its current inferiority and backwardness and walk triumphantly into a new era of renewal, awakening, progress, and glory. Based on this premise, ideas of "Eastern intellectual unity,"[46] of working for the strengthening of "the spiritual bond" among Eastern nations,[47] or of consolidating "a spiritual bond, an intellectual-scientific bond, and an economic-commercial bond" among all the countries of the East[48] elicited considerable verbal support from Egyptian commentators in the 1920s and early 1930s.

But again, as with schemes of political cooperation, these sentiments ran into the same obstacles of fuzziness of definition and difficulty of implementation. Actual attempts to promote Eastern cultural bonds turned out to be efforts that in practice fostered Muslim or Arab interaction. Thus the celebration initiated in 1926–1927 by Ahmad Shafiq to honor the poet Ahmad Shawqi, which was intended by Shafiq to bring together representatives from "the whole East" to praise the prince of poets, resulted in the gathering of delegates only from Arab lands in Cairo in April;[49] the efforts of the Eastern Bond to convene a conference to discuss language reform in 1929 were limited to attempting to organize a meeting of Arabs to consider only the Arabic language (they also were never realized);[50] and when the organizers of the Eastern Student Conference intended for 1932 went abroad to establish contacts with other students, it was only the neighboring countries of Turkey, Syria, Lebanon, and Palestine that they visited.[51]

For all the ambiguity of the Eastern idea, it received widespread verbal support in the Egypt of the 1920s. Notions of Eastern solidarity and interaction received frequent approval and reinforcement in the writings of non-Egyptian publicists both within and without the country. The editor of *al-Muqattam,* Khalil Thabit, constantly extolled the benefits of Eastern cooperation,[52] and the contributions to the Egyptian press by Eastern writers living outside Egypt often praised Egypt's preeminent position among the lands of the East and called on it to assume its responsibilities of Eastern leadership.[53] Several periodicals employing the word "East" in their name and marked by a partially Easternist orientation—"Capital of the East" [*'Asimat al-Sharq*], 1923; "The East" [*al-Sharq*], 1924; "The New East" [*al-Sharq al-Jadid*], 1924; "Bond of the East" [*Rabitat al-Sharq*], 1924; the Wafdist daily "Star of the East" [*Kawkab al-Sharq*], 1924;

"Revival of the East" [*Nahdat al-Sharq*], 1925; "The Near East" [*al-Sharq al-Adna*], 1927; "The Eastern Bond" [*al-Rabita al-Sharqiyya*], 1928; "Light of the East" [*Nur al-Sharq*], 1930—began publication in Egypt in the period from 1923 to 1930. Equally as significant as the appearance of these, however, is that most of them were published for only a brief period, most not lasting out the 1920s.[54]

Proponents of the Eastern idea were found in greatest numbers within two sectors of native Egyptian opinion in the 1920s. The first was among Egyptian publicists and intellectuals of a traditionalist or conservative orientation. This sector itself subdivided into two partially overlapping subgroups, one composed of members of the Egyptian religious establishment, the other of Egyptian notables who before World War I had been supporters of an Ottoman/Islamic orientation for Egypt. It was such Egyptian religious leaders and/or cultural conservatives with prior Ottoman connections who seem to have constituted the leading cadre of organized Easternist activitiy in Egypt in the 1920s. Both groups made up much of the leadership of the main institutional manifestation of the Eastern phenomenon during the decade, the Eastern Bond Society of 1922–1931. It was in the nature of things that most of these religious or previously Ottoman-connected leaders of Egyptian Easternism were older men whose formative experiences lay in the prewar era and for whom Easternism seems to have represented a natural continuation of their earlier inclinations adapted to the post-Ottoman conditions of the postwar era.

The other major sector of organized Egyptian opinion that provided important leaders and spokesmen for Easternism was the Liberal Party. To be sure, Liberal endorsement of the phenomenon was far from universal. Although some Liberal notables (who were also of a religious background) were supporters of the Eastern idea and leaders of the Eastern Bond from the early 1920s, more secular intellectuals associated with the party seem to have remained aloof from Easternism in the early and mid-1920s. The party itself made no reference to Eastern solidarities or interaction in its program of 1922,[55] and in the same year the leading Liberal publicist, Muhammad Husayn Haykal, had declined to become personally involved in the new Eastern Bond Society, both on the theoretical grounds that the "culture and languages and national characteristics" of Eastern peoples were too dissimilar to those of Egypt to warrant such collaboration and because of the more practical consideration that his involvement in the organization would detract from the time and effort that he could devote to Egyptian concerns.[56] By the late 1920s, however, Haykal and some of his colleagues on the staff of the Liberal publication *al-Siyasa al-Usbu'iyya* were becoming powerful advocates of Eastern cooperation.[57] Still, one important Liberal leader continued to reject Easternism as incompatible with his thoroughgoing Egyptian territorial nationalism. The intellectual mentor of the Liberals, Ahmad Lufti al-Sayyid, refused to lend his endorsement to an Eastern Student's Conference organized by students of the Egyptian University in 1932. Rather, he counseled his youthful petitioner to "not waste your efforts . . . your country is more suited for your activity."[58]

Easternism met with a more reserved response from Wafdists. Given both the plasticity of the Eastern concept and the popularity of the Wafd in the 1920s, it is hardly surprising that Eastern slogans and ideas received some sympathy within Wafdist circles. Thus Sa'd Zaghlul occasionally referred to himself as an Easterner as well as an Egyptian;[59] one of the two main Wafdist newspapers of the decade, *Kawkab al-Sharq,* was a consistent supporter of Eastern cooperation, indeed announcing one of its goals to be to serve as "a connecting link between the sons of the East";[60] and even the more Egyptianist Wafdist newspaper, *al-Balagh,* wrote approvingly (if infrequently and briefly) of the need for anti-imperalist political collaboration among Eastern lands. But the Eastern idea remained a remote and shadowy one even to those Wafdists who formally endorsed it in the 1920s. More importantly, the leading Egyptian opponents of Easternism came from within the Wafd. On the intellectual level, the Wafdist journalist Salama Musa was perhaps the most vehement critic of Easternism in Egypt in the 1920s, denying Egypt's historical/cultural affiliations with the East and declaring flatly that "the Eastern bond is nonsense because it is based on a false foundation."[61] Politically, *al-Balagh*'s editor, 'Abd al-Qadir Hamza, and its leading pundit, 'Abbas Mahmud al-'Aqqad, were among the most vigorous exponents of the view that Egypt should concentrate on its own internal affairs and eschew external involvement equally in the Arab, the Islamic, and the "Eastern" regions.

The Eastern Bond, 1922–1931

Many of the difficulties surrounding Easternism in Egypt in the 1920s appear in microcosm in the history of the "Society of the Eastern Bond" [*Jam'iyyat al-Rabita al-Sharqiyya*] of 1922–1931. In November 1921, at a meeting of notables hosted by the Iranian merchant Mirza Mahdi Rafi' Mushki, Ahmad Zaki proposed the formation of a society devoted to promoting friendly ties among Eastern peoples.[62] After exploratory meetings in the winter of 1921–1922, the Society of the Eastern Bond was formally inaugurated on 19 February 1922.[63] "The purpose of the Society," as its founding charter adopted at this meeting stated, "is the dissemination and spread of bonds of knowledge and solidarity among Eastern nations, regardless of race or religion." To achieve these goals, the Society originally intended to sponsor a "General Eastern Conference" every three years as well as to become involved in working for such things as language reform, the standardization of weights and measures, and the promotion of both scholarly and commercial exchanges between Eastern peoples. The Society's charter also specified that the organization would not involve itself in religious or political issues.

The founding meeting of the Society in February 1922 was attended by about fifty people of some prominence in Egyptian cultural, religious, and commercial life. Two princes of the royal family, Yusuf Kamal and Isma'il Dawud, were present. Officers of the Society were elected at the founding meeting of 19 February: as President, al-Sayyid 'Abd al-Hamid al-Bakri, head of the Sufi orders in Egypt (selected only after Prince Yusuf Kamal declined the post);[64] as vice-presidents, Shaykh Muhammad Bakhit of al-Azhar and Muhammad Rashid Rida, the Syrian-born editor of *al-Manar;* Ahmad Zaki as Secretary; the Iranian Mirza Mahdi Rafi' Mushki as Treasurer; and Shaykh Muhammad al-Ghanimi al-Taftazani, Nur al-Din Mustafa, and Muhammad Rida Qazwini as Arab, Turkish, and Persian deputy secretaries, respectively. At another meeting on 7 March 1922, an "Administrative Council" [*majlis al-idara*] was selected, composed of all the above plus the former Palace official and contemporary historian Ahmad Shafiq, Shaykhs Mustafa 'Abd al-Raziq and 'Abd al-Muhsin al-Kazimi, and the secular notables Salih Jawdat,

Habib Lutf Allah, Emile Zaydan, and Dr. Mahjub Thabit.[65] Within a short time Dr. Mansur Fahmi and Shaykh 'Ali 'Abd al-Raziq affiliated with the Society and together with Ahmad Shafiq became its leading spokesmen.

The original leadership of the Eastern Bond is illustrative both of the breadth and the limitations of the organization. Although religious leaders were heavily represented, with four shaykhs and another two non-Azharite religious figures, there were also two Christians among the Society's leaders. Native Egyptians formed barely half of the original leadership; four of the Administrative Council were of Fertile Crescent Arab origin, two were Persian, and one was Turkish. The range of orientations represented on the Council was equally broad—from the Christian and secular editor of *al-Hilal,* Emile Zaydan, to the Muslim and the traditionalist editor of *al-Manar,* Muhammad Rashid Rida; from the brother of 'Ali 'Abd al-Raziq to the man who later became one of his most vehement opponents, Shaykh Muhammad Bakhit. "There was a variety here, at all events."[66] If there was a common purpose among the Society's founders and leaders apart from the anti-imperialist intent their actions were soon to demonstrate, it was the more generalized ideas of reform and revival, of the *nahda* of the previous generation, than it was of any particular external orientation or any consensus on the content of the revival that they hoped to foster. What is missing from the Society's early leadership is also interesting. Although there were people connected with the then emerging Liberal Constitutionalist Party (both Shaykh Muhammad Bakhit and al-Sayyid 'Abd al-Hamid al-Bakri were members of the first Liberal directing council of October 1922,[67] and the 'Abd al-Raziq family were leaders of the party as well), there was no one from the leadership of the Wafd among the original cadre of the Eastern Bond.

Little information is available about the following of the Society. It was largely this group of religious and academic dignitaries, who had founded the Society in 1922, which carried out its activities over the following decade. Throughout its history the Eastern Bond remained an elitist group of notables not unlike a private club, an assemblage of predominantly elderly gentlemen who had associated with each other in past years and who joined together in the 1920s to promote the vague Eastern orientation they all shared.

The Eastern Bond took on tangible organizational body only in the mid-1920s. The Society opened a clubhouse in Cairo in January 1925.[68] In 1927 seven committees dealing with different areas of the Eastern world were established, one each for the (eastern) Arab region, the Turkish-speaking area, the Iranian zone, India, the Far East, the Arab west, and Africa.[69] It was only in 1928 that the Eastern Bond began to publish its own journal, the generally monthly "Journal of the Eastern Bond" [*Majallat al-Rabita al-Sharqiyya*]. Funded in part with contributions from Princes Yusuf Kamal and 'Umar Tusun,[70] the journal was published for most of its duration by Ahmad Shafiq and edited by 'Ali 'Abd al-Raziq.

Through most of the 1920s the chief domestic activity of the Society was the sponsoring of lectures for its members and the general Egyptian public. The topics of these reflect no common approach other than a general interest in Eastern cultural revival. Lecturers included conservatives such as Muhammad Rashid Rida expounding on "Sayyid Jamal al-Din al-Afghani and His Influence on the Eastern Revival," journalists such as Mahmud 'Azmi speaking on "A Trip to Syria," and secularists such as Mansur Fahmi lecturing on "The Eastern Need for Renewal."[71] The influence of the Society's domestic activities upon Egyptian opinion in its early years is problematic. British reports on the organization minimize its impact; an evaluation of 1926 stated that "at no time . . . have the activities of this association been either extensive or very important."[72]

The externally oriented activities of the Eastern Bond in the mid-1920s were probably more significant.[73] Several of the Society's leaders took trips abroad during this time attempting among other things to promote contacts with foreign notables in the hope that non-Egyptian branches of the organization might be established. A commemoration of the life and career of the indisputably "Eastern" Jamal al-Din al-Afghani was held in 1924, and the Society sponsored receptions for Eastern dignitaries visiting Egypt such as those it held for delegates to the Cairo Caliphate Congress in May 1926, for the Indian poet Rabindranath Tagore in November 1926, and for King Amanullah of Afghanistan in December 1927.[74]

Additionally, financial assistance was dispatched to aid other Eastern peoples. Such contributions were made to the Turkish Red Crescent, to victims of Spanish-Riffian warfare in 1925, and to the Syrians during their revolt against the French Mandate in 1925–1926. The Society donated funds to the Persian Nationalist Party in 1923, and in 1924 and again in 1926 it attempted to mediate in the strife in the Arabian Peninsula, first in regard to the war between King Husayn and ʻAbd al-ʻAziz ibn Saʻud, later in the border skirmishes between the victorious Saʻudis and the Yemenis.[75] When rebellion in Syria prompted the French bombardment of Damascus in October 1925, the Society not only sent relief funds but also dispatched protests against French policy in Syria to the French government and to the League of Nations.[76]

Much of this activity obviously involved the Society in politics. But an alarmist report to the British in 1927 to the effect that Ahmad Shafiq and the Eastern Bond were spreading "Bolshevik propaganda" in Eastern lands was properly belittled by British authorities in Cairo. Summarizing the Society's goal as "calling Eastern nations to form one block to oppose European Imperialism," they also pointed out that "members of the Oriental Union Society are of the best in Egypt, mentally, intellectually, and religiously, and Communist principles are not likely to commend themselves to such men."[77]

Three observations need to be made about the early activities of the Eastern Bond. First, the Society had only a limited impact on Egyptian and Eastern public life. It had no branches outside Egypt. Within that country it was closer to a gentleman's club than to a mass movement; its meetings drew a small though select audience, and externally its efforts at mediation or rendering support to other Easterners were of dubious influence on Eastern affairs. Second, however much its leaders may have conceived of their activities as "Eastern," most of their attention was centered on the Arab and Muslim worlds. Although the Society sponsored occasional lectures on areas beyond the Arab and Muslim regions and arranged receptions for notables like Tagore, its leaders were predominantly Arab and Muslim, its cultural activities were overwhelming focused on the Arab and Muslim lands, and it appears to have involved itself only in Arab or Muslim political controversies. As with the Eastern idea generally, the Society of the Eastern Bond was an organization primarily promoting Arab and Muslim cooperation. Third, the Society's declared intention of avoiding religious or political issues was not adhered to. The contacts of many of the leaders of the Society were directed to the political goal of promoting the solidarity of Eastern peoples against the common foe of Western imperialism.

Just as the Eastern Bond was unable to avoid involvement in international political issues, so it did not remain apolitical in regard to Egyptian internal politics. In 1925, at the time of the controversy over 'Ali 'Abd al-Raziq's aggressively modernist and implicitly antiroyalist tract, several of the leaders of the Society drafted a petition to the King defending 'Abd al-Raziq and his book on the grounds of freedom of expression. Although the petition was not officially one of the Society itself, press reports of its composition led to the resignation from the Society of two of its more conservative members, Shaykhs Muhammad Bakhit and Muhammad al-Dijwi.[78] In 1926, prominent figures associated with the Society, notably Ahmad Zaki and 'Ali 'Abd al-Raziq, publicly opposed the Caliphate Conference being arranged by Egyptian *'ulama'* for May 1926.[79] As a result of these interventions in the debate over the question of the Caliphate in the mid-1920s, conservative opinion gradually came to regard the Eastern Bond as a secularist stronghold. As King Faysal of Iraq is reported to have told Ahmad Shafiq in an interview in 1927, the word was out that "it [the Eastern Bond] was an irreligious organization, or that it was French, and that it secretly was something other than what it was publicly."[80]

Sustained internal and public controversy over the direction apparently being taken by the Society erupted in the late 1920s. When *Majallat al-Rabita al-Sharqiyya* began publication in 1928, its editor was the unrepentant modernist 'Ali 'Abd al-Raziq. Although the journal under his direction had no party line and published material by conservatives as well, several of its early contributors were leading Egyptian liberals such as Mansur Fahmi, Taha Husayn, Muhammad Husayn Haykal, and even that self-professed "disbeliever in the East," Salama Musa.[81] All this modernist opinion was too much for another leader of the Society, the redoubtable Muhammad Rashid Rida. He had opposed the appointment of 'Abd al-Raziq as editor of the journal from within the Society, but to no avail.[82] When the contents of the journal confirmed his worst fears, he went public with his criticisms, publishing extended critiques of its early issues that denounced *Majallat al-Rabita al-Sharqiyya* and its editor for being basically "irreligious," for spreading "atheist culture" by publishing the views of such modernists, and for news reports on Eastern regions that contained material sympathetic to the radical modernizing regimes in Turkey, Iran, and Afghanistan.[83] 'Ali 'Abd al-Raziq responded to Rida with a counterattack accusing Rida of seeing "ghosts" in his opposition to the change occurring in Turkey, Iran, and Afghanistan as well as for having misinterpreted the reformist message of their joint intellectual mentors, al-Afghani and Muhammad 'Abduh.[84]

This acerbic public dispute had, as might be expected, negative consequences for an already marginal organization. Internally, it led to debates among the Society's leadership over the contents of its journal, with Rida being the main critic and Ahmad Shafiq the chief defender of its editor. When the supporters of 'Abd al-Raziq were victorious in this debate and the Council of the Society formally passed resolutions approving of the journal's direction under the editorship of 'Abd al-Raziq,[85] Rashid Rida announced his withdrawal from participation in the organization he had helped to found.[86] Press reports spoke of other opposition to the modernist direction apparently being taken by the Society.[87]

The organization's internal controversies of the later 1920s did not immediately affect its externally oriented activities. It continued to receive Eastern dignitaries visiting Egypt, and its own leaders were active in disseminating its message in other Eastern lands.[88] By 1929 the Society's journal is reported to have had regular outlets for distribution in Damascus, Baghdad, and Bombay.[89] The international cultural activities of the Eastern Bond were as varied as they had been earlier, including mediation in a dispute between Javanese and Malayan *'ulama'*, involvement in Arab cultural events such as a commemoration of the medieval poet Abu al-'Ala' al-Ma'arri, and an abortive effort to establish an international Arab academy.[90] An effort to sponsor a general Eastern conference in 1930 also failed, apparently because of lack of support in other Eastern lands.[91] Moreover, the Society continued to involve itself in the political struggles of Eastern peoples in the late 1920s. It protested Italian measures of repression in Libya and anti-Islamic legislation by the French in Tunisia and Morocco, and was particularly active in support of the Muslim position in regard to the Western Wall–al-Aqsa controversy in Palestine.[92]

On the whole, the same Arab-Muslim content of the Eastern Bond's Easternism that the organization had demonstrated earlier in its history continued to manifest itself in the later years of its existence. Its externally oriented activities were directed first to the Arab world, second to the non-Arab Middle East, and finally to Muslims outside the Middle East proper. Although *Majallat al-Rabita al-Sharqiyya* did carry occasional articles about the "revival" in China and Japan or on recent political developments in India,[93] there appears to have been no activity undertaken by the Society that was directed to non-Arabs, non-Middle Eastern populations, or non-Muslims. In practice, the Society's Easternism meant Arab-Muslim activity.

By 1930, signs of the imminent demise of the Eastern Bond had begun to appear. Its journal had never been a money-making operation, and by late 1930 admissions of financial difficulties and appeals for readers to contribute financially to its continuation were appearing.[94] In November 1930 one of the Society's most active leaders, Ahmad Shafiq, was forced to withdraw as publisher of the journal because of poor health.[95] The most serious sign of the Society's problems by 1930 was that it had to give up its clubhouse at the end of that year; the new headquarters of the organization became the mansion of its President, al-Sayyid 'Abd al-Hamid al-Bakri.[96] A British report of early 1931 evaluated the Society's following at that time as "inconsiderable."[97]

The Eastern Bond's demise in 1931 was a case of gradual expiration rather than sudden death. Although a general meeting of the membership was held and a new Administrative Council selected in the Spring of 1931,[98] the latter does not appear to have met beyond that time. The Society's journal ceased publication in July 1931 after only three years of operation and despite the editor's stated intention to resume publication in the fall of 1931.[99] In effect, the Eastern Bond Society appears to have gone out of existence as a result of a combination of factionalism, old age, and disinterest on the part of its supporters. Some of its leaders broke away in disagreement; others faded away; yet others turned to other concerns. All apparently acquiesced in the implicit judgment that the time of an Eastern-oriented organization in Egypt had come and gone. It had lasted for only a decade.

Easternism in Retrospect

The Eastern inclination found in Egypt in the 1920s was a complex but also an elusive phenomenon. In some respects it was anachronistic, representing a continuation of the Ottoman/Islamic orientation of the prewar period but in a decade unconducive to regional sentiment or cooperation. In other ways it was premature, pointing toward the broader sense of Asian-African solidarity that was to blossom into a major current only after World War II. It was definitely a secondary orientation for Egyptians, existing only in subordination to the dominant Egyptian territorial nationalism of the decade. Intellectually, the formulations by Egyptian advocates of the Eastern idea were often either nebulous generalizations or contrived speculations, marked by wishful thinking concerning the East and the nature of the ties among its peoples as well as by exaggerated expectations of the prospects of meaningful Eastern interaction. Programmatically, few detailed or significant statements of Eastern solidarity and cooperation were propounded. And practically, little was actually done to promote real Eastern collaboration.

But for all its limitations, Easternism was not without some importance for an understanding of the development of national orientations in modern Egypt. The very existence of the Eastern idea of an organization such as the Eastern Bond in Egypt in the 1920s is significant. On the one hand, it represents the continuing power of sentiments of external solidarity and affiliation for many members of the Egyptian elite even in the wake of the collapse of the Ottoman Empire and the emergence of an independent Egyptian state. On the other, it demonstrates the beginnings of a newer sense of non-Western sharing in the same destiny that had been produced by the global impact of the West since the nineteenth century and reinforced by World War I and the doctrines of national self-determination and revolution spawned by the war. Even in the heyday of Egyptian territorial nationalism, a partial identification with neighboring lands and peoples could be found within much of educated Egyptian opinion.

More important, the Easternist phenomenon of the 1920s is significant for making a definite contribution to the course of the development of nationalism in modern Egypt. The historical significance of the Eastern idea and the Eastern Bond is in their promotion of Muslim and Arab causes within Egypt at a time when the country's dominant ideological outlook was a secularist and often isolationist Egyptian territorial nationalism. By reminding Egyptians of their links to the Eastern world around them in an otherwise Egyptianist decade, both the concept and the organization contributed in some measure to the later movement of Egyptian opinion toward a greater identification with the Arab and Muslim spheres. In a sense, the experimenting with Eastern notions by Egyptians in the 1920s, despite the failure of their experimentation to lead to anything tangible, may have been a necessary clarification of Egypt's relationship to the world beyond the Nile Valley. An Easternist phase may have had to happen before Egyptians could move on to solidarities closer to home and more concrete in content.

Conclusion: The Triumph of Egyptianism

The evolution of nationalist orientations in Egypt betwen 1900 and 1930 was marked by one central process. This was the ascendancy of the Egyptian territorial nationalist perspective. Despite the theoretical elaboration of the territorial nationalist outlook by Egyptian intellectuals in the early years of the century, even at the time of World War I Egyptianism was still a marginal force without significant impact on either the political or the sociocultural life of Egypt. It was the drastic changes in internal and regional conditions during the years immediately after the war that laid the foundations for the postwar ascendancy of Egyptianism. By the 1920s, not only had Egyptian territorial nationalism become the dominant nationalist outlook expounded by Egyptian intellectuals, but it had also become the central inspiration behind the political, institutional, and cultural life of Egypt.

The dominance of Egyptianism made the 1920s a unique era in the history of modern Egypt. Neither before nor after this period was the dominant elite of Egypt as captivated, in its worldview as well as its patterns of behavior, by a single national perspective. In no other phase of the development of modern Egypt was Egyptianism to enjoy such overwhelming preeminence.

Egyptianism influenced the development of many aspects of Egyptian national life after the Revolution of 1919. In terms of the intellectual development of Egypt, in this period Egyptianism became the major source of Egyptian self-identity, loyalty, and national affiliation. It was the inspiration for a new collective image for Egyptians, one that gave new meaning to the Egyptian past and present. It provided the framework for a radically revised interpretation of Egyptian history as well as for a new vision of the Egyptian future. As elaborated by Egyptian nationalist intellectuals in the 1920s, Egyptianism also stipulated a totally different role of world influence and leadership for Egypt within the world community of nations.

A further function of Egyptianism on the intellectual level was that it furnished a solution to the tension between traditional Egyptian society and Western/modern civilization. It seemed to provide the basis for an acceptable compromise between the desire to preserve a local sense of identity, the validation and continuation of the Egyptian historical tradition, and the emerging awareness of the need to adapt to rapidly changing conditions of the modern era by opening Egyptian life to contemporary influences. Egyptianism offered the prospect of harmony of tradition and change, by providing a coherent answer to both the need for an authentic national identity and the wish to become thoroughly modern and progressive. It promised a way out of tradition as embodied in the historic Muslim community, the Arab cultural legacy, and the Asiatic East as well as a way to reorient Egypt toward its "natural" milieu of the Mediterranean and the West. At the same time, the adoption of the Egyptianist orientation would also provide Egyptians with the means to resume the historical dialogue between Egypt and the world at large, thereby allowing the nation to join the universal enterprise of modernity and progress. Thus Egyptianism could resolve tensions existing between East and West, past and future.

Politically, Egyptianism became the main basis for the creation as well as the operation of the modern Egyptian nation-state. Internally, the Constitution, the Parliament, the country's ministries and bureaucracy, the daily operations of the government, the activities of the new political parties, even the liberal and secularizing values prevalent in the 1920s all reflected the dominant Egyptian territorial nationalist orientation; they derived from it and were intended to further it. Externally, the foreign policy of the new Egyptian state was also grounded in the Egyptianist perspective, viewing Egypt as separate and remote from the backward Islamic, Arab, and Eastern worlds at the same time that it was associated with the dynamic and progressive West.

The impact of Egyptianism was also visible in economic life, serving as the basis for a new economic strategy. It played an important role in defining the nature of new public and private economic institutions created in Egypt in the 1920s as well as in determining the economic relationships among Egypt, the region, and the world. In the cultural realm, Egyptianism provided a new content for Egyptian culture. It served as the basis for a new educational program with a new national curriculum, in the process becoming the source of new symbols, myths, and values for the Egyptian younger generation. Egyptianism provided the framework for the Egyptian literary efflorescence of the 1920s. Through Egyptianism and in order to further Egyptianism, Egyptian writers and artists created new genres and canons to nurture their new artistic tastes. At the same time they devoted themselves to the renovation of traditional literary and artistic techniques in order that they might be made congruent with this new Egyptianist national culture. Egyptianism also became the inspiration for a dynamic new Egyptian journalism, for the emergence of new literary, cultural, and political journals marked by a decidedly Egyptianist flavor. In sum, Egyptianism was the *leitmotif* of the era, the source of most of the main developments occurring in Egypt as well as the central principle animating the national life of the "new Egypt" in the post-1919 era.

The uniqueness of this period in Egyptian history also rested in the ability of the exclusively Egyptian territorial nationalist perspective to neutralize alternative nationalist orientations. Neither before nor after the 1920s had other nationalist orientations been as eclipsed by an Egyptian nationalist worldview. An orientation toward the Ottoman Empire was completely eliminated during this period. Adherence to Islamic traditions and to the Muslim community, although still powerful in Egyptian popular life, greatly diminished among the Egyptian elite and temporarily became only a tangential influence on the political and cultural life of the new Egyptian nation. The Arab legacy came under fierce attack in Egypt in this period and was presented as an un-Egyptian and anti-progressive element in the Egyptian past. Both the creation of a new national order and the achievement of full modernity depended on being thoroughly and exclusively Egyptian.

The total triumph of Egyptianism dictated another characteristic of this unique era in modern Egyptian history. This was the high degree of consensus and perceptual homogeneity found within Egyptian society, particularly among its elite. During this period, Egyptianism both as ideology and praxis provided a unifying framework for the many diverse political and intellectual currents existing within Egyptian society. Egyptianism acted as an integrating force in Egyptian life, bridging the gaps between different political tendencies, personal rivalries, and even social groups. It served as the basis for a national order that, at least in the aura of optimism and expectation that followed the Revolution of 1919, was remarkably unified concerning fundamental national questions. Egyptianism seems to have met the needs of many of the groups making up Egyptian society. The desire for national liberation from foreign domination; the aspiration for collective heroism, sacrifice, and grandeur after centuries of national subjugation and humiliation; the hope for the political democratization and greater social integration of Egyptian life; the wish for social and cultural advance and a progressive national strategy for development: all these appeared to be answered by Egyptianism. To be sure, the period was not without its political struggles, its conflicts among religious and secular circles, economic classes, and generations. But from the broader historical perspective that considers this period in relation to those before and after it, these disputes were less intense than those occurring in other periods. Nor were the conflicts of the decade by and large over the question of Egypt's national orientation: the prevailing Egyptianism of the era was overwhelmingly accepted by the different political and social forces in Egypt.

The explanation of the overwhelming triumph of Egyptian territorial nationalism and the resultant creation of this unique era in the modern Egyptian history is primarily to be found in the relationship of the political and intellectual developments of the period and the historical circumstances surrounding them. The revolutionary changes of the years 1918–1924 generated a completely new historical context and thus a total challenge to the intellectual outlook and political activity of Egyptians. Their response to the new challenge of the post-Ottoman age was Egyptianism. Egyptianism appeared to be the only paradigm with which Egyptian society could adapt itself to the conditions of a new historical era. The collapse of the traditional political configuration, the acceptance of the principle of national self-determination, and the popular Revolution of 1919 all combined to produce the belief that an Egypt based on an exclusively Egyptianist national orientation was the inevitable successor to the old Ottoman/Islamic order.

The Egyptianist filter through which nationalist politicians and intellectuals interpreted the world around them in the postwar era is not to be explained solely in mechanistic terms, however. Egyptians were not merely responding to external events. Driven by the impulse to give coherence to a rapidly changing world, Egyptians went further than the pressures of the moment required. They elevated one particular view of the world, the territorial nationalist perspective, as the unifying framework of their life and thought and action. The past, the present, and the future were invested with Egyptianist meaning, and the Egyptianist interpretation became the conceptual guide for Egyptians' behavior in the world around them. Egyptianism shaped the system of aspirations and expectations that the Egyptian elite defined for itself and determined its theoretical and practical attitudes toward both internal and external issues, its national goals and the tactics it adopted to realize these goals.

Typical of the pervasiveness of Egyptianism in the postwar era was the outlook of Egyptian nationalist intellectuals. Their interpretation of the world around them constantly attempted to give a territorial nationalist and often Pharaonicist meaning to phenomena and simultaneously to deny any "foreign" meanings, be they Arab, Islamic, or Eastern. Beyond this, the passionate desire for modernity, the innovation visible in all spheres of life, the secular radicalism, and the dynamism and nonconformity of the period were all reflections of the new Egyptianist *Weltanschauung.*

Similarly, the attitudes and actions of Egypt's political leadership occurred only within the framework of their Egyptianist worldview. Whether it was their position on internal matters such as Egypt's constitutional development, political structure, and educational system or their outlook concerning Arab, Muslim, or Eastern external issues, their Egyptianist perspective provided the prism through which they viewed the world and acted within it. With politicians as with intellectuals, Egyptianism colored everything.

But the post-World War I historical configuration that had produced Egyptianism was not an eternal one. When it began to give way to new internal and regional conditions from the early 1930s onward, the exclusively territorial nationalist orientation also began to be replaced by alternative nationalist perspectives that were more in tune with current realities. An additional factor eroding Egyptianism was its own limitations and its inability to realize the expectations that had been attached to it. With the development of a new historical context and the relative failure of Egyptianism itself by the 1930s came the emergence of other nationalist orientations and alternative strategies for Egyptian politics.

The following period in Egyptian nationalist development, that of the 1930s and 1940s, was quite different from that of the 1920s. In place of the dominance of one particular nationalist worldview and the relative homogeneity of nationalist attitudes and programs that had characterized the earlier period, the following era was marked by the appearance of new forces in Egyptian society and politics, by the articulation of less Egyptianist and more traditionalist (but by no means merely traditional) nationalist perspectives, and by demands for significant changes in the regional policies of the Egyptian state. The involved permutations of antagonistic social forces, rival nationalist worldviews, and competing proposals for national action made the later evolution of nationalism in Egypt much more heterogeneous, multidimensional, and complex than it had been in the 1920s.

The interplay of these diverse elements in the 1930s and 1940s also led to a very different pattern of nationalist development from that which had occurred in the 1920s. Internally, the exclusive Egyptian territorial nationalism of the earlier period rapidly gave way to more Islamic and Arab-oriented nationalist ideologies. Externally, Egyptian political leaders responded to the new pressures placed upon them by adopting a more Arabic and Islamic foreign policy. The new worldviews and policies of the 1930s and 1940s were a radical break with the prevalent Egyptianism of the post-1919 era. In the fullness of time, these new currents coalesced into a new hegemonic nationalist orientation, that of the Egyptian Arab nationalism that reached its culmination in the revolutionary regime of the post-1952 era.

Notes

Abbreviations of Egyptian Periodicals

AH	al-Ahram
AK	al-Akhbar
BL	al-Balagh
BU	al-Balagh al-Usbu'i
FH	al-Fath
FJ	al-Fajr
HI	al-Hilal
KS	Kawkab al-Sharq
MI	Misr
MJ	al-Majalla al-Jadida
MQ	al-Muqtataf
MSI	Mulhaq al-Siyasa
MU	al-Muqattam
RI	al-Risala
RS	al-Rabita al-Sharqiyya
SF	al-Sufur
SI	al-Siyasa
SM	al-Shubban al-Muslimun
SR	al-Sarkha
SU	al-Siyasa al-Usbu'iyya
US	al-'Usur
WA	al-Watan

Preface

1. Our definition of nationalism is drawn primarily from Anthony D. Smith, *Theories of Nationalism* (New York, 1971), chapters one and seven. See also Ernest Gellner, *Nations and Nationalism* (Ithaca, 1983), chapters one and five.

2. For discussions of nationalism that focus on its ideological aspects, see Hans Kohn, *The Idea of Nationalism* (New York, 1944), passim.; Elie Kedourie, *Nationalism* (London, 1960), passim.; Elie Kedourie, *Nationalism in Asia and Africa* (New York, 1970), Introduction.

3. John Higham, "Intellectual History and Its Neighbors," *Journal of the History of Ideas,* 15 (1954), 339–347 (quotation from 341).

4. Gordon S. Wood, "Intellectual History and the Social Sciences," in John Higham and Paul K. Conkin (eds.), *New Directions in American Intellectual History* (Baltimore, 1979), 27–41 (quotation from 32); see also Murray G. Murphey, "The Place of Beliefs in Modern Culture," in Higham and Conkin, op. cit., 151–166, especially 153–154. For a broader anthropological development of this approach, see Clifford Geertz, *The Interpretation of Cultures* (New York, 1973), 3–30, 87–125, 193–233.

5. Rush Welter, "On Studying the National Mind," in Higham and Conkin, op. cit., 64–82 (quotation from 73).

6. Lovejoy's approach to history is presented in Arthur O. Lovejoy, *The Great Chain of Being: A Study of the History of an Idea* (Cambridge, 1936), Introduction, and Arthur O. Lovejoy, "Reflections on the History of Ideas," *Journal of the History of Ideas,* 1 (1940), 3–23. For critiques of his approach, see Quentin Skinner, "Meaning and Understanding in the History of Ideas," *History and Theory,* 8 (1969), 3–53, especially 4–39; Felix Gilbert, "Intellectual History: Its Aims and Methods," *Daedalus,* 50 (Winter 1971), 80–97; William J. Bouwsma, "Intellectual History in the 1980's: From History of Ideas to History of Meaning," *The Journal of Interdisciplinary History,* 12 (1981–1982), 279–291.

7. Wood, op. cit., 34.

8. Critiques of the overly contextual approach can be found in Skinner, op. cit., 39–48; Higham, op. cit., 341; Dominick LaCapra, "Rethinking Intellectual History and Reading Texts," in Dominick LaCapra and Steven L. Kaplan (eds.), *Modern European Intellectual History: Reappraisals and New Perspectives* (Ithaca, 1982), 47–85.

9. The first quotation is from Higham, op. cit., 341; the second is from Gene Wise, "The Contemporary Crisis in Intellectual History Studies," *Clio,* 5 (1975), 55–69 (quotation from 69).

10. For a classic statement of the necessity for synthesis of the study of thought and the study of society, see Karl Mannheim, *Ideology and Utopia: An Introduction to the Sociology of Knowledge* (trans. by Louis Wirth and Edward Shils: New York, 1936), chapter one.

11. R. G. Collingwood, *An Essay on Metaphysics* (Oxford, 1940), 73.

12. Mannheim, op. cit., 3.

13. On the concept of a "community of discourse," see David A. Hollinger, "Historians and the Discourse of Intellectuals," in Higham and Conkin, op. cit., 42–63, especially 42–45, 55–60.

14. Robert Darnton, "Intellectual and Cultural History," in Michael Kammen (ed.), *The Past Before Us: Contemporary Historical Writing in the United States* (Ithaca, 1980), 327–354 (quotation from 337); for a discussion of the problems of classification in intellectual history, see Roger Chartier, "Intellectual History or Sociocultural History? The French Trajectories," in LaCapra and Kaplan, op. cit., 13–46.

15. John C. Greene, "Objectives and Methods in Intellectual History," *The Mississippi Valley Historical Review,* 44 (1957), 58–74 (quotation from 67).

16. Defined in Collingwood, op. cit., chapter five.

17. Greene, op. cit., 59.

18. Ibid., 60.

Introduction: Nationalist Tendencies in Egypt, 1900–1914

1. Albert Hourani, *Arabic Thought in the Liberal Age, 1798–1939* (London, 1962), 341–342.

2. A stimulating interpretation of the nature of Muslim community loyalties is provided in Ira M. Lapidus, "Muslim Cities and Islamic Societies," in Ira M. Lapidus (ed.), *Middle Eastern Cities*

(Berkeley, 1969), and developed further in his "The Separation of State and Religion in the Development of Early Islamic Society," *International Journal of Middle East Studies,* 6 (1975), 363–385.

3. For a summary of the Empire's pan-Islamic campaign, see Bernard Lewis, *The Emergence of Modern Turkey* (London, 1961), 334–337.

4. The phrase is that of Jacques Berque in his *Egypt: Imperialism and Revolution* (trans. by Jean Stewart: London, 1972), 273.

5. See Hourani, op. cit., 73–80, for an analysis of Tahtawi's political ideas.

6. For anti-Turkish statements attributed to 'Urabi, see Ahmad 'Urabi, ed. and trans. by Trevor Le Gassick, *The Defense Statement of Ahmad 'Urabi* (Cairo, 1982), 18–25; Wilfred Scawen Blunt, *Secret History of the English Occupation of Egypt: Being a Personal Narrative of Events* (London, 1907), 172, 251, 344–345; The Earl of Cromer, *Modern Egypt* (two vols.: London, 1908), I, 209, 324. Pro-Ottoman statements by 'Urabist leaders, including 'Urabi himself, are documented in Alexander Schölch, *Egypt for the Egyptians! The Socio-Political Crisis in Egypt, 1878–1882* (London, 1981), 173, 175, 196, 246, 262, 286 (quotations from 175 and 262).

7. Ibid., 175, 179–181, 238, 247, 263–264, 271, 281–283 (quotation from 238).

8. 'Abd al-'Azim Muhammad Ramadan, *Tatawwur al-Haraka al-Wataniyya fi Misr min Sanat 1918 ila Sanat 1936* (Cairo, 1968), 29.

9. For other discussions of the partially instrumental basis of much Egyptian pro-Ottoman sentiment after 1882, see Dhuqan Qarqut, *Tatawwur al-Fikra al-'Arabiyya fi Misr, 1805–1936* (Beirut, 1972), 245–246, and Hisham Sharabi, *Arab Intellectuals and the West: The Formative Years, 1875–1914* (Baltimore, 1970), 107.

10. Discussed respectively in Muhammad Muhammad Husayn, *al-Ittijahat al-Wataniyya fi al-Adab al-Mu'asir* (two vols.: Cairo, 1954), I, 23–29, 29–33, 35–39, 40–44. See also Mounah A. Khouri, *Poetry and the Making of Modern Egypt* (Leiden, 1971), passim.

11. Mustafa Kamil, "al-Islam," *Majallat al-Liwa',* 15 Nov. 1900, 9–15; Mustafa Kamil, "al-Hukuma wa al-Umma fi Misr," ibid., 15–17; see also Fritz Steppat, "Nationalismus und Islam bei Mustafa Kamil," *Die Welt des Islams,* 4 (1955–1956), 251–266, 281–294.

12. Mustafa Kamil, "Rabitat al-Din wa Rabitat al-Watan," *al-Liwa',* 15 Ramadan 1317, as republished in 'Ali Fahmi Kamil (ed.), *Mustafa Kamil fi 34 Rabi'an* (nine vols.: Cairo, 1908–1911), IX, 249–255 (quotation from 250); see also Steppat, op. cit., 266–283; Faruq Abu Zayd, *Azmat al-Fikr al-Qawmi fi al-Sihafa al-Misriyya* (Cairo, 1976), 59–60.

13. See the recent discussion by Dennis Walker, "Mustafa Kamil's Party: Islam, Pan-Islamism, and Nationalism," part 1, *Islam and the Modern Age,* 11 (1980), 329–388; part 2, ibid., 12 (1981), 1–43; part 3, ibid. (1981), 79–113. (The point is developed particularly in part 2, 2–5, 13–15, 28–32.) See also Steppat, op. cit., 266–297.

14. See Walker, op. cit., part 1, 348; part 2, 3, 9–11, 21–24; Steppat, op. cit., 294–314.

15. See Mustafa Kamil, "al-Dawla al-'Ulya wa Misr," in 'Ali Fahmi Kamil, op. cit., VI, 185–193; see also ibid., IX, 3–5, 77–78, 137–138, 170–176, 215–218; Steppat, op. cit., 287–297; Walker, op. cit., part 2, 10; part 3, 80.

16. Discussed in Husayn, op. cit., I, 6–10; see also Arthur Goldschmidt, Jr., "The Egyptian Nationalist Party, 1892–1919," in P. M. Holt (ed.), *Political and Social Change in Modern Egypt* (London, 1965), 317.

17. Walker, op. cit., part 3, 81, 87, 94–100 (quotation from 96).

18. See A. L. Rizq, "Azmat al-'Aqaba al-Ma'rufa bi-Hadithat Taba 1906," *al-Majalla al-Ta'rikhiyya al-Misriyya,* 13 (1967), 247–305, especially 278, 296; Abu Zayd, op. cit., 152; Afaf Lutfi al-Sayyid, *Egypt and Cromer: A Study in Anglo-Egyptian Relations* (New York, 1969), 166–167; Robert L. Tignor, *Modernization and British Colonial Rule in Egypt, 1882–1914* (Princeton, 1966), 278–279; Uriel Heyd, "Hamashber shel Mifraz Eilat bi-Shnat 1906" (in Hebrew), *Sefer Eilat* (Jerusalem, 1960), 204–206.

19. Quoted in Ramadan, op. cit., 34.

20. Markaz Watha'iq wa Ta'rikh Misr al-Mu'asir, *Awraq Muhammad Farid, vol. I: Mudhakkirati ba'da al-Hijra, 1904–1919* (Cairo, 1978), 63–65; see also Rif'at al-Sa'id, *Muhammad Farid: al-Mawqif wa al-Ma'sa* (Cairo, 1978), 142–155; Anwar al-Jundi, *'Abd al-'Aziz Jawish* (Cairo, 1965), 83–87; Muhammad 'Ali 'Alluba, *Dhikrayyat Ijtima'iyya wa Siyasiyya* (Cairo, 1982), 49–52.

21. Mustafa Kamil, "'Inayat al-Misriyyin li al-Dawla," in 'Ali Fahmi Kamil, op. cit., V, 229–232 (quotation from 231). For further examples, see Walker, op. cit., part 3, 89; Abu Zayd, op. cit., 59; Anis Sayigh, *al-Fikra al-'Arabiyya fi Misr* (Beirut, 1959), 51.

22. Mustafa Kamil, "al-Dawla al-'Ulya wa Misr," in 'Ali Fahmi Kamil, op. cit., VI, 185–193; see also ibid., III, 224–239; ibid., V, 86–94, 153–159, 162–164; Steppat, op. cit., 274–275; Abu Zayd, op. cit., 59–60.

23. Hourani, op. cit., 205.

24. Quotation from *al-Liwa',* 13 Sept. 1906, as cited in Abu Zayd, op. cit., 60.

25. Quotation from *al-Jarida,* 1 Sept. 1912, as republished in Ahmad Lutfi al-Sayyid, *al-Muntakhabat* (two vols.: Cairo, 1945), I, 310; see also Charles Wendell, *The Evolution of the Egyptian National Image: From Its Origins to Ahmad Lutfi al-Sayyid* (Berkeley, 1972), 231.

26. Ibid.; see also Husayn, op. cit., I, 85–86.

27. The first phrase appears in Ahmad Lutfi al-Sayyid, *Qissat Hayati* (Cairo, 1962), 70; the second is from *al-Jarida,* 16 Jan. 1913, as republished in Ahmad Lutfi al-Sayyid, *Ta'ammulat fi al-Falsafa wa al-Adab wa al-Siyasa wa al-Ijtima'* (second ed.: Cairo, 1965), 72; the third is from *al-Jarida,* 21 Oct. 1911, as quoted in Wendell, op. cit., 233.

28. Quoted in Jamal Muhammed Ahmed, *The Intellectual Origins of Egyptian Nationalism* (London, 1960), 69; see also al-Sayyid, *Egypt and Cromer,* 188.

29. See Ahmad Zakariya al-Shaliq, *Hizb al-Umma wa Dawruhu fi al-Siyasa al-Misriyya* (Cairo, 1979), 221, 225–226; see also al-Sayyid, *Egypt and Cromer,* 188.

30. Quoted in ibid., 190–191; see also Shaliq, op. cit., 219–231.

31. Discussed in al-Sayyid, *Qissat Hayati,* 132–133.

32. See Rashid Ismail Khalidi, *British Policy towards Syria and Palestine, 1906–1914* (London, 1980), 33, 35.

33. As quoted in al-Sayyid, *Egypt and Cromer,* 167.

34. Muhammad Husayn Haykal, *Mudhakkirat fi al-Siyasa al-Misriyya* (three vols.: Cairo, 1951, 1953, 1978), I, 20. For a further exploration of the national outlook of this class, see Walid Kazziha, "The Jarida-Umma Group and Egyptian Politics," *Middle Eastern Studies,* 13 (1977), 373–385.

35. Quoted in Walker, op. cit., part 3, 96.

36. Quoted in Sir Ronald Storrs, *The Memoirs of Sir Ronald Storrs* (New York, 1937), 92–93.

37. See Abu Zayd, op. cit., 137–138, 145.

38. Ibid.

39. The main source on this subject is Jamal Zakariya Qasim, "Mawqif Misr min al-Harb al-Tarablusiyya, 1911–1914," *al-Majalla al-Ta'rikhiyya al-Misriyya,* 13 (1967), 306–342.

40. Ibid., 320, 328, 339; Abu Zayd, op. cit., 155–157; Husayn, op. cit., I, 35–39; Sayigh, op. cit., 72.

41. Qasim, op. cit., 335; Taha Husain (Taha Husayn), *A Passage to France: The Third Volume of the Autobiography* (trans. by Kenneth Cragg: Leiden, 1976), 44; John Russell (Russell Pasha), *Egyptian Service, 1902–1946* (London, 1946), 146.

42. Qasim, op. cit., 334–335; Haykal, op. cit., I, 35, 50; 'Alluba, op. cit., 74–75; Qallini Fahmi, *Mudhakkirat Qallini Fahmi Basha* (two vols.: Cairo, 1934), II, 65; Wilfred Scawen Blunt, *My Diaries* (two vols.: London, 1921), II, 367.

43. Qasim, op. cit., 315–320, 325–326, 340; Emine Foat Tugay, *Three Centuries: Family Chronicles of Turkey and Egypt* (London, 1963), 102, 290; Muhammad Subayh, *Batal La Nansahu: 'Aziz al-Misri wa 'Asruhu* (Cairo, 1973), 47. For similar assistance rendered to the Ottomans by Egyptians during the Balkan wars, see Shaliq, op. cit., 234–235.

44. See Haykal, op. cit., I, 50–51.

45. Hourani, op. cit., 80.

46. Ibid., 78.

47. Ibid., 79; see also Wendell, op. cit., 129–130.

48. Quoted in Hourani, op. cit., 79.

49. Quoted in Sayigh, op. cit., 63.

50. Schölch, op. cit., 209, 284, 311–312 (quotation from 284).

51. Mustafa Kamil's speech of 22 Oct. 1907 in Alexandria as given in 'Abd al-Rahman al-Rafi'i, *Mustafa Kamil: Ba'ith al-Haraka al-Wataniyya* (Cairo, 1950), 469; see also Husayn, op. cit., I, 67.

52. Quoted in Abu Zayd, op. cit., 58–59; see also Wendell, op. cit., 250.

53. Quoted in ibid., 267.

54. Quoted in ibid., 247.

55. Quoted in ibid., 267.

56. Quoted in Husayn, op. cit., I, 65; see also Abu Zayd, op. cit., 58–60.

57. See Sayigh, op. cit., 49–50.

58. Hourani, op. cit., 206; see also Steppat, op. cit., 251–258.

59. *al-Jarida,* 2 Jan. 1913, as republished in al-Sayyid, *Ta'ammulat,* 65–68 (quotation from 67); also quoted in Wendell, op. cit., 270. See also al-Sayyid, *Muntakhabat,* II, 117–118.

60. *al-Jarida,* 1 May 1909, as quoted in Wendell, op. cit., 268.

61. al-Sayyid, *Muntakhabat,* I, 170; also quoted in Wendell, op. cit., 8–9.

62. al-Sayyid, *Ta'ammulat,* 17–21; see also Wendell, op. cit., 37.

63. al-Sayyid, *Ta'ammulat,* 65; see also Wendell, op. cit., 238.

64. See al-Sayyid, *Ta'ammulat,* 27–28; Wendell, op. cit., 224–225, 272–278.

65. *al-Jarida,* 23 Aug. 1908, as quoted in Wendell, op. cit., 240; see also Ahmad Lutfi al-Sayyid, *Safahat Matwiyya min Ta'rikh al-Haraka al-Istiqlaliyya fi Misr* (Cairo, 1946), 33–34.

66. *al-Jarida,* 6 May 1911, as quoted in Wendell, op. cit., 239.

67. *al-Jarida,* 9 Jan. 1913, as republished in al-Sayyid, *Ta'ammulat,* 69–70, and quoted in Wendell, op. cit., 259. For a general discussion of this theme, see al-Sayyid, *Ta'ammulat,* 65–74.

68. *al-Jarida,* 2 Sept. 1912, as quoted in Nabih Bayyumi 'Abd Allah, *Tatawwur al-Fikra al-Qawmiyya al-'Arabiyya fi Misr* (Cairo, 1975), 51.

69. For a survey of the *nahda,* see John A. Haywood, *Modern Arabic Literature, 1800–1970* (New York, 1971), chapter three. Pre-1914 proposals for Arabic language reform are summarized in Husayn, op. cit., II, 334–336; Wendell, op. cit., 276–280; and Anwar al-Jundi, *al-Fikr al-'Arabi al-Mu'asir fi Ma'rakat al-Taghrib wa al-Tab'iyya al-Thaqafiyya* (Cairo, 1961), 566–570.

70. For examples, see Khouri, op. cit., 21; Walker, op. cit., part 3, 91; Wendell, op. cit., 125, 157, 248; Akram Zu'aytir, "al-'Uruba fi Misr," *al-'Arabi,* no. 244 (March 1979), 7–10.

71. Cromer, op. cit., II, 216–217.

72. See Husayn, op. cit., I, 204–205; Hourani, op. cit., 196; Wendell, op. cit., 157.

73. Blunt, *My Diaries,* I, 135, 247.

74. Thomas Philipp, *Gurgi Zaydan: His Life and Work* (Wiesbaden, 1979), 30–32, 62, 67.

75. Mustafa Kamil writing in *Majallat al-Liwa',* Oct.-Dec. 1902, 75–78; see also 'Ali Fahmi Kamil, op. cit., VI, 27–29; Husayn, op. cit., I, 204–205; Hourani, op. cit., 208. For the expression of similar attitudes toward the Syrian community in Egypt on the part of Mustafa Kamil's successor Muhammad Farid, see Sa'id, op. cit., 143–145.

76. Husayn, op. cit., I, 207–209; Sayigh, op. cit., 114.

77. Cromer, op. cit., II, 198; Blunt, *Secret History,* 412.

78. Cromer, op. cit., II, 198; for the post-1914 use of the proverb by an Egyptian, see Ralph M. Coury, "Who 'Invented' Egyptian Arab Nationalism?," part 1, *International Journal of Middle East Studies,* 14 (1982), 249–281; part 2, ibid., 459–479 (reference in part 2, 473).

79. Quoted in Walker, op. cit., part 3, 95.

80. Storrs, op. cit., 92.

81. For this interpretation, see Qarqut, op. cit., 199–207, 241–242; Muhammad 'Imara, *al-'Uruba fi al-'Asr al-Hadith* (Cairo, 1967), 271–275; Ahmad 'Abd al-Mu'ti Hijazi, *'Urubat Misr* (Beirut, 1979), 178–183. The most frequently cited "Arabist" statement is that attributed to Mahmud Sami al-Barudi stating that "[f]rom the beginning of our movement we aimed at turning Egypt into a small republic like Switzerland—and then Syria would have joined—and then Hejaz would have followed us"; Blunt, *Secret History,* 344.

82. For Tawfiq's maneuvers (and Ottoman dismissal of the same as being without foundation), see 'Urabi, op. cit., 33, and Schölch, op. cit., 232, 245. Statements contrary to Arab nationalist aspirations or intentions by 'Urabist leaders may be found in ibid., 311–312; Sayigh, op. cit., 42; Sylvia G. Haim, *Arab Nationalism: An Anthology* (Berkeley, 1962), 46; 'Abd al-'Ati Muhammad, "Tatawwur al-Fikra al-'Arabiyya fi Misr," *al-Fikr al-'Arabi,* I, nos. 4–5 (Sept.–Nov. 1978), 295–318, especially 297–299.

83. See 'Imara, op. cit., 331; Bassam Tibi, *Arab Nationalism: A Critical Inquiry* (trans. by Marion Farouq-Sluglett and Peter Sluglett: New York, 1981), 85.

84. See Husayn, op. cit., I, 23–29; Khouri, op. cit., 106–108.

85. For examples, see 'Ali Fahmi Kamil, op. cit., VII, 27–29; ibid., IX, 200; discussed in Husayn, op. cit., I, 6–10, and Hourani, op. cit., 203.

86. See Sayigh, op. cit., 72.

87. Quoted in ibid., 55.

88. Markaz Watha'iq, op. cit., 100–101.

89. Ahmad Lutfi al-Sayyid, "al-Mas'ala al-'Arabiyya," *al-Jarida,* 30 Aug. 1911, as republished in al-Sayyid, *Muntakhabat,* I, 250–251; see also the discussions in Sayigh, op. cit., 59, and Zu'aytir, op. cit., 8–9.

90. al-Sayyid, *Qissat Hayati,* 137.

91. See *al-Jarida,* 2 March 1913, as republished in al-Sayyid, *Ta'ammulat,* 75; *al-Jarida,* 6 Jan. 1913, as republished in al-Sayyid, *Ta'ammulat,* 70 (both also cited in Wendell, op. cit., 230, 260).

92. See Blunt, *Secret History,* 86–87; Hourani, op. cit., 269–270.

93. Ibid., 270; Elie Kedourie, "The Politics of Political Literature: Kawakibi, Azoury, and Jung," in his *Arabic Political Memoirs and Other Studies* (London, 1974), 107–123, especially 108.

94. See Abu Zayd, op. cit., 115–120; Muhammad, op. cit., 299.

95. Markaz Watha'iq, op. cit., 116; Khalidi, op. cit., 226, 234, 239; Elie Kedourie, *In the Anglo-Arab Labyrinth: The Husayn-McMahon Correspondence and Its Interpretations, 1914–1939* (London, 1975), 12.

96. See Markaz Watha'iq, op. cit., 99–100, 112; Blunt, *My Diaries,* II, 390; Qasim, op. cit., 332–334.

97. Information on Misri's prewar involvement in Arab affairs may be found in Markaz Watha'iq, op. cit., 99–101, 116; Khalidi, op. cit., 341–346; Subayh, op. cit., 41–94; Majid Khadduri, "'Aziz 'Ali al-Misri and the Arab Nationalist Movement," in Albert Hourani (ed.), *Middle Eastern Affairs* (*St. Antony's Papers,* no. 17) (London, 1965), 140–163, especially 140–145.

98. The Abbas Hilmi II Papers housed at the Durham University Library contain a file of correspondence between Misri and 'Abbas Hilmi exchanged while Misri was in Libya in 1911–1912 (Abbas Hilmi II Papers, file 112); see also Markaz Watha'iq, op. cit., 110, 116. For Misri's prewar nationalist ideas, see Khadduri, op. cit., 148–149; Muhammad 'Abd al-Rahman Burj, *'Aziz al-Misri wa al-Haraka al-'Arabiyya, 1908–1916* (Cairo, 1979), 69–70.

99. Subayh, op. cit., 62; Zu'aytir, op. cit., 8; Djemal Pasha, *Memories of a Turkish Statesman, 1913–1919* (New York, 1922), 58; As'ad Daghir, *Mudhakkirati 'ala Hamish al-Qadiyya al-'Arabiyya* (Cairo, 1959), 47–48.

100. C. Ernest Dawn, *From Ottomanism to Arabism: Essays on the Origins of Arab Nationalism* (Urbana, Ill., 1973), 152–153.

Chapter 1. Egyptians, Ottomans, and Arabs during World War I

1. Examples of Egyptian recollections of sympathy for the Ottoman cause at the start of World War I may be seen in Haykal, op. cit., I, 55–64; Salama Musa, *The Education of Salama Musa* (trans. by L. O. Schuman: Leiden, 1961), 97; Jamil 'Arif (ed.), *Safahat min al-Mudhakkirat al-Sirriyya li-Awwal Amin 'Amm lil-Jami'a al-'Arabiyya, 'Abd al-Rahman 'Azzam* (Cairo, 1978 or 1979), 78–84; Markaz Watha'iq, op. cit., 168, 199–200. British opinions to much the same effect may be seen in Storrs, op. cit., 145–146; Sir Ronald Wingate, *Wingate of the Sudan* (London, 1955), 205, 210–211, 220; George Lloyd (Lord Lloyd), *Egypt Since Cromer* (two vols.: London, 1933–1934), I, 187–191, 204.

2. See Haykal, op. cit., I, 56; Musa, op. cit., 97; Storrs, op. cit., 146.

3. Sir Ronald Storrs, "Note Respecting the State of Public Opinion in Egypt," 31 Aug. 1914 (FO 407/183, no. 7); see also Haykal, op. cit., I, 63–64; Ramadan, op. cit., 59–60.

4. Mentioned in the "Egyptian Personalities" report of the British Embassy, Cairo, 1938; FO 371/22004, J2184/2014/16.

5. Wingate to Hardinge, 24 Nov. 1918; FO 371/3204, as reproduced in Mu'assasat al-Ahram, *Khamsun 'Amman 'ala Thawrat 1919* (Cairo, 1969), document 14. See also Wingate, op. cit., 205, 210–211.

6. Note from Storrs, 3 Dec. 1914; FO 141/648, 232. See also Markaz Watha'iq, op. cit., 200; Anwar al-Jundi, *al-Imam al-Maraghi* (Cairo, 1952), 112–113.

7. Fakhr al-Din al-Ahmadi al-Zawahiri, *al-Siyasa wa al-Azhar: Min Mudhakkirat Shaykh al-Islam al-Zawahiri* (Cairo, 1945), 165–166; see also Storrs, op. cit., 153.

8. Discussed in Husayn, op. cit., II, 7–14.

9. Cited in Subayh, op. cit., 65.

10. Zawahiri, op. cit., 177.

11. Haykal, op. cit., I, 61; see also 'Arif, op. cit., 78, for much the same linkage of motives.

12. Text in Markaz Watha'iq, op. cit., 176–177; see also the extract from the "El Ittihad El Osmani" of 31 Dec. 1914 as translated in FO 141/648, 232/0.

13. Markaz Watha'iq, op. cit., 171–173, 178–179, 191, 202; FO 141/648, 232/355, 232/356, 232/536.

14. Markaz Watha'iq, op. cit., 181–184.

15. Quotation from a telegram from the High Commissioner, 28 Oct. 1914 (FO 141/800, 248 tels. 1914); see also 'Arif, op. cit., 78–79; Haykal, op. cit., I, 62–63.

16. Djemal Pasha, *Memories,* 154; George MacMunn and Cyril Falls, *Military Operations, Egypt and Palestine: From the Outbreak of War with Germany to June 1917* (London, 1928), 35–36.

17. On British security measures in Egypt in late 1914, see FO 407/183, no. 87; MacMunn and Falls, op. cit., 48; P. G. Elgood, *Egypt and the Army* (London, 1924), 60–61, 82, 87; Isma'il 'Ali Sa'id, *al-Azhar 'ala Masrah al-Siyasa al-Misriyya* (Cairo, 1974), 276–280; 'Abd al-Rahman al-Rafi'i, *Muhammad Farid* (second ed.: Cairo, 1962), 420–421.

18. Sir Ronald Storrs, "Note Respecting the State of Public Opinion in Egypt," 31 Aug. 1914 (FO 407/183, no. 7); see also Storrs, op. cit., 146.

19. See respectively Cheetham to Grey, 18 Nov. 1914 (FO 407/183, no. 49); same to same, 8 Dec. 1914 (FO 407/183, no. 72); same to same, 28 Dec. 1914 (FO 407/183, no. 87).

20. MacMunn and Falls, op. cit., 39–40; Wingate, op. cit., 198–199.

21. This is suggested in Haykal, op. cit., I, 62–63.

22. Ibid.

23. 'Arif, op. cit., 84–86. The campaign in the Western desert is described in detail in MacMunn and Falls, op. cit., 101–145.

24. Ahmad Shafiq, *Mudhakkirati fi Nisf Qarn* (three vols.: Cairo, 1934–1937), III, 58–63; cf. 'Arif, op. cit., 83–84.

25. Quotation from a "Memorandum by Sir R. Graham on Future British Policy with Regard to Egypt," 2 March 1917 (FO 407/183, no. 98); see also Wingate, op. cit., 205, 210–211.

26. Discussed in Shaliq, op. cit., 317–318.

27. Haykal, op. cit., I, 57–58.

28. al-Sayyid, *Qissat Hayati,* 162–164.

29. Shaliq, op. cit., 319–320.

30. Ibid., 320–321.

31. Ibid., 322.

32. FO 141/648, 232/356, 232/536 (1914) and 232/0 (1915); Markaz Watha'iq, op. cit., 176–179, 191, 202–203.

33. Telegram from Foreign Office to High Commissioner (Cairo), 3 Jan. 1916 (FO 141/648, 232/54); Grant Duff (Berne) to Grey, 24 May 1916 (FO 141/648, 232/78).

34. Report on "The Journey of the Khedive to Constantinople," 9 Oct. 1917 (FO 141/648, 232/154); despatch from Rumbold (Berne) to Balfour, 11 Dec. 1917 (FO 141/430, 5411/7).

35. Markaz Watha'iq, op. cit., 192, 292–293; cf. Sa'id, *Muhammad Farid,* 153–154.

36. Quoted from Markaz Watha'iq, op. cit., 192, 280; cf. Sa'id, *Muhammad Farid,* 155–157.

37. Markaz Watha'iq, op. cit., 280.

38. For examples, see ibid., 279–280, 293, 346. By mid-1916, Farid is reported to have become so exasperated by the difficulties he had had in dealing with the Ottomans that he retorted when spoken to in Turkish by a friend, " 'Don't talk to me in that damn language. I am sick of the Young Turks' "; Grant Duff (Berne) to Grey, 24 May 1916 (FO 141/648, 232/78).

39. Markaz Watha'iq, op. cit., 313.

40. Memo to the High Commissioner, 30 June 1916; FO 141/461, 1198/169a.

41. Ibid.

42. "Effect in Egypt of Hijaz News: Second Note," 4 July 1916; FO 141/461, 1198/190.

43. Ibid.

44. For examples of the theme of Ottoman oppression of the Arabs under the Young Turk regime, see AH, 25 June 1916, 1; ibid., 8 July 1916, 1; MU, 23 July 1916, 2; ibid., 26 July 1916, 2; MI, 27 June 1916, 2; ibid., 10 July 1916, 2.

45. MU, 25 July 1916, 1–2.

46. AH, 8 July 1916, 1.

47. WA, 11 July 1916, 3.

48. The first quotation is from AH, 25 June 1916, 1; the second from MU, 7 July 1916, 1.

49. Telegram from High Commissioner (Cairo) to Foreign Office, 3 July 1916; FO 141/461, 1198/169a.

50. See FO 141/462, 1198/463 and 1198/468.

51. "Egypt and the Arab Movement," 14 Aug. 1917; FO 141/783, 5317/1.

52. "Account of a Meeting Held at the Residency," 23 March 1918; FO 141/430, 5411/17.

53. Files FO 141/461, 141/462, and 141/825 are devoted to the repeated requests of Sharif/King Husayn for military aid from Egypt.

54. Telegram from Sirdar (Erkowit) to High Commissioner (Egypt), 20 June 1916 (FO 141/461, 1198/126); telegram from Sirdar (Gebeit) to High Commissioner (Egypt), 24 June 1916 (FO 141/461, 1198/142); telegram from Sirdar to High Commissioner (Egypt), 26 June 1916 (FO 141/461, 1198/152).

55. Ibid.

56. T. E. Lawrence, *Seven Pillars of Wisdom: A Triumph* (London, 1935), 93. For a reference to Sharifian officers being insulted by Egyptians when visiting Cairo, see Haim, op. cit., 47.

57. Markaz Watha'iq, op. cit., 301.

58. Cited in Zeine N. Zeine, *The Struggle for Arab Independence: Western Diplomacy and the Rise and Fall of Faisal's Kingdom in Syria* (Beirut, 1960), 214.

59. Markaz Watha'iq, op. cit., 202, 236; Grant Duff (Berne) to Grey, 24 May 1916 (FO 141/648, 232/78).

60. Rumbold (Berne) to Balfour, 11 Dec. 1917; FO 141/430, 5411/7.

61. See Burj, op. cit., 130–131; Khadduri, op. cit., 151–156.

62. Ibid., 156.

63. Ibid., 152–154; A. L. Tibawi, *Anglo-Egyptian Relations and the Question of Palestine, 1914–1921* (London, 1978), 134–135, 148.

64. Letter from Naval Commander-in-Chief, East Indies and Egypt, 25 Jan. 1917, reporting on a conversation with Misri (FO 141/825, 1198/807); cf. FO 141/462, 1198/613.

65. Burj, op. cit., 133–134.

66. Unofficial diary of Sir Ronald Storrs summarizing a discussion with King Husayn (FO 141/825, 1198/769); see also Storrs, op. cit., 198; Randall Baker, *King Husain and the Kingdom of Hijaz* (Cambridge, 1979), 131–132.

67. Unofficial diary of Sir Ronald Storrs maintained on his trip to the Hijaz of October 1916 (FO 141/462, 1198/613), from which the following quotations are taken. An abbreviated version of the conversation is contained in Storrs, op. cit., 194.

68. For the historical nature and uses of Mahfuz's Trilogy, see Sasson Somekh, *The Changing Rhythm: A Study of Najib Mahfuz's Novels* (Leiden, 1973), 50–51. Somekh's general conclusion about the value of the trilogy for scholars is that "no future student of Egyptian politics, society or folklore will be able to overlook to material embodied in Mahfuz's Trilogy" (ibid., 106). For a detailed analysis of the nationalist perspective found in the work, see Israel Gershoni, "Between Ottomanism and Egyptianism: The Evolution of 'National Sentiment' in the Cairene Middle Class as Reflected in Najib Mahfuz's *Bayn al-Qasrayn*," *Asian and African Studies,* 17 (1983), 227–263.

69. Najib Mahfuz, *Bayna al-Qasrayn* (second ed.: Cairo, 1964), 18.

70. Ibid., 66.

71. Ibid., 311.

72. Ibid., 66.

73. Ibid., 362–367.

74. Ibid., 366.

75. See al-Sayyid, *Qissat Hayati,* 165–170; Shaliq, op. cit., 325.

76. For two examples, see Mansur Fahmi, "al-Umma wa al-Raja'," SF, 18 Feb. 1916, 1; Mansur Fahmi, "al-Jinsiyya al-Misriyya," ibid., 4 April 1916, 2–3.

77. Muhammad Husayn Haykal, "Qasim Amin," SF, part 1, 25 Feb. 1916, 1–2; part 2, 3 March 1916, 2–3; part 3, 31 March 1916, 2–3; part 4, 14 April 1916, 1–2; part 5, 19 May 1916, 1–3. The articles were later republished in Muhammad Husayn Haykal, *Fi Awqat al-Faragh* (Cairo, 1925), 96–131; in the second edition (Cairo, 1968), 91–126. The following references are to the second edition.

78. Haykal, *Fi Awqat al-Faragh,* 91–92.

79. Ibid., 92.

80. Ibid., 92–93.

81. Ibid., 91–97.

82. See the article on Taine by Haykal originally published in SU, 9 June 1928, 10–11, 13;

republished in Muhammad Husayn Haykal, *Tarajim Misriyya wa Gharbiyya* (Cairo, 1929), 243–267 (reference from 246–247). In this article Haykal made a detailed analysis of Taine's critical and philosophical works. For Taine's direct influence on Haykal's theories about the scientific study of literature, see D. Semah, *Four Egyptian Literary Critics* (Leiden, 1974), 70–74.

83. Hippolyte Taine, *Histoire de la littérature anglaise* (four vols.: Paris, 1863–1864), I, "Introduction."

84. See Edmund Wilson, *To the Finland Station* (New York, 1953), 45–54, especially 49.

85. Taine, op. cit., xxii–xxxi.

86. Ibid., xxii–xxv; see also Rene Wellek, *A History of Modern Criticism, 1750–1950: vol. IV, The Later Nineteenth Century* (New Haven, 1965), 27–31.

87. Taine, op. cit., xxv–xxviii.

88. Ibid., xxviii–xxxi; Wellek, op. cit., 31–32.

89. Taine, op. cit., xxviii–xlviii; Wellek, op. cit., 27–57. For Taine's influence on late nineteenth-century European nationalist thought, particularly in France, consult C. J. H. Hayes, *The Historical Evolution of Modern Nationalism* (New York, 1931), 173–184.

90. Haykal, *Fi Awqat al-Faragh,* 98ff.

91. Ibid., 98–99.

92. Ibid., 99.

93. Ibid., 98–99, 109.

94. Ibid., 99–102.

95. Ibid., 100.

96. Ibid., 100–103.

97. Ibid., 101–103.

98. Ibid., 101–102.

99. Ibid., 103–104.

100. Ibid., 101–104.

101. Ibid., 104.

102. Ibid.

103. Ibid., 104–106, 111, 116–117.

104. Ibid., 105.

105. Ibid.

106. Ibid., 105–106.

107. Ibid., 106.

108. Ibid.

109. Ibid.

110. The last two articles in the series apply Haykal's theory of environmental determinism to the life of Qasim Amin; see ibid., 112–126.

Chapter 2. The Revolution of 1919 and Its Aftermath

1. The social basis of the Wafd is discussed in Marius Deeb, *Party Politics in Egypt: The Wafd and Its Rivals, 1919–1939* (London, 1979), 44–45, 68–70.

2. Part and parcel of the 1919 Revolution was the effort of native Egyptian capitalists to create nationally oriented and indigenously controlled economic institutions for Egypt. The centerpiece of this endeavor was *Bank Misr,* the bank established in 1920 under the leadership of Muhammad Tal'at Harb in which both shareholding and participation on the board of directors was to be limited to native Egyptians, and whose founder intended the bank to "work for the interest of Egypt before any other interest" (Harb's speech on the opening of the bank in May 1920; Muhammad Tal'at Harb, *Majmu'at Khutub Muhammad Tal'at Harb* (Cairo, n. d.), 45). Other new economic institutions spawned during the years after World War I were the Egyptian Federation of Industries (1922), which promoted tariff reform and industrialization in Egypt, and the Egyptian General Agricultural Syndicate (1921–1922), which was oriented toward developing a coherent national policy for the production and marketing of Egyptian cotton. On the economic aspects of the Revolution of 1919, see Robert L. Tignor, "The Egyptian Revolution of 1919: New Directions in the Egyptian Economy," *Middle Eastern Studies,* 12 (1976), 41–67; Marius Deeb, "Bank Misr and the Emergence of the Local Bourgeoisie in Egypt," ibid., 69–86; Robert L. Tignor, *State, Private Enterprise and Economic Change in Egypt, 1918–1952* (Princeton, 1984), especially chapter two.

3. Deeb, *Party Politics,* 39–40.

4. For the postwar fate of the Watanists, see ibid., 80–85; Markaz Watha'iq, op. cit., 431–434.

5. Quoted in Jukka Nevakivi, *Britain, France, and the Arab Middle East, 1914–1920* (London, 1969), 50.

6. For a contemporary appreciation of the impact of Wilson's ideas in Egypt, see Muhammad Husayn Haykal, "Tumas Wudru Wilsun," in his *Fi Awqat al-Faragh,* 144–151 (originally published in SI, 5 Feb. 1924). For a more general discussion of the impact of Wilsonian ideas in Egypt at the close of World War I, see 'Abd al-Rahman al-Rafi'i, *Thawrat Sanat 1919* (two vols.: Cairo, 1946), I, 57–60.

7. Wingate to Hardinge, 14 Nov. 1918 (FO 141/773, 7819/3); for later accounts of the meeting, see 'Abd al-'Aziz Fahmi, *Hadhihi Hayati* (Cairo, 1963), 76–89; Wingate, op. cit., 229; Rafi'i, *Thawrat,* I, 70–72.

8. Text in Ahmad Shafiq, *Hawliyyat Misr al-Siyasiyya* (ten vols.: Cairo, 1926–1932), *tamhid* I, 154–156.

9. 'Abd al-Khaliq Muhammad Lashin, *Sa'd Zaghlul: Dawruhu fi al-Siyasa al-Misriyya, 1914–1927* (Cairo, 1975), 178–179.

10. "Les Revendications Nationales Egyptiennes. Memoire présenté par la Délégation Egyptienne chargée de defendre la cause de l'indépendance de l'Egypte;" contained in FO 407/184, no. 66, and in file 35 of the Abbas Hilmi II Papers.

11. Lashin, op. cit., 163; Leland Bowie, "The Copts, the Wafd, and Religious Issues in Egyptian Politics," *Muslim World,* 67 (1977), 106–126, especially 107–108.

12. On Coptic participation in the uprising of March–April 1919, see FO 407/184, nos. 87, 93, 99, 165.

13. See FO 407/184, nos. 152, 178, 191. See also Reinhard Schulze, *Die Rebellion der Agyptischen Fallahin 1919* (Berlin, 1981), 185–186.

14. Sa'd Zaghlul, *Majmu'at Khutub wa Ahadith* (Cairo, n. d.), 69; similar assertions on 7, 16, 166.

15. Bowie, op. cit., 111.

16. Ibid., 112–113.

17. For the former, see Shafiq, *Hawliyyat, tamhid* I, 154–156; for the latter, see Rafi'i, *Thawrat,* I, 76–77.

18. From the Wafd's manifesto of early 1919 addressed to the representatives of foreign powers in Egypt; ibid., 106–107.

19. Ibid.

20. Memorandum from Sa'd Zaghlul, 6 March 1920; FO 371/5019, E1641/1641/16; cf. Ramadan, op. cit., 405.

21. Letter from the "Egyptian Delegation" at Lausanne, 31 Jan. 1922 [*sic:* 1923]; FO 839/13.

22. *Taqrir al-Hizb al-Dimuqrati al-Misri 'an Mashru' al-Ittifaq bayna al-Hukumatayn al-Misriyya wa al-Injiliziyya* (Cairo, 1920), 63–64 (this pamphlet contains the program of the party).

23. Program republished in *al-Tali'a,* I, no. 1 (Jan. 1965), 159.

24. Shafiq, *Hawliyyat, tamhid* III, 335–337.

25. Ramadan, op. cit., 404–406.

26. See their memorandum to the Peace Conference of April 1919 as cited in Rafi'i, *Thawrat,* I, 94–103.

27. Délégation Nationale Egyptienne (Parti National Egyptien), "L'Indépendance de l'Egypte et les interêts des Puissances," contained in FO 839/13.

28. For reports of pro-Ottoman sentiment or Young Turk influence, see FO 407/184, nos. 23, 31, 152, 178, 191. For contrary evaluations, see FO 407/184, nos. 87, 92 (quotations from the latter).

29. Derby to Curzon, Paris, 21 April 1919 (FO 407/184, no. 210).

30. Former reported in Allenby to Curzon, 5 Aug. 1920 (FO 141/433, 10770/47; for the latter, see the secret memo on "Turco-Egyptian Relations," 29 Dec. 1922 (FO 141/514, 12390/53), and Ramadan, op. cit., 409.

31. Quotations are from the "Note on the Egyptian Press, No. 30. Period from the 23rd May to the 5th June 1920" (FO 371/4996, E6478/426/16).

32. "Note on the Egyptian Press, No. 27. Period from the 24th April to the 1st May 1920" (FO 371/4996, E4758/426/16); "Note on the Egyptian Press, No. 30. Period from the 23rd May to the 5th June 1920" (FO 371/4996, E6478/426/16).

33. Ibid.

34. Allenby to Curzon, 16 Sept. 1922 (FO 141/514, 12390/31); memorandum on "Kemalism. Pan-Islamism," 4 Oct. 1922 (FO 141/514, 12390/33).

35. Report on "Kemalist Propaganda," 23 Sept. 1922; FO 141/514, 12390/32.

36. See Husayn, op. cit., II, 17–21.

37. Report on "Kemalist Propaganda," 23 Sept. 1922; FO 141/514, 12390/32.

38. Telegram from Allenby to Constantinople, 18 Nov. 1922; FO 141/514, 12390/41.

39. Husayn, op. cit., II, 17–19.

40. Ibid., 20–21.

41. Ibid., 25–27.

42. Report on "Kemalist Propaganda," 23 Sept. 1922; FO 141/514, 12390/32.

43. Ibid.

44. Report on "Kemalist Propaganda," 18 Oct. 1922; FO 141/514, 12390/35.

45. The first quotation is from the testimony of Mr. R. V. Wild before the Milner Commission, 5 Jan. 1920 (FO 848/6); the second from a "Report on the General Situation in Egypt for the Period March 7 to March 16 [1920] Inclusive" (FO 371/4984, E2897/93/16).

46. For examples, see FO 407/184, nos. 93, 191.

47. Schulze, op. cit., 150–192.

48. Mahfuz, op. cit., 364–374.

49. Ibid., 369.

50. Ibid., 405.

51. Ibid., 463.

52. Ibid., 414.

53. Ibid., 371–372.

54. Ibid., 428.

55. Ibid., 556–557.

56. Ibid., 379–380.

57. See ibid., 375–381, 401–404, 534–544, 553–555.

58. Ibid., 401–402.

59. Ibid., 555.

60. Ibid., 562–565.

61. The first phrase is quoted in Rafi'i, *Thawrat,* I, 107; for references to Egypt's "Arabs," see Zaghlul, op. cit., 69, 121–122.

62. Mahmud Abu al-Fath, *al-Mas'ala al-Misriyya wa al-Wafd* (Cairo, 1921?), 199; see also FO 407/187, no. 279.

63. Allenby to Curzon, [?] June 1920; FO 406/44, no. 341.

64. Storrs, op. cit., 456.

65. Wingate to Hardinge, 14 Nov. 1918; FO 141/773, 7819/3.

66. Unsigned letter from Geneva to President Wilson, 24 March 1919; Abbas Hilmi II Papers, file 106.

67. "Les Revendications Nationales Egyptiennes;" FO 407/104, no. 66.

68. "Memorandum by Sir R. Graham on the Unrest in Egypt," 9 April 1919; FO 407/184, no. 152.

69. Manifesto "To the Members of the House of Commons" from the Egyptian Delegation in Paris, 13 July 1919; contained in the Abbas Hilmi II Papers, file 35.

70. For the limits imposed by postwar censorship on Egyptian commentary on Arab affairs, see FO 141/620, 323/25.

71. MU, 15 July 1920, 1.

72. AH, 26 July 1920, 1.

73. AK, 28 July 1920, 1 (as quoted in the *Egyptian Gazette,* 29 July 1920, 4).

74. "Note on the Egyptian Press for the Period from the 13th to the 17th July;" FO 371/4996, E9611/426/16.

75. For examples, see MU, 21 July 1920, 1; ibid., 27 July 1920, 2.

76. "Note on the Egyptian Press, No. 35. Period from July 28 to August 11, 1920"; FO 371/4996, E10463/426/16.

77. As reported by the British Embassy in Constantinople in March 1920; FO 141/648, 232/181.

78. Report from A. W. Courtney, 2 March 1921 (FO 141/648, 232/231); letter from A. W.

Courtney, 4 May 1921 (FO 141/648, 232/233). Both of the above reports are based on material obtained from Syrian sources in Constantinople.

79. Report from A. W. Courtney, 2 March 1921 (FO 141/648, 232/231); "Activities of the ex-Khedive," 9 Nov. 1921 (FO 141/650, 232/269); "The ex-Khedive," 27 March 1922 (FO 141/650, 232/305); memo from Col. Ryder, 3 July 1922 (FO 141/650, 232/319).

80. Based on a conversation between 'Abbas Hilmi and a British official in Constantinople in 1921 as reported in FO 371/6343, E1393/1393/65; developed in detail in the unsigned document "Brouillon d'une étude sans titre concernant les pays arabes et l'Angleterre" contained in the Abbas Hilmi II Papers, file 37. See also Itamar Rabinovich, "Inter-Arab Relations Foreshadowed: The Question of the Syrian Throne in the 1920's and 1930's," *Festschrift in Honor of Dr. George S. Wise* (Tel Aviv, 1981), 237–250, especially 239.

81. Letter from [name illegible] to Furness, 2 Jan. 1923 (FO 141/650, 232/352); [same?] to same, 4 Jan. 1923 (FO 141/650, 232/353); "Activities of the ex-Khedive," 13 Jan. 1923 (FO 141/650, 232/359). For 'Abbas Hilmi's activities at Lausanne, see Mahmud 'Azmi, *Khabaya Siyasiyya* (Cairo, n. d. [1950?]), 56–64.

82. "Activities of the ex-Khedive in Europe," 19 Dec. 1921; FO 141/650, 232/248.

83. Letter from [name illegible] to Furness, 2 Jan. 1923 (FO 141/650, 232/352); "Activities of the ex-Khedive," 13 Jan. 1923 (FO 141/650, 232/359).

84. See Rafi'i, *Thawrat,* I, 103, 109, for examples.

85. Ramadan, op. cit., 282–283; Tariq al-Bishri, *Sa'd Zaghlul Yufawidu al-Isti'mar: Dirasa fi al-Mufawadat al-Misriyya al-Biritaniyya, 1920–1924* (Cairo, 1977), 99–104.

86. Elie Kedourie, "The Genesis of the Egyptian Constitution of 1923," in Holt, op. cit., 347–361, especially 355–357.

87. Quoted in Bishri, op. cit., 120.

88. Rafi'i, *Thawrat,* I, 109; Lashin, op. cit., 189.

89. Bishri, op. cit., 118.

90. Ibid., 124–129.

91. Ibid., 136.

92. Ibid., 131–132.

93. Quoted in Rafi'i, *Thawrat,* I, 109.

94. Bishri, op. cit., 136.

95. Ibid., 137.

96. *Journel Officiel,* 15 March 1922, as contained in FO 371/7733, E3384/1/16.

97. The text of the Egyptian Constitution of 1923 is available in Marcel Colombe, *L'évolution de l'Egypte* (Paris, 1951), 281–304.

Chapter 3. Egypt and the Caliphate Question, 1924–1926

1. See above, chapter two.

2. "Memorandum—9.11.22. Angora and the Caliphate" (FO 141/587, 545/77); Allenby to Constantinople, 18 Nov. 1922; FO 141/514, 12390/41; letter from [name illegible] of the Cairo City Police to Owen Tweedy, 6 Aug. 1923; FO 141/587, 545/98.

3. For Muslim reactions in general, see Arnold J. Toynbee, *Survey of International Affairs, 1925: vol. I, The Islamic World Since the Peace Settlement* (London, 1927), 62–65.

4. Quoted in Husayn, op. cit., II, 28.

5. MU, 5 March 1924, 3.

6. The quotation is from Shaykh Muhammad Shakir as quoted in Husayn, op. cit., II, 33; the second point was made by Muhammad Husayn Haykal writing in SI, 13 March 1924, 1.

7. AK, 3 March 1924, 3; ibid., 4 March 1924, 3; ibid., 5 March 1924, 3.

8. SI, 5 March 1924, 4.

9. See Husayn, op. cit., II, 29–32, for several examples.

10. AH, 14 March 1924, 4, as quoted in ibid., 34.

11. For instances, see SI, 5 March 1924, 4; AH, 12 March 1924, 1; AK, 6 March 1924, 2.

12. Among individuals, Shaykh Muhammad Shakir in MU, 8 March 1924, 1, and Shaykh Muhammad Bakhit in SI, 23 March 1924, 3. Group declarations of allegiance to 'Abd al-Majid are given in AK, 6 March 1924, 2; ibid., 7 March 1924, 2; ibid., 9 March 1924, 1; MU, 17 March

1924, 2; ibid., 18 March 1924, 2. For the Shaykh al-Azhar's statement, see FO 371/10217, E2322/1752/44.

13. Allenby to MacDonald, 29 March 1924; FO 371/10218, E3098/1752/44.

14. For the reaction of the parties cited, see respectively SI, 7 March 1924, 3; Muhammad Ibrahim al-Jaziri, *Athar al-Za'im Sa'd Zaghlul: 'Ahd Wizarat al-Sha'b* (Cairo, 1927), 210; AK, 6 March 1924, 3; ibid., 13 March 1924, 1.

15. Telegram from Allenby, 15 March 1924; FO 371/10217, E2230/1752/44.

16. "Pan-Islam and the Caliphate," report prepared by the India Office, April–May 1924; FO 371/10110, E3657/2027/65.

17. Toynbee, op. cit., 61.

18. For examples, see MU, 7 March 1924, 2; SI, 10 March 1924, 3; ibid., 13 March 1924, 3.

19. An overview of this activity may be obtained from *Oriente Moderno,* 4 (1924), 222–223.

20. See MU, 5 March 1924, 3; AK, 4 March 1924, 3; SI, 5 March 1924, 3.

21. MU, 6 March 1924, 2.

22. Ibid., 7 March 1924, 2; ibid., 11 March 1924, 2; ibid., 13 March 1924, 7.

23. AH, 21 March 1924, 1.

24. P. J. Vatikiotis, *The Modern History of Egypt* (New York, 1969), 299. The political dimensions of the Caliphate question in the mid-1920s are discussed in Elie Kedourie, "Egypt and the Caliphate, 1915–52," in his *The Chatham House Version and Other Middle-Eastern Studies* (New York, 1970), 177–212; Tariq al-Bishri, "al-Malik wa al-Khilafa al-Islamiyya," *al-Katib,* 13, no. 142 (Jan. 1973), 44–72; Martin Kramer, "The General Islamic Congress for the Caliphate in Egypt," paper delivered at the Shiloah Center for African and Middle Eastern Studies, Tel Aviv University, on 10 March 1982, passim. We are indebted to Dr. Kramer for providing us with a copy of his study.

25. The official response is summarized in Achille Sékaly, *Le Congrès du khalifat* (*Le Caire, 13–19 mai 1926*) *et le Congrès du monde musulman* (*La Mekke, 7 juin–5 juillet 1926*) (Paris, 1926), 7–8.

26. Minute by Furness, 6 March 1924; FO 141/587, 545/127.

27. Reported both in a letter by [name illegible], 7 March 1924 (FO 141/587, 545/128), and in the paper on "Pan-Islamism and the Caliphate" prepared by the India Office in April 1924 (FO 371/10110, E3657/2027/65).

28. The public report on the meeting is in AK, 19 March 1924, 3. The contemporary British report on its substance is given in Allenby to MacDonald, 29 March 1924 (FO 371/10218, E3098/1752/44). Fu'ad's later account is in Percy Loraine to Sir R. Lindsay, 16 Nov. 1929 (FO 371/13756, E6113/6113/65).

29. See the letter by [name illegible], 7 March 1924 (FO 141/587, 545/128); Allenby to MacDonald, 29 March 1924 (FO 371/10218, E3098/1752/44); Henderson to Chamberlain, 24 Aug. 1925 (FO 371/10913, J2461/2350/16); Loraine to Lindsay, 16 Nov. 1929 (FO 371/13756, E6113/6113/65).

30. For examples of pressure in this direction within the *'ulama',* see MU, 17 March 1924, 2; ibid., 18 March 1924, 2; AK, 24 March 1924, 5; *Oriente Moderno,* 4 (1924), 222.

31. Text in SI, 27 March 1924, 5–6; also in Toynbee, op. cit., 576–578; Sékaly, op. cit., 30–33.

32. The invitations and a selection of the responses received are discussed in Mahmud Sharqawi, "Dirasat Watha'iq 'an Mu'tamar al-Khilafa al-Islamiyya 1926," *al-Katib,* 10, no. 113 (Aug. 1970), 115–122; ibid., no. 114 (Sept. 1970), 132–137; ibid., no. 115 (Oct. 1970), 156–161; ibid., 11, no. 119 (Feb. 1971), 151–158.

33. For information on the apparatus of the campaign, see Kedourie, "Egypt and the Caliphate," 182–185; Bishri, "al-Malik," 48–49; Kramer, op. cit., 1–7; Zawahiri, op. cit., 209–210; Lord Lloyd to Chamberlain, 15 May 1926 (FO 371/11476, E3178/1511/65).

34. This is the thrust of Zawahiri, op. cit., 209.

35. On Palace support for the campaign, see Kedourie, "Egypt and the Caliphate," 184–185; Bishri, "al-Malik," 49, 52–53; Kramer, op. cit., 5–7; Sharqawi, op. cit., 10, no. 115, 158–159; Shafiq, *Hawliyyat, 1924,* 118–119.

36. See AK, 29 March 1924, 3.

37. Discussed in Abu Zayd, op. cit., 160–161.

38. For its founding, see AK, 22 March 1924, 3. This committee's orientation and activities are discussed in Allenby to MacDonald, 1 June 1924, (FO 407/198, no. 213); memo on Caliphate Committees, received 3 June 1924 (FO 141/587, 545/201a); *Oriente Moderno,* 4 (1924), 222–223, 292–293; Bishri, "al-Malik," 65–67; Kramer, op. cit., 7–8; "Report on the General Situation in Egypt for the Month of February 1926" (FO 371/11582, J980/25/16).

39. Lord Lloyd to Chamberlain, 15 May 1926 (FO 371/11476, E3178/1511/65); cf. Kramer, op. cit., 8.

40. Cited in *Oriente Moderno,* 4 (1924), 240.

41. See Bishri, "al-Malik," 52, for the former; the latter is cited in Jaziri, op. cit., 210.

42. For Wafdist opposition to the campaign for a congress in 1924, see Kedourie, "Egypt and the Caliphate," 185, 189; Bishri, "al-Malik," 53; Shafiq, *Hawliyyat, 1925,* 1054–1055; Kramer, op. cit., 10.

43. The lukewarm external response to the congress idea is discussed in Zawahiri, op. cit., 211–213; Sharqawi, op. cit., 10, no. 114, 135–137, 10, no. 114, 156–161, and 11, no. 119, 152–158; Kedourie, "Egypt and the Caliphate," 187–188; and Kramer, op. cit., 11–27 (although the latter, in contrast to the first three, holds that internal rather than external opposition was probably the main factor behind the postponement of the congress).

44. Text in *Oriente Moderno,* 5 (1925), 91–92, and in Sékaly, op. cit., 34–36.

45. For general discussions of the work and its significance, see Hourani, op. cit., 184–188; Nadav Safran, *Egypt in Search of Political Community* (Cambridge, 1961), 141–143; Hamid Enayat, *Modern Islamic Political Thought* (Austin, Texas, 1982), 62–68; Leonard Binder, "'Ali 'Abd al-Raziq and Islamic Liberalism," *Asian and African Studies,* 16 (1982), 31–59.

46. 'Ali 'Abd al-Raziq, *al-Islam wa Usul al-Hukm* (third ed.; Cairo, 1925), 12–20.

47. Ibid., 36.

48. Ibid., 83.

49. Ibid., 103.

50. Ibid., 39–47.

51. See Deeb, *Party Politics,* 77, 113–114; Henderson to Chamberlain, 15 Aug. 1925 (FO 371/10913, J2461/2350/16).

52. Muhammad 'Imara, *al-Islam wa Usul al-Hukm, li-'Ali 'Abd al-Raziq: Dirasa wa Watha'iq* (Beirut, 1972), 10–13.

53. KS as quoted in ibid., 12. See also Henderson to Chamberlain, 15 Aug. 1925 (FO 371/10913, J2461/2350/16); Kedourie, "Egypt and the Caliphate," 190–191.

54. For examples, see Shafiq, *Hawliyyat, 1925,* 761–764; 'Imara, *al-Islam,* 15–23.

55. The charges are given in Shafiq, *Hawliyyat, 1925,* 745–746; see also Binder, op. cit., 51.

56. The judgment of the Council is given in 'Imara, *al-Islam,* 72–91; cf. Toynbee, op. cit., 80–81.

57. Minutes on press reaction to the 'Abd al-Raziq hearing, in FO 141/819, 18036; see also 'Imara, *al-Islam,* 15–17.

58. Ibid., 109–110.

59. See Lashin, op. cit., 456; 'Abbas Mahmud al-'Aqqad, *Sa'd Zaghlul: Sira wa Tahiyya* (Cairo, 1936), 518–519.

60. Minutes on press reaction to the 'Abd al-Raziq hearing, in FO 141/819, 18036; Bishri, "al-Malik," 60.

61. Ibid., 60–61; 'Imara, *al-Islam,* 27–28.

62. The Liberal position is analyzed in ibid., 29–34, and in Charles D. Smith, *Islam and the Search for Social Order in Modern Egypt: A Biography of Muhammad Husayn Haykal* (Albany, 1983), 78–79; see also minutes on press reaction to the 'Abd al-Raziq hearing, enclosed in FO 141/819, 18036.

63. On the ministerial ramifications of the controversy see Afaf Lutfi al-Sayyid Marsot, *Egypt's Liberal Experiment, 1922–1936* (Berkeley, 1977), 86–87; Smith, op. cit., 78–79.

64. Bishri, "al-Malik," 63.

65. On the genesis of this assembly, see Toynbee, op. cit., 308–312.

66. Text in Sékaly, op. cit., 37–41; cf. *Oriente Moderno,* 6 (1926), 80.

67. Bishri, "al-Malik," 65; Kramer, op. cit., 8–9.

68. Quoted from a resolution of the committee of February 1926 as contained in FO 141/587, 545/231; see also Henderson to Chamberlain, 9 Feb. 1926 (FO 371/11581, J451/25/16); Shafiq, *Hawliyyat, 1926,* 107.

69. See Bishri, "al-Malik," 64.

70. Ibid., 64–65; Shafiq, *Hawliyyat, 1926,* 107–109, 148–149; *Oriente Moderno,* 6 (1926), 257–258.

71. "Report on the General Situation in Egypt for the Month of March 1926," in FO 371/11582, J1309/25/16.

72. Ibid.

73. Foreign reaction to the summons of February 1926 is dealt with in Lord Lloyd to Chamberlain, 30 April 1926 (FO 371/11582, J1144/25/16); *Oriente Moderno,* 6 (1926), 261–263; Toynbee, op. cit., 84–85; Kramer, op. cit., 13–15, 18, 24–27.

74. Zawahiri, op. cit., 213; Kramer, op. cit., 28.

75. AH, 27 April 1926, 4; cf. Sékaly, op. cit., 42–46; Shafiq, *Hawliyyat, 1926,* 203; *Oriente Moderno,* 6 (1926), 263–264.

76. Attendance at the congress is listed in Sékaly, op. cit., 46–48, 55–57, 64–66, 88–90 and analyzed in Toynbee, op. cit., 85–86; Shafiq, *Hawliyyat, 1926,* 203; and Kramer, op. cit., 28–29.

77. Lord Lloyd to Chamberlain, 22 May 1926 (FO 371/11476, E3304/1511/65). The meetings were held *in camera,* but generally similar accounts appeared *al-Ahram, al-Muqattam,* and *al-Siyasa* (the Wafdist newspapers *al-Balagh* and *Kawkab al-Sharq,* in contrast, did not carry detailed accounts of what they regarded as a trumped-up affair). A French version of the (edited) official proceedings is contained in Sékaly, op. cit., 46–122.

78. Ibid., 120.

79. See SI, 19 May 1926, 5; Sékaly, op. cit., 71.

80. For the dynamics of the congress, see Lord Lloyd to Chamberlain, 22 May 1926 (FO 371/11476, E3304/1511/65); Bishri, "al-Malik," 67–69; Kramer, op. cit., 30–31.

81. Text in AH, 19 May 1926, 5; Sékaly, op. cit., 73–77; *Oriente Moderno,* 6 (1926), 270–272.

82. Text in AH, 20 May 1926, 5; Sékaly, op. cit., 102–110; *Oriente Moderno,* 6 (1926), 272–273; Toynbee, op. cit., 578–581.

83. AH, 20 May 1926, 5, and Sékaly, op. cit., 110–118.

84. Zawahiri, op. cit., 216–217.

85. Lord Lloyd to Chamberlain, 30 April 1926 (FO 371/11582, J1144/25/16); same to same, 15 May 1926 (FO 371/11476, E3178/1511/65).

86. See AH, 12 May 1926, 5; ibid., 17 May 1926, 5; ibid., 20 May 1926, 5.

87. SI, 19 May 1926, 5; KS, 14 May 1926, 1.

88. Lord Lloyd to Chamberlain, 15 May 1926; FO 371/11476, E3178/1511/65.

89. Lord Lloyd to Chamberlain, 22 May 1926; FO 371/11476, E3304/1511/65.

90. SI, 20 May 1926, 5; Sékaly, op. cit., 122; Kramer, op. cit., 31.

91. Hourani, op. cit., 191; but cf. Binder, op. cit., 33–34, for a different interpretation.

92. Quoted in Shafiq, *Hawliyyat, 1926,* 108.

93. The quotation is from a press interview with Zaghlul in June 1924 as cited in Jaziri, op. cit., 210; for Zaghlul's criticisms of 'Abd al-Raziq, see 'Imara, *al-Islam,* 109–110.

94. Quoted in Ahmad Shafiq, *A'mali ba'da Mudhakkirati* (Cairo, 1941), 184–185.

95. For analyses of the arguments offered in defense of 'Abd al-Raziq in mid-1925, see Shafiq, *Hawliyyat, 1925,* 755–761; Bishri, "al-Malik," 58–61; 'Imara, *al-Islam,* 23–35; Smith, op. cit., 78–79.

96. For examples, see AH, 7 May 1926, 1; BL, 11 May 1926, 4; KS, 14 May 1926, 1.

97. Haykal, op. cit., I, 258–259.

98. For examples, see MU, 8 March 1924, 1; AK, 6 March 1924, 2; SI, 23 March 1924, 3.

99. Toynbee, op. cit., 576–578.

100. Ibid., 577.

101. Given in Shafiq, *Hawliyyat, 1925,* 745–746, and in Binder, op. cit., 51.

102. The judgment in 'Abd al-Raziq's hearing is given in 'Imara, *al-Islam,* 72–91 (quotation from 75).

103. Quoted in Bishri, "al-Malik," 64.

104. Text in AH, 19 May 1926, 5, and in Sékaly, op. cit., 73–77.

105. Quoted in ibid., 85.

106. Quoted in Toynbee, op. cit., 88, and in Sékaly, op. cit., 78.

107. Quoted in Anwar al-Jundi, *Ahmad Zaki al-Muqallab bi-Shaykh al-'Uruba* (Cairo, 1964), 233.

108. This was Haykal's approach in 1924; see SI, 13 March 1924, 1.

109. For an example, see KS, 14 June 1926, 1.

110. See *Oriente Moderno,* 6 (1926), 261; Sharqawi, op. cit., 11, no. 119, 154–155; Husayn, op. cit., I, 45–62, for examples of schemes for a modified Caliphate emanating from non-Egyptian authors in the mid-1920s.

111. A. Sanhoury, *Le califat: son évolution vers une société des nations orientale* (Paris, 1926), 570–572.

112. Ibid., 605–607.

113. MU, 21 May 1926, as cited in Shafiq, *Hawliyyat, 1926,* 282; KS, 14 June 1926, 1; ibid., 27 June 1926, 1.

114. SI, 5 March 1924, 4.

115. KS, 21 Sept. 1924, 1; also cited in Abu Zayd, op. cit., 71–72.

116. Sanhoury, op. cit., 572.

117. AK, 3 March 1924, 3.

118. SI, 7 March 1924, 3; ibid., 13 March 1924, 1.

119. KS, 14 May 1926, 1.

120. MU, 7 March 1924, 2.

121. For examples, see ibid., 11 March 1924, 2; SI, 10 March 1924, 1; ibid., 13 March 1924, 1; AH, 21 March 1924, 1.

122. Quoted in Henderson to Chamberlain, 4 Sept. 1925 (FO 407/201, no. 28). This eventually became the position of the Supreme Caliphate Committee headed by Shaykh Abu al-'Aza'im; see the February 1926 manifesto of the Committee contained in FO 141/587, 545/231, and also Henderson to Chamberlain, 9 Feb. 1926 (FO 371/11581, J451/25/16).

123. AH, 28 March 1924, 1.

124. Quoted in Kedourie, "Egypt and the Caliphate," 186–187.

125. SI, 21 May 1926, 1. For a discussion of this Congress, see chapter ten.

126. KS, 14 June 1926, 1.

127. Discussed in Bishri, "al-Malik," 64–65.

128. BL, 11 May 1926, 4.

129. Ibid.

130. Quoted in Jaziri, op. cit., 210.

131. As reported in Loraine to Lindsay, 16 Nov. 1929; FO 371/13756, E6113/6113/65.

Chapter 4. Egyptian Intellectuals and the Formation of a New National Image

1. Friedrich Nietzsche, *Der Wille zur Macht,* in *Friedrich Nietzsche Gesammelte Werke* (Munich, 1920–1929), XIX, 13.

2. Kenneth E. Boulding, *The Image: Knowledge and Life in Society* (Ann Arbor, 1961), 3–18.

3. Ernst Cassirer, *An Essay on Man: An Introduction to a Philosophy of Human Culture* (New Haven, 1948); quotations from 23–26.

4. Boulding, op. cit., 6.

5. Ibid., 6–18.

6. Discussed at length in ibid., 32–114.

7. Mannheim, *Ideology and Utopia,* 49–62.

8. Boulding, op. cit., 64; see 64–81 for a general analysis of the point.

9. Edward Shils, "Intellectuals," in David L. Sills (ed.), *International Encyclopedia of the Social Sciences* (seventeen vols.: New York, 1968), VII, 399–415 (quotation from 412).

10. Ibid.

11. Ibid.

12. Boulding, op. cit., 62. For an extended sociological discussion of "latent" versus "manifest," see Robert Merton, *Social Theory and Social Structure* (expanded ed.: New York, 1968), 73–138.

13. J. L. Talmon, *The Origins of Totalitarian Democracy* (London, 1952), 2.

14. Ibid., 3.

15. J. L. Talmon, *Political Messianism: The Romantic Phase* (London, 1960), 20.

16. Alexis de Tocqueville, *The Old Regime and the French Revolution* (trans. by Stuart Gilbert: New York, 1955), 156.

17. For examples, see Haykal, *Fi Awqat al-Faragh,* 246–325; Muhammad Husayn Haykal, *Thawrat al-Adab* (Cairo, 1933), 5–16, 62–160, 244–253; Salama Musa, *al-Yawm wa al-Ghad* (Cairo, 1927), 229–257; Isma'il Mazhar, *Wathbat al-Sharq* (Cairo, 1929), 3–21; Ibrahim al-Misri, *al-Adab al-Hayy* (Cairo, 1930), 17–25; Mahmud 'Azmi, "al-Tarbush aw al-Qubba'a?," HI, 36 (Nov. 1927), 52–56.

18. The view of Sami al-Jaridini in a symposium arranged by *al-Muqtataf* on the subject of "al-Nahda al-Sharqiyya al-Haditha," MQ, 70 (Feb. 1927), 134; see also Salama Musa, "Ta'rikh

al-Wataniyya al-Misriyya," HI, 36 (Jan. 1928), 270–271; Salama Musa, "al-Lugha al-Fusha wa al-Lugha al-'Ammiyya," ibid., 34 (July 1926), 1073; "al-Turkiya al-Jadida," SU, 3 Dec. 1927, 23.

19. See the report by Ibrahim Zaki (special correspondent of *al-Siyasa al-Usbu'iyya* in Turkey), "Ta'thir al-Nahda al-Qawmiyya fi al-Adab al-Turki," ibid., 2 April 1927, 13; Mahmud 'Azmi, "al-Tarbush aw al-Qubba'a?," HI, 36 (Nov. 1927), 52–55; "al-Tajdid fi Turkiya," MJ, April 1930, 737–741. See also Semah, op. cit., 80.

20. Mazhar, *Wathbat al-Sharq,* 21–61; Isma'il Mazhar, *Mu'dilat al-Madaniyya al-Haditha* (Cairo, 1928), 205–226; Musa, *al-Yawm wa al-Ghad,* 254–255; Mahmud 'Ali al-Sharqawi, "Nahnu wa Turkiya," US, May 1929, 599–600; Ibrahim Zaki, "Tashabuh al-Hawadith fi al-Ta'rikh al-Misri wa al-Turki," SU, 9 April 1927, 13.

21. Muhammad Husayn Haykal, "al-Nahda al-Turkiyya," ibid., 8 Oct. 1927, 10–11.

22. Ibid.

23. Ibid.

24. Ibid.

25. Mazhar, *Mu'dilat al-Madaniyya al-Haditha,* 205–209.

26. Ibid., 206; see also Isma'il Mazhar, "Falsafat al-Inqilab al-Turki al-Hadith," MJ, Aug. 1931, 1212–1228; Mazhar, *Wathbat al-Sharq,* 4–44; see also US, Jan. 1930, 2–16.

27. For examples, see Haykal, *Fi Awqat al-Faragh,* 246–301; Haykal, *Mudhakkirat,* I, 77–79, 93–94, 141–142, 220–222; Haykal, *Thawrat al-Adab,* 5–16; Musa, *al-Yawm wa al-Ghad,* 229–257; Tawfiq Mikha'il Tuwaij, "Tatawwur al-Adab al-Misri wa Aghraduhu," SU, 25 May 1929, 17–18; Ibrahim Ibrahim Jum'a, "Ayna Adabuna al-Qawmi?," ibid., 14 April 1928, 26; Niqula Yusuf, "Misr ba'da Khamsat Qurun," ibid., 7 Sept. 1929, 24–25; Salama Musa, *Ahlam al-Falasifa* (Cairo, 1926), 111–113; Salama Musa, "Ta'rikh al-Wataniyya al-Misriyya," HI, 36 (Jan. 1928), 266–271.

28. See Niqula Yusuf, "Hal Lana Adab Qawmi?," SU, 26 Jan. 1929, 23–24; Hafiz Mahmud, "Misr bi-Majdiha Ula," MJ, Feb. 1931, 474–476; Shuhdi 'Atiyya al-Shafi'i, "Fi al-Adab al-Fir'awni," SU, 31 Aug. 1929, 22; Muhammad Zaki Salih, "Ihya' al-Khulq al-Qawmi," ibid., 15 Jan. 1927, 31; Muhammad Husayn Haykal, "Misr al-Sahira," ibid., 28 Sept. 1929, 3–4; Muhammad Husayn Haykal, "Misr al-Haditha wa Misr al-Qadima," ibid., 27 Nov. 1926, 10–11; Muhammad Amin Hassuna, "Fi Sabil al-Da'wa ila al-Adab al-Qawmi," ibid., 19 July 1930, 9; 'Abbas Mahmud al-'Aqqad, "Fi al-Madi," BU, 11 March 1927, 19–20. The concept may also be found in BU, 21 Jan. 1927, 1; ibid., 10 Feb. 1928, 1–2, 16–20; ibid., 20 April 1928, 1–2; ibid., 25 May 1928, 1–35; US, June 1928, 1122–1128; MJ, June 1930, 913–915; HI, 31 (March 1923), 571–576; ibid., 34 (April 1924), 676–683; ibid., 37 (Feb. 1929), 503.

29. Tawfiq al-Hakim, *'Awdat al-Ruh* (two vols.: Cairo, 1933). Hakim actually completed the writing of the work in 1927, in Paris; see ibid., II, 233; Salah al-Din Dhihni, *Misr bayna al-Ihtilal wa al-Thawra* (Cairo, 1939), 67–68, 174–175.

30. The theme is developed most fully in *'Awdat al-Ruh,* II, 184–221.

31. Ibid., 212.

32. Ibid.

33. Ibid.

34. Ibid., 212–213.

35. Ibid., 214.

36. Ibid.

37. Ibid., 212–221.

38. Mahfuz, *Bayna al-Qasrayn,* 374.

39. Ibid.

40. Ibid., 404–414.

41. Ibid., 408–410.

42. Ibid., 409.

43. Ibid.

44. Ibid., 410.

45. Ibid., 412–413.

46. Ibid., 412.

47. Ibid., 413.

48. Ibid., 414.

49. Ibid., 428.

50. Ibid., 486.

51. Ibid., 569. It is no accident that Fahmi was killed in an "anti-heroic" situation—at a peaceful demonstration celebrating the release of Sa'd Zaghlul from exile—and not in one of the violent confrontations of the Revolution of 1919. While Mahfuz models Fahmi primarily as an embodiment of the new and revolutionary Egyptian generation, a youth who above all identified with the new Egyptian nationalism and was willing to all he could to serve the Egyptian national cause, Mahfuz also introduced less heroic dimensions into Fahmi's character. Doubts and fears concerning his chosen course occasionally occur to Fahmi, reflecting the fundamental tension within him between the traditional world in which he grew up and the new world in which he hopes to participate. By not making Fahmi a stereotyped character, Mahfuz humanizes him and makes him a more persuasive figure. See Somekh, op. cit., 112, 124.

52. See, for example, his first novel, *'Abath al-Aqdar,* which filled the entire issue of *al-Majalla al-Jadida* of September 1939.

53. For examples, see Salama Musa, *Mukhtarat Salama Musa* (Cairo, 1926), 10–11; Musa, *al-Yawm wa al-Ghad,* 231–257; Tawfiq Mikha'il Tuwaij, "Tatawwur al-Adab al-Misri wa Aghraduhu," SU, 25 May 1929, 17–18; Muhammad Zaki 'Abd al-Qadir, "Da'wat al-Adab al-Qawmi," ibid., 12 July 1930, 14; "Da'wa ila Khalq al-Adab al-Qawmi," SU, 28 June 1930, 7; Isma'il Mazhar, *Ta'rikh al-Fikr al-'Arabi* (Cairo, 1928), 91–120.

54. Haykal, *Thawrat al-Adab,* 5–16.

55. Ibid., 9–11; see also ibid., 224–250.

56. Ibid., 10.

57. 'Abd al-Qadir Hamza, "Timthal Nahdat Misr," BU, 25 May 1928, 1.

58. Ibid.

59. Isma'il Mazhar, *Ta'rikh al-Fikr al-'Arabi,* 97–101.

60. Ibid., 99–102.

61. Ibid., 101–102.

62. Ibid.

63. For examples, see Musa, *al-Yawm wa al-Ghad,* 229–257; Ibrahim al-Misri, *al-Adab al-Hayy,* 17–18; Ahmad Dayf, *Muqaddima li-Dirasat Balaghat al-'Arab* (Cairo, 1921), 1–2.

64. Biographical data on Egyptianist intellectuals have been drawn primarily from Yusuf As'ad Daghir, *Masadir al-Dirasa al-'Arabiyya* (three vols.: Sidon, 1956–1972); 'Umar al-Dasuqi, *Fi al-Adab al-Hadith;* (sixth ed.; two vol.: Cairo, 1964); Shawqi Dayf, *al-Adab al-'Arabi al-Mu'asir fi Misr* (second ed.: Cairo, 1961); Muhammad 'Abd al-Jawad, *Taqwim Dar al-'Ulum* (Cairo, 1952); Anwar al-Jundi, *A'lam wa Ashab Aqlam* (Cairo, n. d.); Anwar al-Jundi, *al-Muhafaza wa al-Tajdid fi al-Nathr al-'Arabi al-Mu'asir fi Mi'at 'Amm, 1840–1950* (Cairo, 1961); Khayr al-Din al-Zirikli, *al-A'lam: Qamus Tarajim li-Ashhar al-Rijal wa al-Nisa' min al-'Arab wa al-Musta'ribin wa al-Mustashriqin* (fifth ed., eight vols.: Beirut, 1980); Giora Eliraz, *Egyptian Intellectuals in the Face of Tradition and Change, 1919–1939* (in Hebrew: Ph.D. dissertation, Hebrew University of Jerusalem, 1980); H. A. R. Gibb, trans. and with a supplement on the modern era by Jacob M. Landau, *Arabic Literature: An Introduction* (in Hebrew: Tel Aviv, 1970); Ibrahim A. Ibrahim, "Isma'il Mazhar and Husayn Fawzi: Two Muslim 'Radical' Westernizers," *Middle Eastern Studies,* 9 (1973), 35–41; Safran, op. cit.; interviews with Hafiz Mahmud (19 July 1980 and 21 July 1980) and Husayn Fawzi (20–29 July 1980 and 24–26 Sept. 1980).

65. Edward Shils, "Intellectuals, Tradition, and the Traditions of Intellectuals: Some Preliminary Considerations," in S. N. Eisenstadt and S. R. Graubard (eds.), *Intellectuals and Tradition* (two vols.: New York, 1973), I, 21–34 (quotations from 22 and 24).

66. Shils, "Intellectuals," 410.

67. One omission from this list of prominent Egyptianist intellectuals demands explanation: Ahmad Lutfi al-Sayyid. Although Lutfi al-Sayyid was the intellectual mentor of much of this group, the "teacher of the generation" [*ustadh al-jil*], in the interwar period he published very little on nationalist theory or national issues and so has been omitted from the list.

68. Haykal, *Fi Awqat al-Faragh,* 356.

69. Shils, "Intellectuals," 410.

70. Ibid.; see also S. N. Eisenstadt, "Intellectuals and Tradition," in Eisenstadt and Graubard, op. cit., I, 1–19, especially 18.

71. Lovejoy, op. cit., 20 (quoting George Herbert Palmer).

72. For general evaluations of this school of thought, see H. A. R. Gibb, "Studies in Contemporary Arabic Literature," in his *Studies on the Civilization of Islam* (ed. by Stanford J. Shaw and

William R. Polk: Boston, 1962), 245–319; Vatikiotis, op. cit., 292–312; Majid Khadduri, *Political Trends in the Arab World* (Baltimore, 1970), 219–252.

73. See Deeb, *Party Politics,* 11–12, for an analysis of the term.

74. Ibid., 12 (quoting *al-Misri,* 9 Oct. 1930, 15).

75. J. P. Nettl, "Ideas, Intellectuals, and Structures of Dissent," in Philip Rieff (ed.), *On Intellectuals* (New York, 1969), 53–122 (quotations from 55 and 62); see also Charles D. Smith, "The Intellectual and Modernization: Definitions and Reconsiderations: The Egyptian Experience," *Comparative Studies in Society and History,* 22 (1980), 513–533, especially 530–532.

76. Nettl argues it is less useful in general; see Nettl, op. cit., 58ff.

77. Karl Mannheim, "The Problem of Generations," in his *Essays on the Sociology of Knowledge* (trans. by Paul Kecskemeti: London, 1952), 276–322 (quotation from 304).

78. Ibid., 306.

79. Ibid., 319. Mannheim also notes that not all members of a chronological "generation" become one "generation unit": "within any generation there can exist a number of differentiated, antagonistic generation-units" (ibid., 306). Differences notwithstanding, however, "[t]ogether they constitute an 'actual' generation precisely because they are oriented toward each other, even though only in the sense of fighting one another" (ibid., 306–307). This distinction will be pertinent for our next volume, where the thought and behavior of the opposing, non-Egyptianist, Arabo-Islamic oriented "generation unit" is the subject of inquiry.

80. For information on the publishers and dates of publication of Egyptian Arabic-language periodicals, see Mahmud Isma'il 'Abd Allah, *Fihris al-Dawriyyat al-'Arabiyya al-lati Taqtaniha al-Dar* (Cairo, 1961).

Chapter 5. The Egyptian Nationalist Image of the Arabs

1. Tawfiq al-Hakim, "Ila al-Duktur Taha Husayn," RI, 1 June 1933, 5–8. The following discussion is based on this article.

2. Yusuf Hanna, "al-Da'wa ila al-Adab al-Qawmi," SU, 9 Aug. 1930, 10. For other examples, see chapter six.

3. For examples, see Musa, *al-Yawm wa al-Ghad,* 235–246; Ahmad Durini Khashaba, "Fi al-Adab al-Misri," MJ, Aug. 1931, 1189–1197; Niqula Yusuf, "Hal Lana Adab Qawmi?," SU, 26 Jan. 1929, 23–24; Ibrahim Ibrahim Jum'a, "Ayna Adabuna al-Qawmi?," ibid., 14 April 1928, 26.

4. Hasan 'Arif, "'Arabiyya aw Fir'awniyya: al-Ittijah al-ladhi Yajibu an Tattajiha ilayhi Misr," BL, 11 Oct. 1933, 5.

5. Ibid.

6. The Pharaonic dimension of Egyptian territorial nationalism is analyzed in chapter eight.

7. Hafiz Mahmud, "Misr bi-Majdiha Ula," MJ, Feb. 1931, 474–475.

8. Ibid., 476.

9. Ibid.

10. Ibid.

11. Nashid Sayfin, "Misr Fir'awniyya Lahman wa Damman," part 1, MU, 19 Aug. 1930, 7; part 2, ibid., 10 Sept. 1930, 7; part 3, ibid., 18 Oct. 1930, 7.

12. Ibid., 19 Aug. 1930, 7.

13. Ibid.

14. Ibid.,; see also Musa, *al-Yawm wa al-Ghad,* 233–257.

15. For an example, see Ahmad Husayn, "Misr Fir'awniyya," MU, part 3, 26 Sept. 1930, 11.

16. Nashid Sayfin, "Misr Fir'awniyya Lahman wa Damman," MU, 18 Oct. 1930, 7.

17. Dhihni, *Misr bayna al-Ihtilal wa al-Thawra,* 71–73.

18. Ernest Renan, *Muhawarat Raynan al-Falsafiyya* (trans. by 'Ali Adham: Cairo, 1929).

19. Ernest Renan, *De la part des peuples sémitiques dans l'histoire de la civilization* (Paris, 1862), 10–21.

20. Ibid., 10–19.

21. Ibid.; Ernest Renan, *Histoire générale et système comparé des langues sémitiques* (Paris, 1855), 14–15.

22. Renan, *De la part des peuples sémitiques,* 9–30.

23. Ibid.; Renan, *Histoire générale,* 1–24.

24. Ibid., 10–19; Renan, *De la part des peuples sémitiques,* 17–26.
25. Ibid., 16.
26. Renan, *Histoire générale,* 15–17.
27. Renan, *De la part des peuples sémitiques,* 17.
28. Ibid., 12–13.
29. The classic study of the ideas of the *Shu'ubiyya* is contained in Ignaz Goldziher, *Muslim Studies* (trans. by C. R. Barber and S. M. Stern: two vols.; London, 1967, 1974), I, 137–198; see also 'Abd al-'Aziz al-Duri, *al-Judhur al-Ta'rikhiyya lil-Shu'ubiyya* (Beirut, n. d.); H. A. R. Gibb, "The Social Significance of the Shuubiya," reprinted in his *Studies,* 62–73; Roy P. Mottahedeh, "The Shu'ubiyah Controversy and the Social History of Early Islamic Iran," *International Journal of Middle East Studies,* 7 (1976), 161–182.
30. See Goldziher, op. cit., 137–155, 158–163, 166–167.
31. Ibid., 154–156.
32. Ibid., 155.
33. Ibid., 142–147, 149–150, 152–154, 160–163, 166–167.
34. Ibid., 137–163.
35. Ibn Khaldun, *The Muqaddimah: An Introduction to History* (trans. by Franz Rosenthal: three vols.; New York, 1958), I, lxxvi–lxxxiii.
36. Ibid., I, 89–183.
37. Ibid., I, lxxvi–lxxxiii, 252–253, 308–310; ibid., II, 235–307, 411–463.
38. See the discussion of this point in the Introduction.
39. From an article of 1936 by Sati' al-Husri, as reprinted in his *Abhath Mukhtara fi al-Qawmiyya al-'Arabiyya* (Cairo, 1964), 124–126.
40. For examples, see Tawfiq al-Hakim, "Ila al-Duktur Taha Husayn," RI, 1 June 1933, 5–8; Niqula Yusuf, "Hal Lana Adab Qawmi?," SU, 26 Jan. 1929, 23–24; Muhammad Ghallab, "al-Adab al-Misri," ibid., 21 Dec. 1929, 20; Muhammad Husayn Haykal, "al-Fann al-Misri," ibid., 17 Dec. 1927, 23; 'Abbas Mahmud al-'Aqqad, "al-Shi'r al-'Arabi wa al-Shi'r al-Injilizi," BU, 8 June 1928, 12–13.
41. See 'Abbas Mahmud al-'Aqqad, "al-Nathr wa al-Shi'r," BU, 9 Sept. 1927, 12–13; Ahmad Durini Khashaba, "Fi al-Adab al-Misri," MJ, Aug. 1931, 1189–1197; Tawfiq Mikha'il Tuwaij, "Tatawwur al-Adab al-Misri wa Aghraduhu," SU, 25 May 1929, 17–18; Misri, *al-Adab al-Hayy,* 53–55; "al-Adab al-Qawmi," SU, 19 July 1930, 26–27; Hafiz Mahmud, "Misr bi-Majdiha Ula," MJ, Feb. 1931, 474–476.
42. See Haim, *Arab Nationalism,* 25–34, 78–80; Dawn, op. cit., 138–144; Khaldun S. Al-Husry, *Three Reformers: A Study in Modern Arab Political Thought* (Beirut, 1966), 55–112.
43. Tawfiq al-Hakim, "Ila al-Duktur Taha Husayn," RI, 1 June 1933, 6.
44. Muhammad Husayn Haykal, "al-'Arab wa al-Hadara al-Islamiyya," SI, 3 June 1925, reprinted in his *Fi Awqat al-Faragh,* 368–381; references to the latter.
45. Ibid., 368–371.
46. Ibid., 370–373.
47. Ibid., 370.
48. Ibid.
49. Ibid.
50. Ibid., 370–371.
51. Ibid., 371.
52. Tawfiq al-Hakim, "Ila al-Duktur Taha Husayn," RI, 1 June 1933, 6–7.
53. Ibid., 6.
54. For examples, see Misri, *al-Adab al-Hayy,* 53–55; 'Abbas Mahmud al-'Aqqad, *al-Fusul: Majmu'at Maqalat Adabiyya wa Ijtima'iyya* (Cairo, 1922), 34–40; 'Abbas Mahmud al-'Aqqad, *Muraja'at fi al-Adab wa al-Funun* (Cairo, 1925), 100–108; Musa, *Ahlam al-Falasifa,* 112; 'Abbas Mahmud al-'Aqqad, "al-Nathr wa al-Shi'r," BU, 9 Sept. 1927, 12–13; Tawfiq al-Hakim, "Ila al-Duktur Taha Husayn", RI, 1 June 1933, 7.
55. Ibid., 6.
56. Ibid.
57. Ibid.
58. Ibid.

59. Ibid., 6–7.

60. See Haykal, *Fi Awqat al-Faragh,* 373.

61. Discussed in Semah, op. cit., 3–36, 59–65.

62. See 'Aqqad, *Fusul,* 34–40; 'Aqqad, *Muraja'at,* 100–108; 'Abbas Mahmud al-'Aqqad, *Mutala'at fi al-Kutub wa al-Hayat* (Cairo, 1924), 226–231, 290–299; 'Abbas Mahmud al-'Aqqad, *Sa'at bayna al-Kutub* (Cairo, 1929), 191–194.

63. 'Aqqad, *Fusul,* 40.

64. In an interview in HI, 36 (Nov. 1927), 36.

65. Ibid.

66. Muhammad Ghallab, "al-Adab al-Misri wa Mizatuhu 'an al-Adab al-Samiyya," SU, 21 Dec. 1929, 20.

67. Tawfiq al-Hakim, "Ila al-Duktur Taha Husayn," RI, 1 June 1933, 7; see also Tawfiq al-Hakim, "Min al-Ustadh Tawfiq al-Hakim ila al-Duktur Taha Husayn," ibid., 1 Oct. 1933, 9–13; 'Aqqad, *Fusul,* 34–40.

68. Haykal, *Fi Awqat al-Faragh,* 372.

69. Ibid., 370–375.

70. Ibid., 370.

71. For examples, see Musa, *al-Yawm wa al-Ghad,* 119–122; Misri, *al-Adab al-Hayy,* 53–55; Ahmad Durini Khashaba, "Dirasat al-Adab al-'Arabi," MJ, March 1931, 543–544.

72. 'Abbas Mahmud al-'Aqqad, "al-Nathr wa al-Shi'r," BU, 9 Sept. 1927, 12; Musa, *al-Yawm wa al-Ghad,* 119–122; Salama Musa, "al-Lugha wa al-Adab al-'Arabiyyan," MJ, Sept. 1935, 9–13.

73. See Musa, *Mukhtarat,* 7–11; Misri, *al-Adab al-Hayy,* 53–55; Musa, *al-Yawm wa al-Ghad,* 236–238; Ahmad Amin, "al-Tajdid fi al-Adab," RI, 1 June 1933, 15–17.

74. Friedrich Nietzsche, *The Complete Works of Friedrich Nietzsche* (ed. by Oscar Levy: eighteen vols.; New York, 1909–1924), V, part 2, 16–30.

75. 'Abbas Mahmud al-'Aqqad, "al-Nathr wa al-Shi'r," BU, 9 Sept. 1927, 12–13; Ahmad Amin, "al-Tajdid fi al-Adab," RI, 1 June 1933, 15–17.

76. See Musa, *al-Yawm wa al-Ghad,* 119–122; Misri, *al-Adab al-Hayy,* 54; Ahmad Amin, "Jinayat al-Adab al-Jahili aw Naqd al-Adab al-'Arabi," in his *Fayd al-Khatir: Majmu' Maqalat Adabiyya wa Ijtima'iyya* (ten vols.: second ed.; Cairo, 1946), II, 194–229.

77. See especially Musa, *Mukhtarat,* 7–11, 48–54; Musa, *al-Yawm wa al-Ghad,* 119–122, 231–241.

78. Salama Musa, "Qati'at al-Madi," *al-Hadith* (Aleppo), 1 Jan. 1928, 32.

79. Ibid., 32–34.

80. Ibid., 32.

81. Ibid., 32–33.

82. Musa, *al-Yawm wa al-Ghad,* 119.

83. 'Abbas Mahmud al-'Aqqad, "al-Nathr wa al-Shi'r," BU, 9 Sept. 1927, 12–13.

84. Ibid., 12.

85. Salama Musa, "Qati'at al-Madi," *al-Hadith* (Aleppo), 1 Jan. 1928, 33–34; see also Musa, *al-Yawm wa al-Ghad,* 235.

86. 'Abbas Mahmud al-'Aqqad, "al-Nathr wa al-Shi'r," BU, 9 Sept. 1927, 12.

87. This theme is developed repeatedly in Hakim, *'Awdat al-Ruh,* II, 13–56.

88. Ibid., 21–22.

89. Ibid., 22–23.

90. Ibid., 23–24.

91. Ibid., 24.

92. Ibid.

93. Ibid., 25.

94. Ibid., 23.

95. Isma'il Mazhar, "al-Thaqafa al-Yunaniyya wa 'Alaqatuha bi-Hadarat al-Sharq al-Qadima," US, Sept. 1929, 323.

96. Ibid., 324.

97. Ibid.

98. Reprinted in Haykal, *Fi Awqat al-Faragh,* 368–380.

99. Ibid., 377.

100. Ibid., 375–376.
101. Ibid., 376–377.
102. Ibid., 377.
103. Ibid., 378.
104. Ibid., 379.
105. Ibid., 378–380.
106. See Musa, *al-Yawm wa al-Ghad,* 231–242, for the best example.
107. Ibid., 235–238.
108. Ibid., 236.
109. Ibid., 237.
110. Ibid.
111. Ibid., 244; see also Musa, *Mukhtarat,* 278; Salama Musa, "al-Mujaddidun fi al-Sharq al-'Arabi," HI, 33 (Nov. 1924), 135.
112. Musa, *Ahlam al-Falasifa,* 112.
113. Tawfiq al-Hakim, "Ila al-Duktur Taha Husayn," RI, 1 June 1933, 7–8.
114. Ibid., 7.
115. Hakim, *'Awdat al-Ruh,* II, 24.
116. For an extended presentation, see Mazhar, *Ta'rikh al-Fikr al-'Arabi,* 91–120.
117. Ibid., 95–97, and Isma'il Mazhar, *Malqan al-Sabil fi Madhhab al-Nushu' wa al-Irtiqa' wa Atharuhu fi al-Inqilab al-Fikri al-Hadith* (Cairo, 1924), 128–143; see also Mazhar's translation of Charles Darwin's *The Origins of Species,* entitled *'Asl al-Anwa'* (Cairo, 1918); Mazhar, *Mu'dilat al-Madaniyya al-Haditha,* 1–75; and his "al-Tatawwur wa Atharuhu fi Mustaqbal al-Fikr al-Insani," US, March–April 1930, 337–341.
118. Isma'il Mazhar, "Uslub al-Fikr al-'Ilmi," MQ, 68 (Feb. 1926), 137–145, reprinted in his *Ta'rikh al-Fikr al-'Arabi,* 91–102 (references to the latter); see also Mazhar, *Malqan al-Sabil,* 128–143.
119. Mazhar, *Ta'rikh al-Fikr al-'Arabi,* 97.
120. Ibid., 97–98.
121. Ibid., 97.
122. Mazhar, *Malqan al-Sabil,* 128–130, 137–143.
123. Mazhar, *Ta'rikh al-Fikr al-'Arabi,* 98–99.
124. Ibid., 102.
125. Musa, *al-Yawm wa al-Ghad,* 7.
126. Ibid., 9.
127. Ibid., 7.
128. Ibid., 9.
129. For examples, see ibid., 113–131, 160–165, 229–257; Musa, *Mukhtarat,* 48–54, 261–264; Salama Musa, "al-Misriyyun Umma Gharbiyya," HI, 37 (Dec. 1928), 177–181; Salama Musa, "al-Sharq wa al-Gharb," RS, Dec. 1928, 46–50; Salama Musa, "al-Sharq Sharq wa al-Gharb Gharb," MJ, May 1930, 882–888. Other Egyptian nationalist intellectuals expressed similar ideas in the late 1920s and early 1930s: for examples, see Muhammad Abu Ta'ila, "Misr bayna Hadaratayn," BU, 12 June 1929, 4–5; Mahmud 'Azmi, "Kayfa Amantu bi al-'Ilm Wahdahu," MJ, Dec. 1929, 148–151; Sami al-Jaridini responding to a poll about "al-Nahda al-Sharqiyya al-Haditha," MQ, 70 (Feb. 1927), 133–136; the editorial response to a reader in HI, 38 (May 1930), 886; US, Aug. 1929, 1419–1421; ibid., March–April 1930, 366–374.
130. See Musa, *al-Yawm wa al-Ghad,* 229–234, 241–242, 247–257; Salama Musa, "Ila Ayyahuma Nahnu Aqrabu: al-Sharq aw al-Gharb?," HI, 35 (July 1927), 1072–1074; Salama Musa, "al-Misriyyun Umma Gharbiyya," ibid., 37 (Dec. 1928), 177–181; Salama Musa, "al-Sharq wa al-Gharb," RS, Dec. 1928, 46–50; Muhammad Sharaf, "Taqaddum al-'Ulum wa al-Funun: Laysa al-Misriyyun Samiyyin," MJ, May 1930, 897–900; Muhammad Sharaf, "al-Misriyyun Umma Ghayr Sharqiyya," ibid., June 1930, 961–964.
131. Ibid., 964.
132. Muhammad Ghallab, "al-Adab al-Misri wa Mizatuhu 'an al-Adab al-Sami," SU, 21 Dec. 1929, 20.
133. Ibid.
134. Ibid.
135. Ibid.; see also Muhammad Ghallab, "al-Hayat al-'Aqliyya fi Misr al-Fir'awniyya wa fi Misr al-Muslima," ibid., 10 May 1930, 8–9.

136. Tawfiq al-Hakim, "Ila al-Duktur Taha Husayn," RI, 1 June 1933, 5–8.

137. Ibid., 7.

138. Ibid.

139. The broader meaning of "adab" is "culture" in general; but, in line with the primary focus of Egyptianist intellectuals on the written word in both Arab and Egyptian cultural expression, we will usually use the term in its narrower sense of "literature."

140. Niqula Yusuf, "Hal Lana Adab Qawmi?," SU, 26 Jan. 1929, 23.

141. Ibid.

142. Ibid.

143. Ibid., 23–24.

144. Tawfiq Mikha'il Tuwaij, "Tatawwur al-Adab al-Misri wa Aghraduhu," ibid., 25 May 1929, 17–18.

145. 'Aqqad, *Mutala'at,* 274–275; 'Abbas Mahmud al-'Aqqad, "al-Nathr wa al-Shi'r," BU, 9 Sept. 1927, 12–13.

146. Haykal, *Fi Awqat al-Faragh,* 372–375.

147. Ibid., 372.

148. Ibid., 372–373.

149. The theme is developed at length in his article "Jinayat al-Adab al-Jahili aw Naqd al-Adab al-'Arabi," in his *Fayd al-Khatir,* II, 194–229.

150. Ibid., 201–205.

151. Ibid., 205–207.

152. Ibid., 203–204.

153. Ibid., 205.

154. Ahmad Amin, "al-Tajdid fi al-Adab," RI, 1 June 1933, 15–17; see also Amin, *Fayd al-Khatir,* II, 194–229.

155. See Muhammad Husayn Haykal, "al-'Arab wa al-Hadara al-Islamiyya," SI, 3 June 1925 (reprinted in his *Fi Awqat al-Faragh,* 368–381), and Muhammad Husayn Haykal, "Hal al-Adab al-'Arabi Qadimuhu wa Hadithuhu Yakfi li-Takwin al-Adib?," SU, 21 April 1928, 11.

156. Haykal, *Fi Awqat al-Faragh,* 373.

157. Ibid., 373–374.

158. Ibid., 378–379; see also Muhammad Husayn Haykal, "Hal al-Adab al-'Arabi Qadimuhu wa Hadithuhu Yakfi li-Takwin al-Adib?," SU, 21 April 1928, 10–11.

159. Ibid., 11.

160. Haykal, *Fi Awqat al-Faragh,* 374.

161. Amin, *Fayd al-Khatir,* II, 201.

162. Hafiz Mahmud, "Nahdat al-Qissa al-Misriyya," BU, 13 May 1927, 19.

163. For the anti-Arabism of this group of young intellectuals, see their journal FJ, 27 Jan. 1925, 1–2; ibid., 3 Feb. 1925, 1; ibid., 10 Feb. 1925, 1–2; ibid., 17 Feb. 1925, 1–2; ibid., 6 March 1925, 1; ibid., 3 April 1925, 1–2; ibid., 16 June 1925, 1.

164. Musa, *Mukhtarat,* 7–11.

165. Ibid.; see also Musa, *al-Yawm wa al-Ghad,* 119–122, 235–238.

166. Ibid., 119–122; see also Salama Musa, "al-Dhawq al-Sharqi fi al-Funun: Huwa Dhawq al-Saj'," FJ, 15 July 1926, 1–2.

167. Musa, *al-Yawm wa al-Ghad,* 122.

168. Ibid., 237; Salama Musa, "al-Lugha al-Fusha wa al-Lugha al-'Ammiyya," HI, 34 (July 1926), 1074.

169. Developed in Musa, *Mukhtarat,* 98–103.

170. Ibid., 99–100.

171. Ibid., 99–102.

172. Ibrahim al-Misri, "Falsafa wa Tahlil," in his *Sawt al-Jil* (Cairo, 1934), 88.

173. Ibrahim al-Misri, "al-'Aqliyya al-'Arabiyya," in his *al-Adab al-Hayy,* 53–55.

174. Ibid., 53.

175. Ibid.

176. Ibid., 54.

177. Ibid.

178. Ibid.

179. 'Abbas Mahmud al-'Aqqad, "al-Qadim wa al-Jadid," in his *Mutala'at,* 227–230.

180. Ibid., 229.
181. Ibid.
182. Ibid., 229–231.
183. Ibid., 229–230.
184. ‘Aqqad, *Muraja‘at,* 103.
185. Ibid.
186. Developed in ibid., 102–108.
187. ‘Abbas Mahmud al-‘Aqqad, “al-Nathr wa al-Shi‘r,” BU, 9 Sept. 1927, 12–13; see also ‘Aqqad, *Sa‘at bayna al-Kutub,* 116–118.
188. ‘Aqqad, *Muraja‘at,* 103.
189. ‘Abbas Mahmud al-‘Aqqad, “al-Shi‘r al-‘Arabi wa al-Shi‘r al-Injilizi,” BU, 8 June 1928, 12–13; ‘Aqqad, *Mutala‘at,* 297–299.
190. ‘Abbas Mahmud al-‘Aqqad, “al-Shi‘r al-‘Arabi wa al-Shi‘r al-Injilizi,” BU, 8 June 1928, 12.
191. Ibid.
192. Ibid., 12–13.
193. Ibid.; for a further discussion, see Semah, op. cit., 7–9.
194. ‘Abbas Mahmud al-‘Aqqad, “al-Shi‘r al-‘Arabi wa al-Shi‘r al-Injilizi,” BU, 8 June 1928, 13.
195. ‘Abbas Mahmud al-‘Aqqad, “Bayna al-Siyasa wa al-Adab,” in his *Muraja‘at,* 18–20.
196. Ibid., 18.
197. Ibid.
198. ‘Abbas Mahmud al-‘Aqqad, “Ara’ fi al-Asatir,” in his *Fusul,* 28–40.
199. Ibid., 35.
200. Ibid., 36.
201. Ibid., 34–40; see also Semah, op. cit., 7–8.
202. Tawfiq al-Hakim, “Ila al-Duktur Taha Husayn,” RI, 1 June 1933, 7.
203. Ibid.
204. Ibid.
205. Ibid.
206. Ibid.
207. Tawfiq al-Hakim, “Min al-Ustadh Tawfiq al-Hakim ila al-Duktur Taha Husayn,” ibid., 1 Oct. 1933, 13.
208. Tawfiq al-Hakim, “Ila al-Duktur Taha Husayn,” RI, 1 June 1933, 7.
209. Ibid.
210. Ibid.
211. Ibid.
212. Ibid.
213. Ibid.
214. Ibid.
215. See FJ, 8 Jan. 1925, 1; ibid., 20 Jan. 1925, 1.
216. Ibid., 8 Jan. 1925, 1.
217. Ahmad Khayri Sa‘id, “al-Istiqlal al-Fikri,” ibid., 27 Jan. 1925, 1. See also ibid., 20 March 1925, 1–2; ibid., 17 April 1925, 1–2; ibid., 26 June 1925, 1–2; ibid., 18 Oct. 1925, 1–2; ibid., 13 Jan. 1927, 1–2.
218. Ahmad Durini Khashaba, “Fi al-Adab al-Misri,” MJ, Aug. 1931, 1189.
219. Niqula Yusuf, “Hal Lana Adab Qawmi?,” SU, 26 Jan. 1929, 23.
220. Ibrahim al-Misri, “Fann al-Qasas fi Misr,” BU, 1 April 1927, 23–25.
221. Ibid., 23.
222. For examples, see Salama Musa, “al-Adab al-‘Arabi wa al-Adab al-Misri,” MSI, 14 Oct. 1932, 25; Tawfiq Mikha’il Tuwaij, “Tatawwur al-Adab al-Misri wa Aghraduhu,” SU, 25 May 1929, 17; Musa, *al-Yawm wa al-Ghad,* 119–122, 235–238; Taha Husayn in an interview in HI, 36 (Nov. 1927), 37–38; Salama Musa, “al-Mujaddidun fi al-Sharq al-‘Arabi,” ibid., 33 (Nov. 1924), 134–136; Ahmad Durini Khashaba, “Dirasat al-Adab al-‘Arabi,” MJ, March 1931, 544.
223. For examples, see Ibrahim al-Misri, “Ayna Huwa al-Adab al-Misri?,” ibid., Dec. 1929, 229–233; Musa, *al-Yawm wa al-Ghad,* 235–237; Misri, *al-Adab al-Hayy,* 53–55; Musa, *Mukhtarat,* 48–54.
224. Misri, *al-Adab al-Hayy,* 53–54.
225. Ibid., 53.
226. Ibid.

227. Ibid., 54.

228. Salama Musa, "al-Lugha wa al-Adab al-'Arabiyyan," MJ, Sept. 1935, 13.

229. Ibid.

230. Musa, *al-Yawm wa al-Ghad,* 122.

231. Tawfiq Mikha'il Tuwaij, "Tatawwur al-Adab al-Misri wa Aghraduhu," SU, 25 May 1929, 18.

232. Ibid.; for this argument see also Haykal, *Fi Awqat al-Faragh,* 169–174, 198–207, 246–268.

233. Tawfiq Mikha'il Tuwaij, "Tatawwur al-Adab al-Misri wa Aghraduhu," SU, 25 May 1929, 17–18.

234. Ahmad Durini Khashaba, "Dirasat al-Adab al-'Arabi," MJ, March 1931, 544.

235. Muhammad Husayn Haykal, "Hal al-Adab al-'Arabi Qadimuhu wa Hadithuhu Yakfi li-Takwin al-Adib?," SU, 21 April 1928, 10–11.

236. Muhammad Husayn Haykal, "al-Fann al-Misri," SU, 17 Dec. 1927, 23.

237. In particular, see Ahmad Amin, "Jinayat al-Adab al-Jahili aw Naqd al-Adab al-'Arabi," in his *Fayd al-Khatir,* II, 194–229.

238. Ahmad Amin, "al-Tajdid fi al-Adab," RI, 1 June 1933, 15–16.

239. Ibid., 16.

240. Ibid., 15–17.

241. Amin, *Fayd al-Khatir,* II, 205–206.

242. Ibid., 205.

243. "al-Sihafa al-Suriyya fi Misr," MJ, Aug. 1931, 1177–1180.

244. Ibid.; "al-Katib al-Misri wa al-Katib al-Suri," ibid., March 1930, 591–592; see also ibid., Nov. 1930, 1.

245. "Anta Misri," ibid., July 1931, back cover; see also ibid., Nov. 1929, 1–2; ibid., Nov. 1930, 1.

246. "al-Sihafa al-Suriyya fi Misr," ibid., Aug. 1931, 1179.

247. Ibid., 1177–1180.

248. "Anta Misri," ibid., July 1931, back cover.

249. Ibid.

250. Salama Musa, "Awkar al-Raj'iyya fi Misr," ibid., Feb. 1930, 435; "al-Katib al-Misri wa al-Katib al-Suri," ibid., March 1930, 592.

251. See Salama Musa, "Awkar al-Raj'iyya fi Misr," ibid., Feb. 1930, 432–435; Ahmad Durini Khashaba, "al-Raj'iyya fi Misr wa Khataruha 'ala Nahdatina," ibid., Dec. 1930, 209–213.

252. Salama Musa, "Awqar al-Raj'iyya fi Misr," ibid., Feb. 1930, 434–435; see also Salama Musa, "al-Salafiyyun wa al-Mujaddidun," ibid., Dec. 1929, 145; "al-Katib al-Misri wa al-Katib al-Suri," ibid., March 1930, 591–592.

Chapter 6. The Egyptianist Image of Egypt: I. Environment and the Nation

1. For representative examples, see Haykal, *Fi Awqat al-Faragh,* 246–301, 344–367; 'Abbas Mahmud al-'Aqqad, "al-Wataniyya," part 1, BU, 30 Sept. 1927, 12–13, 18; part 2, ibid., 7 Oct. 1927, 12–13, 22; Haykal, *Tarajim,* 1–26; Tawfiq al-Hakim, "Ila al-Duktur Taha Husayn," RI, 1 June 1933, 5–8.

2. For examples, see Muhammad Ghallab, "al-Adab al-Misri," SU, 21 Dec. 1929, 20; Muhammad Amin Hassuna, "Fi Sabil al-Da'wa ila al-Adab al-Qawmi," ibid., 19 July 1930, 9; Muhammad 'Abd Allah 'Inan, "al-Misriyya: Turath Qawmi Athil li-Misr," MSI, 14 Oct. 1932, 9; Hasan 'Arif, "Shakhsiyyat al-Umma al-Misriyya," BL, 8 Sept. 1933, 1, 8.

3. See Salama Musa, "Ta'rikh al-Wataniyya al-Misriyya," HI, 36 (Jan. 1928), 266–271; Mu'awiya Muhammad Nur, "al-Adab al-Qawmi," SU, 20 Sept. 1930, 23; Hafiz Mahmud, "Misr lil-Misriyyin," MJ, April 1931, 733–736; Muhammad 'Abd Allah 'Inan, "Adab Qawmi wa Adab Gharbi," MSI, 7 Jan. 1932, 5.

4. Haykal, *Fi Awqat al-Faragh,* 178.

5. For examples, see 'Abbas Mahmud al-'Aqqad, "al-Wataniyya," part 2, BU, 7 Oct. 1927, 13; Muhammad 'Abd Allah 'Inan, "Khawass Misriyya lil-Adab al-'Arabi fi Misr," MSI, 29 Nov. 1932, 8; Hasan 'Arif, "Ayna al-Qawmiyya al-Misriyya?," BL, 19 Sept. 1933, 1, 11.

6. See ‘Ali Muhammad Khalil, “Hadarat Misr Thamarat al-Iqlim,” MJ, May 1931, 807–810; Hasan ‘Arif, “Shakhsiyyat al-Umma al-Misriyya,” BL, 8 Sept. 1933, 1, 8; Muhammad Zaki Ibrahim, “Thaqafat Misr Yajibu an Takuna Misriyya,” ibid., 24 Sept. 1933, 1, 9.

7. Ahmad Sabri, *Kahin Amun: Masrahiyya Fir‘awniyya* (Cairo, 1929?).

8. Ibid., vi.

9. Ibid.

10. Ibid, iii–vii.

11. Ahmad Husayn, “Misr Fir‘awniyya,” part 1, MU, 6 Sept. 1930, 7.

12. See Muhammad Hilmi ‘Abd al-Latif, “al-Nafs al-Misriyya bayna al-Hayat wa al-Fann,” SU, 11 Feb. 1927, 16; Hasan ‘Arif, “Mahammatuna ka-Misriyyin,” BL, 17 Sept. 1933, 3, 8; Hasan ‘Arif, “Ayna al-Qawmiyya al-Misriyya?,” ibid., 19 Sept. 1933, 1, 11; Hasan ‘Arif, “‘Abqariyyat al-Bi’a al-Misriyya,” ibid., 3 Oct. 1933, 1, 11.

13. See Shuhdi ‘Atiyya al-Shafi‘i, “Fi al-Adab al-Fir‘awni,” SU, 31 Aug. 1929, 22; Muhammad Husayn Haykal, “Misr al-Sahira,” ibid., 28 Sept. 1929, 3–4; ‘Ali Muhammad Khalil, “Hadarat Misr Thamarat al-Iqlim,” MJ, May 1931, 807–810; Hasan ‘Arif, “‘Abqariyyat al-Bi’a al-Misriyya,” BL, 3 Oct. 1933, 1, 11.

14. See Shuhdi ‘Atiyya al-Shafi‘i, “Fi al-Adab al-Fir‘awni,” SU, 31 Aug. 1929, 22; Hasan ‘Arif, “‘Arabiyya am Fir‘awniyya,” BL, 11 Oct. 1933, 5.

15. Muhammad Husayn Haykal, “Misr al-Haditha wa Misr al-Qadima,” SU, 27 Nov. 1926, 10–11; ‘Abd al-Hamid Salim, “al-‘Unsur al-Misri,” US, Feb. 1928, 636–642; Hasan ‘Arif, “Ayna al-Qawmiyya al-Misriyya?,” 19 Sept. 1933, 1, 11; ‘Aqqad, *Sa‘d Zaghlul,* 5–36.

16. Muhammad Husayn Haykal, “Misr al-Haditha wa Misr al-Qadima,” SU, 27 Nov. 1926, 10.

17. For a forceful summary of this position, see Hasan ‘Arif, “Shakhsiyyat al-Umma al-Misriyya,” BL, 8 Sept. 1933, 1, 8; Hasan ‘Arif, “‘Abqariyyat al-Bi’a al-Misriyya,” ibid., 3 Oct. 1933, 1, 11; Hasan ‘Arif, “‘Abqariyyat al-Umma al-Misriyya,” ibid., 20 Oct. 1933, 1, 11.

18. For the use of these terms in the 1920s and early 1930s, see Muhammad Abu Ta’ila, “Safhat al-Qawmiyya fi Hayat Sa‘d,” BU, 30 Sept. 1927, 3; ‘Abbas Mahmud al-‘Aqqad, “al-Wataniyya,” part 2, BU, 7 Oct. 1927, 12–13, 22; Yusuf Hanna, “al-Da‘wa ila al-Adab al-Qawmi,” SU, 9 Aug. 1930, 10; Salama Musa, “Tahqiq al-Qawmiyya al-Misriyya,” MJ, May 1931, 787–795; Muhammad ‘Abd Allah ‘Inan, “al-Misriyya—Turath Qawmi Athil li-Misr,” MSI, 14 Oct. 1932, 9; Muhammad ‘Abd Allah ‘Inan, “Khawass Misriyya Qawmiyya lil-Adab al-‘Arabi fi Misr,” MSI, 29 Nov. 1932, 8; Hasan ‘Arif, “Ayna al-Qawmiyya al-Misriyya?” BL, 19 Sept. 1933, 1.

19. Ahmad Lutfi al-Sayyid was impressed with the thought of Le Bon; see al-Sayyid, *Ta’ammulat,* 81–83; al-Sayyid, *Muntakhabat,* II, 8–9; and Wendell, op. cit., 286–287. Ahmad Fathi Zaghlul’s first translation of Le Bon was of his *Psychologie des foules* (Paris, 1896), which appeared as *Ruh al-Ijtima‘* (Cairo, 1909); his second was of Le Bon’s *Lois psychologiques de l’évolution des peuples* (Paris, 1895), which in Arabic was entitled *Sirr Tatawwur al-Umam* (Cairo, 1913). The latter appears to have been the more influential of the two in Egypt. A second Arabic edition of each was published in 1921, when Le Bon’s ideas drew the praise of Egyptian nationalist intellectuals; see ‘Aqqad, *Fusul,* 155–166; Taha Husayn, *al-Ayyam* (two vols.: Cairo, 1929, 1939), II, 174–175. Le Bon’s *Psychologie du socialisme* (Paris, 1908) also appeared in a Arabic translation by Muhammad ‘Adil Zu‘aytir as *Ruh al-Ishtirakiyya* (Cairo, 1925).

20. Ghustaw Lubun (Gustave Le Bon), *al-Hadara al-Misriyya* (trans. by Sadiq Rustum: Cairo, 1924).

21. Ibid., 6–15.

22. See Le Bon, *Lois psychologiques,* 7–17; Le Bon, *Psychologie des foules,* 22–64.

23. Le Bon, *Lois psychologiques,* 7–17.

24. Niqula Yusuf, “Hal Lana Adab Qawmi?,” SU, 26 Jan. 1929, 23.

25. ‘Abbas Mahmud al-‘Aqqad, “al-Wataniyya,” part 2, BU, 7 Oct. 1927, 13.

26. Yusuf Hanna, “al-Da‘wa ila al-Adab al-Qawmi,” SU, 9 Aug. 1930, 10.

27. For examples, see ‘Ali Muhammad Khalil, “Hadarat Misr Thamarat al-Iqlim,” MJ, May 1931, 807–810; Hasan ‘Arif, “Shakhsiyyat al-Umma al-Misriyya,” BL, 8 Sept. 1933, 1, 8.

28. See Niqula Yusuf, “al-Adab al-Misri wa al-Wasf,” SU, 2 Feb. 1929, 13; Hasan ‘Arif, “‘Abqariyyat al-Umma al-Misriyya,” BL, 20 Oct. 1933, 1, 11.

29. Tawfiq al-Hakim, “Manabi‘ al-Fann al-Misri,” in Tawfiq al-Hakim, *Tahta Shams al-Fikr* (second ed.: Cairo, 1941), 118–119. The article was originally written in 1933.

30. Hasan Subhi, “Fi al-Adab al-Misri,” SU, 30 June 1928, 4.

31. Ibid.

32. Shuhdi 'Atiyya al-Shafi'i, "Fi al-Adab al-Fir'awni," SU, 31 Aug. 1929, 22.

33. Ahmad Husayn, "Misr Fir'awniyya," part 1, MU, 6 Sept. 1930, 7; much the same argument later appeared in Hasan 'Arif, "'Abqariyyat al-Bi'a al-Misriyya," BL, 3 Oct. 1933, 1, 11.

34. See 'Ali Muhammad Khalil, "Hadarat Misr Thamarat al-Iqlim," MJ, May 1931, 807–810; Hasan 'Arif, "Shakhsiyyat al-Umma al-Misriyya," BL, 8 Sept. 1933, 1, 8.

35. Mahmud 'Izzat Musa, "Bahth fi al-Adab al-Qawmi," SU, 16 Aug. 1930, 10.

36. See Muhammad Husayn Haykal, "Misr al-Haditha wa Misr al-Qadima," ibid., 27 Nov. 1926, 10–11; see also Muhammad Husayn Haykal, "Ta'rikh al-Haraka al-Qawmiyya," SU, 12 Jan. 1929, 3–4; Hafiz Mahmud, "Misr bi-Majdiha Ula," MJ, Feb. 1931, 474–476; Husayn Mu'nis, "Misr wa Madiha," MQ, 89 (Sept. 1936), 1–8.

37. Muhammad Zaki Salih, "Ihya' al-Khulq al-Qawmi," SU, 15 Jan. 1927, 31.

38. For discussions of Egyptian civics education in the 1920s, see "al-Ta'lim al-Qawmi fi Misr," HI, 34 (Jan. 1926), 401–406; 'Abd al-'Aziz al-Bishri, "al-Tarbiyya al-Wataniyya," SU, 28 April 1928, 4; "al-Tarbiyya al-Wataniyya," MQ, 72 (May 1928), 4; Ahmad Amin and 'Abd al-'Aziz al-Bishri, *Kitab al-Tarbiyya al-Wataniyya* (sixth ed.: Cairo, 1934 [originally published in 1925]), Introduction; 'Abd al-'Aziz al-Bishri, *al-Tarbiyya al-Wataniyya* (second ed.: Cairo, 1928), Introduction.

39. Ibid., Introduction.

40. Ahmad al-Nahri and Ahmad Bayli, *al-Mujaz fi al-Tarbiyya al-Wataniyya* (Cairo, 1926), v.

41. Amin and Bishri, op. cit., 1.

42. Ibid., 2–5.

43. Ibid., 2.

44. Ibid., 3.

45. Ibid., 3–5; see also Muhammad Taha Mahmud, *Durus al-Tarbiyya al-Wataniyya* (fourth ed.: Cairo, 1936–1937), 31–36.

46. Bishri, op. cit., 5.

47. Ibid., 5–7.

48. Ibid.

49. Tawfiq Hamid al-Mar'ashli, *al-Tarbiyya al-Wataniyya* (second ed.: Cairo, 1929), 22.

50. Ibid., 22–23.

51. Ibid., 21–25.

52. Ibid., 125–126.

53. Ahmad Husayn, "Misr Fir'awniyya," part 1, MU, 6 Sept. 1930, 7.

54. Ibid.

55. Ibid.

56. Ibid.

57. Hafiz Mahmud, "Misr bi-Majdiha Ula," MJ, Feb. 1931, 474–475.

58. Ibrahim Ibrahim Jum'a, "Ayna Adabuna al-Qawmi?," SU, 14 April 1928, 26.

59. Emile Zaydan, "al-Shu'ub al-Sharqiyya wa Haqq Taqrir al-Masir," HI, 30 (Dec. 1921), 208–209.

60. For examples of the use of the phrase, see Muhammad Zaki Ibrahim, "Thaqafat Misr Yajibu an Takuna Misriyya," BL, 24 Sept. 1933, 1, 9; Hafiz Mahmud, "Misr bi-Majdiha Ula," MJ, Feb. 1931, 474–476.

61. Ibid., 475.

62. Ibid., 474–475.

63. Ibid., 475.

64. Ibid.

65. Ibid., 474–476; see also Hafiz Mahmud, "Misr lil-Misriyyin," ibid., April 1931, 733–736.

66. For Musa's views on this subject, see his *al-Yawm wa al-Ghad,* 229–257; Salama Musa, "Qati'at al-Madi," *al-Hadith* (Aleppo), 1 Jan. 1928, 32–34; Salama Musa, "al-Wataniyya wa al-'Alamiyya," MJ, March 1930, 532–537; Salama Musa, "Tahqiq al-Qawmiyya al-Misriyya," ibid., May 1931, 794; Salama Musa, "Nahnu al-Misriyyun," BL, 8 Oct. 1933, 3.

67. Salama Musa, "al-Wataniyya wa al-'Alamiyya," MJ, March 1930, 532–533.

68. Ibid., 534–537; see also Musa, *al-Yawm wa al-Ghad,* 239–247; Salama Musa, "Ta'rikh al-Wataniyya al-Misriyya," HI, 36 (Jan. 1928), 266–271.

69. Musa, *al-Yawm wa al-Ghad,* 239–240.

70. Ibid., 240.

71. Ibid.
72. Ibid.
73. Ibid., 236–242; see also Salama Musa, "al-Wataniyya wa al-'Alamiyya," MJ, March 1930, 532–533; Salama Musa, "Ta'rikh al-Wataniyya al-Misriyya," HI, 36 (Jan. 1928), 266–271.
74. Tawfiq al-Hakim, "Min al-Ustadh Tawfiq al-Hakim ila al-Duktur Taha Husayn," RI, 1 Oct. 1933, 10–13.
75. Ibid., 11.
76. Ibid.
77. Ibid.
78. Ibid.
79. Developed in Haykal, *Fi Awqat al-Faragh,* 344–356.
80. Ibid., 351–356.
81. Ibid.
82. Muhammad Husayn Haykal, "al-Fir'awniyya wa al-'Arabiyya: Hadir La Madi lahu La Mustaqbal lahu," MSI, 29 Sept. 1933, 24–28.
83. Ibid., 26.
84. Ibid.

Chapter 7. The Egyptianist Image of Egypt: II. Toward an Egyptian Territorial History

1. Haykal, *Tarajim,* 8–10; see also Muhammad Husayn Haykal, "Ta'rikh Misr wa Adabuha," SU, 22 Dec. 1928, 5–6.
2. Haykal, *Fi Awqat al-Faragh,* 246–248; see also Mar'ashli, op. cit., 5–6, 128–129; Ahmad Husayn, *Imani* (Cairo, 1936), 18–32, 50–59.
3. Haykal, *Tarajim,* 8.
4. Ibid., 8–12; see also Muhammad Husayn Haykal, "Ta'rikh Misr wa Adabuha," SU, 22 Dec. 1928, 5–6; Muhammad Husayn Haykal, "Ta'rikh al-Haraka al-Qawmiyya," ibid., 12 Jan. 1929, 3–4.
5. Muhammad Husayn Haykal, "Ta'rikh Misr wa Adabuha," ibid., 22 Dec. 1928, 6.
6. Ibid.
7. Haykal, *Tarajim,* 9.
8. Muhammad 'Abd Allah 'Inan, "al-Adab al-Qawmi Yaghmitu Haqqahu," MSI, 26 Feb. 1932, 7.
9. Ibid.
10. Ibid.
11. Ibid.
12. See Haykal, *Fi Awqat al-Faragh,* 246–287, 344–356; Haykal, *Tarajim,* 5–26; Muhammad Husayn Haykal, "Ta'rikh Misr wa Adabuha," SU, 22 Dec. 1928, 5–6; Muhammad 'Abd Allah 'Inan, "al-Adab al-Qawmi Yaghmitu Haqqahu," MSI, 26 Feb. 1932, 7.
13. Muhammad Husayn Haykal, "Ta'rikh Misr wa Adabuha," SU, 22 Dec. 1928, 6.
14. See Muhammad Husayn Haykal, "Ta'rikh al-Haraka al-Qawmiyya," SU, 12 Jan. 1929, 3–4; Muhammad 'Abd Allah 'Inan, "al-Misriyya: Turath Qawmi Athil li-Misr," MSI, 14 Oct. 1932, 9.
15. Muhammad Husayn Haykal, "Ta'rikh Misr wa Adabuha," SU, 22 Dec. 1928, 6.
16. Haykal, *Fi Awqat al-Faragh,* 352.
17. Ibid., 351–356; see also Mar'ashli, op. cit., 5–6.
18. Ibid.; Muhammad Husayn Haykal, "Ta'rikh al-Haraka al-Qawmiyya," SU, 12 Jan. 1929, 3–4; see also Haykal, *Thawrat al-Adab,* 121–152.
19. See Hasan Subhi, "Fi al-Adab al-Misri," SU, 30 June 1928, 4; Hakim, *'Awdat al-Ruh,* II, 22–24, 37–56; Mar'ashli, op. cit., 125–127.
20. Shuhdi 'Atiyya al-Shafi'i, "Fi al-Adab al-Fir'awni," SU, 31 Aug. 1929, 22; Hakim, *'Awdat al-Ruh,* II, 22–24, 37–56.
21. For a summary of his views, see Hakim, *Tahta Shams al-Fikr,* 116–121; he first dealt with the theme of the relationship of time and place in his dramas *Ahl al-Kahf* [*People of the Cave*] (Cairo, 1933) and *Shahrazad* [*Sheharazade*] (Cairo, 1934).
22. Hakim, *Tahta Shams al-Fikr,* 116–117.
23. Hakim, *'Awdat al-Ruh,* II, 37–56.

24. Hakim, *Tahta Shams al-Fikr,* 117.

25. For examples, see an article of 1924 by Taha Husayn as reprinted in his *Hadith al-Arbi'a'* (tenth ed.: three vols; Cairo, 1976), III, 98–100; Haykal, *Fi Awqat al-Faragh,* 246–268; Muhammad Husayn Haykal, "Misr al-Haditha wa Misr al-Qadima," SU, 27 Nov. 1926, 10–11.

26. See ibid.; Husayn, *Imani,* 18–39, 50–59; Haykal, *Thawrat al-Adab,* 121–139; Hakim, *'Awdat al-Ruh,* II, 22–24, 37–56, 212–221; Muhammad Husayn Haykal, "Misr al-Sahira," SU, 28 Sept. 1929, 3–4.

27. See Husayn, *Hadith al-Arbi'a',* III, 98–100; Hakim, *'Awdat al-Ruh,* II, 212–221; Tawfiq al-Hakim, "Min al-Ustadh Tawfiq al-Hakim ila al-Duktur Taha Husayn," RI, 1 Oct. 1933, 9–13; Muhammad Husayn Haykal, "al-Fir'awniyya wa al-'Arabiyya," MSI, 29 Sept. 1933, 24–28; Hakim, *Tahta Shams al-Fikr,* 117; Husayn, *Imani,* 18–39, 50–59.

28. Hakim, *Tahta Shams al-Fikr,* 120–121.

29. Ibid., 118, 121.

30. Ibid., 121.

31. For examples, see Nahri and Bayli, op. cit., 281–282; Taha Husayn, "Ila al-Ustadh Tawfiq al-Hakim," RI, 15 June 1933, 6–9; Muhammad Husayn Haykal, "al-Fir'awniyya wa al-'Arabiyya," MSI, 29 Sept. 1933, 24–28; Husayn Mu'nis, "Misr wa Madiha," MQ, 89 (Sept. 1936), 1–8. The outstanding expression of these concepts can be found in Muhammad Ghallab's series of articles on "al-Hayat al-'Aqliyya fi Misr al-Fir'awniyya" published in SU between 1 March and 17 May 1930.

32. See Muhammad Zaki Salih, "Ihya' al-Khulq al-Qawmi," SU, 15 Jan. 1927, 31; Hasan Subhi, "Fi al-Adab al-Misri," ibid., 30 June 1928, 4; Hakim, *'Awdat al-Ruh,* II, 23–24, 27–32.

33. See Niqula Yusuf, "Hal Lana Adab Qawmi?," SU, 26 Jan. 1929, 23–24; Yusuf Hanna, "al-Da'wa ila al-Adab al-Qawmi," ibid., 9 Aug. 1930, 10; 'Ali Muhammad Khalil, "Hadarat Misr Thamarat al-Iqlim," MJ, May 1931, 807–810; 'Aqqad, *Sa'd Zaghlul,* 18–43.

34. Muhammad Husayn Haykal, "Misr al-Haditha wa Misr al-Qadima," SU, 27 Nov. 1926, 10.

35. Ibid.; see also Mar'ashli, op. cit., 125–134.

36. Salama Musa, *Misr Asl al-Hadara* (Cairo, n.d.), 9.

37. Ibid., 10.

38. For examples, see Hasan Subhi, "Hadith al-Masa'," BL, 16 Sept. 1933, 1, 3; Hasan 'Arif, "'Abqariyyat al-Bi'a al-Misriyya," ibid., 3 Oct. 1933, 1–11; 'Abd al-Halim Salim, "al-'Unsur al-Misri," US, Feb. 1928, 636–642; Mar'ashli, op. cit., 125–127; Nahri and Bayli, op. cit., 281–286.

39. Muhammad Husayn Haykal, "Dhikrayyat Qadima," SU, 2 April 1927, 10.

40. Muhammad Husayn Haykal, "Ta'rikh al-Haraka al-Qawmiyya," ibid., 12 Jan. 1929, 3.

41. See Haykal, *Tarajim,* 5–26; see also Mar'ashli, op. cit., 5–6, 125–129.

42. As presented in his *Tarajim,* 5–26.

43. Ibid., 10.

44. Ibid.

45. Ibid., 8–15.

46. See Husayn, *Hadith al-Arbi'a',* III, 98–99; Muhammad 'Abd Allah 'Inan, "al-Adab al-Qawmi Yaghmitu Haqqahu," MSI, 26 Feb. 1932, 7; Muhammad 'Abd Allah 'Inan, "Khawass Misriyya Qawmiyya lil-Adab al-'Arabi fi Misr," ibid., 29 Nov. 1932, 8; Taha Husayn, "Da'ira," KS, 28 Aug. 1933, 6.

47. Salama Musa, "Tadris al-Ta'rikh," in his *al-Yawm wa al-Ghad,* 155.

48. Ibid., 154–157; see also Muhammad Husayn Haykal, "Ta'rikh al-Haraka al-Qawmiyya," SU, 12 Jan. 1929, 3–4; Salama Musa, "al-Taqaddum al-Jadid fi Dirasat al-Ta'rikh," MJ, April 1931, 708–710.

49. Ibid., 3–4; see also Haykal, *Tarajim,* 1–13; Mar'ashli, op. cit., 5–6, 125–129; Nahri and Bayli, op. cit., 281–286.

50. Haykal, *Tarajim,* 8.

51. Ibid., 9; see also Muhammad Husayn Haykal, "Ta'rikh al-Haraka al-Qawmiyya," SU, 12 Jan. 1929, 3.

52. Ibrahim Jalal, "Misr al-Mustaqilla qabla al-Fath al-'Uthmani," Hi, 38 (April 1930), 665.

53. Muhammad Husayn Haykal, "Ta'rikh al-Haraka al-Qawmiyya," SU, 12 Jan. 1929, 4.

54. Ibid., 3–4.

55. Mar'ashli, op. cit., 5–6.

56. Husayn, *Hadith al-Arbi'a',* III, 98–99.

57. See Nahri and Bayli, op. cit., 281–286; Haykal, *Tarajim,* 8–26; 'Abd al-Hamid Salim, "al-'Unsur al-Misri," US, Feb. 1928, 637–639.

58. Mar'ashli, op. cit., 6.

59. For representative praise of this period of Egyptian history, see Haykal, *Tarajim,* 10–11; Nahri and Bayli, op. cit., 281–282; Shuhdi 'Atiyya al-Shafi'i, "Fi al-Adab al-Fir'awni," SU, 31 Aug. 1929, 22; Mar'ashli, op. cit., 128–131; Bishri, op. cit., 159–160.

60. See Musa, *Misr Asl al-Hadara,* 5–13; Mar'ashli, op. cit., 130–131; Muhammad Husayn Haykal, "Misr al-Haditha wa Misr al-Qadima," SU, 27 Nov. 1926, 10–11; Muhammad Husayn Haykal, "al-Fann al-Misri," ibid., 17 Dec. 1927, 23; Muhammad Husayn Haykal, "Hal min Khatwa Jadida fi Sabil al-Fann al-Misri?," ibid., 7 Jan. 1928, 10.

61. Mar'ashli, op. cit., 130.

62. Nahri and Bayli, op. cit., 281.

63. For examples, see Muhammad Husayn Haykal, "Ta'rikh Misr wa Adabuha," SU, 22 Dec. 1928, 6; Hafiz Mahmud, "Misr bi-Majdiha Ula," MJ, Feb. 1931, 476; Husayn Mu'nis, "Misr wa Madiha," MQ, 89 (Sept. 1936), 1.

64. Bishri, op. cit., 159; see also Amin and Bishri, op. cit., 199; Nahri and Bayli, op. cit., 282.

65. Ibid., 281–283; see also Mar'ashli, op. cit., 128–132; Amin and Bishri, op. cit., 199–200.

66. Nahri and Bayli, op. cit., 281.

67. For examples, see Mar'ashli, op. cit., 131; Amin and Bishri, op. cit., 200; Haykal, *Tarajim,* 11–12.

68. See ibid., 1–13; Amin and Bishri, op. cit., 200.

69. Haykal, *Tarajim,* 12.

70. Ibid., 12–13.

71. Husayn, *Imani,* 52.

72. Ibid.

73. Haykal, *Tarajim,* 12.

74. Mar'ashli, op. cit., 131.

75. Haykal, *Tarajim,* 12–13.

76. Husayn, *Imani,* 52.

77. Haykal, *Tarajim,* 13–14; see also Bishri, op. cit., 164.

78. Mar'ashli, op. cit., 132; Haykal, *Tarajim,* 13–14; Husayn, *Imani,* 52–53.

79. Haykal, *Tarajim,* 15.

80. Husayn, *Hadith al-Arbi'a',* III, 98.

81. Ibid.

82. Ibid.

83. Haykal, *Tarajim,* 15.

84. Husayn, *Hadith al-Arbi'a',* III, 98.

85. Haykal, *Tarajim,* 14.

86. Ibid., 14–15; Husayn, *Imani,* 52–53.

87. Ibid.; see also Haykal, *Tarajim,* 14–15.

88. See these issues as raised by Muhammad 'Abd Allah 'Inan in his "al-Misriyya: Turath Qawmi Athil li-Misr," MSI, 14 Oct. 1932, 9.

89. 'Aqqad, *Sa'd Zaghlul,* 20; see generally ibid., 18–27.

90. Taha Husayn, "Da'ira," KS, 28 Aug. 1933, 6.

91. Ibid.

92. Ibid.

93. Hafiz Mahmud, "Misr bi-Majdiha Ula," MJ, Feb. 1931, 476.

94. Muhammad Rif'at and 'Abd al-'Aziz al-Bishri, *al-Tarbiyya al-Wataniyya* (Cairo, 1937), 17.

95. Ahmad Husayn, "Misr Fir'awniyya," part 2, MU, 16 Sept. 1930, 3.

96. Ibid., part 3, 26 Sept. 1930, 11.

97. Ibid., part 2, 16 Sept. 1930, 3.

98. For two examples, see Niqula Yusuf, "Misr ba'da Khamsat Qurun," SU, 7 Sept. 1929, 24–25; Muhammad Ghallab, "al-Hayat al-'Aqliyya fi Misr al-Fir'awniyya wa fi Misr al-Muslima," ibid., 10 May 1930, 8–9.

99. Ahmad Husayn, "Misr Fir'awniyya," part 1, MU, 6 Sept. 1930, 7.

100. Muhammad 'Abd Allah 'Inan, "al-Misriyya: Turath Qawmi Athil li-Misr," MSI, 14 Oct. 1932, 9.

101. Ibid.

102. Ibid.

103. Ibid.
104. Ibid.
105. Ibid.
106. Hasan Subhi, "Alfaz Hayya min al-Lugha al-Misriyya al-Qadima," SU, 18 May 1929, 21.
107. Ibid.
108. Ibid. See also Hasan Subhi, "Fi al-Adab al-Misri," SU, 28 June 1928, 10.
109. In a lecture delivered at the Egyptian University as published in *al-Manar,* 19 Jan. 1931, 465–473; excerpts in FH, 12 Rajab 1349, 2.
110. Ahmad Husayn, "Misr Fir'awniyya," part 1, MU, 6 Sept. 1930, 7.
111. Ibid.; for similar views, see Musa, *al-Yawm wa al-Ghad,* 237–238, 251–252; Muhammad Amin Hassuna, "Fi Sabil al-Da'wa ila al-Adab al-Qawmi," SU, 19 July 1930, 9.
112. See Muhammad Husayn Haykal, "Bayna al-Hadir wa al-Madi," part 1, ibid., 4 May 1929, 3–4; part 2, ibid., 11 May 1929, 3–4; see also Muhammad Husayn Haykal, "Misr al-Haditha wa Misr al-Qadima," ibid., 27 Nov. 1926, 10.
113. Ibid.
114. Ibid.; Muhammad Husayn Haykal, "Bayna al-Hadir wa al-Madi," part 2, ibid., 11 May 1929, 3–4.
115. Muhammad Husayn Haykal, "Misr al-Haditha wa Misr al-Qadima," ibid., 27 Nov. 1926, 10.
116. Ahmad Husayn, "Misr Fir'awniyya," part 1, MU, 6 Sept. 1930, 7.
117. Ibid.
118. Ibid.
119. Hakim, *Tahta Shams al-Fikr,* 122–125.
120. Ibid., 123.
121. Taha Husayn, "Ila al-Ustadh Tawfiq al-Hakim," RI, 15 June 1933, 6.
122. Muhammad Husayn Haykal, "Ta'rikh Misr wa Adabuha," SU, 22 Dec. 1928, 5.
123. Muhammad 'Abd Allah 'Inan, "Khawass Misriyya Qawmiyya lil-Adab al-'Arabi fi Misr," MSI, 29 Nov. 1932, 8.
124. Haykal, *Tarajim,* 16.
125. Quotation from ibid., 17; for the perspective in general, see also Husayn, *Imani,* 53–56; Mar'ashli, op. cit., 132–134; Bishri, op. cit., 164–172; Amin and Bishri, op. cit., 201–203.
126. Haykal, *Tarajim,* 17.
127. Husayn, *Imani,* 54–55; see also Haykal, *Tarajim,* 17–18; Mar'ashli, op. cit., 128–129, 133–134; Amin and Bishri, op. cit., 201–203; Nahri and Bayli, op. cit., 282–286; Muhammad 'Abd Allah 'Inan, *Misr al-Islamiyya wa Ta'rikh al-Khitat al-Misriyya* (Cairo, 1931), 3–7, 15–20.
128. Haykal, *Tarajim,* 17; Mar'ashli, op. cit., 123; Husayn, *Imani,* 54; Nahri and Bayli, op. cit., 282–283.
129. See Haykal, *Tarajim,* 17–19; Mar'ashli, op. cit., 123; Husayn, *Imani,* 54–55; Amin and Bishri, op. cit., 201.
130. Haykal, *Tarajim,* 18.
131. See Husayn, *Imani,* 55; Bishri, op. cit., 168.
132. Haykal, *Tarajim,* 18.
133. Ibid.; see also Husayn, *Imani,* 55; Ibrahim Jalal, "Misr al-Mustaqilla qabla al-Fath al-'Uthmani," HI, 38 (April 1930), 665; Nahri and Bayli, op. cit., 283; Muhammad 'Abd Allah 'Inan, *Mawaqif Hasima* (Cairo, 1929), 60–63; Muhammad 'Abd Allah 'Inan, "Fikrat al-Hurub al-Salibiyya," HI, 34 (April 1926), 709–713.
134. Haykal, *Tarajim,* 20.
135. Ibid., 19–23; see also Nahri and Bayli, op. cit., 283–284; Ibrahim Jalal, "Misr al-Mustaqilla qabla al-Fath al-'Uthmani," HI, 38 (April 1930), 667.
136. Haykal, *Tarajim,* 22–23.
137. Ibid., 23.
138. Ibid.; see also Muhammad Husayn Haykal, "Ta'rikh al-Haraka al-Qawmiyya," SU, 12 Jan. 1929, 3–4.
139. Ibrahim Jalal, "Misr al-Mustaqilla qabla al-Fath al-'Uthmani," HI, 38 (April 1930), 666–667.
140. Ibid., 667.
141. Haykal, *Tarajim,* 21–22; see also Mar'ashli, op. cit., 134; Anwar Zaqlama, "Misr wa Urubba fi 'Ahd al-Mamalik," MJ, Sept. 1930, 1323–1326.

142. See Haykal, *Tarajim,* 20–23; 'Inan, *Misr al-Islamiyya,* 31–61, 96–106, 116–146; Taha Husayn, "Ila al-Ustadh Tawfiq al-Hakim," RI, 15 June 1933, 6–7.

143. Amin and Bishri, op. cit., 202.

144. Haykal, *Tarajim,* 19–20.

145. Ibid., 18–20; Nahri and Bayli, op. cit., 283–284.

146. For examples of such praise of the Mamluks, see Bishri, op. cit., 171–173; Mar'ashli, op. cit., 133–134; Amin and Bishri, op. cit., 202–203; Haykal, *Tarajim,* 19–23; Husayn, *Imani,* 55–56; Nahri and Bayli, op. cit., 283–284; Ibrahim Jalal, "Misr al-Mustaqilla qabla al-Fath al-'Uthmani," HI, 38 (April 1930), 666–667; Anwar Zaqlama, "Misr wa Urubba fi 'Ahd al-Mamalik," MJ, Sept. 1930, 1323–1326.

147. Haykal, *Tarajim,* 22–23.

148. Ibid., 24; see also Mar'ashli, op. cit., 134–135.

149. Muhammad 'Abd Allah 'Inan, "al-Misriyya: Turath Qawmi Athil li-Misr," MSI, 14 Oct. 1932, 9.

150. Haykal, *Tarajim,* 24; see also Mar'ashli, op. cit., 134–135.

151. Haykal, *Tarajim,* 24; see also Nahri and Bayli, op. cit., 284–285.

152. Amin and Bishri, op. cit., 203.

153. Mar'ashli, op. cit., 134–135; Haykal, *Tarajim,* 24–25; Amin and Bishri, op. cit., 203–204; Bishri, op. cit., 175–176; Nahri and Bayli, op. cit., 284–285.

154. Haykal, *Tarajim,* 25; see also Amin and Bishri, op. cit., 204; Mar'ashli, op. cit., 135.

155. Muhammad Husayn Haykal, "Ta'rikh al-Haraka al-Qawmiyya," SU, 12 Jan. 1929, 3–4.

156. Haykal, *Tarajim,* 25.

157. Ibid.

158. See Mar'ashli, op. cit., 135–136; Amin and Bishri, op. cit., 204–205; Bishri, op. cit., 176–181.

159. Husayn, *Imani,* 56–57; see also Mahmud, *Durus,* 106–109.

160. Haykal, *Tarajim,* 25–26; Nahri and Bayli, op. cit., 285.

161. See Husayn, *Imani,* 56–57; Mar'ashli, op. cit., 136–137; Amin and Bishri, op. cit., 204–205; Nahri and Bayli. op. cit., 285; Salama Musa, "Ta'rikh al-Wataniyya al-Misriyya," HI, 36 (Jan. 1928), 266–267.

162. Haykal, *Tarajim,* 26.

163. Ibid.; Mar'ashli, op. cit., 135–137; Amin and Bishri, op. cit., 205–210; Bishri, op. cit., 181–184; Nahri and Bayli, op. cit., 287–295; Husayn, *Imani,* 57–58.

164. See Haykal, *Tarajim,* 26; Mar'ashli, op. cit., 141–150; Amin and Bishri, op. cit., 216–220; Bishri, op. cit., 187–193; Nahri and Bayli, op. cit., 295–300; Musa, *al-Yawm wa al-Ghad,* 244–257; Salama Musa, "Ta'rikh al-Wataniyya al-Misriyya," HI, 36 (Jan. 1928), 266–271; Muhammad Husayn Haykal, "Ta'rikh al-Haraka al-Qawmiyya," SU, 12 Jan. 1929, 3–4.

Chapter 8. The Egyptianist Image of Egypt: III. Pharaonicism

1. For pre-1914 Pharaonicist expression in Egypt, see the Introduction. It is worth noting that the objective basis of the "Pharaonic" sentiment found among modern Egyptians was in large part provided by the West: by the emerging discipline of Egyptology of the nineteenth century. For Egyptianists' acknowledgement of their debt to European Egyptology as well as for appeals for Egyptians to play a larger part in the interpretation of their ancient heritage, see Muhammad Husayn Haykal, "Misr al-Haditha wa Misr al-Qadima," SU, 27 Nov. 1926, 10–11; Salama Musa, *Misr Asl al-Hadara* (Cairo, n. d.), 5–13. The history of native Egyptian Egyptology is analyzed in Donald M. Reid, "Indigenous Egyptology: The Decolonization of a Profession?," *Journal of the American Oriental Society,* 105 (1985), 233–246.

2. Ibid., 7; see also Salama Musa, "Dima' al-Fara'ina Tajri fi 'Uruqina Jami'an," BL, 18 Oct. 1933, 1.

3. Salama Musa, "Nahnu al-Misriyyun," ibid., 8 Oct. 1933, 3. For a detailed attempt to demonstrate the physical resemblances between ancient and modern Egyptians, see his "al-Wajh al-Misri al-An wa Ayyam al-Fara'ina," MJ, April 1934, 12–15.

4. Quoted in Husayn, *Ittijahat,* II, 135.

5. Nashid Sayfin, "Misr Fir'awniyya Lahman wa Damman," part 2, MU, 10 Sept. 1930, 7.
6. Muhammad Zaki Salih, "Ihya' al-Khulq al-Qawmi," SU, 15 Jan. 1927, 31.
7. For a classic statement of this position, see 'Aqqad, *Sa'd Zaghlul,* 5–39.
8. Hasan Subhi, "Hadith al-Masa'," BL, 6 Sept. 1930, 1, 3.
9. Ahmad Husayn, "Misr Fir'awniyya," part 1, MU, 6 Sept. 1930, 7.
10. Ibid., part 2, 16 Sept. 1930, 3.
11. Ibid.
12. Ibid., part 3, 26 Sept. 1930, 11.
13. Muhammad Husayn Haykal, "Misr al-Haditha wa Misr al-Qadima," SU, 27 Nov. 1926, 10–11. The article was republished, with several changes, in his *Thawrat al-Adab,* 140–152, under the title "al-Ta'rikh wa al-Adab al-Qawmi." As David Semah has demonstrated, the changes were an intentional attempt by Haykal to moderate his extreme Pharaonicism of the 1920s and to adjust his earlier views to his more Islamic public orientation of the 1930s; see Semah, op. cit., 96–97.
14. Muhammad Husayn Haykal, "Misr al-Haditha wa Misr al-Qadima," SU, 27 Nov. 1926, 10.
15. Ibid., 10–11.
16. Ibid., 10.
17. Ibid.
18. Ibid.
19. Ibid., 11.
20. Ibid. 10.
21. For the contemporary impact, see MQ, 62 (1923), 1–8, 105–109; for the impact of the discovery on younger Egyptians, see the later memoir by Ahmad Husayn, *Nisf Qarn ma'a al-'Uruba wa Qadiyyat Filastin* (Sidon, 1971), 27–29.
22. See the accounts in AH, 5 March 1924, 4; AH, 7 March 1924, 4; AH, 9 March 1924, 1.
23. HI, 32 (April 1924), 677.
24. See the discussion in 'Umar al-Dasuqi, *Fi al-Adab al-Hadith* (two vols.: sixth ed., Cairo, 1964), II, 137–146, 169–173.
25. Khalil Mutran, "Nashid Tut-'Ankh-Amun," HI, 32 (June 1924), 913.
26. Muhammad Husayn Haykal, "Misr al-Haditha wa Misr al-Qadima," SU, 27 Nov. 1926, 10.
27. Muhammad Zaki Salih, "Ihya' al-Khulq al-Qawmi," ibid., 15 Jan. 1927, 31.
28. 'Abbas Mahmud al-'Aqqad, "Tut-'Ankh-Amun wa Rihlat al-Sahra'," reprinted in his *Mutala'at,* 267–269 (quotation from 268). 'Aqqad himself later visited the Pharaonic sites in Upper Egypt; see his article "al-Madi," BU, 11 March 1927, 19–20.
29. Articles describing his trip appeared in *al-Siyasa* in late 1922–early 1923 and are republished in his *Fi Awqat al-Faragh;* references to the latter.
30. Ibid., 251–256.
31. Ibid., 254.
32. Ibid., 255–256.
33. Ibid., 258.
34. Ibid.
35. Ibid., 258–259.
36. See ibid., 263–268.
37. Ibid., 263.
38. Ibid., 265.
39. Ibid., 265–268.
40. Ibid., 265.
41. See ibid., 255–256 and 263–268.
42. Ibid., 256.
43. Ibid.
44. Ibid., 260.
45. Ibid., 264.
46. Ibid., 265.
47. Ibid., 260.
48. Ibid., 261.
49. Ibid.
50. 'Abd al-Qadir Hamza, "Fi al-Aqsur," BL, 21 Jan. 1927, 1.
51. Ibid.

52. Ibid.
53. Ibid.
54. Ibid.
55. Ibid. For another account of such a pilgrimage to Upper Egypt by an Egyptian literary figure, see Mansur Fahmi, *Khatarat Nafs* (Cairo, 1930), 157–163.
56. In his *Imani,* 18–39.
57. Ibid., 22.
58. Ibid.
59. Ibid., 24.
60. Ibid.
61. Ibid.
62. Ibid., 24–25.
63. Ibid., 29.
64. Ibid., 31–32.
65. Ibid., 20–21.
66. Ibid., 21.
67. Ibid., 31.
68. Quotation from Husayn, *Nisf Qarn,* 29.
69. Husayn, *Imani,* 26–27.
70. Ibid., 30.
71. Husayn, *Nisf Qarn,* 29.
72. Musa, *Misr Asl al-Hadara,* 13.
73. Ibid., 5–7.
74. For examples, see Mar'ashli, op. cit., 40–45, 128–132; Bishri, op. cit., 137–138, 147–148, 159–163; Amin and Bishri, op. cit., 169–170, 199–200; Nahri and Bayli, op. cit., 281–283; Mahmud, *Durus,* 31–34.
75. Ibrahim Numayr Sayf and 'Abd al-Hamid Batriq, *Suwar min al-Hadara fi Misr al-Qadima* (Cairo, 1926).
76. For an excellent example, see the series of articles by Mahmud Tahun, "al-Misrulujiyya aw 'Ilm Misr al-Qadima," part 1, BU, 14 Jan. 1927, 20–22; part 2, ibid., 21 Jan. 1927, 3–7. For further examples, see ibid., 11 Feb. 1927, 18; ibid., 10 Feb. 1928, 16–20.
77. See ibid., 1 April 1927, 25–26 (interview with Hasan Subhi); MJ, April 1931, 642–648 (interview with Labib Nasim); ibid., July 1931, 1023–1025 (interview with Sami Jabra).
78. Such as "Fi al-Mathaf al-Misri," BU, 5 June 1929, 22–23; see also Muhammad Husayn Haykal's short story "Ibis," set in the Egyptian Museum (republished in his *Fi Awqat al-Faragh,* 269–287).
79. For examples, see HI, 32 (April 1924), 1; BU, 20 April 1928, 1, 17.
80. Quotation from "Akhnatun: Ahad al-Fara'ina al-Mujaddidin," MJ, Nov. 1929, 42–44; for other discussions of the New Kingdom, see "Tut 'Ankh Amun wa Hal huwa Fir'awn Musa?," HI, 31 (March 1923), 571–576; "Tut 'Ankh Amun wa al-Lurd Karnafun," BU, 21 Jan. 1927, 15, 32; "Makburat Tut 'Ankh Amun wa al-Kunuz al-Jadida al-lati Wujidat fiha," ibid., 10 Feb. 1928, 16–20; "Ra's al-Malaka Nafartiti," MJ, June 1930, 913–915; "Amun Awwal al-Arbab," ibid., Aug. 1930, 1187–1190.
81. For examples, see BU, 7 Jan. 1927, 1, 23; ibid., 8 April 1927, 20–21.
82. See Muhammad Kuta, "al-Kahana al-Misriyyun," BU, 25 Feb. 1927, 42.
83. As in 'Abd al-Rahman Fawzi, "Sirr 'Azamat al-Fara'ina," ibid., 22 April 1927, 15.
84. For examples, see Muharram Kamal's series of eight articles on Pharaonic religion, which appeared in BU between 15 April and 29 July 1927, or "'Aqa'id al-Misriyyin al-Qudama' fi al-Adyan al-Haditha," MJ, July 1930, 1128–1130.
85. See the discussion of his ideas in Fathi Radwan, *'Asr wa Rijal* (Cairo, 1967), 264–265.
86. Musa, *Misr Asl al-Hadara,* 130.
87. Ibid., 135–138.
88. Ibid., 63–68. For further examples, see Muharram Kamal, "al-Mabana wa al-Maqabir al-Fir'awniyya," part 1, BU, 1 April 1927, 21–22; part 2, ibid., 8 April 1927, 20–22; Muharram Kamal, "al-Rasm wa al-Naqsh wa al-Taswir 'inda al-Misriyyin al-Qudama'," ibid., 11 March 1927, 14–15; Muharram Kamal, "al-Tamathil 'inda Qudama' al-Misriyyin," ibid., 18 March 1927, 18–19; Muharram Kamal, "Fann al-Hafr wa Sina'at al-Tamathil," ibid., 25 March 1927, 8–9, 18; 'Abbas Mustafa 'Ammar, "Adabiyyat Qudama' al-Misriyyin," part 1, BU, 13 Jan. 1928, 27–28; part 2, ibid., 20 Jan. 1928, 14–15; part 3, ibid., 3 Feb. 1928, 28–29; Muhammad Lutfi Jum'a, "Hayat al-Qudama' al-Misriyyin

al-Ijtima'iyya," ibid., 23 April 1930, 10–11; Niqula Yusuf, "al-Musiqa al-Misriyya," SU, 16 March 1929, 12; Niqula Yusuf, "al-Musiqa al-Misriyya fi Tariq al-Tajdid," MJ, Nov. 1930, 42–46.

89. Muharram Kamal, "al-Ahram: Bahth Fanni," part 2, BU, 4 March 1927, 41.

90. Hasan Subhi, "Alfaz Hayya min al-Lugha al-Misriyya al-Qadima," SU, 18 May 1929, 21.

91. Hasan Subhi, "Fi al-Adab al-Misri al-Qadim," RI, 1 Aug. 1933, 17–18, 24.

92. Hasan Subhi, "Fi al-Adab al-Misri," SU, 23 June 1928, 10; Hasan Subhi, "Fi al-Adab al-Misri," ibid., 30 June 1928, 4.

93. Hasan Subhi, "Alfaz Hayya min al-Lugha al-Misriyya al-Qadima," SU, 18 May 1929, 21; "al-Lugha al-Fir'awniyya," ibid., 13 July 1929, 22; see also another article by Subhi on the same subject in ibid., 24 Aug. 1929, 22.

94. For two examples, see "Misr al-Qadima wa 'Azamatuha," BU, 7 Jan. 1927, 1; 'Abd al-Rahman Fawzi, "'Azamat al-Fara'ina: Wasf Mawkib Misri Qadim," ibid., 15 April 1927, 34.

95. Ahmad Husayn, "Misr Fir'awniyya," part 3, MU, 26 Sept. 1930, 11.

96. See Salama Musa, "Misr Asl Hadarat al-'Alam," HI, 35 (Dec. 1926), 183–186; Salama Musa, "Muluk al-'Alam min Sulalat al-Fara'ina," HI, 37 (Nov. 1928), 39–42 [republished in his *Misr Asl al-Hadara,* 153–156]; Salama Musa, "Misr Asl Hadarat al-'Alam," MJ, Dec. 1929, 195–198.

97. Musa, *Misr Asl al-Hadara,* 36.

98. Ibid., 11; see also Salama Musa, "Hadith 'an al-Fara'ina," HI, 37 (June 1929), 929–932.

99. Salama Musa, "Hadarat Misr fi al-'Iraq wa Asiya," in his *Misr Asl al-Hadara,* 37–43; see also Salama Musa, "Misr Asl al-Hadara: Hadarat Misr fi al-'Iraq wa Asiya," BL, 30 June 1935, 3; Salama Musa, "al-Misriyyun wa al-Kaldaniyyun," MJ, July 1930, 1065–1067.

100. Musa, *Misr Asl al-Hadara,* 37–43.

101. Ibid., 77–86.

102. Ibid., 14–36.

103. Ibid., 148–152; see also Salama Musa, "Thaqafat Misr 'inda al-'Arab," HI, 37 (Feb. 1929), 426–428.

104. Musa, *Misr Asl al-Hadara,* 139–147.

105. Ibid., 147.

106. Nashid Sayfin, "Misr Fir'awniyya Lahman wa Damman," MU, 10 Sept. 1930, 7.

107. Ahmad Husayn, "Misr Fir'awniyya," part 3, ibid., 26 Sept. 1930, 11.

108. Musa, *Misr Asl al-Hadara,* 131–132.

109. See ibid., 133–138; Salama Musa, "Qimat al-Hadara al-Misriyya wa Hal 'Amalat li-Sa'adat al-Bashar?," BL, 29 June 1935, 3.

110. Ibid.; Musa, *Misr Asl al-Hadara,* 135–138; for similar concepts, see Hafiz Mahmud, "Tatawwur al-Tafkir," SU, 15 Jan. 1927, 3.

111. For examples, see Musa, *Misr Asl al-Hadara,* passim.; Mahmud Shakir, "al-Misaha fi Misr fi 'Ahd al-Qudama' al-Misriyyin," HI, 34 (Jan. 1926), 347–350; Hasan Subhi, "Fi Mudun al-Athar al-Misriyya," BU, 15 April 1927, 10–11; "Hadarat Misr qabla al-Ahram," MJ, Jan. 1930, 308–309; Ahmad Zaki Abu Shadi, "al-Nahala al-Misriyya," ibid., April 1930, 747–750; Muhammad Lutfi Jum'a, "Hayat Qudama' a-Misriyyin al-Ijtima'iyya," BU, 23 April 1930, 10–11; Salama Musa, "Turath Qadim," MJ, June 1930, 1007; "al-Misriyyun wa Ikhtira' al-Sufun," ibid., Feb. 1934, 21–25.

112. Muhammad Lutfi Jum'a, "al-Dimuqratiyya al-Misriyya fi 'Ahd al-Fara'ina," ibid., 15 May 1929, 22–23.

113. Ibid., 23.

114. For general discussions of this, see ibid.; Muhammad Lutfi Jum'a, "Nasihat Rumi lil-Misriyyin," ibid., 29 May 1929, 8–9; "Nahnu wa al-Aghriq," MJ, Aug. 1930, 1125–1127; "al-Mizaj al-Aghriqi," ibid., Aug. 1931, 1200–1202; Husni al-Shintanawi, "Jamal Misr wa Jamal al-Aghriq," BU, 21 Aug. 1929, 2.

115. Musa, *Misr Asl al-Hadara,* 69–76, 96–101; see also Salama Musa, "Misr Asl al-Hadara wa al-Aghriqiyya hiya al-Mahd al-Thani laha," BL, 15 June 1935, 3, 11.

116. Ibid., 3.

117. Ibid.

118. Ibid., 11.

119. 'Abd al-Qadir Hamza, "al-Madaniyya al-Misriyya al-Qadima wa Maslak al-Madaniyyatayn al-Yunaniyya wa al-Rumaniyya ma'aha," BU, 11 March 1927, 3–5, 12.

120. Muhammad Zaki Salih, "Ihya' al-Khulq al-Qawmi," SU, 15 Jan. 1927, 31.

121. Husayn, *Imani,* 55.

122. Amin Wasif as quoted in the collection of Egyptian opinions on Arab subjects compiled by *al-Hilal* in the early 1920s, *Fatawa Kibar al-Kuttab wa al-Udaba' fi (1) Mustaqbal al-Lugha al-'Arabiyya (2) Nahdat al-Sharq al-'Arabi wa Mawqifuhu iza' al-Madaniyya al-Gharbiyya* (Cairo, 1923), 108.

123. Musa, *Misr Asl al-Hadara,* 85–86.

124. Ahmad Husayn, "Misr Fir'awniyya," part 3, MU, 26 Sept. 1930, 11.

125. Muhammad Husayn Haykal, "Siyasat al-Usbu'," SU, 28 May 1928, 14.

126. Ibid.

127. Ibid.

128. Ibid.

129. Ahmad Zaki Abu Shadi, *Akhnatun: Fir'awn Misr* (Cairo, 1927), 4–17.

130. Ibid., 8–9.

131. Ibid., 15–17.

132. Ibid., 17.

133. Ibid.

134. Sabri, *Kahin Amun,* xii.

135. Ibid., xi–xii.

136. Husayn, *Imani,* 28–32, 45–49; Husayn, *Nisf Qarn,* 28.

137. Ibid., 28–29.

138. Hakim, *Tahta Shams al-Fikr,* 116–121.

139. Yusuf Sabri and 'Ali Shahid, *Nafrat aw 'Ashiqat Fir'awn,* (Cairo, 1928).

140. See his stories "Ibis" and "Samiramis" in his *Fi Awqat al-Faragh,* 269–301, as well as his later tales "Izis" and "Afrudit" in his *Thawrat al-Adab,* 161–177 and 195–210.

141. *'Awdat al-Ruh* is analyzed in 'Abd al-Muhsin Taha Badr, *Tatawwur al-Riwaya al-'Arabiyya al-Haditha fi Misr, 1870–1938* (Cairo, 1963), 372–397; Hamdi Sakkut, *The Egyptian Novel and Its Main Trends from 1913 to 1953* (Cairo, 1971), 85–88; Hilary Kilpatrick, *The Modern Egyptian Novel: A Study in Social Criticism* (London, 1974), 41–44 (synopsis 205–206); Somekh, op. cit., 18–19; Pierre Cachia, "Idealism and Ideology: The Case of Tawfiq al-Hakim," *Journal of the American Oriental Society,* 100 (1980), 227–228.

142. See the material in Dasuqi, *Fi al-Adab al-Hadith,* II, 122–158, 187–204.

143. Ahmad Muhammad al-Hawfi, *Wataniyyat Shawqi: Dirasa Adabiyya Ta'rikhiyya Muqarana* (Cairo, 1978), 165–173.

144. Ahmad Shawqi, "Tut 'Ankh Amun," in Ahmad Shawqi, *al-Shawqiyyat* (four vols.: Cairo, 1930), I, 335.

145. See Hawfi, op. cit., 166–167.

146. Ibid., 170–186.

147. Ibid., 162–188.

148. Hawfi's judgment on Shawqi's patriotic poetry of the post-1919 era was that no other Egyptian poet of the period "praised the glory of ancient Egypt as Shawqi did"; ibid., 193.

149. On this, see Dayf, *al-Adab al-'Arabi al-Mu'asir,* 141–142.

150. See ibid., 149–150; M. M. Badawi, *A Critical Introduction to Modern Arabic Poetry* (Cambridge, 1975), 116–119.

151. Muhammad al-Asmar, "Qudama' al-Misriyyin aw Hadarat Tiba wa Manif," SU, 16 April 1927, 7.

152. The above details concerning the monument are taken from Ahmad Lutfi al-Sayyid's article reviewing its genesis and construction (AH, 20 May 1928, 1, 3), and from Prime Minister Mustafa al-Nahhas's speech at its unveiling (US, June 1928, 1122–1126); see also Subhi al-Sharouni, "Mahmoud Mukhtar: A Traditional and Contemporary Artist," *Ur,* 1 (1984), 27–30. Today the monument stands in front of the main entrance to the Egyptian University in Giza.

153. For details, see BU, 25 May 1928, 2, 12–13, 17.

154. Text in US, June 1928, 1122–1126.

155. Ibid., 1122.

156. Ibid., 1122–1123.

157. Ibid., 1123.

158. Ibid.

159. Ibid., 1124.

160. Ibid., 1125–1126.

161. Text in ibid., 1128, and also in Hawfi, op. cit., 158–159.
162. US, June 1928, 1128.
163. See BU, 25 May 1928, 16–17.
164. "Siyasat al-Usbu‘," SU, 26 May 1928, 14.
165. See Dasuqi, *Fi al-Adab al-Hadith,* II, 145–146.
166. ‘Abd al-Qadir Hamza, "Timthal Nahdat Misr," BU, 25 May 1928, 2.
167. Ibid.
168. ‘Abbas Mahmud al-‘Aqqad, "Timthal al-Nahda," ibid., 12–13, 35.
169. Ibid., 13.
170. Ibid., 35.
171. The bulk of the following is taken from the account in ‘Aqqad, *Sa‘d Zaghlul,* 619–624.
172. Ibid., 623.
173. See Shafiq, *Hawliyyat, 1929,* 1249–1250.
174. "Memorandum Respecting the Egyptian Press and Anglo-Egyptian Relations, February 7 to 13, 1930," FO 407/210, no. 30. It is interesting to note that the young Husayn Fawzi, studying in Paris at the time, was both astounded and angered by the position of the Liberals and *al-Siyasa,* which seemed to him to be a betrayal of the earlier Pharaonicist orientation of the party; interview with Husayn Fawzi, 27 July 1980.
175. ‘Aqqad, *Sa‘d Zaghlul,* 619–620.
176. Ibid., 620; see also the account in HI, 44 (July 1936), 1023–1028.
177. ‘Aqqad, *Sa‘d Zaghlul,* 620.
178. Ibid., 619.
179. On the creation of his statues, see HI, 39 (Jan. 1931), 327; HI, 39 (March 1931), front leaf; HI, 39 (June 1931), front leaf. For his nonpayment, see the obituary "Mukhtar," MJ, May 1934, 7.
180. ‘Aqqad, *Sa‘d Zaghlul,* 620–621.
181. Ibid.
182. Ibid.

Chapter 9. The Egyptianist Image of Egypt: IV. Toward an Egyptian National Literature

1. See Ahmad Dayf, *Muqaddima li-Dirasat Balaghat al-‘Arab* (Cairo, 1921), 3–11; Ahmad Dayf, "al-Adab al-Misri fi al-Qarn al-Tasi‘ ‘Ashr," MQ, 68 (April 1926), 401–405; Semah. op. cit., 78.
2. Printed as the opening essay in his *Muqaddima,* 3–11.
3. Ibid., 4.
4. Ibid., 6.
5. Ahmad Dayf, "al-Adab al-Misri fi al-Qarn al-Tasi‘ ‘Ashr," MQ, 68 (April 1926), 403.
6. Ibid., 404.
7. See the Introduction to his *Balaghat al-‘Arab fi al-Andalus* (Cairo, 1924).
8. Republished in his *Fi Awqat al-Faragh,* 344–356.
9. Ibid., 346–347, 350–353.
10. Ibid., 346.
11. Ibid., 347.
12. For his views on this broader subject, see ibid., 344–367; Haykal, *Tarajim,* 152–153; Haykal, *Thawrat al-Adab,* 62–76, 90–110, 121–139.
13. Haykal, *Fi Awqat al-Faragh,* 350–356.
14. Ibid., 351.
15. Ibid., 352–356, 365–367, 380–381.
16. Ibid., 354; see also Muhammad Husayn Haykal, "al-Fir‘awniyya wa al-‘Arabiyya: Hadir La Madi lahu La Mustaqbal lahu," MSI, 29 Sept. 1933, 24–28.
17. "Da‘wa ila Khalq al-Adab al-Qawmi," SU, 28 June 1930, 7.
18. Ibrahim al-Misri, "Ayna huwa al-Adab al-Misri?," MJ, Dec. 1929, 228.
19. "Da‘wa ila Khalq al-Adab al-Qawmi," SU, 28 June 1930, 7.
20. Ahmad Dayf, "al-Adab al-Misri fi al-Qarn al-Tasi‘ ‘Ashr," MQ, 68 (April 1926), 406.
21. Niqula Yusuf, "Hal Lana Adab Qawmi?," SU, 26 Jan. 1929, 18.
22. Ibrahim al-Misri, "Ayna huwa al-Adab al-Misri?," MJ, Dec. 1929, 228.

23. Tawfiq Mikha'il Tuwaij, "Tatawwur al-Adab al-Misri wa Aghraduhu," SU, 25 May 1929, 18; see also Mu'awiya Muhammad Nur, "al-Adab al-Qawmi," ibid., 20 Sept. 1930, 23.

24. See Tawfiq Mikha'il Tuwaij, "Tatawwur al-Adab al-Misri wa Aghraduhu," SU, 25 May 1929, 18; Mu'awiya Muhammad Nur, "al-Adab al-Qawmi," ibid., 20 Sept. 1930, 23.

25. Ibrahim Ibrahim Jum'a, "Nuridu Adaban Qawmiyyan," ibid., 31 Aug. 1929, 8.

26. Salama Musa, "Tahqiq al-Qawmiyya al-Misriyya," MJ, May 1931, 790.

27. Haykal, *Thawrat al-Adab,* 122.

28. Niqula Yusuf, "al-Adab al-Misri wa al-Wasf," SU, 2 Feb. 1929, 13.

29. See Muhammad Zaki 'Abd al-Qadir, "Da'wat al-Adab al-Qawmi: Bayan," ibid., 12 July 1930, 14; 'Ali Muhammad al-Bahrawi, "al-Shi'r al-Misri," *Apulu,* March 1933, 787.

30. Ibrahim al-Misri, "Wa'i al-Bi'a wa al-'Asr fi al-Adab al-Hadith," in his *Wahy al-'Asr* (Cairo, 1935), 9–19 (quotation from 9).

31. Ibid., 17.

32. Ibid., 18.

33. Ibid., 9–19; see also Misri, *al-Adab al-Hayy,* 17–33, 56–67, 104–112.

34. Misri, *Wahy al-'Asr,* 10–11, 15–17.

35. Ibid., 19.

36. Ibid.

37. The appeal was first published collectively under the title "Da'wa ila Khalq al-Adab al-Qawmi," SU, 28 June 1930, 7; much of its text was repeated in a separate article by Muhammad Zaki 'Abd al-Qadir, "Da'wat al-Adab al-Qawmi: Bayan," ibid., 12 July 1930, 14.

38. See ibid., 5 July 1930, 24–25; ibid., 19 July 1930, 26–27.

39. Ibid., 5 July 1930, 24–25.

40. Ibid.

41. Muhammad Zaki 'Abd al-Qadir, "Da'wat al-Adab al-Qawmi: Bayan," ibid., 12 July 1930, 14.

42. Mahmud Taymur, *al-Shaykh Jum'a wa Aqasis Ukhra* (second ed.: Cairo, 1927), 10–14.

43. Ibid., 10.

44. Ibid., 12; see also Mahmud Taymur, "Nushu' wa Tatawwur al-Balagha al-Qasasiyya," the Introduction to his *al-Shaykh Sayyid al-'Abit wa Aqasis Ukhra* (Cairo, 1926), 1–47; Mahmud Taymur, *Nushu' al-Qissa wa Tatawwuruha* (Cairo, 1936), passim.

45. Niqula Yusuf, "al-Adab al-Misri wa al-Wasf," SU, 2 Feb. 1929, 13.

46. Tawfiq Mikha'il Tuwaij, "Tatawwur al-Adab al-Misri wa Aghraduhu," ibid., 25 May 1929, 18.

47. 'Ali Muhammad al-Bahrawi, "al-Shi'r al-Misri," *Apulu,* March 1933, 787.

48. 'Aziz Talha, "Da'wa ila al-Adab al-Qawmi," SU, 19 Oct. 1929, 23.

49. The above contrast between romanticism and realism is based on the following: M. H. Abrams, *The Mirror and the Lamp: Romantic Theory and the Critical Tradition* (New York, 1953), 198–213, 240–244; Rene Wellek, *A History of Modern Criticism, 1750–1950: vol. II, The Romantic Age* (New Haven, 1955), 18, 74–75, 82–83, 144–163; Rene Wellek, *A History of Modern Criticism, 1750–1950: vol. IV, The Later Nineteenth Century* (New Haven, 1965), 28–57; Linda Nochlin, *Realism* (London, 1971), 13–56, 103–137, 209–247. A comprehensive discussion of romantic and realistic influences on Egyptian intellectuals in the interwar period can be found in Eliraz, op. cit., 140–167.

50. Editorial in FJ, 27 Jan. 1925, 1.

51. Ibid.

52. Ibid.

53. Editorial in ibid., 20 March 1925, 1.

54. Muhammad Zaki 'Abd al-Qadir, "Ara' fi al-Adab al-Qawmi," SU, 12 Oct. 1929, 13.

55. Ibid.

56. Ibid.

57. Ibrahim al-Misri, "Fann al-Qasas fi Misr," BU, 1 April 1927, 24.

58. For statements of this viewpoint, see Ibrahim al-Misri, "Fann al-Qasas fi Misr," BU, 1 April 1927, 23–25; Niqula Yusuf, "Hal Lana Adab Qawmi?," SU, 26 Jan. 1929, 23–24; Mu'awiya Muhammad Nur, "al-Adab al-Misri al-Hadith," BU, 6 March 1929, 8–9; Muhammad Lutfi Jum'a, "al-Adab al-Rusi al-Jadid," ibid., 28 Aug. 1929, 8–9; Salama Musa, "al-Adab al-Injilizi al-Hadir," MJ, April 1930, 691–695; Muhammad Lutfi Jum'a, "al-Nahda al-'Ilmiyya fi Misr fi Awa'il al-Qarn al-'Ashrin," BU, 25 June 1930, 14–15, 26; Muhammad Zaki 'Abd al-Qadir, "Da'wat al-Adab al-Qawmi: Bayan," SU, 12 July 1930, 14; Yusuf Hanna, "al-Da'wa ila al-Adab al-Qawmi," ibid., 9 Aug. 1930, 10;

Mahmud 'Izzat Musa, "Bahth fi al-Adab al-Qawmi," ibid., 16 Aug. 1930, 10; Mu'awiya Muhammad Nur, "al-Adab al-Qawmi," ibid., 20 Sept. 1930, 23; Salama Musa, "al-Adab al-'Arabi wa al-Adab al-Misri," MSI, 14 Oct. 1932, 25; Haykal, *Thawrat al-Adab,* 49–76, 83–134, 153–160.

59. Ibrahim al-Misri, "Ayna huwa al-Adab al-Misri?," MJ, Dec. 1929, 231.

60. Muhammad 'Abd Allah 'Inan, "Adab Qawmi wa Adab Gharbi," MSI, 7 Jan. 1932, 5.

61. Ibid.

62. Ibid.

63. Mahmud 'Izzat Musa, "Bahth fi al-Adab al-Qawmi," SU, 16 Aug. 1930, 10; see also "Da'wa ila Khalq al-Adab al-Qawmi," ibid., 28 June 1930, 7.

64. The phrase appeared first in Muhammad Zaki 'Abd al-Qadir, "Ara' fi al-Adab al-Qawmi," ibid., 12 Oct. 1929, 16, and was repeated in 'Aziz Talha, "al-Da'wa ila al-Adab al-Qawmi," ibid., 19 Oct. 1929, 23.

65. Ibrahim Ibrahim Jum'a, "Nuridu Adaban Qawmiyyan," ibid., 31 Aug. 1929, 8.

66. Ibid.

67. Shuhdi 'Atiyya al-Shafi'i, "Fi al-Adab al-Fir'awni," ibid., 31 Aug. 1929, 22; Shuhdi 'Atiyya al-Shafi'i, "Fi al-Adab al-Fir'awni," ibid., 14 Sept. 1929, 27–28; see also Hasan Subhi, "Fi al-Adab Al-Misri," ibid., 23 June 1928, 10; Hasan Subhi, "Fi al-Adab al-Misri," ibid., 30 June 1928, 4; and Muhammad Husayn Haykal, "al-Fann al-Misri," ibid., 17 Dec. 1927, 23.

68. Muhammad Husayn Haykal, "Misr al-Sahira wa 'Uquq Abna'iha min Jamaliha," ibid., 28 Sept. 1929, 3–4; reprinted in his *Thawrat al-Adab,* 121–139.

69. Muhammad Husayn Haykal, "Misr al-Sahira wa 'Uquq Abna'iha min Jamaliha," SU, 28 Sept. 1929, 3.

70. Ibid.

71. Muhammad Zaki 'Abd al-Qadir, "Ara' fi al-Adab al-Qawmi," ibid., 12 Oct. 1929, 13.

72. Ibid., 13, 16.

73. Niqula Yusuf, "al-Adab al-Misri wa al-Wasf," ibid., 2 Feb. 1929, 13.

74. Ibid.

75. Niqula Yusuf, "Hal Lana Adab Qawmi?," ibid., 26 Jan. 1929, 23.

76. Niqula Yusuf, "al-Adab al-Misri wa al-Wasf," ibid., 2 Feb. 1929, 13.

77. Ibid.

78. Yusuf Hanna, "al-Da'wa ila al-Adab al-Qawmi," ibid., 9 Aug. 1930, 10.

79. Ibid.

80. Ibid.

81. Tawfiq Mikha'il Tuwaij, "Tatawwur al-Adab al-Misri wa Aghraduhu," ibid., 25 May 1929, 18.

82. Ibrahim Ibrahim Jum'a, "Ayna Adabuna al-Qawmi?," ibid., 14 April 1928, 26.

83. Muhammad Zaki 'Abd al-Qadir, "Da'wat al-Adab al-Qawmi: Bayan," ibid., 12 July 1930, 14.

84. Musa, *Ahlam al-Falasifa,* 111–113.

85. In BU, 20 March 1929, 5, 7.

86. Ibid., 5.

87. Ibid., 7.

88. Niqula Yusuf, "Hal Lana Adab Qawmi?," SU, 26 Jan. 1929, 23.

89. Ibid.

90. Ibrahim al-Misri, "Ayna huwa al-Adab al-Misri?," MJ, Dec. 1929, 230.

91. Ibid., 232.

92. Misri, *Wahy al-'Asr,* 12.

93. Ibid., 15.

94. Ibrahim al-Misri, "Ayna huwa al-Adab al-Misri?," MJ, Dec. 1929, 233.

95. Ibid., 234.

96. Salama Musa, "al-Fulklur al-Misri wa Ahammiyyatuhu," in his *Mukhtarat,* 191–196 (quotation from 195).

97. Ibid., 195–196.

98. For examples of this worship of the peasantry, see Hakim, *'Awdat al-Ruh,* II, 7–25; Musa, *Ahlam al-Falasifa,* 111–113; Muhammad Hilmi 'Abd al-Latif, "al-Nafs al-Misriyya bayna al-Hayat wa al-Fann," SU, 11 Feb. 1927, 16; Niqula Yusuf, "Hal Lana Adab Qawmi?," ibid., 26 Jan. 1929, 23–24; Shuhdi 'Atiyya al-Shafi'i, "Fi al-Adab al-Fir'awni," ibid., 14 Sept. 1929, 27–28; 'Abd al-Latif al-Saharati, "al-Adab al-Qawmi," SU, 11 Oct. 1930, 23.

99. See Niqula Yusuf, "al-Adab al-Misri wa al-Wasf," ibid., 2 Feb. 1929, 13; Ahmad Durini Khashaba, "Fi al-Adab al-Misri," MJ, Aug. 1931, 1189–1197; Hakim, *'Awdat al-Ruh,* II, 7–56; 'Aqqad, *Sa'd Zaghlul,* 18–67.

100. See Musa, *Mukhtarat,* 191–196; Musa, *Ahlam al-Falasifa,* 111–113; Yusuf Hanna, "al-Da'wa ila al-Adab al-Qawmi," SU, 9 Aug. 1930, 10.

101. See Bishri, op. cit., 1–5; Amin and Bishri, op. cit., 1–17; 'Aqqad, *Sa'd Zaghlul,* 25–27, 37–39, 499–501; and the program of the short-lived "Workers' and Peasants' Party" organized by Isma'il Mazhar and other progressive intellectuals in 1930 (see Isma'il Mazhar, "Hizb al-Fallah," US, May 1930, 10–13; "Barnamij Hizb al-'Ummal wa al-Fallahin," appendix to ibid.).

102. 'Aqqad, *Sa'd Zaghlul,* 28.

103. Ibid.

104. See Musa, *Ahlam al-Falasifa,* 111–113; Misri, *Wahy al-'Asr,* 9–19; Muhammad Hilmi 'Abd al-Latif, "al-Nafs al-Misriyya bayna al-Hayat wa al-Fann," SU, 11 Feb. 1927, 16; 'Abd al-Halim Rafi', "Tatawwur al-Thaqafa al-'Amma wa Atharuhu fi Nishatina al-Fikri," BU, 19 Aug. 1927, 24–26; 'Abbas Hafiz, "al-Wataniyya wa al-Adab: al-Wataniyya al-'Amma wa Wataniyyat al-Siyasiyyin" part 1, ibid., 27 April 1928, 10–11; part 2, ibid., 4 May 1928, 10–11; part 3, ibid., 11 May 1928, 10–11.

105. Tawfiq Mikha'il Tuwaij, "Tatawwur al-Adab al-Misri wa Aghraduhu," SU, 25 May 1929, 18.

106. Editorial in FJ, 18 Jan. 1926, 1.

107. See the editorials in ibid., 24 April, 1 May, and 8 May 1925; Ibrahim al-Misri, "Hawla al-Ta'lif al-Qasasi al-Misri," ibid., 24 Jan. 1926, 1; Hafiz Mahmud, "Nahdat al-Qissa al-Misriyya," BU, 13 May 1927, 19; Tawfiq Mikha'il Tuwaij, "Tatawwur al-Adab al-Misri wa Aghraduhu," SU, 25 May 1929, 18; "al-Adab al-Qasasi fi Misr: Istifta'," MJ, June 1931, 961–970.

108. See Ahmad Dayf, *Balaghat al-'Arab fi al-Andalus,* Introduction, iii; Mahmud Taymur, "Tatawwur al-Qasas wa Nushu'uha," FJ, 24 Jan. 1926, 1; Ibrahim al-Misri, "Hawla al-Ta'lif al-Qasasi al-Misri," ibid., 24 Jan. 1926, 1; Haykal, *Thawrat al-Adab,* 77–110.

109. See Hafiz Mahmud, "Nahdat al-Qissa al-Misriyya," BU, 13 May 1927, 19; Niqula Yusuf, "al-Adab al-Misri wa al-Wasf," SU, 2 Feb. 1929, 13; Tawfiq Mikha'il Tuwaij, "Tatawwur al-Adab al-Misri wa Aghraduhu," SU, 25 May 1929, 18; Yusuf Hanna, "al-Da'wa ila al-Adab al-Qawmi," SU, 9 Aug. 1930, 10; Mahmud 'Izzat Musa, "Bahth fi al-Adab al-Qawmi," SU, 16 Aug. 1930, 10.

110. See FJ, 7 Nov. 1925, 1; ibid., 28 Dec. 1925, 1; Ibrahim al-Misri, "Shakhsiyyat al-Fannan," BU, 11 Feb. 1927, 36; Misri, *Wahy al-'Asr,* 17; Tawfiq Mikha'il Tuwaij, "Tatawwur al-Adab al-Misri wa Aghraduhu," 25 May 1929, 17–18; Yusuf Hanna, "al-Da'wa ila al-Adab al-Qawmi," ibid., 9 Aug. 1930, 10; Mu'awiya Muhammad Nur, "al-Adab al-Qawmi," ibid., 20 Sept. 1930, 10; Mahmud 'Izzat Musa, "Bahth fi al-Adab al-Qawmi," ibid., 16 Aug. 1930, 10; Haykal, *Fi Awqat al-Faragh,* 22–90; Haykal, *Thawrat al-Adab,* 77–110; "al-Adab al-Qasasi fi Misr: Istifta'," MJ, June 1931, 961–970.

111. See his *Thawrat al-Adab,* 77–110 (quotation from 94).

112. Ibid., 91.

113. Ibid., 88.

114. Misri, *Wahy al-'Asr,* 16–17.

115. Ibrahim al-Misri, "Fann al-Qasas fi Misr," BU, 1 April 1927, 24.

116. Ibid., 25.

117. Hakim, *Tahta Shams al-Fikr,* 126.

118. Muhammad Amin Hassuna, "Fi Sabil al-Da'wa ila al-Adab al-Qawmi," SU, 19 July 1930, 9.

119. Muhammad Zaki 'Abd al-Qadir, "Da'wat al-Adab al-Misri: Bayan," ibid., 12 July 1930, 14.

120. See the editorial on "al-Riwayat al-Qasasiyya wa al-Ta'lif al-Masrahi," FJ, 13 Dec. 1925, 1; Muhammad Husayn Haykal, "al-Ta'lif al-Masrahi," in his *Thawrat al-Adab,* 111–120; Hakim, *Tahta Shams al-Fikr,* 116–128; Muhammad Lutfi Jum'a, "al-Ta'lif al-Tamthili fi Misr," BU, 24 April 1929, 22–23; Muhammad Lutfi Jum'a, "Athr Fann al-Tamthil wa Adabuhu fi al-Madaniyyat al-Insaniyya fi al-Sharq wa al-Gharb," ibid., 14 Aug. 1929, 6–8.

121. Muhammad Husayn Haykal, "al-Ta'lif al-Masrahi," in his *Thawrat al-Adab,* 111–120.

122. Ibid., 118–119.

123. Ibid., 119.

124. Ibid.

125. Ibid., 120.

126. Ahmad Durini Khashaba, "Fi al-Adab al-Misri," MJ, Aug. 1931, 1195. For similar views, see Muhammad Husayn Haykal, "al-Fann al-Misri," SU, 17 Dec. 1927, 23; Muhammad Husayn

Haykal, "Hal min Khatwa Jadida fi Sabil al-Fann al-Misri?", ibid., 7 Jan. 1928, 10; 'Ali Mahmud, "Ihya' al-Fann al-Misri," ibid., 7 Jan. 1928, 3.

127. Salama Musa, "al-Dhawq al-Sharqi fi al-Funun: Huwa Dhawq al-Saj'," FJ, 15 July 1926, 1.

128. See ibid., 27 Jan. 1925, 1.

129. Ibid., 1, 4; see also ibid., 3 Feb. 1925, 1; ibid., 10 Feb. 1925, 1; Muhammad Shukri, "al-Inbi'ath al-Jadid," ibid., 17 Feb. 1925, 1; ibid., 18 Oct. 1925, 1.

130. See ibid., 6 March 1925, 1; ibid., 3 April 1925, 1; ibid., 10 April 1925, 1; ibid., 26 June 1925, 1; ibid., 13 Jan. 1927, 1.

131. The concern with music of the Modernist School is discussed in Ahmad Khayri Sa'id, "Shuru' fi Nahda," ibid., 20 March 1925, 1, and was commented upon in personal interviews with Husayn Fawzi in July 1980. See also Niqula Yusuf, "al-Musiqa al-Misri," SU, 16 March 1929, 12.

132. Editorial by Ahmad Khayri Sa'id in FJ, 28 Oct. 1926, 1.

133. Ibid.

134. Ibid.; see also Munir al-Husami, "al-Musiqi al-'Arabiyya wa al-Musiqi al-Gharbiyya," US, 1 May 1928, 997–1002; Niqula Yusuf, "al-Musiqi al-Misriyya fi Tariq Jadid," MJ, Nov. 1930, 42–46; Tawfiq al-Hakim, "Ila al-Duktur Taha Husayn," RI, 1 June 1933, 6–8; Muhammad Husayn Haykal, "al-Fann al-Misri," SU, 17 Dec. 1927, 23.

135. For a detailed analysis of 'Aqqad's critical theory, see Semah, op. cit., 3–65.

136. 'Aqqad, *Fusul,* 265.

137. Ibid., 265–269; see also 'Aqqad, *Muraja'at,* 17–25, 100–108, 273–276.

138. 'Aqqad, *Fusul,* 268–269.

139. See ibid., 267–268.

140. Ibid.; see also his *Mutala'at,* 10–17.

141. Ibid., 12–13.

142. Developed in 'Abbas Mahmud al-'Aqqad, "al-Ihsasiyya fi al-Taswir," BU, 16 March 1928, and reprinted in his *Sa'at bayna al-Kutub,* 289–293.

143. Ibid., 282–285, 289–293; see also 'Aqqad, *Mutala'at,* 208–210, 259–262.

144. For the use of the term, see 'Ali Muhammad al-Bahrawi, "al-Shi'r al-Misri," *Apulu,* March 1933, 787. The concept was discussed intensively by the Modernist School in the mid-1920s (interviews with Husayn Fawzi, July 1980).

145. Misri, *Wahy al-'Asr,* 12–13.

146. Niqula Yusuf, "al-Adab al-Misri wa al-Wasf," SU, 2 Feb. 1929, 13.

147. Muhammad Zaki 'Abd al-Qadir, "Da'wat al-Adab al-Qawmi: Bayan," ibid., 12 July 1930, 14.

148. 'Ali Muhammad al-Bahrawi, "al-Shi'r al-Misri," *Apulu,* March 1933, 787.

149. Haykal, *Thawrat al-Adab,* 68–70.

150. Ibid., 65, 73–74.

151. Ibid., 72.

152. Ibid., 67–76.

153. The following analysis of 'Aqqad's views on the nature and functions of "national" poetry is based on his series of eight articles on "Egyptian Poetry" ["al-Shi'r al-Misri"] published in BU in May–June 1927 and republished in his *Sa'at bayna al-Kutub,* 102–139 (quotations from the latter).

154. Ibid., 121–125; see also 'Aqqad, *Fusul,* 290.

155. 'Aqqad, *Sa'at bayna al-Kutub,* 124–125.

156. Ibid., 121–125.

157. Ibid., 125.

158. Ibid., 123–125.

159. Ibid., 123.

160. Ibid., 106–107, 112–113.

161. Ibid., 104–105.

162. Ibid., 105.

163. Ibid., 106–116; see also Semah, op. cit., 32–33.

164. The most comprehensive source on the language issue in modern Egypt is Nufusa Zakariya Sa'id, *Ta'rikh al-Da'wa ila al-'Ammiyya wa Atharuhu fi Misr* (Alexandria, 1964). For overviews of prewar suggestions for the alteration of Arabic in Egypt, see Husayn, *Ittijahat,* II, 334–336; Jundi, *al-Fikr al-'Arabi,* 564–568.

165. Amin's views on Arabic language reform may be seen in some of the later writings of his colleagues: see Ahmad Lutfi al-Sayyid, "Dhikra Qasim Amin," MQ, 51 (Aug. 1917), 156–162; Mu-

hammad Husayn Haykal, "Qasim Amin," SU, 16 April 1927, 10–11, also reprinted in his *Tarajim,* 152–166; Muhammad Husayn Haykal, "al-Nathr wa al-Shi'r," SU, 13 Aug. 1927, 10, also reprinted in his *Thawrat al-Adab,* 49–61; see Wendell, op. cit., 176–180, for Lutfi's views on language reform.

166. For an overview of the positions taken by Egyptian intellectuals in the interwar period, see Eliraz, op. cit., 115–139.

167. Tawfiq Mikha'il Tuwaij, "Tatawwur al-Adab al-Misri wa Aghraduhu," SU, 25 May 1929, 18.

168. Hafiz Mahmud, "Fal-Tatawwur al-Lugha," MJ, June 1930, 1095–1098.

169. Niqula Yusuf, "Hal Lana Adab Qawmi?," SU, 26 Jan. 1929, 24.

170. Ibid.

171. For examples, see 'Aqqad, *Sa'at bayna al-Kutub,* 134–139; Ibrahim Ibrahim Jum'a, "Ayna Adabuna al-Qawmi?," SU, 14 April 1928, 26; 'Abd al-Qadir Hamza, "al-Lugha al-'Arabiyya wa al-Huruf al-Latiniyya," BU, 1 June 1928, 3–5; Muhammad Husayn Haykal, "al-Lugha wa al-Adab," SU, 1 June 1929, 3–4, reprinted in his *Thawrat al-Adab,* 39–48; Muhammad 'Abd Allah 'Inan, "Tadris al-Adab al-'Arabiyya," ibid., 31. Aug. 1929, 8; Hafiz Mahmud, "Fal-Tatawwur al-Lugha," MJ, July 1930, 1095–1098; Muhammad Isma'il al-Najdi, "al-Lugha al-'Arabiyya wa Adabuha," BU, 30 April 1930, 24–25.

172. Haykal, *Fi Awqat al-Faragh,* 363.

173. Ibid., 367.

174. Ibid., 345–346.

175. Ibid., 346.

176. Haykal, *Thawrat al-Adab,* 42; in general, see also ibid., 39–48.

177. Haykal, *Fi Awqat al-Faragh,* 346.

178. Ibid., 361.

179. Haykal, *Tarajim,* 164; see also Semah, op. cit., 91–92.

180. Haykal had proposed this as early as his article on "Fawda al-Lugha" in *al-Jarida,* 3 May 1913 and reasserted it in his *Fi Awqat al-Faragh,* 357–367.

181. Ibid., 348.

182. Ibid., 361.

183. See ibid., 198–242, 344–367; Haykal, *Thawrat al-Adab,* 90–139, 153–160. See also Semah, op. cit., 83–95.

184. Haykal, *Fi Awqat al-Faragh,* 10–21, 127–142, 170–185, 344–367; Haykal, *Thawrat al-Adab,* 111–120.

185. See his "'Illat al-Shi'r," in *Thawrat al-Adab,* 62–76; see also Semah, op. cit., 94–95.

186. Tawfiq 'Awwan, "al-Adab al-Qawmi Aydan," SU, 31 Aug. 1929, 23.

187. Salama Musa, "al-Lugha al-Fusha wa al-Lugha al-'Ammiyya," HI, 34 (July 1926), 1073–1077 (quotation from 1074).

188. Ibid., 1075.

189. Salama Musa, "Tahqiq al-Qawmiyya al-Misriyya," MJ, May 1931, 789.

190. Musa, *al-Yawm wa al-Ghad,* 251; see also Ahmad Durini Khashaba, "Fulujiyyat al-'Ammiyya al-Misriyya," MJ, Nov. 1930, 66–69.

191. Salama Musa, "al-Lugha al-Fusha wa al-Lugha al-'Ammiyya," HI, 34 (July 1926), 1077.

192. Tawfiq 'Awwan, "al-Adab al-Qawmi Aydan," SU, 31 Aug. 1929, 23.

193. Ibid. For a similar view, see Muhammad Zaki Ibrahim, "Thaqafat Misr Yajibu an Takuna Misriyya," BL, 24 Sept. 1933, 1, 9.

194. Salama Musa, "al-Lugha al-Fusha wa al-Lugha al-'Ammiyya," HI, 34 (July 1926), 1077.

195. See ibid., 1075–1077; Niqula Yusuf, "Hal Lana Adab Qawmi?," SU, 26 Jan. 1929, 24; Muhammad 'Ali Hammad, "'Awdat al-Ruh: Bayna al-'Ammiyya wa al-'Arabiyya," RI, 15 Sept. 1933, 40–42.

196. Salama Musa, "al-Lugha al-Fusha wa al-Lugha al-'Ammiyya," HI, 34 (July 1926), 1075–1077. For a further elaboration of the concept, see his "Tarqiyyat al-Lugha al-'Arabiyya," MJ, July 1930, 1071, and his "al-Lugha wa al-Adab al-'Arabiyyan," ibid., Sept. 1935, 9–13.

197. Tawfiq 'Awwan, "al-Adab al-Qawmi Aydan," SU, 31 Aug. 1929, 23.

198. Muhammad Amin Hassuna, "Fi Sabil al-Da'wa ila al-Adab al-Qawmi," ibid., 19 July 1930, 9.

199. Ibid.

200. Ibid. For similar views, see also Ibrahim Ibrahim Jum'a, "Ayna Adabuna al-Qawmi?," ibid., 14 April 1928, 26; Ahmad Durini Khashaba, "Fi al-Adab al-Misri," MJ, Aug. 1931, 1192–1193.

201. Muhammad Husayn Haykal, *Zaynab: Manazir wa Akhlaq Rifiyya* (second ed.: Cairo, 1929). *Zaynab*'s original date of publication is usually given as 1914, but reviews of the work appeared in late 1913; see Sakkut, op. cit., 12.

202. Gibb, "Studies," 293; For general analyses of *Zaynab,* see ibid., 291–294; Badr, op. cit., 317–333; Sakkut, op. cit., 11–18; Somekh, op. cit., 1–5; Kilpatrick, op. cit., 20–26 (synopsis 200–201).

203. Gibb, "Studies," 294–295, 317.

204. For a summary of this discussion, see ibid., 295–298, and the discussion on the novel held in Egypt in 1931 (participants Ahmad Ramzi, Ahmad Khayri Sa'id, Husayn Fawzi, Mahmud Tahir Lashin, and Zaki Tulaymat); "al-Adab al-Qasasi fi Misr: Istifta'," MJ, June 1931, 961–970.

205. See Muhammad Husayn Haykal, "Hadith Shabab," *al-Jarida,* 11 April 1911, republished in his *Fi Awqat al-Faragh,* 337–342; Muhammad Husayn Haykal, "Hadith al-Shams," SF, 1 Sept. 1916, republished in ibid., 194–197; see also Semah, op. cit., 95.

206. Ibid., 184; Muhammad Lutfi Jum'a, "Muhammad Taymur wa Adabuhu," BU, 14 May 1930, 8–10.

207. See Badr, op. cit., 211–258, on the contribution of 'Isa 'Ubayd.

208. See ibid., 211–260; Gibb, "Studies," 299–318; Gibb and Landau, op. cit., 143–145; Roger Allen, *The Arabic Novel: An Historical and Critical Introduction* (Syracuse, 1982), 35–36.

209. For the early popularity of his stories, particularly those in these two collections, see FJ, 10 Feb. 1925, 3; ibid., 13 March 1925, 3; ibid., 24 April 1925, 1; ibid., 1 May 1925, 1; ibid., 8 May 1925, 1–2; ibid., 26 June 1925, 2; ibid., 24 Jan. 1926, 1–2; ibid., 1 July 1926, 2–4; and Muharram Kamal, "Rajab Afandi: Qissa Misriyya bi-Qalam al-Ustadh Mahmud Taymur," BU, 3 June 1927, 27–28.

210. For examples, see ibid.; Hafiz Mahmud, "Nahdat al-Qissa al-Misriyya," ibid., 13 May 1927, 19; Niqula Yusuf, "Hal Lana Adab Qawmi?," SU, 26 Jan. 1929, 24; Tawfiq Mikha'il Tuwaij, "Tatawwur al-Adab al-Qawmi wa Aghraduhu," ibid., 25 May 1929, 18; Ahmad Durini Khashaba, "Thaqafatuna al-Misriyya," MJ, Aug. 1930, 1237; Hafiz Mahmud, "Kalimat fi al-Adab al-Qawmi," SU, 2 Aug. 1930, 10; "al-Adab al-Qasasi fi Misr: Istifta'," MJ, June 1931, 961–970. See also Gibb and Landau, op. cit., 143–152.

211. Salama Musa, "Tahqiq al-Qawmiyya al-Misriyya," MJ, May 1931, 787.

212. Mahmūd Tahir Lashin, "Fi Bayt al-Ta'a," FJ, 17 Feb. 1925, 3–4; Mahmud Tahir Lashin, "al-Ustadh," ibid., 6 March 1925, 3; on the collections of his stories, see Ibrahim al-Misri, "Fann al-Qasas fi Misr," BU, 1 April 1927, 23. See also Badr, op. cit., 214–233; Sabry Hafez, "The Maturation of a New Literary Genre," *International Journal of Middle East Studies,* 16 (1984), 367–389.

213. Kilpatrick, op. cit., 51 (first published in HI, 41 (June 1933), 1097–1106, and HI, 41 (July 1933), 1241–1256).

214. This was the term later applied by Haykal himself to several of his stories and articles republished in his *Thawrat al-Adab,* 153–243.

215. Many of his short stories are available in his *Fi Awqat al-Faragh,* 269–336, and his *Thawrat al-Adab,* 161–243; for the optimistic tone of one of his short stories of the mid-1920s, see Charles D. Smith, "Love, Passion and Class in the Fiction of Muhammad Husayn Haykal," *Journal of the American Oriental Society,* 99 (1979), 254.

216. See Badr, op. cit., 173–178.

217. Ibid., 177.

218. See FJ between January 1925 and January 1927; see also Badr, op. cit., 221–233.

219. For the impact of *al-Ayyam* on Egyptian fiction, see ibid., 297–317; Gibb, "Studies," 297; Somekh, op. cit., 13; Allen, op. cit., 36–37.

220. Ibid., 37.

221. For discussions of this work, see ibid., 37–38; Badr, op. cit., 333–356; Somekh, op. cit., 14–17; Kilpatrick, op. cit., 26–30 (synopsis 201–202).

222. See above, chapters four, five, and eight. *'Awdat al-Ruh* is analyzed in Badr, op. cit., 372–397; Sakkut, op. cit., 85–88; Somekh, op. cit., 18–19; Cachia, op. cit., 227–228; Kilpatrick, op. cit., 41–44 (synopsis 205–206).

223. See Niqula Yusuf, "Hal Lana Adab Qawmi?," SU, 26 Jan. 1929, 24; Gibb and Landau, op. cit., 143–145.

224. Both are discussed in Jacob M. Landau, *Studies in the Arabic Theater and Cinema* (Philadelphia, 1958), 130–132.

225. For Fawzi's dramas, see FJ, 3 Feb. 1925, 3; ibid., 24 Feb. 1925, 3–4; ibid., 20 March 1925, 3–4. For the plays of Ramzi and 'Alam, see Muhammad Lutfi Jum'a, "al-Ta'lif al-Tamthili fi Misr,"

BU, 24 April 1929, 22. See also Semah, op. cit., 171–186. Abu Shadi's Pharaonic dramas are discussed in Badawi, op. cit., 117–119; Dayf, *al-Adab al-'Arabi al-Mu'asir,* 152; Salma Khadra Jayyusi, *Trends and Movements in Modern Arabic Poetry* (two vols.: Leiden, 1977), II, 377.

226. Landau, *Studies in the Arabic Theater and Cinema,* 82.

227. See "Hadith ma'a al-Ustadh Zaki Tulaymat," MJ, May 1931, 777–780; see also Landau, *Studies in the Arabic Theater and Cinema,* 92.

228. Cachia, op. cit., 226.

229. See FJ, 10 Feb. 1925, 1–2; ibid., 3 April 1925, 1–2; ibid., 13 April 1925, 1–2; ibid., 26 June 1925, 1–2.

230. See Muhammad Husayn Haykal, "al-Fann al-Misri: Juhud Jama'at al-Khayal fi Sabiliha," SU, 17 Dec. 1927, 23.

231. See ibid.; Muhammad Husayn Haykal, "Hal min Khatwa Jadida fi Sabil al-Fann al-Misri?," ibid., 7 Jan. 1928, 10.

232. See above, chapter eight, and also 'Ali Mas'ud, "Ihya' al-Fann al-Misri," ibid., 7 Jan. 1928, 3; "Mukhtar," MJ, May 1934, 7.

233. For detailed discussions of the *Diwan* group and their poetry, see Badawi, op. cit., 84–114; Jayyusi, op. cit., I, 152–175; S. Moreh, *Modern Arabic Poetry, 1800–1970* (Leiden, 1976), 65–81.

234. These points are developed in the discussion of the group in Badawi, op. cit., 89–91.

235. See Hawfi, op. cit., 152–257, 289–310, 337–423; Badawi, op. cit., 30–33, 39; Dasuqi, *Fi al-Adab al-Hadith,* II, 116–122.

236. Badawi, op. cit., 43–46; see also Dasuqi, *Fi al-Adab al-Hadith,* II, 113–116.

237. Published in HI, 32 (June 1924), 913; see also Dasuqi, *Fi al-Adab al-Hadith,* II, 145–146, 169–173; Jayyusi, op. cit., I, 146.

238. Dasuqi, *Fi al-Adab al-Hadith,* II, 122–158; Husayn, *Ittijahat,* II, 129–131.

239. Badawi, op. cit., 109–111.

240. Ibid., 117; Jayyusi, op. cit., II, 377.

241. See FJ, 28 Oct. 1926, 1–2; for Rami's poetry, see also Gibb and Landau, op. cit., 155.

242. Muhammad al-Asmar, "Watani," SU, 9 April 1927, 7; Muhammad al-Asmar, "Qudama' al-Misriyyin," ibid., 16 April 1927, 7.

243. On national anthems, see Dasuqi, *Fi al-Adab al-Hadith,* II, 159–161; the last is discussed in Mahmud Ahmad al-Hanafi, *Sayyid Darwish* (Cairo, 1964), 178.

244. Ibid.

Chapter 10. Egypt and the Arab World in the 1920s

1. See Eric Davis, *Challenging Colonialism: Bank Misr and Egyptian Industrialization, 1920–1941* (Princeton, 1983), 80–85.

2. Harb, op. cit., 137.

3. See his speeches delivered in Beirut and Damascus in July 1925; ibid., especially 131–132, 139–140.

4. For examples, see BU, 12 Aug. 1927, 2; ibid., 29 May 1929, 17.

5. Haykal's ideas on Arab cooperation in the 1920s may be seen in SU, 2 April 1927, 1; ibid., 19 Nov. 1927, 10; ibid., 17 Dec. 1927, 1–2; ibid., 24 Nov. 1928, 5–6; ibid., 8 Dec. 1928, 6.

6. 'Azmi's proposals were developed in detail in ibid., 11 Dec. 1926, 14–15; ibid., 18 Dec. 1926, 14; ibid., 1 Jan. 1927, 14; ibid., 15 Jan. 1927, 14; ibid., 22 Jan. 1927, 14; ibid., 5 Feb. 1927, 17.

7. Several of these are discussed in Shafiq, *A'mali,* 56–74, 154–171, 286.

8. Ibid., 275–278; "Hejaz: Banks and Banking," FO 141/819, 17993.

9. Shafiq, *A'mali,* 285.

10. RS, June 1929, 16–17; "Memorandum on the History and Activities of the Banque Misr," 6 Sept. 1930 (FO 141/560, 1094/1/30).

11. Ibid.; Davis, op. cit., 172–173.

12. Ibid., 174–175; see also FO 141/560, 1094/1/30.

13. Davis, op. cit., 175.

14. For the claim that Egyptian Jews associated with *Bank Misr* eventually came to oppose the idea of a branch bank in Palestine (by implication because of its possible effects on Zionism), see Muhammad 'Ali al-Tahir, *Nazarat al-Shura* (Cairo, 1932), 14.

15. Stonehewer-Bird to Chamberlain, 16 June 1928; FO 406/62, no. 8.

16. Trade statistics and percentages are from the publication of the Statistical Department, Egypt, *Annual Statement of the Foreign Trade of Egypt, 1929* (Cairo, 1930), 16–19.

17. Sayigh, op. cit., 181–182; 'Abd Allah, *Tatawwur,* 68–69.

18. Sayigh, op. cit., 180.

19. Discussed at length in Shafiq, *A'mali,* 56–74.

20. RS, Feb. 1930, 9, contains the first mention of an Egyptian student tour to an Arab region (to Syria and Lebanon for the summer of 1929) which we have been able to find.

21. Discussed in ibid., Feb. 1929, 31; ibid., April 1929, 1–2; ibid., May 1929, 1–5, 51.

22. Shafiq, *A'mali,* 154–161.

23. For a powerful example of this interpretation of Arab unity as anachronistic, see Hasan 'Arif, "'Arabiyya am Fir'awniyya," BL, 11 Oct. 1933, 5.

24. Sami al-Jaridini, "Tariq al-Sharq ila al-Qawmiyya," HI, 33 (May 1925), 857–860 (quotation from 859).

25. For the former, see *Fatawa,* 80–81; the latter comes from an editorial in AH, 5 July 1930, 1.

26. Muhammad 'Abd Allah 'Inan, "al-Misriyya: Turath Qawmi Athil li-Misr," MSI, 14 Oct. 1932, 9.

27. The first reference is from SU, 4 Dec. 1926, 16; the second from ibid., 17 March 1928, 3.

28. Quotations from ibid., 30 June 1928, 15.

29. Ibid., 18 Oct. 1930, 7.

30. For examples, see MU, 3 Nov. 1925, 1; SU, 30 Aug. 1930, 3; Jundi, *Ahmad Zaki.* 236.

31. See AH, 19 Aug. 1924 (as cited in Abu Zayd, op. cit., 128).

32. Coury, op. cit., 462.

33. Attributed to Zaghlul by Khayr al-Din al-Zirikli; see Akram Zu'aytir, "al-'Uruba fi Misr," *al-'Arabi,* no. 244 (March 1979), 12.

34. See BU, 12 Aug. 1927, 2; ibid., 23 Dec. 1927, 2; ibid., 21 Oct. 1927, 2, 35.

35. Quotations from ibid.; for a similar opinion from the Liberal press, see SU, 4 June 1927, 3.

36. See above, chapter three, for several examples.

37. Husayn Mahmud, "Misr wa al-Buldan al-'Arabiyya," MU, 9 Aug. 1930, 1.

38. Ibid. For additional examples of this attitude toward Arab cooperation, see Sami al-Jaridini, "Tariq al-Sharq ila al-Qawmiyya," HI, 33 (May 1925), 857–860; Ibrahim Ibrahim Jum'a, "Ayna Adabuna al-Qawmi?," SU, 14 April 1928, 26; Niqula Yusuf, "Misr ba'da Khamsat Qurun," ibid., 7 Sept. 1929, 24–25; Nashid Sayfin, "Misr Fir'awniyya Lahman wa Damman," MU, 19 Aug. 1930, 3; Ahmad al-Hafni, "Misr wa Kafa," ibid., 15 Oct. 1930, 1; Hafiz Mahmud, "Misr bi-Majdiha Ula," MJ, Feb. 1931, 474–476; Muhammad 'Abd Allah 'Inan, "al-Misriyya: Turath Qawmi Athil li-Misr," MSI, 14 Oct. 1932, 9; Hasan 'Arif, "Ayna al-Qawmiyya al-Misriyya?," BL, 19 Sept. 1933, 1, 11; Mahmud Diyab, "Misr Misriyya," ibid., 6 Oct. 1933, 1; Hasan 'Arif, "'Arabiyya am Fir'awniyya," ibid., 11 Oct. 1933, 5.

39. See Qallini Fahmi, op. cit., II, 73.

40. 'Abd al-Rahman al-Rafi'i, *Fi A'qab al-Thawra al-Misriyya* (three vols.: Cairo, 1947–1951), II, 43–44, 74–75.

41. Arnold J. Toynbee, assisted by V. M. Boulter, *Survey of International Affairs, 1934* (London, 1935), 187.

42. At one point, Egyptian press criticisms concerning French military operations against the Riffian rebels drew an official French protest delivered to the Egyptian authorities; reported in Henderson to Chamberlain, 6 July 1925 (FO 407/201, no. 9).

43. See Kramer, "The General Islamic Congress," 25–27.

44. Allenby to Curzon, 7 Jan. 1924; FO 407/198, no. 10.

45. Clark Kerr to Marquess Curzon, 13 Jan. 1924; FO 407/198, no. 32; see also Shafiq, *Hawliyyat, 1924,* 68–73; Lashin, op. cit., 367–368.

46. Allenby to MacDonald, 7 March 1924; FO 407/198, no. 94.

47. See the review of the border question in Allenby to Chamberlain, 11 June 1925 (FO 407/201, no. 16).

48. For British pressure on the Egyptians, see FO 407/201, nos. 170, 189, 197, 207, 210, 211.

49. See FO 407/201, nos. 231 and 237, concerning the agreement.

50. Material on Egyptian reactions to the Jaghbub issue is available in FO 407/202, no. 187;

Shafiq, *Hawliyyat, 1925,* 209–228, 377–405, 461–470, 1013–1026; Shafiq, *Hawliyyat, 1926,* 98–102; and Muhsin Muhammad, *Sariqat Waha Misriyya* (Cairo, 1981), 154–160.

51. BL, 12 Feb. 1925, as cited in Shafiq, *Hawliyyat, 1925,* 212.

52. AK as quoted in Lord Lloyd to Chamberlain, 12 Feb. 1926; FO 407/202, no. 187.

53. KS as quoted in same to same, 21 Dec. 1925; FO 371/11581, J25/25/16.

54. Allenby to Foreign Office, 28 Nov. 1923, and Foreign Office to Allenby, 3 Dec. 1923; FO 371/8940, E11372/46/91.

55. Reprinted in the Egyptian *Journal Officiel* of 9 April 1925 and enclosed in FO 141/811, 16801/8.

56. "Pilgrimage Report, 1923," in FO 406/53, no. 75; cf. Toynbee, *Survey, 1925,* 290–292; Baker, op. cit., 182; Sir Reader Bullard, *The Camels Must Go: An Autobiography* (London, 1961), 126–127.

57. Quotation from ibid., 136; also discussed in Allenby to MacDonald, 24 Aug. 1924 (FO 371/10016, E7696/7696/91).

58. AH, 4 Oct. 1924, 1; see also SI, 6 Oct. 1924, 1.

59. See Clark Kerr to MacDonald, 5 Oct. 1924; FO 407/199, no. 31.

60. See respectively AK, 7 Oct. 1924, 1–2; KS, 28 Sept. 1924, 1; BL, 6 Oct. 1924, 1.

61. BL, 7 Oct. 1924, 2; AK, 7 Oct. 1924, 1–2.

62. 'Abbas Mahmud al-'Aqqad writing in BL, 19 Oct. 1924, 1; see also AK, 7 Oct. 1924, 1–2.

63. BL, 19 Oct. 1924, 1.

64. AK, 6 Oct. 1924, 1.

65. KS, 29 Sept. 1924, 4; see also ibid., 28 Sept. 1924, 1.

66. SI, 6 Oct. 1924, 1.

67. AH, 7 Oct. 1924; see also BL, 9 Oct. 1924, 2; Toynbee, *Survey, 1925,* 293.

68. The Wafdist attitude toward politics in the Arabian peninsula remained indifferent throughout the 1920s; as late as 1930, then Prime Minister Mustafa al-Nahhas responded to a British inquiry concerning the prospects for Egyptian recognition of Sa'udi Arabia with the admission that "he was not very familiar with the situation in the Peninsula" (memorandum on "Recognition of ibn Saud by Egypt," 12 Feb. 1930; FO 141/501, 583/1/30).

69. Clark Kerr to MacDonald, 11 Oct. 1924; FO 406/54, no. 176.

70. Acting Agent, Jidda, to Chamberlain, 3 Aug. 1925 (FO 406/56, no. 129); telegram from Henderson, 2 Aug. 1929 (FO 371/10809, E4521/10/91).

71. Telegram from Acting British Consul, Jidda, 3 Aug. 1925 (FO 371/10809, E4556/10/91); see also Martin Kramer, "Shaykh al-Maraghi's Mission to the Hijaz, 1925," *Asian and African Studies,* 16 (1982), 124–125.

72. Chamberlain to Henderson, 7 Aug. 1925 (FO 406/56, no. 130); Henderson to Murray, 9 Aug. 1925, (FO 371/10809, E4901/10/91).

73. Henderson to Jordan (Jidda), 14 Sept. 1925 (FO 406/56, no. 148); see also Jundi, *al-Imam al-Maraghi,* 109.

74. Kramer, "Shaykh Maraghi's Mission," 129–130.

75. Henderson to Chamberlain, 6 Oct. 1925; FO 406/56, no. 151.

76. Kramer, "Shaykh Maraghi's Mission," 130–132.

77. Ibid., 131.

78. On Abu al-'Aza'im and his connections with ibn Sa'ud in 1926, see the "Secret Despatch to Jeddah from the British Embassy, Cairo," 29 May 1926; FO 371/11433, E3505/20/91.

79. Zawahiri, op. cit., 241–242; for the Liberal position, see SI, 2 June 1926, 1; ibid., 25 June 1926, 1.

80. Keown Boyd to Hamilton, 22 Aug. 1926; FO 141/792, 18540/5.

81. Sékaly, op. cit., 209.

82. Ibid., 181–182; Zawahiri, op. cit., 244.

83. Sékaly, op. cit., 205–206.

84. See the Egyptian, Sa'udi, and British Legation versions, all contained in FO 141/792, 18512; see also Shafiq, *Hawliyyat, 1926,* 202, 267–271, 283–290.

85. Toynbee, *Survey, 1925,* 319.

86. Lord Lloyd to Chamberlain, 14 May 1927; FO 406/59, no. 39. See also Jacques Jomier, *Le Mahmal et la caravane égyptienne des pèlirins de la Mecque* (Cairo, 1953), 67–69.

87. Henderson to Chamberlain, 21 Aug. 1926; FO 371/11432, E5065/7/91.

88. Ibid.

89. Ibid.

90. Lord Lloyd to Henderson, 15 June 1929; FO 371/13735, E3214/1477/91. For further information on the futile efforts to formalize Egyptian-Sa'udi relations in the late 1920s and early 1930s, see 'Abd Allah, *Tatawwur,* 122–130; FO 141/501, 583/4/30; FO 371/13735, E3214/1477/91; FO 371/13859, J930/49/16 and J1417/49/16; FO 371/14479, E1539/1539/91; FO 371/16013, E63/63/25.

91. Reported in a telegram from Lord Lloyd, 4 March 1929; FO 371/13721, E1173/54/91.

92. Ibid.; Lord Lloyd to Chamberlain, 5 April 1929; FO 371/13721, E1889/54/91.

93. Quotation from ibid.; see also Foreign Office to Lord Lloyd, 15 May 1929 (FO 371/13721, E2392/54/91).

94. AH, 6 Oct. 1924, 1.

95. Allenby to Chamberlain, 5 April 1925; FO 371/10908, J1569/1569/16.

96. For examples, see MU, 20 Oct. 1925, 7; ibid., 25 Oct. 1925, 2; ibid., 29 Oct. 1925, 2; AH, 26 Oct. 1925, 1; ibid., 30 Oct. 1925, 1; ibid., 31 Oct. 1925, 5.

97. Quotations from British evaluations of this Syrian activism are contained in FO 141/585, 13089/33. For French indignation over the political activity of Syrians in Egypt, see telegram from Smart (Damascus), 16 Nov. 1925 (FO 371/10852, E7051/357/89); telegram from Lord Lloyd (Cairo), 8 April 1926 (FO 371/11509, E2288/52/89).

98. Amin Sa'id, *al-Thawra al-'Arabiyya al-Kubra* (three vols.: Cairo, 1934), III, 599–601; see also Philip S. Khoury, "Factionalism Among Syrian Nationalists during the French Mandate," *International Journal of Middle East Studies,* 13 (1981), 441–469, especially 468.

99. Egyptian press reaction to events in Syria is surveyed in the despatch of Lord Lloyd to Chamberlain, 23 Nov. 1925 (FO 407/201, no. 54). For poetry on the subject, see Husayn, *Ittijahat,* II, 118–120, and Samira Muhammad Zaki Abu Ghazala, *al-Shi'r al-'Arabi al-Qawmi fi Misr wa al-Sham* (Cairo, 1966), 67–70.

100. Sa'id, *al-Thawra al-'Arabiyya al-Kubra,* III, 601; SI, 1 Nov. 1925, 2; Shafiq, *Mudhakkirati,* III, 324.

101. The declaration was published in KS, 6 Nov. 1925, 4; see also Lord Lloyd to Chamberlain, 23 Nov. 1925 (FO 407/201, no. 54).

102. See Coury, op. cit., 252.

103. KS, 6 Nov. 1925, 4.

104. Ibid., 9 Nov. 1925, 5.

105. See 'Azzam's later recollections as published in *al-Usbu' al-'Arabi,* 17 Jan. 1972, 43. While 'Azzam did not date his conversation with Zaghlul in the above memoir, he mentioned the incident and set it in its proper temporal context in a private letter to a British official in 1933; see FO 141/744, 834/2/33. For a secondhand account of the incident based on a later conversation with 'Azzam, see Zu'aytir, "al-'Uruba fi Misr," 10–11.

106. Acting High Commissioner Nevile Henderson to Acting Prime Minister Yahya Ibrahim, 6 Oct. 1925; FO 371/10908, J3207/1569/16.

107. See the Egyptian note contained in Henderson to Chamberlain, 7 Feb. 1926 (FO 371/11605, J397/397/16); British acceptance of the reservation is contained in a letter from the High Commissioner to Egyptian Foreign Minister Sarwat (FO 141/664, 8002/32).

108. See BU, 13 Dec. 1927, 2.

109. See Gabriel Warburg, "The Sinai Peninsula Borders, 1906–47," *Journal of Contemporary History,* 14 (1979), 683–684; Kenneth J. Perkins, "Colonial Administration in the Twilight of Imperialism: Great Britain and the Egyptian Frontier Districts Administration, 1917–1939," *Middle Eastern Studies,* 18 (1982), 411–412, 419.

110. Extract from the *Journal Officiel,* 15 Aug. 1927, as contained in FO 141/664, 8002/35.

111. KS, 28 Dec. 1928, as cited in 'Awatif 'Abd al-Rahman, *Misr wa Filastin* (Cairo, 1980), 113–114.

112. Material on Zionist contacts with Egyptian leaders in the 1920s may be found in Frederick H. Kisch, *Palestine Diary* (London, 1938), 67, 109–110, 118–119, 167; Aharon Cohen, *Israel and the Arab World* (New York, 1970), 184–188, 245–246, 299–300; Barry Rubin, *The Arab States and the Palestine Conflict* (Syracuse, 1981), 33–36; Thomas Mayer, *Egypt and the Palestine Question, 1936–1945* (Berlin, 1983), 10–13.

113. Material on Palestinian Arab efforts to attract Egyptian support may be found in Y. Porath, *The Emergence of the Palestinian-Arab National Movement, 1918–1929* (London, 1974), 206, 263–264;

Ann Mosely Lesch, *Arab Politics in Palestine, 1917–1939* (Ithaca, 1979), 138, 158–159; Mayer, *Egypt,* 13–15.

114. 'Abd al-Rahman, op. cit., 119–120.

115. Ibid., 128–131.

116. Ibid., 134–137.

117. Ibid., 143–151.

118. Ibid., 149–150.

119. Shafiq, *Mudhakkirati,* III, 305–307; Porath, op. cit., 206; extract from the Egyptian *Journal Officiel* of 26 Feb. 1929, enclosed in FO 141/513, 12339/27.

120. Allenby to Samuel, 16 June 1923 (FO 141/513, 12339/16); same to same, 18 June 1923 (FO 141/513, 12339/17); Samuel to Allenby, 23 June 1923 (FO 141/513, 12339/20); Kisch, op. cit., 109.

121. Mayer, *Egypt.* 14.

122. Quotation from Lord Lloyd to Chamberlain, 30 April 1926 (FO 371/11582, J1144/25/16). See also Allenby to Samuel, 16 June 1923 (FO 141/513, 12339/16); report from the Cairo City Police, 17 Jan. 1929 (FO 141/513, 12339/26); Shafiq, *A'mali,* 53–54, 70; A. W. Kayyali, *Palestine: A Modern History* (London, 1978), 141.

123. Mayer, *Egypt,* 14–15.

124. Ibid., 13.

125. See the sources cited in note 112, above.

126. Kisch, op. cit., 67, 118.

127. See Tariq al-Bishri, *al-Haraka al-Siyasiyya fi Misr, 1945–1952* (Cairo, 1972), 241; Khayriyya Qasimiyya and B. Nuwayhid al-Hut, "Faqiran Filastiniyyan Kabiran: 'Abd al-Hamid Shuman wa Muhammad 'Ali al-Tahir," *Shu'un Filastiniyya,* no. 39 (Nov. 1974), 143–163, especially 151.

128. See Kisch, op. cit., 167; Mayer, *Egypt,* 12.

129. 'Abd al-Rahman, op. cit., 204–212.

130. Lord Lloyd to Chamberlain, 30 April 1926; FO 371/11582, J1144/25/16.

131. Hoare to Henderson, 31 Aug. 1929; FO 371/13753, E4575/4198/65.

132. Reprinted in MU, 18 Sept. 1929, 1.

133. Almost £E 800 by March 1930; see SM, 1 (1929–1930), 442.

134. See AH, Aug. 31, 1929, 5; MU, 12 Sept. 1929, 6; ibid., 17 Sept. 1929, 5.

135. Their testimony is given in SU, 2 Aug. 1930, 13, 26; ibid., 9 Aug. 1930, 11, 22. For the genesis of their involvement in the issue, see Jundi, *Ahmad Zaki,* 247–250; Muhammad 'Ali 'Alluba, *Filastin wa Jaratiha: Asbab wa Nata'ij* (Cairo, 1954), 37–38. The parallel offer of several prominent Egyptian lawyers to assist in the defense of Palestinian Arabs placed on trial as a result of the disturbances apparently never materialized: see RS, Dec. 1929, 46–48; Mayer, *Egypt,* 19.

136. See SM, 1 (1929–1930), 73–79, 148–150, 211–213, 643, 733, 880; AH, 27 Aug. 1929, 5; ibid., 30 Aug. 1929, 5; SI, 30 Aug. 1929, 5.

137. AH, 27 Aug. 1929, 5; ibid., 31 Aug. 1929, 4; ibid., 11 Sept. 1929, 1; ibid., 19 Sept. 1929, 1; MU, 29 Aug. 1929, 3; SI, 27 Aug. 1929, 5; ibid., 30 Aug. 1929, 5; BL, 1 Sept. 1929, 1; ibid., 4 Sept. 1929, 1.

138. AH, 31 Aug. 1929, 5; ibid., 1 Sept. 1929, 5; BL, 4 Sept. 1929, 1; RS, Nov. 1929, 2–7; ibid., Dec. 1929, 46–48; ibid., May 1930, 53–54.

139. AH, 31 Aug. 1929, 5; see also Mayer, *Egypt,* 18.

140. Ikbal Ali Shah, *Fuad, King of Egypt* (London, 1936), 309.

141. Letter enclosed in the despatch from Loraine to Henderson, 14 Sept. 1929; FO 371/13753, E4860/4198/65.

142. Reported in a letter from Sir George Clerk to Henderson, 3 Sept. 1929; FO 371/13753, E4557/204/65.

143. Reported in Hoare to Henderson, 31 Aug. 1929; FO 371/13753, E4575/4198/65.

144. Palestinian Arab sources as cited in Mayer, *Egypt,* 21–22.

145. Ibid., 22.

146. Russell to Keown-Boyd, 10 Sept. 1930; FO 141/625, 808/4/30.

147. For a general discussion of Egyptian press reaction in 1929, see 'Abd al-Rahman, op. cit., 226–234.

148. See MU, 24 Sept. 1929, 1.

149. See respectively MU, 28 Aug. 1929, 1; SI, 31 Aug. 1929, 1; and MU, 17 Sept. 1929, 1. See also 'Abd al-Rahman, op. cit., 73–74, 128–129, 132.

150. For examples, see AH, 24 Aug. 1929, 1; MU, 29 Aug. 1929, 3; and SM, 1 (1929–1930), 73–79, 880.

151. See the examples in MU, 29 Aug. 1929, 3; AH, 3 Sept. 1929, 5; BL, 4 Sept. 1929, 1. See also Mayer, *Egypt,* 17.

152. Such was the position of the Young Men's Muslim Association and the Eastern Bond Society: see RS, Oct. 1928, 61–64; AH, 24 Aug. 1929, 1; ibid., 1 Sept. 1929, 5.

153. See the editorials in MU, 27 Aug. 1929, 1; ibid., 10 Sept. 1929, 1; AH, 25 Aug. 1929, 3; SI, 31 Aug. 1929, 1; BL, 2 Sept. 1929, 2; ibid., 16 Sept. 1929, 2, for examples of this perspective.

154. The term is quoted in the editorial in BL, 16 Sept. 1929, 2. For similar interpretations, see AH, 25 Aug. 1929, 3; MU, 30 Aug. 1929, 1; ibid., 10 Sept. 1929, 1. See also 'Abd al-Rahman, op. cit., 75, 119–120.

155. BL, 9 Sept. 1929, 2; see also the similar solution proposed in MU, 10 Sept. 1929, 1.

156. MU, 4 Sept. 1929, 1, blamed the problem in Palestine on "the Zionists" and maintained that most Jews disapproved of Zionism.

157. Thus MU published several statements from Jewish writers presenting their interpretations of the controversy; see MU, 29 Aug. 1929, 7; ibid., 3 Sept. 1929, 5; ibid., 20 Sept. 1929, 3; ibid., 21 Sept. 1929, 7.

158. SI, 1 Sept. 1929, 1.

159. MU, 27 Aug. 1929, 1.

160. BL, 9 Sept. 1929, 2.

161. AH, 29 Sept. 1929, 1.

162. SI, 28 Aug. 1929, 1.

163. Ibid., 31 Aug. 1929, 1.

164. Ibid., 4 Sept. 1929, 1.

165. Ibid., 1 Sept. 1929, 1.

Chapter 11. "Easternism" in Egypt in the 1920s

A preliminary version of this chapter appeared under the title "The Eastern Idea and the Eastern Union in Interwar Egypt" in the *International Journal of African Historical Studies,* 14 (1981), 643–666.

1. For Afghani's use of the term, see Hourani, op. cit., 118–119; for Zaydan's, see Thomas Philipp, "Language, History, and Arab National Consciousness in the Thought of Jurji Zaydan (1861–1914)," *International Journal of Middle East Studies,* 4 (1973), 3–22, especially 10–11; for Nadim's, Wendell, op. cit., 157–158. For other prewar usages of the concept of the "East," see Hourani, op. cit., 195; Wendell, op. cit., 222–241, 257–263; Sharabi, op. cit., 44–45, 59–60, 96–100; Donald M. Reid, *The Odyssey of Farah Antun* (Minneapolis, 1975), 98–101.

2. KS, 21 Sept. 1924, as quoted in Abu Zayd, op. cit., 71–72; for a similar interchangeable use of "Easterners" and "Muslims," see SM, 1 (1929–1930), 18–22.

3. This was the prevalent usage of the term by the Liberal publicists Mahmud 'Azmi and Muhammad Husayn Haykal in the 1920s, who, while occasionally referring to a broader "East" beyond the Arab community, more often meant cooperation between the lands of the Arab East when they wrote of "Eastern" cooperation: see SU, 4 Dec. 1926, 16; ibid., 11 Dec. 1926, 14–15; ibid., 11 Feb. 1928, 14, 16. See also Zu'aytir, "Sharqiyyun am 'Arab," 19.

4. Thus the "Eastern" columns or pages of newspapers such as *al-Balagh* and *Kawkab al-Sharq* generally concentrated on material relating to Turkey, Iran, Afghanistan, and the Arab world.

5. Such was the case with the Eastern Bond Society, which is discussed later in this chapter.

6. For the first, see Ahmad Shafiq, "Jam'iyyat al-Rabita al-Sharqiyya: Madiha—Hadiruha—Mustaqbaluha," RS, Oct. 1928, 3–11, especially 11; the latter is used in Jalal al-Din Husayn, "Jama'at al-Rabita al-Sharqiyya: al-Da'wa li-Nahdat al-Sharq," SU, 13 Sept. 1930, 25.

7. For the use of the term "al-wataniyya al-khassa," see Muhammad Husayn Haykal, "al-Jami'a al-Misriyya wa al-Umam al-Sharqiyya," SU, 26 March 1927, 27; for "al-wataniyya al-'amma," see "al-Umam al-Sharqiyya wa Silatuha al-Ma'nawiyya," SU, 4 Dec. 1926, 16.

8. "*al-Siyasa al-Usbu'iyya* fi Sanatiha al-Thalitha," SU, 17 March 1928, 3.

9. "Laysat Misr Qit'a min Urubba," KS, 1 Nov. 1924, 1.

10. "al-Fikra al-Sharqiyya," MSI, 14 Oct. 1932, 17.

11. Ibid.
12. Editorial entitled "al-Wahda al-Sharqiyya," SU, 30 Aug. 1930, 3.
13. Mansur Fahmi, "Safahat Sharqiyya," RS, Oct. 1928, 31.
14. "Mas'alat al-Yawm: Wajib al-Jar ila al-Jar," KS, 6 Nov. 1925, 4.
15. "al-Harb al-Rifiyya wa Sadaha fi Umam al-Sharq," SI, 25 Oct. 1925, 1.
16. "al-Sharq wa al-Gharb," RS, Feb. 1929, 3–11 (quotation from 11).
17. "'Ala Minbar al-Sharq," HI, 38 (July 1930), 1037.
18. 'Ali 'Abd al-Raziq, "Khusum al-Rabita al-Sharqiyya min al-Sharqiyyin," RS, Jan. 1930, 26–27.
19. HI, 38 (July 1930), 1036.
20. Hasan Ahmad al-Banna, "Inna fi Dhalika li-'Ibra," FH, 7 Feb. 1929, 1–2; Hasan Ahmad al-Banna, "al-Sabil ila al-Islah fi al-Sharq," ibid., 25 April 1929, 1–3.
21. Banna, "'Ibra," 1–2.
22. Banna, "Sabil," 3.
23. Banna, "'Ibra," 2.
24. Ibid.
25. Banna, "Sabil," 2.
26. Banna, "'Ibra," 2.
27. Ibid.
28. al-Sayyid 'Abd al-Hamid al-Bakri, "al-Sharq wa al-Gharb," RS, Feb. 1929, 11; for another example from a spokesman of the Eastern Bond Society, see 'Ali 'Abd al-Raziq, "Khusum al-Rabita al-Sharqiyya min al-Sharqiyyin," ibid., Jan. 1930, 26.
29. For examples, see HI, 32 (Nov. 1923), 11–19; MQ, 71 (Aug. 1927), 141; Muhammad Lutfi Jum'a, *Hayat al-Sharq* (Cairo, 1932?), 13–16.
30. HI, 39 (Nov. 1930), 23.
31. Ibid.
32. "al-Islam wa al-Sharq," MSI, 14 Oct. 1932, 16. For similar aspirations, see Ahmad Shafiq, "Jam'iyyat al-Rabita al-Sharqiyya: Madiha—Hadiruha—Mustaqbaluha," RS, Oct. 1928, 11; al-Sayyid 'Abd al-Hamid al-Bakri, "al-Sharq wa al-Gharb," ibid., Feb. 1929, 11.
33. 'Ali 'Abd al-Raziq, "Khusum al-Rabita al-Sharqiyya min al-Sharqiyyin," RS, Jan. 1930, 27.
34. "al-Sharq wa al-Gharb," ibid., Feb. 1929, 1–11.
35. "*al-Siyasa* fi Sanatiha al-Thalitha," SI, 31 Oct. 1924, 1.
36. Prince 'Umar Tusun in his interview entitled "'Ala Minbar al-Sharq," HI, 38 (July 1930), 1036.
37. "al-Haraka al-'Ilmiyya fi Misr wa Atharuha fi Jaratiha al-Sharqiyya," SU, 17 Dec. 1927, 1–2.
38. "Ma Kanat al-Haraka al-Wataniyya al-Misriyya Taba'an li-Qadiyyat al-Sharq, Bal Kanat Qadwatan wa Imaman," KS, 4 July 1930, 1.
39. Ahmad Shafiq, "Jam'iyyat al-Rabita al-Sharqiyya: Madiha—Hadiruha—Mustaqbaluha," RS, Oct. 1928, 3.
40. For examples, see HI, 30 (March 1922), 569–570; "al-Wahda al-Sharqiyya," SU, 30 Aug. 1930, 3; "Mu'ahadat al-Sadaqa bayna al-Umam al-Sharqiyya," BU, 11 May 1927, 8–9.
41. Ahmad Zaki as quoted in Jundi, *Ahmad Zaki,* 236.
42. See "Mu'ahadat al-Sadaqa bayna al-Umam al-Sharqiyya," BU, 11 May 1927, 8–9.
43. Sanhoury, *Le Califat,* 596–604.
44. Ibid., 605–607.
45. Ibid., 607.
46. Ahmad Hafiz 'Awad in an editorial in KS, 21 Sept. 1924, 1, as quoted in Abu Zayd, op. cit., 71–72.
47. "al-Umam al-Sharqiyya wa Silatuha al-Ma'nawiyya," SU, 4 Dec. 1926, 16.
48. "Hawla Da'wa ila al-Rabita al-Sharqiyya," RS, Dec. 1930–Jan. 1931, 7.
49. Discussed in Shafiq, *A'mali,* 56–74.
50. See RS, Feb. 1929, 31; ibid., April 1929, 1–2; ibid., May 1929, 1–5, 51; ibid., July 1931, 6–8.
51. See the biographical sketch of Fathi Radwan in *Majallat al-Jil al-Jadid,* 7 Nov. 1952, 4–7.
52. For representative examples, see MU, 7 Nov. 1925, 3; ibid., 14 Aug. 1929, 1; ibid., 15 Feb. 1931, 1.
53. See SU, 19 Feb. 1927, 15 (reprinting an article from a Syrian journal); ibid., 26 March 1927, 27 (reprinting an article from a Palestinian paper); ibid., 18 June 1927, 4 (printing a letter from a Palestinian Arab).

54. For bibliographical data on these journals, see 'Abd Allah, *Fihris,* 92, 123, 154, 193, 279, 282.

55. Shafiq, *Hawliyyat, tamhid* I, 335–337.

56. Haykal, *Mudhakkirat,* I, 88–89.

57. For examples, see SU, 17 March 1928, 3; ibid., 30 June 1928, 3; ibid., 29 Dec. 1928, 3–4.

58. Quoted in Radwan, *'Asr wa Rijal,* 402–404.

59. See KS, 9 Nov. 1925, 5.

60. Ibid., 29 Sept. 1924, 3.

61. See chapter five for Musa's views on "Eastern" bonds.

62. Allenby to Balfour, 30 June 1922; FO 371/7847, E6907/274/89.

63. HI, 30 (March 1922), 569–570, from which the following is taken.

64. According to Shafiq, *Mudhakkirati,* III, 317–319.

65. HI, 30 (March 1922), 569–570, lists the membership. The date of the selection of the Council is given in RS, Oct. 1928, 4.

66. Berque, *Egypt,* 274.

67. The membership of the Liberal Constitutionalist council is given in Deeb, *Party Politics,* 113.

68. RS, Oct. 1928, 6.

69. Shafiq, *Mudhakkirati,* III, 325–326.

70. According to a report in FH, 17 May 1928, 4–6.

71. From a listing of lectures as given in RS, Oct. 1928, 4–6.

72. "Note on the Rabta El Sharkia (Bond of the East)," enclosed in Lord Lloyd to Chamberlain, 26 March 1926; FO 371/11433, E2219/20/91.

73. Unless otherwise noted, the information in the following two paragraphs is taken from ibid.; Shafiq, *Mudhakkirati,* III, 317–331; and RS, Oct. 1928, 1–11.

74. SI, 23 May 1926, 5; Shafiq, *A'mali,* 134–137.

75. Ibid., 280; Jundi, *Ahmad Zaki,* 243–245.

76. KS, 31 Oct. 1925, 6; SI, 9 Nov. 1925, 1.

77. The report is contained in a despatch from Consul General Parr (Damascus) to Chamberlain, 23 Aug. 1927; FO 37112556, N4338/354/97. The rejoinder came from the Cairo Chancery on 28 Oct. 1927; FO 371/12556, N5239/354/97.

78. Discussed in Shafiq, *A'mali,* 181–184.

79. "Note on the Rabta El Sharkia (Bond of the East)," enclosed in Lord Lloyd to Chamberlain, 26 March 1926; FO 371/11433, E2219/20/91.

80. Shafiq, *A'mali,* 293.

81. Musa, *al-Yawm wa al-Ghad,* 9.

82. According to a report written by a member of the Administrative Council of the Society and published in FH, 19 Jan. 1929, 14–15.

83. See ibid., 31 Jan. 1929, 9–13; ibid., 7 March 1929, 8–12. Cf. Shafiq, *Mudhakkirati,* III, 334–335.

84. "Nahnu wa Sahib *al-Manar,*" RS, Feb. 1929, 17–20.

85. Ibid., March 1929, 47–48.

86. FH, 7 March 1929, 8.

87. Ibid., 7 Feb. 1929, 15.

88. See RS, Oct. 28, 1928, 24–26; ibid., Dec. 1928, 3; ibid., Feb. 1930, 47–48; ibid., July 1931, 24–26.

89. Ibid., Feb. 1929, 80.

90. Ibid., Oct. 1928, 9; ibid., Feb. 1929, 31; ibid., April 1929, 1–2; ibid., May 1929, 1–5, 51; ibid., May 1930, 53–54; ibid., May 1931, 45; ibid., July 1931, 6–8; Shafiq, *Mudhakkirati,* III, 329.

91. RS, Nov. 1929, 27–28; ibid., Feb. 1930, 48.

92. Ibid., Oct. 1928, 61–64; ibid., Dec. 1928, 93–96; ibid., Feb. 1929, 76; ibid., Dec. 1929, 46–48; ibid., April 1930, 53–54; ibid., July 1930, 49.

93. See ibid., Dec. 1928, 1–6; ibid., March 1929, 5–8.

94. See ibid., Oct. 1930, 1; ibid., Nov. 1930, 1–2.

95. Ibid., Oct. 1930, 51; ibid., Nov. 1930, 47–48; Shafiq, *Mudhakkirati,* III, 331.

96. RS, May 1931, 46.

97. Horne to Henderson, 27 Feb. 1931; FO 371/15282, E1205/1205/65.

98. RS, May 1931, 45–46.

99. Ibid., July 1931, 1–2.

Bibliography

Unpublished Sources

Great Britain; Public Record Office; Foreign Office; Series
- 141—Embassy and Consular, Egypt
- 371—General Correspondence, Political
- 395—General Correspondence, News
- 406—Confidential Print: Eastern Affairs
- 407—Confidential Print: Egypt and the Sudan
- 839—Lausanne Conference
- 848—Milner Mission

Abbas Hilmi II Papers (Sudan Archive, Oriental Section, Durham University Library)

Interviews with
- Husayn Fawzi, 20–29 July and 24–26 Sept. 1980
- Hafiz Mahmud, 19–21 July 1980

Egyptian Periodicals

al-Ahram
al-Akhbar
Apulu
al-Balagh
al-Balagh al-Usbu'i
Egyptian Gazette
al-Fath
al-Fajr
al-Hadith (Aleppo)
al-Hilal
al-Jarida
Kawkab al-Sharq
al-Liwa'

al-Majalla al-Jadida
Misr
al-Muqtataf
al-Muqattam
al-Rabita al-Sharqiyya
al-Risala
al-Sarkha
al-Shubban al-Muslimun
al-Siyasa
Mulhaq al-Siyasa
al-Siyasa al-Usbu'iyya
al-Sufur
al-'Usur
al-Watan

Works in Arabic Cited in the Text

'Abd Allah, Mahmud Isma'il. *Fihris al-Dawriyyat al-lati Taqtaniha al-Dar.* Cairo, 1961.
'Abd Allah, Nabih Bayyumi. *Tatawwur Fikrat al-Qawmiyya al-'Arabiyya fi Misr.* Cairo, 1975.
'Abd al-Jawad, Muhammad. *Taqwim Dar al-'Ulum.* Cairo, 1952.
'Abd al-Rahman, 'Awatif. *Misr wa Filastin.* Cairo, 1980.
'Abd al-Raziq, 'Ali. *al-Islam wa Usul al-Hukm.* Third ed. Cairo, 1925.
Abu al-Fath, Mahmud. *al-Mas'ala al-Misriyya wa al-Wafd.* Cairo, 1921?.
Abu Ghazala, Samira Muhammad Zaki. *al-Shi'r al-'Arabi al-Qawmi fi Misr wa al-Sham.* Cairo, 1966.
Abu Shadi, Ahmad Zaki. *Akhnatun: Fir'awn Misr.* Cairo, 1927.
Abu Zayd, Faruq. *Azmat al-Fikr al-Qawmi fi al-Sihafa al-Misriyya.* Cairo, 1976.
'Alluba, Muhammad 'Ali. *Dhikrayyat Ijtima'iyya wa Siyasiyya.* Cairo, 1982.
———. *Filastin wa Jaratiha: Asbab wa Nata'ij.* Cairo, 1954.
Amin, Ahmad. *Fayd al-Khatir: Majmu' Maqalat Adabiyya wa Ijtima'iyya.* Second ed. Ten vols. Cairo, 1946.
——— and 'Abd al-'Aziz al-Bishri. *Kitab al-Tarbiyya al-Wataniyya.* Sixth ed. Cairo, 1934.
al-'Aqqad, 'Abbas Mahmud. *al-Fusul: Majmu'at Maqalat Adabiyya wa Ijtima'iyya.* Cairo, 1922.
———. *Muraja'at fi al-Adab wa al-Funun.* Cairo, 1925.
———. *Mutala'at fi al-Kutub wa al-Hayat.* Cairo, 1924.
———. *Sa'at bayna al-Kutub.* Cairo, 1929.
———. *Sa'd Zaghlul: Sira wa Tahiyya.* Cairo, 1936.
'Arif, Jamil (ed.). *Safahat min al-Mudhakkirat al-Sirriya li-Awwal Amin 'Amm lil-Jami'a al-'Arabiyya, 'Abd al-Rahman 'Azzam.* Cairo, 1978 or 1979.
'Azmi, Mahmud. *Khabaya Siyasiyya.* Cairo, 1950?.
Badr, 'Abd al-Muhsin Taha. *Tatawwur al-Riwaya al-'Arabiyya al-Haditha fi Misr, 1870–1938.* Cairo, 1963.
al-Bishri, 'Abd al-'Aziz. *al-Tarbiyya al-Wataniyya.* Second ed. Cairo, 1928.
al-Bishri, Tariq. *al-Haraka al-Siyasiyya fi Misr, 1945–1952.* Cairo, 1972.
———. "al-Malik wa al-Khilafa al-Islamiyya." *al-Katib,* 13, no. 142 (Jan. 1973), 44–72.
———. *Sa'd Zaghlul Yufawidu al-Isti'mar: Dirasa fi al-Mufawadat al-Misriyya al-Biritaniyya, 1920–1924.* Cairo, 1977.
Burj, Muhammad 'Abd al-Rahman. *'Aziz al-Misri wa al-Haraka al-'Arabiyya, 1908–1916.* Cairo, 1979.
Daghir, As'ad. *Mudhakkirati 'ala Hamish al-Qadiyya al-'Arabiyya.* Cairo, 1959.

Daghir, Yusuf As'ad. *Masadir al-Dirasa al-Adabiyya.* Three vols. Sidon, 1956–1972.
al-Dasuqi, 'Umar. *Fi al-Adab al-Hadith.* Sixth ed. Two vols. Cairo, 1964.
Dayf, Ahmad. *Balaghat al-'Arab fi al-Andalus.* Cairo, 1924.
———. *Muqaddima li-Dirasat Balaghat al-'Arab.* Cairo, 1921.
Dayf, Shawqi. *al-Adab al-'Arabi al-Mu'asir fi Misr.* Second ed. Cairo, 1961.
Dhihni, Salah al-Din. *Misr bayna al-Ihtilal wa al-Thawra.* Cairo, 1939.
al-Duri, 'Abd al-'Aziz. *al-Judhur al-Ta'rikhiyya lil-Shu'ubiyya.* Beirut, n. d.
Fahmi, 'Abd al-'Aziz. *Hadhihi Hayati.* Cairo, 1963.
Fahmi, Mansur. *Khatarat Nafs.* Cairo, 1930.
Fatawa Kibar al-Kuttab wa al-Udaba' fi (1) Mustaqbal al-Lugha al-'Arabiyya (2) Nahdat al-Sharq al-'Arabi wa Mawqifuhu iza' al-Madaniyya al-Gharbiyya. Cairo, 1923.
al-Hakim, Tawfiq. *Ahl al-Kahf.* Cairo, 1933.
———. *'Awdat al-Ruh.* Two vols. Cairo, 1933.
———. *Shahrazad.* Cairo, 1934.
———. *Tahta Shams al-Fikr.* Second ed. Cairo, 1941.
Hamza, 'Abd al-Latif. *Adab al-Maqala al-Suhufiyya fi Misr.* Eight vols. Cairo, 1953–1962.
al-Hanafi, Mahmud Ahmad. *Sayyid Darwish: Hayatuhu wa Athar 'Abqariyyatihi.* Cairo, 1964.
Harb, Muhammad Tal'at. *Majmu'at Khutub Muhammad Tal'at Harb Bik.* Cairo, n. d.
al-Hawfi, Ahmad Muhammad. *Wataniyyat Shawqi: Dirasa Adabiyya Ta'rikhiyya Muqarana.* Cairo, 1978.
Haykal, Muhammad Husayn. *Fi Awqat al-Faragh.* Second ed. Cairo, 1968.
———. *Mudhakkirat fi al-Siyasa al-Misriyya.* Three vols. Cairo, 1951, 1953, 1978.
———. *Tarajim Misriyya wa Gharbiyya.* Cairo, 1929.
———. *Thawrat al-Adab.* Cairo, 1933.
———. *Zaynab: Manazir wa Akhlaq Rifiyya.* Second ed. Cairo, 1929.
Hijazi, Ahmad 'Abd al-Mu'ti. *'Urubat Misr: Dirasa wa Watha'iq.* Beirut, 1979.
Husayn, Ahmad. *Imani.* Cairo, 1936.
———. *Nisf Qarn ma'a al-'Uruba wa Qadiyyat Filastin.* Sidon, 1971.
Husayn, Muhammad Muhammad. *al-Ittijahat al-Wataniyya fi al-Adab al-Mu'asir.* Two vols. Cairo, 1954.
Husayn, Taha. *al-Ayyam.* Two vols. Cairo, 1929, 1939.
———. *Hadith al-Arbi'a'.* Tenth ed. Three vols. Cairo, 1976.
al-Husri, Abu Khaldun Sati'. *Abhath Mukhtara fi al-Qawmiyya al-'Arabiyya.* Cairo, 1964.
'Imara, Muhammad. *al-Islam wa Usul al-Hukm, li-'Ali 'Abd al-Raziq: Dirasa wa Watha'iq.* Beirut, 1972.
———. *al-'Uruba fi al-'Asr al-Hadith.* Cairo, 1967.
'Inan, Muhammad 'Abd Allah. *Mawaqif Hasima.* Cairo, 1929.
———. *Misr al-Islamiyya wa Ta'rikh al-Khitat al-Misriyya.* Cairo, 1931.
al-Jaziri, Muhammad Ibrahim. *Athar al-Za'im Sa'd Zaghlul: 'Ahd Wizarat al-Sha'b.* Cairo, 1927.
Jum'a, Muhammad Lutfi. *Hayat al-Sharq.* Cairo, 1932?.
al-Jundi, Anwar. *'Abd al-'Aziz Jawish.* Cairo, 1965.
———. *Ahmad Zaki al-Mulaqqab bi-Shaykh al-'Uruba.* Cairo, 1964.
———. *A'lam wa Ashab Aqlam.* Cairo, n. d.
———. *al-Fikr al-'Arabi al-Mu'asir fi Ma'rakat al-Taghrib wa al-Tab'iyya al-Thaqafiyya.* Cairo, 1961.
———. *al-Imam al-Maraghi.* Cairo, 1952.
———. *al-Muhafaza wa al-Tajdid fi Nathr al-'Arabi al-Mu'asir fi Mi'at 'Amm, 1840–1940.* Cairo, 1961.
Kamil, 'Ali Fahmi (ed.). *Mustafa Kamil Basha fi 34 Rabi'an.* Nine vols. Cairo, 1908–1911.

Lashin, 'Abd al-Khaliq Muhammad. *Sa'd Zaghlul: Dawruhu fi al-Siyasa al-Misriyya, 1914–1927.* Beirut, 1975.
Mahfuz, Najib. *Bayna al-Qasrayn.* Second ed. Cairo, 1964.
Mahmud, Muhammad Taha. *Durus al-Tarbiyya al-Wataniyya.* Fourth ed. Cairo, 1936–1937.
al-Mar'ashli, Tawfiq Hamid. *al-Tarbiyya al-Wataniyya.* Second ed. Cairo, 1929.
Markaz Watha'iq wa Ta'rikh Misr al-Mu'asir. *Awraq Muhammad Farid, vol. I: Mudhakkirati ba'da al-Hijra, 1904–1919.* Cairo, 1978.
Mazhar, Isma'il. *Malqan al-Sabil fi Madhhab al-Nushu' wa al-Irtiqa' wa Atharuhu fi al-Inqilab al-Fikri al-Hadith.* Cairo, 1924.
———. *Mu'dilat al-Madaniyya al-Haditha.* Cairo, 1928.
———. *Ta'rikh al-Fikr al-'Arabi.* Cairo, 1928.
———. *Wathbat al-Sharq.* Cairo, 1929.
al-Misri, Ibrahim. *al-Adab al-Hayy.* Cairo, 1930.
———. *Sawt al-Jil.* Cairo, 1934.
———. *Wahy al-'Asr.* Cairo, 1935.
Mu'assasat al-Ahram. *Khamsun 'Amman 'ala Thawrat 1919.* Cairo, 1969.
Muhammad, 'Abd al-'Ati. "Tatawwur al-Fikra al-'Arabiyya fi Misr." *al-Fikr al-'Arabi,* 1, nos. 4–5 (Sept.–Nov. 1978), 295–318.
Muhammad, Muhsin. *Sariqat Waha Misriyya.* Cairo, 1981.
Musa, Salama. *Ahlam al-Falasifa.* Cairo, 1926.
———. *Misr Asl al-Hadara.* Cairo, n. d.
———. *Mukhtarat Salama Musa.* Cairo, 1926.
———. *al-Yawm wa al-Ghad.* Cairo, 1927.
al-Nahri, Ahmad, and Ahmad Bayli. *al-Mujaz fi al-Tarbiyya al-Wataniyya.* Cairo, 1926.
Qallini Fahmi. *Mudhakkirat Qallini Fahmi Basha.* Two vols. Cairo, 1931–1934.
Qarqut, Dhuqan. *Tatawwur al-Fikra al-'Arabiyya fi Misr, 1805–1936.* Beirut, 1972.
Qasim, Jamal Zakariya. "Mawqif Misr min al-Harb al-Tarablusiyya, 1911–1914." *al-Majalla al-Ta'rikhiyya al-Misriyya,* 13 (1967), 306–342.
Qasimiyya, Khayriyya, and B. Nuwayhid al-Hut. "Faqiran Filastiniyyan Kabiran: 'Abd al-Hamid Shuman wa Muhammad 'Ali al-Tahir," *Shu'un Filastiniyya,* no. 39 (Nov. 1974), 143–163.
Radwan, Fathi. *'Asr wa Rijal.* Cairo, 1967.
al-Rafi'i, 'Abd al-Rahman. *Fi A'qab al-Thawra al-Misriyya.* Three vols. Cairo, 1947–1951.
———. *Muhammad Farid.* Second ed. Cairo, 1962.
———. *Mustafa Kamil: Ba'ith al-Haraka al-Qawmiyya.* Cairo, 1950.
———. *Thawrat Sanat 1919.* Two vols. Cairo, 1946.
Ramadan, 'Abd al-'Azim Muhammad. *Tatawwur al-Haraka al-Wataniyya fi Misr min Sanat 1918 ila Sanat 1936.* Cairo, 1968.
Raynan, Arnst [Ernest Renan] (trans. by 'Ali Adham). *Muhawarat Raynan al-Falsafiyya.* Cairo, 1929.
Rif'at, Muhammad, and 'Abd al-'Aziz al-Bishri. *al-Tarbiyya al-Wataniyya.* Cairo, 1937.
Rizq, Yunan Labib. "Azmat al-'Aqaba al-Ma'rufa bi-Hadithat Taba 1906." *al-Majalla al-Ta'rikhiyya al-Misriyya,* 13 (1967), 247–305.
Sabri, Ahmad. *Kahin Amun: Masrahiyya Fir'awniyya.* Cairo, 1929?.
Sabri, Yusuf, and 'Ali Shahid. *Nafrat aw 'Ashiqat Fir'awn.* Cairo, 1928.
Sa'id, Amin. *al-Thawra al-'Arabiyya al-Kubra.* Three vols. Cairo, 1934.
Sa'id, Isma'il 'Ali. *al-Azhar 'ala Masrah al-Siyasa al-Misriyya.* Cairo, 1974.
Sa'id, Nufusa Zakariya. *Ta'rikh al-Da'wa ila al-'Ammiyya wa Atharuhu fi Misr.* Alexandria, 1964.
al-Sa'id, Rif'at. *Muhammad Farid: al-Mawqif wa al-Ma'sa.* Cairo, 1978.
Sayf, Ibrahim Numayr, and 'Abd al-Hamid Batriq. *Suwar min al-Hadara fi Misr al-Qadima.* Cairo, 1926.

Sayigh, Anis. *al-Fikra al-'Arabiyya fi Misr*. Beirut, 1959.
al-Sayyid, Ahmad Lutfi. *al-Muntakhabat*. Two vols. Cairo, 1945.
———. *Qissat Hayati*. Cairo, 1962.
———. *Safahat Matwiyya min Ta'rikh al-Haraka al-Istiqlaliyya fi Misr*. Cairo, 1946.
———. *Ta'ammulat fi al-Falsafa wa al-Adab wa al-Siyasa wa al-Ijtima'*. Second ed. Cairo, 1965.
Shafiq, Ahmad. *A'mali ba'da Mudhakkirati*. Cairo, 1941.
———. *Hawliyyat Misr al-Siyasiyya*. Ten vols. Cairo, 1926–1932.
———. *Mudhakkirati fi Nisf Qarn*. Three vols. Cairo, 1934–1937.
al-Shaliq, Ahmad Zakariya. *Hizb al-Umma wa Dawruhu fi al-Siyasa al-Misriyya*. Cairo, 1979.
Sharqawi, Mahmud. "Dirasat Watha'iq 'an Mu'tamar al-Khilafa al-Islamiyya, 1926." *al-Katib*, 10, no. 113 (Aug. 1970), 115–122; 10, no. 114 (Sept. 1970), 132–137; 10, no. 115 (Oct. 1970), 156–161; 11, no. 119 (Feb. 1971), 151–158.
Shawqi, Ahmad. *al-Shawqiyyat*. Four vols. Cairo, 1930.
Subayh, Muhammad. *Batal La Nansahu: 'Aziz al-Misri wa 'Asruhu*. Sidon, 1973.
al-Tahir, Muhammad 'Ali. *Nazarat al-Shura*. Cairo, 1932.
Taymur, Mahmud. *Nushu' al-Qissa wa Tatawwuruha*. Cairo, 1936.
———. *al-Shaykh Jum'a wa Aqasis Ukhra*. Second ed. Cairo, 1927.
———. *al-Shaykh Sayyid al-'Abit wa Aqasis Ukhra*. Cairo, 1926.
Zaghlul, Sa'd. *Majmu'at Khutub wa Ahadith*. Cairo, n. d.
al-Zawahiri, Fakhr al-Din al-Ahmadi. *al-Siyasa wa al-Azhar: min Mudhakkirat Shaykh al-Islam al-Zawahiri*. Cairo, 1945.
al-Zirikli, Khayr al-Din. *al-A'lam: Qamus Tarajim li-Ashhar al-Rijal wa al-Nisa' min al-'Arab wa al-Musta'ribin wa al-Mustashriqin*. Fifth ed. Eight vols. Beirut, 1980.
Zu'aytir, Akram. "Sharqiyyun am 'Arab." *al-'Arabi*, no. 246 (May 1979), 15–21.
———. "al-'Uruba fi Misr." *al-'Arabi*, no. 244 (March 1979), 6–12.

Works in Other Languages Cited in the Text

Abrams, M. H. *The Mirror and the Lamp: Romantic Theory and the Critical Tradition*. New York, 1953.
Ahmed, Jamal Mohammed. *The Intellectual Origins of Egyptian Nationalism*. London, 1960.
Allen, Roger. *The Arabic Novel: An Historical and Critical Introduction*. Syracuse, 1982.
Azmi, Mahmoud. "The Last of the Khedives and the Syrian Throne." *The Arabic World*, 1, no. 1 (16 June 1933), 6–8.
Badawi, M. M. *A Critical Introduction to Modern Arabic Poetry*. Cambridge, 1975.
Baker, Randall. *King Husain and the Kingdom of Hijaz*. Cambridge, 1979.
Berque, Jacques (trans. by Jean Stewart). *Egypt: Imperialism and Revolution*. London, 1972.
Binder, Leonard. "'Ali 'Abd al-Raziq and Islamic Liberalism." *Asian and African Studies*, 16 (1982), 31–59.
Blunt, Wilfred Scawen. *My Diaries*. Two vols. New York, 1921.
———. *Secret History of the English Occupation of Egypt: Being a Personal Narrative of Events*. London, 1907.
Boulding, Kenneth. *The Image: Knowledge in Life and Society*. Ann Arbor, 1961.
Bouwsma, William J. "Intellectual History in the 1980's: From History of Ideas to History of Meaning." *The Journal of Interdisciplinary History*, 12 (1981–1982), 279–291.
Bowie, Leland. "The Copts, the Wafd, and Religious Issues in Egyptian Politics." *Muslim World*, 67 (April 1977), 106–126.

Bullard, Sir Reader. *The Camels Must Go: An Autobiography.* London, 1961.

Cachia, Pierre. "Idealism and Ideology: The Case of Tawfiq al-Hakim" *Journal of the American Oriental Society,* 100 (1980), 225–235.

Cassirer, Ernst. *An Essay on Man: An Introduction to a Philosophy of Human Culture.* New Haven, 1948.

Chartier, Roger. "Intellectual History or Socio-Cultural History? The French Trajectories." In Dominick LaCapra and Steven L. Kaplan (eds.), *Modern European Intellectual History: Reappraisals and New Perspectives* (Ithaca, 1982), 13–46.

Cohen, Aharon. *Israel and the Arab World.* New York, 1970.

Collingwood, R. G. *An Essay on Metaphysics.* Oxford, 1940.

Colombe, Marcel. *L'évolution de l'Egypte.* Paris, 1951.

Coury, Ralph M. "Who 'Invented' Egyptian Arab Nationalism?" *International Journal of Middle East Studies,* 14 (1982), 249–281, 459–479.

The Earl of Cromer [Evelyn Baring]. *Modern Egypt.* Two vols. London, 1908.

Darnton, Robert. "Intellectual and Cultural History." In Michael Kammen (ed.), *The Past Before Us: Contemporary Historical Writing in the United States* (Ithaca, 1980), 327–354.

Davis, Eric. *Challenging Colonialism: Bank Misr and Egyptian Industrialization, 1920–1941.* Princeton, 1983.

Dawn, C. Ernest. *From Ottomanism to Arabism: Essays on the Origins of Arab Nationalism.* Urbana, Illinois, 1973.

Deeb, Marius. "Bank Misr and the Emergence of a Local Bourgeoisie in Egypt." *Middle Eastern Studies,* 12 (1976), 69–86.

———. *Party Politics in Egypt: The Wafd and Its Rivals, 1919–1939.* London, 1979.

Djemal Pasha. *Memories of a Turkish Statesman, 1913–1919.* New York, 1922.

Egypt. Statistical Department. *Annual Statement of the Foreign Trade of Egypt, 1929.* Cairo, 1930.

Eisenstadt, S. N. "Intellectuals and Tradition." In S. N. Eisenstadt and S. R. Graubard (eds.), *Intellectuals and Tradition* (two vols.: New York, 1973), I, 1–19.

Elgood, P. G. *Egypt and the Army.* London, 1924.

Eliraz, Giora. *Egyptian Intellectuals in the Face of Tradition and Change, 1919–1939* (in Hebrew). Ph.D. dissertation, Hebrew University of Jerusalem, 1980.

Enayat, Hamid. *Modern Islamic Political Thought.* Austin, Texas, 1982.

"G." "Textes historiques sur le reveil arabe au Hedjaz." *Revue du Monde Musulman,* 46 (1921), 1–22; 47 (1921), 1–27; 50 (1922), 74–100.

Geertz, Clifford. *The Interpretation of Cultures.* New York, 1973.

Gellner, Ernest. *Nations and Nationalism.* Ithaca, 1983.

Gershoni, Israel. "Between Ottomanism and Egyptianism: The Evolution of 'National Sentiment' in the Cairene Middle Class as Reflected in Najib Mahfuz's *Bayn al-Qasrayn.*" *Asian and African Studies,* 17 (1983), 227–263.

Gibb, Sir H. A. R. (trans. and with a supplement by Jacob M. Landau). *Arabic Literature: An Introduction* (in Hebrew). Tel Aviv, 1970.

———. "The Social Significance of the Shuubiya." In H. A. R. Gibb, *Studies on the Civilization of Islam* (ed. by Stanford J. Shaw and William R. Polk: Boston, 1962), 62–73.

———. "Studies in Contemporary Arabic Literature." In H. A. R. Gibb, *Studies on the Civilization of Islam* (ed. by Stanford J. Shaw and William R. Polk: Boston, 1962), 245–319.

Gilbert, Felix. "Intellectual History: Its Aims and Methods." *Daedalus.* 50 (Winter 1971), 80–97.

Goldschmidt, Arthur. "The Egyptian Nationalist Party, 1892–1919." In P. M. Holt (ed.), *Political and Social Change in Modern Egypt* (London, 1965), 308–333.

Goldziher, Ignaz (trans. by C. R. Barber and S. M. Stern). *Muslim Studies.* Two vols. London, 1967, 1971.

Greene, John C. "Objectives and Methods in Intellectual History." *The Mississippi Valley Historical Review,* 44 (1957), 58–74.

Hafez, Sabry. "The Maturation of a New Literary Genre." *International Journal of Middle East Studies,* 16 (1984), 367–389.

Haim, Sylvia G. *Arab Nationalism: An Anthology.* Berkeley, 1962.

Hayes, C. J. H. *The Historical Evolution of Modern Nationalism.* New York, 1931.

Haywood, John A. *Modern Arabic Literature, 1800–1970.* New York, 1971.

Heyd, Uriel. "Hamashber shel Mifraz Eliat bi-Shnat 1906." *Sefer Eilat* (Jerusalem, 1960).

Higham, John. "Intellectual History and Its Neighbors." *Journal of the History of Ideas,* 15 (1954), 339–347.

Hollinger, David A. "Historians and the Discourse of Intellectuals." In John Higham and Paul K. Conkin (eds.), *New Directions in American Intellectual History* (Baltimore, 1979), 42–63.

Hourani, Albert. *Arabic Thought in the Liberal Age, 1798–1939.* London, 1962.

Husain, Taha [Taha Husayn] (trans. by Kenneth Cragg). *A Passage to France: The Third Volume of the Autobiography.* Leiden, 1976.

Al-Husry, Khaldun S. *Three Reformers: A Study in Modern Arab Political Thought.* Beirut, 1966.

ibn Khaldun (trans. by Franz Rosenthal). *The Muqaddima: An Introduction to History.* Three vols. New York, 1958.

Ibrahim, Ibrahim A. "Isma'il Mazhar and Husayn Fawzi: Two Muslim 'Radical' Westernizers." *Middle Eastern Studies,* 9 (1973), 35–41.

Jayyusi, Salma Khadra. *Trends and Movements in Modern Arabic Poetry.* Two vols. Leiden, 1977.

Jomier, Jacques. *Le Mahmal et la caravane égyptienne des pèlerins de la Mecque.* Cairo, 1953.

Kayyali, A. W. *Palestine: A Modern History.* London, 1978.

Kazziha, Walid. "The Jaridah-Ummah Group and Egyptian Politics." *Middle Eastern Studies,* 13 (1977), 373–385.

Kedourie, Elie. "Egypt and the Caliphate, 1915–52." In Elie Kedourie, *The Chatham House Version and Other Middle-Eastern Studies* (New York, 1970), 177–212.

———. "The Genesis of the Egyptian Constitution of 1923." In P. M. Holt (ed.), *Political and Social Change in Modern Egypt* (London, 1965), 347–361.

———. *In the Anglo-Arab Labyrinth: The Husayn-McMahon Correspondence and Its Interpretations, 1914–1939.* London, 1975.

———. *Nationalism.* London, 1960.

———. *Nationalism in Asia and Africa.* New York, 1970.

———. "The Politics of Political Literature: Kawakibi, Azoury, and Jung." In Elie Kedourie, *Arabic Political Memoirs and Other Studies* (London, 1974), 107–123.

Khadduri, Majid. "'Aziz 'Ali al-Misri and the Arab Nationalist Movement." In Albert Hourani (ed.), *Middle Eastern Affairs* (*St. Antony's Papers,* no. 17: London, 1965), 140–163.

———. *Political Trends in the Arab World.* Baltimore, 1970.

Khalidi, Rashid Ismail. *British Policy Towards Syria and Palestine, 1906–1914.* London, 1980.

Khouri, Mounah A. *Poetry and the Making of Modern Egypt (1882–1922).* Leiden, 1971.

Khoury, Philip S. "Factionalism Among Syrian Nationalists during the French Mandate." *International Journal of Middle East Studies,* 13 (1981), 441–469.

Kilpatrick, Hilary. *The Modern Egyptian Novel: A Study in Social Criticism.* London, 1974.

Kisch, Frederick Herman. *Palestine Diary.* London, 1938.

Kohn, Hans. *The Idea of Nationalism.* New York, 1944.

Kramer, Martin. "The General Islamic Congress for the Caliphate in Egypt." Paper delivered at the Shiloah Center for African and Middle Eastern Studies, Tel Aviv University, 10 March 1982.

———. "Shaykh Maraghi's Mission to the Hijaz, 1925." *Asian and African Studies,* 16 (1982), 121–136.

LaCapra, Dominick. "Rethinking Intellectual History and Reading Texts." In Dominick LaCapra and Steven L. Kaplan (eds.), *Modern European Intellectual History: Reappraisals and New Perspectives* (Ithaca, 1982), 47–85.

Landau, Jacob M. *Studies in the Arab Theater and Cinema.* Philadelphia, 1958.

Lapidus, Ira M. "Muslim Cities and Islamic Societies." In Ira M. Lapidus (ed.), *Middle Eastern Cities* (Berkeley, 1969), 47–79.

———. "The Separation of State and Religion in the Development of Early Islamic Society." *International Journal of Middle East Studies,* 6 (1975), 363–385.

Lawrence, T. E. *Seven Pillars of Wisdom: A Triumph.* London, 1935.

Le Bon, Gustave. *Lois psychologiques de l'évolution des peuples.* Paris, 1895.

———. *Les prémieres civilizations.* Paris, 1889.

———. *Psychologie des foules.* Paris, 1896.

———. *Psychologie du socialisme.* Paris, 1908.

Lesch, Ann Mosely. *Arab Politics in Palestine, 1917–1939.* Ithaca, 1979.

Lewis, Bernard. *The Emergence of Modern Turkey.* London, 1961.

Lord Lloyd [George A. Lloyd]. *Egypt Since Cromer.* Two vols. London, 1933, 1934.

Lovejoy, Arthur O. *The Great Chain of Being: A Study of the History of an Idea.* Cambridge, 1936.

———. "Reflections on the History of Ideas." *Journal of the History of Ideas,* 1 (1940), 3–23.

MacMunn, George, and Cyril Falls. *Military Operations, Egypt and Palestine: From the Outbreak of War with Germany to June 1917.* London, 1928.

Mannheim, Karl (trans. by Louis Wirth and Edward Shils). *Ideology and Utopia.* London, 1936.

———. "The Problem of Generations." In Karl Mannheim, *Essays on the Sociology of Knowledge* (trans. by Paul Kecskemeti: London, 1952), 276–322.

Mayer, Thomas. *Egypt and the Palestine Question, 1936–1945.* Berlin, 1983.

Merton, Robert. *Social Theory and Social Structure.* Second ed. New York, 1968.

Moreh, S. *Modern Arabic Poetry, 1800–1970.* Leiden, 1976.

Mottahedeh, Roy P. "The Shu'ubiyah Controversy and the Social History of Early Islamic Iran." *International Journal of Middle East Studies,* 7 (1976), 161–182.

Murphey, Murray G. "The Place of Beliefs in Modern Culture." In John Higham and Paul K. Conkin (eds.), *New Directions in American Intellectual History* (Baltimore, 1979), 151–166.

Musa, Salama (trans. by L. O. Schuman). *The Education of Salama Musa.* Leiden, 1961.

Nettl, J. P. "Ideas, Intellectuals, and Structures of Dissent." In Philip Rieff (ed.), *On Intellectuals* (New York, 1969), 53–122.

Nevakivi, Jukka. *Britain, France, and the Arab Middle East, 1914–1920.* London, 1969.

Nietzsche, Friedrich (ed. by Oscar Levy). *The Complete Works of Friedrich Nietzsche.* Eighteen vols. New York, 1909–1924.

———. *Der Wille zur Macht.* In *Friedrich Nietzsche Gesammelte Werke* (Twenty-three vols.: Munich, 1920–1929), vol. 18–19.

Nochlin, Linda. *Realism.* London, 1971.

Perkins, Kenneth J. "Colonial Administration in the Twilight of Imperialism: Great Britain and the Egyptian Frontier Districts Administration, 1917–39." *Middle Eastern Studies,* 18 (1982), 411–425.

Philipp, Thomas. *Gurgi Zaidan: His Life and Thought.* Wiesbaden, 1979.

———. "Language, History, and Arab National Consciousness in the Thought of Gurgi Zaydan (1861–1914)." *International Journal of Middle East Studies,* 4 (1973), 3–22.

Porath, Y. *The Emergence of the Palestinian-Arab National Movement, 1918–1929.* London, 1974.

Rabinovich, Itamar. "Inter-Arab Relations Foreshadowed: The Question of the Syrian Throne in the 1920's and 1930's." In *Festschrift in Honor of Dr. George S. Wise* (Tel Aviv, 1981), 237–250.

Reid, Donald M. "Indigenous Egyptology: the Decolonization of a Profession?" *Journal of the American Oriental Society,* 105 (1985), 233–246.

———. *The Odyssey of Farah Antun.* Minneapolis, 1975.

Renan, Ernest. *De la part des peuples sémitiques dans l'histoire de la civilization.* Paris, 1862.

———. *Histoire générale et système comparé des langues sémitiques.* Paris, 1855.

Rubin, Barry. *The Arab States and the Palestine Conflict.* Syracuse, 1981.

Russell [Pasha], John. *Egyptian Service, 1902–1946.* London, 1949.

Safran, Nadav. *Egypt in Search of Political Community.* Cambridge, 1961.

Sakkut, Hamdi. *The Egyptian Novel and Its Main Trends; from 1913 to 1952.* Cairo, 1971.

Sanhoury, A. *Le califat: son évolution vers une société des nations orientale.* Paris, 1926.

Al-Sayyid [Marsot], Afaf Lutfi. *Egypt and Cromer: A Study in Anglo-Egyptian Relations.* New York, 1969.

Al-Sayyid-Marsot, Afaf Lutfi. *Egypt's Liberal Experiment, 1922–1936.* Berkeley, 1977.

Schölch, Alexander. *Egypt for the Egyptians! The Socio-Political Crisis in Egypt, 1878–82.* London, 1981.

Schulze, Reinhard. *Die Rebellion der Agyptischen Fallahin 1919.* Berlin, 1981.

Sékaly, Achille. *Le Congrès du khalifat (Le Caire, 13–19 mai 1926) et le Congrès du monde musulman (La Mekke, 7 juin–5 juillet 1926).* Paris, 1926.

Semah, David. *Four Egyptian Literary Critics.* Leiden, 1974.

Shah, Ikbal Ali. *Fuad, King of Egypt.* London, 1936.

Sharabi, Hisham. *Arab Intellectuals and the West: The Formative Years, 1875–1914.* Baltimore, 1970.

Sharouni, Subhi. "Mahmoud Mukhtar: A Traditional and Contemporary Artist." *Ur,* 1 (1984), 27–30.

Shils, Edward. "Intellectuals." In David L. Sills (ed.), *International Encyclopedia of the Social Sciences* (seventeen vols.: New York, 1968), VII, 399–415.

———. "Intellectuals, Tradition, and the Traditions of Intellectuals: Some Preliminary Considerations." In S. N. Eisenstadt and S. R. Graubard (eds.), *Intellectuals and Tradition* (two vols.: New York, 1973), I, 21–34.

Skinner, Quentin. "Meaning and Understanding in the History of Ideas." *History and Theory,* 8 (1969), 3–53.

Smith, Anthony D. *Theories of Nationalism.* New York, 1971.

Smith, Charles D. "The Intellectual and Modernization: Definitions and Reconsiderations: The Egyptian Experience." *Comparative Studies in Society and History,* 22 (1980), 513–533.

———. *Islam and the Search for Social Order in Modern Egypt: A Biography of Muhammad Husayn Haykal.* Albany, 1983.

———. "Love, Passion and Class in the Fiction of Muhammad Husayn Haykal." *Journal of the American Oriental Society,* 99 (1979), 249–261.

Somekh, Sasson. *The Changing Rhythm: A Study of Najib Mahfuz's Novels.* Leiden, 1973.

Steppat, Fritz. "Nationalizmus und Islam bei Mustafa Kamil." *Die Welt des Islams,* 4 (1955–1956), 241–341.

Storrs, Sir Ronald. *The Memoirs of Sir Ronald Storrs.* New York, 1937.

Taine, Hippolyte. *Histoire de la littérature anglaise.* Four vols. Paris, 1863–1864.

Talmon, Jacob Leib. *The Origins of Totalitarian Democracy.* London, 1952.

———. *Political Messianism: The Romantic Phase.* London, 1960.

Tibawi, A. L. *Anglo-Arab Relations and the Question of Palestine, 1914–1921.* London, 1978.

Tibi, Bassam (trans. by Marion Farouq-Sluglett and Peter Sluglett). *Arab Nationalism: A Critical Inquiry.* New York, 1981.

Tignor, Robert L. "The Egyptian Revolution of 1919: New Directions in the Egyptian Economy." *Middle Eastern Studies,* 12 (1976), 41–67.

———. *Modernization and British Colonial Rule in Egypt, 1882–1914.* Princeton, 1966.

———. *State, Private Enterprise, and Economic Change in Egypt, 1918–1952.* Princeton, 1984.

de Tocqueville, Alexis (trans. by Gilbert Stuart). *The Old Regime and the French Revolution.* New York, 1955.

Toynbee, Arnold J. *Survey of International Affairs, vol. I: The Islamic World Since the Peace Settlement.* London, 1927.

———, assisted by V. M. Boulter. *Survey of International Affairs, 1934.* London, 1935.

Tugay, Emine Fuat. *Three Centuries: Family Chronicles of Turkey and Egypt.* London, 1963.

'Urabi, Ahmad (ed. and trans. by Trevor Le Gassick). *The Defense Statement of Ahmad 'Urabi.* Cairo, 1982.

Vatikiotis, P. J. *The Modern History of Egypt.* New York, 1969.

Walker, Dennis. "Mustafa Kamil's Party: Islam, Pan-Islamism, and Nationalism." *Islam and the Modern Age,* 11 (1980), 329–388; 12 (1981), 1–43, 79–113.

Warburg, Gabriel. "The Sinai Peninsula Borders, 1906–47." *Journal of Contemporary History,* 14 (1979), 677–692.

Wellek, Rene. *A History of Modern Criticism, 1750–1950: vol. II, the Romantic Age.* New Haven, 1955.

———. *A History of Modern Criticism, 1750–1950: vol. IV, The Later Nineteenth Century.* New Haven, 1965.

Welter, Rush. "On Studying the National Mind." In John Higham and Paul K. Conkin (eds.), *New Directions in American Intellectual History* (Baltimore, 1979), 64–82.

Wendell, Charles. *The Evolution of the Egyptian National Image: From Its Origins to Ahmad Lutfi al-Sayyid.* Berkeley, 1972.

Wilson, Edmund. *To the Finland Station.* New York, 1953.

Wingate, Sir Ronald. *Wingate of the Sudan: The Life and Times of General Sir Reginald Wingate, Maker of the Anglo-Egyptian Sudan.* London, 1955.

Wise, Gene. "The Contemporary Crisis in Intellectual History Studies." *Clio,* 5 (1975), 55–69.

Wood, Gordon S. "Intellectual History and the Social Sciences." In John Higham and Paul K. Conkin (eds.), *New Directions in American Intellectual History* (Baltimore, 1979), 27–41.

Zeine, Zeine N. *The Struggle for Arab Independence: Western Diplomacy and the Rise and Fall of Faisal's Kingdom in Syria.* Beirut, 1960.

Index